MUSS

'Impressively researched, splendidly written, sound in judgement, rich in insight and humane in spirit – in every respect a superb study of Mussolini and his Fascist regime.'
IAN KERSHAW, AUTHOR OF *HITLER: HUBRIS (1889–1936) AND HITLER: NEMESIS (1936–1945)*

'…Mussolini is a hard psychological nut to crack. The author wins one over with his many witty asides and insights (and there are not many scholarly biographies where that happens) and there is ample evidence of a subtle and humorous mind at work.'
FRANK McLYNN, THE INDEPENDENT ON SUNDAY

'Mussolini's story demonstrates the limits of his personal power, but also the extent to which he was able to do great harm. It is a credit to Bosworth's biography that he fully gives us both of these sides.'
THE NEW YORK TIMES SUNDAY BOOK REVIEW

'…the definitive study of the Italian dictator'
LIBRARY JOURNAL

'Richard Bosworth has produced a solid, judicious and very readable account of the Duce's life, based on extensive archival research and a well-nigh exhaustive knowledge of the secondary literature.'
NOEL MALCOLM, THE SUNDAY TELEGRAPH

Richard Bosworth is Professor of History at the University of Western Australia and one of the world's leading authorities on modern Italian history. He has been a Visiting Fellow at a number of institutions, including the Italian Academy at Columbia University, Clare Hall (Cambridge), Balliol (Oxford), and the Humanities Research Centre (ANU, Canberra).

for Michal
again

MUSSOLINI

R. J. B. BOSWORTH

First published in Great Britain in 2002 by
Hodder Education, part of Hachette Livre UK,
338 Euston Road, London NW1 3BH

http://www.hoddereducation.com

British Library Cataloguing in Publication Data
A catalogue record for this book is available from the British Library

Library of Congress Cataloging-in-Publication Data
A catalog record for this book is available from the Library of Congress

978 0 340 80988 4

6 7 8 9 10

Production Editor: Rada Radojicic
Production Controller: Iain McWilliams
Cover Design: Terry Griffiths

Typeset by Phoenix Photosetting, Chatham, Kent
Printed and bound in India by Replika Press Pvt. Ltd.

What do you think about this book? Or any other Hodder Education title?
Please send your comments to www.hodderecucation.co.uk

Contents

List of illustrations and maps   ix
Preface   xi
Introduction   1
1 The Furies and Benito Mussolini, 1944–1945   13
2 First of his class? The Mussolinis and the young Benito, 1883–1902   37
3 Emigrant and socialist, 1902–1910   56
4 The class struggle, 1910–1914   76
5 War and revolution, 1914–1919   100
6 The first months of Fascism, 1919–1920   123
7 The Fascist rise to power, 1920–1922   145
8 Government, 1922–1924   170
9 The imposition of dictatorship, 1924–1925   194
10 The Man of Providence, 1926–1929   217
11 Mussolini in his pomp, 1929–1932   241
12 The challenge of Adolf Hitler, 1932–1934   264
13 Empire in Ethiopia, 1935–1936   287
14 Crisis in Europe, 1936–1938   310
15 The approach of a Second World War, 1938–1939   334
16 Germany's ignoble second, 1939–1941   357
17 First fall and feeble resurrection, 1942–1943   382
18 The ghost of Benito Mussolini, 1945–2001   410
Notes   429
Select bibliography   520
Index   565

List of illustrations and maps

Plates appear between pages 270 and 271

PLATES

1 Mussolini at 14
2 Mussolini as wounded soldier
3 Mussolini, November 1922, just after appointment as Prime Minister
4 Mussolini, May 1923, at the conference of the National Alliance for Votes for Women
5 Rachele and Edvige Mussolini, the *Duce*'s wife and sister, 1925
6 Mussolini as fencer
7 Mussolini, April 1926, *en route* to Libya, after Violet Gibson's assassination attempt
8 The *Rocca delle Caminate* above Predappio
9 Edda Mussolini at her marriage with Galeazzo Ciano, 1930
10 Mussolini meeting Ramsay MacDonald, March 1933
11 Mussolini with Fascist Boy Scouts, Rome, June 1934
12 Mussolini meeting Hitler (in a mackintosh) in 1934
13 Mussolini speaking, 1935
14 Statue of Mussolini carved near Adowa, Ethiopia
15 Mussolini in Libya, 1937
16 Party Secretary Starace speaking at Addis Ababa, 1937
17 Mussolini swimming, 1937
18 Mussolini at his desk
19 A small child from the Romagna saluting the *Duce*
20 Galeazzo Ciano handing his son Fabrizio over to the Fascist scouts
21 Mussolini and Neville Chamberlain at the Palazzo Venezia
22 Mussolini visiting Rome University, 1942
23 Mussolini greeted by his son Vittorio in Germany, September 1943

List of illustrations and maps

24 Mussolini on his last speaking visit to Milan, December 1944
25 Mussolini's corpse, carrying sceptre-like a Fascist *gagliardetto*
26 The corpses of Mussolini and Claretta Petacci in the Piazzale Loreto, Milan
27 The Mussolini crypt in Predappio

MAPS

1 The Emilia-Romagna	36
2 Interwar Italy	124
3 The Fascist Empire	286
4 Italy's Second World War	396

Preface

'TOBRUK taken by the Australians, a people who amount to nothing in the history of the world'.[1] So, in January 1941 from his gilded retreat at the *Casa Italiana* attached to Columbia University, Giuseppe Prezzolini, an intellectual patron of the youthful Mussolini, wrote in disgust at the Italian national and Fascist war effort. His words might be read as a dampener on any Australian with the effrontery to seek to understand modern Italian history, let alone craft an account of the *Duce*, Benito Mussolini, leader of Italy from 1922 to 1945. Nonetheless, since the 1960s, it has been my lot to write Italian history and, in many senses, my life work is summed up in this new biography.

As my name indicates, I am an Anglo-Saxon Australian, with few natural connections to Italy. None the less, when, in my teens, I started reading my parents' library, I found among their books *My Autobiography* 'by Benito Mussolini'.[2] Perhaps my father (from 1933 to 1938 a research chemist at the Cavendish laboratories in Cambridge and possessed of vaguely leftist political leanings) had bought it in 1935, prompted by the notoriety come to the *Duce* from Italy's invasion of Ethiopia. My father died, messily, of heart trouble before I was old enough to discuss such matters with him. But my mother later recalled that they had holidayed at Venice in November 1935 (given the sanctions campaign against Italy and the outraged Italian reaction to it, not an ideal moment for such a trip). She added that the imponderable locals had spat at my (fair-haired, blue-eyed, 'English-looking') father and abused him as an 'English dog' when the two went walking in the *calli*, and left her political analysis at that. The holidays they took in Nazi Germany in 1936 and 1937, she remembered more pleasurably; then the beer and cakes were good and the tramping excellent.

We lived in an upper middle class suburb of Sydney, and Italian immigrants, who, in my boyhood, were arriving in Australia in hundreds of thousands, remained for many years well beyond my ken. Although

I had been fascinated somehow by history since boyhood, there was nothing which was as yet destining me to my career as a historian of Italy. When, as an undergraduate, I went to Sydney University in 1961, I did run into interwar Europe, since my most stimulating teacher was Ernest Bramsted, sometime biographer of Goebbels, and one of the few Jewish intellectual refugees from Nazism to find sanctuary in Australia. Bramsted ensured that, when, in 1966, I myself in turn went to Cambridge to do a PhD and work under Harry Hinsley, my research would focus on twentieth-century international relations.

Like many other research students in that decade of 'old-fashioned diplomatic history', I set down to study a small aspect of the coming of the First World War. The 50-year rule was permitting the opening of the archives on that subject, and PhD students were directed to the new material, with the implication that each was colouring in a pebble in the mosaic which would eventually show why there was war in 1914 (and other times). In most ways by accident, among Hinsley's battery of students I received the task of appraising British policy towards Italy. All scholarly decorum, I travelled to the Public Record Office, then still in Chancery Lane, and began to read the diplomatic traffic between London and Rome.

Just in case the 'documents' were not the beginning and end of historical knowledge, Hinsley, in his genial way, suggested that I would benefit from some months in Rome, even though my topic was meant to be 'British', not 'European', history. So, in September 1967, my wife Michal and I reached Rome, with youthful confidence, inadequate Italian and an introduction to Mario Toscano, then Italy's most senior diplomatic historian. He was too grand a figure to spend any time on so humble a visitor, but he did encourage his *assistente*, Giustino Filippone Thaulero, to watch over our lives. For four delightful months, we discovered the *Biblioteca di storia moderna e contemporanea*, other libraries and lots more besides, falling in love with Rome, for us destined to be thereafter the eternal city. Of course, I read mainly on Liberal Italy, but I was tempted on occasion to learn more about Mussolini and Fascism. Now I enjoyed the (highly dubious and ghosted) memoirs of his batman, Quintino Navarra's *Memorie del cameriere di Mussolini* and other such racy works.

My life had reached a turning point. Although I wrote up my Cambridge thesis on the approved topic of 'British foreign policy towards Italy 1902–1915', I had decided to become an Italianist. When, in 1969, I went back to Sydney as a young lecturer, I was determined to write Italian history. I had found an excuse to visit Italy every year, often during the Australian long vacation, that is, over the European winter, always an excellent time to be in Italy, since the Italians are there, the archives are open and the tourists are limited in number.

In thus indulging in autobiography, I am saying that this biography of Mussolini may have been only three years in the making since I signed my contract in 1998. Yet it also reflects work done for a generation. This long-term side of my study means I have accumulated 30 years of debts to many historians, many archives and many libraries. I cannot mention all of these. But one occasion should be recorded. It was 22 December 1970. For the first time, I had ventured to the *Archivio Centrale dello Stato*, redolently placed in its Fascist building 'in the Fascist model suburb of EUR (I had earlier worked in the archives of the Ministry of Foreign Affairs, on the opposite side of Rome, but similarly housed in a Fascist building, with the monumental Fascist *Foro dell'Impero*, now re-named the *Foro italico*, near by). At the ACS, I was reading a dusty file of papers on Liberal Italy, amid the babble of conversation and in the fug of cigarette smoke which distinguish Italian archives from some others. Suddenly scholarly labour stopped. Everybody – students, professors, archivists, document-fetchers – trooped towards a table set up with glasses of *spumante* and slices of *panettone*. A man, whom I later learned was the director, Costanzo Casucci, then gave a speech celebrating us all, emphasising the collective nature of intellectual endeavour and wishing us well for Christmas. In this tiny ceremony I found expressed the humanity in the humanities, and I have never let go my hope in it.

If the ACS is still my special place for a day's archival research, my favourite library is the *Biblioteca Oriani* at Ravenna, with its splendid collection of what might be called *Fascistiana*, and with Dante Bolognesi and his friendly staff. There I did a very great deal of the background reading for this biography. Hell, by contrast, is the *Biblioteca Nazionale* at Rome; its expensive recent technological re-fit has left it still a place where a secret mission statement must pledge that everything will be done to ensure that, from one year to the next, no books are read within its portals.

When acknowledging my debts, it is harder to single out colleagues in the wonderful discipline of history. So many people, be they fellow academics or students or just friends with historical interests, have helped to preserve my passion as a historian. They have written books which I would like to have written and have loved to read. They have thought in ways which I aspire to match and from which I have tried to learn. They have given me hospitality, physical, intellectual and spiritual. Some have even generously striven to polish my writing style and hone my arguments. Any list is invidious but, among those I would especially like to thank, are Roger Absalom, Loretta Baldassar, Tony Barker, Ruth Ben-Ghiat, Judy Berman, Martin Blinkhorn, Judy Bolton, Edmund Bosworth, Mary Bosworth, the late Frank Broeze, Tony Cahill, Paul Corner, Trish Crawford, Gianfranco Cresciani, Patrizia Dogliani, Nick Doumanis, Sheila Fitzpatrick, Frances Flanagan, Oscar Gaspari, Dick Geary, Anthony Gerbino, Grahame Harrison, the Harveys, Marianne Hicks, Reto Hoffman, Ernie Jones, Judith Keene, David Lowenthal, Philippa Maddern, Muriel Mahony, Fabio Malusà, Ben Mercer, the Minellis, Jonathan Morris, Peter Monteath, Michael Ondaatje, Luisa Passerini, Ros Pesman, Lorenzo Polizzotto, David Ritter, Gino Rizzo, Keith Robbins, Giovanna Rosselli, Deryck Schreuder, Enrico Serra, Glenda Sluga, Ed Smith, Jonathan Steinberg, Rob Stuart, Luciano Tosi, Wasim, Graham White and Shane White.

I am similarly indebted to various institutions – St. John's College and Clare Hall, Cambridge, Balliol College, Oxford, the British School in Rome, the Italian Academy at Columbia (where I sought not to be too rude to Prezzolini's ghost) – which have welcomed me as a visitor. While the ravaging of the humanities in Australia by the fans of economic rationalism has proceeded, I have been given a cushy billet through a national Research Council grant, which has exempted me from teaching for two semesters during the research and composition of this book. The writing, which mainly occurred over the Australian summer of 2000–1, was a time of special joy. Can there be anything better than waking up every morning in the endless series of brilliantly sunny Perth days to head for the computer and find that an ancient research technique provides the information and that the mystery of literary creation somehow produces the words? I shall be bereft until I find as challenging a new book to write as this one.

Some readers may be surprised at the gentleness of these sentiments, since I am in some places notorious for having joined academic battles about the interpretation of Italian history with a will (from distant Australia, an expertise in historiography has often been easier of achievement than a knowledge of archival history). As Republican Italy experienced its various travails of leftist hope in the 1960s and 1970s and of rightist return in the 1980s and 1990s, this latter process culminating in May 2001 with the accession of Silvio Berlusconi to the Prime Ministership, it was impossible to do Italian history without some sense of politics. Until the last few years, it was starkly evident that history, and especially the interpretation of Mussolini and his

Preface

regime, its causes, course and consequences, still mattered to a great number of Italians. After all, in my age of innocence, when I published a lengthy but critical monograph on Italian foreign policy before 1914, I found Rosario Romeo, Italy's premier conservative historian, lambasting me in a newspaper review as an 'Italy-hater', one who might be better off assessing his own inheritance from 'Botany Bay' than intruding into discussions about Italian liberalism.[3]

In our time of the 'end of history' (whatever the potential lingering power of irrational fundamentalisms), when ideologies and their meta-narratives sprung from the Enlightenment and its belief in human perfectability through rational knowledge and social action seem ship-wrecked and the market rules all, and when the Italian left seeks to find a 'third way' in an Olive Tree Alliance and with new political groupings called the Daisy or the Sunflower, I struggle against a profound alienation. In these circumstances, it was all the more appropriate when, some time between my signature of the contract and my writing of the manuscript, I was diagnosed with the same cardiac problems which killed my father. Technology having raced ahead, I, as a result, like so many men in their fifties, was physiologically by-passed and now I live with a sense of my bodily good fortune, compared with my father's bad luck. As one who clings to the political ideas and ideals I learned in the 1960s (and which go back to 1789), I am left with the paradox of gratitude about scientific progress mixed with disdain for, and fear of, the hegemonic ideology of the moment, by-passed, but with opposed effect, both in my body and my soul.

I shall leave readers to decide whether any of these events and attitudes can be traced, or are worth tracing, in my prose. I should admit that I have tried to view Mussolini to some extent with 'the eye of pity'.[4] Readers will, I trust, find that I regard him as a bully, a coward and a failure, and that my writing of the biography has not converted me into a worshipper of the *Duce* or of Fascism. None the less, Mussolini, unlike what remains the received understanding of his 'friend' Adolf Hitler, was, I am convinced, a man not so different from many another. In his crass vainglory, his appalling sexism and racism, his innumerable sins of omission and commission, his sad Darwinism, there but for the grace of humanity went numbers of Italians of his generation, and there, with or without such grace, go many of us.

Two final thanks – the first to Christopher Wheeler, the most sensitive and encouraging of editors. The second to Mike whose contribution to the subtlety, range and happiness of my life is infinite and to whom this book is dedicated.

Mussolini is the only person responsible for the major deeds of the regime. However, he is not the guarantor of all the individual undertakings, all the initiatives and all the different ideas which must grow up and flourish around Fascism.

Critica Fascista, VII, 15 September 1929 (editorial).

Yet it seems hardly possible that Mussolini alone has been responsible for the making of all major policies. Rather, it appears that he is essentially the *personification* of Dictatorship. Outwardly he is the inspired autocrat manipulating his puppets, and receiving credit for everything. In practice, however, rule is exercised collectively by a few leading administrators, including Mussolini, and their official and unofficial advisers. Their one basic and constant guiding principle is that their dominance be preserved.

C.T. Schmidt (lecturer in economics at Columbia University),
The Corporate state in action: Italy under Fascism,
London (Left Book Club), 1939, p. 78.

Wasn't Churchill just a Mussolini made over by English society, but not made over too much?

G. Bottai, *Vent'anni e un giorno (24 luglio 1943)*,
Milan, 1977, p. 27.

It is not possible to draw a portrait of Mussolini, without drawing one, too, of the Italian people. His qualities and his defects are not his own. Rather they are the qualities and the defects of all Italians.

C. Malaparte, *Muss. Il grande imbecille*, Milan, 1999, p. 67.
(The sometime radical Fascist, later communist and
eventually Maoist, writer Curzio Malaparte expressed
this view in the summer of 1943.)

Introduction

WHICH European politician of the first half of the twentieth century could be relied on to read the philosophical and literary works of his co-nationals and send their authors notes of criticism and congratulation?[1] Who, at a time of profound crisis and despite his evident ill health, kept on his desk a copy of the works of Socrates and Plato, annotated in his own hand?[2] Who declared publicly that he loved trees and anxiously quizzed his bureaucracy about storm damage to the environment? Who, in his table talk while he was entrenched in power, was fascinated by the task of tracing his intellectual antecedents?[3] Who at least said that he admired contemporary historians for their professionalism and their refusal to bow to fashion[4] and urged that his party's line should be 'indulgence towards professors'?[5] Who seemed almost always ready to grant an interview and, having done so, was especially pleased by the prospect of talking about contemporary political and philosophical ideas? Who left more than 44 volumes of his collected works? Who claimed with an element of truth that money never dirtied his hands?[6] Who could conduct a conversation in three languages apart from his own?[7] Who was warmly solicitous of his daughter, when, after her marriage and in her first pregnancy, she was living in foreign parts, and wrote regularly and personally to her,[8] even if on occasion only to report family pleasure at victories by the national football team?[9]

The somewhat surprising answer to all these questions is Benito Mussolini, *Duce* of Italian Fascism and dictator of Italy from 1922 (or 1925) to 1945 (or 1943). Earlier English-language biographers and many a contemporary concluded that, in essence, Mussolini was both knave and fool. As the very proper English gentleman Anthony Eden put it, with a degree of venom which a gentleman on occasion disgorges: 'Mussolini is, I fear, the complete gangster and his pledged word means nothing.'[10] Promiscuity, boasting, strutting vanity, petty cruelty, incompetence – these were the words most associated with Mussolini, and they have painted him as more a figure of fun than of the sort of dread reserved for his fellow dictators, Hitler and Stalin. These latter were fearful totalitarian tyrants. Mussolini, though it was he who first announced the intention of building a 'totalitarian state', was but a 'Sawdust Caesar',[11] no more than a buffoon.[12]

So, indeed, he was, readers of this new biography may well conclude. Yet, as they commence the pages of this book, they should be cautioned that the long tradition of a critical reading of the *Duce's* career carries more than a little Anglo-Saxon racial prejudice towards lesser breeds outside the law and especially towards 'southerners', 'Mediterraneans', what certain Australians of my acquaintance still call 'Eyetalians'. Assumptions about failure, superficiality and criminality have been a regular part of the English-language discourse on Mussolini, almost as if to imply that such failings are unknown outside Italy. The common assessment that Mussolini was 'no better than third-rate'[13] could seem to suggest that in other, happier, more northern and Anglo-Saxon lands, rulers have been, are, and always will be first-class men (and women).

In Italy, such expressions of effortless superiority have been greeted with some unease. It is true that for a generation the Italian Left, linked in one way or another to the Italian Communist Party (itself enjoying continual growth in electoral support until the end of the 1970s), forged its identity on the 'myth of the Resistance'. By this reading of the history of the twentieth century, Italy, from 1922 to 1945, fell under vicious misrule. Mussolini's dictatorship, so the argument goes, punished the great majority of the Italian people during its generation of power, and its alliance with the ultimate evil of Nazi Germany was natural and inevitable. So, too, was the involvement in apocalyptic war and genocide. Fascism and Nazism, Mussolini and Hitler, were each to be best understood through the 'model of fascism', which brought to light the manifold similarities between the two regimes and their 'charismatic' leaders. It was a model, which had, and has, much to be said for it. Yet, for the post-war Italian Left this interpretation had its greatest use in contemporary politics. It could help check the rapacity of the rich, the sexism of men, the allure of a revived nationalism. It could privilege the working class, trade unions, social humanism, those groups, institutions and ideas which Fascism had opposed and repressed.

Naturally enough, there were plenty of Italians who disapproved of Leftist assumptions about their world and who by no means agreed with the condemnation of all aspects of the Fascist past. From the mid-1960s, what have come to be called the 'Anti-Anti-Fascists' found their champion in Renzo De Felice, the extraordinarily pertinacious biographer of Mussolini. Giorgio Pini and Duilio Susmel, two ex-Fascists, had already in the 1950s written a four-volume study of the *Duce* which is very sympathetic to him (and remains useful to scholars). But in what eventually was a seven-book biography, which ran past 6000 pages, and was published between 1965 and 1997, the last volume posthumously, De Felice provided a massively detailed account of Mussolini's life. De Felice was the epitome of the historian as 'archive rat', to use Stalin's hostile term. He read in depth the government papers typically found in the *Archivio Centrale dello Stato* in Rome – these archives are housed in a building planned for the *Esposizione Universale Romana* (Rome Universal Exhibition), which was meant to celebrate 20 years of Fascist rule in 1942. As it became apparent that De Felice was not as unfriendly to the *Duce* as was the culture of the Left, the *Duce*'s hard-working biographer also acted as a magnet for surviving Fascists who regularly gave him access to their papers and diaries. When his own research was complete, De Felice frequently organised the publication of such works. Both in his prose, however meandering and confused, and in his editorial efforts, De Felice has left a remarkable heritage, one which no subsequent biographer of Mussolini can avoid.

As an interpreter of Mussolini, De Felice needs to be read with greater caution. Especially in the latter volumes, he frequently sought to exculpate the *Duce*, and became savagely dismissive of what he liked to call the journalistic superficiality of the 'Anti-Fascist vulgate'.[14] His own conclusions, he remarked immodestly, were the only possible ones, even when they included a highly contestable emphasis on Mussolini's 'progressive' politics and regret at his bad luck in failing to convert Hitler to the truth that the epicentre of the Second World War lay not on the Russian front but in the Mediterranean. Just before De Felice's death, his version of the past had become grist to the mill of a rising Italian new Right. He was praised by the allegedly 'post-fascist' members of the National Alliance, led by Gianfranco Fini, a man who went on claiming that Mussolini was the greatest statesman of the twentieth century, and by Silvio Berlusconi. This billionaire out-matches Mussolini's own efforts to be a journalist in politics by offering instead the frightening spectre of a media magnate in politics. In contemporary Italy, Berlusconi makes the news in many, too many, ways.

From my distant Australian refuge, I watch these events with the same curmudgeonly discomfort with which I view most contemporary politics. It would be churlish of me, however, not to acknowledge my debt to De Felice's biography. My footnotes certainly betray regular reference to his pages for detail and information. And yet, in this study, my more influential models have been drawn from neither Anglo-Saxon nor Italian biographies of Mussolini (nor from the new, lengthy but 'De Felicean', study by the French historian Pierre Milza).[15] My approach to Mussolini is conditioned by my reading of more general European history.

When Christopher Wheeler kindly raised with me the possibility that I might like to essay a new analysis of the *Duce*, I was doubtful. I had never written a biography before. And I thought of myself, and still do, as more a 'structuralist' or 'functionalist' historian, anxious to explore the 'social roots' of policy than an 'intentionalist' one, convinced that Great Men are indeed great, the dynamos of their times. My surviving interest in these issues shows that I was influenced by the 1980s literature on Nazi Germany. At least in Australia, all who teach twentieth-century European history are to some degree the pensioners of Adolf Hitler; for 35 years, I have smuggled some Italian history into courses which students have volunteered to do because of the terror and the glamour of Nazi Germany. From my immersion in the historiography on Germany I knew that there were fascinating debates about whether or not Hitler was a 'weak' dictator, about what the limits might have been of his power, about the originality or banality of his ideas, and so about the extent to which Nazi practice was an imposition from 'above' or a welling up from 'below'. Since I also had to teach the history of the Soviet Union (being a pensioner of Hitler does not rule out benefit gained from Stalin, too), I was encouraged to consult the fine work of Sheila Fitzpatrick[16] and others on not dissimilar issues in the history of the USSR and notably the functioning of its allegedly 'totalitarian' state amid the complexity and ambiguity of the society of all the Russias.

I therefore began my research by emphasising that I would place Mussolini into his society, commencing with a basic scepticism about the 'Great Man' and the liberal (but also Fascist) idea that every individual is potentially free to follow his or her will. 'My' Mussolini, I was sure (while trying to block out any foolish ambitions to become a 'Great Biographer'), would tell as much about the society of Italy (and the Italies) as it would about the individual peccadilloes of a particular human being.

None the less, to prepare myself for my task, I automatically looked at recent biographies of major twentieth-century politicians. Two especially impressed me. The first was Paul Preston's detailed account of General Franco, with its subtle analysis of how power was exercised in Spain for the lengthy period of Franco's rule. Among the themes which I noted for comparison with Mussolini was Preston's emphasis on the *Caudillo*'s 'inscrutable pragmatism', his 'evasion of commitment and ... taste for the imprecise'.[17] Franco, Preston told me, did not forget to practise obfuscation, the better to confuse later historians —'throughout his life, he regularly rewrote his own life story'. Quite a few Francos thus turn up in his record of the past. (How many Mussolinis might I, then, need to meet, I asked myself.) All the same, at least according to Preston, a real historical actor did exist; Franco's 'powers were comparable to those of Hitler and greater than those of Mussolini'.[18] Protected by his 'ability to calibrate almost instantly the weakness and/or price of a man', Franco, Preston argued, used his power for four decades 'with consummate skill, striking decisively at his outright enemies but maintaining the loyalty of those within the Nationalist coalition with cunning and a perceptive insight into human weakness worthy of a man who had learned his politics among the tribes of Morocco'.[19] Here was a strong dictator, however blindly cruel was his treatment of foes and however unrelentingly barren his view of the world turned out to be. According to Preston, Franco's most telling comments were expressed in 1954, when he informed the Bourbon Pretender Don Juan: 'I never placed my complete confidence in anyone' and this judicious caution had meant that, for him, 'Spain ... [was] easy to govern.'[20] Preston, I reflected, had concluded that a Great (Bad) Man indeed existed in Franco's Spain, one who cheerfully and brutally exercised free will.

Chastened a little in my assumptions and predilections, I then turned to Ian Kershaw's magnificent new biography of Hitler — there were pleasing afternoons when I could abandon the travail of constructing my own prose about Mussolini and read the second volume of Kershaw's study, which reached Australia late in 2000.[21] But when I was planning my biography, it was the introduction to Kershaw's first volume which I found most interesting. Kershaw told me that in shouldering the burden of biography he had come from the 'wrong' direction.[22] His own work was rooted in social history (and I knew, too, that he had written much on historiography). He was associated with members of that functionalist or structuralist school which had spent a generation in debate with intentionalists who thought that Hitler was the supreme historical actor of his era. They believed in 'Hitler's war', 'Hitler's Holocaust' and 'Hitler's Revolution'; they even contemplated Hitler as a 'psychopathic God'.[23] Kershaw and his friends, by contrast, explored the relationship between the German people and Nazi rule, and surveyed the extent to which Nazism won the 'consensus' of the Germans.

Kershaw's intellectual background was one concern. Another was the fact that Hitler seemed to have had no real private life (except that surmised by the psycho-historians). Preston's Franco rejoiced in a wife and daughter, played golf, went fishing, and decayed bathetically under the assault of Parkinson's disease. But Hitler's private world was more difficult to enter, if it existed at all. In the *Führer*'s case, Kershaw lamented, 'there was no retreat to a sphere outside the political, to a deeper existence which conditioned his public reflexes'.[24] In apparent contradiction, Hitler, when acting as an executive, was notoriously fickle, erratic in his attendance at the office, complaisant about his 'artistic temperament' and his devotion to a Bohemian lifestyle. He may or may not have thought that Germany was easy to govern but, frequently, he did not seem to bother to govern at all.

Power in Nazi Germany was centred on the *Führer*. That could not be denied, but Kershaw explained that this power 'derived only in part from Hitler himself. In greater measure it was a social product – a creation of social expectations and motivation vested in Hitler by his followers'. 'A history of Hitler', Kershaw continued, 'had to be, therefore, a history of his power – how he came to get it, what its character was, how he exercised it, why he was allowed to expand it to break all institutional barriers, why resistance to that power was so feeble.'[25] In coping with these questions, Kershaw concluded, Weberian ideas about charisma offered the best conceptual tool, but, he warned, the historical analyst must be as attuned to German society as to Hitler himself.[26] For Kershaw the key phrases in all the history of the Nazi regime were those coined by Werner Willikens, a Prussian bureaucratic expert in agriculture who, unlike the *Führer*, could reliably be found at his desk. In February 1934 Willikens wrote: 'Everyone with opportunity to observe it knows that the Führer can only with great difficulty order from above everything that he intends to carry out sooner or later. On the contrary, until now everyone has best worked in his place in the new Germany if, so to speak, he works towards the Führer'. 'It is the duty of every single person to attempt, in the spirit of the Führer to work towards him', he added.[27] Here, then, was what Kershaw regarded as a new sort of power,[28] under the influence of which Germans sought to express the Word even before it was spoken. They did so in a fog of confusion, miscomprehension, self-interest and fanaticism. Nazi Germany was 'a highly modern state without any central coordinating body and with a [charismatic] head of government largely disengaged from the machinery of government'.[29]

From Kershaw's work came a host of questions applicable to Mussolini. The *Duce* was plainly no exact replica of the *Führer*. Rather like Franco, he did have a private life, a wife and five legitimate children, lots of mistresses, a successful career before 1914 – not yet thirty he was already the editor of the socialist national paper *Avanti!* – illnesses of his own, notably as he aged and his hair grew white. In office, for the most part he was a careful executive, regularly turning up at his desk, conscientiously reading the papers put before him, accepting the forms of office (most ironically a bi-weekly visit to the royal palace to consult King Victor Emmanuel III, the monarch who, throughout the Fascist dictatorship, remained constitutional head of state). There was plenty of evidence that Mussolini knew how to manage and manipulate men (and women). His rule was seconded by a loyalish and largely constant entourage, kept in line by a combination of bullying and blandishments, accepting that they would be regularly berated but also given the opportunity for corruption and for that endemic internecine executive warfare which was the Italian equivalent of the 'institutional Darwinism' historians have discerned in Nazi Germany. It was, in other words, clear that Mussolini was always anxious to govern and to be seen to govern.

Yet, once Mussolini became Prime Minister in 1922 and then dictator in 1925, parallels with Hitler did come to the fore. Despite its bureaucratic aspects, much of Mussolini's governance was charismatic. Indeed, he had been singled out as a bearer of charisma before 1914. Why so? Did Mussolini natively exude leadership? Did he inscribe it on himself? Or, did others forge his character as a *Duce*? Did the charisma change over time? If it was fretted at times of troubles in 1921 and 1924 and then faded into nothingness during the disasters of the Second World War, how and why did these fluctuations happen? Was there another, more personal and 'human', Mussolini somewhere separate from the charismatic *Duce*? How, moreover, did charismatic governance work in Italy? Did it 'revolutionise' Italian society? (Quite a few culturalist historians of Fascism were assuring me that the Italian people had been made genuinely militant by Mussolini's rule, universally ready to march onwards as Fascist soldiers.) Were Italians to a man and a woman true believers in their *Duce*, I mused? Certainly every book published under the regime assured me that the revolution was real and that Italians had been drastically modernised through their good fortune in acquiring Mussolini to rule them. Did they, too, then work towards their *Duce*? Was Mussolini's Italy a replica of what Kershaw has shown happening in Nazi Germany?

A number of matters nourished my scepticism towards this straightforward interpretation of a Fascist 'revolution', led without restraint by a charismatic *Duce*. My first training was in the history of Liberal Italy and I knew enough about that society's rhetoric and practice, especially among the rising generation linked to the Nationalist Association (founded 1910), to be troubled when told of the originality of both Fascist foreign and colonial policies and of the accompanying looser discourse about the 'new Rome' and its *mare nostrum*. I found it hard to believe that Mussolini, at least in the international dealings of Fascism, had been especially 'original'.

Then there was the problem of Italy's special Second World War. In regard to that conflict, I had not been won over by the revisionist arguments of De Felice and some of his English-language admirers who wanted to counter the established conclusion that the Fascist war was a disaster. Rather, I retained the view that, under the 'test' of a second conflict, Mussolini's regime did worse than its Liberal predecessor had done. Liberal Italy was scarcely a place where state and society were reconciled, and yet, from 1915 to 1918, a tough war was fought to victory in a way that proved impossible after 1940, very much to Mussolini's discomfort, given his repeated raising of the parallel. This comparison was so telling that it made it hard to deny that Mussolini's talk about a genuinely 'totalitarian' state and its revolutionised people was, at least after 1940, bombast.

The attitudes and behaviour of Mussolini and the majority of his henchmen were striking in another regard. Even the briefest knowledge of Mussolini himself, of his cynicism, of the crassness of his Darwinist assumption that there was no such thing as society, of his misanthropy, of his half-fearful desire to be left alone, of his eternal scathing condemnation of all he saw around him, of his boasted 'savagery', demonstrated that he was no blindly true believer. Whatever else he was Mussolini was no Hitler impelled by a credo to act in one way and one way only. And what of his entourage? Was his son-in-law and, for quite a while, potential dauphin, Galeazzo Ciano, a Fascist fanatic, this man who trotted off to his golf course for his daily dose of gossip and good times? Ciano seemed more the typical bourgeois playboy (or, in better modern parlance, yuppy), whose adamantinely Fascist phrases were scarcely to be taken seriously. So what of the 'tough guys', Roberto Farinacci or Mussolini's enduring wife, Rachele, were they 'real' Fascists? Again yes and no seemed the only possible answer. Certainly, in some ways, the *Duce* was dependent on them, with their sullen desire that the social order be upturned. They (and Nicola Bombacci, the ex-communist and ex-anarchist who popped back into the *Duce's* life in 1943–45) half convinced Mussolini that, despite his schism from the socialist party in 1914, he had retained some contact with the 'real people'. The word 'half' is important here. Farinacci and Rachele balanced Ciano, the King and the rest of the elite, but their very uncouthness, their crassness, the palpable nature of their commitment to verbal violence (and their own version of corruption), ruled them out as presentable office-holders in the world of compromises and deals which Mussolini believed inevitably constituted 'politics'.

It was a significant inadequacy on their part. When Mussolini admitted, as he sometimes did, that he might not always understand economics, or be fully in touch with society, or altogether comprehend culture, he always maintained that he was the master of 'politics'. To achieve this subtle mastery, he had cast aside his own original earthiness, and outgrown the time of his life when he was just another Farinacci. Sometimes, of course, he acted directly and stubbornly of his own accord (he certainly persisted with the conquest of Ethiopia, for example, against most advice and, a decade earlier, he was equally stubborn in his pursuit of a high valuation of the *lira* on the international currency market). But, rather more frequently, he fudged and waited and 'planned' (always within an elastic time-frame) and watched events, seeking short-term, 'tactical', advantage. 'Totalitarian' seemed, and seems, an inadequate word to describe the nuances of such behaviour.

Similarly troubling was the De Felicean concept of a Fascism possessed of two opposing souls, the radical 'Fascism movement' and the conservative 'Fascism regime'. A Ciano may have been at heart just another European young conservative, a Farinacci may have wanted to burn down the palaces, but Mussolini's retention of a relationship with both indicates that his version of Fascism was not so much split between moderation and revolution as built from these two parts and dependent on them in spite of their evident contradiction. Mussolini, in his preference for tactics over strategy, in his partiality to be confined to mere 'politics', had opted not to choose between this or that 'ultimate' definition of Fascism (or of his own persona). The fundamental point about Mussolini and his regime is that it was, and had to be, both conservative and radical. The threat of the German alliance, present before 1939 but made overwhelming after October 1940, was precisely that it demanded a clear definition of Fascism, an overall strategy, not a set of tactics, an answer, not a gamut of policies. The Mussolinian model had contributed something to the Nazi rise to power, but, in office and as a neighbour, Nazism was too powerful, too demanding, at the same time too similar and too foreign. As an independent entity, Fascism could not withstand its comparison.

Here, then, were major doubts about some accounts of 'Mussolini's Italy'. But my final scepticism was drawn less from history than from my knowledge of Republican Italy, sprung either from the visits I have been lucky enough to make every year since 1967 or from my meeting with Italian immigrants in Australia. Especially from Australian Italians I heard often enough a residual admiration for Mussolini (an intriguing matter that, deserving of analysis), but I was also aware of a shifting and ambiguous world not far below the surface of any Australian Italy. Here 'Italies' were everywhere apparent, and not just the official nation embodied in those somewhat luckless officials sent by the Republic to represent it in the new world or by the local leaders of the 'Roman' Catholic Church. Here, too, was the family in all its power and contradiction.

These Italians of my acquaintance, who had survived the generation of dictatorship and war, were people who preserved difference; I could even sentimentalise them as human beings less impressed by cries for homogeneity, recurrent in 'One Australia', than were many of my fellow citizens. Were not the peoples of the Italies also like that under Fascism? Was not Mussolini, too, a man who incarnated his region and his family as much as he did his nation and ideology? I was willing, of course, to acknowledge that some processes of modernisation and homogenisation were occurring in interwar Italy. After all, they were happening everywhere else. But, I wondered, to what extent did the Italians who experienced Fascism seek to manipulate it to their own advantage, to conceive it in their own way? Were they really a people who had tried to 'work towards their *Duce*', I enquired again? De Felice and others had stated that there was a 'consensus' of some kind in Italy, at least until the fiasco of the invasion of Greece in October 1940. Did approval of Mussolini and his image mean that Italians tried to do his will even before they knew what it was, as Kershaw asserts happened with Hitler and Germany? Sometimes; perhaps. And yet, it seemed to me, more often Mussolini, the 'power holder', worked towards the Italians. Even while he railed against the feebleness of humankind (and by implication cursed his own weakness and back-sliding), he tried to be popular and accommodating. He was at one and the same time a charismatic Fascist dictator and a trimming and cynical politician, peering into the obscurity of the future to find an acceptable present, anxious not to be shown up as too much of a failure, hopeful of getting through another day.

None the less, of course he failed, in almost every sense of the word. The thought *tout comprendre, tout pardonner* is beguiling, but I remain an Anti-Fascist biographer. 'My' Mussolini is not to be celebrated as a Fascist, a dictator, a war-lord or a man. This revived Caesar deserves no historical Roman triumphs. He was cruel (but not the cruellest). He did not really modernise Italy (maybe that is not altogether a bad thing). His Fascism did not in any serious sense pave a third way to the future between liberal capitalism and state socialism. He may have adopted the word 'totalitarian', but his Italy scarcely moved to a single beat, or shook off ancient assumptions about the utility and ubiquity of patrons and clients and family. His belated efforts at autarchy, or economic nationalism, foundered for many reasons, but one was that tourist, emigrant and Catholic Italy could never altogether renounce cosmopolitanism. His empire in Africa was of the old-fashioned, ramshackle, costly variety, familiar from the nineteenth century, and very different from the racial imperium Hitler and his Nazis thought they were destined to construct in the East on the ashes of the USSR and European Jewry. Mussolini's own racism existed, but it was inconsistent, erratic, 'unscientific', never possessing the rigour which might have made him a good recruit for the SS.

In sum, to a considerable degree Mussolini did not even dictate, but, rather, was swept along by a destiny which began with ambition and hope in the provinces and continued with his being the 'first of his class' on the periphery, which took him thence to a blinding but brittle glory, and which ended in squalid and deserved death. Malaparte may have exaggerated, and denied his own complicity and that of his fellow intellectuals when he labelled Mussolini a 'great imbecile', but he was right to declare that, in many senses, Mussolini embodied Italian society after national (dis)unification in the Risorgimento. As a man and a Fascist 'thinker', Mussolini was adamant that he possessed absolute free will. But, in this contention, as in many other matters, he was wrong.

One caution – the first chapter of this book begins the story in January 1944 and proceeds from there to its (seeming) conclusion, the

Duce's death in April 1945. Readers who prefer their biographies to be sequential should go directly to Chapter 2. They should do so, however, with the knowledge that this biographer believes neither in absolute free will nor in absolute determinism. One of the more obvious faults of biography is the assumption, too easily made, that the character being described was always destined to finish where he or she did. Reality is, of course, different. And, in my early chapters, I shall pause from time to time to wonder, in virtual history mode, about a *Duce* as yet only partially made. Turning points where history may or may not turn exist in all our lives, and they certainly did in the flawed life of Benito Mussolini. He may have been dictator of Italy for a generation, but he alone did not craft his career (nor win much personal satisfaction from it).

1

The Furies and Benito Mussolini, 1944–1945

THERE are many books about the Fascist era with wonderful titles, but the best is *Quando il nonno fece fucilare papà* (When Grandpa had Daddy shot), an otherwise trifling memoir by Fabrizio Ciano.[1] The event he describes happened at 9.20 a.m. on the morning of 11 January 1944. An execution had been arranged just outside the gates of Verona, that city of northern Italy which for many centuries had controlled access to the Brenner pass and so stood at the crossroads of the German and Latin worlds. Five Fascist chiefs, found guilty of betraying the *Duce* or Great Leader of Fascist Italy, Benito Mussolini, were shot by a firing squad, composed of young Italians but stiffened by three SS observers.[2] Among the condemned, the most prominent was Galeazzo Ciano, Count of Cortellazzo,[3] son-in-law to the *Duce*. As a camera whirred to record the deaths for a gratified public, Ciano swivelled to face his executioners, more worthy in this last gesture than he had been in most of his life's actions. Six months earlier, on 24–25 July 1943, with Allied forces rapidly pushing back demoralised Fascist defences in Sicily and beginning to target the Italian mainland itself, Ciano and 18 other members of the Fascist Grand Council had voted against Mussolini's continuing as commander of the Italian war effort. It was for this 'treachery' that Ciano, Emilio De Bono, Luciano Gottardi, Giovanni Marinelli and Carlo Pareschi now paid the price. Their blood, it was said, was required as a sacrament for the new *Repubblica Sociale Italiana* (Italian Social Republic) which, since September 1943, had been established to provide some sort of Fascist governance for northern Italy. The matter, the *Duce* had admitted in a moment of frankness, was 'political', not judicial.[4]

Ciano had married Edda, eldest daughter of the dictator, in a lavish ceremony, on 24 April 1930. He was the son of Costanzo Ciano, then

Fascist Minister of Communications, a naval officer, war hero, nationalist, boss of Livorno, and man about town, whose speculations brought him and his family huge profits.[5] In the years after his marriage, Galeazzo Ciano became the most gilded young man of the Fascist regime, thought to be the *Duce*'s anointed successor, neophyte diplomat in China, then Minister for Popular Culture, then Minister of Foreign Affairs and, belatedly, from February 1943, Ambassador to the Holy See. Ciano was a yuppy of his time, as likely to be found at an elegant beach resort or at the bar of Rome's Acquasanta golf course, with its fairways running beside an aqueduct which had once brought water to the first Roman Empire, as at his work-desk. He had met Edda at Acquasanta.[6] Ciano was beloved by the *contessine*, the youthful female aristocrats of the Eternal City, and rumour spread that he bedded them with even greater frequency than that achieved by the *Duce* during his flagrant record of sexual conquests.[7]

Ciano sometimes donned the Fascist blackshirt and the threatening accoutrements of the fanatical *Disperata* squad (he had not actually belonged to it and his party membership had been back-dated).[8] He tried to orate with the best (though hampered by a piping voice).[9] On such occasions he declared himself the servant of, and true believer in, the 'Fascist revolution'. But Ciano also was the Fascist who, on 4 November 1939, having participated in the pompous patriotic ceremonial of Vittorio Veneto Day, the anniversary of Italy's victory in the First World War, repaired to the golf club. There he confided to Giuseppe Bottai, Alessandro Pavolini and Ettore Muti, his fellow Fascist chiefs, that he hoped profoundly that Britain and not Nazi Germany would win the war. Britain, he explained brightly, deserved victory because it stood for 'the hegemony of golf, whisky and comfort'.[10]

However disapproving of Ciano's levity he may have been, Bottai voted with him on 25 July; and by January 1944 was in hiding, awaiting the chance to enrol in the French Foreign Legion.[11] Muti was dead, shot in August 1943 by officials of the royal government as he tried to escape arrest.[12] Pavolini, by contrast, had backed Salò, as the RSI was widely called from the town beside Lago di Garda where some of its ministries were located. According to a sympathetic historian, the fundamental motive for his choice was his admiration for the *Duce*.[13] Certainly, by January 1944, Pavolini, from a class and cultural background in Florence comparable with Ciano's, had turned 'super-fascist'[14] and was loud in his demand that his erstwhile friend pay the ultimate penalty.[15]

One Mussolini, however, tried to oppose such vendettas. Ciano's marriage with Edda may have been 'open', and the couple may have allowed themselves to be raddled by gambling, drink and even cocaine,[16] but, during the crisis of 1943–44, she proved fiercely loyal to her man, the father of her two sons, the husband she still addressed affectionately as *Gallo* (Cock).[17] She stormed and threatened, berating her father for his lack of family sense, his cruelty and his weakness. To the daughter for whom he had always felt affection greater than for his other children, the *Duce* bowed his head, but did nothing to alter Ciano's fate. Another visitor noticed a man who looked 'tired and beaten down'; the *Duce* of Salò kept pressing his stomach against the pain he felt there and would run his finger around his collar as if he had trouble breathing.[18]

Edda did not get far when she tried hysterics on Rachele Guidi, her mother. Rachele had long despised Ciano, the over-privileged *signorino* who was so effete that he played golf.[19] Rachele, despite spending 20 years as the consort of the ruler of Italy, had cherished her image as a woman of the people. In that character, along with homeliness, thrift and commonsense, went her fidelity to her husband, who, she knew, had been betrayed in 1943. Amplifying her determination to be loyal were envy and rancour towards polite society, a brutal acceptance that death must have its day and a determination that traitors should meet their fate. The real 'tough guy' of the family, she let it be believed that she never cried.[20] And the Fascists, those who, like Pavolini, had, for whatever motive, swung behind the Salò Republic, agreed with Rachele. Goffredo Coppola, the rector of the University of Bologna, expressed their attitude when he wrote that the new regime must be cemented by blood and renounce the fondness for compromise indulged in by 'Rabbis, Free Masons and women'.[21]

No doubt the German allies and protectors of Salò applauded his sentiments. They had special reason to condemn Ciano since, from the spring of 1939, the then Foreign Minister had become sceptical about the Nazi world order and had only belatedly and reluctantly accepted Italy's entry into the war. The Nazis were adamant that Ciano, and those of his other associates who had fallen into the RSI's hands, be executed. They must die as a punishment for what they had done, but also in retribution for the humiliating and disgraceful failure of the Italian war effort so far. In other words, they must be liquidated because the Fascist regime, the system for which the word totalitarian had been invented, in which 'all would be for the state, nothing against the state, no one outside the state', had proved hollow and false. Although nobody said so openly (and the matter is not much remarked in current Italian historiography),[22] Ciano was being shot as a proxy for Benito Mussolini, failed totalitarian, failed Fascist dictator, failed leader of his nation, failed warrior for the Nazi–Fascist New Order.

In 1944 those who blamed Mussolini for the disasters all around did not talk about the sins and limitations of their dictator because the propaganda of the Salò Republic was already bent on constructing a fresh Mussolini for the new and terrible times. Even today, some historians[23] aver that, after September 1943, Mussolini courageously offered himself as a shield for Italians against the wrath of their German allies and the horror of the continuing war. The flesh and blood Mussolini, who lived uneasily at the Villa Feltrinelli at Gargnano, was a far less heroic figure. He was ill, tired and depressed. His family squabbled around him. His flabby and pretentious eldest son Vittorio, whom even his father labelled an 'idiot', was belatedly exhibiting an interest in high politics.[24] Vittorio was assisted by his cousin Vito.[25] A number of other more distant relations flocked to the region – one historian has tabulated 200 of them.[26] As an observer commented sardonically, Mussolini felt deep affection for his family, but preferred it when they did not invade his work space.[27] For all his disclaimers, however, Fascism in its death throes was demonstrating through the various Mussolinis and Guidis that the family was one institution which had not fallen victim to 'totalitarian' control.

Rachele, in her private soul, may have been wondering whether her Benito was any more a real man, but she bustled about, impressing visitors with her industry and domesticity. She told a bureaucrat that the problem with her husband was that he believed everybody he spoke to, whereas she believed nobody.[28] Whenever she got the chance, she also cursed her husband for his ongoing relationship with Claretta Petacci,[29] that airheaded and unlosable last mistress, who, after a brief experience of imprisonment in August–September 1943,[30] had taken up residence nearby at the mansion named the *Villa delle Orsoline* for the nuns who had once lived there. And then there was Edda, who came for a last visit on 26 December 1943. She had screamed that the war was lost, that they were all living in utter delusion, that they could not have Galeazzo sacrificed in such circumstances,[31] and then departed for Switzerland, never to see her father again, never again to exchange a civil word with him, indeed declaring herself proud to be the wife of 'a traitor and a thief'.[32] Only the youngest children, Romano and Anna Maria, a childhood victim of poliomyelitis and intellectually slow, were not a major irritation. The second son, Bruno, was dead, victim of a wartime air accident.[33] Bruno's widow, Gina Ruberti, completed the family circle in the Villa Feltrinelli and was favoured by the *Duce*, who perhaps rather admired her openly ridiculing any suggestions that the Axis could still win the war.[34]

In January 1944 Mussolini was trying to keep out of the sight of almost everybody. Most of all he hid from himself while, with profound cowardice, he knowingly let Ciano go to his death in his place. On the night before the execution the *Duce* deliberately and cravenly avoided the chance to exercise the mercy that his position permitted. He did not act because he was aware that the Nazi Germans and the fanatical Fascists were being for the moment satiated by the blood of others and even by that of his daughter's husband. Probably, too, he recognised that, once the sacrifice was made, they would forgive or ignore his own evident inadequacies. No doubt such motives made him the more anxious, after the event, to extract from a friendly visitor the full details of how his son-in-law and his erstwhile colleagues had died. Then, without damage to his own interest, he could piously state that they had not deserved their fate.[35] Still more pathetically, Mussolini tried to blame others for his own refusal to intervene, remarking mournfully that he had suffered a sleepless night on 10 January (he had spent New Year's Day in bed with a fever and stomach pain).[36] Only the malevolence of others had stopped all requests for a pardon from reaching his sympathetic ear.[37] Ciano's mother he regaled with a letter emphasising his own loneliness.[38] When Edda intimated that she was unconvinced by his account of his suffering, with monumental egoism he announced to any who would hear that 'it is my singular destiny to be betrayed by everyone, including my own daughter'.[39] Even in March 1945 he was still talking about the 'atrociously long' 'agony', which he had endured since Ciano went to his death.[40] In his self-obsession, Mussolini tried to block out the reality of the disaster which, for some time, had enveloped Fascism and Italy, and refused to see the Furies gathering about him.

Telling an interlocutor what he wanted to hear, as was his wont, Mussolini contended in the aftermath of the execution of his son-in-law that 'now that we have begun to make heads roll, we must let nothing stand in our way, but go on to the logical conclusion'.[41] And Italy's history from January 1944 to April 1945 was indeed a bitter one, a time when the northern segment of the peninsula was visited both by the passage of the front of the Second World War and by a complex of civil disputes and massacres. By contrast, the 'liberated' south, under the combination of the Allied Military Government and the administration loyal to the Savoy monarchy, experienced the gentler tyrannies of the nation's traditional class, gender and regional differences and the humiliating gap between Italian poverty and the strength of the Anglo-Saxon liberators.[42]

In present day Italy it has become common, at least in some circles, to preach the need to forgive and forget the sins of the Social Republic. At this time, we are assured, Italians,[43] including some prominent historians of the next generation,[44] chose to fight for Mussolini for reasons which deserve understanding and respect. During a 'civil war'[45] in which virtue was not monopolised by either side, many Italians believed that honour and a commitment to the nation were better expressed at Salò than with the invading liberal democrat Allies (and their communist friends).

Pacifying the past is all very well. No doubt it does us all good to confess our sins and to acknowledge our inevitable and manifold transgressions. And yet, it also deserves noting that the RSI was the puppet-ally of Nazi Germany, while that most horrific of modern states continued to exterminate the Jews of Europe and promised, were it somehow to conjure victory from what, by 1944, was looming defeat, to slaughter any ideological or racial enemies in its power. When his forces proved victorious in the Spanish Civil War, Franco, only half a fascist, massacred perhaps 100 000 of his subjects, left another 300 000 as permanent exiles, allowed others to starve and repressed liberty of any serious kind for a generation.[46] What might a Nazi victory in the compendium of second world wars have been like? Would not Mussolini, too, have been driven to a series of atrocious 'logical conclusions', whatever his 'actual' intentions might have been? When an ostensibly respectable intellectual like Giovanni Gentile can be found writing in January 1944 of the urgent requirement that Italy rediscover its soul in the *Duce* who had raised again the national flag, and adding a demand for the 'inexorable punishment' of Anti-Fascists,[47] his words cannot be separated from the context of a world engaged in visceral war. Neither can those of his colleague, Ardengo Soffici, who, despite his own notorious search for funds and status through two decades of Fascism,[48] now inveighed against the 'pustule' of corruption which had somehow grown on the body of Fascism and which must be excised fully and ruthlessly, removing 'the last drop of its corrupt blood'.[49] It has to be assumed that Gentile, Soffici and the other intellectuals who rallied to the RSI, were advocating, and knew that they were advocating, a terrible end for their political opponents. They may have believed that the outbreak of peace would as ever entail presently unspoken compromises, but in cleaving to such traditional cynicism they had not plumbed the nature of the Nazi ally to which they were now committed literally to the death.

No doubt, the number of fighting partisans was actually few until the spring of 1945, and, especially by then, their own motives were not always pure.[50] No doubt, the Resistance, too, included killers in its ranks. No doubt, the Anglo-American bombers were savage in their raids on Italian cities and Allied forces erratic in their civic dealings with liberated Italians. No doubt, good in the ultimate sense did not win in 1945. And yet the victory of the other side, including the victory of the restored Benito Mussolini, would have brought a dark age to Europe, the world and Italy.

In 1944–45 Mussolini scarcely contemplated such a prospect and the difficulties it might have entailed. After all, neither in 1940, nor even in 1935 when Italy attacked Ethiopia, had he set out war aims. As a puppet dictator, his first priority after the killing of his son-in-law and other ex-collegues was to survive. The territory under his purported control continued to shrink, in spite of the slowness of the Allied advance up the rugged Apennines. Naples had fallen on 1 October 1943, Rome followed on 4 June 1944, Florence on 11 August. At least as troubling was the problem of defining the independence left to the RSI by the Germans. The national borders of Italy were a prey to them, too. One recurrent issue was what it was that the Germans intended to do with Trieste and the Trentino, territories governed by the Habsburg empire before 1918 and, from September 1943, returned to 'temporary' German administration. It was all very well Mussolini pompously complaining to his officials about German failure to consult and demanding that Italians rule Italians.[51] In practice, Hitler, alone of the German leadership, favoured any serious resumption of Mussolini's authority in what was left of Fascist Italy. Goebbels, more logical about 'restoring' 'German' control over lands which 'they' had once ruled, instead urged the reclaiming of all Venetia for the *Reich*.[52] Before long the Nazi propaganda minister would jot into his diary what he and his colleagues had long believed: 'Fascism and the social-fascist republic are so impotent that it is fairly immaterial who occupies the various ministerial posts in Mussolini's cabinet'.[53] For the great majority of the Nazi leadership, Mussolini was rather more the puppet and less the dictator.

It was in this atmosphere of German contempt that, in April 1944, Mussolini travelled to the castle at Klessheim near Salzburg for another, the sixteenth, of his meetings with the *Führer*. Although Marshal Rodolfo Graziani, in charge of Salò's formal armies, found the *Duce* nervous and meandering, at the opening of discussions on 22 April Mussolini did argue that his labours were constructing a real government in Italy.[54] However unconvincingly, he was assertive about a series of other matters, including the need to improve the conditions of Italian POWs and work emigrants, from September 1943 kept as virtual slave labourers in Germany.[55] Similarly he wondered whether Hitler could elucidate real German intentions in Trieste and the other border lands. 'The strengthening of the Italian Republic', he urged beseechingly, was 'in the interest of Germany.'[56] With Hitler remaining unaccustomedly silent, Mussolini returned to what, as the war had proceeded, had become his strategic obsession. England, he declared, was the real enemy of the Axis. Could not the USSR be persuaded to accept its old borders and the entire fight redirected to the West?[57]

When he harped on about the idea of a compromise with Stalin, Mussolini was indicating the superficiality of his own commitment to the racist and anti-communist ideals of the Axis. At the same time, he was exhibiting his egregious misunderstanding of the fanaticism about these matters that gripped the minds of Hitler and the rest of the Nazi German leadership. In 1944 Germany was fighting its real war, the most fundamental of all the second world wars, in the East. For an Italian leader to hope wistfully, in the petty interests of his nation, that the Nazis could be detached from this campaign was a delusion of the most profound kind.

None the less, despite the low quality of Mussolini's performance, he did again win over the *Führer*, at least to a degree. Other Germans might comment to each other about Mussolini's feebleness as a negotiator and compare him unfavourably with Vichy Prime Minister, Pierre Laval.[58] However, after technical discussions of ways to stiffen Italian military resistance and some meandering comments from Hitler about the 'unnatural' nature of the Allied alliance and the continuing certainty of Axis victory, the German leader resuscitated his old admiration for the *Duce*. He had decided, he stated bluntly, to have no other contacts with Italy; 'once and for all', he would 'rely on' Mussolini.[59]

As a sign of his refurbished prestige, the *Duce* was allowed to visit a camp where Italian troops of the San Marco division were being trained with German help.[60] He was received enthusiastically and, briefly, his own morale may have risen. However, in what he called 'an almost Socratic dialogue' published immediately after his return to Italy, he was at best measured in his analysis of the likely future. War, he remarked, in hackneyed simile, 'is a great comparative exam for the peoples'. In it, a nation did not always have to win. 'It is possible to lose well; and it is as possible to win badly.'[61] Whenever he surveyed the front, Mussolini's optimism withered.

At Klessheim, Mussolini had insisted that Rome, 'the spiritual centre of Italy', would be defended to the uttermost.[62] By July, when Führer and Duce readied for one last meeting, the Eternal City had already fallen, an event which had prompted Mussolini pathetically to quiz a Fascist colleague about whether this meant that the people of Rome had already forgotten him.[63] Finding a cheering crowd in Italy in 1944 was difficult and so, en route by train to Hitler's headquarters in East Prussia, the Duce stopped off to address soldiers being trained by Nazi experts. He tried to encourage these youths (and himself) with a racism that may not have quite purist enough for any listening Nazi. 'Rome', he proclaimed, 'which, in thirty centuries of its history, has never seen Africans except when shackled to the chariots of its victorious consuls, now has its walls profaned by this uncivilised and bastard race'. 'The multi-coloured enemies' of Italy should realise that the final victory was not yet theirs and that the RSI's troops, like those whom Mussolini was now addressing, would be tough opponents, indeed.[64]

Whether or not he or his audience had their morale raised by these sentiments, with their unwelcome undercurrent of advice that 'America', that ancient paradise sought by generations of Italian emigrants, was now the real enemy, must remain a matter of speculation. At least his speech was better targeted than one by Graziani, who evoked the legions of Varus destroyed by Arminius in 9 CE, only to realise that he was talking about a war in which 'Germans' had exterminated 'Italians'.[65]

Train travel in Nazi Europe by the summer of 1944 was a precarious business and the transit of the delegation was repeatedly delayed by bombing raids and troubles on the line. The Italians were thus not too surprised to find that, just outside Rastenburg, the engine pulled into a siding and sat for an hour without any indication of what was happening. But when the train stuttered to its destination and Mussolini alighted, the Führer, who was wrapped in a blanket, extended his left arm and not his right in greeting.[66] Mussolini had arrived late for the attempt by Klaus von Stauffenberg and what was left of conservative Germany to assassinate Hitler (and pursue a diplomatic ambition to unite with the Western powers in a grandiose struggle against Slavic communism, that is, exactly the opposite of what had become Mussolini's desired war).

In the circumstances, serious conversation between the two battered dictators proved impossible, but the interpreters present depicted for posterity the scene in the room where the bomb had gone off, where, almost as though they were two old men reduced to waiting for Godot, Hitler perched on an upturned box and Mussolini on a rickety stool.[67] Hitler, unsurprisingly, was mainly interested in describing what had happened, in threatening terrible deaths for his failed assassins and in contending that his escape demonstrated that providence was saving him for final victory. Mussolini muttered banalities about his shock and sorrow, although he was secretly pleased to see the German leader taken down a peg. 'We're not alone when it comes to betrayals', he told a Fascist journalist on his return from East Prussia.[68] The two dictators did make a perfunctory effort for a last time to review the situation at the front. Hitler pressed that Florence, the city of *his* dreams,[69] be held. Mussolini asked again that some Italian troops pent up in Germany now be sent south. The distracted Hitler agreed at once.[70] With the *Führer*'s granting of this small concession, any attempt by the RSI to preserve a foreign policy ended,[71] although, back in Italy, Mussolini still found many reasons to squabble with German ambassador Rudolf Rahn.

Five months earlier Mussolini had been jaunty in one exchange with his German minder. On this occasion he took evident pleasure in telling Rahn what he did not want to hear. 'Many Italian industrialists', the *Duce* noted, awaited 'the Anglo-Saxons with open arms.' Many more, he added, had borne responsibility for the Italian abandonment of the German alliance on 8 September.[72] It was time, he implied, for such social forces to be checked and disciplined. It was time to make real the word 'social' in the Social Republic and to give the RSI a popular and 'revolutionary' base of a type invoked before 25 July 1943 but then too often frustrated.

These were the months in which there was much talk of 'socialisation', when Mussolini could happily invoke the Fascism of 1919 in which his programmes had contained radical plans to push society towards equality. Mussolini had, after all, grown to manhood as a socialist, and now, to some extent, he redeployed the vocabulary of his

youth,[73] blessing those of his colleagues who talke
Italy in some way to the Left.[74] As Bruno Spampanato
had been with Mussolini since the 1920s and who,
flirted with the idea of seeking ideological accomm
Fascism and Stalinism,[75] later argued: 'Socialisation
vised. It was rather done with the utmost seriousness, both legally and
practically.'[76]

By the time he was making this case, Spampanato was interested in
giving Fascism a legitimate history and in creating a political space for
postwar neo-Fascism. During the RSI Mussolini's own line on social
revolution wobbled, just as it had done in 1919–20. In any case, his
power and his independence from German control were too slight for
a genuinely radical policy to emerge. Instead, as often in his life,
Mussolini backed and hedged, seeking one day to appease one interlocutor, and the next day another. Thus, to some of his new elite, he
said that any plans for social change were secondary to the requirement that matters return to normality, with an end to violence, and the
nation's regaining its honour.[77] On other occasions he urged haste in
proceeding with socialisation, if only to spite the Germans who
disdained the anti-capitalist rhetoric involved.[78] In seeing contradiction to this promise of a mobilised and egalitarian society, he
instructed his officials not to require party membership from those
who headed financial operations in the Republic.[79] Perhaps the *Duce*'s
real sentiments about all these efforts to earn the RSI a 'place in
history' were best summarised in his bitter comment in August 1944:
'The extent of credulity which can be found in any man of whatever
class or intelligence is quite extraordinary.' In any contest, he went on,
'lies always win against the truth'.[80] No wonder that, shortly after, his
own fudging was apparent when he told an audience of Fascist loyalists that RSI socialisation incarnated a 'human, Italian and achievable'
version of socialism which would somehow eschew social levelling.[81]

Beneath its rhetoric and uniforms – Mussolini required the wearing
of these latter to prevent the spread of 'demo-social slovenliness'[82] –
the RSI lurched along the edge not so much of social revolution as of
anarchy. The question of its armed forces was never fully resolved,
with a party militia, the *Guardia Nazionale Repubblicana*, under
Renato Ricci, contesting the efforts of Graziani to create a 'national',
'unpolitical' armed force of a traditional kind.[83] Only in August 1944
was the GNR finally absorbed into the army.[84] Even then, other independent armed groups continued to flourish. Backed by party
secretary Pavolini, who was locked in personal dispute with Minister

Interior Guido Buffarini Guidi, *Brigate Nere* (Black Brigades) of volunteers grew in number in theoretical imitation of the 'squads' from the salad days of the Fascist rise to power. Just as then, they often embodied a local spirit and shored up the power of a local boss. Their recourse to violence was equally undisciplined and they could even threaten the overthrow of Mussolini himself. The most notorious semi-independent chief was Prince Junio Valerio Borghese, the commander of the so-called *X Mas* (an independent military force),[85] and a naval hero. Borghese did not hesitate to suggest that the *Duce*'s charisma lay buried in the past[86] (the men of Gargnano, he stated loudly, embodied only 'folklore'),[87] and to pursue a sort of independent foreign policy by seeking patrons among the Nazi leadership, whose intervention achieved his release from gaol after his arrest in January 1944. During the early months of 1945 Mussolini was still perturbed by the thought that Borghese might be tempted to mount a coup and sought to defuse his power by promoting him Chief of General Staff of the practically non-existent Salò Navy (and by keeping a secret tabulation of his many adulteries).[88] Similarly, the journalists of the RSI failed to find ideological unanimity, but instead wrangled and plotted against each other.[89] Mussolini's frankest remark about the problem of the armed forces, public order and press opinion in the Salò Republic came when he deplored the death of his long-term (and non-party) police chief, Arturo Bocchini, back in 1940 – 'it just isn't possible to govern without a Chief of Police', the *Duce* murmured sadly.[90]

Meanwhile Italians endured the terror being visited upon them by the Germans and by themselves. In March 1944 a partisan bomb in the via Rasella in Rome, exploded near the palace where Mussolini had once lived, killing more than 30 German soldiers. In retaliation, in the Ardeatine Caves near the Via Appia, the Germans massacred 335 men (including 77 Jews) whom they had summarily rounded up. In June the Hermann Goering division, again reacting to partisan attack, slaughtered more than 200 as it retreated up the Val di Chiana in Tuscany.[91] In September the *paese* of Marzabotto, on the outskirts of Bologna, was similarly visited by condign punishment. In the cities, too, the Germans indulged in terror tactics. In Milan, the public display of bodies at the Piazzale Loreto brought protest from Mussolini who, to Rahn, deplored the damage such acts did to popular morale.[92] In the border territories of Trieste and the Alto Adige, Italy's 'national' prizes from the First World War, present German administration gave every promise of wanting to convert into German rule should a Nazi peace ever be imposed on the region (SS chief, Odilo

Globocnik, transferred from a bestial career exterminating Jews, incarnated at Trieste this potential future).

Throughout his life, and certainly since he had become a Fascist, Mussolini had sown the wind of violence; now he and his subjects reaped the whirlwind. There were plenty of Fascist fanatics who killed with the same will as the Germans (just as there were plenty of non-believers who sought to wait out the catastrophe afflicting Italy). The failings of the Salò government had a more humdrum side. By 1944, food supplies were thin, inflation was rampant and the new government proved as inadequate as the old in imposing any just or credible rationing scheme.[93] Averting his eyes from the catastrophe imploding around him, Mussolini concentrated on self-justification – in June–July publishing in the Milan paper, Il Corriere della Sera, a highly tendentious account of his fall in July 1943.[94] If he could write the history, it might be the more likely to salve his reputation.

At the end of 1944, however, Mussolini did attempt one last mass meeting in which his oratory could amaze and enthuse his people, as once it could be relied on to do. Leaving the greyness of the lakes behind, he came back into Milan and spoke at the Teatro Lirico. He talked about the betrayal by King Victor Emmanuel III and his Prime Minister, Marshal Pietro Badoglio, and the divisive effect of the events of July–September 1943 on the Italian people, whose better elements had nevertheless recognised the need to go on fighting shoulder to shoulder with the German and Japanese allies. The war, he declared, was not yet lost; the pact between plutocracy and Bolshevism must rupture soon. He wanted to revive the spirit of Fascism's early days and was serious about socialisation although he was careful to add an evocation of the golden years of the regime which, he claimed, spanned from 1927 to 1935. He summoned Mazzini again to be the prophet of the times. The new order would favour a united Europe in which Italians 'could feel themselves to be Italian because they were Europeans and Europeans because they were Italian'. It was this amalgam which ensured that they would be steadfast in resisting socialist internationalism and Judaeo-Masonic cosmopolitanism, the 'monstrous' medley of their enemies.[95] Whatever the frustrations of the past the RSI would seek out a 'third way'.

Both the Duce and the audience allowed themselves to be lost in these words and the pleasing re-evocation of a happier time when war could be spoken about but not actually waged. But it did not take long for gloom to return. Mussolini had tried to be a hard-working executive and, in friendly eyes, seemed a competent administrator, 'scrupulous, diligent, attentive' to his advisers.[96] Similarly, on occasion, he could still praise the skill and devotion of the good bureaucrat, so indispensable to any administration.[97] But at his desk, too, his magic was lost – even a friendly observer thought he looked like a provincial lawyer or doctor in the dowdy surrounds of his office at Gargnano, cut off from the splendour of the *Sala del Mappamondo*, his spectacular office in Rome's Palazzo Venezia from 1929 to 1943.[98] He protested that he was bored with what was left of his job (and was, without doubt, bored with himself).[99] The unreality of his position was exemplified in bizarre attempts belatedly to frame a new constitution. Mussolini made a pretence of being interested in the question whether a *Duce* should serve for a maximum of two 7-year or two 5-year terms.[100] Can he have day-dreamed about his own reputation, had he given up his rule in 1936, when Italian troops triumphantly entered Addis Ababa?

Half aware that this was the moment to review his own life, he still gave the occasional interview, speaking warmly one last time about the profession of journalism and recalling that 'to create a newspaper is to know the joy which comes with motherhood'.[101] There were other moments of philosophising. He had always preferred cats to dogs, he said, perhaps thinking of Hitler, Blondi and his 'dog years'.[102] He had made mistakes, the *Duce* confessed, but only when he had obeyed reason rather than being guided by his instinct.[103] Now he had become a prisoner, a toy with which destiny played. But he did not fear death; rather it would arrive as a friend.[104] He believed little or not at all in the creed of Fascism, but only in the goodness of the Italian people,[105] or so he maintained to an intrepid foreign interviewer. To an Italian, by contrast, he urged that Fascism would still be recognised as **the** idea of the twentieth century. In the end history would prove him right.[106] He had only entered the war, he now suggested, to restrain the Germans, and he had early known that the USA was destined to emerge as top nation.[107] At times, too, he claimed that he had always been a socialist at heart, merely one who had adapted socialist thought to reality and so invented the Corporate State.[108] He took pains to deny yet one more time that he had himself been responsible for the murder in 1924 of the socialist deputy Giacomo Matteotti.[109] His work had been beset by 'an ulcer which would have laid low an ox', but his worst fate was the loss of his brother Arnaldo, 'an Italian of the old stamp, incorruptible, intelligent, serene, human', his lightening rod to the people. Towards other figures he had met in his long career, he had rarely found reason for respect. Egoism, after all, was 'the sovereign law'. Men belonged to the animal kingdom. They scratched and killed and deluded themselves when they spoke of their souls.

Ever more sententious and embittered, Mussolini was moving to his end in a way which might be regarded as the quintessence of banality, but for the terror and the slaughter being visited on the peoples of Italy and Europe during those last days of a war which he had done much to unleash. Finding the most predictable of parallels, if one peculiarly lacking in appropriateness, on 15 April Mussolini told an old admirer 'I am crucified by my destiny. It is coming'.[110] The next day, the *Duce* explained to a last meeting of his ruling Council that he would move to Milan, but only briefly, before proceeding to the Valtellina in which Pavolini and his *Brigate nere* were assembling.[111] He would, he added without conviction, 'go to the people' one last time.[112] On 18 April, without consulting his Nazi allies, who were annoyed at the prospect,[113] he left for his final visit to Milan (though, given the coming fate of his corpse, perhaps his journey might be more accurately labelled his penultimate trip there). In Milan, for want of a more fitting setting, he took up residence in the prefecture, where a certain pretence of government survived. By now insomnia had taken deep hold over him. As had been true on other occasions in his life, Mussolini was a prey to nerves and, apathetic about his surrounds, could scarcely eat.[114] Even though he might still state mechanically that the war was a 'great drama', which might not have five, but rather six, seven or eight acts,[115] he had long accepted that all was lost. In that conviction, he began the last week of his life, reduced to the role of a political sleep-walker.

Since September 1943 he had talked from time to time of the heroic last stand which his regime would make should the war go against Nazi-fascism. In February 1945 he had wondered whether Trieste, with its ancient reputation as the prize of Italian nationalism during the First World War, the last citadel of *italianità* (Italianness) against a sea of Slavs (and Germans), ought to be this place of ultimate resistance. But the Nazi Germans, who were very inclined to think that Trieste had come home to the *Reich*, forbade it.[116] And so, instead, the choice fell on the Valtellina, an alpine valley bordering that Switzerland to which the youthful Mussolini had twice emigrated, and near enough to Milan, though otherwise lacking a national past of any fame. As Mussolini told Graziani, another guaranteed to like what he heard, 'Fascism must die heroically.'[117]

Actually, plans for a serious military effort in the Valtellina did not exist[118] and the *Duce* had no will to fashion a grandiose conclusion to his life. As Spampanato commented: 'There's talk about resistance but how and where I do not understand.'[119] Mussolini did not stem the confusion. Rather, on 24 April, he admitted with some relief: 'there are no orders; I can't give orders any more'. There was a time in the tides of men, he pronounced, when you could only be a spectator. His friends must focus on remembering what they had done and not repine about what was to come.[120] Hearing this, Spampanato, at least according to his own account, stooped and kissed his leader's hand.[121]

Such moments of formal piety were fleeting. Once again, Mussolini did not forego the chance to blame others. The Germans, he told any who would listen, had betrayed him as they had done so often before,[122] the implication being that somehow he had not wanted the Nazi-Fascist alliance and the war. Or perhaps the responsibility lay with both the Germans and the Italian people? All had played him false.[123]

Meanwhile, Mussolini tried to make contact with the Anti-Fascist resistance, being especially ready to talk with representatives of the socialist party to which he had belonged before the First World War. The hope of one last deal in which he could out-haggle his rivals subsided with difficulty in this politician's mind. A meeting was arranged for 3 p.m. on the afternoon of 25 April, to be held at the palace of Ildefonso Schuster, the Cardinal-Archbishop of Milan.[124] Schuster, a patriot and anti-communist, had been prominent among the Catholic hierarchy in his endorsement of Mussolini's regime. Its boy scout organisation, the *Balilla*, he had hailed as providing 'a healthy, Christian and Italian education'.[125] The March on Rome, he had argued, saved the nation from Bolshevism, paving the way for the Lateran Pacts, the agreement signed in 1929 between Church and state.[126] Fascism's imperial war, he had celebrated, as the opportunity to 'open the gates of Ethiopia to the Catholic Faith and to Roman civilization'.[127] As late as 1937 Schuster had blessed an assembly of the *Scuola di Mistica Fascista Sandro Mussolini* (Sandro Mussolini School of Fascist Mysticism), pompously named after the son of the Catholic Arnaldo.[128] Only the regime's drift by 1938 into overt racism had prompted Schuster to doubt the superiority of Fascism over other ideologies in the sinful modern world.[129] Hoping with reason in a comforting reception, Mussolini reached the episcopal palace on time. However, the Resistance chiefs were delayed. Cardinal and *Duce* had an hour to chat.

Schuster left behind a wonderfully telling account of Mussolini's last dealing with a member of the hierarchy of the Catholic and Roman

Church.[130] He recalled welcoming the *Duce* with thanks for his 'sacrifice' and his willingness to spend 'a life of expiation in prison abroad in order to save the rest of Italy from final ruin', words which may actually have deepened Mussolini's gloom.[131] The Church, Schuster added, would never forget the service which the *Duce* had done for it in the Lateran pacts. What a shame that Mussolini had himself been served so badly by some of his party chiefs (the Cardinal was an old foe of the radical Fascist, Roberto Farinacci,[132] and had warned Arnaldo about his impiety in 1931).[133] After this scattering of initial comments, the Cardinal noticed that his visitor was depressed and saying little. As a charitable churchman might, he therefore offered Mussolini a small glass of *rosolio* and a sweet biscuit. The conversation still limping, Schuster then asked whether the *Duce* had caught up with his own most recent publication, a life of St Benedict. Mussolini had to confess that he had not read this estimable work. All attention, Schuster then pressed what he said was his very last copy on the *Duce*, insisting that the book would help him understand that 'your calvary amounts to an expiation of your sins before the ever just and merciful God'. In what Schuster discerned as gratitude, Mussolini, again at a loss for words, clutched the cardinal's hands.[134]

The topic of St Benedict allowed the conversation to drift to the sad fate of Montecassino and the abbey where the saint had met the Lombard king, Totila. Each man knew that in 1944 the celebrated Benedictine monument had been reduced to rubble by the invading Anglo-Americans (Schuster had never held back from his denunciations of Allied bombing).[135] With both men warmed a little by this mutual sense of the vice of others, Schuster, ever more palpably in quest of the salvation of Mussolini's immortal soul, raised the story that a priest on the island of Ponza, where the *Duce* had been briefly confined in August 1943, had got some way in 'reviving' Mussolini's religious sense. Mussolini, still uneasy at the Cardinal's rapid fire of conversational gambits and his attempts to plumb his innermost thoughts, replied cautiously that he 'meditated to a degree' on a *Life of Christ* then presented to him. Schuster did not pursue the matter too far, but, again being meaningfully tangential, took his chance to remind the falling dictator of the story that Napoleon on St Helena had found God.[136]

If only to escape from the insistent probing of the state of his soul and the frightening assumptions about his coming fate as a prisoner and exile, Mussolini now stated that, the next day, he would dissolve the armed forces of the RSI and retreat with 3000 men to the Valtellina for a brief last fight. Then he would surrender. Schuster interrupted this account with the shrewd comment that Mussolini would only get 300 to go with him and the *Duce* sadly acknowledged that the assessment was probably true. Aware that he had scored another hit on Mussolini's sagging self-confidence, Schuster turned the discussion back to religious affairs, quizzing his visitor about the Ambrosian rite and later declaring himself astonished to discover that anyone in charge of the destinies of the Italian Church did not have the details of this basic matter at his finger tips. Aware that his attitude was prompting another embarrassment between them, Schuster found safer ground by stating his view that Eastern Orthodoxy should never be confused with 'the real Church of Christ', the Catholic one.[137]

The beginning of a discussion which might have held promise of an agreement between two old men about the sins of Slavs and communists was interrupted by the arrival at last of the Resistance negotiators. In their presence, Schuster discreetly fell silent, but not without hearing Mussolini say that he only believed in ancient history, since the modern version was too skewed by 'passion'. He also remembered the *Duce* complaining that the 'Germans have always treated us like slaves and in the end they have betrayed us.' When the meeting came to a close and Mussolini made ready to leave, the Cardinal did not forget to hand him again that last copy of the *Storia di San Benedetto*, lest the *Duce* in his haste and confusion overlook the precious gift.[138]

Whatever he had thought of the Cardinal-Archbishop's attempts to capture and save his soul, Mussolini now changed direction yet again. With the spokesmen of Anti-Fascism he scarcely negotiated at all, harping instead on German misdeeds. The news had come through that German SS General Karl Wolff had agreed to end hostilities with the Allied forces at 5 p.m. With this prospect so imminent, the discussions broke down, although Mussolini promised the Resistance representatives that he would give them further news within an hour. However, once back at the prefecture, he prepared instead to flee with his immediate entourage to Como, nearer the Swiss border. It was a *sauve qui peut* which bore some comparison with the disgraceful actions of the royal government after 8 September 1943, when Victor Emmanuel III and Badoglio had abandoned Rome and the Italian people to the mercy of the invading Nazi Germans and of those Fascists who chose to go with the RSI.

During the 36 hours in Como the tattered authority of the Salò Republic crumbled into nothingness. At this moment of final crisis,

Mussolini and his advisers could not make up their minds whether to head for the Valtellina or seek the mercy of the Swiss. Before dawn on the morning of 27 April they proceeded up the western side of Lake Como but not heading either towards the boasted Fascist redoubt or for the border. Rachele and the younger children were abandoned at Como. Mussolini sent his wife one last, pathetic, letter, beseeching 'your forgiveness for all the ill I have involuntarily done you. You know that you have been for me the only woman whom I have really loved. I swear it before God and our Bruno at this supreme moment'.[139]

Despite the protestations of enduring love for Rachele, among the convoy were Claretta Petacci and her scapegrace brother, Marcello (poorly disguised as the Spanish consul and his wife).[140] A number of other leading *repubblichino* Fascists, including Pavolini, left Como with them. Present, too, was Nicola Bombacci, a constant associate of the *Duce* in the last days. They had first met in 1910 when Bombacci was a socialist journalist at Cesena, a town in the Romagna just down the railway from Forlì, where Mussolini was then employed. Bombacci had opposed the First World War and, in January 1921, joined the infant Italian Communist Party. But he gradually reconciled himself with the Fascist dictatorship, rallying to the nation over Ethiopia and also enjoying state subsidies for his journalism.[141] After September 1943 he gained a place in Mussolini's entourage and was regularly present at the Villa Feltrinelli. He earned a public presence, too, through his insistence that the new form of Fascism was genuine in its commitment to a version of socialisation.[142] In this time of trouble he almost became a friend for the *Duce*,[143] who had long insisted that he did not, and could not, need friendship. Bombacci's presence at what was to be the very end hinted at the survival of a Mussolini whose roots in the social conflicts and hatreds of the Romagna had never been entirely destroyed.

In the convoy, however, lay another symbolism, one that was less easy to explain away by post-1945 nostalgics. The column of Fascist cars was reinforced by retreating Nazi soldiers, crammed into two armoured trucks and led by Luftwaffe lieutenant Schallmayer, hoping to pass through to the Germanic world by one path or another. The better to conceal himself, Mussolini decided to travel alone with these sometime allies. He donned one of their greatcoats, was given a German helmet to conceal his renowned features, and, in the cabin of the truck, wrapped himself in a blanket against the spring chill. Throughout the countryside between Lago di Como and Switzerland, partisans were active. On the evening of 26 April, in pouring rain, the

52nd Garibaldi brigade had blocked the lakeside road just north of the ironically named *paese* of Musso and south of the slightly larger Dongo. At Puncett, where the hill fell steeply to the lake, the partisans had rolled a great tree trunk, rocks and other debris across the track and waited to see who would try to pass.[144] Eighteen months earlier, when first establishing himself at Gargnano, Mussolini had remarked sourly: 'Lakes are a compromise between a river and a sea, and I don't like compromises'.[145] He had read the omens right. He was destined to die by a lake.

At 6.30 a.m. the next morning, news spread among the partisans that an enemy column was approaching. After a brief exchange of fire in which a stray Nazi bullet killed a marble worker innocently at his labours in the area above the road, the Germans asked to talk.[146] Schallmayer at first tried to tough it out, but the partisans had sent for reinforcements and were soon aware that Bombacci, Goffredo Coppola, Mezzasoma and Ruggero Romano had sought what proved to be unavailing sanctuary with the priest at Musso. By the early afternoon, when Schallmayer accepted the condition that any Italians must be surrendered, the partisans had spotted Francesco Barracu, a fanatical RSI Under-Secretary, and suspected that other Fascists were present in this convoy, too.[147]

At 3 in the afternoon, the column started to move off, slowly, since, to be permitted passage, each member had to present his documents. It was then that a Giuseppe Negri called the partisan leader, Urbano Lazzaro, over, saying with an automatic recourse to local dialect which mocked Fascist efforts to homogenise the nation: '*Gh'è che el crapun!*' (We've got Big-Head). He drew Lazzaro's at first incredulous attention to a figure slumped in the darkness of the back of the truck. The Germans tried to insist that the man was one of them, lying down because he was drunk. But when Lazzaro pulled back the blanket, he knew with whom he was dealing. '*Camerata*', he began (using the Fascist term for comrade), 'Excellency', '*Cavalier* Benito Mussolini'. Only at the last title did a response come. Now Lazzaro snatched off the helmet and the *Duce* was indeed disclosed.[148] 'His face was like wax and his stare glassy, but somehow blind. I read there utter exhaustion, but not fear', Lazzaro later remembered. 'Mussolini seemed completely lacking in will, spiritually dead.'[149] After being disarmed – he had been carrying a machine gun and a pistol which he made no attempt to use – Mussolini was formally arrested and taken to the townhall of Dongo. He spent the following night, his last, in the Dongo barracks. The final visitation of the Furies to his life was to be more prosaic than the various dramatic renditions of the charismatic *Duce* had foretold.

Other prisoners were also being brought to Dongo: the non-Spanish-speaking Petaccis had been unable to preserve their claim to diplomatic immunity. Pavolini had tried to flee, but was dragged in, wounded by shrapnel and terrified at his imminent fate.[150] That evening in Milan, Sandro Pertini, leading member of the Committee of National Liberation (*Comitato di Liberazione Nazionale*; CLN) and eventually president of the Italian republic from 1978 to 1985, broadcast the news that the *Duce* had been captured. Pertini made no attempt to hide his view, shared by his comrades on the CLN, that Mussolini should be shot 'like a mad-dog'.[151]

A rather tasteless controversy hangs over this final twenty-four hours of Mussolini's life. One of the issues is the fate of a leather bag of documents which Mussolini was carrying when he was stopped by the 52nd Garibaldinians (no one seems to have asked whether they included a thumbed copy of the *Life of St Benedict* by I. Schuster). There have been charges and counter-charges about the contents of government papers apparently treasured to the last by the *Duce*. Some have claimed that they contained letters which compromised Churchill and others who wanted no post-war association with Fascism.[152] Except for those who love conspiracy theories, with or without the support of evidence, the speculation has seemed pointless indeed.[153] Others have disputed the exact timing and nature of the events of 27–28 April. The official story was that Mussolini and Petacci were shot on the afternoon of 28 April at 1610 hours beside the Via XXIV Maggio (ironically named for the day in 1915 when Italy had opted to enter the First World War), and just outside the hamlet of San Guilino di Mezzegra. The lovers had been re-united that morning at a nearby peasant house used by the partisans. Shortly after, some communists arrived with orders from Milan to carry out summary justice on the *Duce*. At first Mussolini thought that Walter Audisio, the leader of the execution squad, had come to liberate him and Petacci, who had trouble clambering into Audisio's humble Fiat 1100, hampered as she was by black kid leather shoes with very high heels. But, when the *Duce* was unloaded before the gates of the Villa Belmonte, the actual execution site, he 'obeyed orders docile like a lamb'.[154] When the guns misfired at the first attempt, Mussolini, so Audisio alleged, shook with fear, 'that animal fear which you exhibit before the ineluctable'.[155] Finally, the *Duce* fell, riddled with bullets.

There are several alternative versions. Some say the two were actually shot earlier, probably before noon, and in different circumstances. They were already corpses when hit by bullets at Mezzegra in a staged joint execution. The neo-fascist politician and journalist Giorgio Pisanò has been especially insistent that the two died separately, and that the communists and their partisan friends plotted a mystification of the real story in what he regards as a typically nefarious communist way.[156] The romantic theory has been propounded that Mussolini sprang to the defence of Claretta, about to be abused by her captors, and, a good cavalier at the last, he was shot in the resultant struggle.[157] In this version, she was killed later, unplanned and because there was no alternative. The chief problems with this account are that it lacks any direct substantiation and its most convinced advocates have every reason to wish Mussolini a heroic death.

It is worth underlining the fact that Mussolini's death was not the only one then to trouble Italy. At Dongo the partisans had just shot 15 of those taken at Puncett or its surrounds, including Pavolini, Bombacci and Zerbino (the RSI's last Minister of the Interior). When the corpses were moved to Milan and put on public display they were joined by the bodies of another eight comrades, among whom was Achille Starace, the Fascist party secretary through the 1930s. A less formal reckoning with the two decades of tyranny and five years of world war had begun before the conflict's end and continued for months afterwards, exacting a death toll estimated as approaching 12 000.[158] The war itself, so blithely entered by Mussolini in June 1940, even if it was with the approval of elite opinion, had cost Italy more than 400 000 lives to which should be added those whom the Italians had killed and maimed, during that conflict and in their imperial campaigns in Libya and Ethiopia and in the Spanish Civil War. A still more important context is provided by that complex of vicious battles known to history as the Second World War, the event understood by history through the terrible signifiers of 'Auschwitz' and, after August 1945, 'Hiroshima', terms which express humankind's fall into an all but ultimate abyss.

Aware of such matters, this historian does not regret the death of Benito Mussolini, or want to glamorise the circumstances surrounding it (or exaggerate his uniqueness). All the evidence is that, psychologically, morally and politically, the dictator was dead well before his life was terminated by those final shots. And yet one part of the macabre scene does deserve reflection. Mussolini's demise, both at Mezzegra and in those events which would occur at Milan and which are narrated later in this book, had much that was 'normal' and 'traditional' about it. The failed dictator, fleeing who knows where, had been caught like a rat by his people and by them killed in retribution for his crimes and inadequacies. How different was this from the fate of Hitler, committing suicide amid bombs and fire in his bunker, hidden away beneath the city of Berlin and separate from the terrible sufferings of the city's peoples and the endless travails of those who were conquering it. Different, too, was the death of Stalin, expiring after a stroke in his *dacha*, an object of terror beyond his death both to his people and to his henchmen. These last assembled nervously around his death-bed, trying to make up their minds whether their boss was really dead and whether it was safer to acknowledge the fact sooner or later. The final act of the lives of Hitler and Stalin is enmeshed with the horror of a modernity gone to ruin (and with their coming historical status as Great, if Evil, Men).

Not so the death of Benito Mussolini. Yet, Fascism, too, shed an excess of blood. In its rise to power, during the solidification of the Fascist regime, through its frequently retrograde domestic policies, in Libya and Ethiopia, in its meddling in the Spanish Civil War, and then in its own special Second World War, Mussolini's Italian dictatorship must have sent early to the grave at least a million people, and probably more. It is a cruel record and it ensures that this biography is self-consciously Anti-Fascist in its intent. No doubt I must also admit that, in the catalogue of the crimes, follies and tragedies of humankind which was so expanded during the history of the twentieth century, Mussolini occupies a relatively banal place and was no more than the least of the tyrant-killers who so scarred interwar Europe. He was the one who well reflected his nation, class and gender, although both Hitler and Stalin can also be effectively approached through 'structuralism' rather than 'intentionalism', to use the ugly jargon of historiography. Very likely, the free will of Stalin and Hitler was often as cribbed, cabined and confined as was Mussolini's by the societies in which they operated. But my task is to write the biography of the *Duce* and not of his more notorious contemporary dictators. I must therefore tell the tale from the beginning, from the relatively, but not too humble, birth of an infant in an Italy which itself had only existed for a generation, and ask how remarkable was the boy, Benito Mussolini?

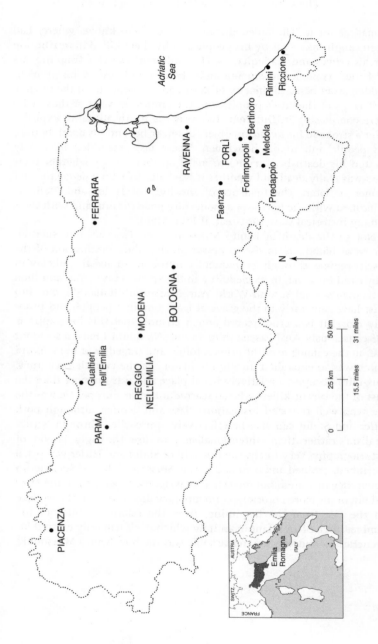

Map 1 The Emilia-Romagna

2

First of his class? The Mussolinis and the young Benito, 1883–1902

O{N Sunday 29 July 1883 at 2 o'clock in the afternoon a son was born to Alessandro Mussolini and Rosa Maltoni. The happy event occurred at the hamlet of Dovia, a scattering of houses lying below the little administrative centre of Predappio, perched on the foothills of the Romagnole Apennines and commanding a back road which ran from the provincial capital, Forlì, to Tuscany.[1] With the northern Italian summer reaching its height, local peasants were no doubt preoccupied with the prospect of the coming harvest, but one Hungarian enthusiast later maintained that, as if to signify the nativity and the national grandeur which it portended, at the hour of the infant's birth a thunder-bolt struck the double-headed eagle of the Habsburgs at the Schönbrunn palace in Vienna and sent it tumbling to the ground.[2] On 30 July the infant was christened Benito Amilcare Andrea Mussolini at the romanesque local church of San Cassiano. A tourist today can find the church (much 'restored' in the Fascist era) and buy a postcard of the baptismal font whose holy waters once anointed the future *Duce*.

Although, as the youthful Mussolini would often tell himself with a characteristic amalgam of anger and ambition, Dovia was not Predappio, and Predappio was not Forlì, and Forlì was not Bologna, and Bologna was not Milan or Rome, and neither of those great Italian cities was Paris, long the metropolis of his dreams, the Mussolinis had a certain presence in their immediate surrounds. They may not have been *signori*, but they should not be confused with, and would not have wanted to be confused with, the lowest stratum of society. The author of one of the numerous hagiographies produced under the eventual Fascist dictatorship struggled to show that the Mussolinis were of noble origin – allegedly, a certain 'Malsomini' had moved from Bologna to Venice in 996; thereafter his family rose socially, undertaking a succession of useful community roles notably in medicine, providing at least one saintly priest and always displaying 'moral and civic elevation', or so the zealous and deferential researcher into Mussolini family history contended.[3] Marriage into the patrician class eventually permitted family usage of the title of count. But, some time in the 1560s, the noble Mussolinis left Venice to return to their origins in the Romagna. Then came a gap, although an English admirer of the *Duce* added the claim that a Mussolini had achieved 'some reputation' as a composer in eighteenth century London,[4] and an Italian expert brought forward what he said was irrefutable proof that the Mussolinis were of genuine Roman descent. Other friends or enemies of the dictator would from time to time aver that he was 'really' Serb, or Macedonian Turk, or Argentinian, or even a Polish Jew.[5]

When, in the late 1920s, the dictator was informed of the more pious research into his ancestry, he was publicly scornful of it, discouraging its practitioners from extending their studies into the more recent past. In a modernising world, a noble inheritance was too much for a *Duce* to bear. Modesty may none the less have had its limits. In July 1943 Egidio Ortona, a young diplomat, visiting the *Rocca delle Caminate*, the restored castle above Predappio which a grateful public had donated to the Mussolini family, noted a genealogy prominently displayed on a wall.[6] Ortona does not specify the detail of this list of family descent and perhaps it only recorded the more historically established fact that the Mussolinis sprang from a family of peasant smallholders who, during the seventeenth and eighteenth centuries, earned their living in the high hill country of the border territory between the Vatican-administered Romagna and independent Tuscany. They generally seem to have worked land holdings, owned by more distinguished locals such as the noble Calboli family. Among them were a Francesco and a Jacobus Antonius Mussolini.[7] By the nineteenth century the family had been forced down nearer to the Po river plain, certainly by the requirement to find paid work and perhaps by the cultural appeal of such growing urban centres as Bologna and Forlì. The first Mussolini to have a serious historical presence was Benito's grandfather, Luigi. Locals remembered him as something of a character, a man who would strut around the town piazza wearing the uniform of the National Guard, which he had first

donned during the political disturbances of 1847–49. He was given to
bragging that he had served a term in the gaols of the Pope-King, Pius
IX, a regrettable fate for one who had for a time received education in
a seminary.[8] In more humdrum matters, Luigi Mussolini was a failure,
however, having been driven by economic need to sell his land to his
brother, Pietro, and being obliged thereafter to sustain himself as a
hired hand.[9] Luigi did not die until January 1908, by which time he
was a decrepit figure in his *paese*. To a degree, therefore, the
Mussolinis were of declining social status, and the personalities of
both Alessandro and Benito owed something to their compelling
desire to restore respect and fortune to their family.

'Benito Amilcare Andrea' – a grovelling biographer would later
state that the *Duce* could dispense with his surname since, plainly, he
was '*ben ito* [well sent] to the Empyrean of Glory, his figure shining
with refulgent light among the stars of the first grandeur',[10] but actually the infant's names were telling in another sense. The family
traditions of the Italian peasantry might have suggested that the child
be called Luigi after his grandfather, but instead the name Benito was
chosen in order to honour Benito Juarez, a Mexican revolutionary
who had ousted and executed the Habsburg Emperor Maximilian. In
the enmity thus declared for the 'German' dynasty, driven out during
the Risorgimento but still installed in Trieste and the Trentino, lay a
hint of patriotism, but Alessandro insisted on adding two other
names, each invoking a prominent local 'socialist': Amilcare for
Amilcare Cipriani and Andrea for Andrea Costa. The baptism of baby
Benito had indeed reflected something of a historic compromise
between the loyal Catholic observance of mother Rosa and the fiery
anti-clericalism and populist revolutionism of Alessandro.

Under the Fascist regime much would be made of the circumstance
that, for a time, Alessandro was a blacksmith – the father forged iron,
his son, it was said, tempered a people.[11] More significant was the fact
that, by 1883, Mussolini's father was already a well-known local
'socialist'.[12] Born on 11 November 1854 at a farm on land still owned
by his father, he had been involved in local political disturbances
while a teenager, and in 1876 had acted as an official delegate for the
paese of Predappio and that of nearby Meldola to the 'Congress of
socialist groups in the Emilia-Romagna'. This meeting of 'subversives'
was held at Bologna, elegantly colonnaded capital of the region and,
for a provincial like Alessandro, doubtless impressive in its 'culture'
and 'history'. Well before his marriage, Alessandro Mussolini was
proud to call himself a follower and even a friend of both Costa and

Cipriani. Each of these men was a key figure in the organising of Italian socialism, with Costa becoming in 1882 the first Italian 'socialist' to be elected to parliament. Alessandro Mussolini assisted his campaign and, it is said, was directly responsible for mobilising some thousand supporters in and around Predappio, votes which proved crucial in the election.[13]

Both Costa and Cipriani were activist rather than intellectual Marxists. Cipriani had fought with Garibaldi at Aspromonte, joined the Greek rebellion against Turkish rule in Crete and rallied to the Paris Commune; his punishment for this last was to be sent prisoner to New Caledonia. He was rather more an anarchist than an orthodox 'legalitarian' socialist, characteristically combining a generosity of spirit with a fondness for ill-prepared insurrection: Michael Bakunin had as much influence on fledgling Italian socialism as did Karl Marx. Costa, too, at least early in his career, made revolution the main plank in his political ideology. Somewhat ironically for a man whose name would be borne by the later Fascist *Duce*, Costa in 1874 declared his political purpose to be 'the destruction of the State in all its economic, political and religious manifestations . . . the abolition of armies, banks and cults'.[14] Later he turned more orthodox, earning fame for the elegance of his dress and the precision of his appearance.[15] He exerted a major influence on the creation of a united Italian socialist party in 1892. Both Costa and Cipriani were by definition also self-conscious internationalists, who looked to the utopia of the brotherhood of man and who, for the most part and at least in theory, scorned the petty interests of the Italian State and nation.

Alessandro Mussolini never made it to the national stage, but he did become a significant political figure in his own region, as early as 1878 attracting police attention as a potentially dangerous revolutionary. In May 1880 he was formally admonished for his threats to property and persons.[16] By the end of his time as an activist, it was reckoned he had published at least 20 articles in the local press, no mean achievement for a man with only a modicum of formal schooling.[17] According to a biography written during his son's regime, he was famed as 'an excoriator of every vice and every corruption' in his neighbourhood.[18] None the less, in 1889 he cooled his revolutionary ardour long enough to favour a compromise whereby his socialists joined with local liberals in order to oust the clerical administration of Predappio. Thereafter Alessandro served on the town council in a variety of positions including, eventually, deputy mayor, sometimes in a junta based on the socialists alone, sometimes in coalition. In 1891 he was sufficiently worldly wise to travel to Milan, and took his eldest son with him, while he arranged to buy a modern threshing machine for his town. Merging ideology with practicality, he was by then sponsoring a co-operative at Predappio, which lasted until 1898.[19] He is also on record welcoming the arrival of the telegraph, favouring the town band, urging the expending of subsidies to meet the medical needs of the local poor and, more surprisingly, in 1900 formally regretting the assassination of King Umberto I. That monarch, he announced, was a 'gentleman' at heart.[20]

Being a socialist in Liberal Italy, however, carried its perils and, in 1902, following a riot in which he did not directly participate, Alessandro Mussolini was arrested and gaoled for six months, 'unjustly' as his biographer would emphasise.[21] Grandfather, father and son Benito would all experience spells in gaol for political reasons, exhibiting a constancy of rebelliousness which must have been relatively unusual in Italian society. Gaol seems to have affected either Alessandro Mussolini's health or his spirit; family matters, and the death of his wife Rosa in February 1905, may have further discouraged him from political activism. Or was it that his position in society had changed? In the years before her death, Rosa had come into an inheritance, producing an elevation in wealth and status which, in the recollection of Mussolini's sister, Edvige, led the peasants of the area humbly to address Alessandro as *Signor padrone*.[22] From 1908, the family rented out some land beside the local river Rabbi for a payment of 490 lire per annum.[23]

After becoming a widower, Alessandro Mussolini retreated from Predappio to take a job as innkeeper on the outskirts of Forlì, detaching himself with seeming deliberation from what had been his political power base. He lived there with a peasant widow, Anna Lombardi (she had reverted to her maiden name), whom he had courted in his youth, and the menage included her five daughters, one of whom was a teenager named Rachele Guidi. This Rachele was soon to be Benito's socialist companion and eventually his church-approved wife. Another of Alessandro's problems may have been drink – one of the first groups to which he belonged called itself the *Società dei bevitori* (Drinkers' club), with a proud slogan boasting that its members intended to 'live working or die fighting'.[24] His son's political enemies had no doubt that Alessandro in old age was an alcoholic, although more charitable onlookers ascribed his health problems to arthritis.[25] Whatever the case, at the inn, named patriotically (and so with a certain lack of socialist internationalism) 'The Bersagliere', Alessandro

Mussolini died in November 1910, aged 56[26] – most of the Mussolinis did not make old bones.[27] Not long before his death, the host of *Il Bersagliere* had cause to see his elder son acting as a waiter there between school-teaching jobs. It was not a sight which pleased him: 'What a dreadful state of affairs! A teacher ... an educated young man, reduced to being a mere servant'.[28] Whatever had once been his revolutionary fervour, in old age Alessandro Mussolini, property owner and small businessman, was moderating his devotion to the principle of equality and had become instead aware of the intricate differences in class and status which characterise the human condition, especially in the imagination of the propertied.

But political contradiction had always hung over the Mussolinis. At least as influential a member of the family was Rosa Maltoni, wife to Alessandro and the mother of the *Duce*. Under the Fascist regime, Rosa Mussolini would be depicted as *La Madre* (The Mother), embodying for her children and especially for Benito 'the most beautiful vision of their past, and a vision which lives on in an eternal present'.[29] Her background and world view were not identical with those of her husband. Rosa Maltoni was born on 22 April 1858, the daughter of a man whom a later biographer pompously called a veterinarian and who humbly did his best to bring some medication to local livestock and some scientific knowledge to local peasants at a village three kilometres outside Forlì. He also owned some land. Whereas all of the Guidi sisters except Rachele were illiterate,[30] Rosa Maltoni's family position a little further up the social scale meant that she received some schooling. Indeed, in 1876, aged 18, she earned a diploma to teach in elementary school; her Fascist biographer celebrated this devotion to 'the most noble calling then available to women'.[31] The following year she was posted to Varano, as the school house for the scattered families of Dovia was called, on a salary of 50 lire per month, a pittance, but more than a peasant, and especially a peasant girl, could expect to be paid. Something of the nature of the school (the Mussolini family would live in the two rooms abutting it) can be seen in a letter Rosa Maltoni penned to the Predappio council in 1894 asking for the windows of the room in which she instructed her pupils to be fixed since wind and snow blew in over herself and her scholars.[32]

It was at Dovia that Rosa Maltoni – to the dismay of her parents, who regretted that their talented daughter was marrying 'down' – met Alessandro Mussolini; in their tiny community they were very likely the only aspirant 'intellectuals'. In January 1882 the couple were

united in marriage, somewhat surprisingly through the religious ceremony which was long avoided by their eldest son and which
Alessandro Mussolini's revolutionary rhetoric was accustomed to
scorn. Rosa Maltoni was known for her piety.[33] Soon she would take
her cherished Benito to the calendar of religious festivals, allowing
him later, when need be, to summon Catholicism as 'the faith of my
infancy'[34] (even if he elsewhere confessed that he had hated the smell
of incense and of the faithful, the guttering of the candles and the
drone of the organ).[35] A biographer later maintained that the young
Duce loved bible reading, at least when he could savour the sonorous-
ness of the lists of names in *Leviticus* or the *Book of Numbers*.[36] In
adulthood, too, his intelligence and understanding were often
sustained by a list and by a (deluded) hope in mathematical precision.

Rosa Maltoni's piety was of a conventional kind and was accompanied by a firm will. Her pedagogical methods were similar. In 1900 she
explained to her superiors:

> In teaching geography I follow the most rational method and avoid the
> formality of complex naming which simply loads the mind with
> abstract, and so useless, ideas. Such concepts hang around for a while
> in a pupil's mind but soon just disappear. In regard to history, I under-
> line the sentiment involved, seeking above all to foster character in the
> children, as well as reinforcing their resolution and determination.

Typically, she added that her instruction would be more effective if
only the lighting available in her school room were not so dim and
unreliable.[37]

One enthusiast eventually averred that Mussolini and that apostle
of hard work and self help, Samuel Smiles, had much in common.[38]
But, among the Mussolinis, it was Rosa Maltoni who was the most
obvious 'Victorian', the upright believer in 'improvement'. She was a
good teacher, but herself did not gain promotion, becoming instead a
local identity and rather more universally admired than her husband.
By the time of her death aged 46, she had sacrificed much to her calling
and her family. Her effort and dedication, and the prestige of the
Mussolinis, were evidenced when her funeral procession drew a
crowd of over a thousand.[39]

By the 1930s Fascist propagandists enjoyed declaiming that 'on
every occasion [the *Duce*] praises Italian women whom he knew
through his Mother and whom he knows through his Woman, both
typical embodiments of the national woman, who lives out her history
between silence and the family hearth'.[40] Another credulous

43

Mussolini

biographer would remember how Rosa had given the baby Benito a
pet white rabbit to which he was attached and which was given to
nuzzling the future *Duce* with its warm pink nose.[41] Such breathless
writers would typically add that, through the presageful events of his
infancy and childhood, Mussolini had mystically absorbed the spirit
of Italian womanhood and could somehow express its essence in his
own erect masculinity.[42] One still more ardent biographer was,
however, dismissive: 'Alessandro Mussolini and Rosa Maltoni only
played the part of a Joseph [and Mary] toward Christ. They were the
instruments of God and history, given the task of watching over one of
the greatest national messiahs. Actually the greatest.'[43] This last,
however, is a decidedly skewed summation of the influence of the
dictator's parents. Rather than being mere sentinels, father and mother
transferred many attitudes, ideals and habits to their son, and some of
the confusion or eclecticism of his ideas in turn reflected the differences which actually existed in the Mussolini parents' view of the
world.

Completing the family and crowding the rooms beside the Varano
school-house were two siblings. The youngest was a girl, Edvige, born
10 November 1888, who would rarely intrude publicly into her elder
brother's life but who was to undertake a supervisory role over the
Duce's children, as befitted an aunt, and who was respected by him for
her capability and her good sense.[44] Far more evident was the middle
child Arnaldo, born 11 January 1885, and thus less than 18 months
younger than Benito. For years the two boys, like many of their class
and nation, slept together on the same iron bedstead (it had allegedly
been crafted by their father and, photos reveal, was ornamented with
putti and grapes).[45] Throughout their lives, the brothers were very
close until Arnaldo's premature death, aged 46 (the same age his
mother had been), on 21 December 1931. Though Arnaldo might
become accustomed humbly to introduce himself as 'Mussolini the
Little',[46] he was often a crucial agent for his older brother – in adulthood, for years they exchanged a phone call each night at 10 p.m.[47] –
and may well have been the only person whom Benito ever trusted.
Certainly Mussolini's eldest son Vittorio was, by contrast, aware that,
whatever the level of his filial respect, he never altogether won his
father's confidence.[48]

Like Benito Amilcare Andrea, Arnaldo was awarded a revolutionary
name by his father, if now one of a greater pomposity, hinting at
Alessandro Mussolini's growth in political experience, worldly status
and ambition. Arnaldo da Brescia was a twelfth-century

anti-hierarchical and puritanical heretic, hanged by the Church for rebellion. In nineteenth-century Italy he had been remembered in anticlerical circles as a somewhat unlikely 'apostle of civil liberty'.[49] Apart from the desire, demonstrated in this naming process, to find inspiration from and connection with history, another sign of the Mussolinis' rise in social status may have been that Arnaldo was not nourished by Rosa, but instead given to a peasant wet-nurse. When he came to write a magniloquent biography of his brother, the *Duce* recalled this matter guiltily and as reflecting an inescapable fate through which the Great Mussolini always overbore the younger brother.[50] Despite the intended resonance of his name, Arnaldo grew up an unheretical child, with an educational curriculum vitae heavily suggestive of maternal influence, but with a hint of his father's presence, too. Rather chubbier than his elder brother, indeed by the 1920s unhealthily puffy-looking, Arnaldo had a higher forehead than Benito, yet his jutting if dimpled chin marked him as a Mussolini.

In 1902 Arnaldo graduated from a college concentrating on agricultural subjects. He was therefore entitled to call himself 'Dott. Mussolini' and duly did so.[51] For a time, Arnaldo followed his brother in emigration to Switzerland, working there as a labourer and gardener. By the end of 1905, drawn back to the family by his mother's death – to his dismay, Arnaldo did not arrive in time to embrace her – and funeral, he was employed to teach a variety of agricultural skills, first at Cesena and then in the emphatically Catholic Veneto. He married in 1909, fathering three children over the next decade. In 1914 he moved from teaching to local administration, obtaining a position as communal secretary. As a result of the battle of Caporetto, however, Morsano, his Friulian township, fell to the Austrians and, in 1918, he was called up (he had not volunteered) for the Italian army. Shortly thereafter he was sent to officers' school, as befitted his educational level and class position. He ended his quiet war as a Second Lieutenant, a rank well above that of Corporal Benito Mussolini.[52]

Whatever the army and its service might have offered him, Arnaldo Mussolini never questioned the fact that the hierarchy of his family mattered more than that of the nation, and he was soon helping his senior sibling, both with the Fascist cause and with more mundane concerns – his elder brother recollected that Arnaldo spent more time looking after Benito's family than did the *Duce*.[53] A Fascist eulogist added that Arnaldo became the shadow who was always there, but who 'did not hamper the bodily movements' of the *Duce*, the 'Great Brother'.[54] Another urged naïvely that only Benito Mussolini understood the Italian people better than did Arnaldo, the teacher of teachers.[55] Actually Arnaldo Mussolini's other identifying factor was his piety. Here was a Mussolini whose politics were markedly clerical. His wife's brother was a priest, eventually employed to give belated baptism to the senior Mussolini children.[56] Analysts still argue about the genuineness of Fascism's thrust towards social and spiritual revolution. It is certainly worth remembering that the mind-set of Arnaldo Mussolini was respectful of the status quo, certainly of the Church and perhaps of the State. Mussolini the Little was no revolutionary. In and around Predappio, he would be remembered as 'the good one'.[57] His elder brother, by contrast, was known as *'e màt'*, the mad one.[58]

Fascist propaganda would love to claim that Mussolini had 'come from the people, sharing in this way all the aspirations of the people'.[59] Of course, the Mussolini family background was a specific one and cannot be generalised to encompass Italians of other classes, regions and times. All the same, any reading of the *Duce*'s personality and mind can easily find there echoes of his family and of the *piccolo mondo* of that part of the Romagna into which he was born.

When Arnaldo and Benito Mussolini engaged in familiar conversation, they, as brothers in Italy might, automatically spoke in dialect.[60] This linguistic preference is a reminder of the novelty and weakness of that Italian nation state which recorded the birth of the two brothers.[61] In 1883 modern Italy had been in existence for less than a generation; its capital had been secured in Rome for not much more than a decade. Similarly the modern Italian language had only recently been invented; linguistic historians nowadays claim that, at the moment of unification in 1860, only some 2.5 per cent of Italians (about 600 000 people) spoke the national language with comfort or pleasure.[62]

Nationalists, then and later, avowed that the unification was natural, and were proudly sure that Italianness or *italianità* was a primordial quality, constituting the eternal identity of the racial stock (*stirpe*) of the peninsula. Reality was different. For all its propagandists' boasts about the eternal nature of Rome and the refulgent glory of the Renaissance, Liberal Italy was a fragile state. Internationally, the nation was required to play the ambiguous and even frightening role of the 'Least of the Great Powers'.[63] Some 14 months before Benito Mussolini's birth, Italy's diplomatists had secured membership of the Triple Alliance with Imperial Germany and Habsburg Austria, a strange pact given that Italian irredentists vociferously maintained that the Risorgimento, or national unification, was incomplete while Austria continued to rule Trieste and the Trentino. Since this was the age of imperialism, men of government mused, perhaps irredentist ardour could be assuaged and European tensions diverted to Africa and the wider world. In 1883 conservative moralist and politician Sidney Sonnino demanded a 'grandiose colonial future' for Italy[64] and the nation's Foreign Minister, Pasquale Stanislao Mancini, a Neapolitan, was actively engaged in the process of planning imperial gain. In January 1885 he sent a battalion of *Bersaglieri* to occupy the Red Sea port of Massawa, thereby initiating a national Italian presence in what would become the colony of Eritrea. From its hinterland beckoned the vast and vulnerable medieval-style kingdom of Ethiopia. Perhaps there, Italy, too, could locate the Glory, God and Gold of modern empire, and prove to Italians that it was better to be the ally of Austria and the Germanic world than its enemy.

As far as the Mussolinis were concerned, these international alarums sounded as yet but fitfully into their daily lives. The domestic travails of Liberal Italy touched them more directly. One prominent issue was the relationship between Church and State. Cavour and his liberal friends had made anti-clericalism a major plank in their programme of 'modernisation', and Italy had been united against the wishes and to the damage of the Vatican under Pope Pius IX (1846–78). By the 1880s the Papacy was in the hands of Leo XIII (died 1903). On election, he appeared an elderly reactionary, and even when his politics proved more ample than expected – in 1891 he published the encyclical *Rerum Novarum* (Of New Things), whose very title promised certainly novelty and perhaps modernity – it was still unclear whether the Church was plotting the overthrow of the heretical or godless Liberal regime which had usurped rule in Rome.

In 1883 Italy's Prime Minister was the cautious Agostino Depretis, a Lombard Liberal and Freemason, who was becoming renowned as the advocate of *trasformismo*, that is, the de-ideologising political practice through which government came from the centre, buying off its 'extremist' foes of left and right through a continuing process of coalition. The best leader was he who could most adroitly offer members of the Chamber of Deputies rewards and benefits (what to some moralists seemed 'corruption') in order to attach them to the governing majority. The legacy of Depretis was durable – in most eyes, Republican Italy after 1946 remained 'transformist' – but, during the 1880s, it also faced critics and challengers. Italy had begun with a tiny and easily manageable electorate, composed of some 2 per cent of the national population. In January 1882 Depretis had acknowledged that social change, which was spreading into the Italian peninsula from the more industrialised Europe to the north, by passing a suffrage reform. It extended the vote to 7 per cent of the population; Depretis had kept the figure low, in a country where the majority of the peasantry remained stubbornly illiterate, by insisting that electors be able to read.

An electorate of that size could still be 'managed' in something like the traditional manner, as successive Prime Ministers – Depretis in the 1880s, Francesco Crispi in the 1890s and Giovanni Giolitti, in the era given his name from 1903 to 1914 – demonstrated. None the less, from the 1880s all Italian politicians were perforce preoccupied with the 'social question', that is, with what to do about that great mass of the population who remained outside the political system. How these masses could be safely 'nationalised' and so converted into loyal Italians was the basic issue in Italian politics until the First World War and beyond.

The Liberal nation seemed to possess two main enemies, each destined to create its own modern mass party. As has been noted, one was composed by those Catholics who yearned either to restore the temporal power of the popes, or to create a Catholic democracy as limned in *Rerum Novarum*. The second was constituted by 'socialists', people like Andrea Costa and Alessandro Mussolini, who preached political and, still more ominously, social revolution. How could they be accommodated in any tolerable system without a descent into 'chaos' and a surrender by the propertied classes of their wealth, lands and expertise? Would drastic solutions prove necessary? After all, as early as 1876 Lombard liberal and financier Marco Minghetti mused about the eventual need for a '*fascio* [union] of all conservative forces' marshalled against the 'ideas of the socialists'.[65]

In the story of the growth of Italian socialism, the Emilia-Romagna, that region which runs from the Po Valley to the Adriatic Sea, was of major significance. Indeed, in 1881 Andrea Costa had founded the 'Romagnole Revolutionary Socialist party' as a first step in his own move from anarchism towards a fully organised state socialism in Italy. Fascist propagandists, too, regularly emphasised the 'Romagnole' character of their *Duce* and his family. Alessandro the blacksmith was thought to be 'a courageous and humble son of the Romagna, thrustful and ardent like its land';[66] Benito was dubbed 'the vehicle of the very soul of the Romagna',[67] and, in the dark days of 1942, an effort was made to cheer the public with photos of the *Duce* and his Romagna, where, it was solemnly explained, Mussolinis had dug for more than three centuries.[68]

What did such grandiose words imply? Partly the answer to that question lay in the past. During the sixteenth and seventeenth centuries, dynastic crises in the various dukedoms handed the rule of territories from the watershed of the Apennines as far as the Po river to the Vatican. However, in many senses, these lands continued to lie 'beyond the mountains'. There was a major climatic difference, with the fogs of the Po valley hovering over the flat terrain for months in winter in a way unimaginable in sunny Rome. Given the weakness of the early modern state – and there were few states weaker and more erratic than the Papacy – the population of such cities as Ferrara and Bologna retained a strong sense of urban identity and a resentment at incompetent, cruel and 'foreign' government from Rome. Romagnoles were thus likely to be dissidents – anarchism did well for a time in the region, while republicanism continued to flourish there throughout the Liberal era.

Economic and cultural developments, however, ensured that 'socialism' was the modern ideology which found most fertile soil in the Romagna. The commitment to revolution appealed to urban intellectuals in the many *città* – a word which more often signified the towns, places with a population of 10 000 or so, than the cities of the region. Not for nothing did Benito Mussolini serve a political apprenticeship editing for a time the earnestly entitled *La Lotta di Classe* (The Class Struggle) in Forlì and, while there, strive for promotion to Bologna. A historian of the region has noted that, by 1900, Bologna had become the 'acknowledged, if unofficial, capital of agricultural Italy',[69] and, as a consequence, the rival of the industrial 'capital' Turin, the financial capital Milan and the administrative capital (and capital in myths) Rome. Predictably, then, Bologna's intellectuals strove to distinguish themselves from their rivals in Turin, Milan, Rome (and Forlì).

But Romagnole socialism was unusual in also penetrating the peasantry in a way which might have surprised that youthful Karl Marx who had declared dismissively that one peasant was separated from another as was one potato from another potato. Po valley agriculture felt the impact of capitalism as early as did any part of Italy. Since the 1880s the Romagnole hinterland had fallen into economic crisis. Old style sharecroppers had been driven either up or, more frequently, down the social ladder as farm production resolved itself into an arrangement between owners (often that now meant anonymous companies) and day labourers. As a modern historian has put it: 'farming in the Bologna plains and to a lesser extent in the foothills, increasingly became an industry like any other'.[70] In this world the socialist message about the steady pauperisation of the working classes, and about an inevitable conflict between bourgeoisie and proletariat, capital and labour, made sense. In 1901 Bologna saw the unification of existing rural groups into *Federterra*, a massive peasant trade union which, within a year, approached a membership of a quarter of a million.[71]

In other words, as the old century passed, both in town and in countryside, any 'new man' of the Romagna was likely to call himself a socialist, and a youthful Benito Mussolini did just that. On 1 May (the day of the workers) 1903, the 19-year-old published a celebratory sonnet to Gracchus Babeuf (charmingly misspelled by Mussolini as Baboeuf), the 'pioneer communist' who had mounted an unsuccessful 'conspiracy of the equals' in Paris in 1796. Babeuf's first name resounded with the clamour of agricultural 'revolution' as once hero-ically pursued in the classical Roman republic, but that was a resonance which Benito Mussolini presently ignored. Instead, the poet sang of the great but sad days of Revolution in Paris, of the betrayal of Thermidor, of the devious plotting of priests, and of the smile of Babeuf at the moment of his sacrificial death. 'Into his dying eyes', the still-not-quite *Duce* wrote, 'travelled the flash of the [socialist] Idea, the vision of the centuries to come'.[72] In his own new century, Mussolini was dreaming of fresh uprisings in which he might be the guiding light. But how had Benito Amilcare Andrea, self-conscious young revolutionary and intellectual, reached this stage of his life?

The upbringing of the infant Benito was inevitably heavily mythol-ogised under his dictatorship, during which an endless stream of servile authors underlined his exceptionality and genius in order to prove that the *Duce* was 'always the *Duce*',[73] and that, from his birth if not before, he had acted 'like a true Roman'.[74] As an old family friend turned hired pen of the Fascist state proclaimed: 'At once the infancy of Benito Mussolini gave unmistakable signs of his great passion for study and spiritual meditation'.[75] Such evidence is difficult to inter-pret and plainly cannot be taken at face value. Rather, the first story about Mussolini as a baby is psychologically intriguing. It was not until after his third birthday that the future orator learned to speak. This delay in maturation so worried his parents that they took him to Forlì to be examined by an ear, nose and throat specialist, presumably a costly trip (and one that a peasant family would not have been able to afford or imagine). Allegedly the doctor told Rosa: 'Don't worry, my good woman, soon he will talk too much'.[76] A modern psychologist might be more worried lest such a delay in maturation suggest that all was not well at home, and it may be wondered just how compatible Rosa and Alessandro really were – after all, even Mussolini's pious socialist obituary of his father admitted that Alessandro had not altogether made a success of life.[77]

For all that, young Benito did not grow up in a way that was exceptional for his class and region. Legend would emphasise his 'wildness', the more to prove his innate quality of leadership. The Fascist image of the boy Mussolini focused either on his commanding of a gang of urchins in its intrepid raids on local farmsteads, or on the Boy-Philosopher, cogitating in the shadow of the ancient oak which grew just outside San Cassiano (vengeful Anti-Fascists cut it down after 1945),[78] or beside the plashing waters of the Rabbi.[79] Mussolini can even be found saying in ultimate cliché that these were the happiest days of his life.[80]

The only real hint of the unusual in the boy Mussolini's behaviour occurred when the nine-year-old, after some family debate, was sent as a boarder to the Salesian college at Faenza, a big school by the standards of the time with 200 pupils aged from six to late teenage, in a town which was the next *città* up the railway line towards Bologna from Forlì. Again, it was a choice of schooling suggesting ambition among the Mussolinis, but with Rosa Maltoni having the greater influence – Benito claimed that his mother had been talked into sending her cherished son there by a 'bigoted' female member of the locally powerful Zoli family.[81] Among the Catholic fathers Benito survived for two years but in increasingly evident travail. There was the problem of religion and, very likely inseparable from it, the problem of class. Certainly in Dovia and probably in Predappio, the Mussolinis were *gente per bene* (respectable people). But the good citizens of Faenza, a *città* with an iron bridge for the provincial to marvel at,[82] did not easily acknowledge inferior beings from a barbarous world outside the city gates. As Mussolini took pains to recall, among the Salesians he was placed in the third and bottom rank, a station which was humiliatingly emphasised during lessons, at school mealtimes, in scholastic dress and in sleeping arrangements. All in all, the fathers of the Catholic order seem to have remembered maliciously the reputation of Alessandro, the blaspheming father of their pupil, and forgotten the piety of his mother. In their conscious and unconscious actions, they made young Benito an object of their dislike and persecution, even though, after some public recalcitrance, he took communion – in the odour of sanctity which briefly clung to him thereafter, he remembered, school food improved.[83]

The outcome of the conflict between boy and teachers was perhaps inevitable. During a petty squabble among the pupils, Mussolini, still short of his eleventh birthday, pulled out a knife and stabbed a class-mate in the hand. There followed a tremendous hue and cry, in which the future *Duce* was told by an outraged Salesian that he had a soul as black as soot, and was then put out to sleep with the school dogs for the night (even if a charitable teacher eventually rescued him from that frightening fate).[84] Deemed violent and uncontrollable, Mussolini was, sometime thereafter, expelled from the school, a circumstance which duly became the stuff of Fascist, Anti-Fascist and sensationalist biographical account, and has remained grist to any analyst deter-mined to prove that only one possible path lay ahead for the future *Duce*.

The problem with drawing too definite a conclusion about his nature from his time at Faenza is that, when, at the end of the summer holidays in 1894, Mussolini transferred to the state school at Forlimpopoli,[85] another but less renowned *città* of the Romagna plain, he became something of a model pupil (despite some trouble occa-sioned by another stabbing incident). At the *Collegio Giosuè Carducci*, named grandly after Liberal Italy's leading (and highly patriotic) poet, and actually headed by the poet's brother Valfredo Carducci, Benito duly passed his exams (if sometimes with a struggle), before matricu-lating in the summer of 1901. A surviving school report shows him doing best in pedagogy, language and literature, and 'morale', and worst in agriculture and maths.[86] He also began to develop what became a lifelong interest in music and even talked about seeking a career as a professional musician – his aim, he said, was to compose a tune which would express 'all the motion of the universe'.[87] In 1899 Mussolini participated in a 'Festival of the Tree' held in the nearby elegant hill-town of Bertinoro and was photographed playing the cornet.[88] It was, then, not just convention which caused the later politician fondly to recall his days at Forlimpopoli.[89] Indeed, the school gave him his first chance to place his name before a wider public. In early 1901 Mussolini was chosen to represent the school in an oration commemorating the death of Giuseppe Verdi, sometime alleged hero of the Risorgimento and composer of universal fame. The socialist national daily *Avanti!* reported the event in a three line piece gravely defining the orator as 'comrade student Mussolini',[90] while the Bologna daily *Il Resto del Carlino* also noted the 'much applauded' speech, even if they thought that the boy who delivered it was 'Benito Mussolino'.[91] Despite the pupil's forensic feat, a few months later the school bursar did not forgo the despatch of an unpaid bill for 22 lire and 68 centesimi to the local mayor with a request that he press payment from the Mussolinis.[92]

An account published in the 1930s by a school-fellow of the *Duce* recalls a proud and generally taciturn boy who sought to mark himself out from the other pupils by his fondness for black clothes (and tie) and by his pallid looks, but he was also known as a passionate and athletic dancer. While still a schoolboy, he boasted of losing his virginity in a Forlì brothel at a cost of 50 *centesimi*, an event which, he said, stimulated both guilt and lust. He told his friends that he was a great writer of poetry, but he always tore up the results.[93] He let it be known that he thought deep thoughts.[94] In his pocket, as his personal talisman, he carried a medallion with the image of Karl Marx on it.[95] Mussolini's prominent eyes grew more burning every day. He began to cultivate a small moustache, which he would keep until the end of the First World War (though it would never grow as luxuriantly as that of his father). Possessed of an excellent memory, he converted the obligatory study of Dante (the medieval religious poet had been installed as the chief cultural symbol of united modern Italian nation and its national language) into a weapon of his own. Thus, it was said, he loved to walk through the dark, silent, streets of Forlimpopoli late at night, shouting the stanze of the *Inferno* or *Purgatorio*. It was as though he was assaulting the walls of the villas which lined his path. And it was the invective of Dante which he especially loved.[96]

When he finished his schooling, Benito Mussolini was young, bright, angry, ambitious, at times violent (as was society around him), disadvantaged in quite a lot of ways, but determined and fortunate to live at a time when his particular talents were beginning to matter. In many ways he was well defined as 'first of his class', though he would not be the only politician in history to deserve that soubriquet. How could he find a way to harness his evident promise, to solace his anger and ambition, and to move from being merely the first of his own small cohort to primacy in some part of that life which mattered? How could he find a path to the great world?

Could teaching be the answer? In his last months as a student, Mussolini was already assisting the staff as a pupil-teacher, notably, it is said, of history, and, in 1901, his mother's vocation seemed destined to be his own (as it would be for a while Arnaldo's). School teaching, at least at the more senior level, could bring considerable respect in *belle époque* Italian society. Some of the atmosphere of that profession is revealed in a ceremony held at the end of school term in May 1910 at Forlimpopoli to honour Valfredo Carducci, 'brother of the poet' as it was inevitably stressed, who had just completed 20 years of service at his school. Benito Mussolini, granted the grandiose title of Forlì correspondent for the socialist national daily paper *Avanti!*, wrote up the event. The mayor, he reported, had presided over the solemnities, which saw Carducci presented with a gold watch and a ceremonial scroll. Ex-pupils had assembled from all around the region, joining their ex-teacher at a banquet, a civic reception and then a concert, held at the elegant *Teatro Comunale* to the benefit of a local sailors' hospice.[97] No doubt plenty of time was left for orations and toasts.

A decade earlier, did the young school graduate wonder whether one day he, too, might expect such honours? In December 1901 Mussolini published in the supplement of a teachers' magazine what seems to have been his first work, an admiring commentary on the Russian novel.[98] For much of the next decade his most likely employment was as a teacher – and, at least if her ghosted memoirs are to be believed, his eventual companion Rachele was expected to address him as *'professore'* until after the birth of their fourth child.[99] But young Benito Mussolini had one other great commitment – politics. The dilemma remained – how could the two vocations be combined?

The ideal solution to this question was local. Young Benito, 'graduate', clutching his 'diploma', sought a post as secretary of the Predappio *comune*, after he had applied for and failed to obtain a series of teaching jobs.[100] His application was taken seriously. The Council voted on the matter, with Alessandro conscientiously retiring from the room during the process. But Benito was too young and too inexperienced a candidate, and was rejected 10 : 4.[101] It would have to be school-teaching, after all. Alessandro allegedly told his son not to be disappointed, but to head out onto the paths of the world. There, he suggested, his son could turn into the 'Crispi of tomorrow'.[102] In February 1902 Mussolini left his parents' house to take up the position of relief teacher at a tiny school at Pieve Saliceto, a *frazione* of Gualtieri Emilia, still in Italy's red belt but more than 100 kilometres from home, where, it was thought, Alessandro's *raccomandazione* (personal reference) had none the less carried weight. Mussolini eventually acknowledged that he did not do especially well in his initial spell as a teacher, but he blamed the reactionary clericalism which, in his opinion, scarred the textbooks even in a socialist *comune*, and explained his failure to foster his pupils' initiative.[103] Others said that, at Gualtieri, he spent too much time drinking and playing cards at the local *Osteria della fratellanza* (Fraternity pub).[104] Moreover, Mussolini's view of discipline, which tended to the libertarian, was rejected by local parents. In June he found that his contract was not renewed, although the reason seems to have had less to do with his pedagogical radicalism than with the public scandal occasioned by his adulterous affair with a local soldier's wife.[105]

In any case, the young teacher was already thinking of sloughing off his commitments to the little worlds of the Po valley. In May 1901 Mussolini had applied for a passport and, because of his family's good financial and civic reputation, had obtained it. As he informed a friend back home in early June, soon he would reside 'no more in the land of Dante, but rather in that of W. Tell'.[106] On 9 July 1902 Professor Benito Mussolini, elementary school teacher, headed for the Swiss border. His mother had transferred funds to him for the trip; they amounted to the equivalent of almost a month's pay. He claimed that the only person to whom he said good-bye at Gualtieri Emilia was 'his woman', whom he would never see again. Since, by his own account, he had once stabbed her in the arm during a quarrel, she may well have been glad to return to her husband.[107] On the slow train Mussolini read in a paper of his father's arrest, but that family crisis did not diminish his determination to shake the dust of Italy from his life.[108] Like millions of other Italians in the decades before 1914 – his train, he recalled, was crowded with others leaving[109] – Mussolini had decided to become an emigrant. He was to celebrate his nineteeth birthday in a foreign clime.

3

Emigrant and socialist, 1902–1910

IN crossing the Swiss border, Mussolini was following a well-trodden path. During the decade from 1896 to 1905, more than 4 million Italians emigrated – during the following ten years the total expanded to 6 million.[1] At first the emigrants tended to come from northern Italy and to expatriate within Europe. However, by the beginning of the new century a wave of departures had begun in the south, with both the United States and Latin America becoming favoured destinations. Furthermore, a massive departure to Switzerland, France, Germany and Austria continued; in 1902, for example, Mussolini was one of 50 233 of his fellow countrymen (the great majority were indeed male) who migrated to the Helvetian Republic.[2] Later in the decade Mussolini also spent time in the Austrian Trentino, and he at least contemplated departure to the USA or to 'Madagascar', this last a somewhat unlikely choice.[3] In 1903 he told one friend that he was mulling over the idea of departure to 'Africa' for 20 years – by residing there he could avoid the national draft.[4] As late as 1910 he and Rachele talked about going together to America, only abandoning the prospect when it became evident that Rachele was expecting a child.[5]

Italian emigrants tended to be young and to be male – between 1896 and 1905, men left at almost five times the rate of women.[6] Those who went generally saw themselves as 'sojourners', or 'birds of passage', working hard and enduring exploitation, not least from those fellow nationals who had departed before them and who now knew the customs and networks of their new countries and could adapt them to their own benefit. Such snares avoided or overcome, the emigrant intended to go home wiser and richer. Often, like Mussolini, Italians emigrated (and returned) more than once, as the spirit of adventure, or need, required. For many, the period of emigration resembled an apprenticeship, or, better, a period of conscription, in which much that happened was cruel or imponderable but during which the life beyond the borders constituted an initiation rite, a necessary service, that eventually set the emigrant, having made a 'fortune', free to return to family, *paese* and full adulthood. Emigration was at its base an act of 'the Italies' and therefore of the un-nationalised masses, behaving as though the modern Italian nation and state were irrelevant to their hopes and fears.

If an ideal of financial and spiritual emancipation was clung to by many an emigrant in desperate times, for each individual the story of migration had its own cast. Experience abroad mostly reinforced the separation of the sexes and shored up the conventional patriarchy – this confirmation of existing habits and beliefs was what happened to the young Mussolini. More striking is the question of identity, an issue which was also of political interest for modernising states, be they the countries which received the emigrants, or Italy itself. Here there was the curious and ironical possibility that the act of migration, despite the apparent accompanying acceptance that the nation-state could provide neither present sustenance nor future opportunity, might actually advance the nationalisation of the masses. Emigration by its definition involved statistics, that process of tabulation and assessment which was so near the heart of the modern state. Emigrants may have left the Italies and their *paesi*, but both the host society and the representatives of the Italian government with whom they came into contact called them 'Italians'. So, too, did the other peoples with whom they mixed. Matters of identity were not always simple. Sometimes 'Latins' would cluster almost as though they were still subjects of Imperial Rome. More frequently, 'Italian' clubs and welfare associations actually turned out to owe allegiance to a region, a town or a village, and members were bound by a classical emigrant 'chain' to the folks back home. Yet, the word 'Italy' could not be expunged from an emigrant's vocabulary. Indeed, as one emigrant put it, it was through going to Latin America that he learned that he was Italian.[7]

Quite a number of important figures in the eventual Fascist regime shared in this honing of their national identity. One was Edmondo Rossoni, for a time Fascist trade union chief. Born in 1884 and so a year younger than Mussolini, and from a *paese* in the province of Ferrara not far from Predappio, Rossoni emigrated to the United States after a brush with the Italian police over his labour activism. There, by 1912, he had become a sort of nationalist, insisting on 'a strictly Italian working-class union' as the best way both to defeat the capitalist bosses and to advance his own career.[8] Another Italian emigrant in the U.S. was Amerigo Dumini, a man who became notorious in 1924 as the leader of the Fascist squad which killed moderate socialist deputy Giacomo Matteotti, setting off the Fascist regime's most public scandal. Dumini was actually a second generation emigrant, born in St. Louis in 1896, but sent back to Italy for some education. Thereafter he learned a nationalist vocabulary (although never forgetting the appeal of the main chance), through the First World War and service in the Italian Army.[9]

Mussolini's own emigrant experience did not at first seem likely to follow such paths. Benito Mussolini was a socialist. His own father, in one of the short articles which he proudly contributed to a local news-sheet, condemned the Italian state for the disgraceful act of driving its citizens out of the country – according to Alessandro, nine families, in total some 50 people, had just left Dovia for Brazil, certain suffering and likely death. Yellow fever, Alessandro warned, stalked the tropics.[10] Likewise, then and later, Marxist theory defined emigration as a process of international exploitation through which the bourgeoisie depressed wages and conditions, both at home and abroad. Indeed, the Emilia-Romagna, precisely because it was 'red', was a region of scant emigration. For most fully aware Marxists, the emigrant constituted a variety of traitor and black-leg who, rather than abandoning his familiar hearth, did better to stay where he could fight the bosses most knowingly and effectively.

In his own mind, Mussolini was certainly not going to Switzerland in breach of the rules of socialism. Rather, his emigration was a variety of exile, a young man's adventure to be sure, but at the same time an expression of contempt towards that Italy which had not found him worthy employment. In his new abode, Mussolini had every intention of remaining loyal to socialist networks – they offered a home away from home. Only weeks after his arrival in Switzerland, he was writing with some regularity in a journal entitled *L'Avvenire del Lavoratore* (The Worker's Future); Mussolini claimed to a friend that he had been made co-editor of the paper along with a Lausanne lawyer, Tito Barboni (indeed the paper's editor and secretary of the Italian Socialist party in Switzerland).[11] Mussolini had not occupied the editor's chair, but he proved a busy scribe, a natural journalist, contributing nine articles in less than six months of his initial residence in Switzerland.

In this regard, Mussolini's emigration was that of an 'intellectual'. In 1902 the institutions of Liberal Italy were notoriously under

challenge from many of the 'best and the brightest' of the new generation, and remained so at least until national entry into the First World
War in May 1915. At the turn of the century critical sociologists were
noting that, in Italy, there were 0.74 lawyers per 1000 inhabitants as
against 0.12 in well-administered and well-ordered Prussia.[12] In 1900
27 of 32 socialist members of the Italian parliament called themselves
professore,[13] meaning that they had graduated in some course and had
the right to teach in school. The pessimistic conservative Guido
Fusinato, who regularly despaired over how Italy might nationalise its
masses, drew the obvious lesson from such detail, inveighing against
'that new form of intellectual proletariat which is even more miserable
and threatening than the economic proletariat, and from which the
extremist political parties recruit many of their shrewdest, most active
and most dubious elements'.[14] Mussolini, of course, was scarcely a
university-trained lawyer, but he claimed the right to be addressed as
professore, boldly asserting the freedoms and duties of an intellectual,
one who was shrewd, active and ready for 'revolution'. His world was,
in his own estimation, a wide-ranging one. Indeed, his initial article
for *L'Avvenire del Lavoratore* contrasted bourgeois Europeans' current
dismay at the collapse of the campanile in Venice (actually, Mussolini
wrote aggressively, the ancient monument was 'artistically of dubious
taste') with their tolerance of the massacre of Armenians in the
Ottoman empire. Violent Kurds, he added with a characteristic hint of
salaciousness, had even tied down Armenian women, committing 'acts
of unspeakable ferocity' on them. When, he asked rhetorically, would
civilization be able to assert itself against such wickedness? He knew
the answer: 'the disappearance of the tyranny which a single social
class, the one with economic privilege, exercises over the other will
signal the end of any fanaticism and racial hatred; then all men will be
united in fraternal solidarity'.[15]

From the very first, then, 'Prof. Mussolini' was pleased to have an
opinion on every issue. In the language of today, he claimed membership of the 'chattering classes', unabashed and determined that others
recognised his presence. His actual education may have been narrow,
but his effrontery knew no limit. Well before his twenty-first
birthday, Mussolini, however callow he was in reality, aggressively
willed himself to be an intellectual among the intellectuals – as one
contemporary noted acutely, he treated 'every other intellectual as an
enemy or a competitor'.[16]

But what did such intellectuality mean?[17] One of the issues of
debate about his period of emigration in Switzerland is whether or

not, in 1904, Mussolini attended the lectures of Vilfredo Pareto at Lausanne university. Pareto was important, as an intellectual of global fame and because his postulation that what he called 'creative elites', that is, men marked by their dynamism and will, were always destined to rule, was eventually declared an antecedent of Fascist ideology. Under the regime, the official line was that Mussolini had heard Pareto, though some have doubted this account, and he certainly did not sit any exams.[18] Perhaps the student's attendance, attention span and comprehension level do not matter very much, except to underline that the ex-school teacher was continuing to absorb the mental world which surrounded him, however unsure his knowledge of the detail of its ideas remained.

Actually, Mussolini the intellectual exile and Mussolini the economic migrant jostle uneasily in any account of his life in Switzerland. Now was the period, to be remembered with advantage at appropriate moments thereafter, in which Mussolini sometimes slept on a park bench, or found precarious work as a builder's labourer, or butcher's or wine-seller's boy (though often he was swiftly promoted to clerical work, and at least one contemporary noticed that this pseudo-worker's hands remained soft and white).[19] On occasion there might be hunger or trouble in finding where to wash – Mussolini recorded his anger at an early employer who complained that his worker was too well dressed.[20] There were debts, not easily repaid, both to friends back in the Romagna and to new acquaintances. There was illness, very likely brought on by the loneliness of exile and the unfamiliarity of his new surrounds – now began rumours, which lasted beyond his death that Mussolini had somewhere contracted syphilis.[21] Anti-Fascists thereafter claimed that there was even thieving on occasion, it being alleged, probably falsely, that Mussolini stole a watch from a friend.[22] There was a somewhat exotic love affair with a Polish medical student. By 1903 there was sex of a less romantic kind in Lausanne with a divorcee, but, as he explained to a male friend, merely 'in order to satisfy the flesh and not the soul'.[23] Finally, there was, from October to December 1903, a hurried trip home, after the news arrived that his mother Rosa was sick. The return visit became the opportunity to look up old friends (and to begin to learn that the stay-at-home world had moved with different rhythms from those of emigration).[24] Time with the family also offered the chance for Mussolini, when he again headed off, to take his brother Arnaldo, now 18, on his emigrant quest.[25] These were not unique choices. The twists and turns of this story, the switching between deprivation and hope, the ties never quite renounced with family, home and *paese* uneasily meshing with the allure of a new world, made up an array of experiences not unfamiliar to other young male emigrants of the era.

To be sure, none of these other emigrants became dictator of Italy and so, however sceptical it is necessary to be about his self-estimation and however self-interested was his hanging out with what have been called the 'vagabonds of intellectualism',[26] Mussolini was beginning to develop a corpus of ideas and a pattern of actions. For this emigrant, socialism, at least verbally, lay at the centre of his being. When Mussolini returned to his mother's bed-side, he explained with self-aggrandising drama to a school-friend: 'By the end of November I'll pack my bags still another time and again head off into the unknown. The [socialist] movement has become a basic need for me. If I stop, I shall simply croak.'[27] Others, too, were beginning to acknowledge his significance. When the Rome liberal paper *La Tribuna* in April 1904 carried a report of one of his conflicts with the police, he was described as the *grande duce* (major leader) of the local socialist group.[28] What were the component parts of the young man's socialism, that ideology which he pledged was his nurturing credo?

The most strident and enduring feature of the youthful Mussolini's belief system was what was then called 'maximalism', a commitment to the act of revolution of the sort which, a generation before, Costa and Cipriani had favoured. Mussolini frequently expressed his scorn, by contrast, for the 'reformist' caution favoured by such moderates as Filippo Turati, co-founder of the Socialist party in 1892 and now a member of the Chamber of Deputies. Turati's respectability and sense of responsibility did not appeal to the dynamic young revolutionary; for him, state authorities were natural enemies.

It was no surprise to find that, among Mussolini's experiences in Switzerland, were trouble with the police, 'arrest, imprisonment, expulsion' from one Canton to the next or, on one occasion, after 10 days pent up in the cells, over the border to Como.[29] There he had promptly bought a train ticket back to Lugano and, though again summoned to explain himself by the forces of law and order, soon took secure refuge with the Barboni family and other socialist friends. Such escapades merely made his allegiance more definite. His first writings in *L'Avvenire del Lavoratore* had set out his line: 'We have no simple formula. We only hope that the party returns to its primordial methods of struggle, and that it directs an implacable fighting spirit against the constituted order, without ever dirtying its hands ... with political or financial deals.'[30] Mussolini was an activist and, in his own mind, a purist one, who deservedly bore the names of Cipriani and the young Costa. In his poetry, he chanted solemn obituaries for fallen comrades, summoning vengeance against their persecutors.[31] He was a Republican; in a paper called *Il Proletario* (The Proletarian), he ridiculed the ways of kings, urging their swift overthrow.[32] Parliament, too, he deemed a farcical organisation, which the virtuous must one day destroy. Those moderate socialists who were trying to make it work in the proletarian interest were deluding themselves.[33]

Most of all Mussolini was an anti-clerical. By the end of the decade, he would write *The Cardinal's Mistress*, a period bodice-ripper in which the Church was portrayed as a place of lust, hypocrisy and murder.[34] In 1910 these were scarcely fresh sentiments in his mind. His first Christmas away from home had stimulated a piece for *L'Avvenire del lavoratore*, in which the future friend or ally of the Catholic Church pondered the gap between the suffering of Christ and the selfishness and corruption of His agents on earth, people whom He would have 'cursed and beaten', had He been given the chance.[35] Some months later, Mussolini's imagination grew more macabre as he moralised about the 'horrors of the cloister'.[36] By contrast, around Dovia, he reported with naïve enthusiasm, socialist baptisms were taking off and very likely would soon replace the religious ceremony.[37]

His orations were filled with similar themes and attitudes (he claimed to devote every Sunday to political speechifying).[38] The strident anti-clericalism, which he had inherited from his father, eventually sparked a public debate, held at the *Maison du Peuple* at Lausanne on 25 March 1904, between Mussolini and a Protestant pastor named Alfredo Taglialatela. In the first moments of his oration, Mussolini found cause to mention Bruno, Leibniz, Robespierre, Bacon, Galileo and a number of other Great Thinkers from the Past.[39] Intellectual precocity was not all, however; it was said that the future *Duce* clinched his argument by presumptuously standing on a table and counting down, for, it was claimed, 5 minutes,[40] while challenging the Almighty to display Himself. God ignored the noisy and blaspheming youth.

The wiser socialists were already arguing that matters of religion were best left to the individual and the tradition of the *mangiapreti* (priest-eater) was becoming outmoded – Mussolini publicly depicted such moderation as time-serving and back-sliding, faring the worse in a confrontation with the older and more experienced Emile Vandervelde, a reformist who eventually became Foreign Minister of Belgium. Certainly the stridency with which the young socialist assaulted the Church and the deity had a troubling side. Would a real intellectual think so crudely? Would a socialist with the welfare of the people at heart be so truculent about the treasured beliefs so many of them held? Did not anti-clericalism, with its conveniently invisible enemy (at least in so far as God was concerned), often cloak ambition, masking a superficial commitment to liberty and equality? These were the questions which underlay the wrangling among socialists about what should be the party line on the relationship between church and state, and between individuals and their religious preference.

If anti-clericalism was one problem for socialist theoreticians, a still greater one involved the nation. Marxist dogma suggested that socialism was by definition internationalist, and maintained that its triumph would free the workers of the whole world. Yet, with every passing decade, the nation became more surely the modern political form, and national cultures were engrained in the peoples of Europe, if not with their mothers' milk, then with that schooling which every state proffered as the obligatory entry gate to modernity. This was the era when peasants (and some workers, too) were 'turning into Frenchmen',[41] Germans, and the rest. For the moment, socialists said that they worked against this tide, condemning jingoism, downplaying nationalist rivalry and even meeting in solemn assembly from time to time as an 'International'. There they promised to blunt any bourgeois drive to war with a general strike; in a better future, workers must not kill other workers. However, not far beneath the surface of socialist thought and practice, the current of nationalism eddied and flowed. Before long, its power would sweep away the leadership of the German Social Democratic Party, the largest and most sophisticated in the world, whose parliamentary membership unanimously voted war credits to the national (and Imperial) German government in early August 1914. How did the young Mussolini define his own posture on the question of the nation?

The answer is, with some innocence, some self-interest and some inconsistency. In theory, as noted above, Mussolini was a fervent internationalist. Nevertheless, despite his Marxist orthodoxy and despite the fact that the processes of the nationalisation of the masses were feebler in Italy than in the countries to the north, a notion of Italian identity seeped into his words and actions. While a schoolboy, Mussolini had been excited for a whole month by the great national crisis occasioned when Prime Minister Crispi's plans for Italian imperial grandeur were wrecked, after Ethiopians routed Italian forces at the battle of Adowa.[42] Rather than rallying to avenge the defeat as other European states had done in other parts of Africa, the Italians thereupon withdrew in bedraggled humiliation from the local emperor, Menelik II's realm.

In Switzerland, too, Mussolini had known the nation. A socialist he may have been, but his accustomed dealings were with those local socialists who, whether themselves Swiss or fellow exiles from Italy, spoke Italian. Language was such a basic matter: 'I had studied French' at school, he mused naïvely, 'but I did not understand it [as spoken around him in Switzerland], given that my ears were not attuned to the sound of a foreign tongue.'[43] At least according to his own account, his oral French soon improved and, throughout his life, he read French often and with pleasure. Yet a foreign air lingered over non-Italian Switzerland and even stained those Swiss who did speak his language. Switzerland was a country naturally given to reformism; the Swiss, he complained, were too cosy in their lives to favour real revolution.[44] They were not his natural bedfellows.

In his uneasiness as an emigrant among the Italian Swiss, Mussolini sought solace as an intellectual exile. Switzerland was after all the home to many such people, Lenin among them, who had fled from the police in their own countries, and who, in relatively liberal surroundings, could now concentrate on planning revolutions as well as on winning out in the endemic factional disputes, recurrent in expatriate intellectual life. Using the spare time in his trip back to his mother's bedside to translate a piece by the Russian anarchist prince P.A. Kropotkin, Mussolini advanced his case to be granted a presence among the exiled dissidents.[45] Once back in Switzerland, Mussolini, with growing aplomb, began to move in the circles of the maximalist Italian socialist Giacinto Menotti Serrati, and his Russian exile friend Angelica Balabanoff, a sprig of the southern Russian nobility.

Mussolini worked with the latter – even if she eventually denounced his treachery to the socialist cause,[46] and bitterly labelled him 'a Hireling, a Judas and a . . . Cain'[47] – on another translation, this time ambitiously of a German work by leading Marxist theoretician, Karl Kautsky.[48] Balabanoff also took time to train Mussolini in basic philosophy through a sort of stimulus and response, rote-learning method. When she provided the name Fichte, he would reply 'thesis, antithesis, synthesis'; Balabanoff: 'Hegel': Mussolini: 'being, non-being, becoming'; Balabanoff: 'Marx': Mussolini: 'need, work, class struggle'.[49] His instructress later remarked of him, with a certain malice and with considerable acuity: 'He thought of himself as an "intellectual", a leader, and the contrast between this conception of

himself and the humilities of his daily life had induced in him an exaggerated self-pity and sense of personal injustice'.[50]

Now Mussolini started reading about syndicalism, a variant of
socialism which flourished in Italy in the decade before the outbreak
of the First World War. He scanned the works of Georges Sorel, the
alienated French bureaucrat who had made himself the renowned
theoretician of these ideas, as well as of the power of 'myth', and so of
the view that the masses could be as easily moved to violent action by
a strategic use of words as by the reality of their own suffering.[51]
Mussolini's mind was still too malleable; his ambition to rise somehow
and somewhere, both culturally and socially, was too naked for him to
be reliably placed as an acolyte of this school or that. None the less, his
last year in Switzerland added syndicalism to the phrases which
would thereafter trace a path in his mind and, on appropriate stimulus, he could regurgitate them with a will.

Suddenly, in the last months of 1904, his Swiss experience came to
an end. Leaving Arnaldo to fend for himself in Berne, Mussolini again
returned home. The reason is still a little unclear. His mother's health
had not improved, and no doubt filial love (Rosa had continued to
send generous subsidies to her emigrant eldest son) gave some impulse
to his decision. The other explanation was more political. With his re-
entry assisted by an amnesty for draft-dodgers, Mussolini had decided
to accept his conscription into the Italian army. In the past, he had
talked about emigration to more distant climes to avoid being called up
and, in March 1904, he had ignored the summons of the Italian state to
Bologna, where he had been condemned *in absentia* by a military court
for evading his national duty.[52] Now, with seeming ease, he sloughed
off his anti-patriotism and anti-militarism, serving his turn as a
bersagliere, and so being inscribed into an elite corps in the Italian
army, with good discipline and even with pleasure.

Again his actions should not be read as too surprising. The Army
did have an appeal to its conscripts, perhaps as the 'school of the
nation' and certainly as an institution which reinforced male values
(and legitimised that violence which was rarely distant from the
poorer, and wealthier, sections of Italian society). Whatever his
reasons may have been, Mussolini remained under the colours for just
short of two years, although, early in his service, he was generously
granted two months leave, a furlough which enabled him to reach his
mother's deathbed.[53] He had been summoned back by a letter from
Temistocle Zoli, warning him that Rosa had contracted meningitis; her
final agony lasted less than a week.[54] Allegedly, Benito knelt,

beseeching forgiveness for his waywardness and blessing for his future. His mother was unable to speak but recognised him through his unusual head-gear, a piece of apparel which she hugged 'many times'.[55] At her death, Mussolini, it was said, felt utterly lost, remarking sadly: 'the only living being whom I had really loved and who had been near to me had been torn from me'.[56] He tried hard to be stoic, however: 'In this hour of pain I bend before the ineluctable law which dominates human life. I would like to find comfort in such fatalism, but the most consoling philosophical doctrines are not enough to fill the emptiness, left by the irreparable loss of a loved being'.[57] More gushingly, Rosa's Fascist biographer declaimed about the sacrifice of her death amounting to a Pact whereby the Mother consigned her Son to Italy, while remaining for all her children 'the most beautiful vision of their past; and a vision which lives on in an eternal present'.[58]

It was said that, before his return from Switzerland, Rosa had written urging her son to settle down. And, for a time, his radicalism did seem to diminish. A week after his mother's death he wrote to his commanding officer expressing his proper patriotic desire to assist as a soldier in preparing the nation against possible invasion by 'barbarians from the north'.[59] When, in September 1906, his term of military service was over, he resumed work as a teacher. In November 1907 he upgraded his qualifications to teach French at secondary level by passing a test set by the University of Bologna, even though, a rebel still, he allegedly provoked consternation among his professors, by entering the exam room smoking and with a louche air.[60] In other ways, his life at last seemed less feckless. Preparing himself to be head of the family, he welcomed the marriage of his sister, Edvige, to a small shopkeeper from the nearby centre of Premilcuore.[61] He evinced more interest than in the past about the financial return being gained from the family land-holding. In some eyes, he was even doing well as a teacher. When, in July 1908 he left his position at Oneglia in Liguria, he was farewelled with a public banquet.[62]

Mussolini was not quite a man of respect, however; the *vie de bohème* was hard to renounce. His sex life remained disordered and, when he went off to teach at Tolmezzo near Italy's northern border, there was rumour of a soon deceased illegitimate son.[63] For the only time in his life, Mussolini drank to excess (as his enemies recalled).[64] He continued to be a socialist (and anti-clerical) activist, although, briefly, the number of his publications declined. His fondness for speechifying did not. The local paper at Udine, for example, was soon describing the deeds of the ebullient revolutionary *maestro* 'Bussolini'. This socialist extremist had improvised a clangorous harangue, lasting for 45 minutes, about the martyred heretic Giordano Bruno. The speech was so inspirational that, at its end, the comrades sang the workers' anthem and finished their demonstration outside the local priests' home by shouting their admiration for Bruno and their undying support for contemporary French anti-clericals.[65]

At Oneglia, Mussolini had an extra reason to revive his political career. The school where he worked was a private, Catholic, one. However, he resided in the town with two of the brothers of G.M. Serrati; Lucio Serrati edited the local socialist weekly, *La Lima*, and, in its pages, Mussolini was soon once more publishing on a wide range of topics. He could still be a naïve provincial, mourning, for example, Edmondo De Amicis, author of the patriotic manual, *Cuore*, which he recalled had been the favourite book of his youth (as it was meant to be for all good Italians).[66] His more accustomed politics, however, were crudely revealed in an article he published at Easter (it cannot have much appealed to his employers), condemning Christian festivals as matters which left real workers utterly indifferent. Only 'idiots', he added, believed Bible stories.[67] Characteristically, he was also quick to defend 'intellectuals' – they were not the ones who brought trouble to socialism; the problem lay instead with 'those who proclaim themselves socialists without really knowing why'.[68] But his most ambitious article for *La Lima* was a lengthy review of Marx on the twenty-fifth anniversary of his death. Here Mussolini celebrated the father of socialism as an activist, as one who was simultaneously 'scientific' and realistic. Marx, he wrote with fervour, had demonstrated conclusively that 'a class will never give up its privileges unless it is forced to do so'. He had proven without doubt that 'the final struggle will be violent and "catastrophic"' because the capitalists would certainly not surrender without a bitter fight.[69]

The message which Mussolini read to himself from such lines was that teaching was a less enticing career than was politics. At Oneglia, his contract was short-lived, as it had been at Tolmezzo, and again he began to think of something better to do. Like many another young man on the make, he remembered his possible patrons, very politely consulting G.M. Serrati about whether he might be thought suitable to edit a paper at Mantova and, if so, begging Serrati to advance his case.[70] In this application he was not successful. Again he was driven back home, there to tell readers of *La Lima* about the revolutionary spirit which, in his surmise, coursed through the Romagna.[71] A strike, some strident orations and a quarrel brought arrest, imprisonment and release on appeal.[72] In the aftermath of these events, and now living in Alessandro's household outside Forlì, Mussolini turned back to culture, writing an exposition of the poetry of Klopstock in the syndicalist journal, *Pagine libere*, and a defence of Nietzsche for the regional cultural magazine, *Il Pensiero Romagnolo*. In this last piece he concluded that Nietzsche was indeed a positive intellectual force; his works resounded with a 'hymn to life'.[73] With an apparent contradiction which he shared with such other nationalisers of the people as Frenchman Charles Maurras, he used the pages of *Il Pensiero Romagnolo* to celebrate local dialect poetry; it displayed 'our people', he explained, and made manifest 'our ethnic and spiritual profile'.[74]

By the time that his readers were digesting this particular idea, Mussolini, now aged 25, had found his best job so far. His patrons, Serrati and Balabanoff, had recommended him as secretary of the socialist organisation in the Austrian-ruled Trentino and editor of the local party paper. On 22 January 1909 readers of *L'Avvenire del Lavoratore* were told to welcome the new comrade: 'Benito Mussolini, besides being a proven fighter, is a fervent propagandist, versed especially in the subject of anti-clericalism. He is a cultured young man, and to the great advantage of our movement, he has a thorough knowledge of the German language.'[75] His most scholarly Italian biographer is more curt: 'Psychologically Mussolini went to Trento, as he had to other jobs, out of a spirit of adventure and a sense of novelty, and also simply to make ends meet'.[76]

Mussolini's own first account of his life in Trent, once city of the Counter Reformation and now a town of 30 000 people, was mixed in its tone. His work, he said, was not demanding. He had to give lots of speeches, but frequently in beer-halls, not venues he liked, given that he had renounced his earlier fondness for alcohol (and, indeed, according to a malicious friend, had turned into something of a hypochondriac).[77] In the town, three journals competed – a socialist paper, a Catholic one and the nationalist *Il Popolo*, organ of the later 'martyr of the Italian nation in war', Cesare Battisti. Mostly the papers used their space to insult each other, Mussolini noted deprecatingly, though he himself did not rule out the possibility of working for Battisti (and was soon writing for *Il Popolo* and for Battisti's weekly, *Vita trentina*). The local socialists, he added, mistrusted his fervour and were not taking to his personality. To fill in time, he was composing short stories 'in the manner of Poe'.[78] He had also put up advertisements round town for himself as a private teacher of French, guaranteeing 'a swift and sure method'. Life, though, had its advantages. One was that the police were less interfering than in Italy. Moreover, he could always spend time in the town library (open from 9 a.m. to 10 p.m., and subscribing to forty dailies and eighty journals in the four main European languages), a place much better than Forlì, ignorant 'town of sellers of pigs and lucerne'.[79]

Trent, or Trento to use the Italian name, was, after all, the biggest centre in which Mussolini had lived. It was also the one most conscious of possessing a culture and a history, destined after 1918 to be the capital of the South Tyrol (or Alto Adige as Italians patriots demanded it be called). Here was a place that mattered in a way that Predappio, Oneglia or Tolmezzo, and even Forlì, did not. Despite standing on the perimeter of Austrian events, the significance of the city was enhanced by contemporary politics. The Habsburg empire of Austria-Hungary was a crucible of *belle époque* European ideas. The leading adherents of 'Austro-socialism', such men as Otto Bauer and Karl Renner, sought a proper line on the great dilemma of how Marxists might relate to the modern state and nation. In the wider intellectual world, figures such as Klimt, Schönberg and Freud allowed the Austrian capital Vienna to challenge Paris as the cultural epicentre of Europe.[80] With his populist and manipulative Anti-Semitism, Karl Lueger, the mayor of Vienna, was pioneering another sort of modernity and winning the admiration of Adolf Hitler (born 1889), who, in 1909, was at the nadir of his fortunes as a failed artist.[81] Hitler and Mussolini did not yet know of each other's existence. Had they done so, there is little doubt that each would have then despised the culture, personality and politics of his later ally.

Although the debates of Vienna grew attenuated by the time they reached provincial Trento, the city embodied a dilemma central to the issue of state formation. Somewhere in the South Tyrol lay the border between the Italian and German speaking worlds, that is, where the dialect of one peasant household had a Germanic base and that of the next some Latinate structure. How, then, should this linguistic border be treated politically? Should it, for example, coincide with state borders? Italian 'irredentists' (those who wanted to 'win back' the *terre irredente* or unredeemed Italian lands) had marked out Trento's significance in 1896 by erecting there a statue to Dante Alighieri, icon of what was called the new, 'Third', Italy. Even the most self-consciously respectable of bourgeois Italians hoped for gain through what they proclaimed to be 'the genius and commitment of their great and inspiring *Duce*', Dante.[82] If this 'ethnic' nationalist thesis was accepted, what did it mean for the survival of the entire multinational Habsburg empire? What, too, did it imply about the fact that Italy and Austria-Hungary were presently joined in the Triple Alliance? How might the national issue be reconciled with other political ideals, the socialist obviously enough, and also the Catholic, since Austria was a place where modern 'Christian Democracy' or 'Christian Socialism' was beginning to flower, and where Italy's future post-Second World War Christian Democrat Prime Minister, Alcide De Gasperi, was commencing a political career and earning Mussolini's ire for his clericalism?[83] Mussolini only stayed 8 months in Trento but, in that period, he both watched and, with his brazen willingness to express a view about anything, participated in the manifold debates which disturbed the city's natural sleepiness.

Over the months which followed, Mussolini dashed off a series of articles on this matter or that, the only real problem for a later analyst being to reconcile what he had to say on various occasions. He did not forget to be an anti-clerical, taking his predilection for blasphemy further than usual when he wrote, with strident cynicism, that 'it was a good bet that many Catholics and quite a lot of priests prefer a good beefsteak to the body of Christ'.[84] Forgetful of his own military service, he now resumed his stance as a convinced critic of militarism, 'that monstrous octopus whose thousand slimy tentacles ceaselessly suck out the blood and best energies of the people'.[85]

He preached socialism. As he explained in a first editorial in *L'Avvenire del Lavoratore*, in phrases which, for all his denials of religion, were indebted to the sermons he had once heard with his mother:

Socialism means the elevation and purification of the individual conscience, and its achievement will be the result of a long series of efforts. Everyone, indeed, from the professional man to the worker, can bring a stone to the edifice, doing a socialist deed every day, and so prepare for the overthrow of existing society.[86]

Actually being a socialist was rather more difficult than was here implied, since factional conflict and schism continued to beset the movement. Once, Mussolini had said that he was a syndicalist, but, in 1907, such supporters of that ideal as Sergio Panunzio and A.O. Olivetti had renounced the mainstream of the Italian socialist party.[87] Now Mussolini decided that he was not a syndicalist, while half fearing and half hoping that syndicalism might prove the way of the future.[88] After all, he explained, Georges Sorel, though difficult to read, was a major philosopher. Unravelling his logic, Mussolini noted disarmingly, was comparable to the trouble it took to find the melodic theme in a musical composition by Wagner. The task was none the less worth the persevering.[89] Roberto Michels, another commentator on the role of elites in moving history, was also to be appreciated.[90] Of course Mussolini treasured Marx; but the father of socialism had an equal, Charles Darwin; each preached 'struggle against tradition, authority, dogma'.[91] In any case, perhaps there was more than one Marx with whom to conjure. The most attractive one was, he declared, the young Marx; he who was 'above all a man of action'; he who preached that 'presently one should not just study the world but rather change it'.[92]

If marking out the proper socialist line had its pitfalls, another matter which could not be ignored in Trento was national difference. On that topic, too, Mussolini's mind flitted from one position to the next. When feeling pious in his socialism, he remembered that Marxists were internationalists, committed to saving the workers of the globe. Patriotism was 'a fetish', manipulated by the bourgeoisie. The true proletariat, he told the audience at one of his speeches, was 'anti-patriotic by definition and basic need'.[93] It was hard, however, to keep such purity unsullied. When the Germanic comrades had to deal with Italians they were not always polite; German socialists were evidently contaminated by nationalism, he wrote, and Germans as a whole underestimated the contribution of Italian emigrants to the working world of Central Europe.[94] A quasi nationalist or racist rejection of German nationalism and racism remained the central issue,[95] but other, similarly ambiguous, generalisations slipped easily into his prose. 'Slavs', in their 'civilization and soul', were given to 'tragedy';[96] Italians, too, were 'sceptical' and 'fatalist', like 'other peoples of the south'.[97] None the less, they had a potentially positive side. When French aviator Louis Blériot flew the English Channel, to Mussolini's eyes the event signalled a triumph of 'Latin genius and courage', as well as providing evidence of the infinite potential of scientific modern man, that blessed being who was rejecting fratricidal struggle in order to win a final victory over 'nature, life and the universe'.[98]

The other great theme of Mussolini's writings, and also a complicating factor in his socialism, was his continuing weakness for intellectuals, and his uneasy desire to cut a figure in their world. As well as maintaining his connection with Battisti, Mussolini exchanged correspondence with Giuseppe Prezzolini, editor of the journal *La Voce*. Prezzolini, a Prefect's son, came from a class and a cultural base well above Mussolini's, even if ultimately he was a journalist whose politics never found a secure ideological purpose; not for nothing would he record his life under the title, 'The Useless Italian'.[99] In 1909 *La Voce* enjoyed great prestige among those dissident young who, as Mussolini put it, viewed Italian Prime Minister Giolitti and his liberalism as 'irredeemably mediocre', an 'anachronism' and national 'shame'.[100] Mussolini took out a subscription to the paper and, in demonstration of his new bond, publicly urged others in Trento to do the same. Prezzolini, he proclaimed, was an intellectual with 'courage', a quality lacking in most of his contemporaries.[101]

Mussolini's correspondence with *La Voce*'s editor was studied in its deference. An appropriate start was to regret that Trento's 'intellectual life' was 'wretchedly discomforting'. When more serious commentary became possible, he tried to explain the intricacies of local politics to his potential patron: the 'Italians' of the Trentino no doubt liked the idea of some autonomy but they scarcely favoured annexation to Italy, he admitted with honesty and acumen. Trieste, too, was neither 'absolutely Italian', nor destined ever to be 'completely Slav'.[102] Nonetheless, what he most admired about *La Voce*, he eventually explained, was Prezzolini's quest to 'make Italy known to Italians'.[103] 'To create an "Italian" soul', he told Prezzolini admiringly, 'is a superb mission.'[104]

After all, Mussolini added in more detail in his own paper, it was clear that socialists, too, did not easily 'abandon their language and culture, the traditions into which they were born and to which they belonged'. They only foreswore 'the bourgeois *patria*'. 'In loving their own nationality, it is not mandatory for them to hate the others. [Rather] harmonic development and the brotherhood of all nations – this is the socialist ideal'.[105]

For some analysts, such comments signify that, by 1909, Mussolini had transmogrified into a national socialist. But it is a mistake to read his views too literally and to regard his course as determined. In corresponding with Prezzolini, he was approaching an acknowledged superior and was palpably endeavouring to be ingratiating as well as respectful and interesting. What his words really conveyed was his thrusting desire to go beyond Trento to some more exciting and important spot: perhaps Florence, perhaps Milan, perhaps Rome. In this poorly cloaked ambition, Mussolini did not confine his world to Italy. Indeed, for him, when imagining a glorious future, the best destination was still Paris, a city, which, he wrote in characteristics phrases in one of his last pieces in *L'Avvenire del Lavoratore*, was 'an immense crucible of passions, hatreds and loves', a metropolis where 'in a relatively small arena world-determining battles are fought out. [There] men multiply their energies a hundred fold in the struggle; [there] they are great in their sacrifice, abject in their vice'. This was the city which contained within itself the 'universe'.[106] In ways not unknown to other contemporary Italian intellectuals – the Futurist Filippo Tommaso Marinetti launched the manifesto of his movement, sometimes deemed nationalist, in *Le Figaro* in 1909[107] – Mussolini's greatest ambition was to be lionised as a 'real intellectual' in Paris.

The track to that summit was not, however, becoming easier to plot. Again a term of employment was to prove short-lived. For all his earlier confident remarks about the relative decency or inactivity of the Habsburg police, the behaviour of the notorious 'subversive' Mussolini had actually been watched from the moment of his arrival in Trento. By the summer of 1909 the authorities had decided to expel him; their search for an excuse became more eager when a visit by Emperor Franz Joseph to nearby Innsbruck prompted a full alert. On 29 August a mysterious theft was blamed on Mussolini, despite a lack of evidence that he was involved. His abode was searched, his writings seized. He himself was arrested yet again, carried off to gaol at Rovereto, with an expulsion order hanging over him. On 24 September he was tried but, to the disgust of the police, acquitted. Still in close confinement, Mussolini went briefly on a hunger strike, but, two days later, Austrian officialdom resolved matters by putting him over the frontier. He carried back to his father's restaurant at Forlì little more than a momentary fame fostered by the ham-fisted nature of his expulsion.[108] The matter was still an object of protest from socialist members of parliament in Rome in March 1910.[109]

For Mussolini, however, the prospects seemed grim. Here he was, again unemployed, again back among the pig-sellers of Forlì, remote from the 'European' intellectual and political world of Trento, and with a decidedly cloudy future. Six weeks after his return he was contemplating another, more distant, emigration. 'I am tired of being in Italy', he wrote to a friend whom he thought might accompany him, 'tired of being in the world (I mean the old world, not [he added pompously] the *lacrimarum valle*). I want to go off into the new. Will you follow me if, as I hope, I make my fortune?'[110] A contemporary recalled a young man who seemed older than his years, unkempt in his appearance, given to sporting a flapping black tie and a tattered 'three day beard', prematurely bald so that his shiny head contrasted strangely with his black chin. His detractors pointed out that his habit of rolling his burning eyes made him resemble the conventional picture of an anarchist avenger of social injustice.[111]

Perhaps this artfully contructed image added to his sex appeal. Certainly Mussolini now found a woman who would share his life. In one of his ample articles for *L'Avvenire del Lavoratore*, Mussolini had expatiated on love, warning against its over sentimentalisation and preaching the need for 'a new law, a new morality, a new religion', which might overthrow the tyrannies of bourgeois and Catholic respectability.[112] Mussolini's own sexual habits remained Bohemian, or 'Latin', throughout his life – one commentator reckoned he slept with more than 400 women.[113] Undoubtedly, there were mistresses, persistent or fleeting, and a number of illegitimate children. There was also the durable relationship with Rachele Guidi, which was in time formalised by marriage, blessed first by the state and eventually by the church, and five legitimate children. Guidi, still short of her twentieth birthday, on 1 September 1910 was delivered of Mussolini's elder daughter, Edda; Rachele was, Mussolini wrote the next year, *la mia compagna* (my female comrade).[114]

Though legends about their relationship abound, the couple first met in Rosa's school room, when Mussolini was standing in for his mother. The schoolgirl Rachele, like many another, was struck by the new young teacher's 'eyes like fire'.[115] For his part, Benito Mussolini may have been attracted by the pupil's blue eyes and blonde hair, ignoring both her squarish physique and her decidedly modest intellectuality. Some 7 years younger than the *Duce*, whom for a long time she would address as *Lei*, using the formal third person appropriate to superiors, rather than the intimate *tu* form,[116] Rachele came from a background poorer than the Mussolinis' and nearer the peasantry. Indeed, in many ways, the most surprising thing about their relationship is that the ambitious Mussolini did not cast her off for a social superior, with whom a personal tie could have brought advantage in wealth, status and connection. As the wife of the dictator, Rachele was not always presentable, or anxious to be presented. But she continued to live with Benito in the somewhat sporadic way that politicians' spouses often do. Unlike Hitler and perhaps Stalin, not to mention many other political leaders, Mussolini had a 'normal' 'home' life, or at least one whose character was shared by millions of his contemporaries and, in his own way, he never ceased to cherish Rachele and to see her as a link to the 'real world' of the 'people'.

Benito and Rachele began cohabiting in early 1910; she must have fallen pregnant at much the same time. Some months before, Mussolini had made her his 'intended', writing properly that he was worried about her moral status while she resided with his father and her mother at the *Bersagliere* inn.[117] Mediterranean issues of 'honour and shame' long played a part in the Mussolini household. Late in 1909 to avoid the perils of life with the ageing Alessandro, Rachele moved to a married sister's home. When Mussolini finally came to fetch her to join him in what would be their tiny flat in Forlì, they walked for kilometres in the rain, because, in Rachele's post-1945 memory, she had not yet comprehended the meaning and purpose of an umbrella. In her mind such contraptions were part of the lifestyle of the flamboyant and spendthrift bourgeoisie and not of people like the Guidis.[118]

Their life was humble – Rachele never forgot her dismay at her companion's habit of wasting money on books.[119] But Mussolini had a job, which again offered the prospect of what Italians are accustomed to call *sistemazione* (a place in life). On 9 January 1910 he had commenced work as editor of the four-page socialist weekly news sheet of Forlì, a task which he combined with the secretaryship of the local branch of the Socialist Party.[120] The paper was called, with Marxist virtue, *La Lotta di Classe* (The Class Struggle). In accepting this post as administrative and cultural leader of Forlivese socialism, Mussolini had come home. Given his talent and enterprise, a future was beckoning in which he would turn into a Forlì notable, a local intellectual certainly, perhaps a potential member of parliament (throughout the history of Liberal Italy, many politicians had commenced their rise that way), and very probably a man of influence. His commitment to revolution and socialism might stand in the way of these prospects, but other youthful ideologues had 'transformed' themselves as they grew older. In early 1910 there seemed quite a chance that Mussolini would soon be smiling at the way he had once so deliberately styled himself a revolutionary. Instead he might soon acquire a paunch, a frock coat and an admiring and importunate set of clients. As he himself argued in his premature account of his brilliant career, he was after all qualified. Since leaving Forlimpopoli, he had imbibed a 'culture', gained a 'knowledge of the world' and mastered a set of 'modern languages'; he had become a man of the world in many senses. Only one matter stood in the way of that resolution of the Mussolini story: 'I am a restless person, with a wicked temperament', he wrote of himself.[121] Forlì would not be enough to satisfy him. Benito Mussolini would want to go further, faster, higher than was possible in the sleepy provinces.

4

The class struggle, 1910–1914

UNDER the Fascist regime, Mussolini declared on occasion that he was a 'child of the last peasant civilization'.[1] This boast was scarcely true (though it may have made sense if redirected to Rachele and her family).[2] Certainly, in January 1910 the last thing that Mussolini was thinking of embodying was an organic relationship with the land. Back in Forlì his interest lay rather in making a splash intellectually and so promoting his revolutionary ideals and himself. There was no need particularly to separate these matters, and historians who try to do so are often guilty of anachronism, and thus of manufacturing a coherent Fascist chief (if there ever was such a person) well before the event. In 1910 Mussolini's imagined itinerary through life remained eclectic. Before assuming the editorship of *La Lotta di Classe*, he had, for example, been an unsuccessful applicant for a job at *Il Resto del Carlino*, the celebrated but liberal conservative Bologna daily[3] and a paper he was soon cheerfully denouncing as a 'factory of lies'.[4] Had he been taken on there, he may well have found reason to moderate his socialism. But in Forlì it was easy to identify with revolution; in a setting like that, it was hard to see an alternative for an aspiring young man of his class and educational background.

Benito Mussolini, editor of *La Lotta di Classe* and therefore chief socialist of Forlì, was not yet 27, and was almost bursting with energy – political, intellectual and sexual. Contemporaries recalled the way in which he liked to go to bed at 3 or 4 a.m., but was always back in the town piazza by 8 a.m., eagerly awaiting the arrival of the newspapers from the greater world outside the town walls. Editing a four-page journal, indeed writing it, since he was *La Lotta di Classe*'s only serious correspondent, and managing the local socialist branch, scarcely constituted a full time job for a man like him. Mussolini spent much of his day leaning up against the kiosk of the *Fratelli Damerini*, esteemed purveyors of papers and of 'all the fresh books which came out on art, science, economics and philosophy'. Whenever such a new work was exposed to the public, Mussolini at once devoured it.[5] In the evening, at 11 p.m., he would ostentatiously take his place at the local coffee shop and commence scribbling his articles for the next edition of *La Lotta di Classe*, all the while gaining fame for the sarcastic retorts which he would throw off about the misdeeds of others.[6] Mussolini, people were beginning to notice, was a man with staring eyes which, if you submitted to his truculent and commanding gaze, could place you in his thrall; his thick lips also expressed a certainty and a dominance, or so his admirers said. All in all, they agreed, he was characterised by 'an extraordinary masculinity'. Soon it would be concluded that Mussolini radiated power, and even now it was clear that he exuded a 'special sense of urgency', was possessed of 'a phenomenal elasticity of judgement', and was a 'journalist born and bred'.[7] By some accounts he was a *Duce* in the making,[8] though such hyberbole might be countered with the equal likelihood at that time that he was just another ambitious provincial, with his destiny as yet uncertain.

At first, after his return from the Trentino, he was only a peripheral figure in the world both of Romagnole socialism[9] and of Romagnole politics. In Forlì the republican movement was at least as strong as the socialist one (and Mussolini was soon acknowledging the influence of a politician whom he saluted as 'the *Duce* of local republicans').[10] In these circumstances of relative anonymity and weakness, Mussolini's task was to campaign on all possible fronts, against the bourgeoisie and the established order, of course, but also against the republicans and, as well, against anyone in the socialist movement who doubted his ideals and methods. Anti-clericalism might still prove a theme worth pursuing. Modestly signing himself 'A Real Heretic', Mussolini was soon telling his readers about the deplorable case of the free-thinker, Francisco Ferrer, executed some months before in Spain, where, Mussolini claimed, the Inquisition still reigned unchecked.[11] In February 1910 he could also exult in legal victory when a case hanging over against him from the previous December was dismissed. For the present unemployed, he had organised a riotous counter-demonstration in a local church after it was announced that the crusading priest, Agostino Gemelli, was intending to preach to the faithful on the extra-scientific virtue of cures at Lourdes.[12]

But anti-clericalism was falling out of fashion and even Mussolini began to recognise the fact. His editorials would have to fix on other matters. A socialist leader, for example, had the task of recording party history and so it was mandatory to write a mournful obituary of Andrea Costa. A few months later he further demonstrated his pedigree by doing the same for his own father[13] – romantic rumour spread that he had sworn an eternal allegiance to socialism on his father's grave.[14] Yet the job had its irritations, too. In a typical piece composed less than a month after taking on his editorship, Mussolini wrote scathingly of the general cultural level at Forlì and especially that to be found within socialist branches. There, on entering the room, a man could expect to see comrades playing *briscola* (a card game), and doing so badly, beneath an obligatory, and presumably frowning, portrait of Karl Marx. The town could not boast one decent bookshop, Mussolini complained despite his patronage of Damerini's; presently one had to ferret out books promiscuously displayed between postcards and perfumes. What was the point of books in Forlì anyway, Mussolini mused bitterly? How could they be discussed rigorously? The locals failed to read serious journals; only four subscriptions could be tallied for *La Voce* and none at all for the syndicalists' *Pagine libere*. His town was a place where 'the people corrupt their brains with pubs, dances, brothels and sport'. 'At Forlì', Mussolini concluded tartly, 'intellectual interests always come last'.[15] The Mussolini who tried to scintillate each afternoon in the piazza was plainly discontented. How could he hit upon a path to greater satisfaction?

To rise was the answer, to redouble his revolutionary rhetoric, to become known not just in Forlì but throughout the region, and even beyond. A Romagnole background might help a man move past the Romagna. On his first speaking appearance as a delegate to the national Party congress in Milan, Mussolini took pains to introduce himself, in what he hoped was a telling fashion, as the messenger of the 'absolute intransigence' of his part of the country.[16] Romagnole spirit meant that here was a young man ready to say openly that 'the Italian parliament is profoundly and irredeemably corrupt'.[17] Here, too, was a spartan spirit not afraid to berate reformists wherever they might be found. He would speak up aggressively when one of their leaders, Leonida Bissolati, controversially agreed, in March 1911, to meet King Victor Emmanuel at the Quirinale, the royal palace in Rome, and give advice on who might serve in the next government.[18] In addition, Mussolini was ruthless in his attacks on the gentlemen of his party, the lawyers for example, men who, like army officers and priests, were, Mussolini wrote evocatively, 'the locusts who fling themselves on the body of a young nation and sap its best energies'; 'lawyers, and priests too', he added, could never be trusted, since they 'had to lie in order to live'. Real socialists they could never be.[19] Similarly, Freemasons were not good comrades, and their ubiquity in Milan made nearby Ravenna a better potential site for a socialist congress.[20] The only crisis to be located in contemporary socialism, he urged, lay among its supporters not in its ideas – he was destined many times to return to this theme of human inadequacy. Real socialist men could see at once that the struggle between bourgeoisie and proletariat was indeed visceral and needed forthwith to be carried to its highest expression – 'total revolution'.[21]

It was the way of the world that, despite his contempt for local life, Mussolini could not avoid the humdrum. His paper, for example, published an effusive report (Mussolini very likely himself wrote it) of a visit which he made in May 1910 to Predappio, by invitation no doubt, but also to shore up his domestic base. He spoke there at considerable length on the theme of 'The socialist and labour movement'. It was a great day. Mussolini's genius had shone through and Predappio could be proud of him. A 'huge' audience had assembled, 'composed of both sexes and of all grades of society'. It was not disappointed. The orator, 'whose name is so dear to our workers', exceeded all expectations in a speech which lasted almost two hours and which, 'with convincing and cutting words and a real oratorical passion, so engrossed the many listeners that they often interrupted him with heartfelt cries of approval, and they saluted him at the end with a wave of applause which went on for quite a few minutes'. The whole event, the correspondent concluded breathlessly, amounted to 'a real intellectual feast'. Everybody in town hoped that Benito Mussolini would soon agree to another speaking engagement at Predappio.[22]

Being lionised by the folks back home must have brought some gratification. But, though not cutting himself free from his base – he never fully did so – Mussolini was still looking out from Predappio and Forlì for wider fields to conquer. Could there be prospects in the editorship of the party newspaper *Avanti!*, a journal reduced in its impact, Mussolini complained with a mixture of disgust and self-interest, because of party factionalism and editorial weakness? From the modest pages of *La Lotta di Classe*, Mussolini began to advocate a drastic solution for the socialists' national daily. Take the paper away from Rome – that city lacked a real working class and was parasitic by definition (whatever later Fascist propagandists might say, Mussolini's soul was not yet altogether Roman). The so-called 'eternal city', he stated in words common enough among all the enemies of the Giolittian Liberal system, pullulated with 'cheap landladies, shoeshine boys, prostitutes, priests and bureaucrats'. Just outside its gates, he lamented, families in the *Agro Pontino* still eked out their survival in straw huts, as though they were primitive beings from beyond civilised Europe. And so, if not Rome, then where? Perhaps Milan, but that was the city of stock-market and business dominance. Florence? But the quality of its existing dailies was too poor. No, the best place for a socialist paper was, it scarcely needed to be said, Bologna, capital of the Emilia-Romagna. There *Avanti!* could be positioned at the 'centre of national proletarian life ... very near the red lands of the Romagna where thousands and thousands of socialists were waiting ready for any sacrifice'.[23] If *Avanti!* was edited there, Mussolini speculated in his secret thoughts, a young and aggressive journalist from Forlì, who had once been rejected for a job with the establishment's *Il Resto del Carlino*, might yet win employment in the numinous regional capital.

Mussolini was constructing himself, then, as 'the extremist', the warrior of Romagnole socialism. As he recalled with some pleasure in May 1911, when reviewing his editorship of *La Lotta di Classe*, he had campaigned with effect not just against republicans but against clericals, anarchists, syndicalists and the mainstream of the Socialist party itself: 'in this ample liberty to criticise, I find my full self-justification'.[24] He had boosted his newspaper's circulation until it sold 1600 copies, with 'about 1000' of those being by subscription. The majority of such loyal readers were, he claimed proudly, 'real workers'. In addition, every Sunday he preached the socialist gospel, either in Forlì or in the smaller towns of the province, whose piazzas and party branches he located with some effort after he tramped down dusty roads.[25] Often he spent the night in down-market provincial hotels – it was in one that he met Leandro Arpinati, destined for a time to be the Fascist boss of Bologna.[26]

By 1911 it could be agreed that he had worked hard and effectively, both in his own estimation and that of others. He loved his infant daughter and continued to live with Rachele. Already his post at *La Lotta di Classe* had outlasted his previous terms of employment and his life had a pleasure and a promise about it which in the past had been lacking. Maybe it was even time to abate his familiar rudeness in dealings with the world and cultivate a certain geniality and sense of humour. And so he expatiated in his own paper about the way in which Romagnoles loved rhetoric, violence and their town *campanile* (bell tower); they rejected emigration and knew only that their *paese* occupied the centre of the world.[27] He was presumably intending to be ironical, but the piece conveys a mixed message, half hostile, half fond, and very much about himself. Mussolini was growing used to being a man who mattered in Forlì.

His accustomed prose remained brusque, sarcastic and churlish. Sorel, whom he had once admired but whose politics had moved rightwards, was now excoriated as 'a pensioner given to sacking library shelves', a covert admirer of the *ancien régime*, an enemy of the French Republic, democracy and socialism.[28] Those intellectuals, who had united at Florence and formed the *Associazione Nazionalista Italiana* (Italian Nationalist Association) and who before long became his crucial allies in the Fascist cause, were the lick-spittles of 'the monarchy, the army and war', 'three words, three institutions, three absurdities'. Acknowledging his own flirtation with Prezzolini and his colleagues at *La Voce*, who themselves looked appreciatively on the Nationalists, Mussolini admitted that once he had sympathised with domestic nationalism and the idea of 'a democratic and cultural movement devoted to the advancement, unification and renewal of the Italian people'. But no more; his socialism was now too stout for further dalliance.[29] Still, there were places worse than Italy, he had to admit, the distant USA, for example. There 'the rapacious property-owning American bourgeoisie admits no limits, possesses no scruples and does not share the fears and the cowardice of our bourgeoisie. [They are] violent, absolute, criminal. When they feel the need, they simply stain their hands with proletarian blood. They lack any human sense. They are only interested in exploitation'.[30] Nor had he broken fully with Prezzolini. Indeed, in March–April 1911 Mussolini humbly asked the editor of *La Voce* for an advance on his royalties for 'The Trentino as seen by a socialist', which was to be published in Florence under Prezzolini's auspices (and with his sub-editorial attention to Mussolini's prose); the death of his father, Mussolini complained, had caused temporary financial embarrassment.[31] Once again the possibility lurked that, somewhere beneath the stormy surface of his rhetoric, Mussolini cherished his Italian identity, and placed implicit limits on his dedication to internationalist revolutionary socialism.

Mussolini, a Socialist Party stalwart? Mussolini, an intellectual patriot? Mussolini, a man of general fame? Each alternative remained alive in his mind. What was not possible was the prospect of Mussolini settling down content in the provinces. His restless search for an extreme line, and for the credit which might accrue from it, had not ceased. Even as, philosophically, he discounted some of his earlier heresies, in practical terms he was stretching his socialist loyalty to breaking point. In April 1911, on his initiative, the Forlì branch declared itself autonomous from the national party organisation. Mussolini justified the decision under the characteristic and heartfelt title 'To Dare': 'We are not talking about raising a new political standard, but rather of saving the old socialist flag from those who have wrapped themselves in its folds.' They stood for compromise and corruption of the ideal; he and his *fascio*, he wrote, perhaps using this word for the first time but without its eventual meaning, instead represented purity. [32]

In this step to outright schism, Mussolini had, however, run ahead of his time (or behind it, since the actions of the Forlì branch with their presumed hypothesis of an eventual Forlì Socialist Republic could be interpreted as campanilism rampant). His maximalist friends in the party were soon engaged in negotiating Mussolini back into the ranks. [33] After all, in the summer of 1911 major issues confronted Italy both at home and abroad, and it was these concerns, as refracted into the Romagna, which were to secure Mussolini's reputation in the party and, over the next 18 months, make him, in some eyes, its coming man.

The years 1911–12 were a watershed for Liberal, Giolittian, Italy. The early part of the twentieth century had been good for a political system which, from 1898 to 1900, under the quasi dictatorship of General Luigi Pelloux, seemed on the edge of collapse. The assassination of King Umberto I by an anarchist emigrant returned from the USA had signalled not reaction but instead an opening of the Liberal regime to emerging social groups. Under Giolitti's clever administration (he was Prime Minister in 1903–05, 1906–09 and 1911–March 1914), the economy for the most part flourished, and such moderate socialists as Turati acknowledged that Italy, too, was a place of 'progress'. In the northern 'industrial triangle', marked out by the factories of Turin, the banks of Milan and the port of Genoa, Italy was rapidly approaching a modernity which in the past had been the privilege of such richer and more powerful countries as Britain, Germany and France. Given this advancement both in reality and in expectation, the state celebrations, planned for the fiftieth anniversary of the Risorgimento in 1911, almost seemed justified. The huge 'refulgently' white Victor Emmanuel monument in Rome, positioned beneath the classical Capitol to claim the inheritance of Latin civilization, was inaugurated to applauding throngs, even if, in March that year, Claudio Treves, the editor of *Avanti!*, was grudging in his admiration of what proper socialists derided as the *monumentissimo*. [34]

Treves' dyspeptic tone expressed the unsurprising fact that

economic growth and social development rarely carry a single message. In 1911 Giolitti, newly returned as Prime Minister, faced a series of dilemmas lying at the heart of Italy's existence as a liberal nation state. There was the division between one part of the country and the other. What should be done with the South, which so far had barely experienced the benefits of economic growth? What should be done with the numerous other pockets of poverty and 'backward-ness'? In a dangerous world of tightening alliance systems within Europe and flaunted imperialism outside it, what should be done to defend or improve Italy's rank as the least of the Great Powers? Furthermore, what should or could be done to nationalise the Italian people, or, to be more precise, the peoples of the peninsula and so of the Italies? How could they be persuaded that official Italy was theirs, too? How, especially, could those dissidents – socialists of all persua-sions, Catholics, Nationalists, intellectuals – who were more and more strident in their attacks on Liberal inadequacy or 'corruption', be 'transformed' into the existing system, without revolution, war or tyranny?

To be sure, Giolitti had an ambitious strategy to deal with these massive issues. Abroad, he planned to seize Turkish-administered Tripolitania and Cyrenaica; these territories could be given the clas-sical name of Libya and, however poverty-stricken in practice, appease the nationalists and raise Italian prestige throughout the world. At home, Giolitti combined welfare (a nationalised insurance scheme) with a large expansion of the electorate – when the vote was next taken in 1913, some 65 per cent of Italian adult males had the right to cast their ballot. In theory the combination looked brilliant, practical liberalism of the most far-sighted kind. In reality it turned into disaster, signalling the commencement of the agony of Liberal Italy. Among those cheering the troubles of the Prime Minister and simultaneously acquiring a new national prominence was Benito Mussolini.

Some socialists were tempted by Giolitti's formula – the cases of Bissolati and Turati were exemplary. They were national figures who, like Giolitti himself, viewed matters from a national perspective. For humbler socialists, indeed for the great mass of the party rank and file, the issues were read differently but seemed no less drastic in their local significance. In the Romagna, for example, the relative economic growth of the Giolittian decade had hardened the lineaments of the class struggle. The modernisation of agriculture simplified the once intricate disparities between various sorts of peasants – large or small landowners, sharecroppers with one rental arrangement or another, and day labourers. More and more, life in the hinterland of Bologna or Forlì became a conflict between wealthy landowners and a peasantry who struggled to make ends meet. Not infrequently the land was falling to limited companies, whose anonymous owners lived far away in Milan or Rome, and whose interests were defended by paid managers, likely to be even more cruel and rapacious than their masters. The great peasant union, *Federterra*, by contrast, continued to grow, notably attracting new members from the poorest peasantry, wage workers on the land. Sharecroppers, too, often in relative decline economically as the pressures of capitalisation bore down on them, were frequently socialists, as, of course, were a number of urban workers and 'intellectuals' of Mussolini's type. They composed an uneasy coalition.

The intellectuals' radicalism and the socialist loyalty of the peasantry were for the moment, however, enhanced by the fact that the landowners, like the industrialists – who, in 1910, established the umbrella employers' body, *Confindustria*[35] – were aggressively forming associations to defend and expand their own interests. In April 1911 the National Agrarian Congress at Bologna was urged to reject the Prime Minister's policies of accommodation of the masses, privileging instead 'the solidarity that unites all those who, in different areas of activity, contribute to the production and development of national wealth at a time when every principle of liberty and justice is threatened with subversion'.[36] In the parliament Giolitti might preach and even practise moderation, compromise and 'national unity', but the reality in the provinces was starker. The rich seemed to be getting richer and more overbearing and the poor poorer but more assertive.

It was a circumstance made for the extremist rhetoric and personal ambition of Benito Mussolini. For some years he had applauded the strikes and other 'social actions' of his region. Now, suddenly, he trod a national stage. The trigger for his elevation was the campaign which, it became increasingly clear in the summer of 1911 as one patriotic anniversary event succeeded another, Giolitti intended to launch against Tripoli. Italian ships sailed to their destination there even before an Italian diplomat presented Turkey with a formal declaration of war on 29 September.

According to socialist theoretics, war, unjust, colonial, imperial war, demanded a general strike and resistance to the utmost from all members of the working class. Mussolini was just the man to urge this case vociferously and without qualification. In his first article about the Libyan question for *La Lotta di Classe*, published on 23 September, he condemned the 'mock-heroic madness of the war-mongers by profession', that is, those nationalists, whose chief ideologue, Enrico Corradini, had been arguing for some time the brazenly anti-Marxist case that Italy was a 'proletarian nation' which should avoid the class struggle and concentrate instead on a fight against the plutocratic nations of Britain and France.[37] Mussolini was not yet sure whether Giolitti was toying with such ludicrous or pernicious sabre-rattlers, but if there was war, he wrote ringingly: 'the Italian proletariat must hold itself ready to effect the general strike'.[38]

When the news reached Forlì that the government was, indeed, intending to act, Mussolini acted also. On 25 September, at his urging, the party branch unanimously voted for the strike; galvanised by speeches from Mussolini and other local leaders, on 26 September socialist cadres sabotaged the back railway line to Meldola, blocking its troop trains and beating off the cavalry attacks which tried to stop them. As Mussolini explained passionately in his report of the incidents for *La Lotta di Classe*: 'the proletariat of Forlì has set a magnificent example. The general strike has fully succeeded'. Reformism, he noted contemptuously, had demonstrated its pusillanimity and irrelevance by doing nothing to block the government's evil course. Real socialists, steeled by the 'new revolutionary mentality' displayed by the comrades of the region, must continue to subvert the war. What had the great French Revolution been, Mussolini added, in a familiar and moving but historically inaccurate parallel, but a general strike which went on for years? Opponents of the strike, be they Sorelians, syndicalists (quite a few of whom had turned patriotic over Libya), socialist members of parliament, orthodox trade unionists from the *Confederazione generale del lavoro*, or any other sort of reformist, must be swept aside.[39] So, of course, should clericals and their reactionary friends.[40] Now was the time of the deed; now might be the hour of the 'revolution'.

A stern response from the government against this fomenting of disorder was not long in coming. On 14 October Mussolini and such associates as the young Pietro Nenni, who, in the 1960s, became Italy's socialist Foreign Minister, were arrested. A contemporary suggests that certain formalities were still observed at this moment. The police located Mussolini sipping a coffee at his accustomed place. 'Professor Mussolini?' they enquired politely. 'You must accompany us to the station'. Mussolini then asked if he could finish his coffee first and was respectfully assured that he could.[41] Only then was he marched off to gaol. On 18 November Professor Mussolini went to trial at Forlì, where he spoke superbly in his own defence as a hero, 'not an evil-doer nor a vulgar criminal, but a man of ideas and of conscience, an agitator and soldier of a faith', who simply demanded respect, if not justice, from the institutions of the king.[42] Listeners were stirred by this rhetoric, but the court, unmoved, found him guilty, and sentenced him to a year's imprisonment. On appeal, however, his term was reduced and, on 12 March 1912, he was let out, jubilant and greatly risen in status.[43] In *La Lotta di Classe*, which kept its readers aware of their leader's sacrifice, the author of an anonymous article in January had been impressed by the power of Mussolini's eyes (as ever 'restless, profound and burning') and of his brain, words and soul; he was possessed of 'a head like that of Socrates'; he was the 'leader'.[44] *La Soffitta*, a socialist journal published in Rome, similarly celebrated his personality; Mussolini, a correspondent wrote, given his deep culture, had undoubtedly become 'one of the most sympathetic and signifi-cant' members of the party.[45] Eventually, *Avanti!*, too, carried a flattering report of the event: 'Comrade Mussolini was released this morning from prison, more a socialist than ever. We met him in his modest house among the family whom he adores and we chatted a little with him. He hasn't suffered physically from his time in prison. A great number of telegrams of congratulations and support were arriving from all over Italy'.[46] Mussolini, it seemed, was deserving of the banquet which the Forlì party membership offered him at the commodious and well-named *Albergo Vittoria*.[47] Unlike his father, he had emerged onto the national political stage, doing so as much through the flagrancy of his actions as the clarity of his ideology.

The banquet over, Mussolini moved swiftly to publicise and rein-force his recent political gains. Now honoured with the title of 'Forlì correspondent' of *Avanti!*, he told readers of his determination to bring out *La Lotta di Classe* in a bigger format and with an almost double run of 2800 copies, transforming it into 'one of the best and most widely-read papers in the Romagna'.[48] He also expanded his intellectual ambitions by beginning to write an extended essay on Czech Protestant theologian, Jan Huss. Though armed with a docu-mentary appendix, *Giovanni Huss il veridico* (Jan Huss the truth-teller),[49] when actually published in 1913, turned out to be a curious work, demonstrating that, whatever else Mussolini may have been, he was no historian. As its author disarmingly confessed in the introduction, Italian libraries contained scarcely any books on Huss, and he himself was not numbered among those few Italians who could read Czech.[50] In great part the book was a slightly genteel throw-back to Mussolini's days as a *mangiapreti* – he wrote again with relish of sex in convents, and papal conspiracy and crime, though he also applauded Huss as a Czech nationalist who resisted 'German' hegemony. In Mussolini's version, the precursor of Protestantism was almost refashioned into a father of the Risorgimento.[51]

Luckily for Mussolini his career was not dependent on such divagations. Practical advantage was coming his way. On 7 July 1912 delegates from all over Italy assembled at Reggio Emilia, just to the west of Bologna, for the Socialists' Thirteenth Party Congress.[52] It was to be an unlucky occasion for the reformists. The year before in Milan they had carried all before them. But the crisis surrounding the Libyan war had heightened social tensions and converted Reggio into a fortress of revolution. When he rose to speak on 8 July Mussolini, still wearing the aura of his heroic exploits over the previous nine months, was very much playing at home.

His speech was a triumph. With studied intransigence, Mussolini signaled to the party faithful and the world beyond that the young editor from Forlì must be acknowledged as a major political figure. The oration began with a root and branch attack on parliament (and socialist parliamentarians), bolstered by an apposite quotation from Marx. Italy, Mussolini proclaimed, was the country where 'parliamentary cretinism ... had reached the ... most humiliating levels'. Giolitti's suffrage reforms were no more than a trick to keep parliament going but the organisation was 'absolutely unnecessary' for real socialists. The record of almost all those elected under the party banner to the Chamber of Deputies was disgraceful. Only Turati (who was attempting a compromise between the warring factions and whom Mussolini did not yet want to antagonise) had remained a real socialist, in his expression of the Italian proletariat's utter detestation of war, for example.

The solution to the problem was simple – expel the leading reformists, Bissolati, Ivanoe Bonomi, Angelo Cabrini and Guido Podrecca. In March a Rome building worker had fired at the King ('Victor Savoy', as Mussolini, no doubt with knowledge of 'Louis Capet' in 1792 and perhaps buoyed by the idea that some saw him as the new Marat,[53] insolently called him). Bissolati and his colleagues had publicly regretted the assault on Victor Emmanuel. But, Mussolini urged, while he did not want to be inhumane towards another human being, it had to be agreed that enduring 'an act such as this is just part of the job of being a king'. The soft-hearted, he ran on, would no doubt argue that the battle should focus on ideas not men. But that was not good enough. Intellectual talk had its limits. There was a time when it was 'logical and humane' to arraign men; 'we should put on trial not an idea but certain specific acts which fall under the party rules, rules which we ourselves have not made', Mussolini declared in the robes of tribune of the people. 'The Socialist Party', he added in a metaphor with a sinister role to play in the tragedies of the twentieth century,[54] 'practises expulsions because it is a living organism. There are socialist antibodies,[55] just as there are the physiological antibodies, discovered by Metchnikoff. If we do not defend ourselves, the impure elements will disintegrate the party in the same way that damaging germs circulate in the blood ... and kill off the human organism.' In sum, new-style political parties in Italy must concentrate on one matter only, the need to bring down the already chaotic and incoherent liberal system, 'assailing it from every side'. That was why a 'numerous and compact' party was required; that was why he carried his list of 'proscriptions', Mussolini concluded with one of those classical references which Italians found so hard to eschew. Real socialists would not want to follow reformists, 'either now, or tomorrow, or indeed ever'.[56]

As far as the party delegates were concerned it was a marvellous speech, learned (there were references to Cervantes as well as to Marx, while Bissolati was blamed for borrowing too much from Sorel), 'scientific' and populist at the same time, a mixture which Mussolini long favoured. The revolutionary from Forlì had made his case in the spirit of the moment. The deputies under attack were expelled (to found their own schismatic Reformist Party). Costantino Lazzari, a friend of Mussolini's old patron, G.M. Serrati, became secretary, while Angelica Balabanoff and Mussolini himself were elected to the party directorate. Moreover, the events in Reggio Emilia echoed resoundingly. The exiled Lenin[57] wrote in *Pravda* of his pleasure that the Italians were taking 'the right road'. The elderly firebrand Cipriani singled out Mussolini for praise in the pages of *L'Humanité*— 'his commitment to revolution', Cipriani declared, is 'just like mine'.[58] The spoils of success were not only verbal. *Avanti!*, party extremists now agreed, could not remain under the editorship of Treves, but must also fall to the revolutionary wing. A journalist, passionate, dynamic, steadfast, was needed to take over. Here stood opportunity even if Mussolini, some weeks after his return from Reggio Emilia, timidly put in an application for another local teaching job.[59]

It was the last suggestion that journalism and politics were not to be his calling. Soon, it was announced that Mussolini was the victorious faction's (interim) choice as editor of the socialist daily. In October 1912, he furthered his cause touring Puglia, his first visit to any part of the Italian south. There he spoke often, and wrote positively of the prospects for socialist conversions among the peasantry, 'a people which feverishly wants to work. A people in other words, not just the plebs'.[60] On 1 December 1912 still more than six months short of his thirtieth birthday, Mussolini took over the editorship of *Avanti!*, having moved his family to Milan from where, since 1911, the paper had been published.[61] Rachele and baby Edda brought with them to a modest flat in Via Castel Morrone, Anna Guidi, who had been left alone after the death of Alessandro. The extended family scrabbled to find an annual rent of a thousand lire.[62]

Favoured by fortune, the rise and rise of Benito Mussolini was continuing at astonishing speed. He wrote in a first editorial of his pride and trepidation in having become spokesman of 'the moral and material patrimony of Italian socialists'. 'After the congress of Reggio Emilia, the victorious group had and has the duty to assume the full responsibility for its own experiment before the Party and the proletariat at large', he explained. Of course he would listen to views from all factions, but he would also be 'more revolutionary'. 'We promise solemnly to demonstrate to the philosophers of bourgeois reaction, to the bloc of hostile parties and to the weak, little instruments of savoy [sic] government, that the vitality of Italian socialism is unbounded.'[63]

Here, then, was Mussolini the militant, pure and ready for any sacrifice to the ideal. Writing anonymously as '*L'Homme qui cherche*', he had told readers of the journal *La Folla* (The Crowd) that party journalists should not think of themselves as working their way up in a career but rather as engaged in battle. (Paolo Valera, the editor of this 'illustrated weekly', remembered his correspondent as possessing 'eyes of fire', and as living with Rachele who was 'a good housewife, and who positively liked their penury'.)[64] None the less, once again, matters were not quite as simple as they might seem. In the very same piece in *La Folla*, Mussolini expressed a curious insecurity: 'I am a primitive. Also in my socialism. I walk up and down in the present market society like an exile. I am not a *businessman* [sic]. I don't have a taste for business'.[65] Nietzsche, he told readers of *Avanti!* at almost the same time, was a name which socialists should not forget.[66] In general, Mussolini was ready to argue, 'it is faith which moves mountains because it gives the illusion that the mountains move. Illusion is, perhaps, the only reality in life'.[67] How 'heroic' and how 'idealist' and 'anti-materialist', Mussolini was asking himself, could and should a socialist be?

Mussolini's intellectual and personal restlessness and insecurity were reflected in a letter which he sent Prezzolini in the immediate aftermath of the Reggio Emilia conference. Its phrases need careful appraisal since, in crafting them, Mussolini was hoping to please the recipient of his note. He was, he confessed, 'a little *dépaysé* among the revolutionaries' (his utilisation of the French *mot juste* doubtless signifying his sophistication). 'Certainly my <u>religious</u> [*sic*] conception of socialism is far from the philistine revolutionism of many of my friends'. Laying it on thickly so that Prezzolini would still want to be his 'friend' and patron, Mussolini mused how 'I need to orient my ideas better and make them more precise', even though he understood the present conflict with the reformists was 'but an episode in <u>the struggle for existence</u>' between the party and those of its organisations more concerned with pay and conditions.[68] 'Sometimes', he explained in a subsequent letter to Prezzolini, 'I have the sensation of shouting in the desert'.[69] A Darwinian? A Nietzschean? A Blanquist? A Vocean? A syndicalist? A journalist who could turn out a good article on anything?[70] Playing the roles of both intellectual and activist was not becoming any easier, now that Mussolini possessed a greater fame, a more immediate importance, and a more pronounced ability to see or to imagine personal opportunity.

Tailoring ideology to action was one problem; sociability was another and sex a third, especially once the Mussolinis were installed in the great world of Milan. The metropolis had so many attractions and there were so many rules to learn. As editor of *Avanti!* Mussolini enrolled in the prestigious *Associazione Lombarda dei Giornalisti*, the local journalists' club, founded in 1890. At its meetings he strove to keep a low profile, although a new colleague remarked sarcastically on the 'embarrassing' inadequacy of his small talk. Mussolini, he remembered, was giving to muttering through his teeth in a way that was hard to hear, and grew rude and ferocious if contradicted.[71] Most of the time, however, the new editor strove to fit in. Gone now was the farouche floppy hat he had sported in the past; its replacement was a bowler. Mussolini also took pains to be seen in the *Galleria*, Milan's most celebrated and elegant meeting place, and tentatively began to enter the city's less costly bars and restaurants, especially if someone else was paying.[72]

The men with whom Mussolini was now uneasily consorting were not like his comrades in Predappio or Forlì. The women of Milan were even more different. Most renowned was Margherita Sarfatti, the art critic for *Avanti!*, born in 1880, married, a mother, Jewish, and presenting herself as a feminist and a new woman. Her husband was a socialist (and Zionist) lawyer; her father had been a reactionary clerical representative on the Venice council; her politics were as potentially elastic as were Mussolini's. Their relationship[73] lingered on until the passage of Fascist racial legislation drove Sarfatti to take refuge (with Mussolini's co-operation) in New York. Earlier Sarfatti wrote an effusive biography of the *Duce*[74] and, though her political role and her influence on her lover should not be exaggerated, she was to achieve some prominence in the regime's cultural policies.

More emblematic, however, was Mussolini's affair with Leda Rafanelli. A woman who paraded her search for meaning between anarchism and 'Arabism', a writer, novelist, journalist and activist, she lived the life of the new woman with greater consistency and conviction than managed by Sarfatti.[75] A wonderfully revealing set of letters written to her by the later *Duce* has survived attempts at their destruction under the regime,[76] and an edited version of Rafanelli's account of their relationship has also been published.[77] Like Sarfatti, Rafanelli had been born in 1880 (at Pistoia in Tuscany), and so was a little older than Mussolini (and a decade senior to Rachele). As a 20-year-old, she had spent 3 months in Egypt and may have had an affair with the Futurist painter, Carlo Carrà.[78] On her return to Italy, she soon made a name for herself, with a variety of opinions which spanned from denouncing clerical lubricity, especially towards minors, to opposing racism and imagining blacks as full participants in society, to endorsing 'free love', even while she believed that the summit of freedom was located in the Moslem world. More conventionally, she pressed that 'mass man' be saved from drink and brothels, and that 'mass woman' not forget or forego motherhood. In uplifting the common people, she declared, a self-conscious elite and avant-garde could build 'the fourth estate', even while she excoriated those who might betray the cause of the workers for the lucre of the bourgeoisie.[79]

Although, throughout his life, Mussolini was the crassest of patriarchs, the new arrival in Milan was easily convinced that he had found a soul-mate when Rafanelli, impressed by a fiery speech he had made about the Paris Commune, introduced herself to him. His ego must have been further stroked when she wrote him up in the anarchist weekly, *La Libertà*, as 'the socialist of heroic times. He is one who still feels, still believes impulsively in a virile and powerful way. He is a man'.[80] In a later novel, Rafanelli described a young journalist 'with big black eyes and a slightly mad look'. Often reduced to nervous silence, he was handsome and yet somehow brutal, but also always ill at ease, readily won by the heavy perfume of his woman. In this man, ambition and sensuality competed in a terrible way; at 25, he looked spent by his internal conflicts. Marriage to a young and beautiful blonde had not requited him; nor had music or writing, even though 'journalism drew him as an electric light draws a moth at night'. This ardent youth wanted passionately to be seen, to be admired, but somehow, for him, satisfaction never came. Only the mysterious allure of a woman in touch with the orient could send him down enchanted paths which might yet lead to happiness. [81]

If this was Leda's literary construction of her friend in 1913 when Mussolini was trying to make Milan sit up and take notice, her admirer for his own part expressed an infatuation with this new woman. Their first problem was how to meet. It was no use trying the newspaper office; there Mussolini was never alone. The café, too, was hopeless, since people crowded around. A better prospect was her home. He could be there at 3 p.m. on Tuesday (the Italian habit of devoting the morning to formal work and the afternoon to other matters was, it seems, Mussolini's, too). 'You have understood me', Mussolini wrote with a lover's platitude, 'and in a way different from the others. I feel that something has begun between us ... or am I just fooling myself? Tell me straight. Wait for me. And I shall wait for you with a strange trepidation'.[82]

A few days later, he wrote again:

Yesterday I spent three wonderful, swiftly-dwindling, hours with you. We spoke about everybody and everything. We have the same sympathies and antipathies, in politics, in art, in philosophy, about the weather. We love solitude. You want to look for it in Africa, I among the tumultuous crowd in the city. The aim is the same. Your little salon has been for me a revelation. It is not like the others. You have given me the illusion of the mysterious and marvellous East, with its violent perfumes, its mad and fascinating dreams.[83]

Mussolini, the provincial, with the dust of Damerini's not altogether brushed from his clothes, was smitten, it seemed, at least for the moment. 'With you, I feel miles from Milan, journalism, politics, Italy, the West, Europe. ... Let's read Nietzsche and the Koran together. Listen. I am free every afternoon. Write to me when I can come and I shall be there, punctual and discreet.'[84]

But finding the high road to love, if that was what the two were imagining, was complicated. Mussolini's life was busier than he had suggested, and soon he was apologising for having been dragged away to Rome, or to Zurich, or for having been taken ill. But when they did meet, it was heaven: 'I seem ten years younger, when I committed any sort of madness.' In his Leda's company, he surrendered to a 'sentiment which I try to define but do not want to define. . . . I shall just leave my days in the hands of destiny'.[85]

And so the story went on. It was a mistake on her part to turn up at one of his meetings, but he was sorry not to have publicly welcomed her there. Could he make up a quarrel on Saturday with flowers? He had left her house at midnight feeling drunk with passion, 'my nerves deliciously aquiver, my heart beating in an irregular fashion as never before, my brain in tumult', and swallowed a large glass of absinthe in order to calm himself down.[86] The dark hours were when he might write to complain of her absence: 'Midnight. I feel I am floating. Full of desire and of nostalgia. I would like to pass on to you a little of the electricity which is coursing through my veins. Who knows why?' But then the commonplace might break in. He had to be away for a few days – it was the middle of July – 'I am taking my domestic tribe, two people, to the seaside'. But he would be back on Saturday. Would she write, 'impenetrable' as she was, 'like an Arab', and so solace his longings?[87]

Matters could turn sour – according to one authority, Rafanelli soon formed another relationship with a Tunisian, 'a co-religionist', and was not at all willing to confine herself to being Mussolini's woman.[88] Now Mussolini wondered if their love was 'morbid'. Did he not on occasion hang around in a square fruitlessly waiting for her: 'You make me like a boy again, that is ingenuous, that is impatient, that is an idiot'.[89] When she announced that their relationship was over, he accepted it as 'destiny', promised to give back her letters and asked melodramatically that his be consigned to the flames.[90] And yet, when, in February 1914, she wrote again, he declared that he had been suffused with joy at the scent of her notepaper: 'You know that strange, magical power which a perfume, your perfume, has on me. It is so penetrating, fascinating, strange, outlandish'. 'You offer me what I cannot find elsewhere [sic]: an hour of peace, of repose. Something entirely different'. For seven times seven years, he pledged fervently, he would wait for her. In the interim, he was off to hear *Tristan* for the first time – even imagined contact with her could put him in the mood to commune with Wagner.[91]

Quarrels recurred. Despite her skill at the 'spiritual game', he feared that she had never quite grasped his nature: 'I am what I am. I, too, have a mask in order to defend myself from indiscreet glances. But under the mask lies the real me which is fleeing from you because you do not want to stop me'.[92] He was still ready for a meeting: 'Dear Leda, you possess something which draws me on, fascinates me, overcomes me'. At 2 a.m., he could smell her perfume, and its memory drove him to scribble one last note to her before he went home.[93] Again at 2 a.m., the thought of her encouraged another bout of philosophising; he wanted to be a modern man, who was therefore all the more engrossed by her 'extraordinary tastes, beautiful moments of madness, discoveries, progress in "Arabism"'. Her special charm made him happy even when he did not really understand what she meant. 'But, above all', he continued, 'you attract me because – with truly remarkable dedication – you have succeeded in making of your life a delightful fiction'. Her commitment was both admirable and seductive. He, after all, was not a cynic; that she must grasp.[94]

Alas for Leda and 'B.', as he had taken to signing himself, the war, the First World War, was coming. She opposed it and wrote against it. He was not so sure. Leading intellectuals like Livio Ciardi and Filippo Corridoni, he complained, had swung around to favour Italian entry into the conflict. The war was 'a contagion which is not sparing anybody'. Before its revolutionary challenge, the proletariat seemed 'deaf, confused, distant'.[95] Mussolini was facing a grave dilemma, and the choice which he would make over it would lay waste his dreams of bohemian love and of intellectual and avant-garde 'vagabondage'.[96] Leda was not to remain his.

What, then, is to be made of the affair? In his maturity, Mussolini was much given to proclaiming that what a man did below his belt was of no interest to anyone but himself.[97] And yet the exchanges with Rafanelli cannot be dismissed. No doubt much of the verbiage which Mussolini deployed was conventional, and, beneath the heartfelt sentiment, was aimed at sexual conquest and little more. Nonetheless, the letters do express the personality of that Mussolini who had just reached Milan. Here was the provincial seeking *sistemazione* in a great city, the man who had never thought that women had minds but now half-hoped, half-feared otherwise, the socialist chief who yearned, almost achingly, to be recognised as a real intellectual, the romantic cynic, the morbid lover, who sighed for what he hoped was the expansive world of love and the intellect, but who lived in a humdrum way with Rachele and Edda and the other children to come, and who would make do with the political.

None of his other women were ever to be as exciting or as frustrating as Leda Rafanelli.

Life in Milan had a mass of problems. For Mussolini's precarious personal finances the transfer to the great city had been expensive. An ingenuous correspondence exists with Cesare Berti, a friend in Forlì, from whom Mussolini had borrowed 100 lire to help with the cost of the train trip, rent and furniture, that debt not being quit until October 1913.[98] To Berti, Mussolini claimed in March 1913: 'Here I work like a dog. I live in solitude. They attack me from all sides; priests, syndicalists and the rest.'[99] All in all, he added a couple of months later, his furious devotion to polemic had rendered him 'the most hated man in Italy' (a phrase destined to recur in his vocabulary about himself).[100]

The solitude, animosity, temerity, the aggressive determination to assume equality but in practice treat most as inferiors, these were now the accustomed postures of a man who grew sure that he was fated to become a leader of some sort. He did well on *Avanti!* – in spite of his disclaimers, he was actually a good and hard-headed businessman. By March 1913 through a series of sackings and some adroit alliance-building, he had eliminated all rivals to his editorship within the paper. At the same time, he was doubling and redoubling the paper's circulation until, just before the outbreak of the First World War, it touched 100 000 copies. He improved *Avanti*'s technology and reduced its deficit.[101] He was also ready to assert brusquely that the paper was all his own work. As he told a colleague: 'I bear the only, sole and absolute responsibility for the newspaper both in regard to the socialists and the public. Moreover, I, without personal preference or antipathy, hand over all the work that is going to the editorial staff simply according to the needs of the paper.'[102] Mussolini had no difficulty in assuming the executive role. Both tireless and ruthless, he was indeed 'one of the greatest journalists of his times',[103] if rather better at the destructive side of the profession than the constructive. Just as a Mussolini who had somehow stayed in Forlì can be imagined taking his place as a local notable, so, without the First World War, Mussolini might have risen in his profession, winning fame as a modernising opinion-maker of the type familiar in the Britain of those days with Lords Northcliffe and Rothermere and in our own with Rupert Murdoch and Silvio Berlusconi.

But editing a paper was not enough for Mussolini. He was anxious to demonstrate his expertise over broader fields. His editorship of the socialists' national daily demanded, for example, that he comment on

those issues of foreign policy which were preoccupying the establish-
ments of pre-1914 Europe. Whether the matter was the actual cost of
the Libyan war (Mussolini thought the imperial adventure had proved
a 'grotesque' waste of money),[104] the spread of the armaments
industry,[105] the detail of happenings in the Balkans,[106] or even the
French colonial programme in Algeria,[107] Mussolini could turn a
phrase and advance an intelligent or peremptory opinion.

Similarly, he could negotiate his way, at least to some extent, among
the bitterly competing factions of Italian socialism, acting at times, for
example, as a friend of the syndicalists, at times as their critic. His
openness or intellectuality he sought to demonstrate through the
holding of a public lecture series on socialist culture at which figures
so diverse as Gaetano Salvemini and Giuseppe Prezzolini eventually
spoke. Aimed, initially, at Milanese workers whom Mussolini hoped to
acquaint with thinkers from Plato to Campanella to Babeuf,[108] the
lectures were subsequently delivered at Rovigo and Florence, in this
last venue with a claimed audience of more than 3000.[109] In 1913–14
Mussolini also found time to put out a theoretical journal, directed not
at the masses but at intellectuals like himself. It was optimistically
entitled *Utopia*.[110] Though proudly claiming on its masthead to represent Italian revolutionary socialism, the journal made much of the
Revolution's French heritage, in its initial issue publishing translated
pieces by Jules Guesde and Auguste Blanqui.[111]

In his editorial Mussolini had explained that *Utopia* had been
created not by the Party but for it. He wanted, he explained, to be
healthily sectarian. There was 'a jealousy over ideas' at the root of
factional difference, he mused, since, 'with ideas as with women, the
more you love them the more they make you suffer'.[112] At much the
same time he told Alceste De Ambris: 'Certainly I am a sectarian. I have
a soul which is narrow-minded, petty, full of sectarian bile. It is so and
I am not ashamed of it ... today, tomorrow or ever.'[113] But in the pages
of *Utopia*, almost become a libertarian, he published syndicalists like
Sergio Panunzio and Agostino Lanzillo, dissident liberals like Mario
Missiroli and friends like Margherita Sarfatti. The Mussolini who now
emerged was the *professore* again, wrestling with a range of ideas and
trying to impress as he did so. Not for nothing would another editorial
in *Utopia* pleasurably mark the fact that the journal had been noticed
by Prezzolini in the pages of *La Voce*. As usual Mussolini switched to
deferential mode in writing about his cultural superiors: 'I am touched
by praise from those whom I esteem intellectually and morally, even if
politics or ideological particularities divide us.'[114]

Actually, *Utopia* never quite made it. Its issues appeared erratically. Its ideological purpose was visibly tainted by its editor's self-aggrandisement. Yet, it had to be admitted that Benito Mussolini was exhibiting a host of talents. He was, for example, an ever more brilliant and persuasive orator. He may have failed in 1913 in his first attempt to stand for parliament – then, at Forlì, he was badly beaten by the local republican[115] – but who could doubt that he would eventually find a place in the national assembly? Certainly he tirelessly practised his speechifying, usually on the party faithful. Mostly, he preached revolution, though, as ever, his version of that desired event was more passionate than clear. In March 1914 for example, he sounded decidedly parochial when speaking at Milan:

> I am a convinced supporter of local government, and I am so precisely because I am a socialist revolutionary and therefore against the state. The municipality is the last bastion behind which the citizen can oppose the steadily increasing invasion from the state.[116]

Later, a close associate would notice the trouble with which Mussolini prepared himself for any speech or meeting. Although exuding spontaneity, he took great care beforehand to craft his phrases, and was very much in control both of his text and his emotions.[117] It cannot be known when such a studied approach became his habit, but it may be assumed that, already while a socialist, he was learning such skills. At the same time, he was growing used to his oratory bringing applause and devotion. He was noticing others, at least as they impinged on himself, his image and 'charisma'. After 1922, he confessed that, as an executive and dictator, he learned as much from the stance and body language of his interlocutors as from their words.[118] He himself certainly hoped to convey as much implicitly as he did explicitly. Later followers would remark on his 'inimitable and incomparable' command of gesture,[119] while a Fascist propagandist, blinded in the war, declared his enchantment just at listening to the *Duce*'s articulation. To his acute hearing, Mussolini had 'more than one voice, or rather spoke with a variety of timbres and tones' – they varied from the sweet and intimate to the stridently powerful – 'which reconfirmed the plurality and multiplicity of his soul'.[120]

Under the regime, of course, Mussolini's charisma was unquestionable and boundless, but, even while he was editor of *Avanti!*, it was building, and he was certainly not averse to its construction. The term *Duce* may have eddied through the vocabulary of the time – in March 1914 the word was even affixed to the studiously prosaic Prime

Minister Giolitti (though the purpose was sarcastic).[121] All the same, the way in which *Duce* began to stick to Mussolini is significant. Whatever the force and the content of his rhetoric about revolution and socialism, it was Mussolini's personality which most impressed his contemporaries. By 1914 many Italians were looking for a 'leader' to cut through the compromise, confusion and corruption which they detected all around and, if doubtless still among a restricted group, Mussolini was becoming known as a potential candidate for this role. His irrepressible dynamism, his unquenchable ambition, the quickness of his thought, his insolent refusal to bow before any odds, his contumely, all were helping to make him into a young man who counted politically, especially if the new world were to be linked somehow to the masses.

A year later, with Italy in the war and with Mussolini no longer a socialist, Torquato Nanni, an old friend from Predappio, at the request of Prezzolini, composed the first of many eulogistic biographies of the *Duce*. In staccato phrases, perhaps even more staccato than those typically used by Mussolini in his speeches,[122] Nanni delineated a 'force of nature', 'the man of action par excellence', who 'had stopped the Italian proletariat from being mere sheep'.[123] If Nanni were to be believed, and behind him Prezzolini and the intellectual establishment, Mussolini was already perceived as having the potential to be the *Duce*.

In reality, at the time Nanni's work was published it is doubtful whether it attracted many readers or whether they were impressed by his case. In 1915 the rise of Benito Mussolini had, for the time, been deflected by events. Moreover, well before Italian entry into the First World War, there were grounds to argue that Mussolini's lightning victories of 1912–13 were looking fragile. It is true that the Socialist Party, at its congress at Ancona in April 1914, had confirmed the domination of the revolutionary faction, strengthening Mussolini's personal position both on *Avanti!* and on the party executive. However, by then it was also becoming evident that the revolutionaries were extremely vague about long-term policy, and basically had no idea either about how their revolution might be implemented or about what it would entail.

Shortly after, large-scale strikes and riots broke out, notably in the Romagna, in what was called 'Red Week'. Mussolini's editorials predictably urged more drastic action, hounding the government and its troops when they attempted to restore order.[124] None the less, the popular discontent was spontaneous, actually taking Mussolini and the rest of the current party leadership by surprise.[125] The inadequacy of their preparation, and their more serious failures, both in tactics and strategy, could not be concealed. By June–July 1914 there were quite a lot of reasons to believe that the next months might restore advantage to the more moderate socialists.

Other, more grandiose, events would in fact decide the destiny of the socialist factions. On 28 June 1914 Archduke Francis Ferdinand of Habsburg-Este and his morganatic wife were assassinated at Sarajevo. Their deaths signalled the collapse of *belle époque* Europe into the First World War. Three years before, Romagnole syndicalist A.O. Olivetti, the scion of a pro-Risorgimento family from Ravenna, had lamented, in phrases typical of the moment, that the society around him in Italy was 'dying for want of tragedy'.[126] Very shortly, Italians and other Europeans were to be accorded tragedies enough to slake any reasonable thirst.

5

War and revolution,
1914–1919

T HE outbreak of the First World War brought grave embarrassment
to the government and institutions of Italy. On 3 August 1914 the
public announcement was finally made that, for the present, Italy,
caught between its membership of the Triple Alliance with Germany
and Austria-Hungary and its 'traditional friendship' with France and
Britain, had opted for neutrality. Given the nation's military weakness
and, behind that, its comparatively feeble economic and industrial
power, staying out of the war was a wise decision. It was, however, a
choice which deepened the numerous fissures in the political and
social bases of the Liberal regime.

Ready to back neutrality was a clear majority of Italians.[1] They
included leading politician Giolitti, the King, important sections of the
Army, big business, Freemasonry, the majority of the bureaucracy,
most socialists, many Catholics including new Pope Benedict XV, the
main part of the peasantry and almost all Italian women. Some of these
individuals and groups themselves differed over whether, or at what
moment, they might accept Italian entry – even Giolitti, whose career
would thereafter be beset by charges of cowardly neutralism, was
happy to contemplate an Italian presence by the side of the winners,
when it was plain who they would be. However, for the moment, he
did not want to force the pace. With a good sense unusual among
Europeans at this time, large sections of the Italian populace were not
victims of a 'short-war illusion' and resisted forecasts that the conflict
would be over by Christmas.

In the end, however, the huge plurality of those opposed to premature Italian entry into the war did not matter. In favour of urgent
commitment were two crucial groups. First was the government itself.
It was a minority administration, more conservative than when

Giolitti was in command, and headed by Southern academic lawyer, Antonio Salandra. This administration, which seemed likely to be short-lived, was given much of its imprint by Tuscan moralist, Sidney Sonnino, who, after November 1914, became Foreign Minister. For more than a generation, Sonnino had combined calls for greater discipline at home (and an end to Giolittian compromise and obfuscation), with a preference for expansionism abroad. The war brought immense opportunity to Salandra and Sonnino. Now they could 'dish the Whigs', whittle away Giolitti's long-standing parliamentary majority, and, as they put it presumptuously, 'enter history'.[2]

Backing this line, if not very fond of the government itself, was another powerful force. It was composed of those intellectuals, especially of the new generation, whose ideas tended to be both expansive and irreconcilable, but who were agreed that they constituted the coming new men without whom a healthy and 'modern' Italy could not prosper. As the so-called *intervento* (the period in-between) wore on, and the treatying by Italy between the Central Powers and the Triple Entente grew more tortuous, Italian intellectuals stentoriously demanded an end to hesitation. And reasonably prominent among them was Benito Mussolini.

Renzo De Felice argued a generation ago that, in the aftermath of the failures of 'Red Week' and just before the onset of the July crisis, Mussolini had glimpsed the future. 'Only Mussolini', De Felice wrote, 'understood that a new era was beginning and that socialism must not continue to be out of step with the times'.[3] Then, and in the months that followed, Mussolini was the socialist who was in touch with the country.[4] It is a curious claim for a historian to make, since it is plain that Italy was manipulated or 'spoken' into the war by a small minority of its population. In any case, the evidence shows that Mussolini, like the overwhelming majority of his contemporaries, was slow to recognise where the July crisis could lead. As a good journalist might, one day after it happened he did report the assassination at Sarajevo. Moreover the event was sufficiently grave for him to speculate about its meaning. The death of Franz Ferdinand, he argued, demonstrated that the conflict between the Habsburgs and the 'Slav world' was profound; the Balkans were being shattered by 'an explosion of national hatred'. As he had learned from his own past experiences in the Trentino, Austrian administration was 'both hateful and hated'. But Mussolini did not laud Serb nationalism either, concluding his piece portentously with the comment that the killing of the Archduke was 'a painful but explicable episode in the struggle between nationalism and central power, which is both the strength and the ruin of that tormented country [Austria-Hungary]'.[5]

Over the next month, he added nothing to this initial appraisal, though he did worry about Greek adventurism as part of a general concern, not unknown among other journalists at other times, that the Balkans could 'burn' at any moment.[6] His major preoccupation remained domestic as he tried to put a positive slant on Red Week, declaring, in a review of those events, that 'revolution' was still imminent locally: 'Italy needs a revolution and it will have one.'[7] Only after the Austrian ultimatum was delivered to Serbia did his attention return to the international scene. Any war, he then suggested, would be at the behest of the 'military party in Austria'. Despite this renewed hostility to the Habsburg regime, Mussolini went on to damn what he feared were secret clauses in the Triple Alliance, insisting that Italy adopt a posture of strict neutrality towards any conflict. The Italian proletariat must not spill a single drop of blood for a cause which was not its own. Socialist policy towards diplomatic scheming must be to insist on the line 'not a man, not a penny' for a war.[8]

When, during the first week in August, the alarums in the Balkans widened into European conflict, Mussolini tended to switch the blame from the leadership of Austria to that of Imperial Germany. The violation of Belgium he deplored as an event which might unite 'all Europe' against the 'Germanic bloc'. Germany, he added, was behaving in an unheard of way. Through its 'brigandage' and 'aggression against Belgium, Germany was laying bare its purpose, its aims and its soul'. 'Prussian militarism and Pan-Germanism' had a sad history; since 1870, Germany had acted as a sort of 'bandit lurking along the road of European civilisation.'[9] These were strong words, and there can be little doubt that they reflected a genuinely emotional reaction by Mussolini against the Central Powers and in favour of France. His 'unspoken assumptions', like the cultural baggage of many Italians, not all on the Left, told him to beware of Austria, the alleged tyrant of the Risorgimento, and to admire France, 'the Latin sister', as it was often called, in somewhat jealous and sensitive affection.

To be sure, too much of the future should not be read into Mussolini's phrases. Until late August he feared that the details of the Triple Alliance were still likely to push the Italian government into the war on the part of the Central Powers.[10] When it became clear that the government was dallying with the other side, Mussolini wrote on a number of occasions in favour of the official socialist line of 'absolute neutrality'. War, he knew from his party's dogma, benefited only the bourgeoisie: 'The proletariat is not disposed to fight a war of aggression and conquest after which it will merely be as poor and exploited as before.'[11] And yet his mind did have trouble in sticking to this line. The German occupation of Brussels was brutal, he reported ingenuously. He was convinced that Imperial troops had shot hostages and used dum-dum bullets. The Triple Entente might well have relative virtue on its side, but did it need Italy at the front and was it not anyway being assisted by Italian neutrality? Trieste might be ethnically Italian, but the city was surrounded by Slavs and the fairest solution for its future was probably internationalisation.[12] Mussolini's thoughts were always likely to range widely, and the new conflict only enhanced this tendency. But, beneath the scatter of his words, he began to perceive that war could entail opportunity, the chance to destroy an old order, the possibility of imagining a new.

With these heresies beating into his mind, by September 1914 Mussolini's adhesion to the official line of neutrality was slipping, even though he still believed that the party's attachment to neutralism was limpet-like.[13] Gradually he began to admit an outright sympathy for the Triple Entente cause. He was aware, too, of the way in which so many leading intellectuals, quite a few of them with political views somewhere on the 'Left', had begun to campaign for Italian entry into the war against the Central Powers. Prezzolini and *La Voce*, the Southernist radical democrat and historian Gaetano Salvemini and his paper *L'Unità*, syndicalists such as De Ambris and Corridoni,[14] his old editor Cesare Battisti – voice after voice – all were bracketing war and modernity. Italy's dissident intellectuals were representing the conflict as the opportunity to cast off the corrupt and time-worn shackles of the Giolittian era and to build a future in which the people would be happier (and their own talents would be better recognised). How could Professor Mussolini not be tempted by their cause?

And so, at first incrementally, he began to retreat from socialist orthodoxy. On 13 September Mussolini explained that he had decided to publish a piece by Sergio Panunzio in *Avanti!* since, after all, 'it would be ridiculous and illiberal to force into silence' those who were backing an Italian entry into the war (although Mussolini then scrupulously reviewed Panunzio's arguments to demonstrate that they were wrong).[15] On 30 September he editorialised about the Italian proletariat's sentimental preference which, like his own, had swung behind the Entente cause, but angrily denied that such sentiment could ever convert workers into 'war-mongers'.[16] Five days earlier he had written privately to Amadeo Bordiga, a Neapolitan engineer and intellectual who was destined to lead the Italian Communist Party, of his sense that neutrality and reformism constituted shabby and unholy allies. The idea of standing pat before great events was, he feared, typical of those who had 'exiled themselves from history'.[17] Deep in the Marxist psyche, after all, was inscribed the idea of the 'locomotive of history', the belief that society was on the move, and that an adroit adept ought to be able to read its course and timetable correctly. Certainly, in Mussolini's mind, a tension was rising to breaking point between the passivity of neutralism and the dynamism of intervention.

And so, on 18 October, he published a crucial article in *Avanti!* It was entitled 'From absolute neutrality to an active and working neutrality'. Mussolini's patience, often precarious, had run out. The socialist party's existing policy was 'cosy', precisely because it was so 'negative'. 'But a party', Mussolini explained in words in keeping with his personality, 'which wishes to live in history and, in so far as it is allowed, to make history, cannot submit, at the penalty of suicide, to a line which is dependent on an unarguable dogma or an eternal law, separate from the iron necessity [of change] over space and time'.[18] In reality, the policy of neutrality had already favoured the Entente and was being nourished by 'a profound hostility to Austria and Germany'.[19] Similarly, it was patently absurd for Italy to stay out of a conflict when the rest of Europe was participating in it. Socialists in France, Belgium and Britain had acknowledged the significance of the 'national problem'.[20] How could Italians not do the same?

Searching for a clinching quotation, Mussolini ended with Marx. The father of socialism, he remembered, had left the message that 'whoever develops a set programme for the future is a reactionary'.[21] Absolute neutrality, he concluded, was by definition 'backward-looking' and 'immobilising'. 'We have the privilege of living at the most tragic hour in world history. Do we – as men and as socialists – want to be inert spectators of this huge drama? Or do we want to be, in some way and some sense, the protagonists'? It would be a disaster to save the letter of the party, he concluded, if that step meant destroying its spirit.[22]

This editorial duly caused a sensation, at least among the socialists and their friends.[23] The heretical sentiments which Mussolini had enunciated were by no means unique, and had occurred to many other socialists, and especially to those who deemed themselves intellectuals. Even Antonio Gramsci, later Communist martyr to Fascism, was tempted.[24] Giuseppe Prezzolini, no socialist but a man honoured and admired by Mussolini, hastened to send his congratulations to this former subscriber to *La Voce*.[25] Such an editorial had other implications, too. On 19 October the executive of the socialist party met at Bologna. Impassioned debate ensued, with Mussolini emphasising that his new outlook was based on principle, reiterating his view that the attacks on him from within the party were 'simply ridiculous'. Nevertheless, his schism was too open, and he resigned as editor of *Avanti!*[26]

Since bureaucratic processes moved slowly, it took another month before Mussolini was formally expelled from the socialist party. His words in his own last defence were dramatic: 'You hate me today because you love me still. ... Whatever happens, you won't lose me. Twelve years of my life in the party are or ought to be sufficient guarantee of my socialist faith. Socialism is in my very blood'. He was, he pledged, still the enemy of the bourgeoisie. When time proved him right on the war, he prophesied, 'you will again see me at your side'. [27]

Mussolini was, of course, not the only dissident ever to leave a socialist party, especially during the trauma of the First World War. In many countries, the great conflict demanded that a choice be made between the ideals of internationalist socialism and those of the nation. Nor was Mussolini the only defector, or 'rat' as they were frequently euphoniously called, to discover that a quarrel which, at the time, had seemed significant but eventually possible to repair, in fact terminated a socialist career. In their insecurity and weakness, socialist parties were given to hating well. Nor, when they hated, was the first charge to be made against a dissident hard to imagine. The 'rat' was likely to be called venal, a Judas who had been bought and sold by the numerous wealthy and powerful enemies of socialism. So, while the interventionist press welcomed Mussolini's conversion to patriotism, and great bourgeois papers like *Il Corriere della Sera* and *Il Secolo* reported the event and sought interviews with the new patriot,[28] a damning phrase began to be bruited abroad among the socialist party faithful: *Chi paga?* (Who is the paymaster?).[29]

In Mussolini's case, there was reason to ask the question. On 10 November, in an interview which he had conceded to *Il Resto del Carlino*, the Bolognese paper, owned by sugar interests and headed by Filippo Naldi, he had a revelation to make. He was not, he stated with accustomed truculence, ready to retire to 'private life'. Rather, buoyed by support from the Francophile Cipriani and other left-leaning interventionists, he was launching a paper in their cause. It would be entitled, with Mazzinian more than Marxist reference, *Il Popolo d'Italia* (The People of Italy).[30] Its initial issue printed on its masthead two slogans, one from Blanqui: 'Whoever has iron has bread' and one from Napoleon: 'The Revolution is an idea which has found its bayonets.'[31] *Il Popolo d'Italia* was also destined to become, from October 1922, the official organ of the Fascist regime.

Although some of the evidence is still disputed, it is clear that by October (if not earlier) Mussolini had been engaged in a double game.[32] He was in communication with Naldi, a notorious advocate of the interests of the local landed elite, who had himself been talking with the highest circles of the government, including the aristocratic Foreign Minister, Antonino Di San Giuliano.[33] Naldi was known for his contacts. Contemporaries remarked on the extravagance of his lifestyle and the way his paper seemed to swing between imminent collapse under debt and sudden bursts of prosperity, which goodtime Naldi would celebrate with 'rivers of champagne'.[34] The result of such dealings was that Mussolini was assured of funding for the new paper. Naldi also promised that the provenance of any largesse would be kept secret, so that it was 'money which I can accept', as Mussolini had put it.[35] The two men had met by arrangement at the Hotel Venezia in Milan, where Mussolini impressed an onlooker with his 'pallid face, and glittering black eyes like those of a porcelain doll'.[36]

Later Naldi and Mussolini travelled to Switzerland in search of funding from the French secret service. In their journey, certain class differences were observed. The sleek Naldi stayed, as he always did, at the best hotel. Mussolini, by contrast, shared a room in a less luxurious hostelry with a journalist acquaintance, Mario Girardon. Naldi was generous enough eventually to take the two out for a final night of drinking, eating, dancing and, by implication, whoring, so presumably some money, or the promise of it, must have passed hands. Amid these events, Girardon, after he fruitlessly began a discussion of Sorel's ideas with his friend, decided that 'Mussolini did not like to get entangled in doctrinal complications. When he likes a theory, he takes it over whole, and then tries to sell it to the public'. Back in the hotel room, he noticed that Mussolini's underwear was torn and his cuffs frayed, and that he shaved himself as though in a fury with hasty and careless strokes. Confined together as they were, Girardon was aware also that Mussolini possessed big feet.[37]

How is this complex story of bribery to be read? In the past Mussolini had not seemed covetous, though he had borrowed from whomever would lend to him and spent what money he had to his own benefit or pleasure. Nor, later, under his regime, was he corrupt, in the sense that General Franco as dictator of Spain became corrupt,[38] or indeed in the way of many a Fascist, Italian and other politician, even if he was not as selfless as official propaganda liked to claim. In accepting the sort of funds which he was now offered – including subsidies from the French embassy[39] and, after 1917, from the British[40] – Mussolini was ruthlessly breaking the accustomed codes of the socialist movement. He was ignoring the fulminations of Leda Rafanelli and many another comrade who had inveighed against the contaminating effects of bosses' gold. He was therefore ensuring that, whatever his revolutionary protestations, he could never go back. If socialist orthodoxy was to fail him, perhaps he could resume an identity as 'Professor Mussolini', that is, as a freelance intellectual, one who had his ideas and, in cavalier confidence, took it for granted that someone else would pay for their publication.

If that was Mussolini's position at the end of 1914, it was a precarious one. The great and powerful had no particular need for him. Marvellous insight into this fact is found in the pages of the diary of Ferdinando Martini, then Minister of Colonies, a Tuscan liberal who had served as governor of Eritrea (there he had carelessly favoured the liquidation of the local population) and who had later tried unsuccessfully to write lyrics for Giacomo Puccini.[41] Martini belonged to the great world. As early as 10 October 1914 he was aware, probably from talks with Naldi, that Mussolini, though still unwilling openly to favour the war, had declared that 'should the war prove necessary, the socialists, too, will do their duty'.[42] Just before Christmas Martini had another meeting with a now annoyed Naldi. The latter explained that he had given money to Mussolini, knowing that the ex-editor of *Avanti!* would bring over to the patriotic cause a whole set of Northern leftists. But, complained Naldi, he could not bear the onerous financial burden of this undertaking alone. And so he had spoken to a lawyer from Bologna, who had seen the local member of parliament, Luigi Fera. He, in turn, promised to alert minister Vittorio Emanuele Orlando, who would then get Prime Minister Salandra to cope with the affair. But, somewhere, the chain of patronage and interest had snapped. Naldi therefore appealed to Martini to intervene himself since a sum of at least 25 000 lire was urgently required.[43] Mussolini, it was plain, could rejoice in his funding and use it the better to preach his cause. However, it was similarly evident that he stood a long way down a complex ladder of patronage, the rules of which all Italian contemporaries understood. His status was scarcely yet that of a potential national leader.

After Naldi's appeal, Martini does seem to have bestirred himself. He continued to keep an eye on Mussolini, even if, by 1916 he regarded him as 'over the top' and even 'mad' in the amplitude of the territorial annexations which he was by then seeking for Italy in the Adriatic. Mussolini's usefulness, Martini recalled, was domestic.[44] Carlo Sforza, another genuine member of the Italian elite, if one who, unusually after 1922, refused to accept the imposition of Fascism, similarly wrote that the key to Mussolini's character was that he was 'a self-taught man, and always a bit above himself'.[45] His comment and the attitude of Martini are a demonstration how Mussolini, in leaving the socialist movement, had cast himself onto seas which he was as yet ill-prepared to navigate. Despite the bitterness and ubiquity of factional fighting within the party ranks, socialism offered its members the comforts of appreciation, a sense of belonging, a place in the world, a path to the future and a reason for optimism. Such advantages were all the more consoling when the social gap between a Martini or a Sforza and a Mussolini, was indeed so yawning. A contemporary remembered Mussolini going to the key meetings of October–November 1914 with an ashen face, trembling with anger.[46] He had reason to be moved. In opting for the war, Mussolini had taken a perilous step, one which in late 1914 seemed unlikely to bring him happiness or serenity, and which may have ensured that he thereafter replaced hope with an ever deepening cynicism about the meaning of his life. Those fellow leftists, who swung over with him and helped to write the first issues of the paper – Sandro Giuliani, Ugo Marchetti, Alessandro Chiavolini, Nicola Bonservizi, Ottavio Dinale, Margherita Sarfatti and Manlio Morgagni – were never altogether cast out from his heart,[47] but perhaps his on-going 'friendship' was nurtured as much by a sense of lost comradeship as by more positive feelings. Some of the disdain which Mussolini evinced, more and more frequently, towards his closest associates may well have sprung from the desperate knowledge that many of them were 'rats', too.

What, then, was the line pursued by *Il Popolo d'Italia*? On 15 November Mussolini proclaimed that, in 'an epoch of a general auction of ideas like the present', the destinies of European socialism were tied up with the results of the war. His opponents, in their intellectual emptiness, stood for death. And so he appealed 'to the young of Italy, the young of the factories and schools, the young in age and the young in spirit, the young of that generation which fate has driven to make history'; to them, he raised the 'fearful and fascinating word: <u>war</u>'.[48] In a second editorial he endeavoured to be more precise. It was in the supreme interest of the proletariat that the war finish quickly – here, after all, was Mussolini's 'short war illusion'. Otherwise, mutual hatreds would penetrate societies too deeply. Germany must be defeated and the influence of Russia on the Entente side diminished. Action was needed, and needed now. 'To de-nationalise the proletariat is wrong; to de-humanise it is a crime', and that was what a policy of absolute neutrality actually proposed.[49]

None the less, Mussolini also devoted many columns in his small paper to strictly personal polemic. He argued bitterly with those who had expelled him from the party. They had begun the fight, he argued stoutly.[50] In any case, he would be a bonny fighter. As he told an erstwhile friend from Oneglia, he personally found solace and instruction in the motto: 'an eye for an eye and a tooth for a tooth'.[51] His enemies had 'stabbed him in the back'; they were 'the worst sort of cowards', no better than '*canaille*'.[52] The ex-comrades from Forlì were especially culpable in his regard. 'Hysterics' and 'cannibals', they might try to stop him speaking, but they would fail and, anyway: 'I am what I was yesterday. . . . a tenacious and disinterested soldier for all the causes of liberty and social justice.'[53] He would sooner or later beat his wretched opponents.[54] 'As long as I still have a pen in my hand and a revolver in my pocket, why should I be afraid of anybody?' he melodramatically asked the presumably startled readers of the conservative daily, *Il Giornale d'Italia*, to which he gave an interview.[55] Actually, it was not entirely a rhetorical question. Duelling remained an acceptable practice of that intellectual-political world in which Mussolini so eagerly participated. Andrea Costa had duelled and, in 1898, the republican, Felice Cavallotti, had died in the course of his 33rd 'conflict of honour'.[56] Even though *Il Popolo d'Italia* took pains to condemn 'disgusting' German-style duelling at university,[57] Mussolini had just the temperament to join in the Mediterranean version of this boy's game, and his expulsion from socialist ranks removed his last reluctance to fight. In February 1915 he engaged in three rounds with Lino Merlino and, in March, he stood for eight with Claudio Treves, his predecessor at *Avanti!* Mussolini was wounded once by the swordplay, Treves three times in a bout which was said to have been conducted with unusual vim and vehemence, and their contest ended without any gentlemanly 'reconciliation'.[58] In lighter vein, contemporaries noticed that, after October 1914, Mussolini transferred his accustomed places of dining up-market and also began to indulge in the expensive hobbies of riding a horse and, eventually, driving a car.[59]

When not sampling the delights of the bourgeois lifestyle, Mussolini sought to rally his friends to his cause – one new associate was Dino Grandi, a Mazzinian law student and occasional journalist for *Il Resto del Carlino*.[60] In early December 1914 Mussolini was already advocating the establishment of so-called *Fasci d'azione rivoluzionaria* (revolutionary groups).[61] On 6 January 1915 *Il Popolo d'Italia* published a draft constitution for the membership. It was not a party, Mussolini emphasised in what would become typical phrasing, but 'a free association of subversives from all schools and political points of view'. It was also republican.[62] The secretary of the *Fasci*, as they were called, was Calabrian Michele Bianchi (he would be a secretary of the Fascist Party, too. Among the directorate were Mussolini's syndicalist contact, Alceste De Ambris, and Giovanni Marinelli, destined, a decade later, to be another prominent early Fascist.

The *Fasci*, Mussolini explained, wanted to teach the 'workers' that only intervention could produce 'social revolution', because such action would tie Italy to France, 'cradle of a hundred revolutions', 'free' Britain and 'generous and heroic' Belgium.[63] Mussolini also spoke of how what he already called 'the Fascist movement' could help spread 'subversive, revolutionary and anti-constitutional ideals' internationally, precisely because it was not bound by 'the rules and rigidity of a Party'.[64]

As yet, however, this verbal elan won few converts and, with the passing months, Mussolini's problems increased. In the debates about whether or not Italy should intervene, *Il Popolo d'Italia* was not finding a political or intellectual space. The paper's readers were told that its funds were running low.[65] On 15 March Mussolini confessed to Prezzolini that the paper could boast only 1600 subscribers, and the great majority of them had paid for a month, not a year.[66] It was all very well expatiating about how the war might bring the 'people of Italy' within the historical process – Mussolini now repeated Prezzolini's worthily didactic claim that winning a war meant for a nation the equivalent of passing an exam.[67] But 'the people' did not seem impressed, and the majority of the populace, like the majority of the members of parliament, continued to prefer neutrality to other alternatives.

In these circumstances, Mussolini's personality led him to rage against the apparent ebbing of enthusiam for war-entry. Before the so-called 'radiant days of May' 1915, when it seemed for a moment that Giolitti might return to government, stimulating nationalist crowds to mobilise in Rome and other cities against this dread event, Mussolini's phrasing was notable in its extremity. In his paper, he urged 'the shooting, I say <u>shooting</u> in the back of some dozen deputies'. 'Parliament', he added, was 'the pestiferous pustule poisoning the blood of the nation. It must be wiped out'.[68] The monarchy, too, if it would not back the war, 'must pay'.[69] To Prezzolini, who as ever did not demur at the junior intellectual's verbal savagery, he suggested that the best way to deal with Giolitti was 'five revolver bullets in the stomach'.[70] In the 'first great war of the Italian people', he urged, the nation must adopt a policy of 'an eye for an eye and a tooth for a tooth'. The Germans aimed at 'exterminating' the Italians. But 'to a war of extermination, we must reply with a war of extermination of our own'.[71]

Whatever the character of Mussolini's nationalism before October 1914, he now found it easy to mouth nationalist phrases. The German Swiss dominated Switzerland and were 'Prussians' at heart; Italians must remember that fact.[72] All foreigners were given arrogantly to viewing Italians as 'strolling musicians, sellers of statuettes, Calabrian bandits'; they must be made to bow instead to the 'new, great, Italy'.[73] Still sensitive to attacks from the socialists, he none the less denied their charge that he had become an imperialist. His present hero was the generous unifier of peoples, Giuseppe Garibaldi, apostrophised in *Il Popolo d'Italia* as 'the *Duce*'.[74] Mussolini saw no reason for Italy to seize the Ticino, Corsica and Malta, though he did not explain why, except to aver piously that, 'like all principles, the principles of nationality must not be understood and practised in an "absolute" sense'. In Dalmatia, he wanted to resist the 'Slavisation' of such 'truly Italian' centres as Zara (Zadar), Spalato (Split) and Ragusa (Dubrovnik), but he could still imagine some compromise arrangement with Serbia over the issue.[75] The Trentino and Trieste, however, were a different matter, since they were 'geographically, historically and morally Italian'.[76]

No doubt Mussolini, for the present, believed in his case, however dubious it seems now. Yet he was giving hostages to fortune if he thought, as he proclaimed, that he was still on the side of revolution. On 24 May 1915, the day that Italy finally declared war on Austria-Hungary, Mussolini wrote in his paper that, for him and all Italians, 'Italy has a historic personality, is alive, possessed of its own body and immortal'.[77] Mussolini may not have signed up for the socially reactionary Nationalist Association, but the gospel which he was preaching, for all its social revolutionary residue, was about as far from socialist internationalism and socialist materialism as it was possible to go.

By the end of May 1915 Italy was at war, a very idiosyncratic war, since the Salandra–Sonnino government tried to restrict the conflict to one with Austria alone, with hostilities not finally being extended to Germany until August 1916.[78] The peculiarities of Italy's war effort have not always been understood by non-Italians, who long have been inclined either to dismiss the campaign, or to assume that what was true on the Western Front must have been true in the 'Italian sideshow'. Militarily, the Italian war was mostly a mountainous one,[79] although the great defeat at Caporetto in October–November 1917 – it roughly coincided with the Bolshevik revolution in Russia – brought Austro-German troops down to the northern plain which ran on to Milan.[80] Between 23 and 26 October of that year the armies of the Central Powers took some 300 000 Italian prisoners of war.[81] Eventually, however, Italian forces, bolstered by their allies, held on the line of the Piave river to the east of Venice and, in the subsequent months, gradually pushed the Central Powers back before the final, if disputed, 'victory' at Vittorio Veneto. On 4 November 1918, a week before the end of the war on the Western front, Austrian forces surrendered.

By then, more than 5 million Italians had seen military service, about the same number as those who had actually voted in the elections of 1913.[82] Throughout the war, Italy suffered a death toll of more than half a million, with a nearly equal number of incapacitated or *mutilati*, to use the graphic Italian word. As had usually been true in the past, the worst of the campaigning was born by the peasantry, that social group which, before 1915, had least embraced the nation. In 1919 an estimated 63 per cent of war orphans came from peasant families, while Professor Salandra set an example of a kind by ensuring that none of his three sons saw service in line of battle.[83]

As with the other combatant states and societies, the conflict made extraordinary demands on the Home Front. In 1919 a leading soldier remarked that, during the war, 'in truth no-one governed Italy,'[84] and it is plain that no Italian equivalent of Hindenburg, Clemenceau or Lloyd George rose above the rest. Neither a general nor a politician dominated the country, power remaining diffused across the various political, military, industrial, landowner, Masonic and bureaucratic elites. Furthermore, the demands of the war effort cut into Italian society as never before. Many did well. With the national government disbursing more in three and a half years of warfare between 1915 and

1918 than it had expended in 50 years of ordinary administration since the Risorgimento, the period saw a massive increase in the bureaucracy, in the profits of industry integrated into close and fruitful relations with the state, and in the size of the working class. Quite a few workers avoided the call-up, since their skills on the factory floor could not be replaced. As a result, this class frequently had a very different experience of wartime from that of the peasantry.

In November 1918 Italy emerged from its military venture with an ambiguous victory. The subsequent peacemaking at Versailles, where Foreign Minister Sonnino showed himself peculiarly ill-adapted to the ideals and hypocrisy of the Wilsonian 'new diplomacy', soon underlined the fact that participation in the war had not amended Italy's position as the least of the Great Powers. Furthermore, Italian society had been radically unsettled by the war effort. In 1919 there was an even more urgent need than in 1914 to find some way of binding the masses to the state system. The vast gap between politics and society was made more emphatic by the events of the last year of the conflict. Between 1915 and the defeat at Caporetto, successive governments, not to mention reactionary and brutal monarchist generals, sought to run a war which was traditional in character. As Salandra put it with his usual crudity: his Italy was fighting for its *sacro egoismo* (sacred egoism), which meant the preservation and enhancement of the interests of the existing ruling elites. Before October 1917 these elites did little to explain or justify contemporary events to the masses. Unlike all the other combatant states, Italy, after the machinations of April–May 1915, had entered the conflict without any *union sacrée*, but rather with the majority of the population at least passively opposed to involvement in the war.

Once Italy was engaged in battle, the requirements of fighting a modern war lessened this gap, with soldiers and their families, and those new social groups benefiting economically and in status from the war, being drawn into seconding the national effort. After May 1915 Giolitti's erstwhile parliamentary majority dwindled to the benefit of the more conservative side of the Liberal groupings. Poor King Victor Emmanuel III had to grow used to being called *Il Re Soldato*, despite his diminutive stature and homely attitudes. But the real move to propagandise the war and to preach that all Italians belonged to the nation only occurred in the last 12 months of the conflict. One who now joined Mussolini in this cause was Roberto Farinacci, once a reformist socialist, then an interventionist and soldier. Summoned back from the front to resume his career as a skilled railway worker, he began to act as correspondent for *Il Popolo d'Italia* in his adopted town of Cremona.[85] Thereafter he became convinced that Caporetto marked the breaking point between the 'old and the new Italy'.[86] As his case suggested, at the end of the war the nationalisation process retained a freshness and a vigour often by then lost in the other combatant states. At the same time, the effect of nationalising propaganda remained circumscribed; not all Italians were ready to surrender their identities to the nation. Rather, in 1919 much of Italian life was defined by a wrangling about the meaning of the war and its implications for the future.

Mussolini's own First World War had two parts, one military, the other political. Though not volunteering,[87] he did accept the draft. On 2 September 1915 he celebrated his induction into the army, in a piece he wrote for his paper[88] (hereafter placed under the management of Manlio Morgagni).[89] The story of Mussolini the soldier became an essential part of the Fascist construction of the *Duce*, perhaps the most essential part. As one windy propagandist phrased it, every 'legionary' of the new Fascist state was both rigidly disciplined and enthusiastically romantic because, in the ranks, his personality merged with that of the great legionary Mussolini, whose spirit was omnipresent and who thus became 'the creator, animator, and infallible guide' of every soldier.[90]

A key source for such ranting was Mussolini's war diary, proudly released in 1923 by *Imperia*, the official Fascist party publishing house, and reverently read by Italian schoolchildren and Fascist loyalists thereafter.[91] It had initially been serialised in *Il Popolo d'Italia* between 1915 and 1917. So much has been made of it that it is hard to read its pages without reference to the later myth of a *Duce*, which was, as yet, by no means fully developed. Nevertheless the diary does contain significant information, both witting and unwitting. *Bersagliere* Mussolini believed in what he viewed as the practical, as a soldier should, expressing his views in lapidary sentences. He was glad to serve at the front: 'It is war time. So you go to war.'[92] 'Trench life is natural, primitive life', even if monotonous at times. 'Rain and fleas are the first enemies of the Italian soldiers. Guns are next.'[93]

War, he explained, was 'grey', constructed from 'resignation, patience and tenacity', accepted by all real soldiers 'as a duty which you don't discuss'. Wartime politics were simple. He said he never heard a mention of neutrality or intervention. Peasant soldiers from the remotest villages very likely could not comprehend such difficult and unaccustomed words.[94] Returned emigrants, especially those from the USA, were the best soldiers, he thought (though he did not wonder whether their power and commitment came from their being nationalised and/or democratised abroad).[95] The villagers near the Isonzo front were, by contrast, enigmatic about the war: 'these Slovenes still do not love us', he noted, while the actual *paese* of Caporetto he dismissed as 'a wretched little Slovene town'.[96] Technology and efficiency were good, but mules were the most useful aides of the Italian army.[97] High on the alpine front (his position was for a time almost 2000 metres up), where soldiers had to combat an 80 per cent slope and could only move roped together, he even had occasion to admire the scenery and philosophise about its attractions.[98]

About different ranks and those matters of class which impinge on other wartime diaries, Mussolini had relatively little to say. Early in his service, he did complain that a colonel could not rouse the troops because he insisted on speaking to them as if they were schoolboys, not men.[99] Similarly, he recorded the suspicion of front-line soldiers that, through the machinations of a 'camorra' of corporals, the best rations were purloined before reaching them.[100] In his paper, he was hailed for his intrepid skills in scabbing for his mates in the trenches copious supplies of chocolate or sardines whenever he had the occasion to visit the company store.[101] But mostly he did not cavil at barriers between the ranks and was more willing to accommodate them than he had been with the differences in class and status in the civil and intellectual worlds. There were moments of vanity – he was pleased to be saluted as 'the interventionist journalist Benito Mussolini'. He had to recognise, none the less, that he was the only soldier in his brigade to read the papers when they arrived sporadically from the plain. The snow and the bitter cold were what mattered most to his comrades.[102]

At times, he was almost deferential, an unusual quality indeed for him to exhibit. In March 1917 he was wounded by shrapnel when a grenade exploded prematurely in an exercise behind the front – one worthy biographer would claim that a piece had been headed for his heart until blocked by a book he was carrying,[103] while his paper contended that he had endured a fever of 40.2 degrees.[104] As a result of his injury, he was introduced to King Victor Emmanuel III, who was on an official visit to the military hospital. They exchanged banalities, which, throughout the Fascist regime, were replayed as grave and significant:

'How are you, Mussolini?'
'Not so well, Your Majesty.'
'Bravo Mussolini! Put up with the immobility and the pain as you must.'
'Thanks, Your Majesty.'[105]

In sum, Mussolini's war diary gained in meaning after its author was elevated to dictatorship. Of course Mussolini the soldier was a patriot. He was moved emotionally when he crossed the border of the Trentino across which the Austrian authorities had once unceremoniously bundled him. On one occasion he rejoiced that the war acted as a melting pot of regionalisms from which a genuinely united Italy could be forged.[106] Similarly, the war experience confirmed his voluntarism, his belief in the triumph of the will: 'The winner of the war will be whoever wants to win it. The winner will be the one who can dispose of the greater reserves of psychic energy and resolution.'[107] No doubt such attitudes are not easy to reconcile with Mussolini's pre-war espousal of socialist materialism. However, on the various fronts of the First World War, they do not really amount to a distinctive credo or set of values. Corporal Mussolini was, in most ways, a soldier like any other.

This normality, often in the past eschewed by the thrusting *Duce*, was being confirmed in his own home. On 17 December 1915 after a bout of typhus earned him first a stay in hospital (and two fraternal visits from younger brother Arnaldo)[108] and then furlough at home, Mussolini formally married Rachele Guidi in a civil ceremony. Nine months later, on 27 September 1916, she was delivered of a son, named, appropriately for the moment, Vittorio. A second son, the conventionally named Bruno, would be born on 22 April 1918. Sister Edvige lived for a time with Rachele during that pregnancy.[109] As ever relieved of domestic duties, Mussolini on occasion had time to play 'some exercises by Liszt' with his young daughter and favourite child, the now legitimised Edda.[110]

It was as well to get these family matters straight, because, on 11 November 1915, Mussolini had fathered another son, called by his mother Benito Albino. This other Benito was, it seems, eventually to be a casualty of the Second World War.[111] The mother of the ill-fated child was Ida Irene Dalser from the Trentino, for a time owner of a beauty salon in Milan which she sold to her lover's benefit and was thereafter employed for a time on *Il Popolo d'Italia*. Her conjugal status, as compared with Rachele's, was sufficiently accepted for Mussolini's commanding officer to send an account of the *bersagliere*'s illness to Ida, not Rachele – some evidence exists that Ida and Benito had undergone a form of religious marriage late in 1914.[112] And Mussolini did acknowledge the liaison and pay Ida a variety of alimony. On becoming dictator, acting as so often through Arnaldo, he also provided a capital sum at 5 per cent for the life expenses of Benito Albino, though he did not bother to see the child.[113] However, the war was ensuring that Rachele would win the contest for Mussolini's affections against her competitor, whom she took to deriding as *la matta* (the mad-woman), ironically visiting on her rival the soubriquet which others had used to describe her husband. Her victory did not curb Mussolini's other amours. According to their biographers, Mussolini remained smitten by Margherita Sarfatti, who had conquered her initial doubts about the war and become a patriot. Her own eldest son, Roberto, died a war hero and his sacrificial death reinforced the political sympathies between Sarfatti and Mussolini.[114] Whatever the character of this office relationship, events had made it clear that Rachele would be Mussolini's legitimate wife and the person who ran his domestic household. In his patriarchal and Mediterranean eyes, there might be other women, but the war had confirmed that there was only one Rachele.

His domestic arrangements might have been becoming somewhat less Bohemian, but, in other ways, the great conflict was complicating Mussolini's life. In 1914, among the socialists, he had seemed a star. But the Italian entry into the First World War, however much desired by Mussolini, had actually dimmed his political influence and authority. During the *intervento* and then in the first years of military campaigning, he had been unable to compete with such grandiose figures as the lush poet and self-proclaimed world's greatest lover, Gabriele D'Annunzio, wealthy man-about-town and Futurist Chief, Filippo Marinetti, and a slew of established Nationalists from philosopher, Enrico Corradini, to journalist and member of parliament, Luigi Federzoni. Compared with such people Mussolini was very much a boy from the back-blocks, sprung from a class well below their own and possessed of a culture to which their natural reaction was scorn. In the estimate of many, Mussolini remained a boorish provincial. It was little wonder that the military authorities, believing that he had not overcome his subversive past, decided not to send him on an officer course.[115] His class and culture, they believed snobbishly, better equipped him for the non-commissioned ranks.

Nor did *Il Popolo d'Italia* fare well while he was at the front. In the weeks before his departure, he had combined vicious attacks on socialists (even Marx and Engels, he now argued, were German nation-alists at heart),[116] with a strident assertion that production would win the war: 'Work and fight: in this formula lies the secret of victory.'[117] The present war, he proclaimed, was a people's war. Italians could be as motivated to win it as were French revolutionary soldiers at Valmy in 1792.[118] But, after he left office, the rhetorical energy of *Il Popolo d'Italia* dissipated. His replacements at the editorial office lacked Mussolini's passion and his journalistic and managerial skills – rather than increasing the paper's sales, his manager Morgagni was rumoured to spend time and money furtively paying off Ida Dalser's hotel bills and other extraordinary expenses.[119] At the same time, the *Fasci d'azione rivoluzionaria* were fading in significance, even though Mussolini wrote from the battle front about their continuing purpose when the age of '"static" parties' was over.[120] By 1917 the paper was tumbling into finan-cial trouble. It was baled out for a while by Cesare Goldmann, a Milanese businessman of Jewish origin, and, later that year, was also assisted by the giant heavy-industrial, ship-building company, Ansaldo.[121]

None the less Mussolini's wounding and hospitalisation occurred at a moment of some opportunity. The surviving journalists at *Il Popolo d'Italia* had made much of their director's sacrifice. He was, they said, the *Duce*, Garibaldi's heir, and, if that proud title was not sufficiently expressive, he was also labelled 'The Inspirer', 'The Inciter', 'Ours'.[122] Others from his circle maintained that he could animate a cause like no other.[123] Such outrageous grovelling seemed justified since, once Mussolini re-occupied his editorial chair in June 1917, the paper quickly regained its initial thrust. Now he insisted that Italians wage what was to be called 'total war'. Though censorship was severe, Mussolini, with his accustomed temerity, began to challenge its authority as he demanded a 'real' government, one that was above all bold and would fight 'the Germans', especially the Imperial Germans, with a will.[124] The pseudo-peacemaking of such feeble men as 'His Holiness Pope Pilate XV' must be rejected.[125] More and better propa-ganda was required to enhance the crucial 'moral health' of the army and so provide it with a 'soul'. Greater impulse was needed to give 'a "social" content to the war effort'.[126] Mostly his language was tough but, on one occasion, Mussolini let slip a residual utopianism; then he imagined an arcadian post-war world, where love would replace hate, leisure suffering and production destruction. With the return of peace, he cogitated briefly, there would be no more 'convulsions', but, rather, a '"détente" of soul and body'.[127]

The battle of Caporetto ended such happy imaginings. Now

Mussolini's most strident past warnings seemed justified as Italy lurched to the edge of utter defeat. Against this threat, he proclaimed, there must be total resistance, 'the Nation must be the army, the army the Nation'.[128] Italians must display the nobility of their stock and march to the beat of 'one heart only'.[129] Socialists and other traitors should be treated without respect or mercy.[130] Frivolity must end, orchestral concerts, theatres, race tracks and coffee shops be closed; the whole people must be militarised and behave with soldiers' discipline.[131] Nor should the peasants be forgotten: '<u>To save the peasantry for the Nation, land must be given to the peasants</u>', he wrote emphatically.[132] The country should be handed over to those who were fighting for it.[133] In sum, he urged, Italy 'requires a government. A man. A man who has when needed the delicate touch of an artist and the heavy hand of a warrior. A man who is sensitive and full of will-power. A man who knows and loves the people, and who can direct and bend them with violence if required'. Under such a ruler – his own choice for the office may be imagined – Italy could wage a 'war which concentrates only on the war'. Then it would at last find a 'government which is also subtle and can adapt itself to circumstances and situations'. Its line would be simple: 'for the ingenuous and ignorant, propaganda; for the *canaille*, lead'.[134]

Mussolini's sentiments were still too extreme for many (and his self-interest was as blatant as usual), but his thoughts were not out of kilter with the times. De Felice perhaps exaggerated a little when he argued that Caporetto converted Mussolini from an agitator into a politician.[135] However, there can be no doubt that the last year of the conflict was fought in a new atmosphere, amounting to a sort of 'people's war'. Such novelty gave potential space to a man of Mussolini's class and culture. In December 1917 more than 150 deputies and 90 senators (including Salandra) joined in a *Fascio parlamentare di difesa nazionale* (Parliamentary union for national defence), again utilising a word which was embedding itself into political parlance. Mussolini duly hailed 'the 152 Fascist deputies' in an article he wrote in January 1918.[136] New Prime Minister, the moderate Liberal Orlando, similarly tried to sound both populist and nationalist, hailing expansionism abroad and social reform at home, and appearing to promise land distribution to his nation's 'heroic' peasant soldiery. Mussolini may no longer have been a Marxist, but again the course of history seemed to be going his way.

He would still occasionally describe himself as a 'socialist', but there were almost always qualifying phrases. His socialism could only be 'anti-Marxist' and 'national',[137] he wrote, since 'to deny the Patria means to deny your own mother'.[138] Now his ancient antipathy for American capitalists was forgotten as he celebrated the arrival of soldiers of the 'New World' in Europe, full of the verve and drive of a 'young stock' (*razza*) and led by 'Woodrow Wilson the wise', a peer-less leader who had demonstrated just how 'holy' the Entente cause was.[139] Mussolini still hankered for a 'dictatorship', which, he argued, could as easily be 'democratic' as 'reactionary'. 'It is only a dictator-ship which can pluck men from where they are and deploy them in the best way possible.' His candidate for this post was, he noted in May 1918, Wilson, the 'noble', the 'sharp and the resolute'.[140] When Wilson spoke, he assumed the part of Moses, translating Europeans to a better world.[141] Even in January 1919, at which time he was urging that 'imperialism is the eternal and unchanging rule of life', Mussolini was still saluting 'Wilson's empire', which, he wrote lyrically, knew no bounds because it expressed 'the needs, hopes and faith of the human soul'.[142] Wilson, his paper proclaimed, was 'the magnificent *Duce* of the peoples'.[143]

Events in Russia, by contrast, appalled. The disgrace of the Treaty of Brest Litovsk was exactly what official socialism offered Italy in prospect.[144] Leninism entailed autocracy, bestiality, terror and chaos,[145] the failure of 'socialism'.[146] As he put it after the war was over, Soviet socialists were no better than murderers.[147] What they were doing in Russia, they would, if given the chance, perpe-trate in Italy as well.

A residue of the dialectic could still be found in his mind, however. At the end of 1917 he had explained more clearly that what he now stood for was the *trincerocrazia* (rule by those who had experienced the trenches). 'Italy', he declared, was dividing into two great parties – 'those who have been there and those who haven't been; those who have fought and those who haven't fought; those who have worked and the parasites.'[148] Production was what mattered most (not, as he might have once thought, pay and conditions). An efficient adminis-tration could easily mobilise 100 000 women to replace physically fit men, presently tied up in the factories.[149] In August 1918 the sub-title of *Il Popolo d'Italia* was changed from that of a 'socialist' paper to one of 'soldiers [*combattenti*] and producers', and Mussolini's editorial declared ringingly that an international of such people was actually being born. [150]

In some other matters Mussolini's line was still inclined to swerve, however. In regard to ambitions in Dalmatia, he was not yet an out and out nationalist, suggesting in April 1918, with a surviving optimism, that 'moral values' could outweigh 'territorial' ones.[151] Similarly he welcomed the suggestion of greater freedom for India, speaking admiringly of what he thought were British 'step by step' plans there.[152] Concerning the League of Nations, whose lineaments were now being sketched, he was more sceptical. The conceptual base of such an institution, he thought, did not fit the Italian *'forma mentis'*.[153] Typically, he preferred realism to idealism. 'The "will to dominate" was', he stated baldly, 'the fundamental law of the life of the universe from its most rudimentary forms to its most elevated ones.'[154] Man was, after all, driven by a 'divine bestiality'.[155] Darwin weighed more heavily on his mind than Marx had ever done.

On 11 November 1918 came the surprise end of hostilities on the Western front, certainly not an event foreseen either by Mussolini or by Italy's leadership. Naturally, *Il Popolo d'Italia* celebrated the victory of the Entente. The fall of the Roman Empire or that of Napoleon, Mussolini wrote with what might seem surprisingly negative or nervous reference, could not compare with its grandeur. Now, he added, 'it makes you dizzy. The whole earth trembles. All continents are riven by the same crisis. There is not a single part of the planet ... which is not shaken by the cyclone. In old Europe, men disappear, systems break, institutions collapse'.[156] Citing Dante, Mussolini orated about the prospect that 'work' could be 'redeemed'.[157] Could the outbreak of peace ensure that real 'revolution' which he had so often exalted?

Actually, of course, the conclusion of the war threatened another dead-end for Benito Mussolini. With the fighting over, what did leftist interventionism now mean? How, still more importantly, could a man who was merely first of his relatively humble class win respect and influence in a world which most likely would return to the hands of the old elites or their sons? It was all very well for Mussolini, still the Francophile, to compare himself with Georges Clemenceau, the French 'Tiger', the Architect of Victory and a Jacobin turned nationalist.[158] But others might not readily accept the parallel. To win the respect he deserved, more political work was necessary, and so, as early as 14 November 1918, Mussolini was trying to organise a meeting of his sort of people: 'if, in a certain sense, the war was ours, so the postwar must be ours', he stated hopefully.[159] They might be called the *Fasci per la Costituente* (Fascists for a Constituent Assembly).[160] His newspaper, he recalled, in new phrases, had been 'virile in the Roman manner'. It had kept alive its 'profound hatreds and loves'. It was ready for future battle and future victory.[161] It could be converted into 'a great news-paper of ideas, news and information'.[162]

What remained imponderable was just who might join Mussolini and to what end. The social policies which he favoured had a radical air. But what would leftists make of his comment in February 1919 that 'the *padrone* ['boss', 'owner'] no longer exists', since the war had demonstrated how Italians must work and produce together. Moreover, Professor Mussolini still had so many competitors in the chaotic ranks of non- or anti-socialist, pro-war, radicalism. Futurists, syndicalists, 'democrats', the *Associazione Nazionale dei Combattenti* (the main returned soldiers' organisation),[163] Nationalists, Gabriele D'Annunzio and many another hoped that the future was theirs, and were convinced that they or their group had played the crucial role in Italy's recent victory, and now knew how best to cash in their part in it.

The political and intellectual world in the early months of 1919 was in flux. Two words, however, were affording some encouragement to Mussolini, and suggesting that a united approach might eventually be possible. They were the obvious word, 'national' and the less familiar but becoming ever more redolent, *fascio*. In February 1919 some 20 *Fasci di combattimento* (ex-servicemen's leagues) had sprung up in places ranging from Venice and Milan, to Ferrara and Florence, to Naples, Messina and Cagliari.[164] On 23 March 1919 Mussolini summoned their representatives and a motley throng of other ex-interventionists to a meeting in Milan.[165] Among those attending were Chiavolini, Farinacci and Marinelli, now joined by Umberto Pasella, Mario Giampaoli, Corrado Pavolini, Cesare Rossi, Mario Gioda, Ferruccio Vecchi, Marinetti and a number of others.[166] All would have roles, though varied ones, to play during the Fascist dictatorship. In a building overlooking the Piazza San Sepolcro, they presently came together to sketch a programme for a national organisation of *Fasci di combattimento*. The Fascist movement was about to be officially born.

6

The first months of Fascism,
1919–1920

WITH the beginning of the first year of peace, Benito Mussolini
stood at another crossroads. He was 35, the father of three legitimate children and the owner-editor of a newspaper which had made
a splash in Milan, Italy's most important city. He had established a reputation as an able journalist and an efficient manager. He was known
to labour and to play hard. A colleague on *Il Popolo d'Italia*, who soon
after would leave the paper, remembered how his editor loved to shut
himself in his office between coffees and threaten to shoot anyone who
interrupted him, a boast which was given a certain verisimilitude by
the fact that Mussolini, the spokesman of ex-soldiers, was always
armed. He worked furiously but without the assistance of notes or
archive. 'Whatever he read went into his brain cells and stayed there.'
Any journalistic underling bold enough to enter his door was attacked
as producing rubbish, a conclusion which Mussolini regularly reached
even when he had not seen the piece in question. Mussolini himself
could write anywhere, and his articles were as likely to be composed
at the theatre or coffee shop, amid gossiping friends, as at the office.
This Mussolini was much given to mood swings, 'a cruel sentimentalist', a man who combined the 'ferocity of a tyrant' with 'the hesitations
of a child'. Altogether he was one who 'never resisted temptation'. He
could also laugh at typographical slips (another journalist remembered
his easy smile[1] and many warmed to his 'geniality'); he joked that his
children amounted to 'the printers' errors of an intelligent man'.
Among his offspring, he added, the newspaper constituted his 'most
perfect child'.[2] As his regime's propagandists would love to underline,
Mussolini honed his knowledge of people while acting as an editor:
'Journalism', he said, 'led me to understand the human material from
which politics is made'.[3]

Map 2 Interwar Italy

A not unfriendly police official reporting in June 1919 to the new Prime Minister, the worthy but unimaginative economist Francesco Saverio Nitti, amplified this picture, observing that Mussolini was of strong constitution. His day began late; usually he did not leave his home until around mid-day.[4] Having departed, however, he was not accustomed to return there until 3 a.m. By the estimate of the time, he was tough and manly, although his sexual conquests and his victories in duels[5] might now be written off as boys' games. He had served in the war, and, at a minimum, not disgraced himself. His experiences at the front made it easy for him to claim to represent Italian soldiery and, in some senses, he did. He could speechify over considerable span, adopting a crudely populist tone on most occasions but also aspiring to intellectual profundity. Whatever the audience, he could be relied on to express views, both spoken and written, on topics which ranged from foreign affairs to Milanese city politics. In every circumstance as a speaker he sparkled. His 'emotionality' and 'impulsiveness' rendered his words spellbinding, even though he lacked the *gravitas* of a real orator. He was, the report ran on, 'at base a sentimentalist and his quality in that regard draws him much sympathy and many friends'. At the same time, he was a ruthless and brutal purveyor of polemic in the debates which were a habitual part of Italian political life, especially when they concerned self-defined members of the intelligentsia. Rabble-rouser, philosopher, factional or party chief, he had sought to master all these briefs, and could make a fist of each of them. He was liberal with any funds which fell into his hands, the police analysis continued, certainly not personally grasping. His conversion to supporting the war, the official believed perhaps too easily, had not been won through corruption, but rather genuinely reflected his ideals. Mussolini rallied behind his friends whatever the cause. At the same time, he was a good hater of his enemies. Very intelligent, he knew how to measure men and swiftly assay their strengths and weaknesses.[6]

In this lengthy appraisal, Nitti was being told that, in the traditions of Liberal Italy, Mussolini was a politician-in-waiting. As the police report reminded the Prime Minister, the editor of *Il Popolo d'Italia* was 'intensely ambitious' and 'did not always stick to his convictions and ideals'; above all, he would not rest content with second place in any ordering of society.[7] De Felice and his followers[8] have argued, with obvious contemporary political motive, that the Mussolini here described still belonged on the left (and always retained a socialist humus for his ideas). And yet, in being so fixated on his alleged ideology, they ignore behaviour patterns familiar in the rest of Italian history. Take the case of Francesco Crispi, an emblematic figure especially because Fascist propagandists loved to depict him as a precursor of the *Duce*.[9] At the peak of his success in the 1890s, Crispi combined hard-line conservative politics at home, in which he did not blanch at summoning the army to shoot peasant protesters, with imperialism abroad (even if it ended in tears at Adowa). In the aftermath of this defeat, Crispi's career collapsed. But more telling is the fact that he had begun his political life in the 1850s as a provincial Sicilian lawyer committed to the 'revolutionary' overthrow of the Bourbon regime. He was, in other words, another ambitious boy brought up far from the centres of power, favouring 'revolution' as a term which more than anything else would guarantee his own elevation. After 1860, in the society of united Italy, he continued to think of himself as belonging to the left. However, his own need for social comfort – a vivid sex life was expensive – and the ordinary processes of *trasformismo* pushed him steadily to the right where greater reward and opportunity lay.

Crispi's case was an extreme one, but as a rough model it illustrates the history of many an Italian politician, both in the Liberal era and in the Republic after 1946. In early 1919 there were plenty of reasons to imagine that Mussolini might find a similar route to 'transformation'. His lifestyle was unthrifty. He had just moved his family to a larger and more commodious flat in the central Foro Bonaparte and he retained a fascination with fast cars (in October 1919 he was lucky to survive a crash at ill-omened Faenza).[10] In 1921 he was to become the proud owner of a new four-cylinder sports Alfa.[11] He continued to take fencing lessons and to duel. He dreamed of flying.[12] Nor was his family cheap. There were medical expenses when, in October 1918, he caught the Spanish flu as did Rachele who suffered the more.[13] The next year baby Bruno almost died from diphtheria.[14] Perhaps his mistress Margherita Sarfatti paid the bills; she was rich enough to do so and, on the edge of forty, she may have been in generous mood. With or without her prompting, as he drifted up-market in his patterns of behaviour, Mussolini began to cultivate a fresh image, shaving off his moustache, wearing collared shirts, and generally aiming at a new elegance.

These personal matters hinted at something more political. There was one overwhelming argument why neither Mussolini nor Italy could resume pre-1915 life – the First World War and all that it implied and had been made to imply. Crispi had twisted his way through the thickets of Liberal factional and interest politics. He existed in a world where the suffrage extended to no more than 7 per cent of adult males and where the great majority of the population was by definition excluded from even a remote influence on the public exercise of power. Already, before 1914, this old world was slipping into crisis, and the war confirmed that its systems no longer worked. The *dopoguerra* or post-war was to be the 'age of the masses', the time when politics were no longer constructed from back-room deals but rather spoken out emphatically to a public who would need the organisation of a mass party and the cultural hegemony of a mass ideology. While Mussolini strove ostentatiously to await his call to 'transform', both he and his social betters glimpsed the reality that 'new', post-war politics must somehow embrace 'mass man'.

In reality the fug of the back-room lingered in Fascist practice (just as it lingers in our own world). However, in terms of presentation and representation – that is, the marketing of politics, both to the people and to financial and intellectual elites – by 1919 it had become necessary to proclaim that politics reflected the masses' will and was rooted in their needs. Moreover, in any attempt to construct a credible programme, recent history, and so the meaning of the First World War, bulked large. All politicians had to take a stance on the war.

Here Mussolini seemed fortunate. In the simplest of understandings, he had been right about the course and the character of that conflict. He had punted on Italy, France and Britain winning it, and the Entente, with the belated help of the USA and the simultaneous defection of Russia into revolution, had done so. The socialists, whom he had abandoned, had tried to pursue an honourable line of 'neither support nor sabotage' towards the national effort, but their policy was too subtle and too virtuous to be explained away polemically. In the post-war era, socialism could only thrive if Italian entry into the conflict was all but universally accepted to have been a disaster. So much human travail had been expended in the fighting that such a renunciation of history, however intellectually convincing, seemed unlikely to appeal to the majority of the Italian populace. In 1919 the forces hostile to socialism could rely on a natural electorate of those who craved a positive memory of the war.

To be sure, the impact of the war was rather more complicated than it might at first seem. After all, the nation-state, Italy, had proved an unreliable victor in the conflict. Indeed, as Foreign Minister Sonnino and Prime Minister Orlando were fumbling their aims and propaganda during the Versailles peacemaking and drastically failing to re-make themselves and their country 'Wilsonian',[15] Italy began to acquire what has been wittily called 'an honorary loser' status in the international sphere of post-war politics. Whatever might be thought of its wartime sacrifice, Italy had again been shown up as no more than the least of the Great Powers and maybe not even that. Mussolini, too, in early 1919 could easily be read as one who had personally snatched defeat from the jaws of victory. Who, after all, constituted his electorate and who were his power brokers? The old elites and their younger comrades in the Nationalist Association had found Mussolini's skills useful throughout the war and especially in the period after Caporetto, when Italy's leaders wanted any help they could get to raise national consciousness and steel the determination to fight. Mussolini had excelled as a drummer for their cause. But did the cause have a future? And how could it be reconciled with Mussolini's own provinciality, his evident limitations as a boy from Predappio who had been merely first in his class? It was not as though Mussolini had been the only propagandist of a nationalised Italian war effort. How could he not now acknowledge the seniority in both class and intellectual terms of D'Annunzio, Corradini, Salvemini and many other potential new politicians, who, however divided one from another, also hoped in the new peace to earn credit from their careers as wartime patriots?

If that was Mussolini's problem 'above', he also confronted evident difficulties 'below'. Whenever he wanted to connect with the masses of a class status inferior to his own, what ideas could he use? Were not the majority of the Italian people, in processes which again had been reinforced by the nature of national participation in the First World War, by now committed either to the socialists, or to the Catholics? The latter had, on 18 January 1919, published a manifesto announcing the formation of a mass party, the *Partito Popolare Italiano* or PPI, to be led, somewhat ambiguously, by a Sicilian radical priest, Luigi Sturzo. The PPI and that ancient anti-clerical Benito Mussolini had little reason to be friends, while the mutual hatreds of the war stood as an impenetrable barrier against any resumption of Mussolini's socialism. As the delegates arrived for the founding meeting of the *Fasci di combattimento* at the building which looked out over the Piazza San Sepolcro (Holy Sepulchre Square), Mussolini must have wondered somewhat despairingly how he might locate a space wherein his promise as a politician could be made good. For the present, and, indeed, for most of 1919, there were many grounds to fear that time was burying him. In the small print, was he about to find that, after all, he had 'lost' his First World War?

Yet a resurrection did lie ahead, and just over three and a half years later Mussolini had accepted his designation as Italy's youngest Prime Minister. During that short period the range of ideas which the *Fasci di combattimento* espoused were hammered into a credible political programme. And the indispensable leader of the *Fasci*, their only plausible national political chief, had become Benito Mussolini. He, and no other, had assumed the role of their *Duce*. How, then, did the fragility and weakness of March 1919 turn into the political triumph of 28 October 1922?

In Mussolini's *Complete Works*, as collected and published by his admirers in the 1950s, the meeting at San Sepolcro is described glowingly as 'the actual birth of Fascism'.[16] This claim is, however, a simplification of the complex state of the Italian new right in the spring of 1919. In the gloom of the Second World War, Mussolini would, with typically savage cynicism, dismiss those who joined him in Milan as men of 'trifling quality'.[17] At the time, however, it was Mussolini himself who was the more obvious bit-player. Among those in attendance, for the moment more celebrated and more active than Mussolini, were Ferruccio Vecchi and F.T. Marinetti. Vecchi was the leader of what he called *Arditismo civile*, that is, a group which strove to chart a peacetime presence for the wartime ideals of the *Arditi*, or crack troops, now discharged from the national forces. Vecchi, too, owned a paper – *L'Ardito* – and viewed the Mussolinian *Il Popolo d'Italia* as just 'another anti-Bolshevik' organ.[18] His movement possessed the smatterings of an ideology – Vecchi spoke of a reliance on youth, a commitment to compulsory military service and a popular army, and a dedication to a reformed education system which would genially split the school-day into three hours of formal lessons and three hours of sport and gymnastics.[19] Others of his ideas were still more idiosyncratic. Vecchi deemed Milan 'the sacred city of *italianità*', and, perhaps to separate himself from Florence-based Nationalists, he even dared to doubt adulation of Dante Alighieri, automatically accepted elsewhere as the poet who first lit the path to a glorious national future. For Vecchi, Garibaldi, a man of action rather than words (and not a Florentine), was 'more of a poet than was Dante'.[20] To make taut their political will, followers of *Arditismo civile*, he said, should adopt the slogan 'first the Patria, then the family, then we ourselves, then the international'. Rather more passionately, the *Arditi* also pledged their utter opposition to socialism, clericalism and all forms of middle-class passivity (*borghesmi*).[21]

Along with a programme went a ritual – Italians, by definition aware of the Vatican and all its works, rarely forbore for long to claim that their ideals were bolstered by a religious impulse from which a ceremonial naturally sprang. So the *Arditi* wore in peacetime the black shirts which had marked them out in war; so, too, they developed the chant *A noi* (which might be best translated as meaning 'Italy belongs to us') meant to signal their unity and their fidelity to the cause.[22] Vecchi was not always a patient lobbyist for his ideals. One unkind critic remembered the *Arditi* wandering from one Milan bar to the next, imposing in their black shirts, but otherwise without an obvious purpose, 'talking loudly until boozed into silence'.[23] By contrast, a more reverent ex-military chaplain wrote in praise of the *Arditi*'s youthfully generous chivalry and willingness to fight to the death against 'barbarian' enemies at home and abroad.[24] Another fan spoke of the the way the *Arditi* embodied 'the unchanging genius of the national stock', exuding an Italian *élan vital* against the leaden heaviness of Germanism. At the front, they had intrepidly engaged in the 'gymnastics of war'; in peace, they would want 'little formal discipline, no bureaucracy, the most flexible of hierarchies'. Manly in every sense, they fused thought, beauty and action; a new aristocracy, they were the enemies of traitors wherever they might hide.[25]

In February 1919, though still believing the Futurists to be too verbal and too detached from the mass of ordinary ex-soldiers,[26] Vecchi had formally met with Marinetti to discuss ways to construct a more practical base for this pot-pourri of ideas. Marinetti was very much an established member of the local intelligentsia, a person with an acknowledged media profile. He was also a man of many contradictions – the revolutionary critic of bourgeois dullness and tedium whose family house was an ornate villa in one of the more sought-after streets in Milan;[27] the bold advocate of phallocracy and the end of marriage who, in 1919, began living with a much younger woman whom he would formally wed four years later and by whom he was hen-pecked;[28] the strident patriot who never quite abandoned the hope of cosmopolitan recognition in Paris. In most eyes, Marinetti's determination to push every issue beyond its logical conclusion as well as his exquisitely bourgeois desire to upset the bourgeoisie, scarcely rendered him a credible political figure. The tone of an article he wrote early in 1919, in which he imagined that the most positive result from the war might be the sudden arrival of men from all over the world and from 'the most diverse races ... uniting in disordered and rapid coitus with just one woman' and thus publicly overthrowing the traditional family, was hardly calculated to win mass appeal.[29] Nor did his demand that the Papacy be expelled from Rome in order 'to free Italy from the Catholic mentality' seem likely to turn into general policy.[30] It made Mussolini, for one, write Marinetti off as an 'authentic buffoon', a man to be disliked and discounted.[31] Given the Futurist chief's vagaries, it is not altogether surprising to find an acolyte of the movement from Rome suggesting that not Marinetti but Mussolini might be 'the new man' of whom the movement had dreamed and wanted to 'adore'.[32]

None the less, among the restless intelligentsia of Milan – people who agreed, or said they agreed, with Marinetti that 'our race outdoes all other races in the huge number of geniuses it produces' – Marinetti retained great cachet. On 15 April he and Vecchi turned some of their words into actions. After meeting at one of the elegant *pasticcerie* in the Milan *Galleria*, and proclaiming their vocation as 'assault journalists',[33] Marinetti and Vecchi marched to the nearby headquarters of the socialist *Avanti!* and proceeded to sack the place, in what was eventually mythologised as 'the first victory of Fascism'.[34] Mussolini himself did not accompany the punitive expedition. However, on 17 April he tried to make the best out of both worlds, explaining in an interview he was granted by *Il Giornale d'Italia*, that, although the attack had been spontaneous, he himself accepted the 'whole moral responsibility for the episode'.[35] The respectable readers of these words were meant to realise that Mussolini was suggesting that he could again become a useful ally for Italy's social elites, a prospect which was reinforced when the police showed little interest in punishing those who beat up unpatriotic newsmen. The socialist press similarly tried to capitalise on the event, preferring to blame the 'rat' Mussolini rather than the more outré Vecchi and Marinetti, even though by doing so they reinforced Mussolini's continuing political presence.

To be sure, doubts lingered about Mussolini's exact political positioning. If, beneath their verbiage, Vecchi and Marinetti belonged to a right of some kind, others among Mussolini's associates in these months were much more likely to talk about social revolution and to sound as if they might mean it. The first secretary of the *Fasci di combattimento* was Attilio Longoni, an airman, but one who had once been a railway-worker and syndicalist. His more active replacement from September 1919 was another syndicalist, Umberto Pasella.[36] Mussolini himself, only two days after the San Sepolcro assembly, announced that 'the hour of syndicalism' had sounded; it was, he said, an ideology which could trace a third way between class struggle and class collaboration.[37] As A.O. Olivetti, a more subtle proponent of this credo, had been stating, syndicalists could find their class identity within the nation rather than in opposition to it.[38] It was unnecessary to be utterly precise ideologically, Mussolini was soon adding, since the Fascist movement was an 'anti-party without a constitution and without rules'. It had as yet no ultimate solution for issues relating to the monarchy or the Church or even socialism – in April 1919 there were rumours that Mussolini had made soundings about his possible return to his old party[39] – or, indeed, any matter. Fascists were practical people who looked to practical choices and foreswore the a priori.[40]

Another way to describe this position is, of course, that it was one of confusion and opportunism. Certainly, compiling a neat account of Mussolini's array of ideas – the journalist kept pumping out his truculent pieces in *Il Popolo d'Italia* – may well be a foolhardy venture. As had been true now for almost a decade, one area of Mussolini's expertise was foreign affairs; those skilled in understanding such matters alone possessed the kudos needed by any leader who aspired to recognition beyond the humdrum world. Readers of the paper could note Mussolini's inveighing against Britain, 'the fattest and most bourgeois nation in the world'.[41] Eire and Egypt, he demanded, should be set free; Malta should become Italian.[42] Woodrow Wilson, whom a few months before he had so admired, was now mocked as fundamentally 'anti-Europe' and 'anti-Latin', at best a muddled professor.[43] The final signature of the Treaty of Versailles, Mussolini admonished in early June, did not mark the end of history. Whatever was presently agreed at Paris, Italians must not renounce the heritage which had come from the decision in 1915 to intervene. Instead, they must proudly recall that the great conflict had represented the first war fought by 'all Italians' since the collapse of the Roman empire.[44] The port of 'Fiume' (or Rijeka) in the north-eastern Adriatic should not be abandoned; whatever the wishes of the new Kingdom of the Serbs, Croats and Slovenes, or of 'international plutocracy', Fiume must remain Italian.[45]

The last reference was not the only hint of anti-Semitism in Mussolini's phrasings at this time, an anti-Semitism which, though infrequently expressed in Italy, could be found more stridently in the pages of *La Vita Italiana*. This journal was edited by 'Dott.' Giovanni Preziosi, an unfrocked priest, and boasted among its regular contributors the economist Maffeo Pantaleoni, business chiefs Oscar Sinigaglia and Dante Ferraris (themselves patriotic Jews), nationalist Corradini, philosopher Pareto, and a number of other intellectuals and politicians of a class and influence superior to Mussolini's.[46] In one of Mussolini's denunciations of 'Leninism' in Russia, he used words which he might have borrowed from Preziosi. 'Eighty per cent' of the Bolshevik leadership, Mussolini remarked, were Jews who, in their secret plots, were actually in the service of the Jewish bankers of London and New York. 'Race', Mussolini wrote in words to be invoked again after 1938, 'does not betray race.'[47]

Those commentators anxious to argue that Fascism, like Nazism, was always committed to 'a war against the Jews', emphasise the fervour of these phrases.[48] More likely, what they signify is Mussolini's chameleon-like ability to take on the colour and tone of the discourse which surrounded him. Indeed, hardly had he exposed these 'Jewish conspiracies' than he was writing in favour of the heavily Jewish revolutionaries of Hungary, where their policies could be read as putting off social revolution while they tried patriotically to defend their country against an invading Romanian army.[49] Nor was Mussolini consistent in his dislike of financiers and businessmen. His first article on the new government attacked Nitti but praised the role taken on by Dante Ferraris, the president of *Confindustria*, the big business league, and a regular and generous contributor to nationalist causes. Ferraris, Mussolini wrote ingratiatingly, was a '<u>self-made man</u>' [*sic*], a man of action who was committed to saving Italy from social disintegration and simultaneously to modernising Italian industry and Italian industrialists.[50] As if in proof of his new interest in such a world, Mussolini, one day in the spring of 1920, braved the floor of the Milan Stock Exchange, with a friendly journalist taking pains to explain the arcane deals going on there.[51]

Despite the breadth and ambition of his commentary on the state of the world, Mussolini's most common phrases were truculently directed at the more homely matter of lambasting the mainstream socialist party. Socialists, Mussolini typically recalled, had, in 1914, taken Italy into a 'civil war', a conflict which had still not ended. It was not a fight between rich and poor as socialists liked to argue, he explained, but rather one between 'national' and 'anti-national' forces, a dispute based not on economics but on mentality.[52] The contest was not material but spiritual.

In other words, despite his yearning for social recognition, Mussolini was at his most verbally consistent in his hostility to socialism. Nevertheless, as the polemics heated up, the initiative in this running dispute seemed to lie not with Mussolini, who, in August 1919, was again reduced to making plaintive appeals for new subscriptions to save *Il Popolo d'Italia* from collapse,[53] but with the socialists. Though they did not cease their cry that Mussolini was a 'rat' who had been bought and sold, another soiled hireling of the bosses,[54] the socialist movement had more than Mussolini on its mind. Nitti's goverment was offering the lack-lustre slogan 'produce more – consume less'[55] to an Italy which was drastically dislocated by the problems of fitting a war economy, society and polity to peace. Could this, socialists asked in hope, and their enemies in fear, be the hour of the revolution when, as the words of a contemporary song ran aggressively, 'we shall do as they are doing in Russia. Whoever doesn't work, won't eat'?[56] New members were flocking into socialist unions and, even if a much publicised strike in favour of Russia failed in July (and was bitterly condemned by Mussolini and his friends),[57] in the election to be held in November the socialist vote promised to be high. It was all very well for the *Fasci* to draft radical sounding programmes involving swingeing taxes on war profiteers, a reduction in the voting age for men and votes for women, an 8-hour day, the abolition of the Senate[58] and many another leftist cause (even refurbishing the ancient catch-cry of seizing ecclesiastical goods).[59] But it was the socialists who, during the autumn and winter of 1919, seemed to be riding the wave of history and who could afford to deride the small and divided *Fasci di combattimento*. A historian tabulated 16 rival groups who, earlier in 1919, had been using the word *fascio* to describe themselves.[60] Ranging from anarchists to restless bourgeois university students, these 'fascists' had nothing in common except their name.

It was true that in August 1919 Mussolini somehow found the funds to float a new journal, entitled *Il Fascio*, whose aim was to help define the movement, and that, by then, the *Fasci di combattimento* were becoming the best known of the competing groups. Even if 'fascism' could be thus confined, an ample political space for its followers was still hard to discern in post-war Italy. One event, however, was about to give a new cast to Italy's postwar crisis and, in the long run, to open important opportunity for Benito Mussolini. On 12 September 1919 poet Gabriele D'Annunzio, saluted by Vecchi as the 'great *Duce*',[61] led a band of what were claimed to be 1000 myrmidons, the same number who had once accompanied Garibaldi to Sicily, to seize Fiume, a humble town of 49 000, which speechifying had converted into a Great National Cause. There, D'Annunzio established what has been called a 'lyrical dictatorship',[62] pledged to defending the city's *italianità* against all comers. He also flirted with social revolution, collaborating with syndicalist Alceste De Ambris in drafting the *Carta del Carnaro* (Carnaro charter), a document destined to be glossed as a precursor of Fascist corporatism.[63] De Ambris himself would soon break with Fascism, writing bitterly of Mussolini's 'monstrous egoism' and his 'crafty political gamesmanship', which had taken Fascism towards a 'reactionary involution', made it an instrument of the landowners, and betrayed Fiume.[64] Oblivious to such bickering, D'Annunzio, with characteristic advertising flair, sought new propaganda techniques to win the souls of the townspeople. According to some historians, the poet was pioneering the coming modern and Fascist worlds.[65]

In retrospect, D'Annunzio appears at least as unlikely a political figure as was Marinetti. The two poets cordially disliked each other and each deprecated his rival's use of words. If Marinetti (born 1876) had tried to be steely, hymning the rise of the machine, D'Annunzio (born 1863) had made a name for himself through the lushness of his language and the arch pornography of his themes. Each had conditioned his commitment to a Great Italy with a love of Paris. D'Annunzio, who had the higher international reputation, had lived for long periods in France. However, he, too, had rallied to Italy's war, been prominent at interventionist demonstrations, and, during the conflict, had completed well-publicised expeditions, notably an intrepid aerial raid on Vienna on 9 August 1918. Whatever the ambiguity of his past role and present lifestyle, D'Annunzio had become identified with the new nationalist cause and was viewed by some, and especially by himself, as a credible national leader.

Not surprisingly Mussolini did not warm to D'Annunzio and his little free state. The class and cultural backgrounds of the two leaders were wildly different. None the less, both now and later, Mussolini sought to utilise any headline which D'Annunzio might stimulate and harness any resulting energy for his own purposes. A version of events common after 1922 would praise the way in which Mussolini and D'Annunzio worked together during the occupation of Fiume in sketching the lineaments of a new politics at home and abroad. In practice, however, Mussolini evinced little desire to join the poet in Fiume, where he had reason to fear that his burgeoning charisma would fall under the shadow of the poet's own and might indeed be blighted for ever. Mussolini's tilting for Fiume was restricted to the rhetorical. In *Il Popolo d'Italia*, he hailed the occupation of the city as a grandiose gesture of revolt against 'the plutocratic Western coalition', 'sharks' every one.[66] The 'pseudo-economist' Nitti, he added, dulled by the Bourbon mentality that could be expected of a man of the South, could never begin to comprehend such grandeur.[67] Mussolini even made a flying visit to Fiume on 7 October. But that trip was designed to publicise a first national congress of *Fasci di combattimento* – with what would become accustomed military vocabulary, Mussolini was calling it an *adunata*, or muster. With the efficient help of Pasella, who did not hide his dislike of D'Annunzio's silliness, this meeting had been summoned to Florence for 9-10 October. There it was Mussolini who was meant to cut a figure in the world of new politics, not D'Annunzio. In language that was still deliberately opaque, Mussolini used the moment to proclaim the rise of a group which was 'not republican, not socialist, not democratic, not conservative, not nationalist', but was young and did believe in the cause of the war. It was destined to unite in 'a synthesis of all negations and all positives', especially as its members campaigned against Nitti, *Sua Indecenza Cagoia* (His Indecency, the Shit-Bag).[68]

Rather than sacrificing all for Fiume, Mussolini was directing his attention to the fast-approaching national elections in which he was standing as a candidate in Milan. In articles and speeches he tried to mobilise support and his singing of the *Arditi* anthem *Giovinezza* at public *adunate* was directed to the same end.[69] Mussolini continued to stress his 'lack of prejudice' philosophically and his determination to solve Italy's problems practically as a soldier might. 'Only the intelligent and the strong-willed', he declared, had 'the right to decide the country's fate'.[70] Ever more blatantly, Mussolini was underlining his departure from his socialist past and his willingness to adapt himself to those social goals which he had once opposed.

For the moment, few listened. On polling day, Mussolini garnered fewer than 5000 votes in his electorate. The anti-war parties, the Socialists and the PPI, were, by contrast, triumphant, winning between them just over half the 508 seats in the Chamber of Deputies. The socialists alone took 156 and, on 19 November, *Avanti!* exulted that 'the Italy of the revolution is born'.[71] Those who wished to save the old social order and those who had favoured Italy's First World War had reason to be depressed, even though D'Annunzio remained in Fiume. There the poet, too, seemed to be yielding to a new radicalism, in what he avouched was 'the city of life',[72] an indulgence in revolutionary rhetoric that distressed such otherwise friendly business leaders as Sinigaglia. Others noticed that D'Annunzio's 'legionaries', as he was pompously calling them, and especially the airmen, sometimes sought refuge from their personal travails in cocaine, a drug which was becoming common among the post-war *beau monde*.[73]

One who refused to bow to what seemed the new reality was Benito Mussolini, even though at the end of 1919 branches of the *Fasci* only maintained a feeble existence in Milan, Turin, Venice, Cremona, Bologna and Trieste.[74] He boldly disguised his electoral rout as 'a political affirmation', 'neither a victory, nor a defeat'.[75] As for the socialists, he prophesied that they would not crow for ever. In the French elections, their comrades had done badly. In Italy, there was a yawning gap between the socialist vote and the socialist ideological penetration of the masses. 'Strike-mania' could not last, and the socialist revolution was far from completion.[76] 'There are victories which are as crushing as defeats', Mussolini concluded,[77] as he optimistically scanned the right for some political space.

Briefly, his enterprise was interrupted when, in the aftermath of the elections, he, along with Vecchi and Marinetti, was arrested on Nitti's orders. The police had uncovered a store of arms which Mussolini and his friends were illegally holding. However, almost as quickly, and again on prime ministerial intervention, the supporters of the *Fasci* were released, and Nitti ignored suggestions from the Prefect of Milan that the weapons-possession charge be prosecuted.[78] Beset by many enemies, Nitti had apparently decided that his sort of liberal should not renounce contact with Mussolini, who could thereby continue to draw advantage from the prospect of his 'transformation'. Though defeated at the polls, Mussolini had not been expelled from the political stage.

Indeed, hardly had the electoral excitement settled than there were momentary suggestions that Mussolini might be just the man to accompany industrialist Ettore Conti[79] on an official expedition to the Caucasus, where it was imagined the nation might be granted a mandate and where local Mensheviks might warm to a personage like him. In the pages of *La Vita Italiana*, Sinigaglia told a nationalist readership that trade prospects were good but blamed Nitti for not pressing ahead with negotiations in that part of the ex-Russian empire.[80] The mission had been put off. Mussolini, by February 1920, with aplomb or effrontery, explained that he was not going to Baku because he had realised that it would be unpatriotic to absent himself from Italy while the Fiume question remained unresolved.[81] Of course he had never dreamed of supping with the despised *Cagoia*.

What the aborted affair of the Caucasus really signified was that the *Fasci*, despite the bleakness of the current political situation, were indeed winning a new set of converts. Among the first was Vincenzo Fani Ciotti, a sickly middle-class littérateur (he lived mostly on the

Riviera) who published under the pseudonym 'Volt'. Fani Ciotti had a background in orthodox nationalism and had truck with the Futurists. But, when he joined Mussolini, he thought of himself as an 'integralist', one who approved of 'the monarchy, religion, hierarchy, a disciplined concord between individuals and classes, a generational solidarity proceeding across time, heredity, family, racial selection, dominion, empire'.[82] The society he most admired was, he said, Japan.[83] All history, he maintained, was dominated by aristocracies and Mussolini was thus 'the *Duce* of an aristocracy which is still to be created'.[84] Fani Ciotti, it was plain, embodied a Fascist right which tolerated with difficulty the radical chic of Marinetti and Vecchi, and which saw little future in Mussolini's own lingering forays into populist syndicalism.

By the end of 1919, then, many factors were driving Mussolini further to the right. The son of Alessandro might retain a barely suppressed resentment towards his social betters, and his wife Rachele, with a never diminished crassness, might endorse such hostility in their domestic conversations, but Mussolini was set on a political course which was, above everything else, anti-socialist. Not for nothing would his new year's message to his readers for 1920 urge 'a return to the individual', which almost sounded as though Mussolini was readying himself for our own contemporary marketised end of history.[85] His friends, and therefore he, too, were determined to crush the socialist movement, both politically and throughout civil society. In 1920 this determination deepened and spread, and 'Fascism', despite being still highly local in its base and organisation, began to exhibit the first signs of a national appeal and purpose.

The Fascist minister, Raffaello Riccardi, later re-invoked these early days of Fascism in the region of the Marche. At his own town of Senigallia, just north of Ancona on the Adriatic coast – and a place of republican traditions but one where the local middle classes deplored what they viewed as socialist violence and lack of patriotism – Fascist supporters began in 1920 to assemble at the *circolo cittadino*, or club for more respectable citizens. Indeed, one imaginative youth, sprung from what Riccardi described as the more manly of the town middle classes, appropriated one of the club's billiard cues to serve as the staff on which to affix the pennon of their infant anti-socialist movement. An ex-member of the *arditi* had purloined a black petticoat from his mother's store and the 'squad', as it called itself, inscribed it worthily with the Latin tag *custodes et ultores* (guards and avengers).[86] As the group's social activities and ambitions grew, Riccardi was selected to travel to Milan in order to meet Mussolini and bring the local into contact with the national. He found the *Duce* furiously scowling while he scanned a newspaper in his office and Riccardi was ignored until he explained that he was a Fascist from the Marche who needed to acquire arms. In response, Mussolini scribbled an address on a piece of paper which he then signed, and promptly went back to his reading. Riccardi noticed the dynamism of his future *Duce*'s eyes, and hurried off to collect two bags of revolvers and grenades.[87] For provincials willing to be star struck, Mussolini could offer charisma, contacts, a ruthless approval of violence and an ability to locate the weapons they needed.

Elsewhere in northern Italy, similar but rather grander events were beginning to occur, if at first slowly. In Trieste, a city where 'Anti-Slav' bands had not been unknown even under Habsburg rule,[88] Francesco Giunta and others were uniting to destroy any opposition which they could find from 'Slavs' and 'communists'.[89] In the Po valley and Tuscany, opponents of socialism grew restive at what seemed to them a violent local tyranny in which the poorest classes threatened to over-turn all 'civilization'. In Puglia in the south memories revived of those squads which, during the first years of the century, already in one town or another were accustomed to stiffen the power of the local landowners.[90] By March 1920 Mussolini admitted that, personally, he did not now mind being labelled a reactionary: 'the title pleases us, because, at the present time, amid the orgy of revolutionary words, to be a reactionary is a sign of nobility ... to a minority movement like our own', even though, somewhat apologetically, he also took the occasion to reiterate his continuing commitment to a series of social reforms.[91] At much the same time, he again summoned the 'freedom of the individual' to his rhetorical cause. The state turned into a 'Moloch', he declared, when it tried to be 'a banker, a lender, a gambling-house keeper, a seaman, a bandit, an insurer, a postman, a railway-worker, an impresario, an industrialist, a teacher, a tobacco shop-owner, a judge, a gaoler and a taxman'.[92] As he adopted one verbal gambit or another, Mussolini's conflict with official socialism became visceral. After a murderous incident at the Piazzale Loreto in Milan, a square destined to play a further part in his history, Mussolini wrote that socialist barbarism had outmatched that of prim-itive tribes and 'cannibals'. 'Those who lynch others', he observed with a menace of his own, 'don't represent the future, but rather the age of primitive man (a time which was healthier than that of civilized man).'[93]

In May, at the second Fascist congress, held patriotically on the 24th, fifth anniversary of the Italian entry into the war, Mussolini concentrated his fire against the socialists, who, he maintained, were guilty of being 'anti-Italian'. From some of his old ideals, he now openly back-pedalled. The Vatican's implicit power could not and should not be denied. Although, personally, he confessed to finding any religion irrelevant, Catholicism could be wedded to the nation and speed the expansion of its power. The monarchy, too, should not be lightly abused; rather, the eventual creation of a republic could be postponed to an appropriate time. Even the bureaucracy, which he had roundly condemned only a month before, had a good side which might be enhanced through a pay-rise for the bureaucrats.[94] Listening to Mussolini's words was a new *Fasci* directorate, which itself had swung openly to the right.[95] Rejecting his new line were such old allies as Marinetti and Vecchi, who failed to renew their membership, with the Futurist being especially disgusted by what he viewed as Mussolini's toadying to the church.[96]

While the *Fasci* thus looked to a fresh political positioning, the Nitti administration had entered its unhappy last days. The Fiume issue lingered. Socialism swept both urban and rural parts of northern Italy, where the poorest peasants extracted improved contractual relations from many a landowner, where the ancient and intricate verities of peasant class differences seemed to face revolutionary overhaul, and where, more generally, the countryside no longer acknowledged the supremacy of the city as all decency and order knew it must. The *Popolari* were proving equally intractable and Catholic trade unions were almost as demanding of improved pay and conditions as were socialist ones. As the economy stuttered, the cost of living spiralled to a level four times greater than in 1913. A union demand for a 30 per cent wage rise grew strident. A failure even in his area of greatest expertise, on 9 June 1920 Nitti resigned. His replacement was Giovanni Giolitti, so dominant and astute a politician before 1914, but now approaching his eightieth year and, in nationalist perspective, damaged beyond repair by his neutralism during the war.

The fires of social crisis burned on. In August–September before he was properly settled back into the Prime Ministership, Giolitti faced the massive problem of the 'occupation of the factories', an action which revolutionaries hoped would amount to an orderly culmination of the summer of deepening social violence. In Turin and Milan, the metal-workers' union FIOM and revolutionary intellectuals like Antonio Gramsci seemed about to convert the rhetoric of social revolution into practice. As one factory after the next fell to their control, at least half a million workers were associated in their cause. So united were the workers that such an emblematic modern industrialist as Giovanni Agnelli of Fiat contemplated accepting some sort of worker control. Confronted by this array of unwonted events, Giolitti behaved with characteristic (and salutarily ostentatious) caution, telegraphing his Prefect in Milan on 11 September with the advice: 'It is necessary to make the industrialists understand that no Italian government will resort to force and provoke a revolution simply to save them money'.[97] The Prime Minister was also known to be pressuring Italy's banks to withdraw their support from the more hard-line industrialists, and, in apparent accord with his fellow Piedmontese Agnelli, talked favourably of workers being granted shares in the concerns which employed them.[98]

As ever, at least in the short-term, Giolitti proved the master tactician. His belief that the social storm would blow itself out and that a Bolshevik take-over was not imminent proved correct. By 25 September the occupations were finished. There had been, and would be, no revolution from the left. Another matter Giolitti did not foresee, however. In little over 2 years there was to be a revolt from the right, when landowners, industrialists, nationalists and those with positive memories of the war united to dispel the spectre of an Italian communism and to revenge themselves on those who had in 1920 seemed on the brink of power. This triumphant campaign was led by Mussolini who, during the months of crisis, had kept up his usual running commentary on events, still, on occasion, sounding as though he had preserved sympathy with the poor, but always ending by rejecting the ideals and actions of the socialists. 'Class struggle', he noted, might be all very well in some utopia but not in an Italy which needed urgently to produce.[99] Fascists as ever emphasised the practical but 'our principles have been and remain these: to defend the national war effort, to enhance the existing victory, strenuously to oppose the imitation of revolutionary Russia indulged in by our home-grown socialists'. 'We are indeed a minority', Mussolini ran on, in words which adapted into one of the slogans of the regime, but 'a million sheep will always be dispersed by the roar of one lion'.[100] All the other anti-socialist parties, Mussolini predicted as the occupation of the factories began, were destined to dissolve, since they could not, and would not, act with leonine courage. Their members must switch instead to the *fascisti*, even if only in a temporary way to achieve a set aim.[101] The best example of this outcome, he added a month later, was already evident in the Venezia Giulia, where a national 'defence' against 'Slavs' and a praiseworthy 'imperialism' abroad, could go hand in hand with an anti-socialist syndicalism that ensured production and class collaboration at home.[102] Mussolini had long thought of himself as a leader; now he was beginning to detect a potential mass of wealthy and influential followers.

As the sun began to shine on his prospects, there was some time to relax. In this summer and autumn of Italian discontent, Mussolini was not just busy as an editor and polemicist. Rather, his life was enlivened by a new hobby and one which could readily be adapted into a new politics – flying. The young socialist who had hailed Blériot's conquest of the Channel now had his own chance to soar into the skies. An infatuation with the cult of the air had lingered in his mind until, in August 1919, he imagined an empyrean future in which the tyranny of distance had been overcome along with differences between peoples. Then, he mused romantically, 'all souls will be fused into a single soul'.[103] At the turn of the next New Year, he excused himself to D'Annunzio for what might have seemed inattention to events at Fiume by explaining that he was contemplating departing on a 'raid' to Tokyo, and preparing for the prospect of such a world-girdling exploit was taking a lot of his time.[104] When, 6 months later, that flight did go ahead without him, Mussolini still waxed lyrical about it. 'A flash of green, white and red, Italian, light will stay in the skies', he pronounced grandiloquently, 'signalling to the infinite what Italy stands for.' 'Flight', he continued, constituted 'the greatest poem of modern times', the contemporary equivalent of Dante's *Divine Comedy*.[105]

Mussolini was not alone in expressing these overblown views. The air, especially while planes offered a cockpit open to the elements, seemed to many a contemporary to exemplify 'reactionary modernism' and appealed to a world-ranging new right which included Hermann Goering, Charles Lindbergh, and a number of Mussolini's Italian friends.[106] Among these last were Giuseppe Bottai, who drifted into the Fascist movement from a background in Nationalism and Futurism helped by his leadership from 1921 of a 'Roman Club of Fascist Flyers',[107] and the Ferrarese *Alpino,* anti-socialist and patriot, Italo Balbo (whose sister had been christened Trieste Maria).[108] Later to be the Fascist Minister for Aviation, as well as the heavily propagandised pilot-commander of intercontinental flights, Balbo had, back in 1911, aged 15, tended fires lit to chart the path of airmen dauntlessly competing in a race from Bologna to Venice and back, and sponsored by Naldi and *Il Resto del Carlino*.[109] By 1921 Balbo was one of the most active and significant of Fascist squadrists. Dreams of flight and of beating up socialists went together because, in the aftermath of the First World War, propagandists were sure that the individual courage needed to conquer the air, as the expression went, was fundamentally 'Anti-Marxist'.[110] Darwinism, too, slipped easily into an aerial vocabulary; and so, despite Mussolini's happy thoughts about a fused mankind, did nationalism. Italy, Mussolini typically began to argue, must aim to achieve 'primacy in the air' and those idiots who objected to such a target or who, like Nitti, were penny-pinching about its cost, should be swept aside.[111] From August 1919 *Il Popolo d'Italia* featured a *pagina aeronautica* which was meant both to favour the cause of the aeroplane and to underline the modernity and technological optimism of the *Fasci*. Mussolini took to defining himself as 'a fanatic for flight'[112] and on at least one occasion aimed to stun a meeting of the *Fasci* by appearing dressed as an airman.[113]

Nor was his interest merely theoretical and propagandist. In July 1920 Mussolini found time from his other affairs to start flying lessons at an airfield at Arcore, on the outskirts of Monza, just to the northeast of Milan. 'Prof. Mussolini' arrived, so his instructor remembered, wearing his editor's get-up: 'a dark suit, a bowler hat, grey spats'.[114] On subsequent flights he used the occasion to bring Rachele and the boys or Edda with him on an afternoon outing. On one occasion he was in a special hurry because he had a duel scheduled shortly after his flying lesson.[115] Over the next year Mussolini completed 18 flights, lasting almost seven and a half hours. In March 1921 he survived a crash at the cost only of scratches to his face and a twisted knee – flying was still a decidedly hazardous undertaking, even if Mussolini's instructor advertised his joy-flights with the comforting advice that 'every passenger is insured'.[116] As a result of his success as a pilot, from May 1921 Mussolini and a Jewish Fascist acquaintance, Aldo Finzi, were gratified by being labelled 'the first flying members of parliament' by the *Gazzetta dell'Aviazione*.[117] Indeed, throughout his life, Mussolini retained pleasant memories of his experiences at this time. Flying had something viscerally Fascist or Mussolinian about it as man flew heavenwards to challenge the very gods. There were times when the working dictator could take control of a plane in which he was travelling. Contemporaries noted how, even during the dark days of the Salò Republic, he sloughed off his usual gloom when again given the chance to be his own aviator.[118] More notoriously, in August 1941 he had insisted on piloting a plane in the company of Hitler, who paled at what he viewed as ludicrous, and dangerous, Latin bravado.[119] Whatever else troubled Benito Mussolini, before and after 1922 it was not a fear of flying. In 1920-21, in the open cockpit, he dared both the elements and those still Marxist dullards who clung to material interests on the ground and swore to strike him down, as, inexorably, he conquered the air, and contemplated the conquest of Italy.

7

The Fascist rise to power,
1920-1922

'INTENTIONALIST' historians, in whose cause biographers are likely to be enrolled, are much given to arguing that dictators dictate. Great Men are great in their possession of free will; it is they who move and shake their societies. Cesare Rossi, an early follower of Mussolini, who broke from the movement and then pursued an ambiguous personal course in the shadowy world of the secret services,[1] has tried to counter such a line. Almost all the most characteristic features of Fascism, he remarked, came from 'below': the use of the Roman salute began at Verona; the solemn appeal to the fallen at Modena; the kneeling before a ceremonial coffin at Florence; the use of castor oil on Anti-Fascists at Ferrara; the employment of trucks to carry Fascist punitive expeditions into the countryside at Bologna; the *Balilla* or Fascist scouting movement for boys at Piacenza. 'The gestures, customs, rites which then spread', he has explained, 'germinated spontaneously.' Their adoption by the wider Fascist movement and party was a matter of imitation. To his list can be added the wearing of the black shirt, the singing of the party anthem *Giovinezza* and the chanting of the slogan *A noi* – all originated with the *Arditi*. Much of the remaining stage-furniture of the regime was invented either by D'Annunzio at Fiume or, more loosely, by the Futurists. The word, *fascio*, was ubiquitous in Italy in the aftermath of the war, while the term *Duce* was by no means at first confined to Benito Mussolini. In sum, what historians these days are inclined to call the liturgy of Fascism, the medium through which it expressed its message, was scarcely inscribed by Mussolini alone.

But the limits of Mussolini's individuality and inventiveness were not confined to dressage. Certainly, no account of the rise of Fascism and of Mussolini to power from late 1920 to October 1922 should assume that the two worked in natural or happy harness. Rather, the relationship between the *Duce* and his movement was a flickering one, in which a unity survived uneasily, while a mutual self-interest continued to curb the many factors which suggested divorce. During these months, so crucial for Italian political history, Mussolini may have been turning into **the** *Duce*, but it was still not altogether clear to what political end and with what social following.

Prime Minister Giolitti was meanwhile working at his accustomed rhythms and with his usual intent. One issue of continuing concern was foreign policy where, he believed, D'Annunzio's posturing at Fiume and a number of other difficulties in the Balkans must end. In August 1920 he found reason to evacuate Italian forces from Albania, where troops had first arrived on Christmas Day 1914 but where the value of a national presence in this poor and unstable land had never been clarified. This withdrawal facilitated more general negotiations with the Kingdom of the Serbs, Croats and Slovenes and, on 12 November, the Treaty of Rapallo was signed. Its clauses demarcated the border between the new Yugoslav state and Italy in the Adriatic. D'Annunzio and Fiume had been by-passed and, on Christmas eve, the Italian army moved against the rag-tag force left in the town. A few casualties were enough to snuff out resistance and D'Annunzio, who had been shouting to the heavens *o Fiume, o morte* (either Fiume or death), found his own third way by fleeing back to Italy on 18 January 1921. This *Duce*, as his admirers had been accustomed to call him, may have possessed 'limitless charm' and a seductive prose style,[2] but he plainly lacked staying power.

Benito Mussolini was an onlooker to these events, well aware that a rival was being weakened and humiliated, if not totally eliminated as a possible leader of the new right. It was true that, later in 1921, a crisis in the Fascist movement would revive suggestions from such local chiefs as Balbo and Grandi, now a lawyer with offices in Bologna,[3] that D'Annunzio head the Fascist movement.[4] Similarly, D'Annunzio's name would resurface in the jockeying for political authority in October 1922,[5] though the poet was then hampered by injuries sustained in a fall from a palace window.[6] In every case Mussolini found the right tactics to counter the poet's allure. After 1922 he would confine him to the Vittoriale, a palace near Salò, where D'Annunzio could architecturally express his syncretic soul, rejoice in his titular elevation to Principe di Montenevoso, and surrender all political influence.[7] D'Annunzio's charisma had wasted while Mussolini's had grown.

In 1920, while the Fiume occupation lasted, Mussolini's approach was straightforward enough. He penned his regular commentaries on foreign affairs, aware that he could not let himself appear as lukewarm as he probably was about D'Annunzio's adventure. Mussolini's rhetoric about foreign affairs was thus sharp and aggressive. Fiume must be annexed; Versailles revised.[8] Italy, he urged, should have the courage to aspire to a 'world policy'.[9] A 'young people' must be 'imperialist'[10] – only Italy had offered the Albanians of Valona (Vlora) some hope; without the Italian presence the locals would return to scrabbling around in the dirt outside their 'primitive huts'.[11] As he had done the year before, Mussolini even dabbled in the vocabulary of Anti-Semitism, narrowing his definition of who might constitute the nation and contradicting his recent enthusiasm for the free individual. 'Italy', he remarked, 'did not know Anti-Semitism and we believe that it will never know it.' However, he continued, Zionism was beginning to threaten this tradition of tolerance. So far, Italian Jews had generally been steadfast in their willingness to sacrifice their blood 'for this our adorable homeland' and probably they would be smart enough always to do so. If they were not, he predicted with a hint of menace, Anti-Semitism would begin to grow 'in the one country where it had never been'.[12]

What is to be made of these last observations? Despite Mussolini's clichéd gainsaying, a latent element of Anti-Semitism did exist in Italy, especially on the Catholic right, and a smattering of prejudice lurked in the minds of many Italians. In what was becoming Mussolini's own circle, *La Vita Italiana* continued to declaim against 'the Jewish international' – in a particularly shrill article in August 1920 editor Preziosi claimed that David Lloyd George was of Jewish origin. If that 'fact' was not disturbing enough, Preziosi went on to retail the story of the *Protocols of the Elders of Zion* which, at that moment, had wide currency outside Italy being, for example, believed by the London *Times*. As far as Preziosi was concerned, the *Protocols* justified his longstanding view that revolutionaries from Marx to Trotsky worked hand in glove with international banking and stock-broking from New York to Warsaw, and all nefariously aimed to victimise Italy.[13] Mussolini never seems especially to have warmed to Preziosi – he was said to have told a friend that the ex-priest was marked by the evil eye.[14] What Mussolini's own Anti-Semitism best reflected was a combination of his conscious desire not to be outdistanced on the right – if nationalist circles were going Anti-Semitic, then Mussolini would move that way, too – and what would become a familiar but less conscious tendency for Mussolini to parrot the ideas and attitudes of those surrounding him.[15] Under the dictatorship, too, his own position was often heavily influenced by the views of his latest interlocutor. Certainly, Mussolini's Anti-Semitism, if that is what it was, settled back beneath the surface of his mind, while the *Duce* proceeded with his love affair with Margherita Sarfatti, his friendship with Aldo Finzi and his welcoming of the considerable number of patriotic and socially conservative Jews who favoured the growing Fascist movement.

Similarly, Mussolini's more general observations on foreign affairs should probably not be taken as seriously or literally as they have been by those critics anxious to prove that, from beginning to end, 'Mussolini meant war'. The first intention of his words remained what it had been when, on *Avanti!* or even at *La Lotta di Classe* in his socialist past, he had striven to make a name for himself by flaunting his expertise about the great world. Politicians of national stature held views about international affairs. Mussolini was, or wanted to be, a politician of national stature. Therefore, he must never forego the chance to express opinions about Italy's place at the tables of diplomacy. In these circumstances, no one should have been too surprised to learn that, despite his fiery nationalist verbiage, Mussolini readily accepted the realism of Giolitti's deal at Rapallo[16] and swiftly adapted to the new arrangements in the Balkans. Without trumpeting the matter, he had opened contact with Giolitti as early as October 1920, and exchanges of ideas continued through Alfredo Lusignoli, the prefect of Milan. Mussolini even met Foreign Minister Sforza, seemingly assuring him that his backing of D'Annunzio had its limits.[17] Italy, he now wrote with a decided switch of tone, had a profound need for peace. Only 'madmen or criminals' rejected this truth and he took the opportunity to berate members of Nationalist Association in Rome who, he charged, were obsessed about sovereignty over every little island in the upper Adriatic. They were anachronistically 'imperialist', he wrote dismissively; by contrast, his Fascists were merely healthily 'expansionist'.[18] The Mussolinian line on foreign policy, Giolitti and Sforza might be expected to understand, could trace many twists and turns.

Whatever he said about the international situation, Mussolini's real concerns were domestic. Trieste and Venezia Giulia, where the intensity and success of 'border fascism' increased every day, provided a meeting between the two worlds. In these newly annexed territories, Mussolini was proclaiming as early as June 1920 there could be no compromises over the political and ethnic victory won in the war. Right-thinking Italians, he urged in phrases which delighted local supporters, must 'energetically clean-up [sic] Trieste'. (Here indeed was a metaphor with a future in the region.) The city so far had not been fully annexed; it must be, through a process of ethnic and class cleansing in which both internationalist socialists and 'Slav' elements should be purged.[19] In September Mussolini gave a major speech at Trieste in which he invoked more stridently than in the past the 'glory that was Rome' and that Italian primacy which was allegedly evident in hydroelectric technology and many other fields. 'Every modern man', he added pompously, as though again donning the gown of 'Prof. Mussolini', had read Cervantes, Shakespeare, Goethe and Tolstoy. But Dante was still the best. Bountifully enriched by past and present, Italians could dismiss from their minds both their own socialists and the Bolsheviks of Russia, whose Soviet regime in reality amounted to 'a dictatorship by a handful of intellectuals', who had nothing in common with 'real workers'.[20]

When, later that day, Mussolini cabled the office of *Il Popolo d'Italia* with news of his visit, he revelled in the 'marvellous' local Fascist movement. In all Venezia Giulia, he declared gleefully, the *Fasci* now dominated local politics; the terrain there had proved 'wholly favourable to ... [Fascism's] development'. To the horror of its socialist or catholic rivals, Fascism's own syndicates or unions were starting up everywhere. The evident advantage gained by the *Fasci* over their rivals owed much to 'the national struggle', to the assertion of Italian-ness over 'Yugoslav megalomania' and 'Slav ... racial rancour'. Ethnic difference, it seemed, possessed propulsive qualities politically which were easier to direct than was class conflict. 'It could well be that the Fascists of Venezia Giulia signal the commencement of a great move-ment of national renewal and constitute the generous and tough vanguard of an Italy about which we dream and for which we prepare'.[21] He did not add that provincial Fascists had been able to rely on tacit support from the local representatives of the Italian govern-ment who had, for example, turned a blind eye when, in July, Fascists burned down the Hotel Balkan, a Slovene redoubt.[22] In their hearts, army, police and prefects agreed with the *Fasci* that violence in the cause of Italian ethnicity was not violence at all. They did not object either when Francesco Giunta justified salutary Fascist violence on the grounds that the national government had 'gone missing' in the newly annexed territories of Italy's north and east.[23]

But what of violence in the cause of class? The failure of the occupation of the factories had brought to the surface that social element which, already before September 1920, had been resentful of socialist gains, be they political, economic or cultural. Now these 'agrarian fascists', based especially in the Po valley, Tuscany and Umbria, where socialism was for the moment powerful and even over-weening – and where a modernised agriculture, ever more ruthless and competitive in its class relations, spread – were becoming Fascism's certainly most numerous and perhaps most influential mass base. Even liberal Luigi Albertini, the editor of *Il Corriere della Sera*, defended 'holy reaction' in such places.[24] So widespread was the sympathy among Italian elites for the move against the socialists that it would be foolish to think that Mussolini himself was in direct control of 'crusades' assembling in Florence, Modena or the rest. His task, rather, was to ride the political groundswell which resulted, and so remain the national leader of what was still overwhelmingly a local movement, or a series of local movements. If he spoke as a convinced nationalist in Trieste, in these other regions he must sound ever more fervently an enemy of peasant socialism and all its works.

In this part of Fascism's rise the examples of Bologna and Ferrara were emblematic. In these two historic centres on the Po plain, Fascism sank early and profound roots. In the latter city, case studies have explained, socialism was destroyed by its success. The region had already been a place of unionism and social violence before 1914.[25] Despite some momentary gains for a 'third way' favoured by Calabrian syndicalist Michele Bianchi, who was active there,[26] a contest was developing between the poorest of the local peasantry, the *braccianti* or landless day labourers, and the landowners, and the crisis re-emerged in the *dopoguerra* worse than before. Complicating the matter were sharecropping and other middling peasants who traditionally had been very aware of the differences in status between their families and those of the *braccianti*. Socialism, especially as embodied in the peasant union *Federterra*, tried to embrace both. In August 1920 *Federterra* claimed 74 000 members in Ferrara province alone, the highest tally in Italy (Bologna came next with 73 000).[27] This mass following was, however, poorly instructed in union principles and practices, and was riven by potential disaccord.

In 1919 Fascism had briefly materialised at Ferrara with syndicalism as its main programme, although a local futurist and *Ardito*, Olao Gaggioli, had acted as his city's representative at Piazza San Sepolcro.[28] By the end of 1919 the Ferrara *fascio* had, however, collapsed. It revived towards the end of 1920, with Gaggioli unrepentantly urging violent retribution against socialist 'robbers'. His Fascists were rich and 'modern' enough to assemble a pool of trucks in which to sally forth from Ferrara in 'raids' against socialist meeting places in the countryside. Local socialists had been intransigent, both in their rhetoric and their tactics, scandalising landowners by strikes at planting time and again when harvest was due. In early 1921 socialist power collapsed before the better armed and more ruthless Fascists and also because of social divisions that remained unresolved among the socialists. The greater matter then became the character of local Fascism, where a contest grew between Gaggioli and the more socially respectable Italo Balbo, who, then and later, got on well with the prominent Jewish community at Ferrara.[29] A dispute also simmered between the movement's local organisation and headquarters in Milan, which strove to limit the almost complete independence of Ferrarese Fascism, and to exact a financial tribute from what was evidently a flourishing movement.[30] The authority of the able, ambitious and cynical Balbo[31] continued to expand, as did a structure of Fascist unions, sometimes composed of unwilling members assembled at gunpoint, but none the less pledged to offer some social 'justice' and not merely to second bullying by the large landowners. The more left-leaning of local Fascists, however, began to find themselves excluded from influence and advantage, and Gaggioli and his friends eventually abandoned the movement. By the summer of 1921 Balbo had turned away from too intense a concentration on native Ferrarese affairs in favour of a 'foreign policy'. His 'squads' now drove their trucks in the Fascist cause over the provincial borders to Venice and Ravenna. On 10 September 1921 the sensational 'March' of 3000 *squadristi* on Ravenna was patriotically timed to coincide with the raising of a monument to the poet Dante who was thought to be buried there, and became the occasion for a brutal cleansing of the city's 'Reds'. To show their mettle, Balbo's men celebrated their victory over unpatriotic socialists by solemnly filing past the poet's tomb.[32] By February 1922 Balbo was loudly demanding that Fascists venture still further afield and 'conquer the nation'.[33]

In Bologna the story was similar. Again a social crisis had threatened before 1914, even though the mainstream of local socialism was responsibly reformist. Dante Ferraris, who, along with sugar interests and arms manufacturers, was prominent locally in right-wing causes provided finance for the Nationalist Association's paper, *L'Idea Nazionale*.[34] In the *dopoguerra*, the social conflict had deepened, especially when the socialists polled 63 per cent in Bologna city in the elections of November 1919. *Il Resto del Carlino* commented meaningfully that the real losers from this figure were 'moderates'; indeed moderation, the paper mused, might no longer be a tenable political stance.[35] Until the election result had its effect, the *Fasci* were pitifully weak, in August 1919 counting 15 members who favoured a still radical programme, and in December numbering as few as six.[36] By the next year, however, the movement had been taken in hand by the activist Leandro Arpinati, an old acquaintance of Mussolini, who could boast of having once been an anarchist and then an interventionist, but who now was willing to do business with local elites.[37] In November 1920 an armed attack on the *Palazzo d'Accursio*, seat of the socialist city administration, underlined what sort of business the *Fasci* meant. The murderous violence involved was endorsed editorially by Mussolini who wrote: 'The reality is this. The socialist party is a Russian army encamped in Italy. Against this foreign army, Fascists have launched a guerrilla war, and they will conduct it with exceptional seriousness.'[38] Thus endorsed, Bolognese Fascism began to bloom, nurtured by both provincial landowners and urban commercial interests, though Arpinati's humble origins – he let it be known that, after his marriage in June 1921, his accommodation still did not include a kitchen and his wife cooked on a portable stove[39] – somewhat restrained the movement's conservative drift. Squabbles recurred between Arpinati, who, in his paper euphoniously entitled *L'Assalto* (Assault), had not ceased to invoke an inheritance for his ideas from Andrea Costa,[40] and the more socially respectable Grandi.

Elsewhere in the Emilia-Romagna, the picture varied. At nearby Reggio Emilia, no class fudging was needed since Ottavio Corgini, the founder of the Fascist movement in the province, doubled as President of the Reggio Chamber of Agriculture.[41] By contrast, in Mussolini's home province of Forlì, the movement was feeble, despite inauguration at a resonant site beside the Rubicon river in April 1921 (Fascist *signorini* had arrived by car and proceeded to harangue the assembled peasantry who seem to have been bemused by the experience); neither Forlimpopoli nor Predappio would have a party branch organised until September 1922.[42]

Anti-Fascist observers of Fascism, both in the region and especially in the city of Bologna, recognised the movement's social conservatism, even while admitting that it attracted 'those who enjoyed carrying arms' and exhibited a certain social and ideological heterogeneity, amounting less to a revolution than 'a convulsion of the middling classes'.[43] As one disillusioned ex-republican Fascist put it in the autumn of 1921:

> Every region, every province, possesses its <u>own</u> Fascism. Most often agrarian in the Emilia, nationalist and conservative in the Veneto, irre-dentist and provocative towards Slavs and Germans in the border territories to the east and north, sparked in many small towns by private vendettas or conflicting local interests, it is nonetheless, either with its syndical organisation or with its squads of thugs, in fact working for the richest part of society.[44]

Its programme might seem to have many colours, but the battle which Fascism waged was fundamentally directed to winning the class war against the socialists.[45]

To the south of these regions, the social crisis was not so acute, the interests of the usual ruling elite not so threatened and Mussolini's own attention was rarely engaged. In the Abruzzi, for example, Fascism was slow to develop. All the same, in 1920 Giacomo Acerbo, later to be a Fascist minister, was emerging as its local chief, a role which would be confirmed by the April 1921 elections. Acerbo (born 1888) was a sprig of a distinguished local bourgeois family, and, before 1914, had been experimenting politically as a Giolittian. He had favoured intervention in the war, however, and was to serve in it with distinction. One of his brothers, a captain in the celebrated Sassari Brigade, lost his life at the front. After 1918 Acerbo participated in the uncertain politics of the *Associazione Nazionale dei Combattenti*, emerging as uncontested leader of the movement in the provincial capital, Teramo.[46] Once an admirer of D'Annunzio, who had been born at Pescara, the regional capital of the Abruzzi, Acerbo now evinced both a fervent nationalism and a relative social conservatism, hostile to those in the ANC who talked carelessly about deals with the socialists. By February 1921 Acerbo was occupied ensuring that his strain of conservative Fascism out-distanced the more radical variety still strong in the rival provincial centre of L'Aquila (where the eventual Party Secretary, Adelchi Serena, was commencing his rise).[47] Local landowners had decided to favour Acerbo's cause and were presum-ably cheered when he organised a March on Vasto, then a socialist stronghold.[48] By 1922 Acerbo was widely acknowledged as the 'new man' of the Abruzzi, although a sceptical historian might doubt most of his claims to novelty, and after 1922 many of the systems and struc-tures of what had once been called *giolittismo* were again evident in what had become his Fascist fiefdom.[49]

Further south still, in Sicily, Fascism was almost non-existent. None the less, there in 1919 Prince Pietro Lanza di Scalea, a member of the local nobility but destined to be a Fascist Minister of Colonies (and rumoured a patron of the Mafia), [50] urged the need for a *Partito economico*, pledged to 'defend to the uttermost' the existing system against any social threat.[51] That year and the next there were some land occupations and other signs of social radicalism in parts of Sicily, with the Catholic PPI being an important local presence. However, in the elections of November 1919, unlike in the north, the old liberal bloc held. During that year, a few Mussolinian Fascists appeared in Palermo under the leadership of a revolutionary syndicalist, but they did not obtain a following and their organisation soon collapsed.[52] By the time of the elections of 1921 a different sort of Fascism had made its presence felt and was led by a lawyer, Gennaro Vilelli, from Messina, and an archaeology teacher from Palermo, Biagio Pace, the latter destined to become a major propagandist of Fascist imperialism.[53] It was still, however, a meagre and divided movement. Social violence in the cause of the existing elite was left in the hands of 'the Mafia'[54] in an environment in which socialists did not exaggerate when they stated that 'it is enough to be a socialist to know that you may not wake up the next morning'.[55] The Sicilian version of liberalism had never flinched from utilising violence in defence of the social order.

In the spring of 1921, then, Fascism, in one version or another, was a rising phenomenon as the tide of socialism was turned back in every locality. By May Fascists controlled most of the Venezia Giulia and the Po valley – in Mantua a student group called *Terza Italia* fused with the more nationalist returned soldiers and turned Fascist.[56] Equally, the *Fasci* had seized authority in the Piedmontese provinces of Alessandria and Novara, and in Tuscany – where, in Arezzo province, motorised squads were known to stay out on their 'expeditions' for five days[57] – Umbria and even Puglia.[58] The casualties of this offensive mounted: between January and April the official total was 105 dead and 431 injured; from April to May a further 102 dead and 388 injured.[59] Notorious was the sacking of Empoli, an industrial town to the west of Florence where, on 1 March, invading Fascists taunted local socialists with the cry: 'Either leave Empoli, or you will stay in Empoli for eternity.'[60]

As the front of this social war moved on, Mussolini's task, as leader of the variegated *Fasci* movement, was an intricate one. The provincials in their energy and determination should continue their quasi-military operations, but they should not forget their obeisance to the one who alone possessed the charisma, the drive and the contacts to be their *Duce*. Simultaneously, the politicians in the great world, and especially Giolitti, should remember Mussolini in their plans and policies. Mussolini would have to speak with many voices. At the same time, he needed to think harder about the institutionalisation of what was after all still a 'movement', not a party, and about its financing. In October 1920 the bourgeois paper *Gazzetta Ferrarese*, in sentiments which expressed a feeling among many of the liberal elite, had yearned for a 'Man' to take the country in hand: 'If this man arises, he will earn for himself a unanimous national consensus.'[61] Mussolini had to ensure that he, and not Balbo or another squadrist chief, or, worse, Giolitti or some old politician, was the figure who was most widely acknowledged as ready, willing and able to assume this role.

There were many reasons, then, why Mussolini's ideological line remained adaptable. He welcomed the new year with another of his disquisitions on economic liberalism. The Italian state, he wrote, in words which must have been, and must have been meant to be, music to those industrialists willing to nourish his movement financially, was overgrown. 'Every state-owned concern is an economic disaster', he declared, again displaying his apparently impeccable economically liberal credentials. The state doubtless needed to run many things, but business was not among them. No doubt, Fascism stood for the reinforcement of the 'political state', but, at the same time, it favoured the 'gradual demobilisation of the economic state'.[62] He, and his backers, also agreed in welcoming the split of the socialist movement. At the Congress at Livorno in January 1921 the *Partito Comunista d'Italia* was born, amid events which demonstrated that the Italian Left had been driven into a new hesitancy and confusion as a result of Fascist assaults.[63] Not even communist ideologue Antonio Gramsci's sarcastic dismissal of Mussolini's movement as composed of 'monkey people', those who 'make news, not history', could conceal the deteriorating condition of the Italian Left.[64]

The problems in the agrarian world also deserved comment. The *Fasci*, Mussolini explained, were indeed committed, eventually, to a solution whereby land was acquired by those who worked it. However, any move towards greater social equality would be slow. It could only be achieved with national agreement and so without any damage to the economy.[65] Meanwhile, attacks on peasant socialism must proceed, not because the Fascist movement was intrinsically violent, but rather 'out of surgical necessity'. 'Chivalry', Mussolini remarked piously, should never be renounced on his side of politics.[66]

The key matter was, however, the elections which Giolitti was calling for May.[67] Our programme, Mussolini announced 'without false modesty', was 'to govern the nation' with those policies 'needed to ensure the moral and material grandeur of the Italian people'. Fascists, the *Duce* again explained, eschewed ideological dogmatism:

> We permit ourselves the luxury of being aristocratic and democratic, conservative and progressive, reactionary and revolutionary, accepting the law and going beyond it, according to the circumstances of the time, place and environment, in a word, of the 'history' in which we must live and act.[68]

One who did not dislike the sound of these words was Giolitti himself. The Prime Minister, rather bemused by the new post-war world of mass politics, had decided to gamble on a loose 'National Bloc' into which Fascist candidates were to be welcomed. Mussolini did not demur, explaining philosphically that 'life for those who do not wish to spend it in some remote lonely ivory tower, demands certain contacts, certain deals and, why not say the terrible word, certain compromises'. Anyway, he added, a National Bloc, stiffened by the presence of Fascists, would soon march to a Fascist rhythm and with Fascist *éclat*. They would no longer be 'Giolittian' in the old sense. Neither the squadrists of Central Italy nor the nationalists of border Fascism had cause to worry about the 'brilliant' arrangement which he had reached. [69]

Giolitti was confident, too, telling Sforza that the Fascists were but 'fireworks: they'll make a great deal of noise but only leave smoke behind'.[70] It was an unjustified confidence. Giolitti's days of managing politics were coming to an end. It was true that, in the elections, the divided socialists lost about 20 per cent of their members of the Chamber of Deputies. But thereafter, sounding a jarring parliamentary note, at least 35 Fascists took seats in Rome (less discordant may have been the fact that 16 of them were lawyers).[71] Among them was 'Professor Benito Mussolini', the fullness of whose 'transformation', it was swiftly plain, was not what Giolitti had wished. No sooner was he elected than Mussolini announced that the Fascists would assemble on the extreme right of the Chamber, while associating themselves with the opposition. As so often, Mussolini tried to convey more than one message. Still 'tending to be republican', his Fascists did not want to be confused with members of the Nationalist Association who, perpetually lacking a mass base, counted only 10 members in the new house.

Fascists, Mussolini pronounced, constituted 'an aristocracy of thought and deed', and, in their bright honour, were outdistancing the class-bound Nationalists; the Fascists, and only the Fascists, were the winning movement of the new Right.[72] The complacent bourgeoisie, he added aggressively, was as much the movement's enemy as were socialists; Fascism, strengthened by its genuine mass base, had 'lead and fire' ready for them, too.[73] After all, Mussolini was soon emphasising, he disliked everything about parliament, its way of seating members, its assumptions about oratory. In its cosy gentlemanliness, it fostered too much 'useless chatter'. Better would be a tribune where a 'tough guy' like himself could ringingly speak his mind.[74] The Fascists were entering the halls of traditional national power flaunting their disrespect. Since they sprang from the soldiers' world in the recent war, Mussolini pledged that they would behave in parliament like a 'homogeneous, organised and disciplined platoon', determined to act rather than talk.[75] If the old elites were intending to welcome Fascism to their bosom, it would have to be on Fascism's terms. The shirt of war could not be doffed; carpet-slippers (the latter remained a pet hatred of Fascist rhetoric concerning bourgeois softness while Mussolini, contemporaries noticed, slept in his underclothes like a real working man and did not own a pair of pyjamas) must now be renounced for ever.[76]

Actually, Mussolini's position was neither as adamantine nor as puissant as he claimed. Often in the past, he had excoriated the corruption and vice of the national capital. But as a member of parliament (even if one patronised by old leaders who on occasion still had difficulty spelling his name),[77] he possessed profound hope that the future would bring still more advantage. In the interim, Mussolini took up residence at the elegant Hotel des Princes in Piazza di Spagna, and began in private to enjoy some of the many flesh-pots of Rome.[78] To personal contradictions were added political ones. In reality, the new Fascist parliamentarians, and the movement as a whole, were anything but united. In the aftermath of their victory, the *Fasci* drifted into crisis. The trouble was to take 6 months to resolve, during which time it did finally become clear that a new party, indeed a new style of party, was coming into existence under Benito Mussolini, and that he was its only credible *Duce*.

Once again, then, it had turned out that the radicalism and intransigence of Mussolini's words were only part of their meaning. There was something to be read between the lines. Having again distanced himself from Giolitti, whose government collapsed on 27 June,

Mussolini had not, however, renounced the idea of finding other friends and allies for his Fascist legions. The moderate Ivanoe Bonomi was the new Prime Minister. During the election campaign he had paid tribute to the 'youthful exuberance' of Fascism, praising the way in which the movement had assisted a 're-birth of the national spirit'.[79] Simultaneously, however, Bonomi had urged an end to violence. And, on 21 July at Sarzana in Liguria, in an apparent sign of a new official will to curb Fascist excesses, the police repelled a squad arrived from Tuscany and intending a violent assault on local Leftists. In thus committing his government to a policy which applied the letter of the law, Bonomi was making it known that the level of violence in 'real Italy' had become intolerable and that he desired some accommodation between Fascism and socialism.

Despite the plenitude of his words since October 1914 and the violence of Fascist deeds in recent months, Mussolini did not find the notion surprising or impossible. Sensing the way the wind was blowing, during the fortnight before 21 July he had already been talking in public and private about the advisability of a 'peace agreement' with the socialists.[80] On the evening of the events at Sarzana, the national council of the *Fasci* met in Rome, engaging in a lively, if confused, debate. Mussolini's own line was, however, clear. For the moment at least, Fascist violence had gone too far. As he editorialised in his paper on 24 July, too many late joiners of the movement had interpreted Fascism in a personal and cynical way, converting it to 'an organisation based on violence in order to be violent'. These misguided newcomers needed to be purged and those who remained must accept the discipline which he implied could only come from bowing to their leader and his will on all occasions.[81]

Many Fascists were appalled by this sudden detour on the political road. Roberto Farinacci, by now established as the *ras* (an Ethiopian word for tribal chieftain come into Italian usage) at Cremona, had just made a splash in the cloakroom of the Chamber of Deputies by beating up a Communist deputy who had earlier opposed the war.[82] Destined to be a major figure in the regime and a never altogether denounced influence on Mussolini, Farinacci, both now and later, maximised his intransigence, while glorying in the right to equality or near equality with his chief. Rather than have truck with 'Bolsheviks', on 23 July he resigned from the national directorate. Seconding him was, among others, economist Maffeo Pantaleoni who, in *La Vita Italiana*, roundly condemned the whole idea of treatying with 'social-Nittian robbers', an action which, he argued, would betray the idealism of those intellectuals and students who had flocked to serve beneath the Fascist banner. Had Mussolini, he wondered with the obsession of his journal, fallen prey to the malign influence of the Jews?[83] Those true believing Fascists who liked to expatiate about their 'crusade' being fought by a militia armed with a divine will and refreshed by a profound religious sense would, it seemed, have trouble fitting the 'pact of pacification' into their creed.

Matters moved quickly. On 2 August the agreement with the socialists and their trade union, the *Confederazione generale del lavoro*, was signed. Mussolini's language the next morning in *Il Popolo d'Italia* was unabashed by the consternation which this reversal in Fascist tactics had produced. The treaty was signed; it had become 'historic'. It safeguarded the nation, and the nation must always predominate over 'faction'. Furthermore, the promise of social peace left Fascism with an 'infinity' of other jobs (though Mussolini, perhaps prudently, did not spell these out). In any case, Mussolini's tone grew personal. 'If Fascism does not follow me, no-one can force me to follow Fascism.' 'The man who has founded and led a movement and has given it all his energies', he ran on uncompromisingly,

> has the right through the analysis of thousands of local matters to make a general synthesis of the whole political and moral panorama. He has the right to see the full horizon from the top of the mountain, and view a world which is not that of Bologna, nor Venice, nor Cuneo, but of Italy, Europe and the world.[84]

Fascism, he implied, could not survive and flourish without a genuine national leader.

In this bold assertion of his own indispensability, Mussolini was trying to head off those who rejected his line. For the moment he did not succeed. The distinguished philosophical 'father of new nationalism', Enrico Corradini, while conceding that 'these *Fasci*' had possessed a 'psychological' value over the last months, took the moment to urge that the fundamental Italian 'problem' remained that of constructing a powerful state. The *Fasci*'s youth and their inheritance from the war had made them a sort of 'militia'. However crusading was not the same as politicking. The national state must take charge of the national destiny, and itself put down the socialists. In the meantime, he continued severely, the situation had been worsened by the 'pact of pacification', since it converted the holy contest between those who incarnated the nation and those who did not into a 'sport' which could be indulged in or abandoned as the pleasure took its participants.[85]

Within the Fascist movement similar sentiments obtained. Vociferous in attacking Mussolini were Grandi of Bologna and Pietro Marsich of Venice. The latter was a left interventionist who himself had pursued a fluctuating course in Venetian politics.[86] There the nub of any action was the ever growing authority of Giuseppe Volpi,[87] a business man, sometime Giolittian, and during the war, so far as Nationalists were concerned, dangerously close to German banking. Volpi had just been appointed Governor of Tripolitania by democrat Minister for the Colonies, Giovanni Amendola, but was destined later to be Fascist Minister of Finance, 'Count of Misurata', head of *Confindustria*, acknowledged 'doge' of Venice and a man Mussolini cheerfully greeted as 'friend'.[88] Spurred by the contest with the politically sinuous Volpi, Marsich strove to embody a pure Fascist radicalism, even daring to announce that 'we are not ready to sacrifice Fascism to Mussolini'.[89] Grandi, too, was scarcely a worshipping Fascist militiaman. Rather, he was ambitious, able and presentable, despite his youth (he had been born in 1895), already imagining a distinguished career for himself. For him, now was the moment to urge that the Emilia was the real 'cradle' of Fascism and therefore to be trusted in the way that pompous Milan could not be.[90] On 16 August Grandi organised a meeting at Bologna of anti-Mussolinian Fascists. Many humble members of the *Fasci* took the occasion to express their local attachments – Mario Piazzesi, a Tuscan youth, characteristically imagined a leadership in the hands of 'Florence, my Florence, always at the head, always first' in denying any deal with the 'bestial' socialists.[91]

In reaction to this bubbling up of a semi-anarchist fondness for little worlds somewhat out of kilter with ideas about national grandeur and unity – Piazzesi loved Florence because he so despised Rome[92] – Mussolini, on 18 August, tabled his resignation from the executive committee of the *Fasci di combattimento*. He could not cope any more, he wrote, with the wave of provincial indiscipline stirred up by the 'pact of pacification'. He would, he said, just become 'a simple follower of the *Fascio* in Milan'.[93] The Fascist movement must do without his 'charisma', which indeed some of his colleagues among the *Fasci* were almost ready to discount.[94]

Mussolini's retreat was a tactical one. Less than a week after his resignation, and now emphasising his surviving dedication to defending the *Fasci* from their enemies both to the Left and the Right, Mussolini urged that it was time to change the movement into a fully organised and fully disciplined party, one that could boast both a 'soul' and a 'programme'.[95] And over the next three months he steadily enhanced his own role in the newly systematised group.[96]

By early November he was ready to mark his 'return'. A party congress was summoned to Rome, emblematic capital of national political power where local Fascism remained weak. (Mussolini limbered up psychologically for the event by fighting another well-publicised duel – Finzi acted as his second).[97] When the meeting in Rome opened, Mussolini was reckoned to have only one-third of the delegates as reliably his own.[98] However, he had already made soundings to Grandi, a man whom he rightly understood was vulnerable to the Fascist version of duchessing. Grandi was offered a prominent role in the new theoretical journal, *Gerarchia*, due to be launched in the following January and probably financed by Margherita Sarfatti, who became its *de facto* editor.[99] Mussolini, it was also understood, was guaranteeing to look after the younger man's future. As the congress proceeded, the *ras* failed to unite or to enunciate a policy. On 8 November Mussolini, Grandi and Marsich embraced before the cheering delegates. (The Venetian Fascist, however, had not been bought off and was not to have a Fascist future, quarrelling with Grandi and leaving the party by the next February.)[100] For this public accord, the price which Mussolini had to pay was abandonment of the 'pact of pacification', although he tactfully delayed its denunciation for a week.[101] In his eyes, the game was worth the fee. Conflicts between the leader and his movement would ebb and flow beneath the surface of the history of Fascism, but, in most senses Mussolini had won a final victory over the *ras*. Fascism could not do without its *Duce*, while Mussolini now knew that he was immensely superior to any party rivals and, even if he never lost his suspicion of them, its members were no more than an entourage, needing Mussolini more urgently than he needed them.

During his months of relative withdrawal, Mussolini had continued to cast around for an ideal programme for the party which was forming. As ever his thoughts ranged widely. Fascism must reflect the 'primordiality' and the eternity of the nation; before such historic grandeur, individuals were mere 'transitory beings'. The state must serve this nation. Fascism would 'restore' it, just as Fascism would sturdily defend the heritage and memory of the First World War. At present, the party was agnostic over the institutional question of a monarchy or a republic, but it would want to establish a *Consiglio tecnico nazionale* (National Technical Council) to sit in parallel with parliament, and serve the practical instead of the wordy. Emigrants should be allowed the vote. As far as economics were concerned, production was what should be favoured most.[102] There might on occasion be need for state protection of industry but as Mussolini, still polishing his contacts with business and finance, re-emphasised to his audience in Rome, 'as far as economics is concerned, we are liberals, because we believe that the national economy cannot be usefully entrusted to collective or governmental and bureaucratic organisations'.[103]

There was no doubt, however, that the real key for the present lay within the party itself. There, if Fascism were to win its battles, discipline must dominate.[104] The borrowing of a military and militant vocabulary, natural enough in every circumstance of the *dopoguerra*, became more institutionalised. During a speech to the Chamber in December Mussolini upbraided his opponents in other parties with the taunt that a military style now had become obligatory for all.[105] To ensure his own command, Mussolini had taken pains to surround himself with reliable and obedient lieutenants. Replacing the too independent Pasella as secretary of the movement was Michele Bianchi, once a colleague on *Avanti!* and long a respectful admirer of the *Duce*[106] – already in August Mussolini had instructed him to develop a clear Fascist philosophy (and, by implication, one that was not too complex or arguable). Those 'soldiers who fight knowing their cause', Mussolini had advised with some pomposity, 'are always the best'.[107] Beneath Bianchi were three Under-Secretaries, Achille Starace, Attilio Teruzzi, and Giuseppe Bastianini; each destined for a long career under the dictatorship, with Starace[108] and Teruzzi[109] being disliked by most with whom they came into contact while also being known as Mussolini's men. Administrator of the party was Giovanni Marinelli, a man who combined bureaucratic efficiency and an ability to manage Mussolini's personal finances. He also had a reputation (to be confirmed in 1944) for cowardice, hypochondria and corruption.[110] Apart from Mussolini himself, the only member of parliament to be granted a place on the party directorate was the now tamed Grandi. A team was being assembled.

Similarly, a method was being invented. The squads were attached to local party branches and made the object of military-style review by a travelling Inspectorate General. Fascist women's groups – nine women had been present at the Piazza San Sepolcro meeting[111] but a distaff Fascism had not taken off in the months which followed – were brought under greater control. Early Fascist women tended to link their feminism with Mussolini's cause but at the end of 1921 the organisation began to make evident its doubts about women's liberation.[112]

In Italy's universities, with their overwhelmingly middle-class student bodies, Fascism was popular, and here, by February 1922, the new party sought discipline through a national Fascist federation of university groups, administered from Bologna.[113]

To add to the efficacy of this structure came words, lots of words, the meaning of which remains a matter of considerable dispute. Historian Emilio Gentile, for example, has argued that the newly disciplined movement possessed a military, mythical and religious character which utterly distinguished it from its competitors. Fascism, he says, embodied a 'new state of mind'.[114] Its adherents were true believers in a 'political religion', adepts of a Fascist 'liturgy', and determined to nationalise or, rather, fascistise the masses.[115] According to Gentile, a party member meant it when he declared that his weapon was

the faithful and inseparable lover of a Fascist. ... Much more than a woman. Women talk too much and never get on with it. ... The Browning pistol. The only thing which a Fascist loves with an almost carnal love. When nothing else is faithful to the Fascist, the Browning pistol is his only and eternal faith. And that's enough.

After all, 'for us the war has never come to an end. We simply replaced external enemies with internal ones'.[116]

In the day-to-day world of ordinary politics, however, such attitudes might be thought hard to preserve, especially after the regime was established and much humdrum governing became necessary. Indeed, even in 1921–22 there were grounds for doubts about the fascistisation of Fascist souls. Too many Fascists, then and later, left space in their holy missions for self-interest and, more occasionally, for self-doubt. And of all the souls in Italy, Mussolini was the least credulous, viewing Fascism, like everything else, in a practical rather than a sacralised fashion.

To be sure, the quasi-military campaign against leftists and non-Italians continued. The Bonomi government had found its own strategy damaged beyond repair by the collapse of the 'pact of pacification'. Early in the New Year, beset by an economic crisis exacerbated by the collapse of the *Banca Italiana di Sconto*, Bonomi resigned. His administration was replaced on 26 February by another coalition, this time headed by Luigi Facta, a Piedmontese subordinate of Giolitti. Everyone assumed it was a caretaker government. The official toughness made manifest at Sarzana was now a memory and, by the summer of 1922, in most of northern Italy, Fascist squads did their violent work without let or hindrance from prefects, police or army. Late in July Italo Balbo led a punitive march like that of Sherman in Georgia through Mussolini's own homelands, travelling from Rimini to Sant'Arcangelo to Savignano to Cesena to Bertinoro, 'destroying and burning all the Reds' houses and all the places where socialists and communists rally'. He boasted in his diary: 'It was a night of terror. Our passage was signed by plumes of smoke and fire. All the Romagna plain up to the hills became prey to the exasperated reprisals of the Fascists, determined to finish for ever Red terror', though, in practice, Balbo admitted, there had been meagre evidence of Leftist resistance.[117] By autumn the Fascists were doing something similar in the Trentino-Alto Adige – anyone who rejected full-scale Italianisation suffered the consequences and, again, the government stood by and did nothing to repel the marchers.

In September the squads had reached Terni and Civitavecchia, which lay within striking distance of Rome. An attack on the capital seemed imminent. Within the Fascist movement, Balbo, Farinacci and even Bianchi grew pressing in their demands for action.[118] Given the breadth of Fascist control of provincial Italy, would the seizure of national power prove 'a fact before it happened', as one Triestine Fascist later averred?[119] How easily could the Fascist victories in 'real Italy' be converted into an occupation of the seat of power of 'legal Italy'?

To answer these questions it is necessary to understand the way in which Mussolini had been reacting to these increasingly impatient demands from 'below'. The deal reached in November 1921 meant that provincial Fascists continued to hail Mussolini as their *Duce*. But for Mussolini such salutes were not enough as he wanted his followers' respect and devotion untrammelled. In September 1922 the new tone expected by the Fascist leader was evident in an account published by the ex-Futurist journalist Emilio Settimelli. The language used to describe the *Duce* had indeed heightened (though it had not yet reached the fervour which became mandatory after the seizure of power). Mussolini expressed a 'force of prodigious variety', Settimelli wrote. It might be true that the lines at the corner of his eyes hinted at his 'subtle sense of irony' and he might still be imagined laughing, and yet his face was that of a man perpetually alone. So, too, his walk, with rapid, hurried, even distracted steps, reflected the profundity of his commitment to his thoughts and to his pledge to re-animate Italy. Here was a man turning, at least in Settimelli's prose, into a god.[120]

And yet a real world had not ceased to exist. In it, squadrists sometimes went too far – Balbo's diary, despite being published under the regime, recalls Mussolini's trying to dissuade him from too precipitate action during the summer of 1922.[121] Around that time rumours resurfaced of the chance of a break between Mussolini and the more intransigent of the *ras*.[122] If he were to contain this latent conflict, Mussolini must preserve his contact with the centres of official authority; indeed, connection with national power continued to underpin any charisma which might be inscribed on the *Duce*. In his articles, speeches and actions, Mussolini needed to make it completely clear that he was the Fascist who mattered, the one who comprehended Rome, Italy, Europe and the world. If he failed in his understanding, if he were shown to be a fool or a dullard, then he might lose his credibility both with the Fascists in the country at large and with those elites who still governed Italy. In every political match in which he engaged he must win.

He needed, therefore, to express an opinion on many matters, and always in a way which was strident and 'revolutionary' but at the same time left him open to compromise and possible negotiation. There was the Vatican, where Benedict XV, a compromised figure on the right because of his doubts about the Italian war, had died on 22 January. Benedict's demise prompted Mussolini to philosophise about the Papacy's Roman inheritance[123] and so remind the Church that his friendship might be possible, despite his ancient anti-clericalism and those more recent disputes which frequently boiled to the surface with the *Popolari*, especially with their most radical elements – Farinacci in Cremona was a *mangiapreti* of the old school who did not hold back in his excoriation of priestly meddling in civil life.[124] As long as Farinacci and his friends were capable of being put back on the leash, there were advantages to be won from the suggestion that the new Pope, ex-Archbishop of Milan, Achille Ratti, who took the title Pius XI, might be tolerant towards the 'better side' of Fascism. Sprung from a Lombard landowning family and fervently hostile to 'Bolshevism' and all its works, Pius XI himself possessed a peremptory personality, and what papal propagandists were soon praising as a love of 'discipline and work', all of which bore some comparison with Mussolini's own qualities and image.[125] Mussolini noticed the parallel, and the panoply with which a new Pope was installed. Here was an example of the inscription of timeless and limitless charisma; Fascism might have much to learn from it.[126] As surprising as it might seem, within the subtle council chambers of the Vatican, Mussolini began to be viewed positively.

A commentary on foreign affairs had to be maintained. *Gerarchia* could be a useful vehicle for expert analysis of such matters.[127] In March 1922 Mussolini felt able to take time off from domestic preoccupations and go on a well-publicised fact-finding mission to Germany where, among others, he met Walter Rathenau. This German Jewish statesman a few months later was murdered by the German Right, a fate which Mussolini claimed, without much evidence, to have foreseen.[128] On this occasion Mussolini gave little indication of any latent Anti-Semitism, and he was at pains to claim that Fascism had nothing in common with the bloody vengefulness of the extreme German Right.[129] At the same time, he noted his conviction that the Weimar republican system was 'completely and historically foreign to the soul of the German people'.[130] A tourist, too, he found the quality of German theatre poor and the *Reichstag* architecturally even smaller and uglier than *Montecitorio*, the seat of the parliament in Rome.[131] Here, his prose was proclaiming, was, in many senses, a man of the world.

Back home again (he celebrated by fighting another duel in which, with his accustomed devil-may-care fierceness, he severely wounded his opponent),[132] Mussolini continued to scan the international horizon for advantage. In the diplomatic arena, he urged, Italians should more visibly stand on their own feet, demonstrating to the British, for example, that they produced more than *gelato*. 'Italy', he added, in phrases borrowed from the Nationalists, 'has come of age and can no longer be treated like a child.'[133] Austria, by contrast, needed Italian backing[134] and so did Kemal Atatürk's regime in Turkey, where Italians must oppose the 'unchecked megalomania of Greek imperialism'.[135] On issue after issue, Mussolini's readers of *Il Popolo d'Italia* and the whole political world were being advised to admire the Fascist chief's range of information and ideas.

Most importantly, there were top people at home to ingratiate himself with or to pressure. In February 1922 the word *Duce* remained sufficiently unsacralised for Mussolini to apply it flatteringly to industrialist Gino Olivetti.[136] But the real targets of Mussolini's rhetoric were other politicians. In their world Mussolini moved every day with greater aplomb and greater potential ruthlessness. One feeble Facta government replaced another, but the 'big men' of national politics remained those who had led during the war. Here was further evidence of the way in which that great conflict still defined most of what happened in Italy, as well as providing pleasing proof to the aspiring Mussolini that, once a leader made it to the top, he could expect to stay there or thereabouts. As the summer of 1922 wore on rumours were rife that Salandra, or Orlando, or Giolitti, was about to make a comeback. As the old chiefs heard the rumours, they girded their loins, tightened their strategies, and sought to defeat their putative enemies before they grew too strong. Towards Salandra, the furthest to the right, Mussolini, through intermediaries, was polite but cagey,[137] and such tactics won a declaration from the ex-Prime Minister in September that he regarded himself as an 'honorary Fascist'.[138] With Orlando, contact was opened in July through Acerbo, but at the time negotiations failed, although not before the Sicilian leader talked of making Mussolini his Minister of Foreign Affairs in a hypothetical new government.[139] No doubt the political world was digesting the new prestige which the boy from Predappio had evidently earned. It remained to be seen whether he would prove to be a coming man, or **the** coming man.

The crucial interlocutor remained Giolitti. Despite his age, he still saw himself as waiting to save the nation, and was in turn regarded by Mussolini as his most dangerous opponent. Early in October the *Duce* told a friend 'either we stuff him now or he and his friends will stuff us tomorrow'.[140] A determination to see Giolitti off, however, did not prevent Mussolini from talking warmly to an intermediary of his desire that the old liberal take the reins again, especially if it meant pre-empting the scheming Orlando.[141] So infinite were Mussolini's skills and so unconfined his effrontery, that Nationalist Luigi Federzoni, another with whom delicate negotiations continued, paralleled Mussolini's bargaining ability with that of Giolitti. Indeed, he concluded, Mussolini had the potential to outdo the old master.[142]

Here, then, was the background to the March on Rome and what the regime later loved to call the 'Fascist revolution'.[143] On 24 October a Fascist party conference assembled at Naples – the South was still largely unimpressed by the Fascist advance elsewhere. The *ras* urgently demanded a March on Rome and, by the morning of 28 October, were mobilising armed supporters. Mussolini, on a number of occasions during the previous months, had himself not ruled out a Fascist *coup de main*.[144] In September he had stated bluntly that 'our programme is simple. We want to govern Italy',[145] even though he had qualified this comment with typical remarks about the childishness of the masses,[146] sentiments which could be as easily directed at the Fascists of the countryside as at the rest of the Italian populace.

At Naples and during the days which followed, Mussolini had not opposed his restless and importunate *ras*. But he had made plain that it was his task to manage the situation, a control which would be most effective in the political and not the social world. Later, the Fascist regime was anxious that the March on Rome be given the title of a revolution but, in October 1922, it was a change in government to be achieved by negotiation at least as much as by naked violence. In the arena of high politics, apart from the politicians, the Army and the monarchy were forces with which to reckon. On 14 October Mussolini sent a warning shot across the bows of Pietro Badoglio, a leading general (although one whose reputation had been besmirched by Caporetto), who was rumoured to have urged military action against the Fascists. Any such move, Mussolini wrote, would precipitate a 'massacre in the grand style', though, naturally, he was sure that his party and the army, which shared so much, would never really be at odds.[147] What of Victor Emmanuel III, the celebrated *re soldato*? For him, the best pressure was to hint that his cousin, the Duke of Aosta, was taller, a better soldier and could make a more manly king.[148] The king, like all the rest, had his weaknesses and could be pressured, bullied and blackmailed into accepting the presence of Fascists in government.

The formula worked brilliantly, even though the marching Fascists proved poorly armed and easily disconcerted by the commencement of autumnal rains and by their lack of good maps. While they organised what they boasted was a pincer movement from Perugia and other centres to the north of Rome, Mussolini remained ostentatiously in his Milan stronghold, unhooking his telephone for three nights in a row while he publicly attended the theatre, demonstrating thereby that nothing could ruffle him. The main politicians eyed each other but could not unite. Salandra, Orlando and Giolitti each awaited his own return to the Prime Ministership, but each indicated a preference that the post be entrusted to the young Mussolini rather than to a hated old rival. The army chiefs enigmatically advised the monarch that their forces were loyal, but that such loyalty was better not put to the test.[149] The Vatican washed its hands. Facta fluffed an effort to impose martial law. On the morning of 29 October Mussolini received the crucial phone call with an offer that he form a coalition government. His press release was emphatic: he was proceeding to the capital 'wearing his black shirt, as a Fascist', and he was backed by 300 000 men, 'organised and faithful to my orders'.[150] Still not hurrying, at 8.30 p.m. he caught the Milan–Rome *direttissimo*, humbly and frugally rejecting the suggestion that a special train be hired for the occasion. Fourteen hours later he reached Rome, where some bedraggled Fascists were organising their victory parade and taking it out on what working-class zones they could find in the capital. On 31 October, aged 39, Mussolini was sworn in as Italy's youngest prime minister. The great majority of people who counted in Italy, excluding the immediate political enemies of Fascism, welcomed the news. But Gaetano Salvemini, the historian and journalist and once the young Mussolini's friend, wrote on the 29th to an acquaintance in Paris that his country was on 'the verge of madness'.[151] More charitably, Margherita Sarfatti surmised that her lover and his Fascists could now 'restore style to the Italian people'.[152] Neither was altogether wrong.

8

Government, 1922–1924

WHEN Mussolini came before King Victor Emmanuel III in order to be entrusted with the task of forming a government, he was said to have declared: 'Sire, I bring you the Italy of Vittorio Veneto.' For all its repetition thereafter by regime propagandists[1] and even by Mussolini himself,[2] the remark was apocryphal; Mussolini mocked it in private as 'the sort of rubbish you come out with in school assemblies'.[3] Nor had the First World War made Mussolini possible in the way that Ian Kershaw has argued was true of Hitler. Without the conflict the later *Führer* very probably would have remained a nobody.[4] Unlike his later German colleague, Mussolini had earned considerable distinction before 1914 and, in some virtual history that omits the war, can be imagined pursuing either an ideological or a political career. And yet Italy's special First World War had indeed reached government at the end of October 1922. The Fascists and their *Duce* embodied it in many ways. There were, for example, the imperial ambitions unleashed after 1915 at the heart of the ruling elite, when liberal fathers passed the torch to Nationalist sons. The new generation was girded by a determination to alter Italy's apparent destiny as the least of the Great Powers. Fascist foreign policy might eventually indulge in aggression in a way which made some liberals blanch, and yet a continuity from Liberal to Fascist ambition in Ethiopia, in the *mare nostrum* (it had been so nominated well before 1918), in the Balkans, in the Eastern Mediterranean and in the administration of Libya, cannot be denied. Still more significantly, Fascism incarnated the new brutalism, the masculine willingness to kill and to maim, the yen for killing machines, the cruel 'mateship', all qualities and attitudes learned or refined at the front and together amounting to that new barbarism which has been identified as a crucial antecedent of Auschwitz.[5] In the Fascist rise, Mussolini had never distanced himself far from violence, the duel fought with maximum roughness and almost to the bitter end, the insulting slap, the forced dose of castor oil, the burning of a newspaper office or a peasant meeting-place, the purchase and provision of pistols and bombs, the sallying forth armed and motorised in a uniformed squad, the slaughter of an enemy.

As if to mark his character in this regard, just before the March on Rome Mussolini had appointed as his personal bodyguard or 'gorilla', the thuggish butcher, Albino Volpi,[6] later to be one of the murderers of Matteotti. In Mussolini's mind, and in those of his entourage and many of his followers, a public approval of violence, a continuous acceptance of the usefulness of its employment, were precisely what made a man a man. Having arrived in Rome, Mussolini may have exchanged a telephone call with his brother in which he humbly gave thanks for the good fortune of his success and expressed gratification at the blessings of the Deity which the pious Arnaldo summoned down upon him.[7] Thereafter he may have ostentatiously gone off to the elegant *Pasticceria Latour* to take his coffee among the best people.[8] He may have sought or received Margherita Sarfatti's advice about how to smoothe his path into the capital's social and artistic salons (he was soon cheering those attending an exhibition by declaring that 'you can't govern without art and artists'),[9] and been solaced by her expressions of love.[10] But the new Prime Minister was a hard man, *un animale poco socievole* as he loved to define himself,[11] a person who, as a contemporary put it, above all lacked any sense of being checked or curtailed by the law.[12] In his youth Mussolini had expressed his attraction to the thought of both Marx and Darwin. By 1922 it was the philosophy of the latter which had taken control of his mind. His Darwinism, like that of many another, was of a bitter sort. Time and again Mussolini might prove he was the fittest in his world, but somehow the victories were never sweet, the final act, he went on fearing, could yet reveal his every triumph had been but momentary and the end was to be dire. Like Shakespeare's Richard III, Benito Mussolini had set his life upon a cast and should stand the hazard of the die, all the time believing that, somewhere, sometime, somehow, fate must run against him.

Contemporary culturalist historians, anxious to paint a thick description of 'fascinating Fascism' in all the *élan* of its advertising and 'spin', obscure the rancour (and the nervous fear) at the heart of Fascism and its *Duce*. Many Fascists were no more than offspring of the liberals of the Risorgimento. But they were sons who had been through the terrible experience of the First World War and were destined never to regain the 'comfort' which had existed for the better-off sections of society during the *belle époque*. Then the fathers had at least talked as though a kind and gentle world might eventually extend to all society. Though Fascist yuppies in time appeared and themselves yearned to be at ease, Mussolini and his regime mostly bespoke an era of mobilisation – the muster, the march, the battle, the liquidation of foes who paradoxically never lost their menace, and the permanent readying for another conflict, another test. As the Fascists began to govern, they revealed that the 'order' to resume in Italy under their aegis was to be an edgy, even frenetic, one, in which, ironically, all successes would themselves prove as hollow or uncertain as had that at Vittorio Veneto.

The Fascist rise to power had been scarred by up to 2000 deaths[13] (the March on Rome had an official toll of three),[14] low figures given the horrors to come in the twentieth century, but at the time a high cost to pay. The casualties of the last two years, and the ambiguous way – half coup, half manipulation – in which power had been achieved gave the new government an urgent need to justify itself. What, then, were Mussolini's intentions, now that he had become Prime Minister? The answer is not at all plain. Here was a politician who, despite his youth, had pursued a twisting path to the *Palazzo Chigi*. He had written (and spoken) a very great deal – 18 of the 36 volumes of the standard edition of his *Opera omnia* are consumed by his publications and statements before October 1922. But he had composed no single work of political philosophy, nothing comparable to *Mein Kampf* or the *Secret Book* (even though the influence on Hitler's course after 1933 and the originality of the ideas in these works are still disputed by historians). Perhaps the squads were already developing a mystical side and their members had adopted a Fascist mentality – some historians say so. Perhaps they were genuinely moved and uplifted by the liturgy of Fascist ceremonial. Mussolini himself, however, went on being the least mystical of men. Balbo might claim in his diary that, when they met in Milan on 6 October, the *Duce* had made their souls 'vibrate in unison', and that Mussolini had been compelling in the clarity with which he foresaw the future.[15] On the detail of this future, however, Balbo had nothing to say. Other more critical contemporaries noticed instead the fluctuations in Mussolini's ideas and the way he preferred to avoid in-depth conversations,[16] sometimes excusing himself by saying that the details should be left to the experts. Here, they discerned, was a leader more interested in imposing his will than in harmonising his attitudes or policies.[17] Here was a politician more interested in seeming to know than in knowing.

Mussolini quickly developed an administrative style which reflected his sense of duty and power, and which possessed a some-what antique air. Using a pen, black ink and a very firm hand, throughout his dictatorship he wrote out most of his speeches and quite a few of his letters and telegrams.[18] Never forgetting the lessons learned in his socialist days that complex issues could be compre-hended in point form, he succinctly enumerated the matters which he thought needed action. Such brief 'orders' exuded a pleasingly mili-tary air, suitable for a dictator who led a militant regime. None the less, one contemporary thought that Mussolini ran Italy as once he had governed *Il Popolo d'Italia*; with his ministers acting as sub-editors, he reserved to himself the task of setting the general tone and crafting the headlines.[19] Appropriate for one who liked to boast of the 'mathemat-ical' ordering of his life, Mussolini had his day punctuated by an endless stream of visitors, who could rarely be dismissed in less than 15 minutes, time that visibly ticked by on the face of a small clock which sat on his desk. Some audiences were granted to key ministers or officials, but quite a few were earmarked for more ordinary Fascists, or for foreigners, never reluctant to spend some happy days in Rome.

Especially for Italians, to win access to the *Duce* was a matter of prestige and gave promise of enhanced authority and the possibility of financial gain.[20] In turn Mussolini mostly had to seem pleased by the visits and always needed to appear knowledgeable about the life and beliefs of his interlocutor. It was a taxing requirement, but one Mussolini proved able at surmounting, even if the inevitable superfi-ciality of his 'knowledge' undermined the chance that he could thoroughly master his brief in more serious matters of government. There was much about Mussolini's role as leader which foreshadowed that world in which political chiefs have turned into travelling sales-people, more fascinated by image and spin than devoted to a deeper comprehension of society.

As he began to explore the surrounds of the Prime Ministerial office and became accustomed to life in the capital which, in the past, he had frequently disdained, Mussolini had plenty of reasons to believe that his struggles were not over and to ask anxiously whether being first in his class at Predappio was sufficient qualification to cope with the manifold political and social quicksands of 'eternal' Rome. Mussolini's private life remained disordered; just surviving was demanding an expenditure of psychic energy which, before long, revealed its fee. Then there was his workaday life. Here, too, the Fascist rise had been more precipitate than planned. Perhaps it was all the more Fascist to work on the run. Certainly, during the early days after the March on Rome, Mussolini administered Italy from what has been called a 'luxury bivouac' in the Hotel Savoia, via Ludovisi, near the Borghese gardens.[21] There he tried to designate a political line on this or that aspect of government. There, too, and perhaps more imperatively, his private secretary, Alessandro Chiavolini, sought the means to fob off the most pressing of office seekers and profiteers, and fruitfully to manage the government's secret funds, once so useful to Giolitti and now available to the Fascist cause.[22]

Petitioners at the Fascist gate were indeed innumerable. Whatever variety of 'revolution' Fascism might be, a throng of importunate clients applauded it. To give but one example, on 18 December 1922 Renato Citarelli, a fledgling engineer from Calabria, opened suit with the *Duce* in a process which, some years later, culminated in his appointment to the consulate in Perth, Western Australia, perhaps the most humble position in all the national diplomatic service, but a position, nonetheless. Citarelli was one of those whose career advanced over the sackings of older diplomats in the so-called 'massacre of the innocents', and he owed his elevation to his alleged Fascist purity. In Perth, he was indeed a fire-breathing extremist, given to evoking Mussolini ('He Alone is the artificer of this our revival and this our grandeur') in almost any circumstance and with unlimited fervour.[23] Perhaps, by then, Citarelli believed what he said and his soul was mystically filled with the Fascist religion. But his initial letter to Mussolini raises some doubts, since it is studded with the forms and processes of ordinary Italian, and especially ordinary Southern Italian, life.

Citarelli's appeal began, ingratiatingly, with an expression of his utter faith 'in the magnificent understanding possessed by Your Excellency through the noble intuition of Your elect soul'. To sentiment were added facts. Citarelli was the son of a Calabrian doctor who had died young, leaving his family in sadly straitened circumstances. Citarelli had fought valorously through two years of the war, losing both his brothers who died as heroes at the front. Thus bereaved and tempered, after the war he moved to Turin to study engineering, there associating himself with the local Fascist Cesare De Vecchi (from 1933, pompously given the right to add di Val Cismon to his name). Together, they sallied forth on squadrist raids against 'reds' in Casale and Vercelli. These punitive expeditions having achieved their purpose, Citarelli went back to his studies. Around this time, he acknowledged, poverty had driven him to approach Giolitti about the prospect of some well-remunerated position, but the old politician, who may have had other preoccupations, did not go beyond promises. They were not enough to save Citarelli's two little sisters from wretched accommodation in a cheap *pensione*. And so, he stated frankly, he was transferring his hopes to Mussolini. He was not a member of the party, he had to admit, but, 'as a child, I learned one religion, that of the *Patria*'; to Italy his devotion could entail 'any sacrifice'; it was 'to the death'. He was only 24, he noted in peroration, but he had suffered so much. So could he see the *Duce* whom he so admired and, more prosaically, be forthwith found a post in which he could offer 'my work, my skill, my passion, my life' to 'beloved and blessed' Italy?[24]

From October 1922 to December 1923 Fascist party membership grew from some 300 000 to more than 780 000, with the influx being especially notable in the South.[25] Many of these new Fascists had motives and world views like those of Citarelli. In their *mentalité* Fascism's entrenchment in office meant advantage, personal advantage, the tawdry as much as the sublime. In 1926 the use of *raccomandazioni* (letters of recommendation) was officially banned,[26] but in practice they remained pervasive in Fascist Italy, indeed it has been reckoned that, once installed in power, the *Duce* himself received daily some 1500 letters requesting favours and support.[27]

In December 1922 Mussolini, learning quickly what it meant to be a dispenser of patronage, transferred his base to the five-star Grand Hotel, which lay just around the corner from Santa Maria della Vittoria, the baroque church which houses Bernini's statue of Santa Teresa rapt in ecstasy, a saint showing herself a true believer either in God or in woman. The possible impact of Bernini's celebrated statue on the new Prime Minister and on his comprehension of Fascist ecstasy was fleeting. In March 1923 Mussolini, assisted by the good offices of Baron Alberto Fassini, a man of many contacts who knew the highways and byways of Rome,[28] moved again, now to a bachelor flat at the *Palazzo Tittoni*, via Rasella.[29] It was a curious site, since via Rasella branches off via Milano and its *Traforo* or tunnel, which skilled engineers in Liberal Italy had dug beneath the royal palace or *Quirinale*. It was almost as though the 'revolutionary' Prime Minister had agreed to live at the palace gate, an impression which was reinforced by the fact that Fassini was *persona grata* in royal circles (themselves not above the search for profit), a natural intermediary between Victor Emmanuel III and the *Duce*.[30] If these networks looked intricate, Mussolini's creature comforts were placed more straightforwardly into the hands of housekeeper Cesira Carocci, a traditionally formidable figure combining utter authority in the 'female zone' with unalloyed personal deference towards her employer.[31]

Rachele, Edda, Vittorio and Bruno were left in their Milan flat in the via Pagano, the family still extended by the presence of mother-in-law Anna. Soon after Mussolini became Prime Minister, however, he was wealthy enough, or had enough access to credit, to purchase *Villa Carpena*, a landholding on the outskirts of Forlimpopoli – can he have delighted in the thought that his grandfather's humiliating cession of family land had now been avenged? The *Villa Carpena* was the sort of estate owned by *signori*, although the Mussolinis did not themselves take up residence there until March 1925.[32] Then and thereafter Mussolini was rarely to be seen in the Italian version of the garb of a country squire, but Rachele cheerfully took on the role and reputation of a woman of respect at Forlimpopoli and in the rest of the Romagna. In matters to do with the exercise of local power and influence, if not in her personal style, image and vocabulary, Rachele had become a *signora*.

In Milan, close to the Via Pagano, was the apartment of Arnaldo Mussolini, his wife and children, in via Massena. Benito Mussolini's rise entailed new prominence for his younger brother. Far off in busy and imponderable Rome, Mussolini badly needed a *uomo di fiducia* (a really reliable person) to oversee the daily running of *Il Popolo d'Italia*, long his special delight and the undergirding of his influence were he ever to be forced back into opposition. Should Mussolini's power be enduring, as he hoped, then the paper must act as the focus of the Fascist regime's propaganda and 'information'. Mussolini needed his man in Milan. It says a great deal about the history of the Italian family, about the eventual limitations of what came to be called a total-itarian state and about Mussolini's fundamental mistrust of his fellow Fascists that Arnaldo, who had been employed on the accounting side of *Il Popolo d'Italia* since his demobilisation in 1919, now took over the editorship of the paper.[33] Journalism apart, in all matters best not exposed to public knowledge or comment, Arnaldo acted as Mussolini's agent and friend. As the *Duce* confided in characteristic phrases to an American journalist: 'I have a deep affection for my brother. To be sure, he is too fat, but that is not his fault. He is, of all men, the one to whom I turn first when I require unstinted devotion and unfettered attachment.'[34]

The younger brother was indispensable. When Arnaldo suddenly died in 1931, his teenage son Vito was made official editor of *Il Popolo d'Italia*. Unsurprisingly, Vito Mussolini, dim and untrained, failed to grow into the job; indeed, he rarely turned up at the office.[35] While he 'matured', the paper was 'temporarily' until 1936 placed under the command of Mussolini's old friend, Sandro Giuliani, and that of the professional journalist, Giorgio Pini, thereafter.[36] As for other, less formal matters, from 1931 Mussolini had to fend for himself in a world that seemed to have become the more bitter and treacherous without his brother.

If these private matters needed some ordering, the new government was, naturally enough, Mussolini's main official preoccupation. The administration which he had assembled was delicately balanced. He himself was Prime Minister, Minister of Foreign Affairs and Minister of the Interior – this last position was one which, as Giolitti had understood, commanded the prefectures and police and so controlled the most significant secret zones of national governance, the funds separate from any budget, the access to telephone taps, the ability to act covertly. Except from 1924 to 1926 and during the Salò Republic, Mussolini retained this ministry throughout his regime. Not even a brother could be trusted there.

Of the Fascists, Acerbo served as Under-Secretary to the Prime Minister and Finzi Under-Secretary to the Ministry of the Interior. Each of these underlings was a friend; neither was a combative *ras*. Neither Balbo, nor Grandi, nor Farinacci, nor Bianchi, none of the more obvious members of the leadership group, was yet elevated to ministerial office. First Michele Terzaghi[37] and, after his commitment to Freemasonry was exposed too blatantly, later, Giuseppe Caradonna, a *ras* from Puglia, undertook the humble seeming task of Under Secretary to the Post Office. No doubt the occupants comprehended that this was a traditional area of 'corruption', a position where monies flowed and contracts were refused or secured, a good place for a Fascist, especially one who was not too credulous about God and man (while Caradonna had been at pains to advise Mussolini that no government, not even a 'revolutionary' one, should exclude representatives from the South).[38]

Telling, too, were the various positions accepted by men from the existing elite who were not yet Fascists but who were certainly willing to fellow-travel with what had become the triumphant movement or with its successful leader. Mussolini may have told Balbo, an alert listener, that, in time, he intended to deal with 'the old aunts of liberalism',[39] but presently he was happy to work with those who would work with him. Giovanni Gentile, one of the nation's two most distinguished philosophers and an intellectual with a genuine international reputation, took on the Ministry of Education, intending to convert his beliefs in a strong and organic state into practice. The two military ministries, those of war and the navy, went to General Armando Diaz, Italy's commander at the end of the great conflict (though illness soon drove him off to hedonist retirement on Capri),[40] and to Paolo Thaon di Revel, who had been Italy's senior naval officer in 1917-18.

Luigi Federzoni, the leading Nationalist member of parliament, was sworn in as Minister of Colonies, a doubly significant role. Since its formation in 1910 the Nationalist Association had been the most fervent proponent of Italian expansionism. Federzoni himself had been a tireless advocate of Italian power in the Adriatic, Aegean and indeed the whole Mediterranean. He also expressed a paranoid concern about an alleged Germanic domination of national culture and finance.[41] Civilization, he proclaimed curtly, could only grow if Italian power was maximised.[42] The Nationalists favoured a highly conservative policy at home, sceptical of the presence of any virtue in the masses and unconvinced by Fascist populism. During the weeks before the March on Rome, the ANI leadership had let it be known that their own paramilitary *Sempre Pronti* squads were ready to fire on the Fascists, should the King summon them in defence of the nation's institutions. Mussolini registered their threat, and in his memory nourished his hostility to such upper-class dalliers with politics and power.

For all the latent conflict, after 28 October compromise between Mussolini and the ANI was swiftly reached. Federzoni took the occasion to pledge the undying 'friendship' of the Nationalists for the 'Mussolinian' cause, a support made certain, he said duplicitously, in gratitude for the profundity of the *Duce*'s 'loyalty' to them.[43] By February 1923 the Nationalist jurist Alfredo Rocco, from 1925 to become a Fascist Minister of Justice, had drafted a detailed set of terms through which the ANI accepted absorption into the *Partito Nazionale Fascista* (PNF).[44] Thereafter, Nationalists would stud the elite of the Fascist regime, leading communist, Palmiro Togliatti, to argue that the movement had as much absorbed Fascism as vice versa.[45] His argument is persuasive to a considerable degree, although Mussolini continued where possible to subvert Nationalist snobbery and arrogance, characteristically confiding to a friend that Federzoni was the sort of old man who put on a dark suit before going out to buy a roll of toilet paper.[46]

The business world was appeased by the appointment of economist Alberto De' Stefani as Minister of Finance, a position which from February 1923 embraced the previously independent Treasury. De'

Stefani was a Fascist, but his formidable personality and his confidence in dealing with the highest intellectual circles[47] made him a notably independent one.[48] His views on economics were orthodox enough, and he was soon urging his leader to lessen journalistic snooping around business concerns and suggesting that the populace at large must tighten their belts rather than rely on state assistance.[49] He also countenanced with aplomb the cutting of military expenditure. Nudged by his advice, the *Duce* spoke up in the Chamber about his commitment to balancing the budget 'at any cost'. History, he added in typical phrases, taught that financial rigour was what saved nations.[50] With De' Stefani in office, Fascism had endorsed the view that what was good for Fiat, the banks and even international capital was good for Italy. In 1924 Mussolini sagely told a visiting correspondent from the *Chicago Daily News* that he and his government stood four-square 'for the greatest economic liberty',[51] and, later that year, De' Stefani, to the applause of the markets, announced that the national budget was in surplus.[52] Mussolini may by then have been engaged in liquidating liberal ideals in the political and cultural worlds, but he was as yet very cautious about the economic one, either because of his own native sense of good housekeeping or his canny realisation that money commanded respect both from a liberal and a Fascist.

The Minister of Work and Welfare was Stefano Cavazzoni, another adroit choice. Cavazzoni was a member of the conservative wing of the PPI and, by April 1923, was urging the party congress to follow his lead in accepting collaboration with Mussolini, a suggestion enhanced by the Fascists' benign treatment of the Vatican's *Banco di Roma*, which had been in difficulties in October 1922, but had been rescued by the government's official and unofficial help. Other Catholic conservatives similarly evinced a liking for dictatorship, since, they averred, a dictator was someone who could be seen taking responsibility and could be relied on to stem the threatening tide of Bolshevism, Freemasonry and that democracy for which sinful man was not morally ready.[53] Pius XI probably did not demur from these ideas and, although Luigi Sturzo for a while was stubborn in his commitment to the survival of his party, by July 1923 he had resigned office. Thereafter, the PPI, unblessed by the Vatican, drifted towards its final dissolution in 1926.

But what of the Fascist party itself? How did its members view the events in Rome and what was Mussolini's policy to be towards his own supporters, whom he knew were likely to be demanding, chary of discipline and hostile towards any return to normality? On 5 November the answer seemed clear as Mussolini telegraphed firm advice to his prefects and police to stop that social violence which 'bloodies and dishonours the nation'. Many participants in Sunday skirmishes had donned an ideological dress, he added, but their real motives arose from 'petty local and personal passions'.[54] It was time to reimpose the authority of the national state against both the enemies of Fascism and the Fascists. Even Gaetano Salvemini, the most purist of Anti-Fascists, now admitted that 'Mussolini is not as mad as the hordes of Fascist youths', or as D'Annunzio, 'the maddest of all', who, he still feared, would try to oust the *Duce* on a 'superfascist programme'.[55]

Salvemini was not reading the political situation with great accuracy or acumen, but it was worth asking whether the instructions to cool the social crisis were likely to be carried out by the officials, or were fully approved by the Fascists in the provinces, or even by Mussolini himself. On most issues the *Duce* continued to speak with two or more voices. In his initial speech to the Chamber of Deputies, he proclaimed roundly that 'the revolution has its rights'. He and his party had overwhelmed their opponents and, if he wanted, he could show just what such supremacy meant, 'converting this dumb, grey, chamber into a barrack for my legions. ... I could shut parliament down and constitute an exclusively Fascist administration. I could, but at least for the moment, I don't want to'.[56] But these were not his only words. On an occasion like the death of Sidney Sonnino, moral leader of Italian conservatism, the new Prime Minister could be all propriety as he urged that 'the interests of the *Patria* must transcend all'.[57] Similarly, he was ostentatiously respectful when he mentioned the Church. His own spirit, he announced, was, contrary to much evidence, 'profoundly religious'; the Catholic religion constituted 'a fundamental force which should be respected and defended'.[58] Pious to the Church, respectful to the King, on many occasions polite to the national establishment,[59] but still the black-shirted Fascist *Duce*, Mussolini kept his options open. When he told some provincial Fascists ringingly: 'I am the trustee of the will of the best young people in Italy, I am the trustee for the passion of thousands of dead, I am the trustee of that great struggle of ideals and power which has been bubbling away in our younger generation',[60] it was unclear whether he was trying to curb or to unleash his listeners' political passions.

Words apart, evidence mounted that a revolution was being

institutionalised. Before October Mussolini had talked about creating a body parallel to the parliament and separate from it. Such an organisation, he had argued, would be more efficient and less given to windy speechifying than was the Chamber or Senate. On 15 December it became clear what he had meant as, the press was informed, the Grand Council (*Gran Consiglio*) of Fascism had assembled (in the *Duce*'s private apartment at the Grand Hotel).[61] At the same time the ordinary Cabinet continued to meet – by the end of the month, it could boast 12 sessions[62] – as Mussolini commenced his Prime Ministerial work 'like a catapult'.[63] In the flurry of administrative activity, however, no attempt was made for the moment to define the relationship between the Cabinet and the Grand Council. All that was clear was that, on the register of the Council's members were the great names of the Fascist movement which had been so notably absent from the Cabinet. The *quadrumvirs*, those who had headed the March on Rome, Italo Balbo, Cesare De Vecchi, Michele Bianchi, Emilio De Bono (from November 1922 Chief of Police), were there. So were Edmondo Rossoni, leader of the Fascist unions, Nicola Sansanelli, a colourless figure soon briefly to replace Bianchi as PNF secretary, Giuseppe Bastianini and Attilio Teruzzi. Aldo Finzi took the minutes. He, Massimo Rocca and party press officer Cesare Rossi were the only ones destined not to have long and distinguished careers under the dictatorship. Present, too, at the second meeting of the Council in January 1923, were Dino Grandi, Achille Starace, Francesco Giunta, Piero Pisenti and a number of others. An entourage was assembling; henchmen were finding a role and the Grand Council of Fascism began to challenge the left-over liberal institutions as the place where key matters were discussed and decided.

The Council's initial act indeed smacked of revolution. The party chiefs had been worried about the way 'best to utilise the Fascists' military organisations'. Their solution was to create the *Milizia per la Sicurezza Nazionale*, soon to be the *Milizia Volontaria per la Sicurezza Nazionale* or MVSN (Voluntary Militia for National Security).[64] Such a body could channel Fascist energy and stand at the ready should any Anti-Fascists seek seriously to oppose the new government. Here was evidence that a Fascist understanding of law and legal process was not what liberals publicly assumed it to be. As the second meeting of the Council was told, the MVSN would be 'Fascist in its essence', designed stoutly to defend the 'revolution of October'.[65] The MVSN would compose the revolutionary guard.

But, again, matters might not be as straightforward as they seemed.

Between these first two meetings of the Grand Council Mussolini had faced a crisis in his relations with the party. For three days just before Christmas 1922 Fascist squads rampaged through Turin, city of Fiat, the Agnelli family and of much industry as well as of Gramsci, his paper, *L'Ordine Nuovo*, the office of which was now sacked, a university where Marxist ideas had possessed considerable influence, and a working class with a decided sense of itself. Here was an Anti-Fascist citadel that had not fallen before the March on Rome. Now the Turin Fascists, led by *quadrumvir* De Vecchi, exacted brutal revenge, at a cost of a dozen lives and much scandal.[66] An analysis of the event reveals two apparent oddities about it. The initiative for the murders and burnings was local. Mussolini did not order them in any direct fashion; indeed, on the first day of the 'action', he wrote to De Vecchi to complain of rumours that the Piedmontese leader had been claiming responsibility for the March on Rome, when he knew very well: 'I planned it, I wanted it and I imposed it.'[67] De Vecchi responded at once, denying everything and pledged sycophantically: 'I am the follower and you are the chief'.[68] However, his actions in Turin implied that his loyalty and deference were not absolute and he was indeed willing to find means to pressure his leader into acknowledging his significance and merit.

But De Vecchi's world did not revolve around Mussolini alone. In the complexity of life, he had other more pressing foes. The Fascism of Turin, like Fascism in most parts of the country, was riddled with factional disputes. Typically, these set radical and *petit bourgeois* Fascists against their more conservative and socially respectable colleagues. In Naples, for example, the charismatic and intransigently radical Aurelio Padovani, who had emerged as the city's Fascist chief in 1921 and was for a time a member of the Grand Council, in 1923 was challenged by forces led by Paolo Greco, an ex-Nationalist with many friends among local businessmen. Greco, it was soon clear, could rely on backing from Mussolini[69] and, amid much toing and froing, Padovani surrendered his political role (and, in 1926, his life when he fell somewhat mysteriously from his balcony).[70]

Similar disputes can be described in every town and city. So, in Turin, De Vecchi's authority was opposed by Pietro Gorgolini and Mario Gioda (this last, the founder of the Turin *fascio* in 1919, was an ex-anarchist), who still espoused the radical ideals of Piazza San Sepolcro. De Vecchi by contrast was a monarchist, with friends among the Nationalists and in the Army and Church.[71] It might have been expected that the raid against the working class of Turin would be the work of the radicals. But, actually, it was the other way round. De Vecchi and his men were responsible for the murders and, indeed, were bitterly criticised by Gorgolini and Gioda for the savagery of their actions. Anti-Fascist Turin may have fallen, but other Fascists opposed the method of its defeat. The results were complex. In May 1923 Mussolini felt strong enough to sack De Vecchi from his govern-mental position and did so with a peremptoriness of phrasing which became his custom.[72] Since, even out of office, De Vecchi retained friends of his own, in October 1923 he was sent to be Governor of Somalia, a distant post in which it was devoutly hoped he would not be a nuisance.[73] This fate, however, did not destroy De Vecchi's influ-ence in Turin. He was destined to be that city's leading Fascist throughout the regime (even though Mussolini regularly practised his wit on his ineffable stupidity).[74] Gioda, by contrast, left the party in 1924. And there was one other paradoxical effect. Turin remained through the Fascist years still its own place; its citizens continued to think of themselves as Torinese, and a slippage among the workers back into their old enthusiam for socialism and democracy was never far from the surface of Fascist and 'totalitarian' life.[75] Turin had gone 'Fascist' in its own manner and in a way which had certainly not been directly planned by Mussolini. Turin was to prove a city highly recal-citrant to any expectation that it might 'work towards its *Duce*'.

The *fatti di Torino* do, however, reinforce the argument that, in the short term, the creation of the MVSN was at least as much directed at calming the Fascists as at pushing the revolution further.[76] Indeed, in June 1923 Mussolini boasted to the receptive audience of the Senate that the gravest issue resolved by his government so far was 'the problem of squadrism' and the squads' resistance to 'the authority of the state'.[77] Local *ras* were not so entranced by such claims and quite a few remained suspicious of the MVSN as an institution designed to centralise and to control.[78] It was useful, of course, in absorbing the Nationalists' *Sempre pronti* squads, though the Army was, unsurpris-ingly, critical of a body which might derogate from its own authority. Still more emphatically, Anti-Fascists regarded the squads, whatever their form, as the epitome of Fascist tyranny. Mussolini, it seemed, was looking for means to govern the country in a more drastic sense than had his predecessors but, in 1923, it was not at all clear that he had found the means fully to bridge the ancient gap between 'legal' Italy and 'real' Italy.

While domestic business was his main concern, Mussolini could not escape foreign affairs. In his first two months in office he travelled to

Switzerland and to London, as negotiations proceeded on reparations and other issues left over from the war. Even before leaving Milan to take up office in Rome, on 29 October he had issued a press release with the somewhat anodyne message that his government would pursue an international policy 'based on dignity, and avoiding both hesitation and threats'.[79] Once appointed Prime Minister, Mussolini added, in a simile common in Nationalist circles, that 'Italy wishes to be treated by the great nations of the world like a sister and not like a waitress'. Characteristically, his first speech to the Chamber of Deputies blew both hot and cold. The *Duce* had promised that the new government would accept all treaties as binding, even though, he added fiercely, 'the revolution has its rights' both at home and abroad. All the same, Italian policy, he promised, would be strictly realist, based on the *do ut des* principle.[80]

The London *Times*, then still the most thunderous of international organs, had suggested that 'the Fascisti', although 'a strange organisation of mixed origin' whose 'violence may too easily degenerate into excess', nonetheless stood for 'a return to the older creative ideals of Italian Liberalism',[81] and so Mussolini wondered if conservative Britain might now respond to an appeal from 'conservative Italy', as he defined his government.[82] *The Times*, which, like many foreign observers, was ready and anxious to believe that Fascism possessed a 'good' as well as a 'bad' side and hoped that Mussolini embodied the former, did worry lest Italian diplomacy go 'wild'.[83] And the paper's fears were shared by the diplomatic world. However, Mussolini's initial threats to pursue a revolutionary foreign policy, if that was what they were, soon subsided. A second speech on the international situation in February 1923 pledged in statesmanlike vein that 'originality is impossible in foreign policy'.[84] British ambassador, Sir Ronald Graham, was soon reporting that Mussolini was 'a statesman of exceptional ability and enterprise',[85] 'if inclined to be hasty and violent'. None the less, he added, Mussolini 'reacts no less quickly [to reality] and is willing to learn by experience'. His 'Fascista government' was doing well abroad and at home.[86] There were days when he fell into 'fits of ungovernable rage' and to some extent the *Duce* was 'a strange man and has lately caused some comment by driving about through Rome in his two-seater with a well-grown lion cub sitting beside him'. However, Graham advised, 'the Italians seem to like this sort of thing', and, after his moments of acting up, Mussolini soon calmed and was then open to sweet reason like any other gentleman.[87] To international observers, the domestication of Benito Mussolini, the adaptation necessary to render him 'one of us', did not look too arduous a task.

Among his own diplomats, any early doubts were also soon overcome. The Italian foreign service was deeply infected with the ideals of the ANI. At the same time, officials were usually suspicious of the populism of Fascism and sardonic about the provincial uncouthness of the new national leader – one of their number took time out to teach the *Duce* the smatterings of official etiquette.[88] Much later commentary has exaggerated the conflict between Mussolini and his diplomatic staff. In reality, right through to 1940 there is far more evidence of a commonality in their views than of profound disputation. The Fascist revolution was not so out of kilter with the unspoken political and social assumptions of diplomacy for the new government to cause any particular dislocation. Only one leading figure resigned – Carlo Sforza, by October 1922 no longer Foreign Minister but ambassador in Paris[89] – and, among the lower ranks of the Ministry, there was only one other case of public dissidence.[90] The diplomats, like the rest of officialdom, were true to the classically bureaucratic principles of ostensible calm, obfuscation and procrastination. The Fascist excitation, they believed profoundly, would not last; things only ever changed to remain the same. As the very experienced Giacomo De Martino explained carefully, crafting his words so that they contained many messages, any sense of alarm felt by elite circles in Britain, where he served as ambassador, had been diminished, as the Fascist government had settled down. The City in particular, he added meaningfully, was ready to approve the Fascist experiment.[91] The Chargé in Washington agreed.[92] So long as their words were understood, such advisers were gently pushing their new Prime Minister towards what they hoped would be a realistic assessment of where power resided and how it was best approached by a nation of Italy's modest international authority. As one of their number underlined in his memoirs, the best sort of Prime Minister fulfilled the role of Naples' San Gennaro, that is was one who agreed to be exhibited once a year and remain a mystery the rest of the time.[93] But would Fascist Italy indeed 'settle down'? Or would Mussolini kick against the pricks? As the first months of 1923 passed, commentators at home and abroad were unclear whether Fascism or Italy, ideological belief or national interest, better defined the new government's comprehension of the wider world.

Expressions of nationalism were hard to restrain and Mussolini was not the only Italian to hope for a grander national presence in the world. Historian Gioacchino Volpe, an intellectual pillar of the regime, wrote in *Gerarchia*, for example, that Corsicans carried 'our imprint in the plainest possible way' and hoped that the French would remember that 'Corsican history is also our history'.[94] Margherita Sarfatti, too, had taken herself off to Tunis where the majority of European immigrants were indeed Italian. The account she prepared in November 1923, endorsed with a preface from her lover under the pompous pseudonym 'Latinus', urged the preservation and development of the *italianità* of the Italians there, even if Sarfatti had to admit that the French were good administrators and failed to avoid the clichéd conclusion that Arabs were 'great big children at heart'.[95]

Italy's relations with the Greater Powers constituted one important issue. But what of the smaller states? Among these the most troubling was Greece, a country frequently lambasted in Nationalist circles. One of the first messages about the international situation which Mussolini received urged him on no account to weaken in the determination to keep the Dodecanese islands, occupied by Italy since 1912 and the object of prolonged international treatying,[96] out of Greek hands. The Greeks, Mussolini was told, were a people incapable of gratitude. Their superior, Italy, must treat them firmly as a good master might.[97]

The rest of the Balkans, Africa, even the world beyond that might raise problems for a patriotic government. So myriad were the international concerns that, on 28 August 1923, Mussolini advised his prefects, whom he had previously urged to ensure their precedence in any issues of local hierarchy over PNF chiefs,[98] again to restrain any Fascist overenthusiasm. 'The most delicate problems of international order', the Prime Minister explained, 'are presently coming to the surface'.[99] A full-scale crisis was brewing between Italy and Greece.

Mussolini's own interventions over foreign questions had been few, and, despite occasional flourishes, had so far scarcely departed far from the Italian norm. But on 28 August Mussolini cabled his minister in Athens, the euphoniously named Giulio Cesare Montagna, urging 'immediate and exemplary punishment' for those who, the day before, had committed a 'barbarous massacre',[100] which had just been reported from the Greek–Albanian frontier. An Italian general Enrico Tellini, heading an inter-allied commission surveying the border, was among those killed.[101] The Greeks blamed bandits, but Montagna suggested that the current Greek government had acted as the assassins' financier or worse and, on 29 August, Mussolini ordered the Italian fleet to ready itself to occupy the island of Corfu, unless the Greeks accepted within 20 hours a stiff set of demands. These even

involved such humiliating pinpricks as the Greek government's attendance at a funeral ceremony in the Roman Catholic cathedral in
Athens, where each minister should publicly honour the Italian flag,
as well as the urgent payment of a swingeing financial indemnity of 50
million lire.[102] In reply, the Greeks were conciliatory, but the die was
cast and, on 31 August, Italian troops landed on Corfu. In the confusion of disembarcation the island had been bombarded without
warning for some minutes beforehand. Fascist Italy was announcing
itself on the international stage with what seemed a replica of the
squadrist raids, so ruthlessly deployed against its socialist and other
domestic enemies.

Then, 'salutary violence', as the Fascists enjoyed defining it, had
regularly brought the collapse of opposition. But the diplomatic world
was more complicated than were the Italian provinces. Once Corfu had
been seized, it was not at all clear what was meant to come next, and
Mussolini was soon circularising his diplomats with the strange advice
that their nation had engaged in a 'peaceful and provisional' invasion.[103] Leading Fascists, even so socially respectable a one as Giovanni
Giuriati, eventually to be secretary of the PNF, were soon suggesting
that Mussolini exploit the opportunity provided, withdraw Italy from
the League of Nations and so proclaim that the revolution was not
prepared to suffer the yoke of international control.[104] By contrast,
some career officials – the wily and experienced Sicilian Salvatore
Contarini, the Secretary General of the Foreign Ministry, had been
driven by the summer heat to absent himself from the capital for the
more pleasant climate on Ischia – were deeply troubled by the precipitate nature of the action and aghast at the failure to anticipate what
might happen thereafter.

Moreover, Mussolini soon found that he was not just dealing with
Greece. In Britain, France and elsewhere, the drastic nature of the
Italian act reminded people not so much of a squadrist raid as the ill-
fated Austrian ultimatum to Serbia in 1914. The unilateral occupation
of Corfu was read as a direct Italian challenge to the newly formed
League of Nations with its untested promises of peace preserved
through collective security. There was much concern, especially in the
press, where the London *Times* was moved to editorialise magisterially
that the fall of Fascism might be bad for Italy, but the fall of the League
would be bad for Europe.[105] In reaction Mussolini raged to his
bemused ambassador in London that 'the utterly unacceptable English
press campaign' was likely to cause permanent damage to relations
between the two Powers.[106] Many historians, convinced that Fascism

of any kind meant war, have agreed that 'Europe was seeing a type of diplomacy which was to reach its zenith and its most cynical form in the coming decade'.[107] 'More than any other individual perhaps', they have suggested, 'Mussolini was responsible for the collapse of the League; [the attack on] Ethiopia [in 1935] was the climax of the erosion begun at Corfu.'[108]

There are, however, some problems associated with the argument that the *Duce*'s little burst of aggression was the act of 'one man alone'. There is every reason to believe that elite opinion in Italy supported the 'firmness' of Mussolini's treatment of the Greeks.[109] Italy's most significant, still liberal, paper, *Il Corriere della Sera*, under its renowned editor, Luigi Albertini, fully backed the government, criticising, for example, the British reaction and generally arguing that Italy was displaying 'moderation' and 'self-sacrifice' towards the 'brutally offensive' Greeks.[110] Antonio Salandra, the conservative who had taken Italy into the First World War and now national representative to the League in Geneva, similarly endorsed Mussolini's decision, praising a government which was willing to bolster national prestige.[111] Thaon di Revel, the naval chief, had been planning an action against the Greeks for months, since a dispute over the ownership of the Dodecanese islands had continued to simmer. Indeed, on 1 August Thaon had advised Mussolini that a full-scale naval war with Greece could earn a 'maximum profit with a minimum of risk' and, parroting the language of the Nationalists, suggested that it should not be long before the Adriatic was made into 'an Italian lake'.[112] Antonio Foschini, the commander who actually landed on Corfu, was, according to his memoirs, much more aware of working under Thaon than of responding to the *Duce* whom he had never met.[113]

In other words, the Corfu incident offers considerable evidence for the Togliatti thesis that, at least in so far as international policy was concerned, the Fascist regime tended frequently to follow where the Nationalists had pointed.[114] Mussolini was not acting in a way that was out of line with their wishes and habits. Nor, should the truth be known, was his critique of the vagueness and confusion of the League of Nations absent from the thoughts of conservatives in such countries as Britain and France. Among the London press, the *Morning Post*, *Daily Mail* and even the *Observer* invoked *Realpolitik* to justify their appreciation of Italy's actions, rejecting the prospect of being dragged into the role of an 'international policeman'. Mussolini's 'virile direction' of his country, they said, was to be applauded.[115] By January, even *Headway*, the journal of sympathisers with the new diplomacy, averred that Mussolini counted 'for something more than Fascism'.[116] Neither in the 1920s nor the 1930s would Mussolini be the only European to doubt the efficacy of the League of Nations.

In any case, the Corfu crisis was proving a short summer storm. On 12 September Thaon had advised his leader that, if events pitted it against the British Royal Navy in the Mediterranean, the Italian fleet could only survive for 'forty-eight hours'.[117] Fifteen days later the Italian occupation of the island ended, and the conflict between Italy and Greece was left to international accommodation. The League, for the moment, had held and Italy had been shown yet again that it was the least of the Great Powers. On the other hand, there was little sign that Mussolini's own image had been damaged by the Corfu crisis. Indeed, on 23 September he was informed by his secret service that the British ambassador in Rome, Sir Ronald Graham, rejected the view that the *Duce*'s actions had been too 'impulsive'; rather, Graham had advised the authorities back in the UK, Mussolini had shown himself to possess limitless 'energy'. The *Duce*'s sceptical realism meant that friendship with his Italy could from now on be based on a rigorous assessment of gain and loss.[118] Nor was Graham Mussolini's only foreign admirer. As early as November 1922 intelligence had been received in Rome that a certain 'Hittler', chief of the Bavarian 'Fascists', was impressed with recent events in Italy and anxious to develop better ties with the new administration.[119] Mussolini showed some interest in the potentially fraternal German movement, but the fiasco of the 'Beer Hall putsch' in November 1923 persuaded him for the moment that Hitler and his associates were 'buffoons'.[120] The more typical foreign sympathiser with Mussolini's policies was presently the Spanish general, Miguel Primo De Rivera who, visiting Rome two months after his September 1923 *pronunciamiento*, was much impressed. 'Your figure', he told the *Duce*, 'is not just an Italian one. You are the apostle of the world campaign against dissolution and anarchy. . . . Fascism is a universal phenomenon that ought to conquer all nations. . . . Fascism is a living gospel.'[121] As slightly double-edged reward, Primo was hailed by his king, Alfonso XIII, as 'mon petit Mussolini'.[122]

Such flattery of the Italian leader was all very well, but foreign diplomats noticed also that the ebullience at Corfu, once it subsided, was not repeated, at least in the short-term. Italian foreign policy possessed some wobbles in the 1920s, but did not again seek to astonish the world. Rather, it was the fate of Fascism domestically and his construction of a regime to govern Italy which had all along been Mussolini's main priority.

In that regard, the *Duce*'s first preoccupation had been a highly practical one, a matter which augmented the tendency of a number of his contemporaries to view him as the new Giolitti.[123] Mussolini wanted to organise some elections. After all, he still was only the leader of thirty-five Fascist deputies in the Chamber. Now he needed to solidify a broad support to ensure that he would, for the foreseeable future, be as politically indispensable as Giolitti had been from 1901 to 1915. Two techniques were employed, one legal, the other more overtly Fascist and revolutionary. Giacomo Acerbo, the respectable Fascist from the Abruzzi, acting on an initial plan by his fellow Southerner Michele Bianchi, had drafted a law which worked its way with some controversy though the parliament during the summer and autumn of 1923. It entailed a reward in terms of seats to be assigned for the largest party which won more than 25 per cent of the total suffrage available and so was directed at the creation of a stable majority in a multi-party system. The Left in great majority opposed the measure, as did Farinacci for different motives among the more intransigent Fascists. But Giolitti, Salandra, Orlando, *Il Corriere della Sera* and, by implication, the Vatican and the King all endorsed it,[124] amid much complacent conservative rhetoric about unifying the nation and refurbishing the authority of the executive. In November the 'Acerbo law' went through the Senate in a single sitting. In January, with the approval of King Victor Emmanuel III, the parliament was dissolved. Elections were scheduled for 6 April.

This much was constitutional; but what of the Fascist party and its activities in the world outside Rome? Social violence had not ceased. The killing of the left-Catholic priest Giovanni Minzoni near Ferrara in August 1923 was only the most notorious of squadrist deeds. In a frequent correspondence with Mussolini, Farinacci, who had assumed the mantle of most Fascist of the Fascists, continued to urge intransigence and to attack the retention of office by any from the old establishment.[125] The *ras* of Cremona remained a zealous advocate of 'the methods of intelligent surgery' against those who evinced lingering doubts about Fascism and its revolutionary victory.[126]

Farinacci's level of ideological sophistication was not high. But Fascism was trying to establish itself intellectually. In June 1923 the Roman, ex-Nationalist, Giuseppe Bottai (born 1895), under Mussolini's spell since they had met in 1919,[127] announced with considerable fanfare the first issue of a journal to be entitled *Critica Fascista* and boasting on its editorial board a roll of honour of Fascists and Fascist sympathisers including Acerbo, Balbo, Bastianini, Bianchi, Corradini,

Federzoni, Forges Davanzati, Gentile, Giunta, Grandi, E.M. Gray, Sergio Panunzio, Rocca, Rocco, Cesare Rossi, and Rossoni. A first editorial explained the need to solidify the 'revolution' by 'stabilising certain political and spiritual values'. The imprint of Nationalism was very strong. Indeed Corradini wrote the first article elucidating 'the historic nature of political doctrines'. Forges Davanzati, another Nationalist who had once been employed to stiffen popular morale after the Caporetto defeat, went on to argue that Fascism should not be regarded as being in government, but instead as having become the government. Having overwhelmed the defeated 'parties', it incarnated a new generation, and must move forward to build a genuine nation-state, stiffened by 'all the best forces' in Italian society. Panunzio, a (Southern) philosopher of syndicalism, added that socialism was now utterly defeated, but that Fascism was rooted in its own unions, which ensured that Fascism and the state were becoming identical.[128]

Here, then, was a limning of matters that would be discussed both under the regime and by the post-1945 historiography. In a second issue of *Critica Fascista*, Mussolini himself wrote an preface, expressing his pleasure at the idea of disciplined criticism. 'Professor Mussolini' once more, he was glad that Fascism could show itself to be intellectually productive and was delighted when Bottai proclaimed Fascism 'intellectual above everything else'.[129] Fascism, Mussolini emphasised, must be 'educational', or it was nothing.[130] In the following months, Bottai and others kept up their demands that the revolution not turn passive. Fascism, Bottai wrote, as 'a revealed religion has reached a point where it must codify itself and build its temples'.[131] In the Grand Council, too, the regime talked about its 'historic mission' to build a 'new ruling class for the nation' and praised the fighting spirit still evident in the MVSN, while adding more cautiously that 'every attempt to separate Mussolini and Fascism is inane and absurd'.[132]

Bottai did not forget respect, either. Local party bosses erred when they grew too independent. They must comprehend that their *Duce* was 'a man full of power and sweetness, who has not forgotten and will not forget that to rule is neither just a matter of convincing people nor of forcing them but rather an exquisite synthesis of both. ... As far as we are concerned Fascists have only one way to be genuinely Mussolinian and that is to live the life of the party intelligently'. Resisting the siren song of those who were 'discontented, deluded, incapable and unworthy', Fascists should try automatically to second the 'struggles and preoccupations of the Chief'.[133] In his continuing programme and mental attitude, Bottai, something of a perpetual adolescent, would spend two generations working towards his *Duce*. But the question remains: how many other Italians were as ready to subjugate their souls to Mussolini as was Bottai?

Nor did expressions of loyalty or love salve Mussolini's own deepening sense of the hollowness of life. As the elections were being held, he published in *Gerarchia* a disquisition on Machiavelli. He had, he remarked, just re-read the Florentine writer's corpus, although, he added modestly, he had not fully plumbed the secondary literature in Italy and abroad. Machiavelli's thought was, Mussolini announced, more alive now than ever. His pessimism about human nature was eternal in its acuity. Individuals simply could not be relied on voluntarily to 'obey the law, pay their taxes and serve in war'. No well-ordered society could want the people to be sovereign. Machiavelli's cynical acumen exposed the fatuity of the dreams of the Enlightenment (and of Mussolini's own political philosophy before 1914).[134]

If dark thoughts about human nature could not altogether be dispelled from his mind, for the present matters seemed set fair for the *Duce*. Addressing party faithful in January 1924 Mussolini warned them against developing ideas about a leader pushed this way or that by good or bad counsellors. Rather, in his 'not at all sociable life', he made his decisions in the solitude of his soul and often late at night. Each morning five or six men came briefly in to instruct him about the condition of Italy. He listened to them, but then made up his own mind.[135] This gospel about his charisma and his 'savagery' continued to win converts. All over the country, men from the elite hastened to join the *listone* (big list), as the government ticket for the elections was called. Arnaldo Mussolini passed on the sage and very northern advice to his brother that, south of Rome, the *listone* should cheerfully accommodate the old elite, since there 'personalities' and not parties were what counted.[136] With the government able to rely on widespread approval from the 'best people', the electoral campaign proceeded in relative calm and, all decorum, Mussolini again explicitly instructed the prefects to suppress violence from whichever part of the political spectrum it originated.[137]

The result was a triumph. The *listone* had not needed the assistance of the provisions of the Acerbo law, since the government won more than half the votes in the North of Italy, 76 per cent in the Centre and 81.5 per cent in the South where, 18 months earlier, Fascism had scarcely existed. Never before in Italian national history since 1861 had there been such a resounding victory. Moreover, in its aftermath, Mussolini sought to take consensus further, coolly reviving the idea of an accord with the moderate socialists. Could reformist leader Filippo Turati and trade union chief Ludovico D'Aragona, it was asked, be 'transformed' into a fully united, national government?[138]

Some on the Left remained determined to oppose the Fascist tide. Among them was Giacomo Matteotti, himself a reformist but a man especially hated by the Fascists because of his class and regional background – his family in Rovigo were prominent in a local bank[139] – and because he had so firmly rejected the patriotic option in the First World War. Matteotti also had excellent international contacts and, in April 1924, he travelled to London and met some Labour leaders. On 30 May, again in Italy, Matteotti spoke up in the Chamber against what he said had been fraudulent elections, in which the level of cynical violence might be compared with Mexico, were it not for the fact that such a statement insulted the Mexicans.[140] More worryingly, it was rumoured that Matteotti had collected damning evidence about Fascist corruption. Vast bribes, it seemed, had been paid by Sinclair Oil, an American company with flourishing ties to such prominent bankers as Samuel Guggenheim, J.P. Morgan and Andrew Mellon, in order to secure the right to control petrol distribution in Italy.[141] There were also tales of illicit arms trading. Arnaldo Mussolini was thought to be implicated in some of the deals,[142] as were others in the *Duce*'s entourage, including Finzi, a very wealthy Fascist from the Polesine and so from Matteotti's immediate world.[143] If its violence had not condemned it, was Fascism about to fall beneath the weight of party corruption?

It was not. On 10 June the sensational news spread that Matteotti had been kidnapped. Armed men had grabbed him while he was walking near his house by the Tiber, bundling him forcibly into their car which had then sped off. The leader of the squad involved was Amerigo Dumini. Born in 1896 to emigrants in St. Louis, Missouri, Dumini had excellent contacts which reached up to the *Duce* himself. Matteotti had been taken on a journey from which he was not destined to return. No news of the oil or other possible scandals was further to disturb the press. But Matteotti's abduction threatened to destroy the edifice which Mussolini had been so adroitly and single-mindedly constructing since October 1922. Would his coalition survive murder not just in the provinces, but on the streets of the capital and where blood seemed to stain the hands of the Prime Minister himself?

9

The imposition of dictatorship, 1924–1925

A T the beginning of June 1924, having established himself as the 'new man' of post-war politics, Mussolini seemed entrenched in a certain sort of power. He had enjoyed administering a nation and had proved lively and adroit in keeping together his coalition of support and, indeed, in expanding it. He had been careful to ingratiate himself with the old Liberals, the most significant of whom had joined his *listone* in the elections.[1] He had continued to harness the 'energy' of provincial Fascism with skill and ruthlessness, deploring 'useless' violence[2] but by no means rejecting the intimidation of his surviving political opponents. 'Order', Fascist order, he was given to proclaiming, was a fundamental national concern; without it, the lira might fall[3] and the nation be unable to assert its proper place in the world. Since October 1922 Mussolini had successfully presented himself both as the Fascist *Duce*, commander of a crusading militia, and as a statesman-in-the-making, in Rome set high above petty local concerns. With his huge electoral victory he had achieved a position of political strength beyond that imagined by Giolitti or Crispi, Depretis or Cavour. Here, indeed, was a man who, had he wanted, could have become a 'parliamentary dictator' with few dangers or threats lurking in his path. In less than two years, Benito Mussolini had made himself the Italian politician of whom everyone, both within his country and without, had heard.

Did he, then, know where he was going? Was he already determined to be a Fascist dictator? Some analysts say so.[4] His personality certainly remained domineering, and his tactical relationship with his own party was such that either he was acknowledged as its unchallenged leader or the Fascist movement was relegated to the provinces and he must find another vehicle through which to obtain power.

Furthermore, he had never hidden his contempt for much parliamentary practice, although the zeal with which he applied himself to managing an election suggested that he had still not discounted the Chamber as a seat of authority. Most importantly, Mussolini was distinguished from his Liberal predecessors in understanding that, even in relatively backward Italy, a successful politician now required a means or a rhetoric which could bind a very considerable percentage of the population to his cause. The depressed democrat, Gaetano Salvemini, may have declared sadly that only some 100 000 Italians really cared about their nation,[5] and it was true that much of peasant and female Italy was politicised in the most marginal of senses and could easily slip back into the patterns of the pre-modern political and social worlds. But Mussolini had recognised that, after the mobilising which had gone on during the First World War, all Italians had to be addressed politically. As never before, they needed to believe that they belonged to the nation-state. In one way or another, as Prime Minister or as dictator, Mussolini would want to press forward with the 'nationalisation of the masses'.[6]

And yet historians need to be careful. Hindsight always smooths the confusions and compromises of real life, locating patterns and inevitabilities where they may not have existed. Whether Mussolini, as yet, knew that he was travelling to a 'totalitarian' end, as it would soon come to be called, and that he was destined to impose a secular religion whose most obvious characteristic would be his own deification, may be doubted. The Mussolini who liked to crash through or to crash seemed balanced by the more machiavellian traditional politician who was at his happiest negotiating deals with all sides. Not for nothing was Mussolini, in the aftermath of his electoral victory, rumoured to be reviving thoughts, expressed three years before in the pact of pacification and never entirely abandoned,[7] that a 'transformation' of some socialists into governmental ranks might yet be possible.[8] In June 1924 Mussolini was still endeavouring to combine the roles of Prime Minister of a coalition administration and Fascist *Duce*.

The kidnapping and murder of Matteotti marked a major crisis in Mussolini's life. Was he responsible for the killing? His Italian biographer De Felice says no, or at least not directly.[9] The most recent historian of the event, Mauro Canali, disagrees, ascribing direct blame to the *Duce*.[10] In Canali's view a *Ceka* had been established in July 1923 as a 'secret criminal organisation at Mussolini's command'.[11] Its creation signalled the commencement of 'totalitarian' state terrorism, even if the killing of Matteotti had been arranged to silence him more because of the practical matter of the oil scandal than as an attack on 'Anti-Fascism'.

Canali's detail is impressive, but perhaps the case against Mussolini remains 'not-proven', to utilise that significant Scottish legal term. There can be little doubt that Mussolini had, on many occasions, condoned and encouraged violence and murder, and that he hated Matteotti.[12] It is clear, too, that the squad led by Dumini planned their attack with the foreknowledge of the highest circles of the Fascist party, and with the direct assistance of such figures as Marinelli, Finzi, Cesare Rossi and Filippo Filippelli, the editor of *Il Corriere Italiano* and a major contact to the financial world for Arnaldo Mussolini.[13] On the night of 9–10 June Dumini and his associates parked their car, which had been obtained for them by Filippelli, in the *cortile* of the Palazzo Chigi itself, with the justification that *Cavalier* Dumini was an assistant of Rossi, engaged on important business in Rome.[14] Equally, the legal processes after the event were designed to avoid any thorough investigation and, though Dumini and other members of the squad did go to gaol, they scarcely suffered the punishment they deserved.

And yet some questions remain. Both Dumini and his enforcer, the butcher Albino Volpi, earned themselves ample files in the *Duce*'s private secretariat. The content is curious. Each, either directly or through family members or friends, wrote to their dictator with a combination of pious respect and an open hint of blackmail. Asmara Norchi Volpi, for example, in May 1929 urged Mussolini's intervention to grant her husband a licence for a new market stall in Milan both because of what she described as the parlous economic circumstances of the Volpi family and because of the 'merit' Albino Volpi had earned (and would always be ready to earn) in the cause of 'Your Excellency and Fascism'.[15] Five years later, business still being bad for the Volpis, a friend reminded Mussolini of Volpi's 'faith, courage and devotion to the *Duce*', while Volpi himself assured the dictator that he did little except call down blessings on him, his loved ones and family.[16]

Still more striking is the correspondence with Dumini who, by 1939, had managed to extract from the regime subsidies which officials tallied in excess of 2.37 million lire.[17] In his letters to his *Duce*, Dumini was much given to asking: 'Can Your Excellency have forgotten what, in the years of danger, Amerigo Dumini did for the Idea'?[18] As he bled his patron, Dumini frequently philosophised about the Darwinian world in which fate might happily allow him to 'see the end of our suffering and the extermination of all those who seek in vain to ruin me and my whole family', malevolent people who pullulated and plotted within the ranks of the party as well as elsewhere.[19] Dumini, in other words, viewed himself much more as a client than as a selfless legionary of the Fascist creed. This impression is confirmed by a letter written by Dumini's mother to Mussolini complaining that the confining of her son to Longobuco in Calabria was intolerable since such a southern *paese* was 'a place for wild beasts, in regard to the climate, the isolation, and the food and lodging'.[20] The Duminis were scarcely convinced that every village in the South was an equal part of the Fascist nation, but they did know that one who assumed the status of a patron had obligations to his client.

The correspondence with the killers of Matteotti thus offers excellent evidence of the lingering of patron–client `relations and a patron–client mindset even in a boasted totalitarian state. But what does it demonstrate about Mussolini's guilt for the actual murder? The messages are mixed. In other regimes, Dumini, Volpi and the rest surely would not have survived their own importunity. Few thought blackmailing Hitler or Stalin a fruitful idea. Compared with the Night of the Long Knives in Nazi Germany, let alone the purges in Stalin's USSR, or the vicious pursuit of republican sympathisers in Franco's Spain, the killing of Matteotti was messy and amateurish, both in the event and after. When Matteotti was bundled into the car, a local *portiere* noted its number-plate[21] and it was soon traced. Did the squad really intend to kill the socialist or was their intention merely to beat him severely? If murder was the aim, the killers were remarkably incompetent in disposing of the corpse, which they eventually left by the road leading from Rome into the Sabine hills. Allegedly they had simply driven their Lancia around until almost out of petrol and then scrabbled a shallow grave at the roadside.[22] No preparations had been made to suppress or answer the inevitable hue and cry which developed over the fate of the disappeared deputy and which continued unabated until the body was found on 16 August. The panicky decision on 12 June to arrest Dumini, for fear that a chain of responsibility might lead to Mussolini, was another leap in the dark, certainly unplanned before the event. Finally, Mussolini himself would go out of his way to send financial assistance to the widow and children of Matteotti,[23] perhaps proof of guilt, but not an act of that cruelty and callousness which other dictators later so readily displayed. A dictator with at least the glimmering of a contrite heart both to his henchmen and his victims, if that is what Mussolini was, is an unusual figure on the brutal stage of twentieth-century history.

In any case, in the short term the greatest significance for Mussolini of the Matteotti murder lay in his political handling of the event. Here, after initial hesitations (both Rachele, his wife, and Margherita Sarfatti did their best to stiffen his morale),[24] Mussolini rose to the occasion and, from the edge of disaster, steered a course which led to his re-affirmation as national leader. Three forces stood in his path, each of great potential menace. How did the old elites, apparently convinced in their allegiance to liberal values and the law, cope with a Prime Minister implicated in murder? How, too, did the more radical opposition approach the occasion which seemed so promising for their Anti-Fascism? And what finally was the attitude of the Fascists of the provinces? Did they not want to use the killing of a socialist to take the revolution further and faster and now liquidate all their enemies, if necessary sloughing off the *Duce* in favour of some more drastically Fascist *ras*?

The King, the Pope, the Army, business, the elites of Italian political and civil society, and many a distinguished foreign observer[25] caused little difficulty. Their attitude to the crisis was well summed up in an editorial in the London *Times* which advised that 'homicide is more common ... [in Italy and its political circles] than in most other civilised states'.[26] The paper, none the less, did not formally condone murder and had harsh words for 'village ruffians' and 'hooligans in the towns who committed crimes on the pretext that they were serving the Fascist cause'. *The Times*' editorials even acknowledged that Mussolini might have 'provoked Nemesis himself'.[27] However, then and later, the paper's editor believed in the Prime Minister's ultimate good faith, backed his victory over 'Bolshevism' and agreed that his fall was 'too horrible to contemplate'.[28]

The Vatican's *Osservatore Romano* was similarly willing to forgive and forget, preaching in predictable parable: 'Let him who is without sin cast the first stone'.[29] The Monarchy agreed. Victor Emmanuel III, some months earlier, had praised Mussolini's 'capacity for work and extraordinary ability at assimilating information', applauding his defeat of the 'low game of the parties'.[30] After the elections, the King's speech to the Chamber had gone out of its way to salute the triumph of 'the generation of Victory [in the War] which now controls the government'.[31] And throughout the Matteotti crisis, Victor Emmanuel resisted calls for Mussolini's dismissal on the conveniently constitutional grounds that he was 'blind and deaf' until the Prime Minister lost his majority in the parliament, while noting in his diary that Salandra, too, was still a supporter of the Fascist chief.[32] The Army leadership, which had gone on disliking the MVSN's ideological commitment, its amateurism and its threat to the Army's own perquisites, took the occasion of the crisis to hand over 100 000 war surplus rifles to the party militia, thus confirming its preference for Mussolini over the alternatives.[33] Some business leaders deplored the murder, with Gino Olivetti briefly nourishing the heresy that 'the black flag may not be better than the red'.[34] However, the majority of Italian industrialists remembered instead their old catch-cry that politics was a dirty business, taking the self-interested line that now was the time to concentrate on their profits and leave others to make the big political choices.[35] Their decision was sweetened in September when Mussolini elevated a score of their number to the Senate.[36] Even liberal philosopher–historian Benedetto Croce favoured the 'best elements of Fascism' and refrained from campaigning against Mussolini.[37]

To be sure the first news of the murder, and Mussolini's initial embarrassment and unease in the Chamber on 11 and 13 June – the *Duce* talked weakly of 'devilish' plots against himself[38] – had worried quite a few liberals. The stock market briefly shook.[39] But, soon after, the crisis turned from being an issue of the law or of the tolerance of social violence to one of a conflict between Fascism and Anti-Fascism. In that dispute, the elites of old Italy knew where they stood.

It was the democratic and socialist left, joined by what remained of the *Popolari*, who had made the choice a stark one. On 13 June some hundred deputies abandoned the parliamentary chamber, branding the government itself unconstitutional. With that love of classical parallels they ironically shared with Mussolini, the Anti-Fascists called themselves the 'Aventine secession' on the model of what, on occasion, the plebs had done in republican Rome. While the King, Army and Pope wavered, the tribunes of the Left had opted for rigour and decency, but their virtue would not save them from defeat.

Mussolini knew how to outflank them. On 17 June he announced that the ex-Nationalist Luigi Federzoni was taking over the Ministry of the Interior, the fount of constitutional discipline in Italy. It was a brilliant choice.[40] Federzoni's respectability dissipated whatever doubts about Fascism and its leader currently afflicted members of the old elite. Federzoni's deference, demonstrated by the ease with which the ANI had accepted the merging of their movement with the National Fascist Party, ensured that he would not himself plot to thwart the *Duce*'s will.

In any case, the Anti-Fascists on the Aventine were finding that their gesture of disapproval and dismay was barren. The passage of time worked against them, bringing their numerous divisions to the surface. By November 1924 communist leader Gramsci had been driven to the maximalist and despairing conclusion that Fascism and liberal democracy were 'objectively' alike. The years of squadrist assault had reduced the working class to 'a disconnected, fragmented, scattered mass' with no energy or purpose. The PC d'I, he complained, had no line or method left through which it could control events.[41] More moderate socialists were appalled by communist intransigence, but their urging of unity at all costs fell on deaf ears.[42] The democrat Giovanni Amendola retreated to an intransigence of his own, deciding that 'we ... the cultivated, middling classes are the last hope of Italy',[43] an attitude ill-calculated to win over those convinced they served workers or peasants. At *Il Corriere della Sera*, Luigi Albertini had ended his earlier flirtation with Fascism and tried bravely if belatedly to reaffirm liberal values, but, though his paper's circulation increased, its editor, too, proposed no real solution to the political crisis.[44] Among the Catholics, Sturzo and De Gasperi wondered whether the ban on alliance with the socialist left should now be lifted, but more authoritative Church spokesmen pronounced that the whole Aventine experiment amounted to a 'grave error'.[45] During the dark days of the regime Anti-Fascists might argue that the Aventine experience had helped to forge their political understanding, but, in the immediate circumstances of 1924, it was soon evident that they offered little threat to Mussolini's retention of authority.

More rumbustious were the Fascists. Their typical figure of the moment was Farinacci. In his paper *Cremona nuova* he expressed an adamantine intransigence. There would be trouble, he warned as early as 14 June, if the party in the provinces believed that the leadership was betraying them.[46] Statesmanlike speeches by Mussolini in Rome were all very well, but Fascism must not resile from 'the full recognition of the rights of the victors over the vanquished'.[47] Mussolini must construct a strong state and a Fascist one, and do so without backsliding or regret.[48]

Mussolini's own tone was more fluctuating, as he sedulously strove to tell his listeners what they wanted to hear. Once he overcame his initial confusion, he instructed his prefects to keep him especially informed about Fascist extremism, although he also organised official Fascist rallies against the opposition and any revival of 'subversion'.[49] As well as continuing to blame dissident Fascists for the murder of Matteotti and to deny any personal responsibility – the act, he wrote in *Il Popolo d'Italia*, was 'barbarous, useless, Anti-Fascist, and, from a political viewpoint, anti-Mussolinian'[50] – the *Duce* used the appointment of Federzoni to assure the Chamber of Deputies that he favoured 'legality' and 'national conciliation'. None the less, he added with a hint of truculence, he had no intention of 'renouncing those principles which we have the sacrosanct duty to defend at any cost'.[51] To the Grand Council, his message was similar. The Nationalists were now fully fused with the rest and, after all, 'Fascism' was 'composed of ex-s' of one kind or another. 'The fascistisation of Italy', he went on, 'must happen but its pace cannot be forced'.[52]

As the weeks slipped by and his government survived, Mussolini augmented his efforts to win over the liberal elite. The new Italy, he declared, stood for peace at home and abroad, but peace based on 'dignity, pride and a sense of discipline'.[53] Collaboration between Fascism and Liberalism was 'possible, desirable, and fertile in its results'. Fascism had transcended the era of the club and castor oil. It was even time to be modest. 'If the nation one day tires of me I shall go without slamming the door and with a tranquil conscience, since so many big and difficult issues in every field from that of banking to those of foreign policy have been confronted and resolved'.[54] These seductive words made it all the more urgent for a man like Farinacci to understand that his own rhetoric must avoid all 'threats and intimidation'. 'You must wave not just an olive branch, but a whole forest of olive trees', Mussolini admonished.[55]

But a second murder now sent the crisis lurching on to another track. On 12 September the Fascist deputy and unionist Armando Casalini was shot down on the streets of Rome. Blood had been, or seemed to have been, matched with blood. Farinacci responded immediately by declaring that enough was enough, demanding that Amendola, Albertini, Sturzo and Turati pay the price for any Fascist sacrifice. Fascists like himself, true Fascists, could no longer tolerate having their hands bound. Vengeance must be theirs.[56] 'The land of Dante and Mazzini must not be consigned to Lenin',[57] he urged, summoning provincial Fascism behind him.

For a while Mussolini resisted, at least in public, the pressure which continued to build from a 'second wave' of squadrism. On 4 October he was careful to state, piously and with an obvious moral for the military chiefs, that 'the day in which the Army becomes seditious, that day the nation runs mortal danger'.[58] Into the bargain, he now took the moment to speak ingratiatingly about poets and intellectuals at the Bocconi university in Milan (and make modest complaint about his own lack of proper academic opportunity so far).[59] He went on official pilgrimage to the *Touring Club Italiano*, patriotic redoubt of the Milanese bourgeoisie.[60] He was all decorum as he mourned the death of Giacomo Puccini, whose music, he said, had brought the nation 'pure and refulgent glory'.[61] He spoke, too, in many a small northern town, never forgetting to praise the locals' own virtues.[62] But still he did not act. Indeed, on 11 November he again assured the Chamber that *rassismo* was in decline and 'Fascist illegality, too, is not only not tolerated but is severely punished'. Otherwise, he joked to the Senate a few weeks later, to the 'opposition of many colours' among the Anti-Fascists might be added a 'Fascist Aventine'.[63]

Action, after all, there was going to be. In December Farinacci was not alone in his mounting impatience to unleash a Fascist offensive.[64] The legal process for the Matteotti murder had reached De Bono and Finzi[65] and again threatened to inculpate Mussolini himself.[66] There were rumours, too, of open dissidence in the cabinet where De' Stefani had sought permission to resign and where a number of ex-liberal and Nationalist ministers, including even Federzoni, were nervous and restive.[67] Among the Fascists, discontent grew, focusing on the position of Federzoni as Minister of the Interior and on what seemed Mussolini's own endless prevarications. Although Farinacci could still warn off potential competitors with the advice that 'only one myth' was tenable in Italy – that of the *Duce*,[68] to his leader, he urged that the tocsin be sounded for the offensive.[69] The Tuscan radical Fascist Curzio Suckert, better known under his pen-name as Curzio Malaparte, was unrepentant in attacking the *Duce* himself, warning him that 'it was not Mussolini who had carried the Fascists to ... the Prime Ministership, but the Fascists who had carried him to power'. Now 'Mussolini must bow to the revolutionary will [of the provincial Fascists] or resign, even if only for a short time, the revolutionary mandate entrusted to him'.[70]

The pressure had built to breaking-point. On 30 December 1924 Mussolini instructed the prefects to convey to deputies home for the Christmas holidays that they must absolutely attend the parliament on 3 January, when the Prime Minister would give a major speech.[71] The *Duce* tried to evince a public calm – the story was spread that, on 2 January 1925, one visitor had a 9 am meeting with the *Duce* so that they could discuss the elegance and meaning of Dante's prose; Mussolini maintained that he disciplined himself to read a Canto every morning and it was implied that his current scanning of the Great National Poet influenced the phrases of the speech to be delivered the next day.[72] There was no doubt, however, that, although he remained nervous at the possible negative reaction of King, Army and old elites to a variety of Fascist coup,[73] he had now been persuaded to step into the open and resolve the crisis.

When he spoke to the Chamber his phrases were plangent. The opposition on the Aventine was damned as 'an anti-constitutional secession, unacceptably revolutionary' in its intent. Mussolini himself was a man of 'reasonable intelligence, much courage and an utter contempt for monetary gain'. If he had wanted to set up a *Ceka*, he would have done so in a whole-hearted manner. In any case, whatever had been planned and plotted in June, now 'I declare, in the presence of this assembly and that of the whole Italian people, that I, and I alone, assume the political, moral and historic responsibility for everything that has happened'. 'If the outbreaks of violence have been the result of a particular historic, political and moral climate, I take the responsibility, because I created this historical, political and moral climate with a propaganda campaign which has run from the *Intervento* until today.' 'When two irreconcilable forces meet', he proclaimed in peroration, 'the only solution is force.'[74] When he fell silent, Farinacci, a rival noticed, strode across the chamber ostentatiously to be the first to shake his hand.[75] On 3 January 1925 the Matteotti affair had found its resolution and Benito Mussolini had announced himself as the Fascist dictator of Italy.

To the words were added deeds. On 12 January the King approved a new cabinet. Gone then or in the next few months were most of the Liberals; by August Mussolini himself was Prime Minister, Minister for Foreign Affairs, Minister of War, Minister of the Navy, Minister for Aviation. Later he would also become Minister of Corporations (1926-29), Minister of Colonies (1928-29) and Minister of Public Works (1929), while in November 1926 he resumed his position as Minister of the Interior. This slew of offices has a curious side; being a Pooh-Bah is not the most obvious way to consolidate individual power. Certainly Hitler, Stalin and Franco never followed Mussolini's course in this regard. Inevitably, the Under-Secretaries of Mussolini's numerous portfolios conducted most day to day business. Here Fascists were now present with Grandi, Under-Secretary at the Foreign Ministry from May 1925, Balbo, Under-Secretary for Aviation from November 1926, Teruzzi, Bianchi and Arpinati, all serving turns as Under-Secretary for the Interior (Bianchi was also for a time at Public Works), Giunta as Under-Secretary to the Prime Minister, Bottai at Corporations and Fulvio Suvich, Alessandro Lessona, Dino Alfieri and De Bono, who had shrugged off the Matteotti affair, acting as Under-Secretaries of this ministry or that. From July 1925 De' Stefani was replaced at the Ministry of Finance by Giuseppe Volpi, the ex-Giolittian, ex-neutralist, ex-target of the Nationalists, ex-Governor of Tripolitania, appointed to that last post by Amendola in liberal days but, from October 1922, willing servant of Fascism. With an ideological practicality which would often characterise the dictatorship, Volpi, who had not taken a Fascist card until July 1923 (but could boast that he served on the board of forty-six companies already in 1922), had his party membership back-dated to January 1921.[76] Lessona, later to be Minister of Colonies, cut his teeth as Mussolini's conduit to the Albanian politician who, president from January 1925, elevated himself in 1928 to be King Zog I,[77] and, as a reward for his skill in bribery and diplomacy, similarly acquired a forged party history.[78]

Along with the new appointments to government came changes in the administration of the Fascist party. Since August 1924 the travail over the Matteotti affair had been reflected in the handing of the party to an emergency directing committee of fifteen. However, on 12 February 1925 Mussolini appointed Farinacci as the sole PNF secretary. The party, it had been announced, would be purged of the corrupt and the lukewarm, the *arrivistes* and the cynics. Its local disputes, Mussolini instructed the new secretary, must remain local and not damage the 'prestige of Fascism and its work of government'.[79] With this charge to discipline the party, Mussolini had, as it were, chosen a thief to catch a thief, elevating a potential opponent, but one whose venality and other weaknesses actually made him easy to control, to a key position in his regime. It was a tactic Mussolini would repeat. Along with the purge also went an expansion – under Farinacci, party membership, which had fallen to below 600 000 in the second half of 1924 rose to 938 000 in 1926.[80] The ranks of the PNF were again opened to those sufficiently clear-eyed to realise the advantage which could spring from their membership, and from being led by a *Duce* who intended a lengthy stay in office.

Mussolini's relationship with Farinacci is a psychologically interesting one, revealing a great deal about both the Fascist government and its leader. Farinacci was an extremist of a kind, winning approval from such diverse Fascist revolutionaries as Malaparte and the fanatically Anti-Semitic Preziosi and his journal, *La Vita Italiana*.[81] Farinacci himself, the ex-railway worker socialist, flaunted his populist crudity, never being happier than when berating priestly piety and deriding any display of manners and decency. His course through Fascism – he remained a leading figure almost to the end –

made him in time a staunch advocate of the alliance with Nazism and an out-and-out racist.[82] And yet Farinacci better resembled a Tammany Hall tough than an ideological fanatic.[83] He was neither a Himmler nor a Goebbels, despite his prominent role in the Fascist press and his effrontery in publicly defending Dumini and the killers of Matteotti.[84] It is hard to see him as a true believer in anything except Roberto Farinacci and in the need to remain angry against all those who blocked his path to wealth and fame.

Mussolini, with whom he exchanged a frequent and often passionate correspondence, well understood that ultimate ideological emptiness, especially because, over time, it became so evident that he shared it. Meanwhile the *Duce* endured, and even perhaps enjoyed, Farinacci's regular pin-pricks about this or that gap between Fascist theory and Fascist practice (and his regular declarations that he was a Fascist who told the truth), rather as he enjoyed occasional contact with his similarly down-to-earth wife. Alone among Mussolini's associates, Farinacci confessed that he thought of the *Duce* as a 'brother' and a 'friend'.[85] Just in case fraternal amity should have its limits, Mussolini treasured in his private files a piece of evidence which could rein in Farinacci. The rough and tumble boss of Cremona had plagiarised, in the most straightforward fashion, the thesis which earned him the right to a well-remunerated career as a lawyer,[86] amending the title of another's work and repeating it word for word. The *Duce* amplified his version of these texts with a formal note stating that, legally, Farinacci's deed was punishable with 6 months of gaol, 'being mandatory in all universities in the kingdom where university exams are concerned'.[87]

The PNF apart, other social forces needed adjusting to the patterns of open dictatorship. Although the crucial appointment was not made until May 1925, Mussolini quickly looked to the military, knowing only too well that, in any society, power potentially grew out of the barrel of a gun. The Isonzo stalemate and Caporetto defeat had left major stains on the Army's record. In the *dopoguerra* experts were bitterly divided over how the armed forces might be made more modern and efficient, with radicals pressing for a populist *nation armée* (*nazione armata*), though always remaining a little vague about the detail. The numerous generals (from 176 in 1914, they numbered 556 in 1919)[88] were more circumspect about change since, above all, they were unwilling to accept any whittling down of their own status and influence. During the Fascist rise to government, the Army debate focused on questions of pay and conditions for officers as a whole, and the lack of resolution on such humdrum matters was symbolised by the successive appointments of four Ministers of War in the course of 1922.[89] The Army leadership was, to say the least, highly tolerant of most Fascist attacks on the ex-'defeatist' Left in the provinces. The army paper, *L'Esercito italiano*, on 31 October 1922 hailed 'our revolution', even if it then explained that Fascism had won 'precisely because [this revolution] had nothing really new to show to the Italian people'.[90]

From 1922 to 1925 Diaz presided over a restructuring of the military forces, but it was very much a conservative one, all the more because De' Stefani had severely trimmed the defence budget.[91] Nevertheless, money was found to increase officers' and, especially, generals' pay; while from November 1924 the new senior rank of Marshal was established (enabling Italians, it was implied, to match the Napoleonic system in France and so avoid the 'dishonour' of lessened status at international meetings).[92] In 1924 the lax traditionalism of Diaz was being widely attacked, notably by such rival generals as Antonino Di Giorgio and Gaetano Giardino. Relations with the MVSN remained delicate.

Mussolini the dictator cut a tangle of Gordian knots. His choice for the co-ordinating position as Chief of General Staff was Pietro Badoglio, who had held the same position under Nitti and Giolitti from 1919 to 1921. One of the great stayers of the regime, Badoglio hung on to his office until after the disastrous military failure in Greece in the autumn of 1940. To be ennobled as Duke of Addis Ababa, Badoglio sprang from a Piedmontese *petit bourgeois* family, with impeccable liberal antecedents. His father and grandfather had been mayors of Piedmontese towns.[93] Blamed in many quarters for direct responsibility for the Caporetto fiasco,[94] as well as being highly reluctant to implement any thorough investigation of the Army's planning, logistics and morale,[95] Badoglio was a monarchist who, on the eve of the March on Rome, had made no secret of his willingness to fire on the Fascists if called upon to do so.[96] None the less he readily accepted the Fascist government and, perhaps archly, in 1923 chose *Cremona nuova* to express his admiration for the 'healthiness' of the effect of the new regime.[97] That did not mean that he had become an advocate of radical military reform; rather the reverse. The appointment of Badoglio as Chief of General Staff signalled a quietist army, whose main preoccupation would be to look after its own (while Badoglio rarely avoided personal opportunity for venality).[98]

Lest Badoglio were more ambitious than he seemed, Mussolini

constrained him by appointing to the new position of Deputy Chief of General Staff, Francesco Saverio Grazioli, an ostentatiously pro-Fascist general, but one known to be inconstant and unreliable, and to be hated by Badoglio. Mussolini's own accession to the Ministry of War made the theorem perfect. As Giorgio Rochat, Italy's brilliant military historian, has put it, Mussolini's stratagems had created 'an army with too many officers, too few soldiers, inadequate material reserves and an antiquated structure, costly in its management and with excessive ambitions', while also, given Fascism's silencing of an 'Anti-Fascist' press, easily able to avoid criticism.[99] Rochat did not need to add that this Army would, unless there was complete disaster, be loyal to Mussolini, though remaining in its ultimate disposition more friendly towards the King and Italy's old institutions than to the Fascist party and its purported 'revolution'. In 1925, its most significant leaders thought with considerable justification that they had adapted the *Duce* to their own cause.

The Matteotti murder and its aftermath, and the tumultuous road which had led both to the acceptance of dictatorship and this rash of new appointments had, it now became clear, exacted a price from Mussolini. At 4 a.m. on the morning of 15 February, only three days after he had entrusted the PNF to Farinacci, the *Duce* who, until now, had seemed so robust, so intrepid, so bold, so unbowed, so jaunty, the man whose charisma had indeed been constructed on a version of brutal manliness, was suddenly taken ill. The crisis was severe. In his flat in the Via Rasella, he vomited blood and his housekeeper urgently summoned doctors to his bedside.[100] They diagnosed an ulcer, counselled quiet and proposed a change in diet. Mussolini withdrew from the limelight for a number of weeks and put up with the rumours zealously collected by the police that he was dangerously ill and that Federzoni was talking to Salandra and Giolitti about a moderate triumvirate which could replace him and simultaneously beat off the threat of the Fascist trio of Farinacci, De Vecchi and Giunta.[101] Even after he recovered Mussolini subsequently ate little meat and drank sparingly. The school-mate of one of his sons later remembered the *Duce* waxing sententious about the curative virtue of yoghurt for lunch.[102] Admiring visiting journalists, especially if they were female, were likely to be regaled with accounts of Mussolini's preferences in fruit and veg and his noble abstinence from meat, wine and coffee.[103] He also took time to send the teenage Edda a clipping of a newspaper article entitled 'Nicotine makes you ugly and damages your health'. During the war, he admitted, he had smoked 'innumerable cigarettes', but they had worsened his ulcer and his daily catarrh. 'You pay for everything in life', he concluded with paternal sententiousness.[104]

In the spring of 1925, the doctors had wondered whether an operation was needed, but this solution proved unacceptable to Mussolini. The whole event was hushed up. It is likely that not even Rachele was kept fully informed about the breakdown in her husband's health.[105] At this stage in their marriage, their contact was infrequent and Edda, their daughter, would even later allege that her mother for a time solaced herself with a lover from Forlì,[106] a claim which, if true, cannot have lessened the tension in the *Duce's* life. Mussolini might concede to the more perceptive of his interviewers that he was 'living on his nerves',[107] but his public image could not be infringed by an admission of weakness on any front. Indeed, Mussolini had just published in *Gerarchia* a 'eulogy to his loyal followers', in which he ascribed the victory over the Aventine and the Fascist dissidents to himself; the obedience of the trenches, he demanded, must be replicated in that Fascist militia which he, and he alone, commanded.[108] From 1925 Mussolini the man and 'Mussolini', the vehicle certainly of charisma and perhaps of power, the *Duce* in a newly absolute sense, began to follow different paths.

It was round about this time that Rachele moved the Mussolini children to the *Villa Carpena* and there her mother Anna died. It had been a difficult few months for that side of the family, since, during the previous year, Rachele had lost two sisters. Pina, at 35, was a victim of cancer, leaving seven children to mourn her; Giovanna, already a mother of fourteen, died in childbirth.[109] When, on 28 December 1925 Benito and Rachele were finally married in a church and had their three children baptised (officiating was Arnaldo Mussolini's brother-in-law), there were political ramifications, as rumours began to circulate of a compromise deal between Catholic Church and Fascist Italian state. But another reason for the wedding may have been the new sense of the fragility of life which the Mussolinis had begun to experience.

To be sure, the extended family had not overlooked the advantages of being related to Benito Mussolini. They, too, knew something about patronage and clientship. A characteristic document survives from 1927 in which Arpinati, the Fascist boss of the region, wrote to the municipal authorities at Predappio with the news that

the *Duce* is literally besieged with requests for subsidies on the part of his relatives. The matter is becoming annoying, even indecent. Go back

to Predappio. Do the fullest documentary search in the communal regis-
ters and the baptismal files. Then distribute the attached sum in as
equal and speedy a way as possible. You will find 60 000 lire in bank-
notes. The *Duce* will be profoundly grateful at the service you will thus
render to him and to the decorum of the Fascist revolution.[110]

A malicious historian has tabulated 334 relatives who, by 1943, had
extracted government aid from their ties to Mussolini, 105 being from
Rachele's side of the family, 229 from Benito's.[111] Such tawdry matters
remained officially secret, although doubtless there were those in the
know, especially in the Romagna; they believed that such was the way
of the world.

At a public level, the Mussolinis were becoming ever more
respectable – the *Duce* was not above cosy talk about his *casa* (house)
at Carpena.[112] Romano Mussolini, with his evocatively imperial first
name (and highly banal later personality), was born in September
1927, Anna Maria in September 1929 (each presumably conceived
during the Christmas break of the year before). Almost alone among
the Fascist leadership,[113] the Mussolinis were doing their best for
national demographic growth (and for Catholic propriety). Moreover,
just after the Matteotti crisis began, Edda Mussolini had been moved
from a high school in Milan to Italy's most prestigious academy for
young ladies, the *Santissima Annunziata* college at Poggio Imperiale
near Florence;[114] even there, however, rumours spread that she outdid
in wildness those sprigs of the aristocracy who were her class-mates.[115]
In 1928 she was packed off on a tour to India.[116] Soon she would be
needing a husband (and candidates for her hand would have their
characters, prospects and politics reviewed by the police). At her
father's instruction, all mail to her was opened before delivery.[117]

Her brothers grew towards their adolescence, on occasion
photographed with their father while they picnicked or played some
family sport. Actually, Mussolini remained a distant father, remembered as one who preferred stroking the family cat to cuddling his
own offspring.[118] As if in reaction, Vittorio and especially Bruno
turned into wordless youths, unlikely to star as leaders of any new
ruling class. On the rare occasions on which he did show up at home,
the *Duce* preferred to eat alone. Contemporaries noticed that the
Mussolini family was not given to chat.[119] Perhaps those stomach
pains, which, after 1925, were always likely to recur, reinforced
Mussolini's known dislike of most forms of physical contact.[120]
Perhaps, too, the suppressed physiological suffering – from 1925 there

would always be moments when Mussolini pressed hard on his lower abdomen to relieve a flash of pain[121] – along with the psychological tenseness and probable sense of inadequacy, as well as the boring diet and the array of tasteless foods which featured in it, ensured that the *Duce*, despite all the revolutionary rhetoric, 'in his heart, believed in nothing'.[122] Somewhere beneath the pomp and show a bleakness lingered and grew.

Mussolini's private life may have been in most ways banal, but, through these years, the manufacture and reinforcement of his charisma proceeded apace. Already in 1923 Arpinati had thought it appropriate to fete a visit to Bologna by obsequiously greeting the *Duce* with the resounding triumphal march from *Aida*.[123] Thereafter no limits could be set to the leader's grandeur. The celebration of Holy Year (*L'Anno Santo*) in 1925 brought advice in tourist guides that Mussolini himself was among the sites to visit.[124] As one American journalist remarked: 'everyone who came to Rome wanted to have an interview with Mussolini. To see him was as much a part of the long-planned trip to the Eternal City as it was to visit the ruins or to walk over the places where the heroes of antiquity had once walked'.[125] Now the slogan, invented by Leo Longanesi, a journalist recommended to the *Duce* by Arnaldo, that *Mussolini ha sempre ragione* (Mussolini is always right), began to be heard.[126] An imaginary Mussolini began to penetrate people's minds and find a presence even in their dreams. One Fascist propagandist maintained that villagers were growing sure that Mussolini, a Santa Claus for all the year, had, on one night or other, passed by their home on a solitary excursion by motor cycle or car.[127] Vigilant, ubiquitous, immanent, this Mussolini was acquiring the qualities of saint or god.

Nor were the humble public alone in experiencing it. Politicians grew ever more expert at grovelling. Giuseppe Bottai, in his own eyes[128] the most intellectual of the Fascist leadership, again underlined his infinite '<u>faith</u> in your thought and method'. He and his friends knew they worked '<u>in Fascism and for Fascism</u> and, above all for You, whom we acknowledge as the spiritual chief of our generation'. Bottai then contrasted Mussolini's virtue with the 'chronic rebelliousness' of less worthy party members like Farinacci.[129] Federzoni was another to register his 'infinite personal devotion' when addressing the *Duce*; his leader must look to his health since 'it is not just yours, but all of ours. It belongs to the entire Italian people'.[130] Even Farinacci agreed that 'more than the rest of us, you have great duties. Your life does not belong to you, but to the whole

Italian people'.[131] The tone of Farinacci's correspondence with Mussolini none the less was not reliably respectful. When the *Duce* reacted angrily to a Farinacci warning against risking his life flying, Farinacci wrote back sarcastically, 'from now on, I'll change tack and always tell you to go off and fly, and, why not, urge you to drive your car at least 150 kms per hour'.[132]

In this construction of a *Duce*, sport, with its combination of masculinity and modernity, was an insistent theme (however much, in practice, many areas in the peninsula were still devoid of the fields, courts and halls which might be utilised for leisure activities).[133] Once sport had seemed 'made in England', a commentator noticed, but now the *Duce* was himself the complete sportsman 'in the idea, in the discipline, in the act'.[134] On a typical day, readers were assured, he would rise at seven, take a cold bath, scoff a glass of milk and then proceed to an hour's riding, leaping onto his horse like 'a born cowboy'.[135] That exercise over, he might proceed to fence. He preferred the most manly and brutal weapon, the sabre, and, with his teeth set in grim determination, typically fought 'with a style that was totally personal, full of clever ruses, sudden counter-attacks, blows unexpected to the logic of his adversary, which the *Duce* launches like the punishment of God'.[136] Similarly he was a devoted swimmer, and had just told an American journalist that he yearned also to have time to practise football, tennis and even golf.[137] No wonder that the first issue in 1928 of the journal *Lo sport fascista* saluted the '*Duce*, aviator, fencer, rider, first sportsman of Italy'.[138]

Along with the indulgence in sport went the photographs. Already in the 1920s one observer suggested that Mussolini had become the most photographed man in history.[139] Images of him were distributed to the Italian people through the press, or the postcard. Well before 1922 Italians had grown accustomed to collect likenesses of the innumerable saints of the peninsula as mementos of a visit and as an aide to piety. Now an estimated 30 million pictures of the *Duce* in up to 2500 different poses began to circulate[140] in what was a curious example of the sacralisation and commercialisation of political life. In 1926 a 14-year-old fan, Claretta Petacci, daughter of the Pope's doctor, papered her room with such images,[141] impelled by those motives which, some decades later, persuaded her successors to treasure the pictures of pop stars or football players. The young Petacci was so stirred by the photographs on her wall that she wrote personally to her *Duce*, enclosing some stanzas of her adoring poetry.[142] That year, too, reverent readers learned from one priest, who had discovered, before the papal hierarchy did, how to mesh Catholicism and Fascism, that Mussolini was a sort of re-born St Francis of Assisi.[143]

One notable and humanising feature of Mussolini's image, a matter to which we are now accustomed but which was new at the time, was his public or photographed extrusion of bodily liquids. Mussolini sweated, shook off water after a swim and doffed his shirt when about to ski (or join the harvest) in a way unimaginable for most of his political contemporaries. His body left 'after-images' of itself to console or arouse the faithful.[144] Hitler, Stalin, Lenin, Baldwin, Chamberlain, Roosevelt, Blum and Franco were not visibly 'men' in this way. Less expansive than the *Duce* they timidly kept their bodies as private concerns.

Similarly, Mussolini's alleged sexual prowess,[145] however actually curtailed by his doubtful health, was never denied by the regime but, rather, was linked to his image and charisma. Here, after all, were more personal fluids to 'share' with his public. If the regime's propaganda was deifying Mussolini and, as the dictatorship wore on, becoming more insistent that the *Duce* be 'granitic',[146] a 'man alone',[147] necessarily without friends,[148] elevated far above ordinary emotions, nevertheless, through the omnipresence of his body, a human side kept peeping out. It was this idiosyncratic mixture of the divine and the profane which presumably explained a letter sent to Mussolini by a teenage female admirer. She confided that she had just taken communion for the first time. As she had done so, she had been filled with the hope she could 'receive' both Jesus and Mussolini. 'Both of you will be there on my tongue, will repose on my breast, will rest on my poor heart. How good you will be!'[149] Transubstantiation, fellatio and more ordinary loving congress mingled in her mind; here, indeed, was what would later be called sex appeal. It even extended to the wives of foreign politicians. Clementine Churchill, who met the *Duce* in March 1926, found him 'quite simple and <u>natural</u>, very dignified ... [with] beautiful golden brown, piercing eyes which you can see but can't look at', all in all, 'one of the most wonderful men of our times'. She was delighted to take away a signed photo in memento.[150] Lady Asquith more briefly expressed her delight in Mussolini's 'muscles' and 'extraordinary vitality'[151] (quite a change no doubt from her husband). Lady Ivy Chamberlain, wife and later widow of Sir Austen, was an enduring fan, delighted, it seemed, to be given her own Fascist party badge to treasure.[152] Lady Sybil Graham, the wife of the British ambassador,[153] was rumoured to be equally charmed by the *Duce*. During the next decade, too, many a dowager warmed to the thought of tea with Mussolini.

However emphatic, the *Duce*'s charisma was never unchallenged. Italy, after all, remained a monarchy. Predictably, attempts were made to sell the image of King Victor Emmanuel III, even though his short stature – Margherita Sarfatti maliciously remembered him as an enthroned king whose feet never reached the ground[154] – parsimony and homeliness must have made early paladins of the advertising trade shudder at their task. All the same, some play was made of the 'Fascist King', notably on the occasion of the jubilee of his reign in June 1925.[155] Victor Emmanuel, some propagandists believed, might be 'the best custodian of the national will', the 'first soldier of Italy'.[156] The best known school manual that appeared during the regime, ex-Nationalist Roberto Forges Davanzati's *Il balilla Vittorio*, naturally imagined its hero star-struck by a glimpse of the *Duce*,[157] but 'Vittorio' shared a name with the King and did not forget to show him reverence, too.[158]

When he came to Rome to learn about the great imperial capital, 'Vittorio' had another obligatory respectful visit to make, and that was to the Vatican. Pope Pius XI remained another competitor in the charisma stakes.[159] The Pope could even be portrayed as a *sportivo*. His fans never forgot that his devotion to tramping in the Alps meant that he could be denominated the *Pontefice alpinista* (the mountaineer Pope).[160] The durable historical resonance of the papal office, bolstered by the complex stage furniture of modern Catholicism, was a permanent, if often forgotten or underestimated, part of the history of the construction of *mentalité* in Fascist Italy. Propaganda might ensure that Mussolini was the name on everyone's lips, but the Pope, his cardinals and bishops, his saints and martyrs, preserved a sacred place in many Italian hearts. The boast by a Fascist journalist in 1928 that 'the Mussolinian cult is now thoroughly rooted in the Italian populace'[161] thus possessed an equivocal side; since the cultic ideal retained the smack of the Church, its unspoken assumptions did not renounce religiosity. As one clerical fascist had put it happily: 'Italian imperialism is beginning to recognise ... that the only genuinely universal idea alive in Rome is Catholicism'.[162]

From time to time, there were even hints that lesser Fascists could become vehicles of charisma. Mussolini was not alone in spawning gushing biographies, although the appearance of such a work often foretold trouble for an overambitious *ras*. Both Giampaoli[163] and Arpinati[164] ended in gaol not long after their followers had played up their appeal.

Discussions about the internal discipline of the PNF were not ended by the speech of 3 January 1925. But, for the moment, Mussolini concentrated on the repression of the Anti-Fascists. He may have formally distanced himself from any recurrence in squadrist violence, reacting sharply, for example, when Farinacci openly endorsed the murder of Matteotti, censoring his phrases and declaring that Fascism was achieving its victories in spite of the Matteotti affair rather than because of it.[165] But this advocacy of legality did nothing to prevent the brutal and, ultimately fatal, beating of Giovanni Amendola in July 1925, replicating what had been done to the younger 'liberal socialist' Piero Gobetti in September 1924. Those who could began to flee abroad as the only way to escape Fascist attacks,[166] historian Gaetano Salvemini for one departing in the summer of 1925.[167] Then, and on all occasions, Mussolini was glad to learn that life was being made difficult for his opponents.[168] Also in exile were Nitti and Sforza, thus to be numbered among the few liberals who opted for liberty rather than the Fascist alternative.

Repression of opponents went hand in hand with the construction of a Fascist state. It was not Mussolini's work alone. Rather a key figure was the Minister for Justice, Alfredo Rocco, an ex-Nationalist of reactionary cast.[169] On 2 October 1925 the Palazzo Vidoni pact represented the triumph of his version of social policy. In its brief clauses, Fascist unions replaced what was left of their socialist and Catholic rivals and were recognised as 'the exclusive representatives of the workers' by *Confindustria*, the Big Business League, which had been established in 1910 and was headed until 1934 by Gino Olivetti, from the great Piedmontese and Jewish entrepreneurial family. In return, the 'Confederation of Fascist corporations' acknowledged the supremacy on the employer side of *Confindustria*.[170] In practice, it went without saying, the industrialists retained great freedom of action. Any idea that a fair and equal system of arbitration was being born was false, though Mussolini would, before long, take care to distance himself to some degree from Italy's business and banking chiefs.

Another matter for urgent attention was the press. As early as 1923 the important daily *Il Secolo* had been won over to the Fascist cause with the lure of government subvention.[171] Now pressure built for other papers to reflect the unity which Fascism intended to impose. Mussolini the journalist was making sure that no one under his governance could possess the freedom to write phrases which had once served him so well. When, on 4 November 1925, seventh anniversary of triumph at Vittorio Veneto, a socialist deputy Tito Zaniboni and a retired general Luigi Capello were arrested and accused of plotting Mussolini's assassination (the police had been following their plans from the beginning),[172] the desire to curtail the liberty of the press became overwhelming. By the next month the wealthy Crespi family, owners of *Il Corriere della Sera*, Italy's best-known paper, had bowed to reiterated demands that their liberal editor Albertini be sacked.[173] Other papers acted similarly, being especially gratified when they received the promise of government money to assist any restructuring.[174] They were pushed by a new press law which converted journalism into an activity supervised by the state. As Mussolini explained in a speech on 11 December in which he reviewed the labour situation: 'I consider the Italian nation in a situation of permanent war. I have already said and I repeat that the next five or ten years will prove decisive for the destiny of our people'.[175]

Since the Corfu crisis, the domestic situation had been so fluid that Mussolini had devoted little time to foreign affairs. Mostly, he had left diplomacy in the hands of the experts in the Foreign Ministry, ever alert, however, to detect any hint of Anti-Fascism on their part.[176] He was alive to the 'damage' the unguarded phrases of Farinacci might wreak on Italy's international position.[177] In his more expert hands, ideology had not been allowed to stand in the way of Anglo-Italian relations after the Labour (and wartime pacifist) leader Ramsay MacDonald became Prime Minister of Great Britain in the spring of 1924.[178] Mussolini had been similarly realistic in his dealings with the USSR. Despite Fascism's declared intention to extirpate communism at home and Mussolini's own frequent attacks on Bolshevik policy in Russia, a treaty of commerce and navigation, signed on 7 February 1924, restored formal relations between the two rival 'revolutionary' states. Then and thereafter, Fascist Italy made little diplomatic attempt to launch an international crusade against the Soviet state.[179]

The most important diplomatic activity in which Italy was engaged during 1925 was the preparation of the Treaty of Locarno, signed on 1 December. By this pact Germany was restored to the comity of nations and, in return, promised formal acceptance of its western borders as reached at the end of the First World War. It gave no guarantees about its eastern borders, nor its southern ones (as a historian of these events has noted, Locarno did nothing to change the fact that 'The [German–Austrian] *Anschluss* remained for Italy the problem of problems').[180] During the Locarno treatying, Mussolini had indulged in an occasional rhetorical flourish (and firmly underlined his view that an *Anschluss* was intolerable and would signal the 'revival of the war').[181] Basically, however, he did nothing to indicate that his Italy would not replicate the patterns well established in the foreign policy of the least of the Great Powers. It was only when he talked at home that it seemed there might be something different about Fascist diplomacy; when he suggested, for example, that the war had never ended. As he had put it in that same speech of 11 December, this time using a characteristic sporting simile, 'In politics, it is sometimes necessary to endure blows as you would if you were in the <u>ring</u>. The essential thing is not to be knocked out, and that we shall not be'.[182] Just what that severe determination to fight on might imply was to be left for later definition.

For the present, Fascist rule did not alarm the chancelleries of Europe where Mussolini was thought no doubt rather Italian in his indulgence in emotional outbursts, but not a leader of untoward ambition. So, too, at home, the great majority of Italy's intellectuals had, along with the rest of the elite, accepted the regime and begun to seek favour from it. Most influential was philosopher Giovanni Gentile, who, having ended his term as Minister of Education, joined a Committee of Eighteen, ordered to review the constitution in the light of recent events.[183] In April Gentile published a manifesto in favour of Fascist order. Its clauses sufficiently annoyed purist liberals for Benedetto Croce to produce 'The manifesto of Anti-Fascist intellectuals' on 1 May, and thereafter to retreat to a gilded internal exile in his family palace in Naples, there to preach liberal ideals to visiting and respectful students. Other, less purist, intellectuals read politics as others were doing, and sought to fasten themselves to a well remunerated patron–client relationship.[184]

By now Gentile was given to celebrating Fascism's 'total' conception of life, and 'total' was the word which was gaining a new prominence in the vocabulary of Fascism. On 22 June, in a speech to the PNF congress in Rome, Mussolini announced his determination to 'fascistise the nation'. 'Our ferocious totalitarian will', he ran on, 'shall be pursued with a still greater ferocity. ... The first watchword for the day, Fascists, is this: absolute ideal and practical intransigence. The second is all power to all of Fascism'.[185] The words were still not quite emerging in the lapidary way 'history' required. But Mussolini was announcing the Fascist determination to build a 'totalitarian state', a new system in which individuals served the united nation and in which classes dissolved. On 28 October 1925, in the luminous surrounds of *La Scala* opera house, the *Duce* hardened his phrasing for the third anniversary of the March on Rome. Fascism, he proclaimed in words his propagandists would henceforth endlessly repeat, was bent on establishing a regime in which 'all would be for the state, nothing outside the state and no-one against the state'.[186]

10

The Man of Providence,
1926–1929

IN July 1925 Mussolini had responded to the birthday wishes trans-mitted to him by Rachele with the wry comment that, at 42, he was feeling 'both very young and very old'.[1] His ambivalence about the meaning of life was not surprising given the breadth of Fascist activity and the pretensions of the Fascist regime to be a total one. That totality, naturally enough, made remarkable demands on Mussolini. The propaganda statement, retailed to the *Balilla* or party boy scouts, that he invariably worked 14 or 16 hours each day,[2] may be discounted. However, his chief Italian biographer has asserted that he did pursue his political labours for 'ten hours or more every day',[3] and he certainly never shared Hitler's fondness for pointless chat. A younger colleague recalled that 'bureaucratic papers were his joy; the clear chronology, the able synthesis, the telling detail, the essential reference – these were what gave him delight'. Extemporising, speaking before he was fully informed, he disliked, and he always preferred to have on his desk, and for his eyes only, a written account of what was to happen at any meeting.[4] He understood that a totali-tarian dictator had to be, or to seem to be, expert in everything. When Farinacci suggested that, elevated to Rome, Mussolini could no longer see what was happening among the groundlings in the provinces, he felt affronted.[5] Especially in these years of the creation of the Fascist system, no matter was too small for the dictator's interest – in January 1926 he even remembered officially to instruct newspapers to avoid stories about suicide and crime, since such reports merely offered bad models to 'the weak or the weakening'.[6]

Cowing the press was only one part of the building of a totalitarian dictatorship. Between 1926 and 1929 Mussolini tried, with lesser or greater success, to bend labour, capital, the peasantry (and thus the

South), and the Fascist party to his will. He negotiated a deal with the Catholic Church, and, however circumspect his foreign policy remained in practice, boasted that Italy was becoming a 'world power, that is, one with interests not curtailed by sector or continent'.[7] The real novelty of his ambition lay in his pretensions to enter the hearts and minds of his subjects, and so install Fascism as a political religion. While the word totalitarian steadily expanded in meaning after its first usage in May 1923 in Amendola's *Il Mondo*, when it meant merely the desire for overwhelming electoral victory,[8] Mussolini, at least for a time, hoped to establish a fully organic relationship with the Italian people. For all the cynicism which, almost against his will, kept creeping back into his heart, he aspired in these years to be a revolutionary of a new sort and find a political formula which would outmatch the socialism of his own youth and of many of his Anti-Fascist enemies.

His ideals, none the less, if that was what they really were, did not run free. The cornerstone of the new Fascist state was repression. In this regard, events helped to justify a new rigour in policing Italy. Now was the moment of opportunity when Mussolini could put into practice what he had outlined to Farinacci as his preferred tactics: 'suddenly take the initiative and strike my adversaries at the time of their greatest disorder and panic'.[9] The assassination planned by Zaniboni and Capello in November 1925 was followed by other attempts on the *Duce*'s life. At 11 a.m. on 7 April 1926 an upper-class Irish woman, Violet Gibson,[10] shot at Mussolini while he was emerging from a hall at the *Campidoglio* in the centre of historic Rome, where, ironically, he had just inaugurated an international surgeons' conference. Her bullet merely nicked the bridge of her target's nose and Mussolini took the opportunity to spin the affair in his favour by being photographed shortly afterwards continuing his work and with just a small facial plaster to hint at his brush with death. Indeed, by 4.30 p.m., still sporting his bandage, Mussolini was orating to a meeting of party officials and government workers. In a dramatic peroration, soon adopted as one of the slogans of the regime, he urged the need for all to ' "Live dangerously". Indeed, I say to you like an old soldier: "If I go forward, follow me. If I retreat, kill me. If I die, avenge me." '[11] When later that night a crowd assembled at the Palazzo Chigi, Mussolini emerged onto a balcony to tell them: 'I am one of your generation. That means that I am the newest sort of Italian, one who is never thrown by events, but rather proceeds always straight down the road assigned by destiny.'[12] With less spartan emotion, Arnaldo rang from Milan in tears – his phone was tapped and policemen recorded the event. Mussolini told his brother to stay calm; the murder attempt had only affected him for 'an instant', he said, although Arnaldo, as usual, took occasion to thank the Lord for having saved the *Duce* from a worse fate.[13]

Miss Gibson was diagnosed as mentally unstable and soon expelled to Great Britain, whose diplomats had intervened on her behalf[14] (although Fascist newspapers did not miss the chance for xenophobic tirade, *La Vita Italiana* inveighing against the 'female foreign devil').[15] However, a third effort at assassination brought more direct response from the Fascist authorities. On 11 September Gino Lucetti,[16] an anarchist returned from a period of emigration in France, threw a bomb at Mussolini as the *Duce* drove up to the *Porta Pia* and towards his office; Mussolini was not wounded but eight bystanders were. The scandal caused by this act resulted in the appointment of a new Chief of Police, Arturo Bocchini, from the pre-fectural service. Before Bocchini had fully mastered his brief, on 31 October a teenage boy from an anarchist family, Anteo Zamboni, tried to shoot the *Duce* as he drove through the streets of Bologna. Zamboni was lynched on the spot by enraged Fascists, and a contro-versy has continued to circle over the affair, with suggestions that either Zamboni was not the real perpetrator or the assassination plan had been plotted within dissident Fascist circles in Bologna, whose *ras*, Arpinati, eventually fell foul of the Fascist state.[17]

What was really important about the Zamboni affair, however, was Mussolini's reaction to it. He now took the brakes off state repression, on 6 November stripping the moderate Federzoni of the Ministry of the Interior, which returned to his own hands, and pressing forward with other legal changes. Although the actual legislation was drafted by Federzoni and Rocco, each an ex-Nationalist rather than a fanatical Fascist, it was now that opposition parties, unions and associations were formally banned, and Italy became a one-party state. The Aventine secessionists, who had been left in limbo since January 1925, were finally deprived of their seats in parliament. The death penalty, the abolition of which the Grand Duchy of Tuscany and then United Italy had pioneered in Europe, was re-instated for political crimes. On 25 November a Special Tribunal for the Defence of the State (*Tribuna speciale per la difesa dello stato*) was instituted, and given a party gloss, since most of the judges who served it were drawn from the MVSN. Clandestine emigration was blocked with greater energy – the days when Salvemini could be smuggled over the Little Saint Bernard Pass while the border guards ate a long lunch[18] were over, theoretically at least.[19] Italy was to be converted into a Fascist fortress.

Conditioning the ideological thrust of these decisions was the selection as Police Chief of Bocchini, a man who, until his death in 1940, would seem to some 'the occult and extremely powerful dictator of the dictator'.[20] Bocchini's background was that of the Southern bureaucrat, such a classic figure in Italian history after the Risorgimento. He had been born in 1880 at San Giorgio del Sannio in the province of Benevento amid the hills to the east of Naples.[21] After taking out a law degree, in 1903 he had joined the state service. He was the son of a landowner and had a number of brothers who viewed themselves as agents of his local influence. Installed in office, he made himself into the boss of the Benevento region and it was thought that no development occurred there without his approval and gain.[22] His career had blossomed after 1922, with his appointment successively to be prefect of Brescia, Bologna[23] and Genoa. In these posts he was known as one who would repress dissident Fascists with the same firmness with which he would deal with any opponent of the state. Indeed, in 1926 his name had been advanced first by Federzoni. He was also well regarded by Augusto Turati, the *ras* of Brescia who, in March, had replaced Farinacci as PNF secretary.[24]

Throughout his career, Bocchini was anything but a fanatical believer in the Fascist revolution. Well known for his wanton appetites, he would laugh that he was only a Fascist as far as his belt.[25] A German contact remembered him soothing 'his nerves with lobsters, oysters, capons and vintage burgundy'.[26] His death, on 20 November 1940, was occasioned by a succulent dinner at the *Albergo Ambasciatore* in Rome, followed by a tryst with the 25-year-old Maria Letizia De Lieto Vollaro, from a Benevento noble family. Her family provoked gossip after the event by their shameless pursuit of his rich inheritance, justified by what seems to have been a hasty marriage between Maria Letizia and a moribund police chief.[27] Bocchini had made feeble attempts to disguise his traditional views on 'corruption', expecting those who sought his patronage and favour to proffer gifts of a suitable value.[28] He also enjoyed access to a secret police budget, which he treated as his own. Mussolini benignly required no audit of his expenditure from it.[29] Bocchini was equally a *furbo* (smart one) in the regularity with which, despite Fascist rhetoric about national unification, he deployed southern policemen to watch over northern Anti-Fascists.[30] He did nothing, either, to change his juniors' existing habits of tapping the phones of leading Fascists, not excluding Mussolini and his brother (and, later, his mistress).[31]

Here, then, was a Fascist non-believer who better resembled a Scarpia brought to life than a Heinrich Himmler. By the late 1930s Fascist and Nazi police had to meet quite often and Bocchini had no difficulty in smoothing his relationship with Himmler, even if in private he mocked the Nazi 'hyena'.[32] The solemn attendance at his funeral of both Himmler and Heydrich may have allowed him a posthumous moment of ribaldry, all the more because he had been associated with the group around Foreign Minister Ciano, who feared the implications of the German alliance and wanted to delay entry into the war.[33] Bocchini was also a foe of 1930s Party Secretary Starace,[34] whose (self-interested) true belief in Fascism and its revolution he must have found droll. Their attitude may have been enhanced by the fact that Starace came from Gallipoli, further to the south and a place which Bocchini knew in his heart to be more rustic than Benevento. In sum, Bocchini was an Italian from that world where 'patronage was an integral dimension of ... life at every level of society, including the modern state itself',[35] incarnating much which was the exact reverse of a 'Fascist new man'. He embodied the structures of the history of the Italies far better than he represented the Fascist revolution.

Furthermore, he got on extremely well with the *Duce*, who saw him almost every day. Indeed, it was their collaboration which earned Mussolini the encomium from an Anti-Fascist historian of being one of the greatest Ministers of the Police in history.[36] By May 1927, in his Ascension Day address, which was arguably the most significant speech he ever made, Mussolini publicly expressed his pleasure at the reforms to the police service over which Bocchini had so far presided. 'Did not the policeman', Mussolini asked to the amusement of his deferential Fascist audience, 'take historical precedence over the professor?'[37] The re-organised police, he boasted, were winning the battle against crime, both petty and organised. They had defeated Anti-Fascism. They were a model of intelligence.[38] Thereafter Mussolini continued to heap praise on Bocchini and to enjoy his robustly cynical company. When Fascism was at its last gasp, Mussolini would claim one reason for its final feebleness was the premature death of Bocchini.[39] The police chief was just the man not to be too taken in by easy rhetoric about charisma, and Mussolini's fondness for him suggested that the *Duce*, too, knew that deeds sometimes mattered more than words and images.

One of the creations of these years was the secret police, or Ovra, whose name was apparently chosen for its sinister resonance rather than because it stood for something. Bocchini was certainly efficient in patrolling and curtailing any who plotted against his master, filling files on 130 000 Italians.[40] He was still more successful in what a post-modernist would call controlling the discourse, sponsoring an often convincing image of the 'degeneracy' of Anti-Fascism and, simultaneously, over and over again penetrating the political resistance with his own agents and so enhancing the fear, suspicion and self-hatred which, in any case, tended to colour exile life. The censorship of the press ensured that the younger generation of Italians frequently did not even know the names of those Anti-Fascists who had fled abroad or who were in *confino*.[41] Bocchini achieved his success in this policing, despite the fact that, compared with other authoritarian regimes and even with our contemporary society, his staff at Ovra of some 375 in 1940 was small.[42] No doubt, its size hints at the actual narrowness of the political class in Italy and the superficiality of the penetration of Fascism, Anti-Fascism or any modern ideology as political religions into the great majority of Italian lives.

Equally paradoxical was the frequently used punishment system of *confino*, inherited from the Liberals but now expanded. In it, political dissidents (a number of whom were Fascists) were transferred from their homes to some remote village, always in the South (and notably on the islands of Lipari, Tremiti[43] and Ponza), where it was assumed by all that civilization and so, presumably, the nationalisation of the masses were lacking. A number of political dissidents reported that their gaolers would automatically address them as *professori* or *commendatori*, imponderable beings from a foreign and literate class, who had somehow fallen foul of the imponderable system.[44] Ironically, the more humble staff of Mussolini's office were said to regard the events which occurred there somewhat similarly.[45]

The success of Bocchini's policing, and the full backing which Mussolini gave it, ensured that the Special Tribunal was relatively mild in its recourse to capital punishment. From 1927 to 1943 the regime imposed 42 death sentences for political crimes, of which 31 were carried out, 22 of these during the Second World War. The group to be most insistently persecuted were the Slovenes on the north-eastern border – a priest could be sent to *confino* merely on the suspicion that he had celebrated a mass in Slovene.[46] In 1927 Mussolini was sufficiently paranoid about the 'Slav threat' to assure Giuseppe Volpi that plans had been worked out to repel any military-style invasion from that direction.[47] Overall, the Special Tribunal successfully prosecuted 13 547 cases and imposed 27 742 years of gaol.[48] To these totals need to be added the tens of thousands who were sent to *confino*, restricted to their homes or otherwise put under surveillance.[49]

After 1945 the most celebrated martyr of Fascism was the communist historian and politician Antonio Gramsci,[50] brought before the Special Tribunal in 1927 and singled out by Mussolini who intervened with the judges to ensure 20 years of imprisonment. Beset by illness, Gramsci survived 10, before dying on 27 April 1937, a few days after being released from gaol.[51] He was 46 years old. To many, Gramsci's fate reflected the general assault by Mussolini on the working class, its representatives and institutions. In the understanding of Marxists and those influenced by them, Fascism was impossible to analyse without some acceptance that Mussolini had become the agent of the bourgeoisie.[52] This charge was always a particularly bitter one for the *Duce*, given his memory of his own socialist youth, and he frequently sought to rebut it. Rhetorically, he could be relied on from time to time to excoriate the irresolution and languor of the bourgeoisie, people, he complained, who loved to ape the manners of the French, English and Americans, while denying influences rooted in the soul and soil of Italy.[53] Similarly, he was emphatic that Fascism, with its own syndicates or unions, did not intend to abandon the working class, but, while also not infringing property rights and the national interest, would, on all occasions, defend them.[54]

Syndicalists never ceased to play a role among the Fascist ruling elite, and their continuing presence has encouraged some to aver that Mussolini's regime always possessed a more socially radical side than did Hitler's.[55] From 1922 to 1928 the leader of Fascist syndicalism was Edmondo Rossoni, an old Romagnole associate of the *Duce*. Rossoni's emigrant experience had not been in Switzerland or Austria but in the USA, and it was amid the evident poverty and exploitation there that he came to the view that unions must accept the nation. A revolutionary interventionist, Rossoni had, by 1921, drifted into the Fascist movement. With the March on Rome, he was at once designated Secretary General of the *Confederazione delle Corporazioni fasciste* (Confederation of Fascist Corporations). In November 1926, with the dissolution of its surviving Marxist and Catholic rivals, this body was renamed the *Confederazione nazionale dei Sindacati fascisti* (National Confederation of Fascist unions). It would, the regime proclaimed, act as a sure shield for those who produced the nation's wealth. Fascism, Mussolini told a visiting British journalist, was 'a method, not an end. If you like, it is an autocracy with democratic overtones'.[56]

Perhaps buoyed by his leader's populism, Rossoni continued to press for workers' rights. However, he viewed with disfavour the fact that most of the arbitration legislation now being created was drafted by the reactionary Rocco,[57] and was unconvinced by the claim that the simultaneous banning of both strikes and lockouts was proof of the regime's even-handedness on class matters.[58] He was no less sceptical when Mussolini began talking about the institution of a 'Corporate State' – the *Duce* had taken on the new Ministry of Corporations in July 1926.[59] In this system, parliamentary representation was to be channelled through the corporations, bodies on which delegates of capital and labour would sit, it was said, in social equality and with full dedication to the cause of the nation and Fascism.[60] Not even the trumpeted drafting of a Labour Charter in April 1927, with its assertion of the complete freedom of 'professional and syndical organisation', reconciled Rossoni to the new structures of the Fascist state.[61]

Mussolini had himself played a minor part in the framing of that crucial statement, leaving the matter to debate between his keen (and reliably deferential) Under-Secretary at the Ministry of Corporations, Bottai, and Rossoni and Rocco.[62] Bottai was the quickest to realise what was wanted, publishing in *Critica fascista* an article by a young Fascist urging all Italians to 'imitate' Mussolini's way of life. 'To know and profoundly understand Mussolini, to obey him conscientiously', readers were told, 'means to understand the great cause of Fascism in the best possible way. Only a fanaticism for the *Duce* will accelerate the march of Fascism'.[63] Bottai may have thought that the Labour Charter meant a confirmation of Fascism's social purpose and embodied 'the supremacy of the ethical principle in the economic order',[64] but Rossoni saw instead a diminution of the power of the workers and a favouring of the bosses. No amount of verbiage about the mystical allure of the *Duce* could disguise that fact. When he reviewed the issue, historian Renzo De Felice agreed that the Charter did little to improve Italians' working conditions. Its real effect was merely to enhance Mussolini's own authority.[65]

One result of these events was the fall of Rossoni, who, in November 1928, found his position at the head of the Fascist unions abolished (he was replaced by seven heads of the Corporations of Industry, Agriculture, Trade, Transport, Banking, Professionals and Artists, Seamen and Airmen). This adjustment in the ordering of labour affairs occurred amid rumours that Rossoni had dared to talk about the fall of the *Duce*.[66] Certainly Mussolini began to keep a file on his old friend's acts of alleged corruption, which included land deals conducted in his father's or uncle's names and promiscuity, while a rumour that his gauche wife had once been a Rome prostitute was also recorded.[67] These matters did not prevent Rossoni's eventual return to a minister- ial post – from January 1935 to October 1939 he held the Ministry of Agriculture and Forests, a somewhat ironical fate for a workers' leader. By then he was thought to be a sardonic observer of the Nazi Labour front and still a self-conscious 'Fascist of the Left', although, having learned the lessons of seven years out of office, he took pains to emphasise that he was, above all, 'a Mussolinian'.[68] Throughout the regime, syndicalism was entrenched in the vocabulary of the *Duce* and the other Fascists, remaining a target of an imagined revolutionary future, though never ceasing to be, in practice, more intellectual construct than social reality.

During the building of the *stato totalitario*, it was none the less true that not just labour but also industry and finance felt the effect of Mussolini's power. Until 1926 Mussolini had done little to challenge the authority of the business world. He had sought to check muttering among the more militant Fascists about the behaviour of the wealthiest sections of society, officially upbraiding Farinacci when he attacked the selfishness of the banks or made other financially risky state- ments.[69] On most occasions, Mussolini defended the orthodox approach to economics of De' Stefani and Volpi, enjoying the view that his 'peasant good sense' made him natively wary of overindulgence in government expenditure.[70]

One special feature of Fascist economic policy had been the solic- iting, by Mussolini and his agents, of foreign loans to help the Italian economy recover from the war. Success had been greatest with the United States, suddenly elevated by 1918 to be the world's greatest source of capital. As early as May 1923 Mussolini had met T.W. Lamont, the new senior partner of the Morgan Bank,[71] and, despite certain difficulties during the Matteotti affair, contacts continued. After his appointment to the Ministry of Finance, Volpi, who boasted long experience of the highways and byways of international finance, travelled to the US in October–November 1925 in search of further loans, as well as a better resolution of the continuing issues of Italian war debts to the US and awaited reparation payments from Germany.[72] All went well, with Italy rising to be the second beneficiary, behind Germany, of US credit between 1924 and 1929. Access to foreign funds also helped defend the value of the lira, treated by the *Duce* as a talisman of Italy's international prestige.[73]

To enhance the happy friendship with J.P. Morgan and the other American bankers, Volpi, in summer 1926, made ready to visit the US again. However, on 8 August he abruptly received a memorandum of instruction from Mussolini. An attached letter explained:

> The notes which follow are the result not so much of deep study of the problem which has troubled us all for quite a few months, but rather the result of intuition. In so far as I am concerned, [this intuition] is almost always infallible.[74]

The crafty Volpi may have blanched at the crudity of this explanation of his *Duce*'s thought processes. When he read on, he found that the big issues had become not so much the winning of further loans, as stabilising the value of the national currency. The lira was now not so much a talisman as the heart of Fascism at home and abroad. Mussolini's tone was dramatic. 'The fate of the regime is tied to the fate of the lira', he wrote emphatically. 'It is necessary therefore to consider the battle for the lira as absolutely decisive.' As 'totalitarians', the Italians found themselves 'alone' in a vicious world; they must not bend their heads beneath the 'golden yoke of the Anglo-Saxons'; instead they should stand on their own two feet and 'act in the Fascist way, that is, with great audacity and breadth of vision'. The value of the currency was not so much an economic issue as a psychological one. Italy must be strong enough to achieve a triumph of the will.[75] Ten days later, Mussolini made the matter public in a speech which he gave at Pesaro, announcing 'battle' and proclaiming that 'the Fascist regime, from its chief to its most humble follower is ready to impose the sacrifices needed, so that our lira, which is itself a symbol of our nation, our wealth, our efforts, our strength, our sacrifices, our tears, our blood, is and will be defended'.[76] In the *Duce*'s mind, it seemed, the currency had become the incarnation of both Italy and Fascism.

Over the next 16 months, Mussolini refused to budge from this line, in December 1927 formally setting the value of the lira at 19 to the American dollar and 92.46 to the British pound and reattaching the currency to the gold standard.[77] Many commentators, Volpi among them,[78] believed that the lira was being overvalued, but Mussolini stuck to his tough deflationary line, perhaps hoping further to impress his American banking friends with his rigour and determination.[79] A.S. Benni, spokesman of the more modern industrialists in Italy, adapted to the new valuation by extracting from the *Duce* a wage reduction for the great majority of Italy's workers.[80] Those of them not yet rendered docile by Fascist repression were silenced by an accompanying rise in unemployment which, even according to official figures, trebled between 1926 and 1928.[81]

Was the Fascist regime, then, just another way of doing business? One of the most persistent claims of admirers of Mussolini is that he presided over a 'developmental dictatorship', one committed to 'modernise' Italy.[82] The evidence supporting this view from 1926 to 1929 is, however, mixed. The centralisation of the issue of Italian currency to the Banca d'Italia in July 1926 and the stripping from the Banco di Napoli and the Banca di Sicilia of their surviving right to print notes were indeed acts of firmer government control. However, at much the same time, the regime bowed to pressure from the representatives of small shopkeepers, a number of whom figured as leading Fascists, and instituted a licensing system which protected the retailers from the ravages of supermarkets and other modern sales systems.[83] In so far as his economic policies were concerned, one Mussolinian line looked modernising, the next traditional.

Typical was the story of the Banca Nazionale del Lavoro e della Cooperazione, created from a merger of previous co-operatives in May 1927, and destined to play a major part in Fascist rule both at home and abroad – in this latter case, it followed the national flag to Ethiopia and the empire and to Spain during the Civil War, and also accompanied the Axis to the European New Order.[84] In 1925 the co-operatives had been taken from the hands of Paolo Terruzzi, a Milan radical Fascist until then blessed by Mussolini himself, and placed under the direction of Arturo Osio. Though his background among the Catholic *Popolari* seemed paradoxical,[85] Osio was adroit enough to know, in his dealings with those on high, that the patronage of Farinacci might outweigh the hostility of Volpi.[86] From September 1926 Osio began regular meetings with Mussolini[87] and it was under the *Duce*'s direct aegis that he rallied the cooperatives' fortunes and converted them into a modern bank, one which would outlive Fascism. Osio cemented his ties with Farinacci[88] and also accepted the patronage of Bottai, Rossoni, Ciano and Thaon di Revel, although, when asked, he averred circumspectly that his task in life was simply to make his bank prosper. In January 1942 he was suddenly sacked by Mussolini, amid rumours that, maladroit in the end, he had earned the enmity of the Petacci family.[89] In victory and defeat, Osio was yet another leading servant of the Fascist regime who knew as much about patron–client networks as about ideology, and who happily manipulated each to his own ends.

Meanwhile, the Italian economy was exhibiting only the first signs of recovery from the deflationary effects of the high valuation of the lira when, in October 1929, the world was struck by the Wall Street collapse. During the 1930s Mussolini adopted new policies to try to combat the Great Depression as its groundswell hit Italy, too. In the short term, however, after the flurry of intervention in 1926–27, he displayed little overt interest in national economic matters. Indeed, Angelo Mosconi, who replaced Volpi[90] as Minister of Finance in July 1928, remembered Mussolini as a calm and sensible executive who always listened to frank advice and made it easy for his Minister to pursue careful and healthy policies.[91] Although the *Duce* remained alert to any matter which might damage national prestige – Giuseppe Belluzzo, the Minister for the National Economy, was persuaded publicly to retract an incautious statement that Italy still lacked sufficient raw materials[92] – having flexed his authority over bankers and industrialists, Mussolini left the experts to get on with their work. It was a method he used often.

In these circumstances, Italian business had many reasons to applaud Mussolini's rule. But what was the *Duce* to do about agriculture, still the greatest employer of Italians? Telling evidence about the limitations of the Fascist achievement in modernising Italy and in improving the lot of his subjects could be found in the continuation of poverty and disease, especially in the countryside. On a table of European states, Italy lay 18th in calorie intake, perhaps the starkest of all indices of popular well being.[93] The most wretched conditions were to be found in rural Italy. What was to be done to amend them?

One answer to this question was verbal. As early as 1924, Mussolini had told his party that 'the Italian people is predominantly rural. ... The Fascists of the countryside are the most solid; the rural militia the most disciplined'.[94] In June the following year he announced, with the characteristically militarist reference: 'I have formally opened the campaign for the battle for grain and I have already prepared a general staff to conduct it.'[95] Thereafter he frequently urged the 'ruralisation' of Italy. As he put it in his Ascension Day speech, cities and industrialisation led to sterility, both spiritually and physiologically, and only the fostering of agriculture could really prepare Italy for empire.[96]

In fact, rural Italy had adapted to Mussolini's regime with its own rhythms and regional variations. As late as June 1921 the prefect in one Calabrian town was predicting that Fascism, like 'genuine socialism', could not take root there 'for many years', because the local social circumstances were so alien to mass parties.[97] After 28 October

1922 disputes, usually between grouplets of original Fascists and late joiners, simmered in the rural world, as they did elsewhere in the country. At Catanzaro, one clear-thinking prefect noted that the *fascio* which had sprung up in the town was composed of those ex-members of the old ruling parties who had now donned a black shirt.[98] His comments were seconded by a visiting American anthropologist who, completing field work on a village in Sicily in 1928, argued that the 'high-sounding names' of national politics were used by nobody in common speech. Fascism, totalitarianism, corporatism, syndicalism – each was still an utterly alien concept. Where members of local elites did deploy such terms, it was to win advantage for their 'faction', since the *paese* had, in living memory, always been factionalised.[99] The peasants were cautiously ready to tell any questioner that Mussolini was 'a saint out of paradise',[100] and, in the 1929 referendum, voted unanimously for the regime, marching to the polling booth to the strains of the town band, which promiscuously played *Giovinezza* and the royal anthem, the *Marcia reale*.[101] But *Duce*, King and Pope impinged little on the peasants' ordinary lives, which were defined by the ecology of their agricultural surroundings and the power of the landowners. Their ignorance or cynicism about the great world was such that they believed even the god-like Garibaldi had only offered a choice between *culera o leve* (cholera or conscription).[102] Whatever else Fascism had achieved in this southern village, it had not brought social revolution, or even allowed the possibility of its imagining.

The Southern Fascist leaders seemed equally ready to stain their ideological purity with habits and attitudes from the past, finding more familiar the practice of a Bocchini than what became the theory of a Starace. In September 1924 Acerbo, for example, wrote complainingly to Mussolini of the obscure plots which eddied about him whenever he came to Rome. Could, he asked, somewhat ingenuously, conspiracy be the reason why a distant cousin of his in the Abruzzi had had his career wrecked by being dropped from his party job. 'After this ringing triumph of my enemies and those of the regime, I can't go back to the Abruzzi', he stated regretfully. Could Mussolini intervene? If he did not, he would find that 'after me, the Abruzzo will descend into chaos or worse'.[103]

Mussolini duly provided the necessary backing and Acerbo remained the leading Fascist of his region until the end of the 1930s, regularly passing on his 'recommendations' to his leader, who could rely on the fact that 'I <u>am and always will be, your devoted soldier, ready for any service</u>'[104] (so long, he meant, as his regional power did not shake and Mussolini remained an appropriately generous patron). Similarly, in 1924 Michele Bianchi summoned Mussolini's help to dispel malicious rumours about his womanising, which, he believed, were being spread by anonymous rivals within the party. It would be an 'ingratitude', he added with his own hint of blackmail – the Matteotti crisis was at its worst – if such hostility were not checked. 'Remember, *Duce*, that I was at your side, always utterly disinterested, and especially in all the saddest and most difficult moments' of the rise to power. Could Mussolini not treat him as a friend must treat a friend?[105] Again Bianchi's petition achieved its desired result and he was shored up as a prominent figure in the regime, though not without Mussolini preserving in his ever fattening file on the dalliances of his henchmen the allegation that Bianchi encouraged his aristocratic Calabrian mistress to hand out for a fee well-remunerated local appointments.[106] In turn, Acerbo, Bianchi[107] and the other southern Fascists had their own clients who treated them in much the same way as they approached their *Duce*.

This survival of an eternal South was certainly not a part of Fascism's self-image, nor did it fit the party line about the totality of Mussolinian control. Rather, another feature of the construction of the totalitarian state was the 'battle against the Mafia', in the past a particularly notorious symbol of the weakness and inadequacy of Liberal rule. In this conflict, Mussolini's agent was Cesare Mori, another state official, who, like Bocchini and Badoglio, had no special connection with the Fascist party. Though he was careful to note that he worked in the 'name and by the will of the *Duce*',[108] Mori was permitted to publish an account of his campaigns from 1925 to 1929, in which he was not at all modest about his 'victory'. He particularly emphasised that the Mafia, rather than being a single vast criminal organisation, was more a 'morbid' attitude of mind, which in turn would be overcome by the superior spirit of Fascism.[109] Historians have been sceptical about the boasted Fascist triumph. They have noted instead both the way in which Mori actually protected the power of the old landowning class[110] and the ease with which Sicily slipped again into a backwater – in the 1930s, we are told, 'in some towns the *fascio* only opened on public holidays'.[111] By that decade Mussolini, following the patterns established by his Liberal predecessors, removed Sicily from his normal itineraries. After his successive visits in 1923 and 1924, he only came again in 1937, then to talk vacuously about converting the island into an agricultural paradise.[112] In reality, his policy had been directed far more at pacifying the place than at instilling its inhabitants with a modernising and nationalising revolutionary *élan*. The payment for this failure actively to mobilise the island's citizens was drawn in the summer of 1943, when Sicilians treated the arriving Americans as scarcely more foreign, and much more temptingly rich, than their Italian rulers. Then Sicilians sloughed off Mussolini's rule without a backward glance (even if, during the post-war years, neo-fascism would develop, and retain, a popular base on the island).

Another group whose fate was being decided in these years was Italian women. Fascism possessed a mixed history on the gender question after a first female *fascio* was organised at Monza in March 1920.[113] The initial programmes of the *Fasci di combattimento* gave the issue of votes for women some prominence.[114] In office, Mussolini announced in May 1923 that no obstacle stood in the way of female suffrage and suggested that a start would be made in administrative elections.[115] He even contemplated women being assigned a role in the MVSN.[116]

However, before long, there were problems for Fascist feminism in the fine print.[117] As leader Mussolini turned out to be just another pillar of the patriarchy. Women did not gain the vote locally because local elections were abolished. As part of the new repression, in 1926 elected mayors were replaced throughout Italy by nominated *podestà*.[118] It was true that the regime expanded welfare programmes for women, establishing in 1925 the *Opera nazionale per la maternità ed infanzia* (ONMI; the National Agency for Maternity and Infancy).[119] The achievements of this organisation were conditioned by its Fascist purpose, since, in his Ascension Day speech, Mussolini placed demographic growth at the centre of the regime's programmes: 'It is necessary to watch over the destiny of the race with utter seriousness. It is necessary to make the race healthy, beginning with issues involving mothers and infants.' There were presently only 40 million Italians, Mussolini warned; how could they compete against 'ninety million' Germans and 'two hundred million' Slavs. If Italy wanted to flex its muscles in the world, it must grow to 'sixty million' by 1950. Only when they were demographically fertile did 'empires' survive and flourish.[120] And, as a symbol that breeding must proceed, on 19 December 1926 Mussolini introduced a 'bachelor tax'. Five years later homosexual acts among adult men were made illegal.[121] As Turati put it: 'The family is the basic cell of the State, the Nation and the people. It is the only possible safeguard, the only trench defending us against the corrosion coming from the various amoral, immoral and dissolvent social forces around.'[122] In a Fascist world, except when she had to turn up on parade,[123] a woman, it seemed, was to be confined to kitchen and bedroom.

As the years passed, Mussolini's personal misogyny deepened. 'Love', he told a young admirer, could only be fleeting and was not to be viewed as a sensible guide to life.[124] Women shared with priests the habit of grabbing an arm when offered a finger.[125] Strong men had to avoid their influence, since 'woman must play a passive part. She is analytical, not synthetical. During all the centuries of civilisation, has there ever been a woman architect?' he asked an interviewer rhetorically.[126] Sarfatti's influence was waning, and Mussolini showed few signs of seeking for long the company of intelligent women. As he grew older, he was reduced ever more to being a man's man.

Meanwhile the Fascist regime moved more aggressively than in the past to control education of both girls and boys. In December 1925 the use of the 'Roman' salute was made compulsory in schools and, from October 1926, the Minister of Education, Pietro Fedele, officially proclaimed the anniversary of the March on Rome a day of national rejoicing.[127] In 1928 it was decreed that textbooks were to be placed under strict state control (although the actual commission charged to supervise this process did not properly meet until 1939).[128] In the semi-official pages of *Gerarchia*, the ex-Nationalist Roberto Cantalupo expressed the view that Fascism's key task had become the creation of a new 'ruling class',[129] and during the 1930s this issue would indeed be a central one in Fascist debate. However, for the moment it was Mussolini's supremacy which mattered most. It was typical that, when, in January 1928, the *Duce* was sent a flattering account of his political thought written by the Under-Secretary for Education, Emilio Bodrero, another Fascist from a Nationalist background, his reply was abrupt. The work, Mussolini agreed, was 'interesting and at bottom right. You could add that my culture is not general, let alone generic. Rather it is <u>systematic</u> on every issue. Precisely because culture serves me and I don't serve culture. The means, not the end. An arm, not an adornment'.[130] Despite such bravado, to any who thought about the matter, his cultural pronouncements could at times be odd – what, for example, was a maker of the Italian nation and a Fascist proponent of hierarchy doing proclaiming the German fan of the French Revolution, Beethoven, the 'greatest' of all composers, the person whose music transported a man out of himself?[131]

The greatest arena of potential contestation of the *Duce*'s overweening authority remained the Fascist party and it is no surprise to find the *Duce* curbing it, too, as part of the construction of a 'totalitarian' state. One step was the sacking of Farinacci, who was replaced as PNF secretary by Augusto Turati on 30 March 1926. Farinacci was scarcely pleased to be dropped and, now and later, did not refrain from bombarding the *Duce* with complaints about his successor[132] and such other leading Fascists as Balbo, Federzoni, Bottai and even Arnaldo Mussolini, in his view constant plotters of knavish tricks against his Fascist virtue.[133] From time to time Mussolini exploded in response to Farinacci's needling: 'Everyone inside Italy and out knows, and you do, too, that, if the regime survives and wins the tremendous battles which lie ahead of it, it is because I am alive and work sixteen hours a day, like a black [for it].' 'The problems within the party', he went on savagely, 'originate in great part from your attitude of spiritual indiscipline, your attempts to monopolise a position as the pure saviour of the party, and your unceasing launching of vague and general accusations which are never followed up with proof.' Too many of his friends talked too much, Mussolini charged. Farinacci should forthwith reconcile himself with Federzoni and Balbo and accept the Turati secretaryship. There was no point in strutting around in the garb of an 'Antipope just waiting to be called'.[134]

Turati had been, and remained, close to Arnaldo Mussolini and, when the Secretary undertook another purge of party members, he favoured the more socially conservative supporters of the regime. In his own speeches he promised a new prurience as he chided Italians who drank too much or danced the Charleston and other 'negro dances'.[135] His construction of history was also conservative. Both he and the party embodied the spirit of the wartime trenches. They knew best about order and discipline.[136] The Labour Charter, he was anxious to add, underlined the complete antithesis between 'Rome and Moscow'.[137] Even if, less threateningly on one occasion, he suggested that Fascism should rule 'as much by the force of a smile as the force of the fist', he was sure that the regime should press ahead with unifying state, nation and race.[138] Developing an educational system which would mix sport and the positive inheritance of the war, Fascist teaching would now forge a 'new ruling class'.[139]

But Turati's greatest task was to discipline the party and make its members accept that Mussolini alone ruled Italy. The Fascists should not get above themselves. They should acknowledge that they, too, served the state. Therefore, when petty disputes between *ras* and state officials arose, they must result in precedence being given to the bureaucrat rather than the party member.[140] Had not the *Duce* told Farinacci firmly, 'either no one speaks, or I speak, because I know how to speak better than anyone else'.[141] Turati understood that he was Mussolini's choice as PNF secretary. He knew that his job was to ensure that Mussolini was acknowledged by all as 'the dictator over the party'.[142]

Mario Giampaoli in Milan became the most celebrated case of this disciplining of the Fascists. In the financial capital of Italy, Giampaoli commanded the forces of radical Fascism, editing a monthly entitled *1919* as a symbol of his commitment to the revolutionary thrust of the movement's early years. Even though that journal was anxious to underline that Mussolini was the 'greatest genius of the epoch', it dared to add that Fascists were needed, too.[143] By 1926 Giampaoli was already in bad odour with Arnaldo Mussolini, who feared that Farinacci would ally with him in any relaunch of the ex-secretary's influence.[144] During the next year a catalogue of sins was ascribed to the Milan *ras*. He was sexually and financially corrupt. He lived with three women, one of whom he married hastily in 1926 in order to legitimise a son. At that time he took presents of a million lire by putting pressure on local industrialists. He curried the favour of old squadrists with his populist speeches and appearance of culture (despite his lacking formal qualifications – he had begun his working life as a postman).[145] He lost heavily as a gambler and took money from a prostitution ring. He contemplated setting up his own praetorian guard and did not mind if Milan was publicly split between his supporters and those of the *Duce*'s brother.[146] He alienated Milan's intellectuals and professional classes and, indeed, the whole local bourgeoisie.[147] With such a catalogue of sin reaching Mussolini's desk, only one result was possible. Giampaoli was expelled from the PNF and *1919* was suppressed. Victory in Milan went to Arnaldo Mussolini, Turati and a coming man, Achille Starace, deployed by the other two to oust Giampaoli.[148] The defeated Milan *ras* did not quite disappear from Fascist annals. He kept up a correspondence with Mussolini, proclaiming his own injured virtue and beseeching his *Duce* to restore his patronage to him. In 1938, for example, Giampaoli believed that only the machinations of Jews were stopping his happy *sistemazione* in Naples[149] and, in 1940, with the rallying effect of the onset of war, he regained his party ticket.[150] The police continued their surveillance, however, noting his still extravagant lifestyle and ruthless exploitation of contacts.[151] A last letter survives from May 1943, in which Giampaoli begged to be restored as *federale* or party chief in Milan. He would soon sort out the current decline in morale, he promised his adored *Duce*.[152]

The most unrelentingly critical correspondence to reach the *Duce* came, predictably, from Farinacci, who never accepted the promotion of Turati and who also disliked the pieties of Arnaldo Mussolini. With his unfailing ability to pick on the adjustments and adaptations Mussolini had made but preferred not discussed, Farinacci was not, for example, slow to remind the *Duce* of his anticlerical past. With the Fascist version of wit, he wrote that a cardinal, possessed of a social conscience, had been visiting Cremona, preaching religion and chastity to the workers, even though he ought to have known that in Farinacci's town a renunciation of sexuality was 'as rare as the Arabian phoenix'. Could the worthy prelate not be sent on mission abroad, Farinacci asked, tongue in cheek? 'If I am not mistaken, there are 1 300 000 000 people on earth, of whom 300 000 000 are Catholics. Why not bring to God and Paradise the other 1 000 000 000?'[153] Mainly, however, Farinacci concentrated his fire on his perceived enemies within the PNF. They falsely painted him as an enemy of the *Duce* and were unceasing in their conspiracies against Farinacci and his friends and associates. Their deviousness was enough to convert him into 'a Fascist anarchist', even though his circle was composed of 'Fascists of a genuinely Fascist temper'[154] – Mussolini should accept that 'a real Fascist' was a man 'never afraid to tell his Chief the truth'.[155]

Farinacci viewed the world as a place where interests and individuals were locked in perpetual conflict. The Fascist party might issue appealing statements about national and ideological unity and even decree that Italians blindly serve a totalitarian state. But in this Fascist's mind, conflicts eddied and spread and Farinacci knew that whoever wanted to master his society had to be perpetually alert to present friends and enemies.[156] At the same time, although Mussolini was frequently annoyed with Farinacci, he never broke with him. The *ras* of Cremona bore too much of Mussolini's own radical and 'savage' past to be ignored or denied.

The concept of 'institutional Darwinism' has proved a fertile one for understanding of the administrative processes of Nazi Germany, providing important evidence of political activism occuring on its own, or at least without immediate direction from the dictator. In the battles of Turati, Farinacci, Giampaoli and Starace, the shadow of such Darwinian or Machiavellian conflict can be detected in Italy, too. Nor were these four the only Fascist chiefs to engage in constant struggle one against the other and to do so without Mussolini's immediate behest. All the evidence is that, among the elite (and probably elsewhere in society), such activities never ceased. Reports about Fascists on the rise typically underlined those who favoured them and who opposed them.[157] An ability to read the endless shifts in the alliances and opportunities of a self-interested world remained at the heart of the human condition under Mussolini's rule. The contradictions of any dictatorship, it is plain, the gap between what the dictator claims to know and what he can know, the secrecy or opacity of the decision-making process, the nature of charismatic rule, enhance the belief in Darwinism, though the sceptical historian might add that such attitudes and behaviour patterns are not unknown in alleged democracies and flourish especially in our contemporary 'de-ideologised' world.

If cynicism was not confined to the mind of the *Duce* under Fascist governance, throughout his period in office Mussolini rarely missed an opportunity to ingratiate himself with the Church authorities. It may be true that in 1925 he smiled a little when he formally reproached Farinacci at the intolerable prospect of a recrudescence of squadrism during *L'Anno Santo*.[158] However, any Italian leader, and especially one committed to nationalising the masses, was naturally aware of the presence of the Vatican on Italian soil. A genuine totalitarian should have wanted to uproot it. Certainly, the issue of the relationship between Church and State had been at the heart of the Risorgimento. The Liberal state had been created through the seizure of Papal territories, including the allegedly sacred 'donation of Constantine'. In turn, the modernising principles of liberalism had been anathemised by Pope Pius IX in the *Syllabus of Errors* (1864). For the next half century, somehow resolving the 'Roman question' was a prime matter for any Italian politician who wished to make a historical mark.

During the war and its aftermath, Orlando and Nitti had moved towards an accommodation with the Church only to be blocked by King Victor Emmanuel III, whose mistrustful personality endowed him with a lifetime scepticism about religion.[159] As Fascism rose towards power, Mussolini had rapidly cloaked his own anti-clericalism and done his best to curb the expression of such ideas within the PNF. One of the first public campaigns of the Fascist regime was directed at the suppression of Freemasonry, since 1789 regarded by the Church as its implacable enemy. The victory over 'atheistic socialism' gave the Church hierarchy still greater reason to applaud the new system that was developing in Italy. Equally, the more conservative sympathisers with Fascism were now able to preach that Mussolini should 'openly recognise religious values' and give the divine a presence in the 'national drama'. Fascism, they said, was the natural ally of a Catholic Church which was not by accident Roman.[160]

In May 1926 talks between Church and regime began seriously, when Mussolini authorised Rocco to meet Cardinal Pietro Gasparri, the papal Secretary of State, saying that a separation of Church and State was as absurd as a split between spirit and matter.[161] By August Francesco Pacelli, the lawyer brother to the later Pius XII and member of a family closely linked to the Vatican-owned Banco di Roma, a crucial engine of finance in Fascist Italy, joined the negotiations. His presence was further evidence of the role of brothers in the Italian dictatorship, since Arnaldo Mussolini was one of the most prominent clericals in the *Duce*'s entourage.[162] Blessed by fraternal favour, by November 1926 a draft agreement was reached.

However, its signature was delayed, and then delayed further, when Pius XI took umbrage at Fascist education policies – the aim of the *Balilla* to become a totalitarian organisation, entailing the abolition of Catholic youth groups with which it competed, was rejected by the Church. Among the Fascist leadership, Gentile, Balbo and Farinacci (though for diverse motives) tried to slow too rapid an accommodation with the Vatican, while the King and such surviving Liberal senators as Croce and Albertini similarly counselled restraint.[163] In 1928, however, talks resumed, with discussions coming to a climax in January 1929. As the final clauses – notably those on the exact financial compensation to be granted to the Church in recompense for its territorial losses in the past – were hammered out, Mussolini himself joined the negotiating team. Here, indeed, was a matter important enough for his direct attention. On night after night he worked to the small hours; the last reading of the terms on 31 January, for example, occupied him from 9 p.m. until 1.15 a.m.[164] Finally, even the exact monetary arrangements were approved. Ironically, with that survival of a continuity from the Liberal past so typical of Fascism, two old servants of Giolitti, Bernardino Nogara, in charge of Vatican banking,[165] and Bonaldo Stringher, the head of the Banca d'Italia, were left to finalise the methods and channels of payment.[166]

All then was ready for a great public display, which would be the more exhilarating because the negotiations had been kept secret. On 11 February 1929 in an opulent ceremony at the Lateran Palace, Mussolini signed the various protocols. The Vatican City became a fully independent enclave within the city of Rome and its citizens were exempted from Fascist law. In return the Church recognised that the territorial settlement of the Risorgimento was final. Further clauses returned Catholic authority over marriage, restored compulsory religious education and allowed the Vatican better to discipline dissident priests. Historians have generally concluded that the Vatican had negotiated toughly in the Lateran pacts and had seen its power enhanced in many aspects of Italian life.[167]

For Mussolini, however, these were matters which could be left to history; the short-term rewards for him were huge. His brother Arnaldo spoke of his 'highest delight' at the thought of an Italian people who could now reconcile their everyday inspiration from Catholicism with their nation state.[168] Similarly unstinting in his praise, Pope Pius XI eulogised the *Duce* as the 'Man whom providence has sent us'. The papal paper, *L'Osservatore Romano*, applauded a pact whereby 'Italy has been given back to God and God to Italy'.[169] The Jesuit journal, *Civiltà Cattolica*, in March 1929 agreed that Fascism incarnated 'the restoration of a Christian society'.[170] In 1932 Pius XI even for a time favoured something which he called 'Catholic totalitarianism'.[171] Catholic publicists applauded Mussolini and Pius XI as 'the two greatest men in modern Italy'.[172] A police report on Italian opinion similarly acknowledged 'the unparalleled success of the *Duce*'s genius', although the nation's Jews were thought somewhat troubled by the potentially negative implications of conciliation for them.[173] Abroad, there was similar approval, especially in circles friendly to the causes of the Church. The British Catholics' mouthpiece, *The Tablet*, celebrated the 'great-hearted' and 'great-willed' Mussolini, who had shown himself an 'intellectual giant' in defeating those Italians who wanted a 'Derided Church in an Atheist state'.[174] *The Times*, too, hailed the Concordat as 'very great news indeed', proof of Mussolini's 'great daring and great statesmanship',[175] even if *The Economist* more sceptically argued that an alliance between two autocracies should scarcely give surprise.[176] Although non-Catholics soon turned their minds to other issues, the Catholic press, and Catholic opinion in general, never forgot the Lateran Pacts, and the great majority of Catholic commentators were willing to forgive Mussolini much else because of 'his' resolution of the Roman Question. It was in the troubling days of March 1942 that Mussolini sought to raise public morale by authorising Carlo Biggini, later a Minister at Salò, to collect a full documentary account of an event still allegedly approved 'unanimously' by Italians. Biggini knew the phrasing expected of him. The framing of the Concordat had, he said, been a time when Mussolini 'had been [unequivocally] right'.[177] Certainly there were many Catholics outside Italy who were still impressed with the deal. Even in September 1943 the Irish-Australian Archbishop of Melbourne, Daniel Mannix, described Mussolini as 'the greatest man living today', head of 'the greatest government Italy has ever had'.[178] In such Catholic eyes, the accommodation with the Church had indeed made Mussolini for ever a Man of Providence. It is no wonder that a historian, reviewing the state of Italy in 1929, has argued that the Italian dictator could then rejoice in a fuller consensus than ever before.[179]

To be sure, ironies abounded in the Lateran Pacts. The 'revolutionary' Mussolini had reached accord with the most powerful conservative force in Italian society. The *Duce* who boasted of his total power and infinite charisma had acknowledged that an equal (and potentially greater) power and charisma was incarnated in the Pope. In his heart, Mussolini might retain the atheism of his youth (mixed with a certain superstitition, typical of many of his countrymen, which urged that, despite the irrationality of His being, God might yet exist). Notwithstanding the *Duce*'s occasional railing against his fate, Mussolini's dictatorship had not, would not, and could not storm the citadel of Catholicism.

Such carping thoughts were not, of course, to be expressed openly. Rather, in 1929, as a symbol of the refulgent national glory of the Fascist regime, from the *Rocca delle Caminate*, the much restored, indeed decidedly fake,[180] medieval castle set above Predappio and granted to the *Duce* and his family by a grateful public two years before these momentous events, now radiated the green–white–red light of the Italian tricolour. It could be seen across the countryside and well out into the Adriatic.[181] More privately, the economic fortunes of the Mussolini family had done well from royalties and other arrangements. As late as 1926 Arnaldo had feared that debt would overwhelm *Il Popolo d'Italia*.[182] However, backers had been found and the paper made an instrument of the totalitarian regime. Moreover, to the Carpena estate and the Caminate castle was added a beach house at Riccione, a Romagnole resort to which the *Duce* often repaired in summer. Although he had taken to declaiming against excessive public adulation,[183] Mussolini had become a man of property. As if to indicate his new social status, after his triumph over the Lateran Pacts Mussolini left his quarters in the Palazzo Tittoni to move to the Villa Torlonia, an opulent eighteenth-century palace, on the Via Nomentana, beyond the Porta Pia and the Aurelian wall. The Villa's princely owners held land in many parts of Italy, were not advocates of social revolution, and certainly expected that their new tenant, to whom they had offered a generous rental, would understand their world and its terms and conditions. On 15 November 1929 Rachele and the children moved into this palatial home with its extensive gardens, making the Mussolinis resemble, at least at a superficial glance, the ideal Catholic family as never before. As a demonstration of her own authority in the capital, Rachele sacked Cesira Carocci, her husband's housekeeper since 1923 (though the loss of employment was sweetened in a characteristic Fascist way when Carocci was accorded a pension by the Fascist state; in 1944, she was still sufficiently remembered to be granted an extra payment at a time of need).[184] Mussolini might rule in Rome; but his wife, a traditionalist in her way, had not surrendered her power on the home front. Buoyed by friendships with princes of Church and State, Mussolini had come a long way from Predappio. The only drawback for the Man of Providence was the lurking possibility that these deals and arrangements, rather like those that had promoted Bocchini, Badoglio, Osio and the rest, were leaving certainly the Fascist revolution and perhaps the *Duce*'s power still a mirage.

11

Mussolini in his pomp,
1929–1932

THE triumphant deal with the Catholic Church seemed to translate Mussolini to a new summit of power. While, with the collapse of Wall Street in October 1929, other politicians found their lives full of pitfalls and their futures dim, Mussolini's image shone brightly throughout Italy and beyond. Arrangements had, with patience and skill, been reached with every segment of the old, pre-Fascist, elite. The Pope and the King, industrialists, bankers and landowners, Army, police and officialdom, the great majority of intellectuals (an exception were a few recalcitrant dissidents, most of whom had been chased abroad), all seemed delighted to work with the *Duce*. So, too, did foreign governments, whose expert advisers, during these years of Mussolini's pomp, were increasingly likely to counsel study of the Italian model. Economists, for example, ever more dismal about their inability to block the inroads of the Great Depression into their own societies, were ready to believe that Fascism had inoculated Italy against the unemployment and the collapse of prices and production occurring elsewhere. As Paul Einzig of the *Financial Times* mused after a visit to Italy in 1932: 'The Italian nation has become disciplined beyond recognition, and ... has developed the mentality that places cooperation for the common good above selfish considerations.' The Corporate State, he urged, deserved detailed review, while Mussolini's authority had him in awe. It was 'an amazing mass psychological phenomenon'. The *Duce*'s 'strength and statesmanship' were, he concluded, limitless.[1]

The Fascist party, once so fretful, had been chastened and harnessed during Turati's secretaryship. It might be acknowledged that leading Fascists still squabbled endlessly among themselves. As Mussolini explained in his usual tone, the trouble with revolutions was that the revolutionaries survived them.[2] But scoring cynically witty points was the more pleasant an activity because nowhere among the party chiefs could anyone be imagined contesting the *Duce*'s role and charisma. Within the Fascist regime Mussolini was, or seemed, confirmed as a ruler possessing all but imperial powers. Mussolini had not followed the example of Ahmet Zogu, who had raised himself to become King Zog I in client Albania. But the *Duce* did cherish parallels perceived between himself and Napoleon Bonaparte[3] (who, according to Nationalist commentators, although a Corsican, was 'really' an Italian).[4] The more grovelling biographers added that Mussolini should not be limited by the comparison with one emperor alone;[5] actually, he was the amalgam of all the worthy emperors who had ever been.[6] As if to point the way to such assessments, in 1928-29 Mussolini found time to collaborate with dramatist Giovacchino Forzano on the text of a play about Napoleon,[7] and permitted himself to be cited as co-author when it was performed outside Italy (it did very well in Budapest).[8] The Forzano-Mussolini Napoleon was a great man, prescient and heroic, but destined, none the less, to be betrayed: 'When I am gone, you will hear me defamed by every obscene tongue in France. The men I made, the men in whom I kindled greatness, the men I redeemed from squalor – there is no dishonour that they will spare my name.'[9]

If this passage gives any insight into the *Duce*'s mind, it suggests that a darkness had not dissipated from it. However, for the present, foreboding could be easily confined to Mussolini's private thoughts. Newsreel shots of him at this time show a leader both mobile in his expressions and gestures and ready to smile; the *Duce* visually was a man of charm and panache. Equally, in 1929 the Italian people appeared cheerful and tranquil, with few exceptions fully reconciled to the dictatorship. Propaganda said that they were being persuaded to place Fascism at the centre of their identities. Historical analysis, by contrast, reveals that Catholicism, the family, the *paese* and region, patron–client networks, gender attitudes and many another lingering structure of the histories of the Italies actually distracted the populace from too fervent a Fascist religiosity. For all that, the masses were indubitably quiet and respectful, and, in the referendum of 24 March, gave overwhelming support to the regime and its policies, especially its accommodation with the Church. More than eight and a half million Italians voted yes in support of the regime; only 135 000 voted no, with 8092 spoiling their ballot.[10]

Symbolising his elevation to such unchallenged grandeur, on 16

September 1929 Mussolini moved his office from the Palazzo Chigi to the Palazzo Venezia. There he was ensconced in the Renaissance *Sala del Mappamondo*, built for Popes in the fifteenth century and recently restored. The room measured 18 metres by 15, with a ceiling that was twelve metres high.[11] Footsteps resounded evocatively as visitors timidly trod the vast distance between office door and *Duce*'s (often cluttered) desk. The heart of Rome lay just outside the palace: there stood the Capitol of classical times, and the Victor Emmanuel monument, grandiose symbol of the ambitions of the Liberal era. Soon the balcony of the Palazzo Venezia, the place where Mussolini now gave his most significant or populist speeches, would have a view of the Colosseum, freed by ruthless Fascist urban renewal from its medieval accretions.[12] The wide new avenue which led to the great arena past the classical forums was named the *Via dell'Impero* (Empire Street). Here was a setting where echoes of the First and Second Italies resounded for the Third (even though one cheeky and self-confident young Fascist, who simply walked past the 'lax' guards into the *Duce*'s office, noticed that, like many another, Mussolini kept a photo of his parents on his desk, with images of himself playing the violin and a picture of his 'magnificent angora cat' furnishing other corners of the room).[13]

Luisa Passerini has commented that the first purpose of Mussolini's stream of visitors was to have their dreams confirmed.[14] But it would be more accurate to remark that the *Duce* could inspire both dreams and dread. The *Sala del Mappamondo* was designed to intimidate, almost as though the austerity of the 1920s, with its Roman Republican or early imperial motifs, had been ousted by a Byzantine desire to set the dictator apart from his subjects.[15] From a Coriolanus, one of the Gracchi or a Julius Caesar,[16] Mussolini had been transformed into a Constantine or a Justinian, a semi-deity whose refulgence blinded the dwarfish thieves of ordinary humankind. Marking this lofty eminence, the rhetoric about the *Duce*'s charisma changed direction. The emphasis grew insistent that he was and must be alone. During the 1920s he had, on occasion, complained about his isolation;[17] in the 1930s it became, or was said to have become, a natural part of himself. In April 1932 he told an admirer:

One must accept solitude. . . . A chief cannot have equals. Nor friends. The humble solace gained from exchanging confidences is denied him. He cannot open his heart. Never.[18]

By now Mussolini ostentatiously refused to exchange house visits with the families of Fascist ministers; sociability was not for the likes of him.[19] Innumerable photographs fashioned this newly 'granitic' image into every watcher's mind. By the mid-1930s a stern, unsmiling, thin-lipped and shaven-headed *Duce*, as likely as not equipped with a military helmet, became the ubiquitous image of the dictator. No doubt encroaching baldness was one reason for the headgear (and the fact that what hair he had was turning white another),[20] but Mussolini the marble or steely soldier, Mussolini the human machine, now replaced the more nuanced images of the past.

Had Mussolini, then, in the happy years from the Lateran Pacts to the *Decennale*, or tenth anniversary celebrations of the March on Rome, acquired total power? Was he now a dictator untrammelled by any serious opposition, a man who could by himself chart the fate of Italy and even aspire to transform the world? Was all as it seemed in the structure of authority and decision-making in Fascist Italy? Did Fascism, as one historian has put it with a surprising archness, now possess 'the appearance of a perfectly solid totalitarian system'?[21] After all, not quite everyone altogether and always believed what they saw. In 1927 a police report stated that Aldo Lusignoli had complained to his friends about the ubiquity of police in the Fascist state; their daily meddling outdid the 'wretched record of the Bourbons or the Austrians' before the Risorgimento. But what was the repression for, Lusignoli asked? Had he wanted to, Mussolini could have eliminated that violence and corruption among the Fascists which put its critics out of countenance. 'But', said Lusignoli, 'given his mentality and his innate fear of the stronger, I do not believe and shall never believe that Hon. Mussolini will sweep away his friends, those who have made a myth of him in order to control the whole ramshackle edifice'.[22] Turati, who was suddenly dropped as PNF secretary in October 1930 after rumours of homosexuality and paedophilia were spread about him (belying his official image of spartan incorruptibility),[23] in retrospect agreed. Writing after 1945, he recalled a *Duce* who had 'a terror of his own inadequacy'. Having resolved an issue, Mussolini, he claimed, appeared serene, the better to conceal his often justified fear that he had in the process allowed himself to be dominated by his inferiors.[24] Tullio Cianetti, an Umbrian Fascist enthusiast on the rise in the Fascist union movement, took a different tack. He noticed the uplifting effect of every speech the *Duce* gave. It was only after the euphoria lessened that questions occurred. Just how were the policies so sonorously proclaimed to be carried through? There was the rub, since no one knew how to respond,[25] except with a catch phrase about 'Mussolini's gradualism', polite words to describe the actual stasis which often survived somewhere beneath the rhetorical charge.[26]

The words of Lusignoli, Turati and Cianetti raise intriguing questions, ones present in the historiography of other dictatorships. How did the *Duce* rule? What were the limits, if any, of Mussolini's power?[27] Was he, in any sense, a 'weak dictator'? Were the characteristic features of the Fascist regime imposed from 'above' or 'below'? Had Mussolini mastered Italy, as propaganda loudly contended, or had Italy mastered him?

One arena in which these matters might be measured is foreign affairs. From the beginning of his career, Mussolini had most directly expressed his aspirations to be a 'Great Man' by advertising his expertise in international relations. Similarly, both contemporary and later commentators proved anxious to talk about 'Mussolini's Roman Empire'[28] and 'Mussolini's wars'. Among present-day historians, Macgregor Knox has been especially keen to link *Duce* and *Führer* in what he interprets as a natural 'common destiny'; in his view, each headed the interwar version of what present parlance calls a rogue state. Moreover, as far as Knox is concerned, Mussolini's programme of aggression was 'fixed in all essential details' by 1926,[29] or maybe before that since, he argues, 'war, a very great war, was from the very beginning the essence of Mussolini's program'.[30]

Other historians are less convinced, with Ennio Di Nolfo remarking shrewdly that Mussolini 'backed the revision of the Versailles treaty, but did not actually want its revision'.[31] Contemporaries were similarly unsure. British Foreign Secretary, Austen Chamberlain, who had frequent dealings with the *Duce*, noted: 'I doubt very much whether Mussolini himself knows exactly what he wants his relations with France to be.'[32] A sabre-rattling speech at home would be succeeded by much more rational behaviour in the world of diplomacy. For all Mussolini's rhetoric, Fascist Italy sent dutiful representatives to serve on many committees of the League of Nations and the Italian appointees, in turn, were not treated by their colleagues as men dominated by ideological fanaticism.[33] Fascist Italy even signed the Kellogg-Briand 'Peace' Pact in 1928, although, in a speech to the Chamber of Deputies, Mussolini occasioned knowing laughter from his listeners when he dismissed this agreement as 'so sublime that it should be called transcendental'.[34] All the same, while the pact was being negotiated, he had accepted that there was no point in unilaterally rejecting it.[35]

At the centre of any attempt to define Mussolinian diplomacy in this and other instances is a philological question, typical of the discipline of history. How is a contradiction between words and deeds to be read? Take the question of personnel. When it came to staffing the Foreign Ministry, Mussolini's behaviour appears more radical than it was towards the Army or police. He began 1926, for example, by proclaiming it Fascism's 'Napoleonic year'. 'From today', he promised, Italy 'will begin to have a moral and material place in the world' fitting its increased and increasing power.[36] Apparently true to his word, in September he allowed Contarini to retire from his position as Secretary-General of the Foreign Ministry[37] and, lest a successor match Contarini's alleged moderation, from 1927 any nomination to the Secretary-Generalship lapsed. Under Fascism, politicians, it was clear, were to rule within the Ministry, not bureaucrats.

In 1928 Mussolini and his ambitious Under-Secretary, Dino Grandi, followed up by pushing a score of senior diplomats into early retirement, while simultaneously changing the rules of entry to the Ministry to allow a 'Fascist call-up'.[38] Quite a bit has been made of this purge of the diplomatic staff (and another in 1932), all the more because, after 1945, such emphasis could cloak the extent to which Mussolini's foreign policy, throughout his regime, had either been unoriginal or had been greeted with applause from most members of the national elite. A sense of context is necessary; Mussolini was not the first to fail to nominate a Secretary-General. Crispi had done the same in 1888.[39] Nor were Liberal ministers at all backward in employing their own patronage among neophyte diplomats, who duly cleaved to certain ideological beliefs. In 1914 the Italian diplomatic service was strongly coloured by the unspoken assumptions of the Southern landowning class which largely staffed it, and younger diplomats were likely to approve the ideas of the new Nationalist Association and hope that a Greater Italy could somehow be conjured into existence. It was true that ideology had to bend itself to the practices and customs of the Ministry -- the expression of too overt a passion was inevitably regarded as bad form in such a place. But this reality was true of Italian diplomatic staff after 1928. With the occasional exception, the attitudes of the 'Fascist *leva*' are impossible to distinguish from those of their colleagues who continued in the service from Liberal days. Similarly, few staff backed Salò, and not all of them were excluded from diplomatic careers after 1945.[40] One who, in 1943, opted for the monarchy was Franco Farinacci, the son of the *ras* of Cremona and, before then, vice-consul in such ideologically acceptable places as Hamburg and Seville.[41] He did not retire from the Italian diplomatic service until 1973.[42]

Another instructive case was Grandi, promoted Foreign Minister in September 1929, retaining that office to July 1932, and thereafter, until 1939, ambassador in London.[43] Although his class background always hinted at eventual respectability, Grandi had risen as a radical Fascist, one of the leaders of the opposition to Mussolini over the pact of pacification with the socialists in 1921. He had also been early to dismiss the League of Nations as no more than a coalition of over-rich victors and to demand the revision of the Treaty of Versailles.[44] By 1922, however, Grandi's view of the world was moderating. He was one who could easily adapt himself to office, especially while he remembered to salute his *Duce* as 'a genial statesman armed with an all but supernatural instinct';[45] Mussolini, he agreed, was '<u>the Synthesis of the life of the State</u>' [*sic*], 'infallible in his realism'.[46] Handsome, debonair and urbane, Grandi was a man whom international diplomacy understood, treasured and believed (rightly) it could seduce.[47]

If the personnel of Mussolini's Foreign Ministry did not look as though they embodied a complete break in national continuity, what of actual policy? The Fascists had some zones of special interest, a number inherited from their Liberal predecessors. A weather eye was kept on East Africa and its surrounds, as had been done, with varying results,[48] since the 1880s. Mussolini might declare that, of all the Great Powers, Italy had the most interest in Yemen;[49] he might wonder if more direct advantage could be wrung from Ethiopia.[50] But no drastic action followed, with the *Duce* approving the rise of Ras Tafari to become Emperor Haile Selassie I and signing a friendship treaty between the two states in 1928.[51] In this part of the world Mussolini still went with the flow. A diplomat posted to Addis Ababa remembers a farewell meeting with the *Duce*, full of pleasantries and banalities and ending without Mussolini issuing any instructions or in any way suggesting a revised national line.[52]

When, in 1931, Ethiopia surfaced again as an issue in Rome, it was because the French Prime Minister, Pierre Laval, raised the possibility with Grandi that Italy might be granted 'compensation' there.[53] Laval's initiative was appraised in detail by Raffaele Guariglia, the career diplomat who would be first post-Fascist Minister òf Foreign Affairs after July 1943.[54] Despite his traditional background, Guariglia was delighted to contemplate a means by which 'the generation of Mussolini' could purge the 'stain' of Adowa from the national record. Ethiopia, he advised, was 'the only demographic and economic outlet still open to us. To penetrate it, we'll need money; to take it, probably war. But you don't get anything in this world without effort and strife. If we want an empire, we must find the means to get it'. However, he cautioned, when Italy engaged in African action, its leader should not forget the nation's fundamental interest, 'the only grave, if not mortal danger threatening our country'. That strategically ominous event was an *Anschluss*, that is, a German takeover of Austria. Guariglia counselled a further improvement of Italian ties with France in order to block any German advance.[55] In all this discussion, Mussolini played no part, except as a passive reader of official papers. Ethiopia was not yet significant enough a problem for his independent interest.

Rather than an imagined thrust into Africa, during the first decade of Fascist rule the most immediate diplomatic question was Italy's relationship with the new state on its north-eastern borders coming to be called Yugoslavia. Events during the 1990s might make Fascist policy seem less the actions of a rogue state than those of a prophet of NATO virtue, but Mussolini, despite his public approval of the Treaty of Rapallo, never ceased to meddle in the murky domestic politics of his neighbour. His intrigues brought no protest from Italian diplomats, who instead saw a continuity with what Liberal Italy had been doing since Albania began its uneasy existence in 1913. Italian patronage of King Zog[56] was filled with anti-Yugoslav intent, and Mussolini similarly sent subsidies[57] and smiles to localist 'Moslem' forces in Kosovo.[58] In October 1926 he suddenly suggested to Badoglio that Italy should develop a full-scale invasion plan against Yugoslavia[59] – was this idea an example of what contemporaries understood by the *Duce*'s 'intuition'? However, although Mussolini briefly urged that 'there was not a minute to lose', the matter was not followed up, at least in the 1920s.

Still more damaging to the construction of a united Yugoslavia was Italy's fostering of Croat separatism through the nationalist politician and eventual murderous fascist, Ante Pavelić.[60] When Yugoslavia itself opted for a more authoritarian (and Serb) constitution in 1929, Croat dissidents were given asylum and military training in Italy, helped by the patronage of the ex-Nationalist, Roberto Forges Davanzati,[61] and nourished by a monthly subsidy of 70 000 lire from secret Ministry of Foreign Affairs funds.[62] In February 1929 Pavelić launched with an Italian interlocutor (but not Mussolini) the idea of organising the assassination of the Yugoslav King, Alexander.[63] For the moment the Italians did nothing in response except record the idea, and Grandi remarked complacently that Croat enthusiasm should not be mistaken for the genuinely 'revolutionary instinct' of Italian Fascism.[64] In sum,

Fascist Italy was a bad neighbour to Yugoslavia, but it was not yet plotting with any zeal or consistency the outright collapse of the Yugoslav state. There is also very little evidence that Mussolini's own ideas in the area were either original or especially influential. For many Italians, the Yugoslav question was inextricably tied to the demographics of the Venezia-Giulia and the nationalist determination to deny or to cancel the 'Slav' minorities who lived there. Mussolini scarcely broke with tradition when, in April 1929, he peremptorily ordered the prefect of Trieste to ensure that 'no Slav newspaper' appeared on the streets of that avowedly Italian but naturally polyglot city.[65]

What, then, of the ideological image of Mussolini's regime internationally? The institution of the dictatorship and the subsequent creation of the totalitarian state touched off a debate about the potential place of Fascism in world history. Contributors to *Critica Fascista* and other journals were alert to indications that foreigners were entranced by Italian events. Georges Valois and his *Faisceau* in France,[66] the dictatorship of Miguel Primo De Rivera in Spain,[67] the paramilitary *Heimwehr* in Austria,[68] rightists in Lithuania,[69] Fascists in Japan or Albania or Great Britain[70] (and British pro-Fascists living in Italy),[71] an Australian Prime Minister allegedly gone Fascist in his legislation[72] – the deeds of each won approving mention in the pages of the Fascist press as apparent proof of what were habitually labelled the 'universal aspects of Fascism'.[73] A belief that the Fascist message could be carried across the border was widespread, although Margherita Sarfatti sentimentally sought to explain that a Fascist advance would amount to 'a pacific imperialism through the great exchange of ideas and profound spiritual revolutions'.[74] None the less, for all these hints of ideological expansionism, in a speech to the Chamber of Deputies in March 1928, Mussolini stated firmly that Fascism was 'not a matter for export'.[75]

What is to be made of this statement? The only sensible conclusion is that Mussolini and the rest of the ruling elite had not yet decided on the meaning of universality for a dictatorship in the least of the Great Powers. After all, at the very time when Mussolini was claiming that Fascism was for Italian eyes only, his brother was averring that the Italian model of government had exportable features. In March 1928 Arnaldo pronounced Fascism universal in the sense that it embodied a new type of civilization, sprung from the war, and contrary to the 'aridity' of Anglo-Saxons and the 'barbarity' of Bolshevik Russians.[76] Arnaldo also patronised Berto Ricci, a young Fascist of philosophical and radical bent, who wanted to carry the regime further and faster towards empire and towards the fascistisation of the world.[77] In January 1931 Ricci began publishing a journal entitled *L'Universale* to spread such ideas. The following year the Fascist government favoured the prospect of a fascist International,[78] although the rise of Hitler and the Nazis in Germany was by then making it unlikely that too many ambitious foreign 'fascists' would look to Rome rather than Berlin for intellectual and financial support. Perhaps the most confused position was held by Sarfatti who, in 1932, declared that 'Mussolini, in the name of Italy, has taken on the *leadership* of the world; but there assumes a higher task still which is to defend the Western civilization of the white races'.[79] Whether or not she reflected a confusion in her lover's mind must be left to speculation.

It is plain, certainly, that Arnaldo Mussolini was not without contradictions. From his power base of Milan, he had, for example, looked graciously on the arrival of Rotary in Italy, himself accepting membership of that body.[80] Rotary's liberal internationalism raised some Fascist hackles, but, in 1929, Alessandro Pavolini took time to explain the proper Fascist line: 'in regard to international bodies and associations, like Rotary, which have sprung from a mentality uncongenial to ours as Fascists (for example from democratic, or pacifist, or Protestant, or Jewish mentalities), the Regime has generally followed the policy of being present. It has simply had itself represented by its own men'.[81] The story of the Kellogg-Briand Pact and the League of Nations was being repeated. Fascist spokesmen continued to stress the radical coloration of their dictatorship within Italy, but, at least for the present, they were willing to compromise with the Greater Powers abroad and to some degree adapt themselves to their fashions. Mussolini gave no sign of objecting to such tactical subtlety.

The same attitude recurred in the regime's policies with regard to disarmament, which appeared such a crucial issue in Europe from 1929 to 1932. In his heart, Mussolini undoubtedly viewed the whole idea as 'a tragi-comedy' as he once described it to Austen Chamberlain (who may not have disagreed).[82] However, although the *Duce* was verbally obstreperous in demanding that Italy get, or seem to get, the best in any deal on disarmament,[83] he did not withdraw Italian representatives from Geneva. He just pursued a double line, registering his approval of ingratiating advice from Grandi that the continuing fiasco at the League of Nations would make it easier to persuade Italians to accept 'new sacrifices' for an eventual rearmament[84] (even though there was little sign of such a modernising of Italian arms actually happening – Badoglio advised that any contemplation of a two-front war against France and Yugoslavia would amount to 'our suicide').[85] Indeed, in October 1930 Mussolini told party officials: 'Italy will disarm, only if everyone disarms. ... However, we must also be clear that we arm ourselves materially and spiritually for defence not aggression. Fascist Italy will never start a war'.[86]

It is unlikely that the clauses debated and re-debated at Geneva were Mussolini's first preoccupation. Rather he better displayed his real sensitivities when he rebuked Grandi for writing directly to Farinacci, who, as a result, had published an article in his paper *Il Regime Fascista* praising Grandi.[87] Could there have been somewhere in the process a whiff of mutiny, the *Duce* asked himself, a rival construction of charisma? In Mussolini's mind, all roads traversed by his underlings should lead to Mussolini. This was the leader, alert to even a zephyr of complaint or doubt, who Fulvio Suvich, a Triestine Fascist promoted to be his Under-Secretary when Mussolini resumed the Ministry of Foreign Affairs in July 1932, remembered saying on a number of occasions: 'The Fascists won't like this.'[88] Until the rise of Hitler and the Nazis, worrying about his image, fencing off his charisma and managing the PNF remained for Mussolini more significant matters than charting a new and independent foreign policy.[89] The *Duce* might zealously or dutifully read the diplomatic traffic, and profusely underline the texts of the telegrams and despatches which flowed in great number across his desk, especially because the absence of a Secretary-General had reduced the chance of serious bureaucratic appraisal of information before it left the Ministry. Just occasionally, though increasingly as the 1930s wore on, he might list a set of priorities to be followed in one or other policy area. But, to 1932, Italian diplomacy under his dictatorship remained more Italian than anything else; in so far as foreign affairs were concerned, Mussolini administered a system rather than crafting a new policy of his own free will.

One area of international dealing which might seem to counter this conclusion is emigration. There, by the end of its first decade in power, Fascism appeared to have made a difference. Whereas before 1914 Italians had been abandoning their country at a rate inexorably approaching one million per year (prompting Nationalists to bewail a 'haemorrhage of lost blood'),[90] by 1934 the number leaving had been cut to 68 461.[91] Confirming what looked a drastic turn in national policy, in 1927 Grandi announced that the word 'emigrant' had been cancelled from Italian vocabularies. Similarly, the revived imperialism of the 1930s would seek its justification in demographics.[92] Since the

Italians were a 'prolific people', unlike their French and some other neighbours, this argument proposed that they be appeased with territorial gain. Behind such rhetoric was a new bureaucracy, notably the so-called *Fasci all'estero* (Fascists Abroad). Building on a Liberal structure of *Istituti coloniali italiani* (Italian colonial institutes), which had, however, never functioned effectively, the *Fasci italiani all'estero* promised to inculcate both Fascist ideals and *italianità* among Italians resident abroad. Generous official funding ensured that they could publish a journal, from June 1925 euphoniously entitled *Il Legionario* (The Legionary), full of stories of national triumph and pushing the ideal of an 'heroic and religious' empire.[93] In some accounts, the *Fasci all'estero* constituted another piece in the edifice of a genuinely Fascist and totalitarian society.[94] Might their combined interest in welfare and national glory also explain why, after 1945, memories of Mussolini were happier in most Italian emigrant communities than they were in Italy itself?[95]

Perhaps. But it is hard to accept that the *Fasci all'estero* changed the world. In practice, the migration policy of Mussolini and his regime was reactive rather than original. In 1923 Mussolini had been ready to agree that emigration was 'a physiological necessity for the Italian people'. In 1924 he told the Senate that 'one cannot and must not think about wars to win territory to colonise'.[96] Only in 1926 did he shift ground to state that he was 'no longer an enthusiast' of emigration, revisiting what had once been his Marxist charges against the exploitation which was allegedly the inevitable lot of those who departed their country.[97] His new position was occasioned not so much by his own ideologically impelled beliefs as by the more restrictive attitudes of host societies, and especially the USA, against Italian immigrants. Even then Mussolini remained careful. When the *Fasci all'estero* grew too pushy, they were rebuked in much the same way that radical Fascists experienced at home. Fresh statutes, framed in 1928, emphasised that the *Fasci all'estero* must not infringe the laws of the foreign countries where they operated.[98] Thereafter government money was regularly found to pay for Fascist propaganda among emigrants and, through such bodies as the *dopolavoro* (afterwork) clubs and while Fascism won its wars, converts flocked to its ranks. However, Fascism never resolved the fundamental dilemma at the root of any thoroughly nationalist, let alone racist, Italian foreign policy, which might seek genuinely to nationalise the emigrant masses. If Italy were ever really to imitate Nazi Germany and aspire to bring all Italians home to its *Reich*, then it needed to plan the urgent seizure of New York, Buenos Aires and many another city in the New World. Instead, it sought advantage in Ethiopia and Libya, already populated African territories of little allure to any sensible Italian emigrant. Even at its most aggressive, Fascist Italy behaved as though it were a nineteenth-century power, replicating the grab for Africa indulged in by the Greater Powers at that time. Neither Mussolini nor any other Italian Fascist succeeded in finding a way to give expansionism a 'mass base' and, as a consequence, in its aggression, Fascist Italy never acquired the murderous determination (and notoriety) of its Nazi ally.

There are some ironies in this situation. The worst killing fields of Fascist Italy were within its empire, much of that territory inherited from its Liberal predecessors and all constituting only a small chapter of the European overcoming of the world beyond Europe. In most senses, Italy was not only the least but also the most belated of the European imperial powers. Historiographical relativities and those of power in the world since 1945 have combined to hide the imperial chapter of Fascist history and Mussolini's place in it. None the less, it is a sad and an instructive tale, worth recounting.

In 1922 an Italian writ uneasily covered the colonies of Eritrea and Somalia, acquired in the 1880s, the territories of Tripolitania and Cyrenaica with the desert ex-vilayet of Fezzan, together renamed with classical Roman reference Libya, and won through conflict with Turkey in 1911-12. Italy also governed the Dodecanese islands, seized during that war and retained thereafter, despite considerable international pressure that the Greek populace be handed over to Greek rule. Of this dusty imperium, the most significant part was Libya. During Italy's First World War, Liberal governments had done little to maintain what had always been a fragile national conquest there. In 1921 eighty-nine allotments for a total of 2500 hectares were the extent of Italian agricultural development in the colony.[99] Nevertheless, by then, the Liberal government had determined on Libya's 're-conquest', under the aegis of Giuseppe Volpi, Governor of Tripolitania from July 1921, and Giovanni Amendola, Minister of Colonies from February 1922 and destined to be a 'martyr' to Fascism. Somewhere in the background was the assumption, registered in 1911 by Maffeo Pantaleoni, eventual co-editor of *La Vita Italiana*, that 'the bastardised local population, composed of a mixture of the most disgusting of races, must be repelled and destroyed and replaced by good Italian blood'.[100] Italian imperialism was inevitably similar to that which would lead, or had led, to the decimation of indigenous peoples in many a land annexed by a metropolitan power.

When they thought about a resumed conquest of Libya, neither the trimming Volpi nor the liberal democrat Amendola blanched at 'firmness', a word whose practical significance was often murder. Fascist governance thus offered only a partial break in continuity, with Mussolini's own line on the empire summed up by its leading historian as 'vague, changeable and sometimes contradictory'.[101] Volpi, who remained as Governor until August 1925 and could rely on the backing of Federzoni and Scalea, his Nationalist ministers, and, less directly, of the *Duce*, tried to foster capitalist development, preferring such investment to ideas about a more populist immigration. Volpi typically laboured to produce reports about colonial developments which emphasised his own skills, while downplaying those of others, except for the military victories of the young soldier, Rodolfo Graziani,[102] sent by him into the interior.[103] Graziani, it was soon clear, believed that the best way to win was to be vicious and that meant eliminating old men, women and children, as well as 'rebels' armed against Italian authority. On the Roman model, Graziani habitually defined Libyans as *barbari* (barbarians); in his mind they were people without rights or future.[104]

Volpi's replacement was Emilio De Bono, whose appointment might be read as a signal of a new impulse to fascistise the empire – Mussolini went on a much publicised visit to Tripoli in April 1926, shortly after Violet Gibson's assassination attempt. De Bono was joined by Attilio Teruzzi, designated Governor of Cyrenaica, while another ex-quadrumvir, Cesare Maria De Vecchi, had run Somalia since October 1923. (De Vecchi composed a rhodomontade about his dubious achievements there, mimicking Julius Caesar's use of the third person in his accounts of his military campaigns.)[105] The most celebrated imperial appointment of a Fascist during the regime was that of Italo Balbo to be governor of Libya as a whole in January 1934, while De Vecchi went to be governor of the Dodecanese islands in November 1936, with his usual aggressive incompetence soon undermining[106] what had been the relative contentment until then of at least the poorer local inhabitants with Fascist imperial rule.[107]

The conquest of Ethiopia in 1935-36 entailed a vast expansion of the Italian empire and a new attempt at its Fascistisation and it will be considered below. All the same, the death toll there, however deplorable, never matched that which occurred in Libya during pacification from 1928 to 1933. This period coincided with the appointment of Badoglio to be Governor of Tripolitania and Cyrenaica combined. Part of the story is one of in-fighting. Badoglio was a rival of Graziani, who was made deputy Governor of Cyrenaica in March 1930. Both hated De Bono, Minister of Colonies from September 1929 to January 1935. Graziani was much inclined to underline his commitment to Fascism, and Badoglio rather less so, but the two combined, from June 1930, in a policy of ethnic cleansing of the interior which drove out a population of 100 000.[108] Badoglio endorsed a policy of utter brutality, telling his men that they must be 'ferocious and inexorable' in expelling every family they found.[109] The refugees were pent up in a series of concentration camps near the coast, and there frequently allowed to die of hunger and disease (Fascist rule had killed some 90 per cent of livestock owned by the population of Cyrenaica).[110] When the camps were broken up in September 1933, only about half the original deportees survived.[111]

Until his capture and execution after a mock trial in September 1931 (he was publicly hung as a 'bandit'),[112] Omar el-Mukhtar led a local rebellion. In combating his tenacious forces, the Italians did not hesitate to bomb their enemies with poison gas,[113] a prospect lightly endorsed by Italo Balbo in 1927 when, as Under-Secretary for Air, he welcomed the 'natural marriage between chemical weapons and the sky'.[114] One of the targets of gas attack in Cyrenaica was the 'holy city' of Cufra,[115] with the Italians displaying that determination typical of many imperial powers to wipe out by the most vicious methods possible any version of history in the area which might contest their own. Gas would also be ruthlessly deployed in Ethiopia.

After 1945 an admission of these crimes was wrung with great difficulty from official Italian historians, even though they were serving a Republic and not a Fascist dictator.[116] A silence remains (just as it does over the liquidation of many colonial peoples at the hands of their 'civilised' metropolitan masters). In the literature on Nazi Germany, Omer Bartov and others have been convincing in their arguments that the unimaginable 'barbarisation of warfare' on the Eastern Front was the achievement of the traditional German Army as much as it was of fanaticised Nazis.[117] Kershaw suggests that it was another result of the Germans' determination to work towards their *Führer*. The murderous violence of Italian imperial warfare raises a similar issue but produces a different answer. Mussolini may have always endorsed the most atrocious policies when they were reported to him. But it was Badoglio, Graziani and others who took the initiative, not the *Duce*. Very likely, to some degree, they were influenced by the 'unspoken assumptions' of a new savagery, approved by Fascism and incarnated in Mussolini's personality. However, Badoglio was an officer of the Royal Italian Army, and fully identified himself as such. His imperialism was more traditional than it was 'Mussolinian'. Moreover, there were critics of the cleansing and the concentration camps, notably De Bono and Roberto Cantalupo, the ex-Nationalist journalist who, by then, was Italian minister in Cairo.[118] The motivation for this criticism was more personal (especially for De Bono) and tactical (Cantalupo was trying to pursue a rapprochement with Egyptian nationalists) than ethical. Whether Fascist or not, elite Italians gave few indications of regarding the native inhabitants of their empire as their human equals (whatever may have been the attitude of more humble Italians who experienced life there).[119] However, they sought more to mimic the French and British colonisers of the nineteenth century than the Nazi ones of the years about to come.

If both Mussolini and his educated subjects still dreamed of empire in 1932, their country had a humbler but better remunerated way of connecting with the world – tourism. Totalitarian states open to mass visitation by independent foreigners seem a contradiction in terms (and the suspension in Nazi Germany during the 1936 Berlin Olympics of that regime's more overtly malign activities is well known). But Italy, beautiful, artistic, 'historical' Italy, was indeed a treasured holiday site for many a non-Italian. And Fascists debated what to do about this fact, especially because the Nationalists had repeatedly urged that tourists, questing the Renaissance or summer peaches, actually degraded present-day Italy. Marinetti, as ever, took matters to the extreme by suggesting the aerial flattening of Venice and Florence as the best way for Italians to advance towards modernity and greatness. Such hostility pained thrifty economists, who underlined the fact that tourism was Italy's most flourishing industry. Did Mussolini have an opinion on the matter?

Any attempt to answer this question is complicated by the fact that the administration of tourism was contested by a number of organisations, some of which had a direct continuity from the Liberal past while others were more strictly 'Fascist'.[120] The Corporate State embraced tourism, but it did so with some ambiguity. With genial approval from the Duce, a new organisation, the *Direzione Generale del Turismo*, was created, and subsumed into its own ranks the earlier quarrels which were never fully resolved. During the Second World War, the more prominent officials involved in tourism showed a marked reluctance to abandon their jobs and accept service at the front; they preferred to dream of luxurious hotels even in the dark days of 1942-43. Tourist organisation under Mussolini's rule remained both Liberal and Fascist, but, above all, bureaucratic.

One of the agencies, begun under the Liberals and destined to survive past 1945, was the *Touring Club Italiano*, proud of its base in Milan and in many ways the typical organisation of the Italian middle classes (and determined to nationalise them, if in a somewhat equivocal way).[121] Its history during the dictatorship is revealing. The TCI endured increasing Fascist intrusion which culminated in 1937 with the forced 'Italianisation' of its name; the TCI was meant to become more Fascist as the *Consociazione Turistica Italiana*. The TCI/CTI did, however, successfully resist efforts to transfer its head office to the 'imperial capital', Rome. Moreover, when asked, Mussolini told the CTI's director that all he wanted of the body was that it continue the patriotic work which had always been its purpose.[122] Others, more fanatical and less realistic than himself, he implied, were responsible for the annoyance which the worthy chiefs of the TCI had suffered. He was as ready to work towards the TCI and approve its *mentalité* as he was to require it be adorned with the gloss of radical Fascism.

The greatest tourist event, ostensibly the key moment so far in the Fascistisation of Italian society in the early 1930s, was the *Decennale*, the tenth anniversary celebrations of the March on Rome planned for 1932. There the *Duce* proudly proclaimed that the inevitable fascistisation of Europe was an expression of the light which always shone from Rome.[123] But Mussolini remained aware that he was not the sole interpreter of a Roman inheritance The Lateran Pacts may have been signed, but tiffs with the church had not ceased. Unhelpfully, Mussolini's version of religious history had an impious bent, notably when, in May 1929, he told the Chamber of Deputies that Christianity 'was born in Palestine, but had become Catholic in Rome'. If it had not had the good fortune of a meeting with Rome, he went on aggressively, it would in all likelihood have remained 'an obscure local sect like the Essenes' and 'would have just exhausted itself without leaving a historical trace'.[124] The Lateran negotiations, he concluded, with a hint of less consciously heretical thinking about the nation, had happened because the present Pope was 'really Italian', a typical 'Lombard' in his practical sense and willingness to take initiative.

During the next two years, there were a series of spats between church and state, with the extent of Fascist control over education being a particularly vexed issue. Pius XI had frequently described himself as the 'Catholic Action Pope', and certainly took special pastoral interest in the spiritual and welfare activities of the network of *Azione Cattolica*.[125] Catholic clubs and associations sat badly with the idea of a totalitarian state (even if *Critica Fascista* was willing to acknowledge confusingly that the church was equally totalitarian in its way).[126] Faced with a stubborn opponent, Mussolini gave vent to his habitual misanthropy and malice, qualities which bolstered his nagging sense that he might not be grasping real power. Hearing rumours that the Pontiff had been diagnosed with prostate cancer, Mussolini asked De Vecchi, who had become his ambassador to the Vatican, whether it was true that, within the Sistine Chapel arrangements were made to drain the Pope of urine even while he was celebrating mass.[127]

In May 1931 the Fascist regime banned Catholic Action youth organisations and Pius XI replied with a stern encyclical with the meaningful title *Non abbiamo bisogno* (We have no need). According to their most recent historian, 'Italo-Vatican relations [now] reached an all time low'.[128] Perhaps the dispute was more superficial than profound, however, since Pius XI and Mussolini and their advisers knew that the Lateran Pacts had been a good business deal for both Church and State. By the end of summer a compromise had been reached, with Mussolini acknowledging that he was 'well disposed to the Church playing a greater part in the organisation of the regime'.[129] Papal Secretary of State Pacelli, who was to become Pius XII in 1939 and was already identified by De Vecchi as a prelate of promise and sympathy, was reported to be 'radiant' at the news.[130] In February 1932 Mussolini, despite fears that he was 'going to Canossa' or, worse, seeming to go to Canossa,[131] made a formal visit to the Vatican. Although some churchmen and some Fascists were more suspicious than others, Mussolini and Pius XI accepted that church and state shared enough in their views of the social and gender order at home and in regard to Malta, the USSR and a number of other issues abroad for accommodation to remain the best policy. Fascism, the Pope said, stood for 'order, authority and discipline; none of them contrary to Catholic ways of thinking'.[132]

The party and its role in the further construction of the Corporate State were other areas to occupy the *Duce,* since wrangling among his underlings had scarcely ended.[133] The fall of Turati was followed by a curious interregnum in which, from October 1930 to December 1931, the Party secretaryship was held by Giovanni Giuriati.[134] The new secretary came from a background in border nationalism;[135] he had joined the Fascists in 1921 after being elected a deputy. Intelligent and activist, Giuriati later claimed that he was troubled by Mussolini's increasing isolation and his evident superficiality – Giuriati was unimpressed when Mussolini said he read thirty-five newspapers each day (or at least their headlines and editorial conclusions).[136] Giuriati also found it annoying that Mussolini wanted 'the people to believe that he not only conducted the orchestra but also played all the major instruments',[137] even while, in private conversation, he was most alert when regaled with the details of the latest scandal involving a Fascist.[138] (Mussolini may have enjoyed a straightforward telephone tap of a conversation between Farinacci and General Zoppi of the Ministry of War which reached him in October 1932:

> Farinacci: 'I have a brother who is about to take the exam to be promoted to captain. . .'
> Zoppi : 'Your brother won't run any risks. Leave it to me. I'll fix it.'
> Farinacci: 'We'll have to do it quickly, Zoppi, because the exams are already starting.'
> Zoppi: 'I'll fix it.'
> Farinacci: 'Thanks.')[139]

This almost salacious observing of scandals carried a hint of actual political weakness (rather as Lusignoli had suggested in 1927). When Giuriati planned a serious purge of the corrupt and non-believing from the PNF,[140] Mussolini told him cynically: 'I'll put up a monument to you if you manage to get rid of as many as ten thousand'.[141] Giuriati was similarly frustrated when he tried to extend party control over the armed forces.[142] On most issues he found the *Duce* obstructing his plans to give greater 'reality' to the Fascist revolution and he claimed to have been glad when his resignation was accepted.[143] Certainly, he was not one of those Fascists who returned to office.

Giuriati was replaced by Achille Starace, a Southerner who, a generation after the war, was allegedly still honoured in his home town of Gallipoli as 'Don Achille'.[144] Starace's more common notoriety springs from Mussolini's comment to Arpinati that he had fixed on Starace since he was 'a cretin, but an obedient one'.[145] Certainly Starace was another Fascist around whose family, and especially whose brothers, rumours of rich and illicit deals multiplied. He boasted great military achievement in Ethiopia in 1935–36,[146] but his brutality dismayed his more gentlemanly Fascist colleagues – he was alleged to have shot prisoners out of hand, alternating their hearts and their genitals as his targets.[147] De Felicean historians have been less dismissive about him than has been the convention, underlining, for example, his experience in the party (he was Vice-Secretary, 1921-23; 1926-31) and his nearness to the moderate but believing Fascists of Milan, whose most public figure was Arnaldo Mussolini.[148] Starace took pains to distance himself from Farinacci, telling Mussolini that the *ras* of Cremona, reported to be still critical of aspects of Mussolini's rule, was 'an individual who had completely lost the plot'.[149] Starace would make the party more populist – by autumn 1931 Mussolini had taken to declaring that now was the moment 'to go decisively towards the people'[150] – and vastly expand its membership (from 825 000 in 1931 to 2 million in 1937).[151] Starace became identified with the evolution of the choreography of the regime and the deepening effort to detach the *Duce*'s image from any base in reality. On 12 December 1931 Starace instituted the ritual *Saluto al Duce* (Salute to the *Duce*) at the start of all meetings.[152]

This promulgation of a newly reverent (and absurd) liturgy coincided with tragedy in Mussolini's family life. On 21 December Arnaldo died suddenly of a stroke, aged 46. He had been ailing since the death from leukaemia in August 1930 of his eldest son, Sandro, whom he sorely missed.[153] Mussolini, who, in Rome, may just have received moral uplift through a respectful visit from Mahatma Gandhi,[154] rushed to his brother's death-bed and spent the night of 22 December watching over the corpse and shedding what he would say were bitter and copious tears.[155] He soon composed a solemn memoir of his brother,[156] and the book and Arnaldo were duly hymned by the press. Even *La Vita Italiana*, which was now directly linked to Farinacci's newspaper interests,[157] remembered to eulogise Arnaldo, expert journalist, Fascist man of action and perfect brother.[158]

Actually Arnaldo played another role in the *Duce*'s life, receiving, as he reported in May 1930, 'an infinity of people who beg favours, subsidies and recommendations from me'.[159] Arnaldo was, at *Il Popolo d'Italia* and in Milan, city of the stock market, his brother's man of business. Just before his death, Arnaldo endorsed the choice of Starace for the secretaryship on the grounds that he was 'frank, open, loyal ... a soldier who knows how to obey without mental reserve', a Fascist well regarded by the Milan which mattered.[160] Mussolini would badly miss his brother and, despite the praise, Starace proved no substitute.

Although a mindless populism had taken hold as the recipe for the decade, in *Critica Fascista* Bottai continued to suggest that debate had not been outlawed in Fascist Italy. 'Mussolini', he noted, 'has sole responsibility for the great acts of the regime but he is not the guarantor of every deed, every initiative, every opinion which germinates within Fascism.'[161] As a follow-up article explained, there was no contradiction between discipline and discussion so long as the latter did not become too metaphysical.[162] *Critica Fascista* itself fostered debate about the meaning of art. Of greater potential radicalism was their appraisal of the USSR, which journalist Bruno Spampanato urged was a state that should be assessed with 'Fascist clarity' rather than just being demonised.[163] Bottai, who in the past had contemplated whether Fascism could be a 'permanent revolution',[164] was still confident that the Fascist party must evolve, and do so in a creative way.[165]

It is doubtful whether Mussolini was much impressed by such lucubrations. Was it now that he decided that Bottai had the mentality of someone who 'read too many paperbacks'?[166] After all, who could out-think Mussolini? It was, indeed, in July 1932 that Mussolini published under his name, but with the assistance of philosopher Giovanni Gentile, an entry summarising the 'Doctrine of Fascism' for the new national Encyclopedia.[167] The authors emphasised the 'spirituality' of Fascism and its endorsement of the idea that 'man' improved himself only through struggle. A totalitarian intent was reaffirmed. Individual freedom was a delusion; reality only entered through dedication to the state. Fascism was as anti-liberal as it had been anti-socialist. It believed war fostered moral grandeur and proclaimed that Italy must continue to expand. An empire must be constructed. In sum, Fascism was 'the characteristic doctrine of our time'. The future belonged to it.

As revelatory of the *Duce*'s thought as the *Decennale* approached was a set of interviews which Mussolini granted in March–April 1932 to the journalist, Emil Ludwig (eventually labelled 'a dirty and pretentious Jew', after Mussolini decided belatedly that he did not like what Ludwig had recorded).[168] Ludwig contended that 'in conversation Mussolini is the most natural man in the world',[169] and his Mussolini spoke more personally and less intellectually that the Mussolini of the Encyclopedia article, impressing Ludwig who called him a great statesman, good humoured and a master of detail.[170] Perhaps with the prospect of the *Decennale* on his mind, Mussolini discussed a Fascist liturgy: 'Every revolution creates new forms, new myths, and new rites; and the would-be revolutionist, while using old traditions, must refashion them. He must create new festivals, new gestures, new forms.'[171] However, Mussolini's summary of Fascism was neither taxing nor pretentious: 'When, recently, a Finnish thinker asked me to expound to him the significance of fascism in one sentence, I wrote:

"Life must not be taken easily."'[172] As was so often his habit, Mussolini, smoothing the way with his interlocutor, denied that races existed, arguing anyway that 'national pride has no need of the delirium of race'.[173] He even contended properly that a good ruler should cling to a sense of compassion towards a weak and sinful human kind.[174] Ludwig noticed that, when Mussolini was asked to talk more intimately about himself, he changed the subject, going no further than to state that 'fundamentally I have always been alone'.[175]

It was neither to Ludwig nor the readers of the Encyclopedia but rather to an old friend that Mussolini, around this time, confessed that he found the Italians endlessly 'contradictory'.[176] Could such a people really be dragooned into being the adepts of a new, totalitarian, political religion, especially if their leader himself remained a sceptic in his heart? This question hinted at some bafflement lurking in the *Duce's* mind about the nature of power. Mussolini's own evident surviving doubts suggest that the *Decennale* was an event that can be read in more than one way. There were ceremonies enough to satisfy any student of webs of significance and any believer in the primacy of words and images.[177] However, there was also much that was deliberately superficial about the great celebration. Other regimes had known something about bread and circuses. The developing world of capitalist consumerism understood rather more about hegemonic propaganda than Mussolini did. In fact, Italian state finances were not doing so well; at least a million were unemployed, real wages were down, the Corporate State remained largely on the drawing board,[178] and experts were beginning to argue about the ideal level of state interference in the economy.[179] But the *Decennale* was not scheduled to be a time of analysis of what Fascism had done and what it should do. Instead it was to be a celebration of the *Duce* and only of him. As one of the senior journalists of the regime summed up the message of ten years of Fascist rule, 'the new Italy is called Mussolini' after its 'infallible Chief'; 'the Exhibition of the Revolution is Him: Mussolini'.[180] Another major writer of the regime declared that now 'an imaginary Mussolini operates in the minds and hearts of the people as much as the facts do'. 'The name of Mussolini', he added in explanation, 'is known everywhere ... as a synonym of power and perfection.'[181] Mussolini, said a more provincial commentator, was by now 'omnipresent' in the world.[182]

The massive displays, the fervent eulogies, the apparent solidity of the regime at home and abroad, might seem sufficient to chuff any politician. But happiness and satisfaction continued to elude Benito

Mussolini. The line between power and impotence remained blurred. Moreover, Arnaldo was dead. Correspondence with Edda after her marriage on 24 April 1930 – the event was much trumpeted though the actual ceremony was held in the modest San Giuseppe, the parish church nearest the Villa Torlonia[183] – the birth of Fabrizio, his first grandchild, on 1 October 1931,[184] and the move of his sister, Edvige, to Rome in September 1932[185] offered only feeble compensation. As he approached his fiftieth birthday, Mussolini was reminded by his whitening hair that most of the Mussolinis did not make old bones, and the banning of any discussion of his age in the press scarcely got around the problem.[186] Only the propaganda of the regime hid the fact that the *Duce* was facing a mid-life crisis. In 1933, the unlikely duo of Adolf Hitler and Claretta Petacci were to enter his life, never to leave it until he was dead.

12

The challenge of Adolf Hitler, 1932–1934

On 30 January 1933 Adolf Hitler, *Führer* of the National Socialist German Workers Party (NSDAP), acceded to the Chancellorship of Germany. It was a momentous event. However banal most of his ideas, however tedious his personality and however erratic his work practices, Hitler in office at once altered the unspoken assumptions which underpinned life in Europe and the way diplomatic business was transacted there. One person drastically affected by the change in German leadership was Benito Mussolini.

As has been noted, towards the end of his life Mussolini would wonder whether a future constitutional *Duce* should rule for 14 years or 10.[1] Unwilling, like many an old politician, to abandon a jot or tittle of even imaginary power, Mussolini opted for the longer period. However, had he thought harder perhaps he should have chosen two five-year terms for a *Duce*. After all, had this rule been applied to himself, he could have retired on 28 October 1932, no doubt with the grand and petty failures of a dictatorship on his record, with its repression of social and political liberty and with a terrible death toll in Libya to explain away. His responsibility for the tyrannies and casualties of his regime had not been total, and he might have entered history as a figure of some light and some darkness, a man who had scarcely benefited his people as a whole but had at least administered them for a decade without committing too many unforgivable crimes. From 30 January 1933 things were to be different. Fascist Italy's relationship with Nazi Germany was to be the prime reason why the Furies came for the *Duce* in 1943–45, and the most obvious, if not perhaps the most powerful, justification for his damning[2] in most subsequent historiography.

In our de-ideologised present, some analysts are inclined to discount the model of fascism. They reject that interpretation of the interwar era which once confidently linked the Nazi and Fascist regimes, each seen as a version of 'nationalist socialism', especially designed to thwart the appeal of internationalist, Marxist, socialism. Renzo De Felice led the way in avowing that Fascism and Nazism were radically different regimes, socially, culturally and even in foreign policy. In his view, Fascists always looked to the future and were driven by a fundamental optimism, absent among the Nazis.[3] These arguments are as may be, though it is very hard to believe that the Fascist Mussolini was any kind of optimist. But what matters most in a review of the last 12 years of his power is that, from 1933, Mussolini could less and less deny the appearance of a linkage between his Italy and the new Germany. In the world beyond the two dictatorships, his contemporaries assumed almost automatically that the Fascist and Nazi systems were akin.

The inescapability of this assumption in turn brought new insecurity to Italian Fascism and its place in the world. Irritation, imitation, evasion, each became imbricated into Mussolinian Italy's relationship with Hitlerian Germany. The one position which was impossible was to ignore the fact that something bearing a resemblance to the regime in Rome had taken root in Berlin and, with every passing day, was more evidently activist and fanatical, ready and willing to do what Fascists promised they would do, and do it now. As the decade of the 1930s passed, the glow of Nazi success lit up the edifice of Fascism and, to the careful onlooker, exposed the cracks in Mussolini's construction.

There were matters which cloaked this reality. A significant one was Hitler's own language. From the beginning of his political career, Hitler admired the Italian *Duce*, was flattered when commentators compared the two men,[4] ever hopeful that Mussolini would deign to offer a subsidy or grant a meeting.[5] Some contact between the two movements had existed even before the March on Rome and, immediately thereafter, Mussolini was told that the Nazis' plan was 'in great part taken from the Italian *Fascio*. To restore the authority of the state; to abolish strikes, corruption and waste; to cut the bureaucracy. In a word to restore order. This is their programme'.[6]

The failure of the Beer Hall *Putsch* and Hitler's consequent imprisonment undermined schemes for further collaboration. To an Italian mind, the Nazis blurred into but one of a promiscuous group of European rightist petitioners seeking funds and favour, scarcely likely to emerge from the ruck and master history in the way the Fascists asserted that they had done. In so far as Mussolini himself was concerned, there is no reason to believe that he had any special tenderness for the infant NSDAP, while, in the pages of *Critica Fascista*, the prominent Triestine political commentator Attilio Tamaro sharply separated Italian Fascism from its alleged German admirers. The Anti-Semitic *hakenkreuzler* movement, he warned, was monarchist, revanchist and pan-German, while its obsession with the Jews was in bad taste and politically stupid. Hitler may have tried to urge that the Alto Adige (Süd Tirol) should be left to Italy, Tamaro acknowledged, but the rest of his followers had overwhelmed him with their hostility. The plain truth was that this sort of German Right would never give up its desire for Italian territory.[7]

The majority of this Right, like the majority of the Nazi movement after 1933, had three main reasons to be suspicious of Italy. Their racial theory led them to believe that Italians belonged to the 'Mediterranean' race, allegedly the third and worst of the blood groups who coagulated in Europe. Taking matters beyond the extreme, Anton Drexler, one of the founders of National Socialism, announced that Mussolini was 'probably' a Jew and diagnosed Fascism as a Jewish movement.[8] Other, less dotty, Germans nonetheless knew that Italians, given their racial weakness, were likely to be fickle and feckless, corrupt and corrupting. Such deplorable qualities had, in this view, been fully confirmed by the events of the First World War. Then, Italy, although legally tied to the Triple Alliance, had betrayed its Germanic partners to fight on the Entente side. Being a traitor and being Italian went together. Additionally, Italians were, by definition, bad soldiers, a failing they disgracefully demonstrated at Caporetto (just as they had done during the Risorgimento, when they had purloined territory better ruled by Germans). Finally, Italy, another of the grasping victors at Versailles, had seized purely Germanic soil in the South Tyrol, as well as the port of Trieste, a city which geopolitics meant to be the Germanic outlet to the southern seas. When one matter was added to another, German Nationalists had almost as many reasons to plot the downfall of Italy as they had to plan the demise of Czechoslovakia or Poland. Hitler alone was different. Fanatically driven by Anti-Semitism, Anti-Communism and Anti-Slavism, Hitler had no room among his prejudices to be Anti-Italian as well. Ready to worship the 'incomparable' Mussolini[9] and, simultaneously, to delight artistically (from a distance) in the 'blue skies' and cultural heritage of Italy, the *Führer* of the NSDAP was not a simple or usual Nationalist.

For much of the 1920s the enthusiast for a bond between Fascism and National Socialism was therefore Hitler, and Hitler alone. In the origins of the Axis, the individual did matter, and it might be agreed that Hitler was the first explanation why Italy and Germany fought the Second World War as allies (even if, as shall be seen, neither leader really understood the other's war). In *Mein Kampf*, for example, Hitler argued that geopolitics destined Italy to be Francophobe and so a potential ally of Germany.[10] Giving the lie to Tamaro's suspicions, Hitler continued stubbornly to argue that his friends should accept that the 'reconquest of the South Tyrol ... [is] impossible'. Nationalists who disagreed, he contended, were being led astray by the Jews.[11] In every matter, he stated, Fascism was on the correct ideological line. Its attacks on Freemasonry, the supra-national press and Marxism were directed, however 'unconsciously', against 'the three main weapons of the Jews'.[12] Almost alone of Germans, in 1926–27 Hitler did not complain about the Italianisation policies in the Alto Adige, pursued with Mussolini's personal endorsement[13] and with that Fascist method well defined as the policy of 'open conflicts openly arrived at'.[14] In his *Secret Book*, prepared in 1928, Hitler reiterated his advocacy of an Italian alliance. Indeed the work began with a statement about the need to approve Fascist rule of the South Tyrol, in the interests of winning an Italian alliance against France.[15] Imperial Germany, Hitler added, had committed a fundamental error in concentrating on its ties with the moribund Habsburg empire and so in ignoring the more promising Italy.[16] How much clearer the situation was now, he urged, when Italy was benefiting from the guidance of that 'brilliant statesman', Benito Mussolini.[17]

Later, during the Second World War, in those rambling conversations recorded as his 'table talk', Hitler admitted that he had framed his programme in 1919 without knowing about the *Fasci*. However, he quickly added: 'Don't suppose that events in Italy had no influence on us. The brown shirt would probably not have existed without the black shirt. The March on Rome, in 1922, was one of the turning points in history.'[18] Ian Kershaw dates Hitler's conversion to the idea that he was a *Führer* to the time shortly after the March on Rome, and believes that the image of the *Duce* was partially plagiarised by the leader of the still tiny and fractious NSDAP.[19]

Hitler's determination to be friends did eventually catch the eye of Italian experts. In 1927 an Italian diplomat stationed in Munich drew his superiors' attention to the way Hitler stood out among the German Right in his praise of Italy.[20] Hitler, he reported, 'ended up by saying that, confronted by a petulant and aggressive France, Italy and

Germany must be indissolubly united'.[21] As a result, at the villa of his own good friend Frau Bechstein in Berlin, Hitler met an Italian journalist who heard the *Führer* predict that the NSDAP, which seemed to be languishing politically as the Weimar regime moved towards greater prosperity and stability, was destined before long to advance to centre stage. A new crisis, Hitler prophesied, would be bound to strike Germany, and then his hour would come.[22]

Sure enough, from 1928 the Nazis began to emerge as serious contenders in Weimar electoral politics and the Italians fitfully took notice (though their more direct contacts were with the para-military *Heimwehr* in Austria,[23] whose anti-communism, anti-socialism and anti-parliamentarism they could endorse without fears that an eventually rightist Austria would one day pursue irredentist policies towards Italy in the way that a rightist Germany might do). In May 1929 the Vienna correspondent of *Il Popolo d'Italia* met Hitler and was impressed by him, even believing that the Nazi movement had moderated its Anti-Semitism. The Nazis would limit themselves to reviewing the civil rights of Zionist Jews, he predicted. On his part, Hitler had pledged his determination 'to create in the [German] people sympathy for Mussolini and Italy'. The *Führer*, alert to what he viewed as mistaken Italian priorities, also took the occasion to dismiss the *Heimwehr* as 'too bourgeois'. The journalist was impressed and reported to Rome: 'Hitler is anything other than the clown depicted by his enemies.' His passion and conviction rather suggested that 'he is a man apt to win over the masses'.[24]

The news was registered by the Fascist government that the Nazis were becoming the most significant party of the German Right. As the elections to be held in September 1930 approached, agents – notably Major Giuseppe Renzetti, then president of the Italian Chamber of Commerce in Berlin but later to be inducted as a reliable Fascist into the diplomatic service – predicted gains for the Right, though without at first much distinguishing between Hugenberg, the Stahlhelm and the Nazis.[25] *Gerarchia*, a journal meant to speak for the *Duce* himself, reported the Nazi's winning of 107 seats under the heading 'Hitler's triumph' and declared him 'partially fascist', proof that 'the fascist idea is moving ahead in the world'. The tone was not simply celebratory, however. The Nazi rise was 'full of warning' for the world, the account continued, since it signalled a full German return to power politics. The Austrian Hitler would be sure to raise the *Anschluss* issue.[26]

More secret contacts with the Nazis, still at a relatively junior level in the Fascist hierarchy, gave similarly mixed messages. Hitler continued to flatter every Italian he met, telling another journalist from *Il Popolo d'Italia* that he accepted that Fascism was not for export but only in a 'technical sense', since 'the general concept behind it has international value'. Hitler, the reporter wrote, went out of his way to acknowledge the primacy of Italian Fascism, but, he added, 'the same cannot be said about some people near him'.[27] German events retained a perplexing side. As if to underline the matter, in May 1931 Grandi explained to his chief: 'One day the *Anschluss* will happen. Unity is the law of many races but especially it is the law of the German race. In so far as Italy is concerned, the task is to delay the inevitable process as long as possible.' In 'a generation', Grandi thought, Italy could 'resolve the problem of the Alto Adige' and reinforce its interests along the Danube. Then it might be able to cope with an expanded Germany.[28]

But the Europe of the 1930s, with its tumult and stress, was not going to wait for a generation. Even though Mussolini, with his continuing preference for domestic issues, would on one occasion minute jokingly: 'The Fascist regime wishes – if possible – to live in peace with all States, even including the Vatican City State',[29] he could not ignore Hitler. Berlin was ever more the focus of the gathering storm. Symbolising the unusual nature of any dealings with the Nazis, Renzetti now became Mussolini's private, extracurricular, contact with Hitler and Goering, meeting the Nazi chiefs on a regular basis, reporting straight to the *Duce* and evading the orthodox diplomatic channels. Yet, for all the unorthodoxy of the method, the character of Fascist–Nazi relations did not alter much. Hitler stressed his admiration for Mussolini and his determination to ally with Italy.[30] Mussolini graciously accepted words of homage from the German leader and passed on advice – for example, in November 1931 warning Hitler against allowing possible coalition partners to distract him from the rigour of his own beliefs and policies.[31] There was frequent reference to Hitler's desire to meet the *Duce* face to face, but, whether from the Italian or the German part, the meeting was always postponed.[32] Nonetheless, as Hitler promised fulsomely in October 1932, once he got into power: 'National Socialist Germany and Fascist Italy will be friends for tens and tens of years or at least until I die.'[33]

The Italian press approved the rise of the Nazis, though not uncritically. In a cultural–political monthly entitled *Augustea*, Franco Ciarlantini admitted that it used to be said that Fascism was not for export, but criticised those who 'did not interpret Mussolini's thought intelligently'.[34] 'To think, as many do, that Italy can remain with its Fascist organisation only a silent example of discipline, will and power is an illusion and, worse, an anti-social wish which we do not approve'.[35] It was true that Hitler had an inspirationally life-sized bust of Mussolini in the *Braun Haus* at Munich, and Italians must view the expansion of their ideals with joy, in the prospect of a continuing spread of Fascist influence in 'Europe and the world'.[36] Another journalist agreed that the Nazis' entry to government should be applauded as an Italian triumph, a demonstration that Fascism was at one and the same time 'the Italian revolution and a universal doctrine'.[37]

Most accounts carried somewhere in their lines a hint of lingering concern, nonetheless. Even Farinacci suggested that it would be 'perilous' to assume too automatically that the Nazi and Fascist movements were identical, just as once before it had been a mistake to be too approving of Primo De Rivera's rule in Spain. When, in the November 1932 elections, the Nazis temporarily suffered an electoral setback, Farinacci was happy, declaring complacently that it was not easy to make a revolution, enjoying the idea of the Nazis falling at the last hurdle.[38]

Other articles in *La Vita Italiana* were more predictably delighted at the rise of Anti-Semites to power in Germany.[39] However, the majority of Italian commentators remained troubled by the evidence of Nazi fanaticism on the 'Jewish question'. The cliché held that Anti-Semitism was a foreign import – *Enciclopedia Italiana* in 1932 notably failed to endorse German ideas on race. Some commentators did not hesitate to argue that the Nazis were going too far and that their Anti-Semitism corroded what might otherwise have been positive features of their creed. Asvero Gravelli, an enthusiast for the universality of fascism, called Italian Fascists 'the protestants of the religion of race. We deny this faith and believe rather in the reality of facts and not in a presupposed reality which does not correspond to the truth'.[40] A more common position was held by Renzetti who, in *Gerarchia*, explained away Nazi Anti-Semitism as the product of specific features of German history. Renzetti predicted that, in office, the Nazis would be bound to moderate on the race matter, since they would have so many more serious issues to confront.[41] When, shortly after January 1933, the Nazis began to persecute the Jews, Mussolini, perhaps counselled by Renzetti, averred in *Il Popolo d'Italia* that events should not be taken out of context, suggesting that easy moralising was to be avoided.[42] No country was perfect, the *Duce* contended sagely. Mussolini also hindered attempts by his new Under-Secretary for

1 Mussolini at 14

2 Mussolini as wounded soldier

3 Mussolini,
November 1922, just
after appointment as
Prime Minister

4 Mussolini, May 1923, at the first session of the conference of the National Alliance for Votes for Women

5 Rachele and Edvige Mussolini, the *Duce*'s wife and sister, looking respectable at Predappio, 1925

6 Mussolini as fencer

7 Mussolini, April 1926, *en route* to Libya, but with the sticking plaster still on his nose after the assassination attempt of Violet Gibson

8 The *Rocca delle Caminate*, the Mussolini 'heritage' castle above Predappio

9 Edda Mussolini saluting at her marriage with Galeazzo Ciano, in the lovely spring of 1930

10 Mussolini (with visibly whitening hair) meeting the British Prime Minister Ramsay MacDonald, March 1933

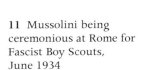

11 Mussolini being ceremonious at Rome for Fascist Boy Scouts, June 1934

12 Mussolini meeting Hitler (in a mackintosh) in 1934

13 Mussolini speaking, 1935

14 Statue of Mussolini carved near Adowa, Ethiopia

15 Mussolini in Libya, 1937

16 Party Secretary Starace orating fearsomely at Addis Ababa, 1937

17 Mussolini swimming, 1937

18 Mussolini at his desk

19 A small child from the Romagna saluting the *Duce*

20 Galeazzo Ciano handing his son Fabrizio over to the Fascist scouts

21 Mussolini showing British Prime Minister Neville Chamberlain the arms collection at the Palazzo Venezia

22 Mussolini visiting Rome University, 1942

23 Mussolini greeted by his son Vittorio in Germany, September 1943

24 Mussolini on his last speaking visit to Milan, December 1944

25 Mussolini's corpse, photographed lying almost on top of his mistress, carrying sceptre-like a Fascist *gagliardetto*

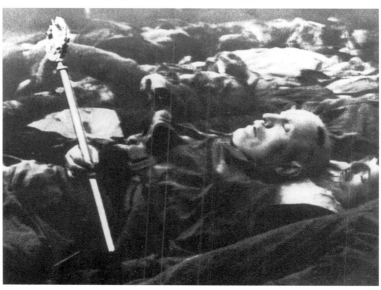

26 The corpses of Mussolini and his mistress Claretta Petacci strung upside down in the Piazzale Loreto, Milan

27 The Mussolini crypt in Predappio

Foreign Affairs, the Triestine and Germanophobe Fulvio Suvich, to curtail the work of Renzetti and restrict German–Italian relations to diplomatic networks alone.[43] At the same time, Mussolini wrote privately to Hitler warning that 'egregious' Anti-Semitism was fuelling foreign criticism and hampering the progress of the Nazi revolution.[44] He also told Bottai with some animus in July 1933 that it was time the Germans really understood 'our order and our doctrine'; once they had grasped Italian Fascism they 'might be convinced that they have nothing to invent'.[45] Glimpses of the *Duce*'s own line on the new Germany showed it to be as ambiguous as was the varied commentary in the Fascist press on the matter.

What, then, was Mussolini's own attitude to race, now that the racial issue was becoming so central to debates about European politics? It is true that a trawl through his numerous speeches and statements can harvest a certain amount of Anti-Semitism.[46] Moreover, he, the censor of so many newspapers, did not stop the publication of *La Vita Italiana* or end Preziosi's tirades against the Jews. On occasion, his regime expressed major doubts about Zionism and its alleged requirement that Italian Jews craft 'double loyalties'.[47] He was similarly not above private complaints about the number of Jews (Catholics and Anti-Fascists) to be found in Italian universities.[48] However, there is scarce evidence that the *Duce* held views on any aspect of the Jewish question which were not shared by other members of the Italian ruling elite. He regularly repeated his scepticism about the claims of racial science; in fact, he maintained, 'race is rather a vague entity given the numerous mixing which has occurred over the centuries'.[49] Indeed, when the *Duce* and Pope met in February 1932, it was the Pontiff who was the more openly racist. In Pius XI's opinion, all the troubles of the Church, in the USSR, Mexico and the new Spanish republic, were 'underpinned by the Anti-Christian spirit of Judaism. When I was in Warsaw' (as Papal Nunzio in 1920), he went on, 'I saw that all the bolshevik regiments, all the male and female commissars, were Jewish'. In case his listener blanched at what almost sounded like sentiments drawn from the pages of *La Vita Italiana*, the Pope at once added: 'In Italy, however, the Jews are an exception'.[50]

It was true that, in his Ascension Day speech and on many other occasions, Mussolini had urged that demography should become the fulcrum of his regime's social programmes (even if the national birthrate actually continued to fall).[51] No doubt, too, he expatiated frequently on the need to educate a Fascist people in warlike values;

only the stern, fit, upstanding and united were ready for empire. Mussolini very much saw himself as the *Duce* of 'one Italy'. Yet, to his way of thinking, the union of Italians was forged by the will to be Italian, and not by the invisible effects of blood. Mussolini would never be a 'scientific' racist, and probably never understood just how purist Hitler and the rest of the Nazis were on the issue. One reason for the confusion was the fact that, deeply set into his mind, was the belief that people were indeed distinguished one from another and that some were undoubtedly 'inferior'. Like the great majority of interwar Europeans,[52] Mussolini assumed without saying so that extra-European peoples, especially blacks and other coloured groups, were 'uncivilised' and stood at the bottom of any hierarchy of achievement or prospect.

When it came to assessing the more familiar world, Mussolini's racism was of the kind still parroted at many a club bar or on many a phone-in radio programme (he would have made a good talk-back host). This is a racism which, with a ready assumption of knowledge where knowledge is lacking, swiftly sketches an unflattering portrait of a national type. For Mussolini, 'democracy for Slavs was like alcohol for blacks'.[53] The 'racial delirium' of the German nationalists was hard to comprehend; however, they did have the excuse of innumerable 'Slavs' on their border.[54] None the less, he told a visitor in May 1940, the Germans were natural 'sadists'.[55] England was damp and grey and the English formal and repressed, too phlegmatic for their own good.[56] The Americans were rapacious and yet to become fully civilised;[57] their capitalist puritanism was riven by hypocrisy.[58] The French were perfidious, arrogant and a prey to their stomachs.[59] Moreover, everything was arranged in a hierarchy (though its ordering could always fluctuate):

> With a Frenchman [Mussolini was talking to a French journalist], we Italians can at once speak with full confidence and comprehension; with an Englishman, we must make quite an effort to understand and be understood; with a German, the difference deepens further, and a real abyss separates us from a Russian.[60]

At the same time, the negativities of most of these views could easily enough be reversed. Russians could be stubbornly brave, Americans entrepreneurial and entertaining,[61] the French cultured.[62] As for the Jews, it was clear that they were not automatically barbarous in the way that blacks and Arabs were deemed to be; they were 'European'.

Mostly they were good people, especially if they were Italian. As Mussolini stated in 1932, local Jews 'have always behaved well as citizens and fought courageously as soldiers'.[63]

The Jews were not the only inhabitants of the country about whom Mussolini liked to pronounce. In his mind, unchanging cultural types may well have been more common within Italy than outside and the accompanying hierarchy all the easier to see. Despite his proclaimed efforts to nationalise the Italian people and even while he knew automatically that one Italian was worth 'three' foreigners,[64] Mussolini did not hesitate to talk about a Genoese 'race',[65] a Piedmontese people (whom he wanted to breed faster – he was speaking to a Piedmontese),[66] and the timeless virtue of his 'own people' of the Romagna.[67] In his opinion, Venetians could not help being Venetian.[68] Further south, racial or cultural groups could also be found, though their behaviour might be less praiseworthy. 'The Florentines' were trouble-makers by nature; their Fascism was given to mutiny and dissent because it was Florentine.[69] Neapolitans were feckless and undisciplined, and nothing could be done to amend their failings, which were primordial;[70] in 1936, Mussolini suggested one day organising a 'March on Naples' so he could 'sweep away guitars, mandolins, violins, folk-singers etc.'[71] Once again, these assumptions were not original – after Senise succeeded Bocchini as Chief of Police, Ciano, maximising every northern cliché about a man from the south, summed up the new Police Chief as 'a Neapolitan, a queer mixture of intelligence and ignorance; he follows his natural instincts and is a black-mailer; fundamentally he is easy going, a chatter-box, superficial and a gesticulator'.[72] Mussolini, like almost all Italians, believed that not all the inhabitants of his country were Italian in the way that he was; that conclusion was very likely the strongest part of his 'racial' credo. In so far as his dealings with the Nazis went, the problem was that his racial understanding was both voluntarist and nuanced, two ideas which radically separated him and other Italians from the racial utopia planned, in Nazi eyes 'scientifically', by the terrible simplifiers of Berlin.

In the practice of diplomacy with the new Germany, Italy tried to take the lead. The initial plan was to frame a 'Four Power Pact', or *Patto Mussolini* as it was frequently called in Italy,[73] to be signed between Britain, France, Germany and Italy. Raised by Mussolini in March 1933 successively with German, French and British authorities, the agreement was signed on 15 July. Overtaken by events,

Mussolini

however, it was never ratified,[74] despite Mussolini's efforts to sell it as
an arrangement which could provide Europe with a decade's breathing space.[75] The other parties to the Pact had expressed doubts about
it early on; in April Mussolini had expostulated to the German
ambassador: 'the idea started off as a boy; the English tried to turn it
into a hermaphrodite; while, in the hands of the French, it would
become nothing but a girl'.[76] The real problem for Mussolini was,
however, that European attention was more and more obsessed with
Germany. The very friendly retiring British ambassador, Sir Ronald
Graham, might stress to London his admiration for Mussolini's 'nous'
and 'guts', his belief that the *Duce*'s foreign policy was 'on the whole
justified and useful to Europe' and his certainty that 'there is no false
race-ism here, and no anti-Semitism to speak of'.[77] But, in the greater
capitals of Europe, the seeming urgency of finding the right line to
Berlin was beginning to preclude much solicitude being wasted on
the secondary dictator.

In any case, for liberal democrats a number of problems were
implicit in the *Patto Mussolini*. Why just four powers? Why the omission of Poland and the USSR (or the USA and Japan)? Why, too, an
apparent return to a Concert of Great Powers, a prospect which sat
uneasily with the 'new diplomacy', learned from Woodrow Wilson
and beloved by liberal democrat opinion, if not necessarily treasured
in their hearts by French and British diplomats? Was Mussolini
striking at the very idea of a League of Nations? The implication of the
Pact was that the four Great European Powers would thereafter come
together to review the Versailles settlement and, very likely, organise
treaty revision, as, for example, the Congress of Berlin had, in 1878,
managed the 'Eastern Question'. They might therefore be expected to
impose an arrangement on Czechoslovakia, a country which Mussolini
was ready publicly to call a 'hybrid abortion',[78] or Lithuania, or
Poland, without consulting the lesser powers. They also might constitute an 'anti-communist', anti-USSR, bloc.

The Four Power Pact continues to have a positive image in Italian
historiography. Rosaria Quartararo, whose work was extensively used
by De Felice,[79] has argued that sensible contemporaries viewed the
suggestion as 'the greatest personal triumph of the *Duce*'.[80] Only
purblind or Italophobe policies and attitudes wrecked the scheme,
which, she avers, was never wholly abandoned by Mussolini and his
advisers. Reasonably wanting Italy to be the *peso determinante* (decisive weight)[81] in a troubled Europe, right up to 1940 they half
expected their own realism to convert others.[82] This conclusion is in

striking contrast to British interpretations which relegate the Pact to being a minor issue, if not proof of a malevolent early wish by the *Duce* to pave the way for a Munich-style agreement to the advantage of Nazi Germany.[83]

Yet there does seem much that is classically Italian about the Four Power Pact. What could be more typical of the diplomacy of the least of the Great Powers than a scheme which prescribed hard borders behind which Italy was accepted as one of them?[84] Moreover, there is quite a bit of evidence that the idea was not some prelude to the Axis. Indeed, it was during the months of the framing of the agreement that Mussolini assumed the role of patron of Engelbert Dollfuss, the diminutive Christian Social Chancellor of Austria (a man willing to drift towards some form of clerical fascism but a reliable opponent of Austrian Nazis).[85] In April 1933 Dollfuss and Mussolini met, and the *Duce* concluded: 'Dollfuss, in spite of his miniscule size, is a man of ingenuity, possessed of real will. Together these qualities give a good impression.'[86] Mussolini had by no means yet accepted that an *Anschluss* was inevitable and there is reason to believe that, as Suvich asserted, the Four Power Pact was directed at containing Germany through the tried and true methods of the old diplomacy, rather than at some warmongering 'fascist' end.[87] Suvich also remembered Mussolini telling him bitterly around this time that he found Nazi racial ideas 'a colossal joke'[88] (which was what Suvich thought them to be).

In 1933–34 the Austrian question was not the only international issue over which Fascist Italy tried hard to be realistic in the traditional sense. One of the rhetorical tropes which Mussolini, not alone in the twentieth century, could turn off and on at will was anti-communism. Many admirers and imitators of the *Duce* thought they were crusading against Bolshevism, just as Fascism went on claiming it had done so victoriously. This ideological war, however, was by no means allowed to damage the bilateral relationship between Fascist Italy and the USSR. A new commercial agreement between the two states was signed in September 1933.[89] Nor had Fascist Italy rejected the idea of arms deals with the USSR, in 1931–32, for example, engaging in lucrative aircraft sales[90] and later accepting contracts to build Soviet naval craft in Italian dockyards, in spite of the prospect of their ending up firing on Fascist Italians in Spain or elsewhere.[91] Italian publicists were by no means universally convinced that the USSR was a natural enemy of Italy and even wondered whether Stalin was not himself transmogrifying into a fascist.[92] It is well known that, during the latter stages of the Second World War, Mussolini on a number of occasions tried to win over Hitler to the idea of a separate peace with the USSR, so that the Axis could concentrate on repelling the 'Anglo-Saxon' menace in the Mediterranean. Although taken seriously by De Felice,[93] this was a lunatic idea to advance to the Nazis, who were almost as committed to the ideal of liquidating communists and Slavs as they were to the 'final solution' of the Jewish question. Mussolini's anti-communism was thus comparable with his racism, in being never total. In the *Duce*'s mind no idea was so powerful that it should blind a man to other, better, avenues to the main chance. Not for nothing was Mussolini to say, in June 1933 as on other occasions, that he had been re-reading Machiavelli.[94]

Then there were the powers outside Europe, notably the USA, where Franklin Roosevelt had assumed the presidency only a few weeks before Hitler became German Chancellor. The Fascist press commented frequently on the New Deal,[95] Mussolini himself arguing in June 1933 that Roosevelt had dictatorial powers which exceeded his own,[96] and there were continuing suggestions that the USA, too, was finding a path to fascism.[97] Japan, by contrast, was not yet a natural ally in Mussolini's mind; rather, in January 1934 he warned about further Japanese penetration of China (where his son-in-law[98] and daughter still represented Italy and so gave proof of Italy's lingering sympathy towards Jiang Jieshi and other Chinese nationalists;[99] might they, too be fascists at heart?).[100]

While he was pondering the darkening horizon of international relations, Mussolini, who had celebrated his 50th birthday a fortnight after the signature of the Four Power Pact and who was ever more inclined to fib about the effects of age,[101] met his last mistress. In September 1933 he could still write to Edda that, 'as in your adolescence when times were tough, so today, you were and are the special favourite of my soul'.[102] Actually, by then, Edda had a female competitor, Claretta Petacci, born 28 February 1912 and from the comfortable Rome bourgeoisie (her mother claimed to be a distant relative of Pius XI, in whose medical service Francesco Saverio Petacci, Claretta's father, worked).[103] The 21 year old was 2 years younger than Edda, although her attentions would be valued rather more by Mussolini's body than by his soul. The two encountered each other, or so the story goes, by accident, on 8 September 1933. Petacci, whose family was wealthy enough to have given her a sports car on her eighteenth birthday,[104] had gone to the beach at Ostia and met the *Duce* who was driving around himself with little or no escort. The young woman seized the opportunity to murmur breath-lessly that it had been her 'dream' to glimpse her leader in the flesh and that she had sent him her poetry, a gift which Mussolini pre-tended to remember.[105]

Within three days the predatory *Duce* was on the phone to her house, where he spoke initially to her mother, who may well have possessed predatory instincts of her own – the greed of the Petacci family became notorious. When Claretta got to the phone, Mussolini asked politely whether she would like to continue their conversation. If she did, a pass to the Palazzo Venezia was waiting. She went the next morning and saw the *Duce* in a little room he kept for naps, just off the *Sala del Mappamondo*.[106] It is unclear whether they had sex straight away;[107] De Felice says that a regular relationship between the two did not commence until October 1936.[108] By then Petacci had a flat in the Palazzo Venezia and had become a sort of *maîtresse en titre*. She would arrive at 2 p.m., have a quick smoke (hiding her habit from the disap-proving *Duce*), and then make ready to greet her lover.[109] Her telephone now began to be tapped by the regime's assiduous police,[110] a surveillance of which she was presumably unaware. She was accus-tomed to return home to mother at around 8 p.m. By 1936 she was a *signora* and not a *signorina*, since, in June 1934, she married Riccardo Federici, an officer who, in 1936, was sent as Air Attaché to Tokyo, where he stayed until 1945.[111] The wedding had occurred with all appearance of solemnity and the couple had been personally blessed by Pius XI.

Telephone taps did not forbear to record Mussolini's conversations with his young friend. His amatory rhetoric remained banal: 'I love you so much, so much. I don't know why I love you like this. I only love you! The perfume of your kisses stuns me, kills me. When I look into your eyes I read to the bottom of your soul! The world vanishes and I forget everybody and everything.' Moreover, as he thought a man must be, he was jealous; just what had she been doing that day?[112] On another occasion the power relation between the two was empha-sised more starkly when Claretta promised 'Ben' a kiss for every gift she had received and was told: 'Don't exaggerate. What you give me more than compensates.'[113] Rome society began to notice the affair. Mussolini might sweep past onlookers alert to gossip, doused in cologne (he preferred this traditional way of combating body odour to new-fangled showers).[114] Or Claretta might appear in public, there to suffer severe appraisal from the envious eyes of higher society dames. As one recalled cattily:

Miss Petacci, his last lady love, although she had beautiful legs and unbelievably small feet like her predecessors, was hardly a fitting companion for a chief of state. I saw her once at the opera and found her very attractive in a certain way. She had too many curls[115] and her make up was unnaturally heavy. Her mink coat was too big; her jewels too showy; but it could not be denied that she attracted attention.[116]

Petacci must have provided some evidence that Mussolini, despite the ageing of his body and the continuation of his stomach pains, had not lost his sex appeal.[117] One observer found him at the beginning of 1934 chubbier (the result very likely of the central place of milk in his diet), but full of vim.[118] He continued his sporting life, in January 1934 being much photographed ski-ing at the new Terminillo resort, high in the Apennines to the east of Rome[119] (a place destined to re-enter his life in 1943). However, when he went home at night to the Villa Torlonia, Rachele and the children, life was humdrum. Guests noticed the heavy and ill-fitting furnishings,[120] the way the *Duce* would repair to the cinema which had been installed and, on evenings off, watch American comedies (like most of his contemporaries, he loved Mack Sennett, Charlie Chaplin and Laurel and Hardy).[121] Visitors also recalled his permanent desire to detour around family hassles. He was a distant father to his two older sons who, as school and police reports indicated, were fond of truancy, sport, fast cars and women of loose morals.[122] When the *Duce* showed up once to watch Bruno play basketball (the boy had been made captain of his team), it was a big surprise.[123] Perhaps these were small mercies. Fabrizio Ciano remembered his more self-consciously upper-bourgeois father summoning him as a quite small child to interview, ordering him to stand to attention and then slapping him in the face, just to be going on with.[124]

Both private and public life still stubbornly refused to bring contentment. Sex with a very much younger woman only confirmed Mussolini's classical view that women were the ones who really enjoyed coitus. 'Voluptuousness', he said, 'exalts the woman, fills her, satisfies her.' Her poor lover was left instead 'empty and disappointed'.[125] In any case, man in general, he confided to a colleague, always kills what he most loves.[126]

Such bleakness was in striking contrast to Starace's populist design for the Fascist party and the razzmatazz which had now become a perpetual part of Fascist rule. Yet, the accompanying reiteration of the ubiquity and omniscience, at times the godlike immanence, of the

Duce concealed his deepening isolation. At times he himself seemed to concede the limitations of charismatic 'power' when he remarked that his absolute authority imprisoned him and even confessed that he on occasion gave orders because it was expected that he do so rather than with a sense that anything would be achieved.[127] Less and less did he bother to summon the Grand Council – it met 106 times between 1923 and 1929, 56 times between 1930 and 1936 and 23 times between 1937 and 1943.[128] By the mid to late 1930s, when the Council did assemble, Mussolini mostly just harangued it; discussion more and more appeared the equivalent of treachery.

In this atmosphere, the more independent thinkers among Mussolini's henchmen were faring badly, especially whilever Starace determined political fashion. Balbo, at best an erratic analyst of anything but, if only from envy, not always quiescent before the *Duce*, was rusticated to Tripoli in January 1934, much to his own disgust.[129] The main victim of the period was, however, Arpinati, who was suddenly sacked as Under-Secretary for the Interior in May 1933 (his replacement was Guido Buffarini Guidi, a Tuscan who was to be one of the stayers of the last decade of the regime and holder of the key Ministry of the Interior during the Salò Republic). In July 1934 Arpinati was arrested,[130] stripped of his party membership[131] and hustled off to *confino*, where he stayed until 1940.[132] The downfall of Arpinati was the work of Starace,[133] with the alleged backing of Giacomo Suardo, A.S. Benni and the business world,[134] and indicates a great deal about the state of the Fascist party in the mid-1930s.

Starace told Mussolini that Arpinati, who had not forgotten his radical youth, had scandalously attacked corporatism and the government's bailing out of banks and industries in trouble as a result of the depression. Arpinati had allowed the number of subscribers to *Il Popolo d'Italia* in the province of Bologna to decline to 36, despite an official campaign to garner 100 000. He was corrupt, guilty of nepotism and worse.[135] His friends used cocaine, exploited prostitutes, corrupted minors, gambled to excess, and denigrated Fascist achievement.[136] He had said in public that the PNF was no more than 'a jumble of buffoons'. He did not mind being thought the 'Black Pope' or, perhaps, the 'Stalin of Fascism'. Worst, he had openly and violently attacked Mussolini's own speeches.[137]

Starace took to purging with a will, suggesting that he was the potential Vyshinsky or Yagoda of the Fascist regime. Just as the official history of the USSR stripped Bukharin and the other victims of the 1937 purge of the capitals of their names while it reduced them to 'white guard insects', so Starace took to writing about 'arpinati', or his accomplice 'iraci',[138] and hoped that they could be 'eliminated from history'.[139] Nothing is known of Mussolini's reaction to the destruction of his old friend, aside from the fact that he stood by and accepted it.[140] Somewhere in his mind he may have agreed with Farinacci,[141] who, once again the voice of a Fascism which had been, told the *Duce* that he did not believe Starace's charges and that, in any case, Arpinati was 'a gentleman'?[142] If so, the nature of Mussolini's charismatic 'power' meant that he had to set aside such secret doubts until the wave of patriotism occasioned by the onset of the war allowed him to retrieve Arpinati from his relegation to the Lipari islands.[143] Mussolini learned that rumour said that Fascism in his cherished Emilia Romagna never recovered from the fall of Arpinati.[144] The party's popularity in the Po valley may not have been enhanced by a speech Starace gave in Mantua in which he boasted that he 'never slept, and worked even in bed', adding that women who wanted to try him out could come backstage.[145] Such domestic travails were beginning to seem side issues compared with the menace which the solidification of Hitler's regime was bringing to international relations.

The initial stage in the Nazi–Fascist relationship climaxed with three major events in the summer of 1934. First was the long heralded meeting between *Duce* and *Führer*, held, on 14–15 June 1934, in Venice, a place ideally suited, it seemed, to cheer the artistic Hitler. The Fascist press advertised the event as 'the encounter between two revolutions'.[146] There were grounds for doubting that the two dictators would warm to each other, however. During the previous months, Mussolini publicly opposed any idea of an *Anschluss*, saying that 'Austria knows that, in its defence of its independence as a sovereign state, it can rely on us.'[147] The Fascist press had echoed its master's word, with Farinacci scorning the Nazis as 'social-nationalists', people possessed of 'the fascist label but not the Fascist substance'.[148] Mussolini again did not hesitate to speak out against Nazi racism: '100% racism. Against all and everybody. Yesterday against Christian civilization; today against Latin civilization; tomorrow, who knows, against the civilization of the whole world.' So 'obscurantist', 'exclusivist', 'chauvinist' and 'imperialist' a policy was, he argued, impossible in the twentieth century.[149] Even in *La Vita Italiana*, the Nazi racial philosopher Rosenberg was damned as 'Anti-Christ'; his 'vacuous' ideology, a commentator wrote dismissively, amounted to 'a pseudo-philosophy of Russian origin'.[150]

Perhaps, then, it is no surprise to find that, at Venice, most things went wrong. The first meeting in the villa at Stra, which had once been Napoleon's, was ravaged by mosquitoes – one memoirist claimed that they were as big as quails.[151] The next at the Venice golf club planned a few years earlier by Volpi and Henry Ford,[152] was scarcely congenial to the two dictators, each (unlike Franco) too traditional a figure to understand that golf and 'statesmanship' went together. In between, Hitler had been taken on a visit to the Art *Biennale*, finding to his disgust that Fascism did not ban the display of modernist – in his view degenerate – paintings, whole rooms of them.[153] On every occasion, Hitler, who came in civilian dress, looking, said Mussolini, 'like a plumber in a mackintosh', talked on and on in German, boring the *Duce* with his diatribes, or perhaps baffling him, for Mussolini liked it to be believed that he understood German without difficulty,[154] but the *Führer*'s garrulity, then and later, tested his comprehension.[155]

As so often, contemporaries did their best to see what they wanted in the meeting. Renzetti reported that Hitler had come home 'radiant', flatteringly convinced that a Mussolini was only born once in every century.[156] The *Führer* remarked that he could discuss things with Mussolini which he could not raise with even his closest German collaborators.[157] Suvich wrote to Dollfuss more tartly that Hitler had gone on and on talking about his *Weltanschauung*, even though it was 'more or less known'. He had been unconvincing over the *Anschluss*, and Mussolini had not weakened in his opposition to it.[158] Mussolini himself told De Vecchi, his by now highly pious representative at the Vatican, that Hitler sounded like a broken record when he raged about the Jewish Christ and the nefarious activities of Germany's Catholics. The *Duce* hoped that he could calm the *Führer* in his Church policy, but he was glad, he added, that Fascist Italy remained 'politically and ethically' in tune with Catholicism.[159]

Whether invigorated by his contact with the *Duce* or not, Hitler went home determined to act. On 30 June he organised the 'Night of the Long Knives', in which Röhm, the SA leadership, and a number of anti-Hitler rightists were murdered, some by accident and some by planning. Between 150 and 200 people died.[160] The Italians were bemused by such open and widespread violence, which had no parallel in their own rise. Even their more Germanophile press tried to explain that Hitler's regime was in 'psychological crisis', occasioned by a weakness for 'intellectualising' and a consequent failure to grasp the 'Latin clarity' embodied in Mussolini.[161] The *Duce* himself used the occasion to prompt the Austrians into being more rigorous in their confrontation with 'terrorism'.[162]

His advice was too late, however. On 25 July Austrian Nazis murdered Dollfuss in a bungled *coup* attempt, brutally leaving him to bleed to death on the Vienna Chancellery floor. The Austrian chancellor only weeks before had written to Suvich of his pleasure at a planned meeting with Mussolini at the beach resort of Riccione,[163] and, on the day of his death, his wife and children were already holidaying with the Mussolini family;[164] indeed the *Duce* had the unenviable job of reporting to them what had happened.[165] To the applause of his press,[166] Mussolini reacted firmly to the killing, even to the extent of mobilising four divisions and moving some equipment to the Brenner frontier.[167] On a more personal level Mussolini also seemed troubled by the murder of a politician he viewed as his Austrian client. His protection of Frau Dollfuss continued in March 1938 when he helped to win her sanctuary in Switzerland[168] and, in the interim, he was solicitous in ordering the purchasing of 'Baby Bugatti', model electric cars for the Dollfuss children[169] and the sending of a *Portrait of Engelbert Dollfuss*, currently exhibited in the Austrian pavilion at the Venice *Biennale*, to the widow.[170]

In his political commentaries, the *Duce* had little reason now to restrain his hostility to Nazi Germany. The 'Social Nationalists' had so many absurd ideas, even when they were drawn from 'Hitler's *New Testament*', as he sardonically labelled *Mein Kampf*. It would take six centuries to breed a pure German race, and so, he added still more sarcastically, 'there was plenty of time to talk over the matter with calm and quiet'.[171] Anyway the Germans themselves were split into at least six races. Their sterilisation programmes were almost as deplorable as was their racism.[172] All in all, he wrote, the Germans were world experts in faithlessness and cynicism.[173] Before an audience at Bari, his contempt towards his alleged imitators in Germany knew no bounds: 'thirty centuries of history allow us to look with utter disdain on certain doctrines from the other side of the Alps which are espoused by the descendants of people who were illiterate at a time when Rome had Caesar, Virgil and Augustus'.[174] In the autumn of 1934 Nazi Germany and Fascist Italy by no means appeared natural allies.

In some senses, Mussolini protested too much, however. Germany was not alone in fostering political terrorism in Europe. Mussolini had regularly incited Dollfuss to domestic repression, whether of Austrian Nazis or of Austrian Social Democrats,[175] who had been cruelly attacked in February 1934 (in notorious incidents, tanks had been used to bombard working-class housing in the city of Vienna itself).

Mussolini was also the patron of Gyula Gömbös, the far-rightist Prime Minister of obsessively revisionist Hungary, and perpetually tried to nudge him towards a more 'fascist' organisation of Hungarian life.[176] The Spanish republic was similarly numbered among the enemies of Fascist Italy. The Italian press gave space to the cloudy ideas of Ernesto Gimenez Caballero, a self-styled potential Spanish fascist chief. The more practical dealings of the Fascist leadership were, however, with dissident generals and monarchists. Italy provided arms and assistance to the attempted coup of General José Sanjurjo in 1932.[177] Two years later, Mussolini and Balbo met General Emilio Barrera and other exponents of the Right and again promised them funds and the delivery of rifles, machine guns and grenades, now to be secretly shipped through Tripoli, with a view to the launching of another coup. 'When I help someone', Mussolini boasted, 'I help them, as Austria knows well.'[178]

Even if the *Duce* remained prickly about the Italophobia always likely to surface in Croat nationalism,[179] the Fascists had not ended their patronage of Pavelić and his *Ustasha* movement. On 9 October 1934 a Croatian fascist, trained in Italy, assassinated King Alexander of Yugoslavia and French Foreign Minister, Louis Barthou, who had been meeting in Marseilles.[180] The deed did not occur at an ideal moment for Italian diplomacy, which had a number of reasons to favour rapprochement with France. None the less, Mussolini told Gömbös aggressively, he would certainly not express public regret over the matter but rather be studied in his indifference.[181] He informed Kurt von Schuschnigg, the successor of Dollfuss, that he had no intention of agreeing to the extradition of Pavelić and his aides (and then pressed the Austrian Chancellor to hasten the fascist-style regimentation of his country).[182]

By 1934 Italy was certainly not a straightforward backer of the status quo in Europe. Quite a number of dissidents, both on the Right and on the Far Right, took Fascist money and, in return, were usually fulsome in their expressions of gratitude towards Mussolini.[183] Italy is, of course, not the only country in world history to look for clients abroad (while, before 1914, Liberal diplomatists had imagined a future in which national largesse could bind foreigners to the Italian cause, surmising that they would thus catch up with the arrogantly superior French).[184] The problem with such a search is that the weaker the power involved the more untrustworthy the clients and the more likely, too, that they will behave in ways which richer powers regard as unacceptable.

In any case, by the end of 1934 Fascist policy was turning its eyes away from Europe to the longstanding national target of Ethiopia. 'Planning' for Fascist action there had been an on-again, off-again matter since Laval and Guariglia[185] raised the issue in 1931–32. One problem was that, as had on occasion been pointed out to Mussolini by such interested parties as Minister of Colonies, De Bono,[186] Fascist rule had done little to alter the sleepiness of the existing East African colonies of Eritrea and Somaliland, unrewarding places even for the most enthusiastic or naïve imperialists. By the end of 1932 De Bono was pressing for a more activist policy towards Ethiopia (and an enhanced budget for himself),[187] if only because as Minister he had to advocate something.

In early February 1934 Mussolini had become more attracted to the idea than in the past[188] and a certain degree of military preparation had begun, though no date had been set. In May Badoglio was still convinced that a conflict would be 'terribly burdensome', advising cautiously that, in most colonial acquisitions, the game was not worth the candle.[189] The murder of Dollfuss similarly acted as a brake, with Mussolini declaring in August that the European situation was too uncertain for Italy to be diverted to an African adventure.[190] However, the reluctance of the liberal democracies to resist Germany with any firmness was now clear. Germany had a case for appeasement, it seemed. Italy did not. After the Dollfuss murder and when Italian troops moved to the Brenner, *The Scotsman* was typical of the British press in reminding its readers that the 'ruthless' Mussolini had once brutally assaulted Corfu. Morally speaking, the paper concluded, 'there was nothing to choose between Italy and Germany',[191] and therefore no likelihood that Italy could expect any backing if it did come to open conflict with Germany. Moreover, in Mussolini's mind and those of his colleagues in the Fascist leadership, there was every reason to think that the European situation was bound to deteriorate further, since Nazi Germany showed few signs of curbing its revisionist intent. The years of stability were over and, if Italy, the least of the Great Powers, wanted any reward, it would have to act promptly and, very likely, ruthlessly as well. In rather similar circumstances in 1911, 3 years before the outbreak of the First World War, Giolitti had seized Libya, fulfilling a longstanding Italian ambition. In 1935, 4 years before the Second World War Ethiopia was to be the national target.

On 30 December 1934 Mussolini issued a directive on the Ethiopian question. Its first paragraph was clear: 'The problem of Italo-Abyssinian relations has moved in most recent times onto a new plane.

From a problem of diplomacy it has become a problem of force; a "historic" problem which must be resolved by the only means which ever resolve such problems – the use of arms'. The *Duce* went on to explain that Emperor Haile Selassie had been more successful than expected in constructing something approaching a centralised state in Ethiopia. His achievement meant that 'time is working against us'. The longer Italy waited the tougher Ethiopian resistance would prove. 'We must therefore deal with the matter as soon as possible, that is, when our military preparations make victory certain.' 'Having opted for war, the aim can only be the destruction of the Abyssinian armed forces and the total conquest of Ethiopia', Mussolini continued. 'An empire cannot be made by other means.' France's policies against Abd el Krim in Morocco had indicated the way forward; then the French had 'profited from a moment when Germany was still unarmed or almost so'. Italy needed Europe to be 'tranquil', believing it could rely on peace surviving until 1937, but not thereafter. Italy's improved current relations with France could check German ambitions against Austria for that period. Italy must urgently build up a massive military supremacy and 'following the Japanese fashion, it won't be necessary to declare war and we can just insist that we are acting defensively'. 'No one in Europe will raise difficulties', he argued, 'if the military situation is resolved speedily.' In any case, Italy had treaty arrangements with Britain and France over Ethiopia and should emphasise that it did not intend to harm those powers' interests. Any embarrassment for the League of Nations would be of minor significance.[192] Italy's long wait to be the ruler of Ethiopia was over. However much reflecting both Italian history in East Africa and the current atmosphere of international relations, Mussolini had decided on the first of 'his' wars.

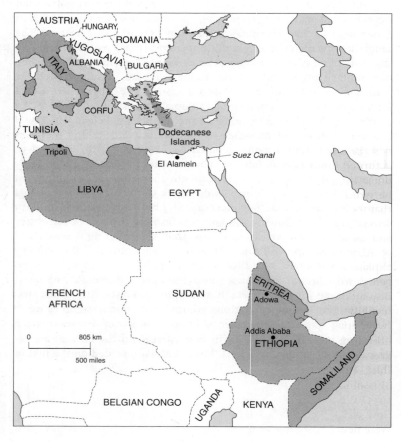

Map 3 The Fascist Empire

13

Empire in Ethiopia,
1935–1936

IN the last paragraph of his directive of 30 December Mussolini had turned his mind back to the situation within Italy. His account of domestic opinion was characteristic. 'The leftovers of the old world', he wrote, 'still fear what they call an adventure because they think that the war will be carried out according to their models. But they are wrong', he added, 'and, any way, they count for nothing politically and socially'. Even though this was to be a war to seize 'the last piece of Africa which is not under European rule',[1] it would, the *Duce* explained, more importantly be the occasion in which the 'younger generation' could demonstrate their superiority over their elders, and display the *élan* which they had acquired as the children of the Fascist revolution. To a realistic eye, imperialism in Africa might seem old, a twentieth-century replication of the habits of nineteenth-century liberalism. But a war fought under the aegis of a Fascist *Duce* would be dressed up as new and 'Fascist'. The war, as it were, would don a black shirt. How, then, had the Fascist revolution been going? How did Mussolini understand its progress and prospects at the beginning of 1935? What had been the effect of his policy of 'going to the people'? How was his choice, Achille Starace, performing as Party Secretary? Were new Fascist men, backed at home by new Fascist women, ready to serve and conquer as the dauntless legionaries of a Fascist empire and the faithful cohorts of their *Duce*?

One matter which Mussolini had typically avoided on 30 December was the budget for the war. He cheerfully advised the deployment of overwhelming force, the arming, dispatch and supply of 'at least 300 000 men', without any attempt to cost the matter. The official line was that the *Duce* was an economic genius, 'both theoretically and practically, with a perfect fusion of thought and action'.[2] By himself, it was said, he was 'the creator of the economy', an 'Economist' in capital letters, unusual among statesmen in his training in the subject and unparalleled in his skill at managing the national finances.[3] In private, Mussolini's subordinates were less convinced about these claims. Suvich for one recalled that the *Duce* normally displayed little interest in financial and economic details, at most, as with many other issues, setting a tone rather than precisely defining policy.[4] However, a disjunction between what was said and what they knew to be true did not seem to matter too much, because, after the flutter over the valuation of the lira, the *Duce* had generally accepted the economic advice of his technocrats and rarely interfered with their day-to-day activities.

Nevertheless, by the mid-1930s the state of the economy was again becoming an important backdrop to political events, because, however belatedly, Fascist Italy was feeling the effects of the Depression. Difficulties were evident on many fronts. The stock market lost a third of its value from 1929 to 1932.[5] The banking system stuttered and gold flowed out of the country.[6] Production and exports fell and unemployment remained uncomfortably high for a regime which preened itself over its solicitude for its workers[7] – in 1935 official figures still disclosed more than three-quarters of a million without work.[8] Real wages fell.[9] Tourism, greatest of Italy's invisible assets, fared poorly, despite the Vatican's promotion of a supernumerary Holy Year in 1933.[10] Emigrant remittances, that other traditional salvation of the national economy, more than halved between 1929 and 1932.[11] Italy even did badly relatively, with its share of Western Europe's output declining from 8.2 per cent in 1929 to 8 per cent in 1937[12] (from 1922 to 1938 Fascism achieved a growth rate of only 1.9 per cent annually, below Liberal Italy's 2.7 per cent between 1897 and 1913, as well as failing to match Britain's 2.2 per cent, Germany's 3.8 per cent and Sweden's 4.1 per cent).[13]

Even by the most generous estimate, Mussolini's management of the economy was not scintillating at a time when the deteriorating international situation was threatening to make unprecedented demands on the nation (and indeed, from 1934 state spending spiralled up,[14] with one technocrat remarking sardonically that the national finances had entered 'the phase of heroic remedies').[15] Mussolini had placed Italy's fortunes in the hands of two technocrats, Guido Jung, an unusual figure, being both Sicilian and Jewish (he was Minister of Finance, July 1932 to January 1935) and Alberto Beneduce, and he usually let them get on with their work. It was their collaboration which, with Mussolini's approval, produced in January 1933 the *Istituto di Ricostruzione Industriale* (the Institute of Industrial Reconstruction or IRI).[16] This organisation, technically 'provisional' until 1937 when Beneduce became its president, engaged in considerable state intrusion into the economy, with three major banks and a number of other industrial concerns being bailed out by public money. IRI was a herald of what would later be called the policy of 'autarchy', that is, of Italy turning its back on international trade and purporting to run an exclusively national economy (even if the dependence on tourism and emigrant remittances belied that claim). In his speeches Mussolini painted autarchy as a major strand of the newly radicalised Fascist revolution.[17] However, most historians argue that IRI, even at the end of the 1930s, continued to be manipulated by private interests and was never honed into a sleek instrument of totalitarian control. One analyst has concluded tartly that autarchy meant the control of everything except profits.[18]

Rather than pushing drastic change in the way business functioned, Mussolini preferred, as so often, to direct his own control and 'authority' into compiling files of gossip about the industrial and financial elite. His secretariat gleaned the information, for example, that Giovanni Agnelli of Fiat had no intention of allowing IRI to become a conduit through which rich men like himself would lend money to the government and also that he had expressed a preference for collecting US dollars rather than lire.[19] Reports of cynicism and greed in turn confirmed Mussolini in his usual view of the world. He remarked in 1937 that 15 years in office had taught him that 'our financiers tire themselves out in their efforts to defraud the state and to stop anyone apart from themselves from making money'.[20] Such angry misanthropy may have been consoling for one who kept telling himself that he (and any real Fascist) had been 'born subversive',[21] but it did not lead to action. Agnelli, for example, remained the real boss of Turin and no Fascist revolution dented his prestige and power.[22] As Mussolini admitted in a moment of some frankness in December 1934:

No state is more totalitarian and authoritarian than the Fascist state; no state is more jealous of its sovereignty and prestige. But it is precisely because of this that the Fascist state does not feel required to interfere in matters beyond its competence and foreign to its nature.[23]

Although never officially stated, throughout Mussolini's rule this exemption from the full rigour of Fascism was frequently understood to have been granted to the biggest businessmen and the highest financiers. Political control might reside with the *Duce*; economic and social power remained more diffuse.

The elite of the financial order aside, the fostering of industrial growth in the most modern sectors of the economy squared uneasily with the populist 'corporatism' which regime propaganda vaunted as lying at the base of the Fascist rule. In the pages of his journal *Critica Fascista*, Bottai led the way in ringing endorsements of corporatism. It amounted, he wrote, to 'a revolution in the revolution'. It was what made the Fascist revolution 'perennial, permanent and inexhaustible'.[24] Mussolini, too, frequently evoked a corporatist present and future. In November 1933 he even went so far as to announce the death of capitalism: 'Today we can state that the system of capitalist production has been surpassed and with it that liberal economic theory which has illuminated it and acted as its apologist.' 'Corporatism', Mussolini went on, 'has defeated both socialism and liberalism and is creating a new synthesis.' For the moment Italy might retain some capitalist leftovers, he acknowledged; after all, he did not run an absolute state, but rather 'an organic and human state, which wants to remain in touch with the realities of life'. None the less, corporatism was the highway to the twenty-first century.[25] The totalitarian state, with its exaction from the populace of a 'greatly heightened moral and intellectual tension', would end by 'burying economic liberalism'.[26] Fascist businessmen would learn to become 'comrade businessmen'.[27]

As if to demonstrate its determination to impose state control over the economy, the Fascist regime had committed itself to a raft of welfare and development schemes; they were another characteristic feature of Mussolinian rule, as well as a reason why he was remembered by a not always ungrateful public after 1945.[28] One of the more lauded of areas of government action was the *dopolavoro*, or after-work organisation, devoted to channelling worker leisure into activities which were worthy, healthy and guaranteed, in theory, to stimulate greater identification with the regime. The original plan did not spring from the *Duce*'s mind, but had been borrowed from the more modern sectors of American business.[29] The concept was then adopted by Rossoni and his syndicalist friends as proof that they were committed to improvement of the workers' lot and that Fascism therefore constituted a genuine 'third way'. Mussolini's most obvious contribution to the system lay in propaganda – the various branches of the *dopolavoro* were, he stated, 'among the most vital and important institutions of the regime' — and in assigning managerial roles.[30] He also curbed the most ambitious ideals of the syndicalists, granting the moderate Turati, while he was PNF secretary, special control over the *dopolavoro*. Turati was keen to prick any syndicalist plans to give the organisation too evidently a socially radical thrust.[31] Even so, membership in the party leisure structures grew steadily, with 2 376 000 being enrolled by 1935; that was the equivalent to some 20 per cent of the industrial workforce and 7 per cent of the peasantry.[32]

The paltry size of this last figure (as well as the continuing relative absence of sports fields and other essential infrastructure throughout the South) exposed another contradiction in the Fascist revolution. The country which was about to wage war, what it proclaimed was an overwhelmingly modern one, on the 'barbarous' and 'backward' Ethiopians was also a place whose *Duce* was much given to orating about the need to 'go back to the land'. Peasants, he was accustomed to proclaim, were people who 'detested those who wanted to stuff their heads full of complicated ideas', whether philosophical or technological. Although each village should, under his regime, get 'electricity, the telephone, the cinema, the radio and proper roads',[33] the peasants were precious to the nation and its stock because of their primordial virility and love of work. Fascist modernism may not have been reliably 'reactionary', but, in a way shared by the Nazis,[34] Fascists, Mussolini included, balanced their enthusiasm for scientific progress with constant evocations of a world destined to be lost.

The most trumpeted rural programmes were those to do with the draining of the Pontine and other marshes and the establishment of model agricultural settlements such as Littoria (today Latina) south of Rome, or Mussolinia, an early 'garden town for peasants' in Sicily.[35] Regime propagandists loved to cite the *Duce* as the inspiration of the schemes — he had provided the slogan: 'to reclaim the land, and with the land the man, and with the man, the race'[36] — but the actual architect of reclamation was Arrigo Serpieri, a technocrat inherited from the liberal past.[37] Furthermore, a case study of the experience of families from the Veneto who transferred to the area outside Rome has concluded that the whole deal was 'a fiddle', at least for the peasants, who from their move south gained neither prosperity nor a reduction in the intricate class variations of rural life.[38] An account of an accompanying campaign, the battle against malaria, has come to similar conclusions. Begun by the liberals, the drive after 1922 to eliminate this ancient scourge of the countryside succeeded only fitfully because the processes involved were top-down and authoritarian, easily manipulated to the benefit of wealthy locals, and obscure and costly to those actually afflicted by the disease. In any case, when, after 1935, the regime had to pay for foreign adventures, expenditure on medical welfare was swiftly downsized.[39] As a result of the cuts, and the war across the Italian peninsula, by 1945 malaria had returned to most of those areas from which the regime claimed it had been eradicated.

In sum, for all the talk about a return to the land (and for all Rachele Mussolini's efforts to prove a modern scientific landholder at the *Villa Carpena*), the *Duce* failed to suture the traditional gap in wealth, influence, status and understanding between city and countryside. In the more remote areas, life went on almost as though the feeble and distant government in Rome was irrelevant to ordinary lives.[40] Just as their fathers had done in 1915, peasants from the Piedmontese mountains thought they had entered paradise when they were conscripted in 1935, because military rations included meat.[41] In the northern Alps, those who stayed at home told an interviewer with some wistfulness in the 1970s: 'Fascism brought us neither gain nor harm. It is as though it had never been.'[42]

The crucial agent of government activity, or inactivity, under the dictatorship was as often the state bureaucracy as the Fascist party. Mussolini's own attitude towards the clerks of the public administration fluctuated. He could be hostile, claiming that one of the essential purposes of his regime was to purge a corrupt, inefficient and flaccid Liberal state, and replace it with the more mobilised and achieving Fascist version. In 1928 he announced that 'the regime must definitively resolve the bureaucratic problem'[43] and, ten years later, he still suggested that personally he was 'anti-bureaucratic by definition'.[44] However, when that rough and tumble economist, Alberto De' Stefani, came up with a plan for drastic change in bureaucratic selection and work methods, Mussolini told him that he lacked political sense. The Fascist regime could not, the *Duce* explained, risk alienating the Southern middle classes; the 'hunger of intellectuals' from there was 'the most difficult of all to placate'.[45] More and more frequently, Mussolini turned his early theses around, hailing his bureaucrats as superior in knowledge, effectiveness and probity to their counterparts in other countries. 'In the great army of the Italian bureaucracy', he averred, 'black sheep are very rare.'[46] They need suffer no drastic amendment of their habits and mentality. As the 1930s wore on and, especially because of autarchy, an array of semi-state bodies multiplied, those who worked for them could often more readily claim a dedication to the revolution than could the more strictly professional officials. According to the historian of Italian white-collar public servants, the overall effect of the Fascist mix of policies and attitudes was neither to purge nor to modernise the state bureaucracy, but rather to leave it 'confused, depressed and cautious', believing glumly that it had been given the task of applying rules in a world where rules did not reliably exist.[47]

Farinacci would remark on one occasion that Mussolini was too given to crawling to 'professors': 'I show them to the door, but you kneel before them. The professors kill you and you just thank them for it.' Who, the *ras* of Cremona concluded with his usual lubberly bravado, 'gives a stuff about Fascist culture'?[48] Such words were designed to annoy and disturb the man who cherished his title as 'Prof. Mussolini'. The *Duce* never ceased to flaunt philosophical interests. Indeed, he almost seemed to yearn for the contemplative academic life when he told a fan: 'whoever really devotes himself to study must avoid too much truck with ordinary men'.[49] Despite the fullness of his political schedule he loved to exhibit his knowledge of Plato, Kant, Nietzsche, Emerson, William James[50] and Machiavelli, although on occasion he would qualify his alleged appreciation of their texts with the more down-to-earth advice: 'today philosophy should be practised in the midst of everyday life'.[51]

Certainly these were the years of the trumpeting of Fascist zeal in education. In 1936 Fascist doctrine was made a compulsory part of all philosophy courses,[52] and Mussolini's thought, Italians were obsessively told, could take an equal place among that of the greatest sages of the past.[53] As one admirer put it, with some opacity: 'his thought we call Italy'.[54] Another more simply stated that, although the *Duce* had not written a study of pedagogy, he was none the less the greatest of pedagogues.[55] Still another urged that Mussolini possessed the span of Leonardo da Vinci, a quality he especially demonstrated through his thought about corporatism.[56] Boasts about supremacy were one thing but Fascism did not intend to preside over a free market of the intellect. In October 1931 university professors had been forced to take an oath of allegiance to the regime (only a sprinkling refused). In 1933 membership of the party became obligatory for new teachers in the tertiary and secondary sectors, while, the following year, it was decreed that teachers had to wear the uniform of some Fascist institution on every official occasion. University students were expected to enrol in the *Gioventù Universitaria Fascista* (University Fascist Youth), both as an entry point to a career and for its present advantages – these included much sporting activity,[57] half-price entry to all cinemas and, if a member joined the related militia, avoidance of immediate military service and a three-month reduction in requirements after call-up.[58] De Vecchi, Minister of Education from January 1935 to November 1936, talked about the Fascist *bonifica* (reclamation) of culture,[59] using the same metaphor as that deployed over the land schemes in the Pontine marshes.

More directly targeted at the masses was popular culture, organised, from 1934, by an Under-Secretariat for Press, Propaganda and Tourism, raised to a ministry in June 1935 and, in both cases, placed under the rule of Galeazzo Ciano (until the summer of 1936). In May 1937 this organisation was expanded to become *Minculpop* (the Ministry of Popular Culture).[60] The sloganeering of the 1920s spread, with Mussolini himself in May 1932 launching the phrase *meglio vivere un giorno da leone che cento anni da pecora* (better to live one day as a lion than a hundred years as a sheep), claiming that it had originally been a password (if rather a long one) at the Battle of the Piave in 1918.[61] The most ubiquitous slogan – *Credere, Obbedire, Combattere* (Believe, Obey, Fight) – had allegedly been coined by Starace, but it was taken up by the *Duce*, when, in 1932, he urged: 'The Fascist Party is an army or, if you wish, an order. You only enter it to serve and to obey.'[62]

It was also emphasised that Fascism must inspire, and be renewed by, youth – Mussolini's own elder sons turned 18 in 1934 and 1936 respectively. At the *Decennale*, Mussolini had spoken of the requirement that 'in the second decade of Fascism we make room for the young. We want the young', he ran on, 'to take up our torch, flaming with our faith, and to be alert and committed in continuing our labours'.[63] To assist in such indoctrination there were the regime's various paramilitary organisations and a more elite 'School of Fascist Mysticism', established in Milan in 1930 and given the ostensible advantage of having Vito Mussolini, Arnaldo's surviving son, as its first president.[64] The historian of this last body has concluded that it exerted 'rather little' influence on the populace at large.[65] More generally, contradictions can easily be found in the regime's cultural politics. One obvious area is film, a form of communication of ever greater popularity, as was demonstrated by the *Duce* in his nightly watching (even though his official line began to deprecate the American films he actually loved).[66] In 1938 343 million tickets were sold to Italian cinemagoers; with war, the total increased to reach 469 million in 1942.[67] Among the Mussolini family, during the latter part of the 1930s Vittorio sought to make a name for himself in the industry and become the leader of the gilded and aristocratic, if raffish, framers of the national cinema. Of the Fascist leadership, Bottai was the chief theoretician of film, suggesting, as early as 1926, that it might prove the 'most Fascist' of all the arts.[68] He was reluctant, however, to implement too overt a control, remarking that the public went to the cinema to be entertained and arguing that they would be put off by too crude an attempt to propagandise them.[69]

The economic crisis and the narrowing of political options during the 1930s gradually brought tighter state controls (and a greater effort by the Vatican to impose its own censorship), but Fascist Italy never became as intrusive as was Nazi Germany in the production and distribution of films. Vittorio Mussolini, after an international tour, returned home in late 1936 to advise what many senior figures in the film industry had thought all along, which was that Italy should avoid 'heavy handed' German methods and opt instead for the 'technical virtuosity and fluid narrative styles' of Hollywood.[70] Mussolini, with his old yearnings, never quite satiated, to gain a comprehension of the great world beyond Predappio (or Rome), expressed a wish to be able to view foreign films so long as they expressed something of the social customs of other countries.[71] He, too, was not by nature an adamantine censor.

A cultural studies expert of the 1990s has suggested that Fascism's 'original totalitarian culture' was what drove Mussolini and his regime to its 'energetic discharge in African soil' in 1935.[72] 'The spectacle of fascism exuded war and narratively prefigured the imperialistic outcome of the totalitarian state's aims', she adds.[73] With less strained but more predictable metaphor, Emilio Gentile has argued that, by the 1930s, 'people and nation were bound in a thick web of symbols'.[74] Were they, it may be asked, or – more appropriately for a biographer – was Mussolini impelled to an imperial act because of his place, both designed and undesigned, in Fascist culture? Was he going to Ethiopia not so much kow-towing to professors of philosophy as satisfying the ambitions all but unbearably heightened in the masses through their absorption of a militant Fascist culture? After all, a regime propagandist asserted manfully: 'the *Duce* guides his totalitarian people [into war] with an intimate but irresistible enthusiasm, almost exploding into colonial expansion'.[75]

No doubt words always matter to some extent, but the medium was not the only message in Fascist Italy. Even in the arenas of culture and propaganda, all was not as it seemed. The ideas of patronage and clientship had not, for example, been purged from Italian minds, despite the puffing of a mystical national and, soon, racial unity. Indeed, the 1930s became a decade of opportunity for what has been called 'the state cultural impresario',[76] in other words the adroit middle man who had somehow won for himself the chance to distribute state largesse to artists and performers. The assumptions which lay behind such a role seemed little changed by Fascist pretensions to a new morality. Mussolini was, for example, in 1934 sent a police report about the always importunate composer, Pietro Mascagni, who liked to think of himself as a heroic leader of the national musical industry. Mascagni had been overheard explaining that he had become a Fascist spontaneously out of the spiritual impetus given by 'a Man whom I love and shall always love'. What, however, was the point of fealty to the *Duce*? he had asked. In Cremona, for example, all musical performance was controlled by Farinacci, who was having the gall to celebrate Ponchielli's anniversary with a staging of Bizet's *Carmen*. 'A foreign work to commemorate a *maestro italianissimo*? And no protest! ... My God, how shameful. And I, the pupil of Ponchielli, excluded from the ceremony!'[77] As he read these phrases, Mussolini had the chance again to register the fact that vanity, opportunism, greed – indeed all human failings – had not been swept away by the Fascist cultural revolution.

When he dined at home, can the *Duce* have heard the same news? Certainly Vittorio Mussolini told a teenage class mate, who, with adolescent hope and ambition, was trying to map a path to radical social change which he still planned to be 'Fascist': 'It's useless. Fascism is nothing but a "bluff". Daddy hasn't managed to do anything he wanted to do. The Italians are Fascists out of cowardice and don't give a stuff about the revolution.'[78] Doubtless Vittorio was exaggerating to some extent, as well as expressing ideas about filial revolt and trying to make a splash with his friends in a way not unknown among other teenagers. But the evident sense of self and family, the maleness (even though his words may hint that Vittorio at home had been listening more to his mother than his father) and the effort to gain kudos by dropping English words into his conversation indicate that Vittorio Mussolini was another Italian who had not subjected his mind to totalitarian cleansing.

A generation ago, De Felice wondered whether domestic concerns might have motivated Mussolini to attack Ethiopia. In his view, it was the failings of Fascism at home and not its success which were the greater prompting force. Basically, however, De Felice maintained,

Ethiopia was an external event and its fundamental context was Fascist or Italian foreign and colonial policy.[79] An Italian 'grab for Africa' was not really an aspect of a Fascist cultural revolution. If De Felice is to be believed, the detailed paragraphs of the directive of 30 December 1934 about the international situation are the real key to the planning of the Ethiopian war. The selling at home of the conflict may have been natural and the excited response to the selling influential. But in recounting the events of 1935, the history of foreign policy should not surrender on every front to the history of advertising.

Before narrating the international crisis, however, a final point is worth raising. An imperial war between a metropolitan power and colonial peoples, even if they were partially assembled into a modern state under Haile Selassie, was radically different from Nazi racial conflict. To a large degree, Mussolini in East Africa was still seeking 'Glory, God and Gold', just as his predecessors in other European countries had done in the world beyond their continent during earlier centuries. A demographic emphasis[80] that Italians could eventually settle the Ethiopian highlands gave some contemporary coloration. However, the campaign of 1935–36 was not identical with the world or European war, launched fully by the Nazis only in 1941. Then the Germans wanted to conquer *Lebensraum* contiguous with the existing nation-state, saving any German 'blood' locatable in the East, as well as exterminating Jews, Slavs and communists. The Italians wanted to colour the map green (or whatever colour geographers assigned to Fascist imperium). In 1935 the spirit of Baden-Powell, Teddy Roosevelt and Marshal Lyautey was as powerful an accompaniment of the Italian armies as was that of Adolf Hitler.

Is there another comparison which makes better sense when assessing the context in which Mussolini worked? What of the Liberal Giolitti's attack on Ottoman 'Libya' in 1911–12? Then the Italian war was much criticised in European chancelleries and among the 'best and most enlightened' of the British press, where it was deemed 'immoral'. Nonetheless, Giolitti gave short shrift to any idea of compromise. He sent troops to Tripoli before actually declaring war on Turkey (and eventually utilised a blatantly trumped-up case to justify the attack). His forces having landed in the territory, he quickly decreed its annexation to the nation. Having taken this uncompromising position, Giolitti stood firm against his more timid contemporaries in the government who believed that he had gone too far.[81] In a number of instances, it might be argued that Giolitti in 1911–12 was tougher in his will and more clear-sighted in his decision-making than was a Fascist *Duce*, except that the Liberal Prime Minister sought victory not so much at the battlefront (he made little attempt to hide his view that soldiers were idiots) or in the public relations sphere as on the tables of diplomacy. There his Italy did indeed win, after the fragile Turkish empire was harried by the outbreak of the Balkan wars, fostered to some extent by Italian monetary and military backing of 'terrorist', or nationalist, Serbs, Greeks, Bulgars and Romanians. In winning imperial lands, Mussolini would not of course invoke the achievement of one deemed as an 'Anti-Fascist' liberal, just the sort of feeble or degenerate politician Fascism boasted it had swept into the ash can of history. But, if truth were told, the Italian war of 1935–36 had quite a lot in common with the Italian war of 1911–12.

Mussolini began the new year with his own effort to master the tables of diplomacy. A campaign in Ethiopia, he hoped, could be won without alienating the 'Locarno powers' and old wartime allies, Britain and France. In early January the French Foreign Minister, Pierre Laval, came to Rome. Mussolini, during a shared *spumante* toast (the *Duce* took just a sip), hailed the visit as 'a concrete indication of the rapprochement' now apparent between the two countries. Laval replied more cautiously that 'all those animated by an ideal of peace today turn their eyes to Rome'.[82] Over the previous decade Italo-French relations had often been tense, and they would soon be so again,[83] but Mussolini and the rest of his diplomatic staff now maintained that these had been merely surface irritations. The activism of Nazi Germany was concentrating minds in a way unnecessary before 1933, and the threat of an *Anschluss* and other revisionist disturbance meant that Italy and France should forgive and forget their past bickering, as well as such drastic events as the recent assassination of Barthou (who actually himself had been an Italophile Foreign Minister).

True to their words, Mussolini and Laval had no difficulty in reaching accommodation on a series of matters, including such hardy perennials as Tunisia, where Mussolini was anxious to assure his French colleague that Italian meddling was over. German rearmament was noted, with Mussolini remarking with his usual preference for saying out loud what others thought but preferred not to verbalise: 'We can't turn back. There is only one way to destroy armaments, and that is to do so physically in war.'[84] According to Italian memoranda, in discussions both on 5 and 6 January Mussolini raised the issue of French *désistement* on Ethiopia, where he was happy to pledge, then and later, that coming Italian action would not infringe French interests. The final communique, at least as reported by Mussolini in *Il Popolo d'Italia*, was plain enough: 'Friendship must not remain mummified in diplomatic protocols, but must be active as in life'. 'The crucial new year', he went on, 'begins under the propitious auspices of the Franco-Italian accords.'[85] Mussolini believed he had won approval for something approaching an alliance with France,[86] and was underlining his intention to claim that backing for a push forward in East Africa. As if in confirmation of his interpretation, over the next months he encouraged Badoglio to go deeper and deeper into military exchanges with the French, giving every indication that he would approve the idea of a full-scale anti-German military pact.[87] Simultaneously he disbursed an alleged sixty million lire to the more venal sections of the French press in the hope that he would thereby ensure a public opinion friendly to Italian ambition.[88]

What of Britain, that country with which, unlike France, a 'traditional friendship' had operated without much check under Fascism? Mussolini was unsure.[89] And so he began a policy of half hints, which, in retrospect, must be blamed as heavily responsible for the wrecking of the longstanding accord and the drift of Italy to its wartime fate as Nazi Germany's 'ignoble second'. The British, too, bore quite a bit of responsibility for the rending of Anglo-Italian relations. Although they would spend most of 1935–36 boosting the virtue of the League of Nations, in their hearts many Tories, actually the dominant element in the so-called National government, and more of their bureaucrats in the Foreign Office,[90] disliked 'Genevaism' as much as did Mussolini. Moreover, the British, contrary to their alleged faith in collective security, were commencing a unilateral policy of appeasement towards Germany, which, in Italian eyes, seemed a combination of *Realpolitik*, weakness and hypocrisy. Would Britain backslide when Germany again raised the *Anschluss*? Probably – what did Foreign Secretary John Simon's visit to Hitler in March 1935, the Anglo-German naval agreement of June 1935 and the British acceptance of the German re-militarisation of the Rhineland in March 1936 mean if not that? If a deal with Germany revising the terms of the Treaty of Versailles was just around the corner, why should not Britain give poor Italy something like Ethiopia for example, 'really' just another slice of Africa, a frippery for an empire on which the sun still did not set? And yet a full-scale quarrel with Britain was a serious matter; as Mussolini was told by his naval authorities in March 1935, it could mean Italy would become an 'out' power, no longer part of the entente which guided Europe.[91]

War in Africa might entail a Fascist leap in the dark which could only find a foothold in Berlin.

The questions were asked and the answers known. But they were not brought out into the open, proof no doubt that Mussolini knew that, in pressing on with an adventure in Ethiopia, he was risking much. The lack of detailed planning was also evidence of the inadequacy and danger of charismatic decision- (or non decision-) making; in 1935 too many crucial issues were less than half thought through, and no mechanism existed to appraise them further. The Grand Council was not asked for advice, ministers avoided cooperation one with another,[92] all idea of a meshing of political and military processes was avoided, while the King was confined to being no more than an onlooker, later to mutter darkly in his repressed way that he had found the *Duce* 'impetuous' during the crisis.[93] Margherita Sarfatti was rumoured to be trying to restrain her old lover, but her influence, sexual and intellectual, had long since waned.[94] Such 'planning' for a war as existed fell to the hands of Mussolini and his man on the ground, the fussy, elderly, white-bearded, half-soldier, half-Fascist, Emilio De Bono.[95] At no stage, was there any detailed investigation of what to do with the territory to be conquered, whatever that was going to be[96] (but Giolitti had been similarly reticent in 1911–12).

An illustration of the *Duce*'s line and method was displayed in a telegram he sent on 25 January to his ambassador in London, and frequent interlocutor on the framing of policy, the mephistophelian Dino Grandi. Mussolini assured Grandi that the French had approved Italy's intention 'to resolve the Ethiopian problem in a radical fashion, either by undertaking direct rule, or in some other way which events counsel'. It was time, the *Duce* wrote, to sound out the British more fully on the same issue. Simon should certainly not be primed with all Italian military planning. Yet he should know enough of the likely future for his country not to want to 'block' Italy but rather offer it 'sympathy'. Simon, Mussolini advised, should be informed that it would be Ethiopia whose intransigence prevented any moderate solution and forced Italy to deal with the issue 'in an effective way, and in ours and the general interest'.[97]

Grandi was soon reporting to Rome his efforts to elicit some acknowledgement from Simon or his officials that they understood this truth that none yet dared to speak. Did Simon get the message when Grandi spoke evocatively of the distinction between a civilised European and a barbarous African country?[98] Was he impressed when Laval showed up in London, to greet Grandi with a Fascist salute as they met for a dinner at the Savoy and to gush that he had been over-whelmed by his Rome days with Mussolini?[99] Sadly the only possible conclusion was no; 'these English dopes', Grandi wrote, in phrases designed as ever to ingratiate himself with his leader, would not confront reality. They were at one and the same time pandering to the whims of their electorate and running to Berlin; 'their policy is as hard to pin down as their fog', he commented.[100] This was ominous news, but it did not discourage the *Duce*. On 8 March Mussolini told De Bono, who, in Eritrea, was organising the unloading of men and equip-ment, that he must be ready to manage an invasion force of 300 000 men by September or October that year.[101]

In April a last chance presented itself to preserve an Anglo-Franco-Italian front. Between 11 and 13 April Mussolini was due to confer with Laval, Simon and the French and British Prime Ministers, Pierre-Etienne Flandin and James Ramsay MacDonald in the delightful surrounds of the Villa Borromeo at Stresa.[102] In his newspaper Mussolini tried again to set the tone of the event on his own terms by producing a little list. What was needed, he wrote, was that '1. Germany must be declared what it is. 2. France must appreciate Italian friendship. 3. England must quickly grasp the state of mind of conti-nental Europe.'[103]

Despite the spring weather, at Stresa fog did not dissipate. The eventual resolution of the assembled statesmen spoke worthily of a desire for peace and a commitment to the League of Nations, and Mussolini signed it along with the rest. Later, he claimed to have inserted the phrase 'in Europe' in the sentence about supporting collective security, and to have done so with a nudge and a wink and the clear implication that such virtuous practice was not to be expected in 'Africa'.[104] But once again, the British would allege that they had not understood.[105] Facing such studied indifference to his needs and ambitions Mussolini was growing irritable, in a way that worried the more cautious of his advisers such as Suvich and Guariglia.[106] On 18 May the *Duce* telegraphed De Bono with the news that France was being 'correct, if very reserved' and Britain was 'agitated'. None the less, he declared, he intended to press on 'at any cost, even if the cost means a break with England, even in the extreme hypothesis of war with England'.[107] By 'October' De Bono must be ready with stockpiled supplies for three years and plans to cope even if the Suez Canal were blocked.

The words were drastic, but should they be read literally? – after all, Mussolini was trying to bestir the not always efficient De Bono to action. Had the *Duce* now really decided without any possibility of retreat that he intended to conquer all Ethiopia by military force? Historians convinced of his 'rogue' wickedness (and of the moral rectitude of their own societies)[108] say yes; that is what you must expect of a 'terrorist' Fascist. Mussolini was certainly resolved to sound as though only war would content him. Dissatisfied by Stresa, he had instructed Grandi to tell Simon that there was no way Italy would accept Geneva's arbitration of the Ethiopian matter and to add meaningfully 'our intention is absolutely firm not to allow our pursuit of Italy's vital colonial interests to be stopped by extraneous matters'.[109] In a speech to the Chamber of Deputies, he warned the French government that it could not expect Italy to stand 'like a stone' on the Brenner and absent itself from the rest of the world.[110] At home the propaganda machine of Fascism worked overtime to demonise the Ethiopians and to excite Italian lust for empire, with constant reference to the humiliations of the past and the need to avenge them.[111] Fascism was doing its very best to display to itself, Britain and the world that it was hell-bent on Fascist war in Africa.[112]

And yet there is reason to question this notion of Mussolini turned warmonger at any cost. After all, the efforts to appease him and his nation were so feeble. In 1935 Italy's precarious position as a power on the edge of relegation (a metaphor Mussolini used more than once) was never more evident. From Austria came secret service reports that Italians were all but universally hated there, and the future of Italian patronage of the regime in Vienna looked dim.[113] The more general context was bleaker. As an American diplomat put it, but the generalisation holds for Great Britain, too: Mussolini's 'enterprise' in Ethiopia was 'regarded as a detail', while Germany 'remained the key to the whole European situation'.[114] The French general Maurice Gamelin felt the same: 'For us Italy is important: England is essential.'[115] The structure of international relations, put under stress by the Nazis in Berlin, simply refused to fall into a pattern which would benefit Italy or satisfy Mussolini. When, in June 1935, an initiative was made to appease the Italian dictator, it was derisory indeed.

The carrier of the deal was Anthony Eden, the elegant, young, ambitious but nervy British Minister for League of Nations Affairs, a newly minted post unlikely to be applauded in Rome. The offer was of an exchange of territory whereby Italy would gain land in the Ogaden desert, and Ethiopia an outlet to the sea at Zeila in British Somaliland.[116] It bore a rough relationship to a plan ventilated in 1913 for an expansion of Italian, British and French control in the region,[117] though with a reduced advantage to Italy. When he laid out the scheme, Eden found himself confronted by an incandescent *Duce*. In retrospect the reaction of the Italian dictator does not seem surprising,[118] but Eden had not been briefed to cope with it. With studied intransigence, Mussolini confirmed that, if there were to be peace, Italy required all non-Amharic territory won by the Ethiopian empire over the last century, plus *de facto* 'control over the surviving nucleus'. If there were war, he announced brutally, it 'would mean the eventual cancellation of Ethiopia from the map'.[119] Already, the *Duce* maintained, grabbing his statistics from the air, Italy had 680 000 men under arms; a million would be ready soon.[120] He did not say, and perhaps he had not noticed, that among his papers was a note from Renzetti who had just seen Hitler privately. The *Führer* had expressed his confidence that Italo-German relations could regain their old lustre. He had, he said, never intended to annex Austria.[121]

In the quarrel between Italy, Britain and the League, there was to be no going back. The British press expressed outrage at events, with *The Times* contending that 'the issue of peace and war is at stake, and of the whole future of the League of Nations'.[122] Grandi assured Mussolini that Eden would be bound eventually to back down after the 'thumping' the *Duce* had given him at Rome.[123] But, as the summer slipped by, the crisis worsened and, at whatever cost to his international image, Mussolini held ostentatiously firm.

The tender sensibilities of Eden left him with the impression that Mussolini was 'a complete gangster', the 'Anti-Christ',[124] a view which he never abandoned and, in 1956, transferred to that other 'Mediterranean' tough guy, Gamal Abdel Nasser.[125] In general, the approach of the Ethiopian war and its prosecution ended the love affair between foreign journalists and Mussolini (if it ever really existed). Once, a posting to Rome had been treasured and Mussolini's office had been besieged by foreigners requesting interviews.[126] Now, some more critical journalists were peremptorily expelled,[127] and publishers found a ready market for books 'exposing' the sins of Fascism. Among a plethora of works, the one with the catchiest title and the most durable influence was George Seldes' *Sawdust Caesar*. The moral of his study was sweeping: 'Reactionary dictators are men of no philosophy, no burning humanitarian ideal, nor even an economic programme of any value to their nation or the world.'[128] They were 'gangsters' more than anything else.[129] Foreign political leaders had always tended to view Italians as the undeserving poor; now Mussolini acquired a common image as an unshaven thug, the worst and least appeasable of the dictators. In London's *Evening Standard*, David Low had long used a yapping terrier called 'Musso' to comment in his cartoons on Italian politics. In October the dog sent a telegram to the *Duce*: 'Intend change my name to Haile Selassie, when you change yours to Spot or Rover.'[130] Back in July, Colonel Blimp had snorted: 'Gad, sir, Mr. Eden is right. We should offer Mussolini Central Africa on condition he stays there.'[131]

To improve their deteriorating image, the Italians funded friendly journalists. In London Grandi had *carte blanche* to pay for sympathetic explanations of Italy's imperial thrust into Ethiopia. However, the ambassador's leading pensioner was the far right commentator, E. Polson Newman, an author of favourable tracts about Italy since the 1920s.[132] Between August and October 1935 Newman was given an all expenses paid trip to East Africa and, on his return, justified the Fascist cause, while loudly condemning the 'barbarism' of the Ethiopians.[133] His influence was nil. Grandi was left to whine that the only people who would show up at the pro-Italian talks he organised were those same 'elderly widows and elderly deracinated ladies' who had long aspired to hand a slice of seed-cake to the *Duce*.[134] Mussolini complained back to him that British hostility was threatening to drive Italy out of the League and fracture the global cause of the white race.[135]

As the world shut against him, the only slight hope for Mussolinian diplomacy was France, where Laval remained slippery, but in his heart undoubtedly willing to hand Ethiopia and more to Italy so long as it manned the Brenner. In a series of meetings with the French ambassador, Charles Chambrun, Mussolini confirmed that his first negotiating position was that which he had explained to Eden, in other words, annexation of large sections of Ethiopian border territory on a model which, Mussolini explained, might imitate Morocco, Egypt, Iraq and, with the most menacing contemporary reference, Manchukuo.[136] Laval often sounded as though he wished to be accommodating but, as he confessed in a metaphor destined to acquire a diverse resonance, in the final analysis French policy was 'tied in an axis to the League of Nations'.[137]

The League session which opened on 9 September produced a further closure against Italy, with British Foreign Secretary, Samuel Hoare, belying the 'realism' of his secret service and imperial past by speaking strongly, if tonelessly,[138] for collective security. Sanctions, it was now agreed, would be imposed once Italy invaded Ethiopia. But even though Grandi for one showed signs of developing cold feet,[139] the *Duce* shrugged off this potentially devastating threat to the national economy and was instead confirmed in his belief that what was to be done was best done quickly. On 29 September De Bono learned that the date for action was 3 October,[140] and at dawn that morning Italian troops crossed the border. Aircraft hurried to bomb Adowa, that settlement from which Italy had been thrown back in 1896.[141] Fascist Italy had engaged itself in colonial war. As Mussolini stressed in his 'speech of mobilisation', it was not only an army which had moved 'but a whole people of forty-four million souls'.[142]

Or was it Mussolini's personal colonial war; was 'one man alone' its cause? Certainly the *Duce* had not yielded during the months of crisis. Rather, he had told himself some months before that the conduct of policy was, above everything else, a psychological matter. A man who possessed the will, like Napoleon or himself (or the unmentionable Giolitti),[143] was destined to triumph. Many of his closest colleagues were less sturdy. So notable a Fascist intellectual as Agostino Lanzillo[144] and so prominent a businessman as Alberto Pirelli[145] were sure that Italy's limited gold reserves would dribble away, especially when sanctions began to bite. The usually unctuous Volpi allowed himself to remark that the *Duce* had gone mad.[146] Neither the King nor Badoglio had hidden their doubts about the colonial adventure. It was all very well invoking Crispi and the dead of Dogali and Adowa,[147] but most Italians remembered these past defeats more with fear than with a spirit of revenge. It was equally predictable that Bottai should stress that the war was a spiritual and revolutionary event and therefore could not be measured in monetary terms.[148] But even Mussolini knew that some bills had eventually to be paid and, in December 1935, he appointed the astute and independent bourgeois economist, Felice Guarneri, to a new post as Under-Secretary for Exchange Controls, with Guarneri's reports to go directly to the *Duce*. Somewhat whimsically the dictator tried to cheer his new agent with the prediction that tourism was about to revive and would plug any present leakage of funds.[149]

To be sure, there were always suggestions that Mussolini's own intransigence could be subject to detumescence, if a suitable offer were made. When, after the initial seizure of Adowa and some other border towns, the Italian advance slowed and both De Bono and Graziani, who was based in Somalia, began to exhibit that caution and immobility which had become typical of Italian military chiefs since the disaster in 1896, Mussolini hinted that a compromise of some sort was imaginable. For all the Fascist tirades which issued from one side of his mouth (including, for example, unlikely threats to take on the British Navy in the Mediterranean),[150] from the other he had never ceased to suggest that his Italy was the natural associate of Britain and France in Europe, committed to blocking any convulsion from Berlin.[151] Moreover, Laval continued to maintain that he was willing to talk[152] – Mussolini was informed that the Pope, speaking as 'a good Italian', had blessed the *Duce*, agreed Italy needed territory to expand and had been unfairly treated at Versailles, but also suggested new conversations with the French.[153] Mussolini's demand to De Bono that he hurry up and occupy territory because it was only possession which was of use in negotiation[154] hinted that he was indeed open to proposals. Suvich, who was trying to convert his Under-Secretaryship for Foreign Affairs into the advisory position once filled by the Secretary-General, meanwhile reminded Mussolini of the lingering potential of the Four Power Pact. In his view, it was still the most 'solid, rational and realistic' way to confront crisis in Europe.[155]

The message from Rome was heard and understood in both Paris and London. First 'experts', then Hoare and Laval themselves, began to frame a plan. Mussolini was encouraging, telling Grandi of his 'maximum' demands (they were as expressed to the French in September), but thereby implying that less than the maximum might be possible.[156] The French even began to pressure Haile Selassie to agree to something approaching an Italian mandate over his country.[157]

This treatying was, however, destined to come to naught. In Paris the plan leaked to the press. Hoare broke his nose skating in Switzerland, was delayed in his return to London and feeble when he addressed the Commons about the infringement of League solidarity. A violent press storm blew, with *The Times* choosing Friday 13 December to pronounce that the 'good name' of Britain was at risk in the Hoare–Laval Pact, which it damned a few days later as a scheme to buy off the noble Haile Selassie with a 'corridor for camels'.[158] Low, whose cartoon terrier was now indeed called Haile Selassie, placed the Anglo–French deal in 'a gallery of double-crossing'.[159] Although Mussolini, on two or three occasions over the next months, again let it be known that compromise was not out of the question, Fascist Italy was not fated to negotiate an end to its Ethiopian war. Instead, shrugging off the inconsistent threats from Geneva to impose 'military sanctions' against the aggressor, Italy moved to overwhelming military victory.

'Implacable', 'inexorable', 'inflexible' were words which Mussolini readily invoked about the African campaign.[160] In November he had replaced De Bono with Badoglio and the career soldier led his troops to Addis Ababa by 5 May. Italian casualties amounted to just over a thousand. Ethiopia, by contrast, was overwhelmed by bombing and massacre[161] – Badoglio took the initiative in again using poison gas, despite Italy's treaty obligations to avoid it, and was duly backed by Mussolini.[162] Graziani adopted the slogan: 'The *Duce* shall have Ethiopia with the Ethiopians or without them, just as he pleases'.[163] Most sinisterly, Indro Montanelli, a young Fascist journalist destined to become the most celebrated conservative commentator in the Italian Republic after 1946,[164] wrote of his fellow soldiers' utter contempt for the Ethiopians. But, he urged, Italians would need to augment their sense of 'racial dignity'.[165] Of course, their racism would not mimic that of 'the blondes beyond the Alps'. Furthermore, he concluded, 'we shall never be dominators if we don't have an exact consciousness of our destined superiority. We do not fraternise with blacks. We cannot. We must not'.[166]

Members of Mussolini's own family were also hearing the gospel of race and finding their minds penetrated by those concepts which elsewhere in European-ruled Africa led to Apartheid. Among the Italian forces were Vittorio and the 17-year-old Bruno Mussolini. Their father was given to telegramming them with congratulations on their bombing prowess (and suggestions they not forget to write to their mother).[167] After the victory Vittorio published his laddish *Voli sulle Ambe*, which came complete with a rugged photo of the hero studiously concealing his unmilitary puppy fat. The *Duce's* son conceded that he was a little disappointed by his first aerial bombing raids, since he had hoped to generate explosions of the sort he was accustomed to view on American films. Sadly the fragile Ethiopian huts had just tumbled down when struck by his bombs.[168] He admitted a sneaking attraction to tall, lithe, lissome, local women, who possessed 'sex appeal' [he used the English term]; but he claimed, with unlikely virtue, that it dissipated when he got up close.[169]

The arrogance, brutality and insouciance of Vittorio Mussolini and Montanelli were matched by older Fascist chiefs, despatched by their leader to be part of the war. Bottai was the most philosophical about events;[170] Farinacci the least, though he lost a hand while fishing with a grenade on a lake near Dessié.[171] More significant was the home front. Whatever the initial doubts there, they were quickly assuaged by a series of headlines blazoning military victories, the tiny cost in Italian lives and the fumbling of those who from Geneva invoked sanctions. For all the Fascist fanfare, many Italians read the Ethiopian war and the proclamation of the empire as a national triumph. A number of stubborn Anti-Fascists, from Orlando to Croce, rallied to the nation, sacrificing their medals and jewellery, as requested by the regime in a sanctions-busting scheme marketed by propaganda as patriotic ceremony. At one such event, in Rome just before Christmas 1935, Queen Elena presented her royal wedding ring to the national and imperial cause.

But the real winner in Ethiopia, the leader of the united and victorious nation, was Benito Mussolini. De Felice did not exaggerate when he wrote that, as the armies advanced to Addis, 'unimaginable exaltation' was visited on the *Duce*.[172] The intimidated British ambassador in Rome was reduced to telling Eden that Mussolini was 'not a man whom one could ask for an interview in order to pass the time of day. He expects the visitor to state his errand and then he replies', although always likely to take the chance to 'inveigh against diplomatists who waste his time'.[173] For the Italian elite, a happy phrase was easier to find. Philosopher Giovanni Gentile emphasised that the return of empire to 'the fatal hills of Rome' entailed the commencement of 'a new history of Italy.' 'Mussolini today', he explained, 'has not just founded empire in Ethiopia. He has made something more. He has created a new Italy'. Buoyed by the Duce's mystical fusion of 'thought and action', Italians could now become people with a 'new style, new men'.[174] In many minds, triumph at Addis Ababa – few noticed that two-thirds of the vast Ethiopia empire remained to be occupied, and the rest was scarcely pacified[175] – meant that the *Duce* commanded as none had before, and so had imposed what might be deemed a 'Mussolinian revolution'.

Later historians have sometimes agreed. De Felice controversially labelled the acquisition of empire 'Mussolini's masterpiece', adding that it was the sweeter since the *Duce* believed in the project more than in any of the other programmes of his regime.[176] Certainly, apart from the psychological cost of toughing it out, Mussolini had had an easy war. An opponent armed in September 1935 with 371 bombs and eleven slow aircraft (of which three could not take off)[177] had scarcely challenged Fascist military power. The *Duce*'s generals may have bickered among themselves, while those in the know gossiped about Badoglio's notorious vanity,[178] venality and fondness for nepotism,[179] and told themselves that the *Duce* hated upbraiding soldiers and was easily intimidated by them.[180] His underlings in the party may have continued to look for advantage one against the other,[181] and not always been as courageous as their words had promised.[182]

His son-in-law Ciano may have now begun to polish an image of world-weary, mondaine and bourgeois cynicism, in a way scarcely appropriate for the seemingly designated leader of the younger generation of Fascists.[183] Plans for what was actually to be done with the territory may have been non-existent. The flaunted brutality of Italian actions before and during the crisis may have given the Fascist dictatorship a far worse image abroad than ever before. Contacts with Nazi Germany may have been increasing[184] and acquiring an evident logic if Italy were to become a pariah power, and Mussolini may have begun to associate his own name with ideas about a *rapprochement* with the 'other' 'fascist state'.[185] Military and other governmental expenditure[186] may have ballooned in what a thrifty economist would say was an unsustainable fashion. However, his own job had proved to entail little more than giving rousing speeches as required and from time to time, from the safety of Italy, instructing his soldiers to get on with it. In the short term at least, dictating an imperial triumph had proven the easiest of tasks.

Back in November 1935 Mussolini had seen Bottai before the minister's departure to the front. The *Duce* had entered his office 'out of breath', as though he had run up the stairs, with the face, Bottai noticed, of 'a fat man made artifically thin', and with a tight stomach. Detail, the *Duce* said, with a rush, interested him not a jot. 'Too much ratiocination! We should rather concentrate on instinct! My instinct tells me that this is a revolutionary war. And that's enough!'[187] No doubt his words had been chosen beforehand to impress the credulous Bottai. Yet, throughout 1935–36 Mussolini shut his eyes to many things and brought off a victory. Now not even his father's ghost could deny that his son was a greater man than Crispi. On 9 May 1936 with King-Emperor Victor Emmanuel III almost smiling on him and to the all but universal joy of the Italian people, the *Duce* set aside his usual anxious contempt for the world around him and proclaimed, with just a hint of uneasiness, that 'Italy finally has its empire. . . . It is a Fascist empire, an empire of peace, an empire of civilization and humanity'.[188] He could not have known at the time, but he was fated never to visit Ethiopia, and the Fascist revolution would only scratch its immemorial soil. Mussolini had become the *Duce* of one of the most fleeting empires in history.

14

Crisis in Europe, 1936–1938

WITHIN Italy, the proclamation of the empire raised Mussolini's reputation to empyrean heights. Grovelling panegyrists oscillated between hailing his apostolacy[1] or his godhead. As the unheroic journalist Asvero Gravelli summarised it in his study of 'spiritual interpretations of Mussolini': 'Homer, the divine in Art; Jesus, the divine in Life; Mussolini, the divine in Action.'[2] Or was the *Duce* some sort of Apollo? – the parallels were growing ever more syncretic. 'Mussolini's smile', Gravelli wrote, 'is like a flash of the Sun god [*sic*], expected and craved because it brings health and life'.[3] 'To whom does he compare? No-one. The very act of comparison with politicians from other lands diminishes Him [*sic*]'.[4] Other propagandists were similarly unrestrained: 'He is always alone like every founder of a religion. The name of this religion is Italy';[5] 'He' was 'infallible', 'ineluctable', a 'Titan', a 'Genius', 'divine'.[6] Looking at him was like looking at the sun; the man could not be seen but rather 'an immense flood of radiant vibrations from the ether'.[7]

If the plaudits were enough to satiate or to gag,[8] the private Mussolini soon found the gloss of Ethiopian triumph wearing thin and his usual pessimism about life confirmed. In June 1936 it became clear that his youngest child, Anna Maria, aged only six, was stricken with poliomyelitis. For more than a week her death seemed imminent and Mussolini abandoned his office to watch at her bedside.[9] Alessandro Lessona, the new Minister of Colonies (June 1936 to November 1937), remembered finding him at the Villa Torlonia one morning 'worn out, unshaven, with red eyes, sporting an old jacket tossed over a crumpled shirt'.[10] As with Shakespeare's Julius Caesar, for those who could see, this god did shake.

With other members of his family, relationships remained imperfect. In July 1936 following pompous attempts to depict him as a journalist of youth,[11] Vittorio became co-editor with the renowned film expert and director of the *Istituto Luce* news service, Luciano De Feo, of a new theoretical journal entitled *Cinema*.[12] His father was momentarily proud of him.[13] However, the *Duce*'s eldest son had trouble concentrating and, with his younger brother Bruno, was thought to spend a lot of time in high-class brothels.[14] Bruno also had to fob off a claim by a poor Roman girl that he had seduced and abandoned her.[15] When, one rainy day in February 1937, Vittorio married a Milanese bourgeoise, Orsola Bufali, in a joint ceremony at St. Peter's with his cousin Vito (who espoused Silvia Tardini), the event was none the less given royal treatment in the Italian press.[16] Such lionising could not disguise the fact that Vittorio was a political cypher. So, too, was Bruno, whose love of fast cars perhaps explained the death of Teresa Velluti, an elderly woman pedestrian crossing a Roman street (even though the official report on the incident concluded sagely that the fault lay entirely with the victim).[17] Bruno, whose career as a pilot meant his lionisation by the press, married Gina Ruberti, the daughter of a school inspector and granddaughter of a Catholic-Fascist Minister of Finance, in October 1938.[18] Soon, the couple produced a daughter; and, not long after, Bruno accepted the presidency of the Italian Boxing Federation.[19]

Rachele, when in Rome, kept herself to the Villa Torlonia, nurturing her homespun image – it was said that she never visited the *Sala del Mappamondo*[20] and that the more fastidious of visitors tried to avoid eating the poorly prepared food[21] served at her table.[22] Sexually, Mussolini had now commenced his dalliance with Claretta Petacci, even though she was not always fun – she would moan about her body, her teeth, her health and the size of her breasts, and stay in bed all day eating chocolate if given the chance.[23] Soon to make a name for himself, at least in scandal, was her elder brother, the euphoniously named Marcello Cesare Augusto Petacci, born 1910, and doubtful incarnation of the imperial hopes of the Rome bourgeoisie.[24]

The only star in the Mussolini family was Galeazzo Ciano, Edda's husband, on 11 June 1936 promoted to become Foreign Minister of Italy. He was then thirty-three, by a great margin the youngest such office-holder in Europe. Ciano was a highly paradoxical figure to be thus elevated to the edge of power and apparently anointed as **the** Fascist of the new generation. Scarcely the child of revolution, he was rather a *figlio di papa* in every sense of that Italian term, inadequately translated as 'Daddy's boy'. His father, Costanzo, a Nationalist and admiral, had been Mussolini's Minister of Communications from 1924 to 1934, serving the longest uninterrupted stint of any Fascist minister (except Mussolini). Among many interests in his home city of Livorno, Ciano senior was the owner of its important and relatively independent newspaper *Il Telegrafo*.[25] Early in charge of Fascist finances,[26] in 1925 Costanzo Ciano was elevated to the nobility as Count of Cortelazzo. The title allowed his son also to call himself 'Count'.

Galeazzo was a brilliant young man, in 1921 graduating second among high-school students on a national list.[27] As Foreign Minister his smartness would make him a sparkling contrast to the flighty Eden, the lugubrious Halifax, the shifty Bonnet and the dire Ribbentrop and Molotov. In his youth his ambition had lain in the composition of light poetry and he could be tracked down to the *Caffè Aragno* in Rome, haunt of aspirant litterateurs. Among his juvenilia was a play with the arch title *La felicità di Amleto* (Hamlet's happiness). Somewhat reluctantly Ciano undertook the exams for the diplomatic service in 1924, entering the Ministry of Foreign Affairs the next year twenty-seventh out of thirty-five graded candidates.[28] Duller contemporaries, and some later historians, would write him off as a 'snob',[29] a man for whom the superficial was the only delight and the only purpose. They were also likely to be enviously critical of his 'open marriage' – Edda told any who asked that she took lovers but made sure that the children were Ciano's.[30]

As Foreign Minister, the *Duce*'s son-in-law was most frequently to be found not at his desk but rather beside the bar at the elegant clubhouse of the Acquasanta golf course, Rome headquarters of the *crème de la crème* of society. There and elsewhere, he held forth to what Bottai called belittlingly his *circoletto*.[31] He also followed his father's habits in accumulating funds, with his punting on Albania's oil industry[32] being a notorious accompaniment to Italy's invasion of its erstwhile puppet in April 1939. A censorious contemporary from the armed forces dismissed him as 'stocky, flabby, swarthy in colouring, with a night-club complexion and patent-leather black hair'. Ciano, the account ran on, 'possessed the character and moral outlook of a professional gigolo. ... He was vain and giddy, utterly charmed with himself, his own self-importance and success'.[33] And yet perhaps, on occasion, Ciano can be assayed with a more forgiving eye. Certainly his celebrated diary[34] remains the best single source on Mussolini's Italy and much else besides; it is studded with conscious wit and less conscious insight.

But what was such a person doing as the young man being groomed, it seemed, to succeed that rough and tough *animale poco socievole*, the *Duce*? If Fascism was a revolution designed to oust the bourgeoisie from their haunts of power and to cut to ribbons their demeaning fondness for slippers and the quiet life, how could Ciano embody it? Was there ever anybody more bourgeois than he? The glaring contradiction of the son-in-law was never resolved; Ciano went to his death aged forty as punishment for being 'Mussolini's shadow',[35] but one who, in the eyes of the Nazis and any other true believers in a universal fascist revolution, grotesquely distorted all that the *Duce* represented. Yet the young man may well have fulfilled an important role for the *Duce*, by the late 1930s confined more and more rigorously by the need to be or to appear 'solitary'. At least for the *Duce*'s private self, some countering to the deluge of deification which washed over him came through such contradictory alter egos as the worldly Ciano and the vulgar Farinacci. (Rachele, who was always scathing about her effete, stuck-up, golf-playing, son-in-law, replicated at home many of the attitudes and 'truths' which Farinacci expressed in the political arena.) Somewhere in the cracks of such ties, in their blatant but unspoken contradiction, Mussolini could aspire to retain a sense of humour[36] and an independent existence as a human being. A Mussolini could survive even his own charisma, knowing that on the borders of his own personality lay both a Farinacci or a Ciano. He could have been each but was neither.

Even armed with this psychological escape clause, for Mussolini to be always the *Duce* was taxing. As he confessed in one moment of depression in 1938, he had become 'a prisoner' of himself, 'of others, of events, of hopes and illusions'. Today, he went on, in words which must often occur to politicians but probably should be eschewed by a *Duce*:

> I must often think what I do not say, and say what I do not think. Yes, there is a real gap between the two Mussolinis. Sometimes it is profound and terrible. Perhaps, one day, one of the two will beg an armistice, break his sword and submit. I still don't know which one.[37]

Nevertheless, part of the job was to speak as though he were supremely confident all the time. In February–March 1937 he gave 'personal' interviews to Ward Price of the *Daily Mail* and Webb Miller of United Press, designed not to reveal too much. His diet, he stressed, was composed of a sparing amount of meat, consumed infrequently, but lots of fresh fruit and vegetables. His two daily meals were 'peasant-style'. He drank neither tea nor coffee, and took only the occasional sip of wine, though, 'like the last of the peaceloving bourgeois', he welcomed a camomile tea each afternoon. He did not smoke. He fitted in 30–45 minutes of exercise daily, and slept readily from 11 p.m. to 7 a.m. He worked 12–14 hours every day, and managed to read about seventy books each year, preferring 'novels and history books. Classics and the occasional romance'; he also liked to stay up to date with the latest publications. 'I read in French, German and also English', he said. He enjoyed Verdi, Wagner and Rossini, but also liked jazz, especially when he could dance to it. The key to his life as an administrator lay in his 'precision and diligence' – 'I boast that I am a first class bureaucrat. I sack any collaborators who are disorganised, confusing and time-wasters'. He was, he concluded, a Taylorised worker.

> I have organised my activity through a division of labour, and a struggle against the dispersal of energy and other time-wasting. It is this that explains the volume of work I get through and the fact that I am never tired. I have turned my body into a motor, which is under constant review and control and which therefore runs with absolute regularity.[38]

In reality, of course, it was not quite like this, even though his under-lining of documents and his scribbling of his unmistakable 'M' on a page to indicate that he had read and absorbed a piece of information do show that he, unlike Hitler, was an assiduous executive. He shared with his German colleague an excellent memory,[39] especially for detail – he would tell a friend of his attention to 'little things', matters which, he said, were 'like fleas that make you scratch your head'.[40] If you did not deal with them worse would follow. His fondness for seeing visitors remained time-consuming, however, as he on occasion acknowledged.[41] It was politic for a *Duce* to be prepared for every new interview – young intellectuals were easily impressed if the dictator knew the title of their latest book,[42] and all visitors were especially happy if they were sent away with approval to do something, even if, generally, they would then have to work out how it might be done. But there were also perils, especially as the 'sacramental' side of Fascism became more arcane and intrusive. Starace had banned the handshake as effete, bourgeois and English, but Mussolini always shook hands with a visitor.[43] In his uniform, haranguing a doting crowd from a balcony, Mussolini looked like a militant *Duce*. In his office, chomping an apple,[44] wearing a battered blue suit[45] or shirt-sleeves,[46] and vainly doffing his glasses as the visitor approached,[47] the

Fascist chief was reduced to being just another man in his fifties. As one disillusioned young visitor put it when he saw Mussolini engaged in ordinary work, he felt 'defrauded of the mythical image of the *Duce*'.[48]

Being an unalloyed vehicle of charisma, 'keeping the spectacle going' for ever, 'keeping people coming to the window to watch the parade'[49] had its treacherous aspects, and Mussolini was glad sometimes to immerse himself less in public relations and more in 'policy-making'. In this regard, the months which succeeded the victory in Ethiopia demonstrated the complex nature of international politics in the late 1930s. Mussolini's belief in 1934 that Europe would stay quiet till 1937 proved overly optimistic. On 17 July 1936 generals in the Spanish Army launched a coup against their democratic government. They did not expect it, but the result was three terrible years of civil war, a conflict which would be understood by many contemporaries as a straight fight between left and right, the cause of socialism or communism or liberal democracy in bloody battle with the ideals of Church, Army and international fascism. The major foreign participant in this Spanish Civil War was Mussolini's Italy. How did this situation occur?

The answer, at least in so far as short-term causation is concerned, is a case study in accident and in the limitations of charismatic decision-making. From the moment the monarchy was ousted in 1931, Fascist Italy became the patron of the enemies of the Spanish Republic. Mussolini had denigrated the new regime from its inception:

> The Spanish Republic is not a revolution but a plagiarism. A plagiarism that arrives a good one hundred and fifty years late. To found a parliamentary republic today means using an oil lamp in the era of electric lights.[50]

Thereafter, a number of dissidents on the right could rejoice in subsidies from Rome, with such career officials as Guariglia, ambassador in Madrid 1932–35, and such Fascist bosses as Balbo enjoying the chance to patronise needy and grateful foreigners. The initiative in such matters rarely came directly from Mussolini,[51] who showed few signs of thinking of Spain as anything other than a far-off and backward country, of little significance either to the international fascist cause or the national interest.[52] Moreover, José Antonio Primo de Rivera, son of the ex-dictator and 'poetic fascist' *Jefe* of the tiny Falange, was, by 1933, one of those extremists who preferred the new model in Berlin to the older dictatorship, once so admired by his father, in Rome.[53] Guariglia encouraged Primo de Rivera junior to meet Mussolini, but the two were never close, even though, by June 1936, José Antonio could exploit part of the modest monthly fund of 1000 pesetas distributed to Italy's friends by the new ambassador, Orazio Pedrazzi.[54]

Although in the summer of 1936 Italian diplomats were alert to the likelihood of a rising against the embattled Republican government,[55] they had no ties with Francisco Franco, the commander of the army in Morocco and the man destined, largely by accident, to emerge as *Caudillo* of a 'new' Spain. The killing of right-wing politician José Calvo Sotelo on 13 July encouraged Pedrazzi, who had retired to summer quarters at the modish resort of San Sebastian, to predict that a *pronunciamento* was imminent.[56] However, the actual rising took the Italians by surprise, even though Pedrazzi telegraphed his new minister in Rome that he was sure that any military dictatorship would possess 'a distinctly corporative character and be highly anti-subversive'.[57]

It was Franco who petitioned Rome, sending his agent Luis Bolín there on 19 July, as well as speaking to the Italian military agent at Tangiers about a loan of aeroplanes in order to assist in the transfer of his troops across the straits of Gibraltar to European Spain.[58] Exiled King Alfonso XIII – Spanish monarchists had developed excellent contacts in Italy – also sent an appeal directly to Mussolini.[59] To Franco's disgust – he bewailed the 'political myopia' of Rome[60] – the Italian authorities at first rejected every request for help,[61] although the inexperienced Ciano flirted with the idea of approving some assistance.[62]

When talking to Italian agents Franco grew effusive about his determination to establish a government of 'the Fascist type'.[63] Whether or not won over by such evident special pleading, Ciano did agree that the planes were available, but he wanted to be paid for their hire up front.[64] He also anxiously circulated his agents in Spain for their assessment of the possible success of the rising.[65] However, before that matter was fully plumbed, crucial secret information came through that the French were going to allow the private export of arms and supplies to the republican government, itself a 'Popular Front', like that now ruling France.[66] The French Prime Minister, Léon Blum, was said to have stated curtly: 'I shall refuse to have any dealings with Matteotti's murderer', when contact with Mussolini was suggested,[67] and, in response, Mussolini used *Il*

Popolo d'Italia to condemn Blum rudely as 'one Jew who did not possess the gift of prophecy'.[68]

The planes now took off from airports in Sardinia for what today might seem the easy hop to Spanish Morocco. But, Rome was soon hearing, only nine of the twelve got there.[69] One ended in the sea and two crashed in French Morocco, where the pilots were arrested, thereupon unheroically confessing their mission. The French press, convinced by Ethiopia if not before that Mussolini was an international rapist, waxed wrothful. The Fascist press replied in kind, and was joined by Catholic papers long hostile to the Republic – *Osservatore Romano* thought the choice in Spain lay between 'humanity and those excluded from it.'[70] With no clear decision-making process and with no serious appraisal of the financial, political and economic costs and implications, Fascist Italy was allowing itself to intervene in a foreign civil war, an action which almost all diplomatic history counselled against, and which military advisers opposed. On 21 July General Mario Roatta told his leader presciently: 'Spain is like a quicksand. If you stick in a hand, everything will follow. If things go badly, they'll blame us. If they go well, they'll forget us.'[71] But such advice disappeared into the air. By early August Italian and German experts were meeting over such detail as the supply of petrol to the insurgent forces led by Franco.[72] By October Italian ground troops were stiffening Franco's armies as they began an unsuccessful assault on Madrid[73] – early in 1937 almost 50 000 'volunteers' were serving in Spain in the so-called *Corpo truppo volontario* or CTV, and they were bolstered by vast and expensive stocks of *matériel*.[74] The Italian leadership had been sucked into becoming the major contributory foreign power to what would eventually in March 1939 be Franco's bitter victory. By then official figures admitted 3819 dead, about 12 000 wounded, the loss of 157 tanks and a cost of eight and a half billion lire.[75]

The Italian version of the Spanish war became another link in the chain which was inexorably reducing Mussolini's freedom to manoeuvre on the international stage as he himself found ever more compelling reasons to work with his German friends.[76] One contributory factor was the Battle of Guadalajara in March 1937, begun with the boast that a small push by Fascist forces would see Madrid fall. In fact the Italian advance was stymied and then repelled in a defeat which, however partial, easily revived memories of Caporetto and the pervasive foreign stereotype of Italians as poor fighters. Lloyd George talked wittily about the 'Italian skedaddle'.[77] Less wry commentators noted that interrogation of prisoners made it 'abundantly clear that the Italian troops included not only Fascist Militia, but regular units of the Italian Army',[78] a fact which mocked the official Italian line that they were not officially intervening in Spain. As in Ethiopia, Fascist actions confirmed Italy's reputation as the worst of contemporary bullies. Even the Spanish populace were said to have transposed the meaning of CTV to *Cuando Te Vas*? (When are you going home?).[79] The Spanish general, Gonzalo Queipo de Llano, had already commented: 'The Germans behave with dignity and avoid showing off. The Italians are quarrelsome and despotic bullies'.[80] Mussolini, who took the defeat as a personal humiliation,[81] may have assured Grandi in late March 1937: 'there is no way that I shall withdraw any men from Spain until both the military and the political failure of Guadalajara is avenged'[82] and talked cruelly of ordering all Italian 'Red' prisoners to be shot,[83] but, in practice, Italy had suffered an irreparable propaganda loss.

Among the Republican troops victorious outside Madrid were Italian members of the 'Garibaldi brigade', Anti-Fascists who had rallied to the leftist cause and chosen a name for their forces which contested the Fascist version of history and claimed the Risorgimento hero for their cause. Later historians would tally 3354 Italian volunteers for the fight against Franco.[84] They were heartened by a slogan: 'Today in Spain; tomorrow in Italy',[85] coined by the patriotic democratic socialist, Carlo Rosselli, leader of an Anti-Fascist movement based in Paris and called *Giustizia e Libertà* (Justice and Liberty).[86] Within Italy, organised opposition to the regime was still feeble, closely watched by Bocchini, depressed by the rallying to the nation over Ethiopia, and, as ever, divided into a variety of squabbling ideological factions – the Sardinian radical Emilio Lussu was right when he remarked that Italian enemies of Fascism had more reason to go to Spain than the Spanish Republic had need of them.[87] However, Mussolini, who was always hypersensitive to the merest hint of popular Anti-Fascism,[88] took the message that a real opposition still existed and was afraid.

Action followed. On 9 June 1937 Rosselli and his brother Nello were bailed up while driving in Normandy, and then brutally stabbed to death by *Cagoulards*, members of one of the many French fascist groups.[89] After the war a complex series of trials demonstrated that the killing had been sponsored by Ciano and his close friend and assistant, Filippo Anfuso. Some witnesses denied that Mussolini was directly involved, though it is hard to absolve him from some responsibility.[90]

In one way, the murder of the Rossellis was a recrudescence of the Fascist way to eliminate enemies, common enough before the regime settled down into its 'totalitarian state'. In another, it showed that world-weary bourgeois 30-year-olds, prematurely in 'power', could plan murder as coldly as could any squadrist. Above all, the event indicated that savagery lurked not far beneath the surface of any who thought themselves to be 'working towards their *Duce*'.

Yet, all things are relative. One somewhat unlikely personage was reporting in 1937 that, among their other sins, the Spanish were unwontedly brutal. Just before the Battle of Guadalajara, Roberto Farinacci arrived in Spain, charged by Mussolini to meet Franco and to report on the civil conflict. He was unimpressed by what greeted him. Franco, he found 'timid' and manifestly 'lacking the qualities of a real *condottiero*'. Worse, he warned, the *Caudillo* was ideologically unprepared:

> He has no precise idea of what the Spain of tomorrow should be like. He is interested only in winning the war, and then for a long period after in how to impose an authoritarian, or, better, dictatorial government to purge the nation of all those who have had any contact, direct or indirect, with the Reds.

Franco did not understand corporatism and had no desire to embrace the working class. His friendship with Italy was quite possibly insincere and he had not abandoned a residual Anglophilia. As fighters, the insurgent forces were in no hurry and were indifferent to the appalling daily death toll. 'To tell the truth, Red and Nationalist barbarity is equal. It's a contest between massacres, almost become a sport.' But, then, such brutality was what could be expected of the Spanish, Farinacci concluded. General Emilio Mola, who seemed brighter than Franco, talked cheerfully of eliminating 'one million Reds', once the victory was his.[91] Italy, the *ras* of Cremona feared, had been dragged into a vicious and imponderable world, with values foreign to its own.[92]

Another reason why Mussolini was so annoyed about the setback at Guadalajara was that, in the very days of the battle, he was engaged in what was meant to be a triumphant tour of Libya, his second visit to that colony and the last which he was fated to make to an intact empire. On 18 March 1937 in a ceremony at Tripoli, he unsheathed the 'Sword of Islam', promising that Fascism would defend its Moslem subjects and help them to greatness.[93] What, then, had been happening in the Fascist empire since the fall of Addis Ababa?

In July 1936 Mussolini had instructed Marshal Graziani, appointed 'Viceroy of Ethiopia', that he should adopt 'a systematic policy of terror and extermination against rebels and any in the population who favour them'.[94] Six months later the *Duce* felt able to announce the 'integral occupation' of Ethiopia: 'the gigantic Italian expedition' there, he boasted, had been 'a masterpiece of ardour, military science and political skill', and now victory was won.[95] But Mussolini's timing was again unlucky. On 19 February 1937 Ethiopian partisans lobbed ten or more grenades into an official group celebrating in the capital the birth of a son to Crown Prince Umberto. At least 30 people were injured, among them Graziani. In reaction, the local Fascist chief, Guido Cortese, told his men they had three days to 'destroy and kill and do what you want to the Ethiopians'.[96] Estimates of the resultant carnage vary from 3000 to 30 000 deaths,[97] with the history of colonialism suggesting that the lower figure is an underestimation. Fascists also took pains to murder the monks at the monastery of Debra Lebranos, 'sacred to the nation', and to burn the holy records of Ethiopian history conserved there.

Genocide might seem to have been in the wings. Graziani could contemplate it, but in time was discouraged by the *Duce*.[98] Indeed, this outbreak of rage was followed by greater calm. In December 1937 Graziani was replaced by the somewhat surprising choice of Amedeo, Duke of Aosta, the head of the cadet branch of the royal dynasty.[99] Aosta was thought to favour closer ties with surrounding British colonies,[100] and he certainly gave Italian imperial rule more of an English or a military than a fanaticised fascist air. Some of the arriving bureaucrats were also anxious to emphasise the propriety of their career choice and differentiated themselves from 'the Fascists', whom they deemed corrupt, brutal and incompetent.[101] Mussolini himself, typically enough, let matters ride.

Actually, times were not good for the 'development' of Ethiopia. By 1941 only some 3200 Italian peasants had settled there and, despite the greatest possible restraint in government expenditure, the Fascist administration ran at a loss. The more honest colonial officials were soon noting that the locals knew far more about what was really going on in any settlement than did the colonial 'masters'.[102] In the backblocks of Ethiopia, with unreliable communications to the next town, let alone Rome, the servants of Fascist empire, like many another metropolitan bureaucrat cast into the heart of Africa, sought to make do in a perplexing world.

Again Farinacci was Mussolini's most direct and honest source on the failures of the new empire. In December 1938 he sent his leader a devastating ten-page report of a visit he had made to *Africa Orientale Italiana* (AOI), as the united colonies of Eritrea, Somalia and Ethiopia were called. There was, he began, a yawning gap between the promise of the empire and the men who had actually arrived there. Among the leaders the only serious activity was backbiting, with each man saying: 'if only Mussolini knew and saw what was going on'. Waste and corruption were endemic. 'Too many people, too many business firms, suck criminally from the breasts of the *madre patria*.' Officials set themselves up in luxury, while ordinary immigrants and common soldiers were reduced to living in huts with the Ethiopians. 'In so far as budgetary matters are concerned, I have the impression that, down there, no one understands or wants to understand anything.' Real experts like Volpi or Cini should be deployed to assess the problem. But there was no reason to be optimistic. 'If everyone keeps telling you that things are fine, they actually engage in the grossest betrayal of you and your tireless work.'[103] If Farinacci were to be believed, the building of a serious empire in this place where Roman legions had never trod before had scarcely begun.

Farinacci's news about corruption, exploitation and infighting ought not to have surprised Mussolini. One individual who sought to do well out of empire was Ferdinando Boattini of Predappio. Police reports into his activities noted that Boattini had only joined the Fascist party in 1936 and soon thereafter had gone to AOI. There, he organised a trade in skins, smoothing his path through his contact with Rachele Mussolini and Edda Ciano, to each of whom, in April 1937, he gratefully gave five prime quality leopard skins in return for a right to purchase four Fiat trucks for his transport needs in the empire.[104] It was alleged that Boattini had made a profit of 3 million lire on his deal, keeping 500 000 for himself and distributing the other five-sixths among his helpful but somewhat greedy contacts.[105] When the war began Boattini also knew how life worked. Called up on 3 January 1941, within five days he was comfortably ensconced in Bologna hospital,[106] and had arranged a complete discharge by 18 January. He retained his ties with Rachele, and they were of further use in the summer of 1942, when Boattini was picked up by the *carabinieri* when they disturbed an illegal gambling ring at Predappio. 'Her Excellency Donna Rachele' intervened in his favour and the zealous arresting officer was promptly transferred from Forlì to a distant posting at Cefalù outside Palermo.[107] This poor policeman's lot was indeed an unlucky one.

But then stories of corruption were always hitting the Duce's desk. In 1937 the most public one precipitated a violent quarrel between De Bono and Lessona, each in his time Minister of Colonies. Lessona, who had risen to prominence in Fascist Italy amid stories of dubious business deals and lubricity[108] and who also possessed contacts with circles near the monarchy, was thought to have pressed Mussolini to drop De Bono as military commander in Ethiopia in favour of Badoglio.[109] The openness of Lessona's attacks on De Bono induced the latter to appeal to Mussolini and so display nakedly the nature of patron–client relationships during the Fascist regime. The matter most under debate was the contract approved over a road constructed between Massawa and Asmara, which Lessona alleged to have been tainted. De Bono was outraged, besieging Mussolini with missives asserting his own probity and demanding that the *Duce* intervene on his behalf. In February 1937 Mussolini responded by declaring:

> I am sure that Marshal of Italy De Bono is above suspicion. From the very beginning I shall punish anyone who dares to spread calumny about him. If the road from Massawa to Asmara was sent for tender without the proper bureaucratic formalities, that was occasioned by my orders because it was necessary to hasten matters in order to win the war.

If, he added, there had been cost over-runs, the issue could be judged by the 'competent authorities',[110] in other words be sent off to one of those classic bureaucratic reviews destined never to report.

The dispute did not end with this sage Mussolinian intervention, however. By July 1937 De Bono, who had also been Chief of Police during the Matteotti murder, minced no words in another of his letters to his leader. He had waited and waited, he fumed, and now: 'I'm stuffed about being taken for a fool, and it is you [De Bono used the familiar '*tu*' form in corresponding with the *Duce* and underlined the more emphatic parts of his prose] who have taken me for a fool and abused my goodness. Given my limitless and affectionate devotion to You', De Bono continued, 'on which I trust I am casting no doubt, I have put a brake on my emotions. But now my cup runneth over; I am at the end of my tether. I have menially drunk too much olive oil and it has brought on intestinal inflammation. Enough.' The plotting of so 'vile, crude and sinister' an individual as Lessona was what could be expected of him. But perhaps Mussolini had not reckoned with the fact that 'in my veins there is not a drop of servile blood and neither in my heart nor in my kidney is there a grain of fear. I repeat to you once more what I have already said and written: <u>I am afraid of nothing and nobody</u>. I am also ready for anything and you should not marvel at what I can do'. His enemies were many; Balbo and De Vecchi were pulling the strings behind Lessona. However, remembering the Matteotti affair, Mussolini should concentrate on him.

> <u>It is you</u> who has <u>the obligation</u> to look after me who has always been really <u>one of your men</u>. Hence if you don't do anything, I shall find justice for myself in a way that is most secure and convenient. It would be well for you to have no doubts about it. I shall act when I see fit and do so exclusively in my own interests.[111]

As he reiterated in a subsequent letter, if matters did not go his way, Mussolini would soon see how the '<u>good</u>' De Bono could become '<u>bad</u>'.[112]

The threats, however empty they may have been – Mussolini told an acquaintance that De Bono was an old and embittered boor[113] – did have some effect. Lessona was dropped as a minister and reduced to being a professor of political science at Rome university. His appeal for ennoblement was rejected, and his wife was left to complain on her tapped telephone that the family had been driven to sack their maid and cook and were facing penury.[114] Although Lessona tried direct protests of his own to the *Duce*, he was not destined to recover office.[115]

While the conflict was at its height, a police report told Mussolini that the affair was viewed in elite society with 'disgusted stupor',[116] but, for the *Duce* it seems merely to have been further proof of the weak and sinful nature of humankind. After all, Mussolini had long believed that the world was divided into 'friends' and enemies. His off-the-cuff conversations were much given to defining men as 'friends', with that elastic category including the Duke of Pistoia, Preziosi, E.M. Gray, Volpi, painter Mario Sironi, Ezra Pound and a number of others.[117] Police reports continued to remind Mussolini that not all 'friends' were reliably faithful, however. Balbo, for example, back from Libya for a while and staying in the opulent surrounds of the Hotel Excelsior in Rome, was overheard complaining about a gamut of matters which ran from Fascist brutality in Spain, to the inadequacy of the Corporate state, which, he said, in practice was overwhelmed by bureaucrats whose mentality was a world away from that of genuine workers. Balbo added his view that the fault lay in the fact that officials were appointed from above. 'I tell you very frankly that I prefer elections for a number of reasons, including public order.

Elections act as a thermometer, and measure the temperature of public spirit.'[118] The Governor of Libya, it seemed, alternative in many eyes to Ciano as imaginable successor to the *Duce*, had reverted to being a liberal and, if these words meant anything, no longer sounded like a sword-bearer of the Fascist revolution, but rather one who was working away from his *Duce*. With these and other reports before him,[119] and with his meetings with the studiously cynical Bocchini continuing almost daily, no wonder that Mussolini was entrenched in his belief that 'man is an absurd animal'[120] and that choosing a good man was about as likely as winning the lottery.[121] No wonder, too, that he soldiered on with his accustomed administrative work, privately sceptical about whether his regime had changed the behaviour patterns and attitudes of its subjects. Coping with foreign affairs, however complex and menacing, might well seem a relief compared with the task of imposing the doctrine of totalitarian Fascism on Italians.

As Mussolini's own directive of 30 December 1934 had promised, once the empire was conquered, his attention would shift back to Europe and its now recurrent international crises.[122] While Ethiopia and then Spain had occupied the headlines, what of the *Anschluss*, what of Germany, Nazi Germany? What, too, of 'universal fascism'? Was the Italian model going to be the political system which dominated the twentieth century, as Mussolini boasted it must?

In regard to this last question, there were quite a few superficial grounds for optimism. Rightist dictatorships were no longer restricted to Italy – indeed, in 1938–39 the betrayal of Czechoslovakia was to eliminate the last State in Europe which, apart from Britain and that Atlantic fringe running from France to Sweden, preserved some semblance of liberal democracy. One new dictator had taken power in Greece, where, in August 1936, General Ioannis Metaxas, with royal approval, had swept aside surviving liberal constitutionalism. Mussolini hastened to send his endorsement of the coup, urging Metaxas in characteristic phrasing as soon as possible:

> 1. to organise a single governing party. 2. to create a single organisation of Greek youth. 3. to create a single organisation of employers and workers, recognised by law and entailing a collective work contract with legal standing. 4. to create a *dopolavoro* on the Italian model.[123]

There have been many complex, not to say baroque, attempts to define 'fascism', but, in 1936, this simple formula (plus a role for the dictator-*Duce*) might reasonably be accepted as Mussolini's version of what his ideology and its 'revolution' meant.

Mussolini also suggested that this list should be adopted in Austria, where, however, Schuschnigg never expressed friendship for Italy with quite the warmth that Dollfuss had done and where the fully 'authoritarian' regime which Italy desired failed to materialise.[124] Even the Germanophobe Suvich, in one of his last attempts at summarising Italy's diplomatic options before he lost office in July 1936, admitted that the Austrian situation was 'difficult'.[125] In early June 1936 Mussolini met Schuschnigg at the *Rocca delle Caminate* and assured him that 'Italy's attitude in regard to Austria is unchanged'. Over-friendly talks between Schuschnigg's supporters and Austrian Nazi sympathisers were, he warned, a *modus moriendi*.[126] He similarly informed the British that they should not be alarmed by the appearance of a thaw in Italo-German relations which was merely prompted by events. None the less, the tone of the relationship between the two dictatorships was changing, and no sooner had he met Schuschnigg than Mussolini told his ambassador in Berlin, with a striking reversal in metaphor, that, 'in great part', he was now favourable to Austria fixing on a *modus vivendi* with Germany.[127] It was as well to have come to such a conclusion, because, on 11 July, an accommodation was reached between the two Germanic powers, suggesting at a minimum that Schuschnigg had accepted a fate which would see his country drift ever more obviously into the Nazi orbit.

Confronted by such a prospect and by the surviving reluctance among the British leadership, and especially by Eden, to acknowledge that Italy had conquered Ethiopia,[128] Mussolini slackened his efforts to preserve an anti-German front. 'The two beauties', as a wry bureaucrat denominated the *Duce* and *Führer*,[129] were entering each other's field of force. It was true that Mussolini continued to assure any who would listen that absorbing Ethiopia was the task in hand for Italians who could therefore again be listed among the 'satisfied peoples'.[130] However, at virtually the same time, he lectured Fascist officials on the need to reignite the spirit raised by successful war and underlined the requirement that 'we develop our policy of economic autarchy as far as possible'.[131] By September 1936 Mussolini was telling the Austrian Foreign Minister that Italo-German relations had steadily improved since the Germans had refused to join the sanctions bloc. Now, between the two countries, a 'parallelism' was growing in the international arena. How long would it last? That, said Mussolini, depended on Britain, since France's internal crisis had reduced it to a country with which dialogue was presently impossible. Italy was concerned that Britain and Germany would come to some arrangement. But then Spain was also hardening the 'parallelism' (Mussolini repeated the term) between Rome and Berlin. 'In Spain, Germany and Italy are acting in accord, with both backing the Francoist revolution.'[132] Later that month, his sentiments had firmed further. It would be good for him to go on an official visit to Germany as the Nazis were suggesting. Such an event, he surmised, 'will be clamorous. It will represent the meeting of the Chiefs of two similar movements and philosophies'. It must be fully prepared, since it would 'signal not just the solidarity between the two regimes but also [the adoption of] a common policy by the two states which must be clearly delineated towards East and West, South and North'.[133]

In fact the first visitor was Ciano, who, at this stage of his career, was a fervent advocate of closer ties with Germany. On 24 October Ciano met Hitler at Berchtesgaden and the two happily agreed on the perfidy of the British – Ciano had brought a dossier prepared by the Italian secret service in proof of the malevolence of London towards the Nazi regime – and on the need to oppose Bolshevism. To Ciano's apparent approval Hitler stated that now was the time for Italy and Germany to 'become more active', and 'move over to the attack' in their dealings with the liberal democrat states. 'The Mediterranean', he said,

is an Italian sea. Any future modification of the balance there must tilt in favour of Italy. So Germany should have freedom of action to the East and the Baltic. By orienting our mutual dynamism in exactly opposed directions, we shall avoid any conflict of interests between Italy and Germany.[134]

The inexperienced Ciano, who, despite his pose of world-weariness, was easily star-struck, had gone very far. He was not, however, checked by his father-in-law. Rather, on 1 November in a speech delivered from a podium set up outside the Milan *Duomo*, Mussolini proclaimed in words destined to become famous: the 'entente' now reached between Germany and Italy was 'not a diaphragm, but rather an axis around which all European states, animated by a desire for collaboration and peace, can revolve'. Britain, he added, must accept that, though the Mediterranean sea might be its road to India, for Italians it represented 'life itself'. Italy could not endure suffocation there. Mussolini also took occasion to re-assert Fascism's revolutionary watchwords: 'We are not those who embalm a past. We are those who anticipate the future'. Fascism was building a 'real civilisation of work', in which the corporate system would soon reach 'its definitive realisation'.[135]

Historians differ in their interpretation of what was happening by the end of 1936 to Italian or Mussolinian foreign policy. Italian diplomatic historians, who tend to be influenced by old or new nationalism, often argue that the accommodation between Germany and Italy was the fruit of 'realism' and reflected the pursuit of traditional national interests rather than being the product of ideological similarity or dictatorial will.[136] Macgregor Knox, by contrast, sees the Axis as 'a goal for which Mussolini actively strove' from January 1936, if not before, as part of his unquenchable purpose 'to smash the European balance' and constitute 'an Italo-German revolutionary alliance against the West'.[137]

The evidence suggests, however, that each of these views is too extreme. It is true that the Fascist Italy which now was engaging in rapprochement with Nazi Germany was a state that, from time to time, jostled the status quo. In 1937–38 Mussolini and Ciano cheerfully slipped subsidies to the fascist Rexists in Belgium,[138] and to anti-British nationalists in Malta,[139] Egypt[140] and other more far-flung parts of the British empire.[141] They continued to back Croat terrorists in Yugoslavia and began to contemplate converting Albania from a client state – in 1936, Mussolini defined it as 'an Italian province without a prefect appointed to it'[142] – to one under direct Italian rule.[143] They talked portentously to each other about how Switzerland lacked a rosy future, given the utterly Italian character of the Ticino.[144] They laughed together when Mussolini declared that the English were people 'who think with their bums' and that the United States was a 'country of niggers and Jews', with which real mutual comprehension was out of the question.[145] They agreed as well that Italians could only be kept up to the mark by being regularly engaged in fighting[146] and that local capitalists were given to fearfully protecting their profits rather than heroically contemplating war.[147]

Nor did these sentiments merely amount to chat. Despite occasional murmurs about Francoist tardiness, ingratitude[148] and bloodiness,[149] Italy continued to be the power most involved in Spain. Because of that and its other activities, between 1935 and 1938 Italy spent almost as much of its gross national product on military matters as did Germany and around double the percentage of Britain and France.[150] From 1934 to 1940 the military and colonial budgets took 51 per cent of Italian government expenditure.[151] Besides, Mussolini on a number of occasions stressed his determination to avoid *giri di valzer* (about-turns at the waltz),[152] the term which had become associated with Liberal Italy's diplomatic inconstancy in pre-1914 Europe.

All the same, somewhere beneath the strenuous verbiage, oscillations continued. Was Italy now fanatically anti-communist? Perhaps. Certainly, when dealing with the Germans, Mussolini, Ciano and others of the Fascist leadership did not forget to say so. Moreover, the purges did prompt Mussolini to condemn the USSR as a place of 'famine and terror' which only a 'cretin' could admire.[153] As if in proof of a new commitment to international anti-communism, on 6 November 1937 Italy joined with Germany and Japan in the 'Anti-Comintern pact' and curtailed what had been, until 1936, relatively warm bilateral Italian–Soviet relations.[154] Apologetics in the Fascist press which, until only a few months before, had continued to wonder if the USSR was evolving in a nationalist, corporative and 'fascist' direction,[155] now ceased. Yet, somewhere beneath the surface, an Italo-Soviet *rapprochement* remained imaginable. It is striking that, when Ribbentrop came to Rome for the Italian accession to the Anti-Comintern pact, Mussolini talked to him less about the USSR than about Spain, Austria and the Mediterranean. Fascist Italy was a prac-tical member of the anti-communist alliance and not one driven by ideology alone.[156]

Had Italy, at the same time, become the sworn enemy of Britain and its empire? When Mussolini was impressing Ciano, it sounded as though Italy had 'inevitably' joined the anti-British bloc, and such talk possessed the further advantage in that each could outbid the other in being mean about ambassador Grandi, who, they were given to complain, had turned half-English.[157] Back in April 1936 Mussolini had already told Grandi that the sanctions campaign had left Italians with a profound hatred of Britain: 'we are now launched, and we shall overthrow anyone who endeavours to stop us, both with force and with diplomacy'.[158] The Axis showed where diplomacy could lead. Likewise, the quarrel with Eden remained personal and profound (on both sides), and Mussolini and his colleagues rejoiced when, just before the *Anschluss*, the Foreign Minister fell. Dealing with the British Prime Minister, Neville Chamberlain, who acceded to his office in May 1937, was, however, another matter. Grandi, Ciano and the *Duce* were ready to listen to sounds of the appeasement of Italy deliv-ered by such personal agents as Adrian Dingli, a lawyer, and Sir Joseph Ball, a Tory party bureaucrat.[159] According to Grandi,

Chamberlain had expressed the wish for a 'totalitarian' solution to Anglo-Italian quarrels.[160] The Prime Minister himself wrote directly to the *Duce* of his desire for an accord, summoning in his support the ghost of his brother, Austen, who, he said, had always viewed Mussolini as 'a good man to do business with'.[161]

In response, Mussolini was ready to concede that the interests of the two states were not in fundamental collision, 'either in the Mediterranean or elsewhere'.[162] For the moment an accord was neither reached nor ruled out,[163] but Italy continued to be the most bumptious of the powers involved in Spain, where the misnamed 'Gentleman's agreement', signed in January 1937 between Britain and Italy to limit intervention, was ostentatiously ignored by the latter. Moreover, in December Italy announced its intention to leave the League of Nations, with Mussolini excoriating 'the Geneva Sanhedrin manœuvred by occult forces against our Italy and our revolution'.[164] The *Duce*'s words were growing ever more rumbustious and, seemingly, ever more Nazified, but, as yet, nothing irrevocable in fact separated the once 'traditional friends'. Their future relationship would be governed not so much by their own actions as by what Nazi Germany was to do to Europe over the next months and years.

The most dramatic sketch of a new course in Italian foreign policy was painted by Mussolini during his first official visit to Germany from 25 to 29 September 1937. That trip culminated in a speech which Mussolini gave in German, haltingly as well as in a downpour before an estimated crowd of 800 000 people in Berlin. He spoke of the similarities between the Fascist and Nazi systems which were, he stated, actually 'the greatest and most authentic democracies existing in the present day world'.[165] The Germans had pulled out all the stops in trying to impress the Italian dictator,[166] and they succeeded. None the less, the *Duce* as yet made no definite commitments, and Goebbels was left to remark that everyone would have to 'wait and see' what was to be the long-term effect on Italo-German relations.[167] Mussolini did, however, return home proclaiming that he was now more sure than ever that 'the future of Europe will be fascist'.[168]

What, then, by the end of 1937, was Italy's exact line on Austria? After all, the issue which Mussolini and his advisers had long regarded as fundamental for Italian diplomacy was the *Anschluss*. Already in November 1936, the *Duce* underlined to his cabinet the 'implacable' and 'historic' nature of Austrian 'hatred' for Italy.[169] Here, it seemed, was a client which could never learn gratitude. As if in reaction, in April 1937 when Mussolini again met Schuschnigg, he proffered the contradictory message that 'Italy still pursues its direct policy to maintain the independence and integrity of Austria, synchronising and harmonising this situation with the Rome–Berlin Axis.' Europe, he added, was 'characterised by the political existence of two blocs which have come into being automatically out of ideological commonality' and through joint work in Spain. Nevertheless, aware of Austrian clericalism, he explained with another twist in his argument, the two totalitarian states were distinguished on the religious question: 'We are Catholics, proud of our religion and respectful of it. We do not accept racial theories, especially when they are given legal consequences. Even our economies are not the same.' What Fascist Italy and Nazi Germany did undoubtedly share was 'the same enemies'.[170]

Mussolini was regularly fond of crafting his words to suit his audience. However, his last phrase may have been a telling one. It does not mean that the Italo-German friendship was only caused by accident, since international Anti-Fascism had been largely prompted by the violence and aggression of Nazi Germany, Fascist Italy and those minor fascist movements which were still plotting their track to power. But it does mean that Mussolini and the rest of the Italian leadership still did not positively endorse an *Anschluss*. They did not regard it as a clearing of the decks which could permit further mutual aggression. Rather, the problem of Austro-German relations was, for Mussolini, another case of shutting his eyes and hoping that, somehow, the worst would not happen. So, early in 1938 he told Ciano that Austro-German union was inevitable but that he preferred that it be delayed.[171] As late as 27 February Mussolini, characteristically reviewing the Austrian question by making a numbered list of the key factors involved, was still convinced that 'it is in the interest of Italy that Austria remains independent'. Such interest, he added, was not so great that it should be defended militarily or by 'a complete reversal of our political relationship with Germany'. Since Italy did not possess the power to stop the *Anschluss* – Mussolini continued to be impressed by reports of the overwhelming Germanophilia within Austria[172] – then Italy must ensure that it did not suffer from an Austro-German union. Ominously, he noted, 'the mass of Germans will weigh on the Brenner and that situation can have hostile ramifications'.[173] Despite the Axis, Italian diplomacy was still facing in more than one direction, with Ciano listening to friendly noises from the new Yugoslav strongman, Milan Stojadinovic, and remarking brightly that Italy could always establish a 'vertical Axis' to balance its existing 'horizontal' one.[174]

Events, however, were destined to outrun such scheming. Although Goering among others had promised that Germany would never act in Austria without previous mutual agreement with Italy,[175] on 10 March 1938 Hitler decided that it was time to move against Austria. An invasion force crossed the border on Saturday 12 March. The day before the *Führer* had sent Mussolini a handwritten note arguing that the situation had become impossible and that the *Duce* would not have behaved differently 'if the destiny of Italians was in play'. The Brenner, Hitler pledged, was the permanent border between the two nations – 'this is a decision which I have not come to in 1938 but rather immediately after the end of the First World War and I have never made a mystery about it'.[176] When Italy did not react, Hitler sent a shorter message stating simply: 'Mussolini, I shall never forget this.'[177] The next day, Mussolini replied politely that his tolerant reaction was an expression of the friendship between the two countries 'consecrated to the Axis'.[178] His colleagues, however, found him grumpy at events.[179] His speech to the Chamber, justifying the act as 'predestined', was embarrassed, especially when he urged that 'for us Fascists, all borders are sacred. They are not discussed; they are defended'.[180] To Ciano he confessed that the *Anschluss*, though 'inevitable', gave him no pleasure and would be bound to be followed by a German push against Czechoslovakia, Switzerland and Belgium, in that order.[181] Italy would have to adapt its policy to such a rocky, but potentially rewarding, future and, in the interim, Mussolini ordered a speeding up of the construction of border fortifications in Italy's north-east.[182] Ciano noted that he and his father-in-law were now bombarded with anonymous letters bewailing the *Anschluss* and Italy's craven acceptance of it.[183] Some later commentators thought that in March 1938 Italy lost its independence and the history of 'real' Fascism came to an end.[184]

The pace of international relations continued to accelerate as one crisis lurched into another, with Nazi Germany always acting as the disturbing power. It was a sign of the new times that American ambassador William Phillips reported that Mussolini seemed to be losing his English;[185] his world was more and more circumscribed by Berlin. In April the *Duce* may have complained that a recrudescence of German nationalism in the Alto Adige, if backed by Hitler, could see the Axis 'blown sky high', and he may have then talked also about reaching an accommodation with the British.[186] Some of his journalists may have continued to stress that, even if the *Anschluss* had been only 'logical', Fascist Italy and Nazi Germany were by no means identical regimes.[187]

But subtle solutions were becoming less and less available to Mussolini and his regime.

The next crisis followed hard on the heels of the *Anschluss*. In early May Hitler came on his second visit to Fascist Italy, a much more celebrated figure than he had been in 1934.[188] It was true that the trip had its down-side – as constitutional head of state, King Victor Emmanuel III was thrust into the *Führer*'s company too often for the contentment of either. It was said that the King asked Hitler unavailingly how many nails could be found in the German infantry boot, and then illustrated his own pedantic knowledge of detail by explaining that in the Italian, there were 74 (22 in the heel and 52 in the sole).[189] In 1942 Hitler was still recalling that he had 'never seen anything worse' than the lugubrious courtiers he met.[190] The Vatican was also touchy about the visit, with Ciano agreeing to eliminate the Via della Conciliazione outside St Peter's from Hitler's parade in Rome, when Pius XI made difficulties about providing illumination for one he condemned as 'the greatest enemy of Christ and the Church in modern times'.[191] Meanwhile knowing Germans laughed at an Italian military exhibition in Naples where quadrupeds vastly outnumbered tanks,[192] while Bocchini took the occasion to sound out Nazis whom he thought might be in the know on the exact nature of Hitler's relationship with Eva Braun. In regard to more serious matters, the Germans were fobbed off when they hinted at the creation of a full-scale military alliance with their Axis 'partner'.[193]

Once back from his Italian tour, Hitler, as in 1934, was spurred to act, with the victim this time to be Czechoslovakia. The German army was ready with an invasion plan but, in the event, they were frustrated when the Czechs proved determined to resist. Although Mussolini told Ciano that he had detected the *Führer* wearing rouge during his visit in order to ward off his habitual pallor and the two agreed that meeting Ribbentrop was a vexing experience,[194] Mussolini also stated that, if war broke out over the Czechs, he would enter the conflict 'at once on the side of the Germans'.

The pledge was, of course, merely verbal and, during the summer of 1938, the Italians did not concentrate on the continuing cold war between their German friends and Czechoslovakia. On 19 August Ciano was astonished to hear that the Nazis were preparing for military action sometime in the next month.[195] Although Mussolini speechified against 'Czecho-Germano-Polish-Hungaro-Rutheno-Romano-Slovakia',[196] when he reappeared in the international limelight during the latter stages of the Munich crisis, he was reduced to acting as Hitler's second. He did confide to Ciano that, if war between Germany on the one side and the USSR, France and Czechoslovakia on the other resulted, he would stay neutral, but he would enter a conflict if Britain did, since, he averred, in a full-scale ideological conflict, 'Fascist Italy cannot stay neutral.'[197] With a cavalier failure to plumb the issue, he even said that he welcomed the prospect of Japanese intervention in a general crisis, whether or not such a move brought in the United States.[198] At the same time, Alberto Pariani, the Under-Secretary for War, conforming to the new belief in *Blitzkrieg*, lightly urged the 'large scale use of gas', even against modern fortifications, though he and his fellow soldiers had made no attempt to assess the likely military, let alone the political, value of such an act. In practice, luckily for Mussolini and the rest of the Fascist leadership, the Munich crisis did not debouch into war.[199] Rather, the *Duce*, for the last time seeming a statesman of global significance, became the conduit for the 'plan' which finally resolved the conference peacefully, even if Ciano noted that his chief was in a bad mood during the last discussions in Munich because he was 'bored by their vaguely parliamentary air'.[200]

In reporting Mussolini's return from Munich, Fascist photographic journals displayed a *Duce* who was 'the Saviour of Europe', and among the crowds true believers carried placards saying: '*Duce*, you are the father of humanity.'[201] Mussolini himself talked about bringing home 'peace with justice', and Italians celebrated as they had not done since the conquest of Addis Ababa. The hailing of their leader was so overwhelming that Mussolini reacted against it.[202] Back in February he had formally adopted the goose-step,[203] with the comment that 'it is a step which the sedentary, the fat, the stupid and the so-called shorties [his audience would have recognised an impolite reference here to King Victor Emmanuel III] will never be able to manage. We like it because of that. Our adversaries', he went on belligerently, 'state that this parade-step expresses an authentic militarism. We are happy about that.'[204] Yet, in October 1938 the Italian masses were evincing anything but a militarist urge as they rejoiced at the preservation of peace in their time. Mussolini, it seemed, would have to find yet another issue through which the people could be mobilised as new men and women. It was time for Italy, as never before, to go racist.

15

The approach of a Second World War, 1938–1939

IN July 1938 Mussolini met the prominent Italian anthropologist Guido Landra[1] and disclosed some personal news. The Mussolinis, the *Duce* stated, were 'Nordics'. They had nothing in common with the French; instead they shared a lot with the English and the Germans. As proof, Mussolini cited the marriage of Edda to a 'Tuscan' and Vittorio to a 'Lombard'. These choices, the *Duce* said, were demonstration 'of the constant instinct of his family [to ally with] people who were purer from a racial point of view'. Talk about being 'Latin' or 'Mediterranean', he added, broadening his theme, must now cease in his country, and be replaced with a privileging of the 'Aryan'. *Romanità* could, however, remain a feature of a newly mobilised Fascist Italy.[2]

There were many ironies in this attempt by the Italian dictator to read his family history in racial terms. After all, it was not so long since Mussolini had derided the 'anti-scientific drivel' of the Germans, itself based, he then took pleasure in pointing out, on the ideas of 'the Frenchman Gobineau'.[3] In those days he had cheerfully told his acquaintances that Hitler was 'a muddle headed fellow. His head is just stuffed with philosophical and political tags that are utterly incoherent'.[4] Following words with action, in the early years of Nazi persecution the *Duce* allowed some 3000 German Jews to find sanctuary in Italy.[5] In 1936 he was still capable of intervening personally to support foreign Jews whom he regarded as 'friends'. Historian George Mosse, member of a wealthy and distinguished German-Jewish family with wide-ranging publishing and newspaper interests, half-remembered Mussolini at that time ringing his mother in Florence to assure her that she and her family 'would not be touched and ... could stay as long as [they] liked'.[6]

Even so, over the previous couple of years Mussolini had been talk-ing more dismissively of the Jews than ever before – in November 1936 he suggested to his cabinet that it was time to introduce racial matters into Fascist discourse and doctrine.[7] One notable radicalising influence was foreign press hostility to the Ethiopian war; the *Duce* began to notice a large Jewish presence among such commentators. As he told Paul Einzig, an economist still friendly to the Fascist regime: 'World Jewry is doing bad business in aligning itself with the Anti-Fascist sanctions campaign against the one European country which, at least until now, has neither practised nor preached Anti-Semitism.'[8] Already in 1935 the police demolition of a *Giustizia e Libertà* cell in Turin had revealed quite a number of Jews among its members, while in Paris[9] Carlo Rosselli continued to provide combative leadership of the non-communist wing of the Anti-Fascist cause.

Rosselli was murdered during the Spanish Civil War, and that con-flict, which pitted the forces of 'order' against those of 'subversion', gave extra impulse to contemplate the role of Jews in leftist revolu-tionary movements, beginning with Marx himself. Mussolini's perpet-ual sensitivity to what was happening in France, that country which had once been his ideal and never ceased to be his measuring stick, was further exacerbated by Léon Blum's leadership[10] of the 'Anti-Fascist' Popular Front and by the prominence, at least according to the Fascist press, of French leftists in giving comfort to the Republican side. Mussolini's attitudes and reactions were not unique. After all the Jesuits' journal *Civiltà Cattolica*, impassioned in its commitment to the Francoist cause, praised the Anti-Semitic legislation so far introduced in Germany, blessing the assistance given to the Insurgent 'crusade' by the Axis.[11] For many Europeans at the time politics were reducing to a choice of two. If Jews were detected on the Left, Anti-Semitism fol-lowed automatically on the Right. On almost every contemporary horizon, there were issues – the deepening quarrel with the British over the Mediterranean,[12] Spain,[13] the noisy attacks on the Jews in Germany (and the rise of a more public Anti-Semitism in Poland, Romania, Hungary, each a country with which Fascist Italy had friendly relations) – which demanded that Mussolini focus on race.

One specifically Italian concern epitomised this situation. In the aftermath of the Ethiopian war, the young historian Emilia Morelli suggested that the real message for Italians was to unite 'against one enemy only, the foreigner',[14] but the acquisition of empire added a problem beyond the simple one of xenophobia. Mussolini was not the first to raise the matter, but, as he complained to Ciano in January

1938: 'the behaviour of many of our men is making the natives lose their respect for the white man'.[15] Two months earlier he had firmly instructed the Duke of Aosta to impose 'racial discipline' on the Italians resident in the empire.[16] A sense of racial hostility towards 'blacks' could draw on a long history in Italy as elsewhere – it could rely on a 'mass base' in a more profound fashion than was true of Anti-Semitism.[17] In the years after 1936 there was quite a lot of discussion about the racial ramifications of empire and exclusionary legislation began to be developed there (though scarcely by the direct edict of Mussolini).[18] However much sponsored by the spirit of the times, ideas about specific racial legislation entered the Italian agenda through Addis Ababa.

In March 1937 Mussolini used his visit to Libya to proclaim a positive policy towards the Arab inhabitants of his empire and their ethnic cousins elsewhere, whose 'Pan-Arab' nationalism made them Anti-British and therefore pro-Italian on the ancient principle that the enemy of my enemy is my friend. This policy, even if pursued somewhat erratically, had racial implications of its own, since Jews had constituted more than a quarter of the population of Tripoli at the moment of Italian occupation[19] and, after 1922, local Jews remained rich and influential. They got on especially well with Balbo when, in January 1934, he arrived as governor with the aim of launching a major immigration scheme for Italian peasants and generally modernising the colony. Though fans of modernity, Libyan Jews were suspicious of Arab nationalism,[20] and so the formula which had made Mussolini speak of befriending local Arabs contained potentially menacing implications for local Jews.

At the end of 1937 it was still possible to be sceptical as to the reality of a full-scale Italian conversion to Anti-Semitic racism. Ciano jotted into his diary the allegation that Italy's Jews feared that he had been persuaded by the Nazis to persecute them. 'Wrong', he commented.

> The Germans have never raised the matter with me. Nor do I believe that we should unleash in Italy an Anti-Semitic campaign. The problem just doesn't exist here. The Jews are few and, but for some exceptions, good. Moreover, it is never a good idea to persecute the Jews as such, since an act like that will provoke solidarity among all the Jews in the world. They can be struck by lots of other mechanisms. But, I repeat, the Jewish problem just doesn't exist here. Perhaps, in small doses, the Jews are needed by society in the way that yeast is needed in bread.[21]

It may well be that Ciano was writing out in more detail the sentiment earlier expressed by his father-in-law that he did not really like Jews, but that this dislike did not convert him into a practising Anti-Semite.[22] Befitting the curious mutuality of their relationship, on February 1938 Mussolini almost repeated his son-in-law's words back to him, stating that he did not want to foment trouble where none existed. On this occasion, however, there was a hint of menace at the end of Mussolini's remarks. He intended to pour cold water on those fanatics enflamed by Anti-Semitism, he said, 'but without quite putting the fires out'.[23] The mobilising power of racism, displayed every day more starkly in Nazi Germany, could, the *Duce* was half persuaded, assist him and his cause. In October 1937 Mussolini had asked one of Landra's young assistants to prepare a full-scale academic brief on the Jews of Italy from the point of view of 'racial science'.[24] Not quite ready to ape Nazi Germany, Mussolini was none the less giving greater indication than before that he might be won over to the view that some form of Italian Anti-Semitism was possible and necessary.

And so he flew a kite about the matter, publishing anonymously in *Informazione diplomatica* an article which he told Ciano amounted to 'a masterpiece of Anti-Semitic propaganda'.[25] He began with another denial that Italy was 'on the point of initiating an Anti-Semitic policy'.[26] He went on to argue that the best solution would be the creation of a 'Jewish state', adding, however, that it could not be in Palestine, an Anti-Zionist conclusion which Ciano seconded, since, otherwise, the young Foreign Minister could not 'safeguard our relations with the Arabs'.[27] But it was in the last paragraph of his article that Mussolini really ventured onto new ground. The Fascist regime, he stated, did not want the influence of Jews, and especially immigrant Jews, to become 'disproportionate'.[28] How to check such excess, for the moment he left to the imagination of his readers.

As the diplomatic crisis moved its epicentre from Austria to Czechoslovakia, Mussolini's oratory grew shriller about many aspects of Italy's relationship with the world. On 14 May 1938 speaking at Genoa from a podium constructed to resemble the prow of a battleship, Mussolini told Italians, in what would become another of the slogans of the last years of the regime, *Chi si ferma è perduto* (Whoever stops is lost). To drive his people on, he invoked the xenophobic vocabulary first coined by the Nationalists and now in greater circulation, urging that 'foreigners' misunderstood Italy when they maundered on about the greatness of its past; any real friend of Italy should instead be alert to present evidence of 'arms and work'.[29] On 4 July, before an audience at the 'new town' of Aprilia, he excoriated what he rudely called 'the great demoplutocracies'; they were, he added flatly, the 'enemies of Italy'.[30] The new tone of exasperation in his words worried members of the Italian establishment, but Mussolini, taking his temerity one step further, now told Ciano (of all people) that the 'defeatist' bourgeoisie needed to be brought into line by a 'third wave' of Fascism. The *Duce* even declared himself determined to establish a network of 'concentration camps', where life would be made tougher for inmates than it was for those currently in *confino*. The path to such places, he said truculently, would be lit by 'a pyre of the writings of Jews, Masons and Francophiles'. 'Jewish writers and journalists' were to be banned. 'The revolution', he argued a little tardily, 'must now make its mark on the habits of Italians'. They must stop being '"sympathetic"', and instead become tough, implacable, hateful. In other words: the bosses'.[31]

For once, the *Duce* was not just sounding off. On 14 July the regime published what was called its 'Manifesto of Racial Scientists', a document to the writing of which Mussolini himself made major contribution.[32] Additionally, to choose Bastille Day on which to publish this document, which rejected so much of the Enlightenment with its optimistic comprehension of humankind's potential, was yet another flagrant attempt by the *Duce* to counter the moral and intellectual superiority which he always knew resided in Paris. In the Mussolini manner, the document was arranged as a list of ten points, a set of commandments inscribed from on high about race. Among key sentences were the statements that 'the people of Italy are of Aryan origin and their civilization is Aryan', and that 'the Jews do not belong to the Italian race' (and neither did other 'Orientals' or 'Africans'). Despite the overwhelming evidence of the rich historical variety of Italians – a matter regularly admitted by Mussolini in the past and not always to be denied in the future – he now argued that 'a pure "Italian race" is already in existence' and that the vast majority of this stock had inhabited the Italian peninsula 'for thousands of years'. In a subsequent piece in *Il Popolo d'Italia*, Mussolini hammered home his themes: 'To call ourselves Aryans means to declare ourselves as belonging to a group historically defined by race; [we belong to] the Indo-European group, the ones who have created world civilization. Without a clear, certain and omnipresent racial consciousness, empires cannot be held. This is why some problems which were once left in the shadows have become of burning relevance since 3 October 1935 [the date of the invasion of Ethiopia]'.[33]

With their opinions illuminated in this way, the Fascist press swung behind their *Duce*. In *La Vita Italiana*, Preziosi took the occasion to argue that he, too, had been always right, by providing a list of quotations illustrating that Mussolini had been driven by a sense of race since at least 1921.[34] To signify his approval of this reinterpretation of his life story, Mussolini set aside his previous dislike and formally received Preziosi who, in edifying homage, presented the *Duce* with a complete set of the journal.[35] Giuseppe Bottai characteristically tried to intellectualise the new policy. Italian racism involved more than just 'science', he wrote. By rejecting materialism, it could up-date that strand of humanist thought which ran from Machiavelli through Mazzini to Mussolini. 'The real bases of Italian racism in fact are and must be eminently spiritual, even if they fortunately spring from some purely biological data.' Racism should be deployed to resist Jews ('the General Staff of international Anti-Fascism') and Africans.[36] It could simultaneously eliminate that 'idiot and criminal, mainly foreign, pseudo-literature' – for Bottai, too, Nationalist words were now refurbished – which depicted Italians as 'sentimentalists, undisciplined, indolent people, tied to the idea of *dolce far niente*'. The Fascist intelligentsia, Bottai charged, should mobilise itself to bruit these matters from the Alps to the islands.[37] The regime had taken on a new cause, and its impulse must start in the schools, extending from there to all aspects of Fascist education.[38]

When the broad brush was abandoned and some effort made to examine the detail, the theory of Fascist racism remained confused – no one could clarify just what voluntarist racism might mean and how such voluntarism could intersect with the history of an allegedly primordial Italian race. Similarly the dilemmas of imperial rule, an avoidance of miscegenation in the empire and Anti-Semitism were regularly intermeshed without explanation or justification. The assertion that Fascism had always been racist was unconvincing, except in the sense that every European society, and certainly the liberal democratic ones in Britain and France, carried the potential to be overtly racist. The nervous reiteration of the idea that Italy was acting independently and not demeaning itself by mimicking its German Axis friend – a claim disbelieved by the populace whatever the press said[39] – and the assertion that the Italians needed again to be radicalised so that a Fascist revolution could at last be carried through were equally riddled with contradiction. Mussolini's own uneasy demand that 'concentration camps' spread across Italy – a decision weakly carried out in practice[40] – was as much proof as was needed that he had grown restlessly envious of the once junior 'fascism' in Berlin and was seeking to force his Italy to catch up with its neighbour (in a way bearing comparison with the desire of Crispi and others in the Liberal era that their Italy adopt policies which might convert it into a really Great Power). The Nazis themselves were surprised by the swift Italian adoption of racial ideas[41] (and secretly astonished that so racially corrupt a people could be so bold), but Nazi influence had indeed trickled down into Italy.

Whatever the exact role of the German model, in August–September 1938 while the Munich crisis beset Europe Mussolini's attention was in great part directed at proselytising his racial 'revolution' at home. There, the very inchoateness (as well as the inhumanity) of the ideas were precipitating opposition, and there were few things which annoyed Mussolini more than overt criticism. Back from a tour of duty in Libya, Balbo took the opportunity to moan to Ciano about the German alliance and about what Starace was doing to Italy and the Fascist party. When the son-in-law maliciously hastened to pass on the news of such truant attitudes to the *Duce*, then holidaying at Riccione, he set off a tirade from his father-in-law. If Balbo 'moved a finger', Mussolini swore that he would arrest him. Balbo was not the only nagging problem, however. Autarchy must be made more 'intransigent'. The Monarchy was a sagging weight on the regime. The royal family might have to be eliminated and the occasion could come with victory in Spain. 'Italy will never be Prussianised enough', concluded the *Duce* (showing by his word choice that he had not understood the modernity of Nazism). 'I'll never leave the Italians in peace even when I'm six feet under', he concluded, with a belligerence which at least impressed Ciano.[42]

And then there was the Pope, who had long been a severe critic of Nazi Germany and was now put out of countenance by Italian Anti-Semitism. 'A nod from me', Mussolini boasted, 'and the anti-clericalism of the people can be set flowing. They swallow with difficulty the idea of a Jewish God'. 'It is for this reason', the *Duce* continued, evidently enjoying the sound of his words, that 'I am a Catholic but an anti-Christian one'.[43] A few weeks later, again trying very hard to be wicked, he suggested to Ciano that the Jews might be despatched to a concession in Somalia, an area 'with lots of natural resources which the Jews could exploit. Among the rest, a shark-fishing industry which would be especially good because a lot of Jews could be eaten up'.[44]

To diatribes in his study were added speeches to the people. In the middle of September Mussolini journeyed to the north-eastern borders. In these areas his subjects had not altogether salved their wounds from both the First World War and the conflicts of the Risorgimento, and hostility to Germany had a mass base (and had been a crucial catalyst of 'border fascism'). Mussolini's major speech was delivered at Trieste – a Slovene onlooker remembered, despite her best efforts to remain detached, how 'irresistibly magnetic' the *Duce* appeared amid the cheering crowd.[45] After running over the historical background, Mussolini loudly justified the German alliance. If the crisis over Czechoslovakia lurched into armed conflict, then 'Italy's place has already been chosen' at the Germans' side, the *Duce* affirmed. Having so carelessly opted for war, Mussolini switched his commentary to the main domestic debate, which was about race. The 'racial problem', he maintained, had not arisen suddenly. Rather, it was a necessary part of imperial rule where race carried precise implications. But, he abruptly added, the Jewish question lay at the heart of the issue. If Fascism lowered its guard, Jewry, a piratical crew, were perpetually ready to board the Italian ship of state and sack it. Action was needed. Therefore, the regime was moving to a 'policy of separation', although exceptions would be made for Jews with 'irreproachable military or civil merits', either to Italy or Fascism.[46]

In practice, a process of the legislative exclusion of Jews from Italian life had begun, with the banning of foreign Jews from schools on 3 August.[47] Peace at Munich did not arrest this campaign. In a speech to the Grand Council on his return from Germany,[48] Mussolini was even more insistent in demanding a combined attack on the bourgeoisie and the Jews. Telling Bottai that he had been meditating on the Jewish question since 1908 (and so readjusting his own history with his usual aplomb),[49] Mussolini argued that the classical Romans had been racists to a man. All of Italian history, he went on, needed to be understood as the story of a race which was 'Aryan of the Mediterranean type, purely so'. It had been 'mathematically certain' (in that favourite phrase which almost always signified statistical imprecision), he explained, that the British and the French would not fight for Czechoslovakia, since they were spiritually hamstrung by their declining birth rates and racially exhausted. Italians, by contrast, could be 'militarised' further, and they would be.[50] When, on 12 November, the news of *Kristallnacht* arrived, Mussolini announced to Ciano that he 'unconditionally approved' the murderous Nazi pogrom: 'He said that if we were in an analogous situation, we would do the same'.[51] However, the next day (perhaps in receipt of information that Italian opinion was disgusted by events in Germany),[52] he backed off a little, describing the fine imposed by the Nazi government on the Jews as 'absurd' and worrying about the tendency of the German regime to pick a fight with the Catholic Church. The Axis, he warned, could not survive if the Nazis moved against German Catholics with the same ferocity as they had attacked their Jews.[53]

There were familiar suggestions here that Mussolini had not plumbed the nature of German racism. However, Fascist Italy still moved ahead with its own version of a war against the Jews. On 17 November legislation was promulgated in the style of the Nuremberg laws.[54] The first clause began: 'marriage of an Italian citizen of Aryan race to a person belonging to another race is prohibited'. There followed detailed measures entailing the exclusion of Jews from the military, education,[55] banking and insurance, the bureaucracy and Party, and any but small-scale business and agriculture, bans which were to some extent weakened by a series of exemptions for those who had served the nation and Fascism, and their families. A press campaign proceeded. Telesio Interlandi,[56] Preziosi's rival as the country's most durable racist and preacher of the idea that 'the intimate logic of Fascism' was racist,[57] was given his own fortnightly, *La difesa della razza* (Defence of the Race), to edit. He attracted to his staff such youthful Fascists as Giorgio Almirante, a man who, during the post-war era, was to be the leader of the neo-fascist MSI.[58] Italy had indeed gone racist and, to some degree, it stayed that way until Fascism fell.

Yet, just as the arguments launched by the *Duce* and others with such fury were fretted with hypocrisy and confusion, so the practice of Italian Anti-Semitism and other forms of racism was never tempered into steely consistency. Italy's road to Auschwitz was not just twisted, but studded with detours. Until 1943 Italian Jews were persecuted in ways which they had not imagined when, in considerable majority, they approved Fascism; they were not, however, killed. Back in August 1938 Farinacci, yet again, had tried to get his leader to examine the reasons which lay behind policy. He began in inimitable style by softening up the *Duce* with a delicious rumour that the Pope's mother was Jewish – what a laugh that would be, Farinacci pointed out in his rowdy way. One nod from the *Duce* and he could unleash a press campaign from Cremona that would make the Vatican blush.[59] But Farinacci had other, more serious, issues in mind. What did racism mean in Italy? 'To be frank', he stated,

> I have never been persuaded by the anthropological line on the racial question. Rather the question is overwhelmingly political. Indeed, I am

even more convinced than before that, when scientists are brought into political matters, they only compromise the situation. In the arenas of philosophy and science, it is always possible to argue; where reasons of state arise, one must just act and conquer.[60]

Not for Farinacci doubtful claims of Aryan blood coursing through the veins of his own family; rather, he preferred the practical approach (claiming it was naturally Fascist).

To be sure, there was a complication in Farinacci's rough and tough comprehension of racial theoretics. Like many Italians, Farinacci had 'his' Jew, a loyal secretary named Jole Foà. The *ras* of Cremona objected to the idea that she be removed from his office. She was, he explained with no sign of embarrassment, about fifty, a spinster who looked after a sister; she was capable and efficient, a good worker. Summarily to sack her would create a bad impression. 'I am happy to approve the extermination of all the Jews', Farinacci wrote in his usual vein, 'but before getting to the humble and innocent, we must start by striking those at the top'.[61]

This idea of being merciful to an extensive list of special cases easily entered Italian minds[62] – perhaps it was part of what has been termed the 'banality of good'.[63] Certainly the possibility of exception and exemption was the opposite face of Farinacci's advice to be racist tactically, and not out of fanatical 'scientific' belief. For all his lucubrations about the quality of Aryan blood possessed by the Mussolinis, the *Duce* did not really demur, or did not do so with any consistency. Despite the angry fervour of his words in 1938, he had not been converted into an acolyte of racism in the German style. Instead, his understanding of life remained complex, even within the Villa Torlonia. In his own home, he acknowledged late in 1941, by which time the Germans were imposing the final solution in the territories they had seized from the USSR: 'My sons staunchly protect their Jewish friends. They threaten to provide a bed for them in their own rooms unless these friends are allowed to emigrate or otherwise can legally and durably find a settled place for themselves' within Italy. In any case, Mussolini meditated in a self-justification of his paternal weakness which would not have been heard with much patience on the Eastern front, a little bit of Jewish blood would do future Italians no harm. Moreover, he could 'never forget that four of the seven founders of Italian nationalism were Jewish'.[64] Envy at German military success and humiliation at Italian military failure no doubt fed his continuing private deprecation of Hitler, but it was the *Führer's* fanaticism about racial ideology which made Mussolini think of him still as a man with 'an abstruse brain', who resembled 'a quack or market-square philosopher'.[65] Besides, his sons may have hinted when they spoke up for their Jews, had not the *Duce* behaved the same way as they did or Farinacci wanted to do? In November 1938 Margherita Sarfatti had been spirited away from Italy and, later, with the direct assistance and advice of her old lover, was taken from Portugal to sanctuary in the USA.[66] Mussolini may have talked racism, and done so with special vehemence when he was trying to convince himself and others that Italy had become a stalwart brother-in-arms of Nazi Germany. But, after a raft of Anti-Semitic legislation in 1938 and some follow-up in 1939,[67] the pace of official persecution in Italy slowed. Moreover, on race, as on so many other issues, the official line adopted in 'legal Italy' was not always followed in 'real Italy'; whatever the case may have been among Germans, the Italians showed few signs of being the 'willing executioners' of Jews.[68]

To absolve Mussolini from any responsibility for the Holocaust as some Fascist nostalgics have done[69] is absurd. To understand him as a philosophically convinced Anti-Semite or any form of racist[70] is equally implausible. As Farinacci had the gumption to reveal, Fascist racism was more opportunist and short-term than fanatical. It was as hollow as were many other aspects of Mussolinian administration.

This hollowness was revealing itself more and more as the 1930s drew to a bloody close. One of the few Fascists who almost always tried to work towards what he imagined were the ideas of his *Duce*, Starace had been an innovative Party Secretary, introducing a series of measures designed to radicalise the populace. In June 1936, the *sabato fascista* or Fascist Saturday promised a weekly mobilising parade or sporting endeavour and, the next year, legislation was introduced to ensure that any bureaucratic job could only be gained by an applicant who was a member of the PNF.[71] Starace tried to amend Italian linguistic habits by banning the usage of the polite form *Lei*, somewhat ironically condemned as a Spanish accretion, and requiring its replacement by the second person plural *voi*.[72] He was seconded by such ex-Nationalists as the distinguished geographer Giotto Dainelli, eagle-eyed in a way more familiar among French linguistic purists about 'foreign' hotel names and other unhealthy influences from beyond the border. There were some droll results. The President of the Touring Club tried to argue that the origin of the name of his organisation lay in the Latin words *globus* and *tornus*.[73] The owners of the *Hotel Anglo-Americano* in Florence had a sisyphean task. In 1940 they changed the name of their hostelry to the *Albergo America*; in 1941 to the *Regina*; in 1943 to the *Mercurio* and in 1944 back to the *Hotel Anglo-Americano*.[74]

In this jousting with words, Mussolini's main role was to coin still more of the slogans which Starace tried to make the political equivalent of those advertising jingles that were already becoming such a brain-numbing part of the universal triumph of consumerism. Mussolini, the leader who was always right, had persuaded his people they were lost if they halted; they must live their day as lions and not waste a century as sheep, but above all they must believe, obey and fight. *Con libro e moschetto, fascista perfetto* (With book and rifle, perfect Fascist), they must proclaim: *Noi tireremo diritto* (We shall forge ahead). Stimulated by the sounds of such chanting, the *Duce* now at least verbally opted for the most 'totalitarian' line on the majority of issues. Starace apart, his most enthusiastic aide was Bottai, who in November 1936 had replaced the blustering De Vecchi as Minister for National Education. Bottai came up with a slogan of his own, even if it was not the catchiest. 'The school', he pronounced, 'acts as the thermometer of the moral life of the country.'[75] To further this revived interest in the verbal control of Italians, in 1939 Bottai published *La carta della scuola* (The Education Charter),[76] its title portentously echoing that of the *Carta del Lavoro* of the previous decade. Education, he proclaimed, had remained a redoubt of the 'bourgeoisie', but now at last it could be taken from their hands and placed under the control of the Fascist state and people.[77] Like racial policy, he explained, this switch was another natural result of the conquest of empire.[78] Education was the essential tool for forging newly imperial men and new women. It was what allowed Mussolini to preside over a 'permanent revolution'.[79]

In spite of such fervent words, somehow the battle to create a Fascist culture was in retreat. The new generation of educated youth was watching American films and reading American novels,[80] as well as consuming in the American manner when they got the chance – Edda Ciano, a highly contradictory social model for young women near the elite, learned, when posted with her husband to Shanghai, that it was chic to drink Coca-Cola.[81] Out in the countryside, illiteracy remained common[82] – Fascist educational policies to overcome this traditional scourge were feeble compared with those adopted in the USSR, for example. Starace's dumbing down, which so annoyed sections of the elite still self-conscious about their intellectuality, was too literary for many peasants, whose cultures had been scarcely amended by two decades of Fascist 'revolution'. Both 'above' and 'below' the Fascist thrust was growing blunt. How did the *Duce* react to this plethora of evidence about the gap between Fascist theory and practice?

A member of the Grand Council remembers Mussolini's deepening 'anger' during these years.[83] This emotion, always been a prominent part of the *Duce*'s reaction to life, was now enhanced by a frustration at the evidence, coming both from within Italy (and within his own family) but most irritatingly from Germany, that he had not been an iron-hard engineer of human souls.[84] And some of the recipients of the perpetual rancour were unimpressed. Vito Panunzio, the son of a leading Fascist ideologue, remembers, for example, how by 1938–39 he and his university friends became given to complaining heretically about Starace and the German alliance. They were also distressed by Mussolini's evident contempt for humankind, mutinously wondering if 'their' Fascism might not prove better than 'his'.[85] The police still functioned with great efficiency and there was little evidence as yet of a popular revival of Anti-Fascism,[86] but, as the Danzig crisis deepened, there was a feeling that the regime was running out of steam. Mostly, the new flaccidity was blamed on 'the Fascists' (especially the sweatily unattractive Starace) and not Mussolini.[87] However, in the secrecy of his diary, one intellectual recorded the rumours that the *Duce* rang the doctors every day to check on his health and that his prowess as a swimmer was less than officially claimed.[88] Although the official verbiage about the *Duce*'s 'bronzed physique', 'rippling muscles' and Stakhanovite work-rate grew ever more intense,[89] somewhere, in some minds, the thought was planted that this god might have feet of clay.

Nor were doubts about Mussolini's sporting skills the only issue. Turned 55 in July 1938 the *Duce* was indulging his sexual peccadilloes for some to see. For those in the know, the problem of the Petaccis was becoming insistent. During the balmy summers of 1938 and 1939 the family took up residence in the delightful setting of the Grand Hotel at Rimini (which director Federico Fellini was to fill with meaning in his magnificent film study of Fascism, *Amarcord*). At this opulent retreat, the Petaccis were conveniently near the *Duce*'s holiday house just up the Adriatic at Riccione and rumours were soon circulating about the coquettish way Claretta reacted when summoned to the phone by her lover.[90] In her golden recollections prompted by the experience of imprisonment in 1943, she recalled one dawn when they had met on a deserted Adriatic beach, and he had called her 'Baby' and said he loved and adored her: 'You are the most beautiful part of my life. You are my youth', she remembered him saying.[91] Worse than her gushing were the scape-grace activities of her brother Marcello, who brazenly organised his success in surgery exams through 'recommendations' rendered unchallengeable by his tie to the *Duce*. So ruthless was he in the matter that he earned himself the craven approval of professors chosen to assess him and a wry commentary from the bureaucrats who facilitated and recorded proceedings.[92] His loutish behaviour in Rome had also won him notoriety; an incident in which his dog had bitten a journalist on the ear was reported with ostentatious anonymity in *Il Messaggero*.[93] An air of 'corruption' had never dissipated from Fascist Italy, but, as the regime and the *Duce* aged, venality and lubricity spread.

If control over the people's thoughts was not total, what of the legal bases of the regime and its ideally permanent revolution? The crises of the late 1930s prompted another examination of the very constitution of the Fascist state. Did it need amendment? The official answer to this question was yes; the revolution must be given new impulse everywhere. Indeed, since September 1924 at Mussolini's behest a wearisome series of commissions had examined Fascism's institutional structure.[94] Repeatedly, their reports were barren. Only in March 1939 did action ensue, when the Chamber of Deputies was abolished and replaced by a *Camera dei fasci e delle corporazioni* (Chamber of Fascist branches and corporations). The members, however, remained largely as before and, in still odder compromise, the Senate survived unamended. Descriptions of the new structure as 'real democracy'[95] were unconvincing, as was Mussolini's justificatory observation that 'the Senate is Roman, but the Chamber is Anglo-Saxon'.[96] The *Duce*'s version of permanent revolution, it was increasingly plain, was more a story of his own permanent sense that the rest of humankind was not made in his own image (an arrogance which only partially cloaked his own sense of inadequacy and root fear that Fascism had never quite achieved the intellectual rigour of that socialism he had abandoned so long ago).

The place of the King was a further topic for discussion, with Mussolini privately belittling the monarch as another who symbolised the unheroic character of Italians and who was lukewarm about the Axis – on a number of occasions Victor Emmanuel did counsel against it,[97] largely on the old soldier's classic ground that the allies in the last war should be eternal. In March 1938 the quarrel deepened between monarch and *Duce* when it was suddenly announced by Costanzo Ciano that Mussolini was to be raised to the rank of *Primo Maresciallo dell'Impero* (First Marshal of the Empire), a post without precedent and with at least potential semi-regal implications.[98] Mussolini was to be the official commander of the Italian military in wartime, a task previously reserved for the King.

Victor Emmanuel made plain his regret at this loss of royal prerogative, provoking Galeazzo Ciano and Starace to careless talk about the need to establish a Fascist republic some time in the future.[99] Mussolini took evidently malicious pleasure in transmitting to the King a report by a Fascist jurist justifying the legality of the new position which 'I, however much a layman, consider exhaustive'.[100] For all that, content as so often at having made a gesture, the *Duce* soon let his relationship with the King slip back into its old groove. Years before he had said that the two shared a bedroom but without a double bed in it,[101] and it was not a bad definition of what had been and remained their relationship. Each man sought refuge in a misanthropy and a misogyny which only deepened over time – Mussolini must have nodded when he heard that the King believed women were 'only good for mending socks and taking to bed'[102] and that the monarch esteemed the Chief of General Staff, Badoglio, a man with 'the brains of a sparrow and the hide of an elephant'.[103] Bottai may have thought he had found a clever formula when he talked about Victor Emmanuel having become the 'King of a Totalitarian State, embodiment of an organised people',[104] but monarch and *Duce* each went on suspecting that, just like every product of humankind, words were dross.

Duce and Emperor were at one also in their mutual dislike of priests. The last years of the pontificate of Pius XI, who died on 10 February 1939, produced some tension between Church and State. In his encyclical *Mit brennender Sorge* of January 1937 Pius had attacked the Nazi regime, condemning it as the near equal in evil to communist Russia as a state, an ideology and a morality. Fascism was always exempt from this condemnation: the Church leadership did not endorse the 'model of fascism', but Pius XI rejected the racial campaign, was doubtful about the Axis and not chary of letting his objections be known to Mussolini. In reaction, the *Duce* gave frequent vent to his dislike of the Pontiff and was peevish in his refusal to mourn the Pope's death; the Vatican, he implied, was too puny to win much recognition from a granitic warrior like himself.[105] None the less, the elevation of Pius XII was welcomed among the Fascist leadership,[106] as it should have been, given the new Pope's family background in Italian high finance, fervent anti-communism[107] and preference for Fascism over other modern ideologies which kept in thrall a sinful humankind. Despite further jars with Mussolini, in his occupation of the papal chair Pius XII heralded no rupture in the cohabitation between Church and State in Fascist Italy.

By 1939 testy complaints about the inadequate revolutionary ardour of Fascists at home were threaded through the *Duce*'s conversation. International affairs, however, dominated the headlines and were, by necessity, Mussolini's priority as an executive. In that regard the months after Munich were enlivened by newly vociferous Fascist demands for reward or payment. The target was France; the desired gains Nice, Corsica, Savoy, Tunis and Djibouti.[108] It was at this point that Mussolini told Claretta Petacci that the French were just the sort of people who were always trying to waylay him and that they must be made to pay for their habitual perfidy.[109] But just how serious was Fascist blackmail of France? Not very, since military preparations against Italy's north-western neighbour were fundamentally defensive and plans for Italian operations against Corsica or Tunis remained notional. Instead, the *Duce*'s exchanges with Ciano illustrated the limitations of charismatic rule, while showing again that, for Mussolini, almost anything was negotiable. Savoy,[110] he thought, could always be swapped for the Ticino.[111] But just how far would the *Duce* go for Djibouti? Or was the real purpose of the campaign, as Mussolini on occasion boasted, craftily to act as a smokescreen for a coming Italian assault on Albania? Yet, even for that long contemplated event, preparations remained primitive.[112] Perhaps the most illuminating comment on the spat with France came from the King, who mused happily that 'destiny' might yet hand Corsica to Italian power, especially in a 'big crisis'.[113] The monarch's greed demonstrate that it was not necessary to be a convinced Fascist for an Italian leader to retain ambitions on a territory which even Ciano admitted was a place where a Corsican irredentism did not exist.[114]

In the New Year the press scolding of France rumbled on, but Italian policy shifted its attention to Britain. Neville Chamberlain and his Foreign Secretary, Lord Halifax, visited Rome in January 1939 – Mussolini found the latter a 'funereal' personality, who spread 'melancholy' wherever he went.[115] The British Prime Minister, who had been impressed by what he thought was the *Duce*'s 'quiet and reserved manner' at Munich,[116] was trying to utilise the good offices of the Italian dictator to reach what he hoped was the enigmatic Hitler with a last plan for appeasement. Chamberlain remained optimistic, easily appeased personally by small gestures as, for example, when Mussolini turned out at a banquet in evening dress rather than uniform.[117] The *Duce*, he reported, looked 'well' and was possessed of 'a strong sense of humour and an attractive smile', while being 'pleasant' in conversation. However, he 'had remained throughout absolutely loyal to Hitler'.[118] Ciano less charitably summed up the exchanges as amounting to a 'nil–all draw'.[119] Chamberlain had brought nothing concrete to offer the Italians.

In any case, before, during and after the visit, the real attention of Mussolini and Ciano was being paid to the ever active Germans. Ribbentrop had suggested that the Anti-Comintern Pact should be converted into a full-scale alliance, and the Italian leaders liked the idea.[120] Once again, however, their enthusiasm was limited. In January–February 1939 Mussolini rejected suggestions by his military chiefs that they should formalise a military treaty with Germany. The soldiers' fear of imminent French invasion was not shared by the *Duce*.[121] He even tried to whistle in the wind about the Germans, telling Ciano on 10 March that they were a military but not a warlike people; give them enough 'sausage, butter and beer, and a people's car', Mussolini declared, and they would cease troubling the world.[122]

Not for the first time, Mussolini's sentiments were peculiarly inapposite. On 15 March Hitler seized the rump of the Czech lands, while also acting as the patron for the priest Jozef Tiso, who became the somewhat unlikely clerical–fascist ruler of Slovakia. No attempt was made to warn the Italian leadership whom these developments took by complete surprise. A chagrined Mussolini muttered: 'The Italians will laugh at me. Every time Hitler takes a country he sends me a message.'[123] At the Villa Torlonia, Ciano found the *Duce* sullen, tired, old and convinced that no one could stem the German advance to hegemony in Europe.[124] Shortly after, the Grand Council reviewed the issue – momentously, the British had by then decided to oppose Nazi Germany should Poland be its next target and so set the conditions of the coming 'war for Danzig', the first of the second world wars. Bottai's description of events at the Council is telling. The members began by reviewing foreign press accounts of the international situation, but Mussolini took over the meeting as he vented his 'irony, anger, boredom, disgust, contempt'. These emotions then spread to the rest of the Grand Council. Just as a splenetic response to the demoplutocracies seemed imminent, in a less ebullient tone the *Duce* began to review German power. Here the evidence was salutary. The Germans were overwhelmingly strong militarily and demographically – 'eighty million' Germans outweighed 45 million Italians, Mussolini said ruefully. In any case, he repeated in what was becoming his *idée fixe*, there could be no more *giri di valtzer*.[125]

Like it or not, Fascist Italy was bound both ideologically and practically to the German side.[126]

One sphere of German superiority to which Mussolini referred with characteristic brevity was the economic. German industrial production, he noted, outperformed Italian by 12 to one. Mussolini loved to proclaim, as he informed a leading industrialist in 1937, that 'an economic issue has never stopped history'.[127] However, over recent years, processes had been underway which were binding Italy in trade of goods and men ever more tightly to the Nazi juggernaut, a fate which had been confirmed when a new commercial treaty was signed between the two totalitarian states in February 1939.[128] Of greatest significance for propaganda was the transfer of what ultimately totalled 500 000 Italian 'guest workers' to Germany.[129] The story of these emigrants from a country which had banned the word 'migration' from its vocabularies to a country which was pledged to become racially pure has much that is hallucinogenic about it. But there were also practical effects of the most alarming kind. The Italians in Germany were allowed to become hostages to fortune in many senses. Could the Fascist regime, which typically sent the workers off with great fanfare, hereafter contemplate a U-turn on this matter, or, indeed, on any aspect of Axis policy? What would it signify about the Italian dictatorship, if the workers did not come back? With its export of manpower, had Italy not become the 'first satellite'[130] of Nazi Germany?

Once again nightmares could not be cancelled from Italian imagining. As a Romanian diplomat brilliantly discerned:

> Mussolini had challenged Fate too long not to feel the threat of an ever-possible reverse. Like the too happy Polycrates, warned by gloomy forebodings, he seemed anxious to escape destiny. His association with Hitler, who could call on infinitely greater forces, was not without elements of uneasiness. He saw himself being dragged along the very road he had opened, a prisoner of the system he had created, and of the passions which he had unleashed – towards a goal which seemed to him to be at least uncertain. Having sowed the wind, he feared the whirlwind – a whirlwind over whose approach he had no control. He still hoped that his momentum would carry him safely between the rocks. His instinct, contrary to Hitler's, was not to charge headlong at obstacles; he wanted to avoid them with profit; but his consciousness of danger did not free him from the powers which had taken hold of him: old grudges, violent irritations, and constant surges of self-esteem. In face of the misfortune which he somehow perceived, his trouble was daily to become more emphatic.

Besides, a sense of personal inadequacy was interlarded with the ever more ominous international situation. Mussolini, the account concludes, 'was to tolerate at his side [Ciano] this lucid young sensualist as a warning that power was slipping from his grasp'.[131]

It was to dispel demeaning thoughts of any kind that the Mussolinian regime now finally invaded and absorbed Albania. It did so in as thuggish a manner as possible, attacking on Good Friday,[132] the day after Albanian Queen Geraldine had been delivered of a baby son. The prospect that Italy could obtain a protectorate without an act of force was rejected by Mussolini,[133] but he had left most preparation to Ciano and his circle. They did not do well. Despite the absence of any politicised opposition, the Albanian populace by no means surrendered their hearts and souls to Italian rule, knowing even better than Sicilians that regimes pass but everyday life continues. Victor Emmanuel acquired another kingdom for his crown, an Albanian Fascist party was soon organised, but Fascist rule remained superficial and costly. Even though Albania was in Europe, and Fascist aggression there assumed a sinister Nazi air, the territory rapidly assumed the character of another imperial outpost, scarcely absorbed into the 'totalitarian' state and left to languish in its dusty 'backwardness'.

The *Duce* should have been accustomed to the idea of bitter triumphs, but Albania stimulated an attack of pettishness. A peace plan drafted by Roosevelt, Mussolini remarked spitefully, was the product of 'galloping paralysis'.[134] Yet being mean to distant Americans solved little. The continuing crisis and the manifest inadequacies revealed when Italian forces tried to land in Albania – military observers talked about 'childish dilettantism' displayed there[135] – at last prompted some review of national armed might. After the German move on Prague, Mussolini had declared: 'The order for the day is this: more cannon, more ships, more planes. At whatever cost, by whatever means.'[136] However, 6 weeks later, Ciano admitted that Italian military power was 'a tragic bluff'. There were no reserves, and equipment even for defence was antiquated or non-existent. The *Duce*, he alleged sadly, had been gulled by the military.[137] Not long after, similarly depressing news about Italy's international balance of trade came from Guarneri[138] – the Minister for Exchange Controls had long been sceptical about his nation's ability to afford grand gestures in foreign policy and had passed on his advice to a *Duce* whom he deemed 'domineering', but 'open to reality'.[139] Empire of any kind, Guarneri warned, would simply 'swallow up Italy' with the expense involved.[140] The racial laws and the constant round of diplomatic crises were, for example, bad for tourism, the national treasure-trove, which fell by what he estimated was 60 per cent during the first six months of 1939.[141] Italy's economy was, in sum, 'precarious';[142] it could not absorb any more shocks; it could not sustain an international conflict.

A yawning gap between words and deeds was hard for the Fascist leadership to deny, and yet events were hurrying on. Mussolini was still talking belligerently about the 'inevitability' of war, but, somewhere in the fine print, he was trying to write in an admission that Italy needed peace for 'three' years or more (the number was meaningless, the chance to remain elastic everything).[143] Meanwhile, Ciano had journeyed to meet Ribbentrop in Milan and, at Mussolini's direct orders on 7 May, signed an alliance with Nazi Germany, the so-called 'Pact of Steel'.[144]

This major step taken, drift resumed. The King warned that, as soon as the Germans believed that they did not need Italy, they would show themselves to be 'the wretches they are'.[145] In response to such dismal prophesy, Mussolini remarked angrily: 'I am like a cat, sensible and prudent. But when I jump, I'm sure to land where I wish.' Could this be the moment, he wondered again, to suppress the House of Savoy?[146] And yet the *Duce* was not exactly himself ready to march. On 30 May he sent Hitler a meandering account why, though war was 'inevitable', it must be postponed until 'the end of 1942'. Italy had some minor tasks to complete, he admitted – the systematising of Libya and Albania, the pacification of Ethiopia, the transfer of its war industries from the Po valley to the South. It needed six new battleships, better artillery, improved morale (in this regard, he noted, with a last attempt to be patronising, the Germans would be sensible to calm relations with the Vatican). Autarchy must be refined further. Perhaps, he suggested, in the early stages of the future war, in 1942 or whenever, Italy could provide men, while Germany gave the means?[147]

Hitler did not demur, remarking politely how pleasant it would be again to meet the *Duce*. And so the last summer of European peace began to pass, with the Italian leadership doing little to change its behaviour or to amend the blatant deficiencies in the process of modernising either their military machine or their society. The Italian ambassador in Berlin was reporting that Stalin had no intention of pulling others' chestnuts from the fire and that the Soviet chief viewed with increasing impatience the patronisingly tardy Anglo-French attempts to reach an arrangement with the USSR.[148] There were pleasant exchanges with the victorious Franco, who did not hide his view that 'in its present state, Spain could not face a European war'.[149] In reply, Mussolini, himself only too ready to patronise any he could deem his inferiors, urged the *Caudillo* to 'go decisively towards the people', adding an invitation for Franco to visit Rome when he saw fit.[150] Then there was the Polish issue. On Danzig, Mussolini had every confidence that another arrangement could be reached, as it had been at Munich, though of course he swore that Italy would intervene should Britain launch a general war.[151] But, to Italian eyes, all seemed quiet enough on the northern front and Ciano jotted into his diary sarcastic asides about the 'alarmism' of some of his diplomatic staff.[152]

How false his optimisim was Ciano discovered on 11 August when he met the egregious Ribbentrop at Salzburg. Ciano had arrived bearing a message from the *Duce* that general war would be 'disastrous for everyone'.[153] But, in response, Ribbentrop and, behind him, Hitler and the rest of the German leadership were 'implacable'.[154] An interminable ten hours of discussion with Ribbentrop and a meeting with the *Führer* did not even minimally change the Germans' minds, or deflect their decision that now was the appropriate moment for war. It did not matter that Italy disagreed, or that the Germans had said in the past that they would wait for some years before touching off a general conflagration. Ciano returned to Rome, convinced, somewhat petulantly, that he had been 'betrayed', and suddenly converted into a Germanophobe.[155] Even greed was now held in check. Only sheer terror of the Nazis could justify the survival of the Axis. Fascist foreign policy, at least as managed by the son-in-law, had collapsed.

But what of Mussolini? When, on 13 August, Ciano went to see him at the Palazzo Venezia, the *Duce* 'was varied in his reactions. First he agreed I was right. Then he said that honour forced him to march alongside the Germans. Finally he contended that he wanted his part of the booty in Croatia and Dalmatia'.[156] Although Ciano did not remark it, Mussolini's singling out of these territories contained some irony, since his choice seemed to imply the creation on Italy's northeastern borders of a bulwark against Germandom.[157] Over the next days, while the *Duce*'s mind flickered from one possibility to another, 'fear of Hitler's ire' was hard to suppress. What, Mussolini asked Ciano, if Italian backsliding induced the Nazis to give up on Poland and 'settle accounts with Italy'?[158]

Certainly, at this time of extreme crisis, the decision-making process, or lack of it, under charismatic rule was plain. Some months before, Mussolini had boasted that Ministers in his government were the equivalent of 'electric light-bulbs which I turn on or off as I wish'.[159] Now there was no process by which the international situation could be properly illuminated and reviewed, no way to reach the future except by stumbling into it. Leading members of the *Duce*'s entourage remained in the dark about what was happening over Danzig, although the allegedly intelligent Bottai wondered unhelpfully whether a conflict had surfaced between the 'Dionysian and Nietzschean' spirit of Berlin and the 'formalist and juridical' essence of Rome.[160]

When Mussolini and Ciano met, their discussions developed a pattern which would continue for some months. Ciano, outraged by German bad faith, rejected the idea of being their ally in war. Mussolini, however much he might twist and turn, could see no alternative to accepting the German alliance.[161] He approached Hitler with a tortuous case to the effect that Italy was not ready to join a general war prompted by a German invasion of Poland but that, if Germany was driven to act after negotiations failed through the 'intransigence of others', 'Italy will intervene on the German side'.[162] In practice, Nazi Germany had further shocks for its hapless ally. On 21 August the Ribbentrop–Molotov pact was announced (it was signed two days later), yet again with no prior information having been sent to Rome.[163] Vittorio Mussolini later claimed that, when he saw the news in *Il Resto del Carlino*, he thought it must be a typographical error.[164] Ciano believed the deal was 'undoubtedly a master coup' which had 'turned the European situation upside down'. In his mind, the stocks of the Axis rose a little. He hoped other matters need not be precipitated but now he, too, was anxious to grab 'booty in Croatia and Dalmatia'.[165]

Cooler thoughts soon revived, as Italy's military chiefs were emphatic in their delineation of the country's state of absolute unpreparedness. The King, too, expressed his sympathy for 'neutrality' (but he did not forget to request a military command for his son should there be war).[166] Mussolini was left to explain to Hitler that, although he 'completely approved' of the Ribbentrop–Molotov pact and agreed with the German position that Polish intransigence was not to be tolerated for ever, Italy could only intervene speedily if Germany sent a massive amount of 'war supplies and primary products'. They would be needed, Mussolini added disingenuously, so that Italy 'could resist the thrust which France and Britain will direct primarily against us'.[167] Ciano sardonically observed that, if the Germans granted the Italian wish list,[168] the transport would require 17 000 trains, hauling 170 million tonnes of goods, and expressed his pious amazement that the Germans could think of taking on Britain and France when their own reserves were so slight.[169]

On 26 August Mussolini wrote again to Hitler, beseeching the *Führer* to imagine his 'state of mind at finding himself forced by influences superior to his will' to stay out of the great conflict.[170] Hitler in reply asked for more immigrant workers and sought the *Duce*'s 'psychological backing' as the crisis evolved.[171] Mussolini did try to nudge the Germans towards a peaceful resolution of the Danzig question[172] and may have briefly dreamed of resuming the role he had played at Munich.[173] Ciano still anxiously watched his mood swings – one day reconciled to events, the next day restless for action.[174] Above all, the *Duce* was adamant that there be no reiteration of the word 'neutrality', so resonant of 1914 and Liberal foreign policy. But Fascist Italy, too, was not destined to enter a second world war at its beginning. Mussolini may have made the trains run on time, as his propaganda declared, but wars, it seemed, were a different matter.

Bocchini let the Vatican know that he had told his chief that 'all Italy loathes war and the people do not want to fight for the Germans'.[175] Of the other leading Fascists, only Starace flirted with favouring immediate entry, though even he pulled back when he discovered, to his amazement, that the rationing plan which, he had boasted, could be applied at a moment's notice actually did not exist.[176] Franco and Salazar, the clerical dictator of Portugal, approved the prospect of Italy standing on the sidelines.[177] Beset by such voices, Mussolini bowed to the inevitable. As Ciano described it, on the night of 2 September:

> The *Duce* is convinced of the need to remain neutral but he is not pleased about it. Every time he can, he refers to the possibility of action on our part. The Italians, by contrast, are in absolute totality happy about the decisions which have been taken.[178]

Two days later, with Britain, France and Germany now legally at war, Mussolini fretted anew about the 'common destiny' which, he was sure, bound Nazism and Fascism.[179] The conflict was of course a curious contest which had pitted the Nazis against the reluctant Western powers, a war well described as 'phoney' for all but the suffering Poles, who were being so brutally overrun in a Nazi *Blitzkrieg*. Was Italy's non-belligerency (as it was perforce to be called to avoid the word neutrality) equally phoney? Or were Fascism and the *Duce*-dictator the real phoneys? A generation earlier, Nationalists had talked cheerfully of Liberal Italy's need to undergo the 'test' of the First World War and had won 'Prof. Mussolini' to their side. How might the Fascist regime survive the test of a fresh conflict? Could it, or should it, seek to reckon the advantages of this side or that? Or was Fascist Italy inevitably required to join Nazi Germany in upholding the murderous cause of universal fascism?

16

Germany's ignoble second, 1939–1941

WHEN, in the aftermath of his meetings at Salzburg, Ciano was trying to push the *Duce* in an anti-German direction, he warned him that he had become Hitler's *secondo poco brillante* (less than smart second).[1] The reference was to a comment which Kaiser Wilhelm II had made about his Austrian ally in the First World War – the sentiment was intended to be friendly but was at once taken as demeaning. Ciano's phrasing was meant to counter those frequently expressed worries of his father-in-law that Fascist Italy had resumed that diplomatic dance in which Liberal Italy had engaged only to cut a poor figure with its promiscuous *giri di valtzer*. Mussolini and Ciano were not the only contemporaries to notice that history was bidding to repeat itself, and any later historian must be alert to the structural implications of possible repetition. In September 1939 world war (of a kind) broke out. Italy did not enter it. In August 1914 world war had begun and Italy stayed on the sidelines until May 1915. When it joined the conflict, its enemies were Germany and Austria-Hungary, in July 1914 its associates in the Triple Alliance (and in an accompanying series of military arrangements). At the time of the First World War ideology and economic interest may have tied Italy to France and Britain, but, during the nine months of the *intervento*, it was possible to imagine Italy uniting with either of the competing blocs (or staying out of the war altogether).

Was the same to happen in 1939–40? The answer, of course, is no. But did Fascist Italy on 10 June 1940 enter its Second World War for structural reasons to do with its position as the least of the Great Powers? Or, rather, did Mussolini unite with Hitler out of common ideological fanaticism and passion for war? Or was everything decided by events? Long-term versus short-term causes, the role of the individual compared with society and *mentalité*, the issues surrounding Italy's involvement in the Second World War are the classic ones of historical causation.

Italian entry also raises major questions about documentation, given the central role of Ciano's *Diary* in any recounting of the story. Ciano paints a vivid picture: on one side the *Duce*, who, as another diarist put it, wanted 'war as a child wants the moon';[2] on the other side, Ciano, a youthful Laocoön, struggling as long as he could to restrain his father-in-law and resist the fatal attraction of Hitler and his Nazi forces. Perhaps this epic conflict is what actually happened. Nonetheless, an analyst needs to be careful before being transfixed by Ciano's words and images. During the history of Fascism, rhetorical meaning should rarely be assumed to be simple and singular. No doubt, from September 1939 to June 1940 Mussolini and Ciano occupied their rival corners and spouted their conflicting words. Yet, each was in a way an *alter ego*; they incarnated the two faces of Italian Fascism. In any case, when they were not phrase-making, each waited and watched the battlefront. The context of years of verbal and real warmongering, and of Mussolini's linking of his status and personality to the idea of Fascist revolution, mattered, but so, too, did the problem of discerning who would win the war, when and how, with the least threat and the greatest advantage to Italy.

The first days of non-belligerency saw a pattern emerging. Italian public opinion rejoiced at the decision to stay out of the conflict.[3] After a brief rush on the banks,[4] the stock market rocketed up.[5] The Vatican was pleased.[6] Bocchini, Bottai and Federzoni made no secret of their relief that Mussolini had not opted for war.[7] Lanzillo wrote sentimentally of the allure of 'serene neutrality'.[8] Farinacci, by contrast, inveighed against 'cretinous' opponents of the Axis, and bitterly opposed the idea of joining the war against Germany in a cause which he described as that of 'international Anti-Fascism, runaways and the Jews'. But even he did not think that the quality of what was on close examination no more than Italy's 'toy army' permitted present engagement in the war.[9] Franco and Metaxas sent less flamboyant notification of their approval of the Italian line.[10] Even German crowds lacked enthusiasm, as Massimo Magistrati, the brother-in-law of Ciano stationed at the Berlin embassy, told him: 'Except for the issue of the Polish corridor, this is a war fought for essentially negative ends and it is dangerous for all'.[11] Only Mussolini, it seemed, was on tenterhooks, as ever grumpy at mention of the parallel to 1914–15,[12] unconvinced by the efforts of Ciano – the son who never was – to persuade him that the war would be long, arduous and won by the British,[13] anxious to do something or to be seen to be doing something. What would the Germans think, he asked before trying to persuade Hitler (and himself) that 'the attitude of Italy which is not a neutral attitude is more useful than our actual intervention'. Had Italy entered the conflict from the start and been at once attacked by the full fire-power of Britain and France, he reasoned, then the trouble which would have resulted 'would probably have annulled the effect of the success of the Germans in Poland'.[14]

Later in the same letter, Mussolini remarked that at least Italy could keep the Balkans from roiling out of control, before underlining that he currently preserved 'a certain latitude on the political and diplomatic terrain which could be of great benefit also to Germany'.[15] Mussolini, in other words, was wondering whether the formula utilised at Munich could not be resuscitated,[16] even after the outbreak of war. Ascribing to the *Führer* his own mentality and method, he continued to expect that Hitler would soon unveil a major peace initiative.[17] Again he was wrong; and neither did Ciano's scheming about a bloc of Balkan neutrals get Italy far,[18] all the more because the Minister of Foreign Affairs and, presumably, the *Duce* could still scent 'booty' in Croatia – Ciano ingenuously imagined obtaining it with Anglo-French approval sprung from an understanding that Italy was blocking a German move south-east.[19] It was all very well Mussolini telling party hierarchs that now was the moment for 'the most ruthless political realism. The era when we helped others is over. The world starts and finishes with us'.[20] But the problem remained to find the policy which was best for Italy, Fascism and Mussolini himself.

In that regard Ciano saw intriguing possibilities opening up when, on 30 November, Soviet forces launched their 'Winter War' against Finland. The sudden and unexplained signature of the Ribbentrop–Molotov pact continued to rankle in Italy, where, in re-evoking anti-communism, Ciano could seem to be both a good Fascist and a good bourgeois. Even Mussolini agreed crossly that the German smashing of Poland was only doing Stalin's work for him.[21] Ciano's friends at the golf club were ready to believe that poor little Finland was the object of barbarous assault, and the nation's gilded university students were also reported to be much moved by the fate of the Finns.[22] So, in early December, Ciano accepted the idea of sending up to fifty Italian planes to the Finns through Germany, and there was talk of Fascist 'volunteers' heading for Helsinki.[23] In the end, these schemes were barren, although Ciano only reluctantly bowed to the

German blocking of the consignment of aircraft,[24] while continuing to lecture the Soviets on Fascist Italy's longstanding ideological commitment to anti-communism.[25] As if trying to justify a major move against the USSR (as a proxy for the real enemy, Nazi Germany), Ciano asked his ambassador, Augusto Rosso, to weigh up Stalin's foreign policy, to try to detect how longstanding the friendship with Germany might be and to assess the motivation behind Soviet 'expansionism'.[26] In reply, Rosso offered sage advice about the Russian national self-interest which conditioned the ideological commitments.[27] But his more telling reaction was to note with some bitterness the fact that, for the first time in three years at his post, he had been asked some intelligent questions and requested actively to participate in the framing of policy.[28] Between the lines of his response, it was plain that he was another who feared that Ciano was very young, and very inexperienced in the real world, and who knew that Mussolini did not take his professional diplomats seriously.

For all the well-founded ambassadorial whinges, the most important Italian relationship remained the bilateral one with Germany. In this regard the war quickened efforts to deal with the problem of German-speaking people living in the Alto Adige. Mussolini and his regime had frequently expatiated on the need to Italianise these border lands, and they could claim that, as far back as 1866, Mazzini had set the Brenner watershed as the border between the German and Italian worlds.[29] In 1939 it was estimated that 95 per cent of public posts in the area were in Italian hands, though Germans composed 75 per cent of the population.[30] Hitler apart, German nationalists were at least as uncompromising as the Fascists on the issue, with President Hindenburg, for one, having saluted 'our co-nationals beyond the frontier indissolubly bound to us'.[31]

Shortly after the *Anschluss*, Goering launched the idea of salving the Axis in this regard through a 'population transfer', or what is today called ethnic cleansing.[32] By May 1939 Himmler had drafted a plan to resettle up to 200 000 South Tyrolers in the Nazi Reich, describing it as a 'perhaps historically unique, generous procedure'.[33] Mussolini was at first somewhat embarrassed by the thought of expelling part of his populace, and the Germans, despite Hitler's regular assurances that the Brenner was Italian 'for ever', also moved slowly.[34] None the less, the idea of a racial removal to be measured 'scientifically' (a 'final solution' to the Tyrol problem) well fitted the Nazi *mentalité*. The Germans of the Alto Adige became the prototype for the massive population moves planned and partially achieved by the Nazis once the war began.[35] By 21 October, after much hard bargaining over detail, an agreement was reached. In a subsequent plebiscite in which German propagandists were said to have threatened German-speakers that, if they did not opt for Germany, they would swiftly be relegated to Albania or Sicily, some 185 000 chose to be moved to the Reich, while 82 000 wanted to stay where they were.[36] The execution of the scheme was not easy, however, and, by September 1943, only 130 000 had actually taken out German citizenship and 52 000 of them were still in Italy.[37]

Ciano had been distracted from these events because of the illness and death of his sister Maria. However, on 25 October he was displeased to learn that the *Duce* was having another bout of Germanophilia and was 'proposing to write a letter to Hitler, saying that, in the present state of play, Italy can act as a moral and economic reserve for Germany, but that as a follow-up it can also take on a military role'. Mussolini, his son-in-law noticed apprehensively, again wanted 'to do something', being emphatic that 'the Axis and the Pact of Steel still exist and indeed function fully'.[38]

Yet, on most days, Ciano's stocks seemed on the rise. On 31 October Mussolini indulged in what he liked to call another 'changing of the guard', that is, a reworking of his government. The great loser in this re-shuffle was Starace, replaced as Secretary of the Party (a position which, since 1937, had been granted ministerial status) by Ettore Muti, a political unknown aged 37.[39] From a humble background in Ravenna, Muti had married a shipbuilder's daughter and become a local notable.[40] To Mussolini, Muti had the virtue of being a Romagnole; to Ciano, he seemed encouragingly hostile to Germany, and a man 'who will follow me like a lamb'.[41] Starace was briefly given an appointment in the MVSN,[42] but soon rusticated altogether, and left to bewail his fate in a regular but unanswered correspondence with his *Duce*. Mussolini refused point-blank to see his old agent, and Starace, deprived of the warmth of the charisma in which he, of all Italians, most genuinely believed, faded into a pathetic old man, chivvied by his surviving acquaintances and utterly deprived of a purpose in life.[43] Muti, meanwhile, was soon at sea in his new office – by January 1940 secret memos emphasised the failure of party propaganda to create 'a proper political consciousness' among the people and the special opposition to the idea of war entry among Italian women, who were resentfully hoarding supplies of oil, beans, rice and soap.[44] Shortly afterwards, another report detected that attendance at Church services was up, and Catholic belief was everywhere augmented by fear of the continuing war and the possibility of Italian entry.[45]

Apart from the elevation of Muti, the most important change in the government was that Alessandro Pavolini took over the Ministry of Popular Culture, commencing his own rise to become a fanatical upholder of revolutionary Fascism. In 1939, however, he was still regarded as one who questioned the German alliance[46] and who belonged to Ciano's circle – the Foreign Minister's considerable vanity was enhanced by a description of the new government as 'the Ciano cabinet'. Ciano noted with some satisfaction that job-hunters now flocked to his door.[47] Three other changes in the government worth recording were the replacement of Guarneri by the Fascist economist, Raffaello Riccardi,[48] and the appointment of Generals Ubaldo Soddu[49] and Francesco Pricolo[50] as the new Under-Secretaries of War and the Air. Each of these three appointments gave promise of a new fervour in war preparation.

After all, Mussolini had not ceased to nourish his frustration at Italy's continued exclusion from 'great events'.[51] Bocchini dared to wonder out loud if the *Duce*'s fidgets were inspired by the damage done to his psyche by a youthful bout of syphilis.[52] Yet a spurious medicalising of matters did not really help analysis, and the war situation remained ominous. Italian observers in Germany freely admitted that they 'hated' the Germans, but nevertheless believed that Hitler would win the war.[53] The peace might be another matter since, ambassador Bernardo Attolico reported, German 'terror' in Poland was so bloody that it would take at least a generation to repair.[54] In almost every way charting the ideal path was difficult. With the receipt of contradictory and alarming news, Mussolini was not the only member of the elite to fluctuate in his views. The hide-bound little King, for example, might intimate to Ciano that he was a convinced 'neutralist', but, shortly afterwards, he confessed he did not like the French either.[55] The monarch was expressing the eternal problem of the least of the Great Powers – how could a crisis be milked for advantage cash down and at no cost to Italy?

Mussolini, arguably more tough-minded than the rest, could see only one real answer to Italy's national dilemma and that was Germany. To the disgust of Ciano, who had convinced himself that entry into the war on the German side would be 'a crime and a piece of idiocy' which must not happen,[56] Mussolini, in the New Year, wrote at length to his 'friend', the *Führer*. Probing for a weakness, he began with a long excursion into the interpretation of the

Ribbentrop–Molotov pact and its reception in Spain, Britain, Finland, and elsewhere. Any further tightening of Soviet–Nazi ties, he warned, could have 'catastrophic repercussions in Italy where Anti-Bolshevik unanimity, especially among the Fascist masses, is absolute, granitic, and goes without discussion'. Contrary to what would become his position in 1942–43, for the present Mussolini had no qualms in telling Hitler: 'The solution to your Lebensraum is in Russia and not elsewhere'. He also remembered that a dose of Anti-Semitism was bound to please his colleague, so he reminded Hitler that Nazism could not lower its 'Anti-Bolshevik and Anti-Semitic flag'. He fully approved the idea of Poland being cleansed of its Jews and praised 'your project of assembling them all in a great ghetto at Lublin'. And yet what, he asked, about some realism on Poland? Could not a 'modest, disarmed' Poland be reconstituted in a way that might allow peace to return. The USA (another subject on which the *Duce* proved highly erratic over the years) would never permit the 'total defeat of the democracies', he warned. As for Italian preparations, their pace could not be forced, but the *Führer* could be sure that Italian entry would occur at the 'most profitable and decisive time'.[57] Having crafted his words with what he must have thought was a fine Italian hand, Mussolini sent a briefer, six-point, summary to Ciano. His key conclusion, the *Duce* wrote, was that, 'unless Germany commits irreparable errors, we shall not denounce the alliance'. There was no way Italian interests could be served by a switch to the other side. By the coming summer, Italian preparations ought to have reached a level capable of having 'a decisive influence'.[58]

Despite such hints of future action, the news remained grim for any leader seeking to assert a major role for Italy. Ciano was sure that, rather than preparing militarily, Italian improvidence was actually increasing and had become 'absolute'.[59] Badoglio,[60] choosing a date sufficiently far into the future as to be meaningless, maintained instead that Italy might be ready in '1942', and, by mid-January, even Mussolini was ready to acknowledge Italy's weakness in arms.[61] Bocchini, whose reputation as a trencherman may have made him especially alert to such matters, thought that even basic foods were becoming scarce.[62] Riccardi expressed his fear that Italy would soon dribble away what was left of its foreign currency reserves,[63] and not all his colleagues were convinced by Mussolini's announcement to cabinet that 'financial problems do not exist for states. States rise and fall after they are afflicted by defeat in war or by internal disintegration'. When Paolo Thaon di Revel, the Minister of Finance, tried to turn discussion onto the historical precedent of the French revolution and its disastrous printing of paper money, Mussolini responded: 'A revolution must be intelligent. Eventually the French revolution stopped being intelligent.' However, to Bottai's naïve dismay, he did not explain further just what he understood was the ideal method of financing a Fascist war effort.[64] To display Fascist bravado on his own part, Thaon di Revel scandalised Ciano by talking cheerfully about the way Italy could always overcome any balance of payments difficulty through a firesale of its infinite supplies of 'priceless' works of art and, not to be outbid in cynicism, Mussolini thought his Minister had come up with a good idea.[65]

Domestic opinion might ebb and flow, but the real problem was still Germany and the auguries in Berlin continued to be very hard to read. What did it mean that Hitler, Ribbentrop and Goering had been closeted for five hours to discuss Mussolini's letter and as yet had still sent no formal reply?[66] If, as Attolico advised, Hitler was not 'a normal chief but an abnormal one', where might his whim take him, especially now that his entourage did not hesitate to display profound 'reserve' about Italy?[67] And what was happening at the front? What if, as the King wondered to Ciano, the onset of spring brought German gains and German victory?[68] What, too, about 'booty'? Should Italy ignore the plots of the Croatian fascist chief Pavelić, whose present blandishments included Italian advantage in Kosovo, a full union between 'Catholic' Croatia and Italy, and the consequent blocking of German penetration of Italy's north-eastern frontier?[69]

With these and other predicaments confronting him, it was little wonder that Mussolini again began to complain of stomach pains[70] and to rail against the Italian people. As he told Ciano savagely, in words which were disguised to conceal his own evident failings (and those of his son-in-law): 'The people must be kept lined up and in uniform from daylight till dusk and given a thumping and then another one, just to be going on with.'[71]

At this difficult juncture, in late February 1940 the Italian leadership was visited by Sumner Welles, the personal agent of US President Roosevelt, on a 'peace mission'. Welles was greeted by a friendly Ciano who remarked: 'No country would want to have Germany as a neighbour. Italy now has her as a neighbour and we must do the best we can to get on with her.'[72] Mussolini was more overtly depressed. To Welles,

he seemed fifteen years older than his actual age of fifty-six. He was ponderous and static rather than vital. He moved with an elephantine motion; every step appeared an effort. He was heavy for his height, and his face in repose fell in rolls of flesh. His close-cropped hair was snow white.[73]

If Welles is to be believed, here was a *Duce* visibly suffering from being the leader of a non-belligerent Italy, a country with no place to go. To be sure, in his own accounts, Mussolini was equally scathing about Welles and his President, dismissing the exchanges with his visitor, since, he said in one of his characteristically rapid summations, Americans were eternally superficial, while Italians judged matters in depth.

After his trip to Rome, Welles went off to the other European capitals, only returning to Italy in the middle of March. Now he found Mussolini much recovered physically and psychologically,[74] and talking expansively but without precision about a revival of the Four Power Pact.[75] In the interim the *Duce* had received another visitor, Ribbentrop, hated by Ciano who decamped to his golf course, but, on this occasion at least, welcomed by the *Duce*. To Mussolini's relief, Hitler had finally replied to the letter of 5 January and done so in friendly vein. Germany's flirtation with the USSR had its limits, Mussolini learned, as he read over the note three times, and the *Führer* went on regarding Mussolini and Italy as his real friends. Really nothing had changed – Germany and Italy were still the twin 'totalitarian states' which Britain and France were determined to destroy. The Axis continued (and Germany would be helpful over coal supplies; negotiations with Britain had done nothing to overcome Italy's perpetually pressing need for secure energy imports).[76]

In lengthy meetings on 10 and 11 March Ribbentrop repeated these sentiments and added the tantalising news that a German military initiative was imminent. Hitler wanted to see the *Duce* very soon to say more; an appointment was made for the next week at the resonant site of the old Austrian border. Relieved of his worry that the German alliance had collapsed and Italy lost appeal compared with the USSR, Mussolini declared at his second meeting with the German Foreign Minister that 'it is practically impossible for Italy to keep out of the conflict. At the right moment, it will enter the war and do so on Germany's side, but in a parallel way, because Italy has its own problems to resolve'. Italy, he added, must 'have free access to the [Atlantic] ocean'; its war should be a Mediterranean one. The *Duce*'s confidence had revived sufficiently for him to make snide references to the diplomatic 'slowness' of the Japanese and to boast that the island of

Pantelleria, Italy's outpost in the Sicilian straits, was 'impregnable'.[77] Late at night he rang Claretta Petacci for some phone solace, admitting that he was 'utterly tired out from the talks', but stating that the 'die was now cast'. No doubt pleased to be impressing somebody, he prophesied that Germany was about to win the war through its power, its military training and its 'dumfounding weapons', the terror of which would soon be revealed.[78]

Was this, then, the final decision for war, and, what is more, for Italy's own *guerra parallela* (parallel war)?[79] Maybe yes, but more likely no. Once Ribbentrop had gone back over the Alps, Mussolini again fell prey to 'nerves'. Just what had he said (the King was wondering about that, too, and had it suggested for the first time since 1925 that a future without the *Duce* might be imaginable)?[80] By 16 March Mussolini had diluted his promise to one of 'potential solidarity' with the Nazis. For now, he stated, he would not enter the war.[81] But that resolve was as equivocal as any other.

On 18 March the *Duce* travelled to the Brenner border, where, unlike sunny springtime Rome, it was snowing. The *Führer* arrived and proceeded to dominate the conversation (as was becoming his wont). Germany would win the war, he was adamant about that. 'The fates of Italy and Germany were indissolubly bound', he added. The pact with the USSR had only been good politics and, anyway, Russia was maturing in a 'Slav–Muscovite direction, and moving away from Judeo-internationalist Bolshevism'. Mussolini was left to nod his agreement and affirm that he had been the first to want to deal with the USSR on realistic grounds.[82] According to Ciano, the *Duce* also acknowledged his 'fascination' for the Nazi leader.[83] But he did get back to Rome without having made any ultimate commitment. On 31 March he told Ciano, the King and his military chiefs that the current situation was still 'extremely fluid'. Once again about to be proved wrong, he doubted the present practicality of a German offensive. If Italy did not want to end up like Switzerland, it must eventually enter the war, and logic still decreed that would be on the Nazi side, since, if Italy swung over to the other grouping, it would draw down on itself a German attack, which it would have to resist alone. What Italy really wanted, Mussolini concluded in words which had occurred also to Liberal leaders before 1922, indeed to virtually every Italian politician since Cavour, was to enter a short war and to have its entry prove decisive.[84]

With the onset of spring even in northern climes the fog of the war began to lift. On 1 March Hitler had given the order to prepare an invasion of Norway and on 9 April the attack was launched. In subsequent weeks, British landings at various Norwegian North Sea ports proved unavailing. Buoyed by the easy victories, Hitler wrote at once to his Italian colleague, both to claim victory and to hail 'a great success for our [mutual] Cause'.[85] Mussolini's first reaction to the news was sullen, again giving little sign that the *Duce* was impelled by his commitment to 'universal fascism' (although, in early April, he did make an another attempt to co-ordinate his possible policy with that of Franco).[86] Rather than wasting time congratulating the Nazis, the *Duce* homilised on the shift he now detected in Italian opinion. The people were 'a whore', he concluded darkly, who simply ran after a 'conquering male'.[87] When translated into a letter back to the *Führer*, the alleged state of national public opinion was converted into a 'staunch *Stimmung*, hostile to the Allies'.[88]

There was no doubt that the German triumphs were having an effect on Italians of whatever class or politics. Although Carlo Favagrossa, to be appointed Under-Secretary for War Production (reporting directly to the *Duce*) on 23 May, warned that Italy had made no serious preparations for any but the briefest campaign,[89] the ministers in charge of finance had swung behind the Germans, as had Muti.[90] Mussolini was as calm as any, saying on 22 April that Italy might enter the war in '1941',[91] and, three days later, that Fascism would join the conflict, but only when it possessed 'the mathematical certainty of winning'.[92] Ciano was rapidly becoming isolated in his surviving hostility to Germany. Secure among his friends at the golf club, he was indiscreet enough to wonder what occasion might demand the arrest of his father-in-law[93] and, on 17 April, horrified Bottai by suggesting that Mussolini was only a little man, especially compared with Hitler. As Bottai confided to his diary, in phrases cribbed from a schoolboy's religious manual (and perhaps meant eventually to reach his *Duce*):

> I stayed silent. I did not dare to confess the pain at the centre of my being. Our generation gets everything from Mussolini. It is Mussolini. It is not possible to compare him apart from us. [It can only be done by acknowledging that] he is in us and we in him.[94]

While Bottai, in his ingenuous way, was clinging to a Fascist ideology or belief system of some sort, events were propelling the nation towards a decision. With the barely contested Nazi occupation of Norway, both the King and Badoglio began to reconstruct themselves as 'not anti-German',[95] and their surviving caution was blasted by further changes at the front. On 10 May German armies swept forward across the Low Countries and France, with Hitler informing his Italian colleague in appropriately Caesarian words that the advance amounted to his 'crossing of the Rubicon'.[96] Italian intervention was now all but certain and yet Mussolini was still on occasion indecisive. On 10 May he thought the Germans had won; on 11 May that it might be better for Italy to wait.[97] He could also savour digression, blasting the Papacy to Ciano as 'a cancer which gnaws at our proper national life'. All he needed to do, he said in one of his studied bursts of rhetorical savagery, was to summon the men of the 'seven cities' of his Romagna, and King and Pope could be hunted out together and for ever.[98] That tirade out of the way with no indication that it was meant to be followed by action, in regard to the real matter of the war on 17 May Mussolini again underlined the need for calm (and present inaction).[99] Yet, on the previous day, he had given a speech about the penalty of Italy being reduced to a 'second rank power' if it did not enter the conflict.[100]

But the options for the Italians were narrowing into non-existence. As if to cancel his recent past, Ciano slipped away to his virtual fiefdom in Albania,[101] to be greeted by cheers for *Duce!* Ciano! which Bottai maliciously thought he heard as *Duce* Ciano![102] Somewhere in the opaque administrative processes of Fascist Italy a decision was being made. On 29 May Mussolini met Badoglio and the other military chiefs, having privately informed his Chief of General Staff that he was sure the war would be over by September and that Italy needed 'a few thousand dead to be able to attend the peace conference as a belligerent'.[103] In the more formal surrounds of the meeting, the *Duce* summoned the spirit of the King to his side, urging that Italy could not stay out of the war. Ordering his thoughts with unconscious meaning, Mussolini underlined the fact that 'we absolutely cannot avoid the war; we cannot fight it with the allies; we can only fight it alongside Germany'. Germany possessed an overwhelming ground and air supremacy which not even untoward behaviour by the USA could check. As for the Italian army, its preparation might not have been ideal, but it could serve. War would commence 'across every frontier' on 5 June.[104]

The following day Hitler was sent the same news, with Mussolini emphasising that 'the command of all armed forces will be assumed by me'.[105] Badoglio and Favagrossa retained doubts about having to participate in any serious fighting[106] and, with German approval, the entry was put back another five days. However, finally, late on the afternoon of 10 June Mussolini spoke from the balcony of the Palazzo Venezia to the crowd which had been hurriedly assembled – the order approving the demonstration had been given only the day before.[107] 'Destiny', the *Duce* announced, had decreed war: 'We go into the field against the plutocratic and reactionary democracies of the West, who have repeatedly blocked the march, and even threatened the existence of the Italian people'. 'Our conscience', he said, is 'absolutely clear'. 'Honour, self-interest and the future' could not be ignored. Mixing his metaphors, he explained; 'we want to snap the territorial and military chains which suffocate us in our sea. A people of forty-five million souls cannot really be free if it does not have free access to the Ocean'. Moreover, the *Duce* added, combining the rhetorics of Fascism and Nationalism,

> this gigantic struggle is only a phase in the logical development of our revolution; it is the struggle of a poor people against those who wish to starve us with their retention of all the riches and gold of the earth. It is a struggle of the fecund and young peoples against barren peoples slipping to their sunset. It is the struggle of two centuries and two ideas.[108]

From Spain, Franco sent his cordial approval and the promise that he would at once alter Spain's position on the war to one of 'non-belligerency', with an implied promise that, for Spain, too, the present would prove just a staging post before entry on the (victorious) Axis side.[109] More soulfully, Ciano jotted into his diary his reaction to the turn of events: 'I am sad, very sad. The adventure begins. May God help Italy.'[110] With still greater insight, a retired liberal and nationalist diplomat wrote: 'Strange to say, the general feeling is one of relief. The trying period of uncertainty is over. The die is cast for better or for worse.'[111] Or was the most telling omen the fact that 10 June 1940 was the sixteenth anniversary of the murder of Giacomo Matteotti? Mussolini had chosen to enter a perilous war with the incarnadine stain of that notorious crime still unwashed from his hands. Blood was indeed destined to call for blood.

Six months after Italy's entry into the war, the British Prime Minister Churchill declared, for blatantly tactical reasons, that the responsibility for the Italian choice was borne by 'one man alone'. This phrase has echoed through the historiography, all the more because ascribing 'guilt' to Mussolini has so fitted the self-interest and the ideology of a range of historians (whose interpretation is bolstered by the graphic detail of Ciano's *Diary*). Given that the Italian war effort was soon shown to be a disaster, and one which culminated in the embarrassing and cynical *sauve qui peut* of the old ruling elites of the nation on 8 September 1943, when Badoglio and King Victor Emmanuel bungled an attempt to change sides, there has been every reason for Italians to single out Mussolini for blame. Indeed, it is hard to find an Italian historian who does not accept the intentionalist position that the Great Man was here decisive. The revisionist De Felice, for example, agreed that 'one man alone' had taken Italy into the war, although, in his opinion, Mussolini's motivation was at least in part the creditable one of a suspicion of Nazi Germany and a desire somehow to restrict its hegemony.[112]

Yet there are grounds for doubting the totality and singularity of Mussolini's power, as my account of the swerves of the *Duce*'s political line through the period of non-belligerency has indicated. For all the verbal discomfort Mussolini expressed about continuing peace, he did not actually enter the war until it indeed seemed won by his fearsome German ally. Measured mathematically (to adapt a cherished Mussolinian metaphor), Fascist Italy watched the front more carefully than Liberal Italy had done in 1914–15. Would any Italian leader, it may be asked, who believed in the myth that Italy was or ought to be a Great Power, have waited longer than Mussolini did? Counter-factual history is hard to disprove. However, the question remains a significant one, all the more because there is plenty of evidence that other Italians, great and small,[113] were ending their doubts about war entry and disguising their dislike of Nazi Germany in the weeks of the Fall of France. By June 1940 even the Catholic Church was reconciled to the idea of a brief Italian participation in a victorious war.[114] There is every reason, in other words, to think that, in the special circumstances of mid-June 1940, Mussolini had made a 'decision' from which few demurred.

Unarguable, however, is the fact that the war entry was proved with astonishing swiftness a mistake. The 'test' even of Italy's relatively peripheral and undemanding Second World War graphically illustrated the limitations of Fascism and the superficiality of Mussolini's purported revolution, just as it made manifest the fatuity of the ambitions for international 'greatness' which had been nurtured in the minds of educated members of the Italian nation since the Risorgimento. Quite a few nations had the hollowness of their political and ideological beliefs savagely exposed by the war – fallen France and devastated Poland were premier examples. But no participant revealed a more profound gap between ambition and practice than did Fascist Italy. For this disastrous 'failure', the *Duce*, Benito Mussolini, must take much of the historical blame.

Yet again the historiography needs to be read with care. Whatever their ideological provenance, quite a few accounts of Italy's military, social and cultural failures at war are posited on a curious comparison between Italy and its 'betters'. The three societies which performed most 'heroically' were, on the losing side, Nazi Germany and Imperial Japan, and, on the winning, the Stalinist USSR.[115] Can it really be agreed without discussion that history should lament the inability of the Italian nation, or the Fascist 'revolution', or Mussolini, to reach the standards of such states? Though many a military historian will bridle at the thought, maybe losing wars is not always the worst option.

Portents of defeats to come reached Italy almost at once. In the Mediterranean HMS Decoy, alerted to Fascist naval moves by British signals intelligence which had been reading Italian cyphers for some months, attacked an Italian submarine two hours before the war declaration was formally delivered.[116] From 11 June Allied aircraft bombed such northern cities as Turin and Genoa, leaving the population depressed at the total inadequacy – exposed by Favagrossa before the war entry – of national anti-aircraft defences.[117] Public opinion only cheered up when, on occasion, it heard rumours of imminent peace.[118] Italian armed forces advanced reluctantly and tardily over the French borders, and, when opposed, were given to ignominious retreat.[119] In Libya, on 28 June Italo Balbo became the first significant casualty of the Italian war, shot down by his own nervous men in mistake as he flew above Tobruk[120] – a few months later Mussolini typically let it be known that his old colleague had been riddled with 'exuberant defects', and had been a prey to a clique of 'vain imbeciles and profiteers', cheerfully reducing the *ras* of Ferrara to just another sometime 'friend' to be readily forgotten.[121]

Behind the events and attitudes of the early months of the Italian war lay the massive structural failure of Fascist modernisation of either arms or society. For all Mussolini's careless talk of 'eight million bayonets' and a fully militarised people, the Army officer corps had remained a caste, detached from the rest of the population. Its officers were loyal certainly to themselves and perhaps to the institution of the monarchy. The rest of the country was beyond their ken. The officers' culture was vastly separate from that of their soldiers, who, given the survival of dialect as the preferred method of discourse for most Italians, often literally spoke another language.[122] Class was everywhere evident, with Italy's overwhelmingly bourgeois university students largely exempt from military service.[123] The requirements for service were flexible for other social groups, too, and many Italians, rejoicing in friends and recommendations, could find justification for ignoring the call-up.[124] In September 1940 the Ministry of War still closed at lunchtime, given the requirement that its bureaucrats have their daily siesta, while in that month hundreds of thousands of peasant conscripts were demobilised in order to carry out their ancient task of bringing in the harvest.[125] This lingering agrarian *mentalité* may help to explain why the Italian army stubbornly refused to become mobile in a modern sense. For different reasons, officers and men both preferred horses or mules to trucks.

The Airforce, in many societies a redoubt of those better attuned to modern technology, retained an artisan character in Italy. It was not a place of mathematical precision, with its officers notoriously multiplying its available planes by tenfold in their tallies, until the real inadequacy of available aircraft was revealed in 1939. Once the war began, Italian production remained derisory; in 1942 the USA could turn out from its factories in a week more planes that Italian industry could manufacture in a year, a statistic which made only one result possible in the battle between the two.[126]

The Navy might have been efficient by comparison, but the sinking at anchor of three battleships at Taranto in November 1940, and the loss of three heavy cruisers at Cape Matapan in March 1941, persuaded Italy's naval leadership that discretion was the better part of valour. Thereafter the Fascist navy was very suspicious of being drawn into any serious contest with the British and other Allied forces.[127] Finally, there was no attempt to co-ordinate the different services – the naval chiefs had scorned what they condemned as the modish virtue of the aircraft carrier – and Mussolini had always been jealously hostile of any attempt at discussions that threatened to by-pass him. Even in war, the command structure remained tattered, with the *Duce* intervening erratically, but enough to satisfy himself that he was indeed in charge. Graziani, in command in North Africa, remembered being received by his commander-in-chief with a 'knowing half smile' but leaving the interview none the wiser about what policy was to be applied.[128] In his diary, Bottai depicted a war leader whose administration grew steadily more 'approximate', with the *Duce*, a 'man of the banner headline' at heart, now bored by detail or discussion and preferring to 'let things run on of their own accord'.[129] Meanwhile, the military chiefs bickered and plotted one against the other, anxious not to lose individual ground in an endless contest for status and recognition. By December 1941 a report suggested that 'the whole of national life is dominated by a conflict of personal egoism',[130] and certainly this generalisation was true of those who were meant to organise the national war effort. Mussolini, unable to work out a system of military and economic priorities, at a loss about how to connect the military and industry, which remained laggard in its production (even of chemical weapons),[131] spent time instead on his language lessons, settling down to do a translation of the lengthy Risorgimento novel, *I promessi sposi*, into German.[132] Can he have been hoping that his consequent mastery of the German language would help him to interrupt more effectively in future meetings with the garrulous *Führer*?

Mussolini's methods of administration as a military commander did nothing to overcome national inadequacies. Typically he would call his military leaders together and then provide a general and superficial review of the war situation. The meeting might conclude with some suggestions for an amelioration of the Italian situation, for example the upping of plane production to 500 per month, but with no indication of how this rise could be achieved and with a looseness of statistical information, a mathematical imprecision that had long been typical of the *Duce*'s rhetoric.[133]

With little but occasional goading from the dictator, the Italian Home Front was proving equally unable to adjust to total war. Early in 1941 workers were reported still to be admirers of their *Duce*, but they believed that 'the war was a private business of the Fascists', a category which did not include themselves.[134] In Autumn 1940 tens of thousands of Italians were still unemployed, even in industrial cities like Genoa, Milan and Bologna, despite the alleged marshalling of a war economy.[135] Food supplies were erratic and sparse, with the family ration from 1941 to 1943 matching that of Poland under German occupation.[136] The official, who was, suddenly after June 1940 charged by Mussolini with organising rationing, remembers having to start by locating some office space for himself, only to be blocked by one meticulous bureaucrat or another.[137] Even in well-off Venice, Prefect Benigni reported in March 1941 that the poorer classes were running out of such basic products as bread, pasta and oil.[138] The sinews of war remained feeble. Steel production fell far below that needed by a genuine Great Power and has been called 'risible' by one historian.[139] Alone of the combatants, Italy did not manage to increase its GDP between 1940 and 1942, and thereafter production fell.[140] In January 1941 the Germans estimated that Italian industry was working at only

25 per cent of its limited capacity.[141] Italian weaponry was antiquated or mis-designed – the Italians throughout the war failed to produce a tank of any quality.[142]

In sum, as the usually credulous Bottai recognised during the first weeks of the war, all was dominated by 'a failure of preparation' and by 'improvisation'.[143] Mussolini himself was a prisoner both of his myth and of the fact that every little matter had to pass his scrutiny. At least until October 1940 he clung to a short-war illusion, allowing Fascist officials happily to plan their activities in the post-war period rather than focusing on the travails enveloping Italy and the Fascist regime.[144] With planning riven by this fundamental confusion, the *Duce*'s reaction, Bottai complained, was, 'if things go well, to take the credit; and, if they go badly, to blame others'. This, Bottai concluded, had become the real meaning of the formula: 'Mussolini is always right'.[145] A soldier summed it up more succinctly. The Italian war effort was sheer 'anarchy'.[146] Here, it seemed, was a dictatorship so weak that, under the first test of war, nobody seemed to control it.

The rumblings about back-stabbing and discontent grew so insistent that it was decided to stage a sporting event, demonstrating that the *Duce* was indeed in superhuman form, still so much the manly embodiment of the Italian 'race' that he could sweat in public. In the event, however, the demonstration was less than successful, in spite of the appearance of a throng of twenty-three foreign correspondents, who assembled in the gardens of the Villa Torlonia. First Mussolini, wearing a white athletic singlet and bare-armed, was viewed going over a set of jumps on his horse. To enhance the journalists' wonder, the *Duce*'s combined riding and fencing instructor regaled them with details of Mussolini's fondness for pasta with butter, garlic and cheese, and his delight in broccoli and zucchini.[147] Then came tennis. An American onlooker remembered:

> The dictator, garbed in a beige polo shirt and shorts which revealed the scar of the wound he had received in the thigh during World War I, was playing doubles. He was serving underhand like a novice, and he violated every tennis rule and tradition by walking at least two steps beyond the base line to serve. Even so, the two athletes who were playing against him – Mario Delardinelli, Rome's leading professional tennis player, and Erlado Monzogoio, a member of Italy's national soccer team – had difficulty in returning his soap bubble serves. Whenever the ball was returned, it floated slowly up so that a lame man with a broken arm could have hit it. Il Duce lobbed, smashed, and smiled, pleased with his triumph.

None the less, some points, some games, did slip away, and the journalists noted that Mussolini and his partner, Lucio Savorgnan, had lost the three sets they watched. They were therefore disconcerted when Alessandro Pavolini, no less, stated that the final result had been a 7–5 set victory for the *Duce*.[148]

But propaganda of this kind was unable to hide the fact that the real catastrophe for the regime lay at the front. On 28 October 1940 with a fortnight's military preparation,[149] Italian forces tried to launch a *Blitzkrieg* on the Nazi model against Greece, using the bases in Albania as a jumping-off point. The result was disaster. An order from Mussolini on 10 November 1940 to raze all Greek cities with a population of more than 10 000[150] was less another example of his habitual careless savagery than a gesture of increasing impotence. Not only did Athens not fall within days, as Mussolini and the rest of his leadership had expected, but soon Greek forces counter-attacked, crossing the Albanian border and threatening to drive the Italians into the Adriatic sea. An inspecting officer, sent to list military deficiencies, found uniforms which disintegrated in the rain, a complete lack of mechanical and medical logistical support, and plummeting morale among both officers and men.[151] Back home, in December 1940 there were reports that newsreel images of the *Duce* were now received with critical silence.[152] Six weeks into what was meant to be a stroll to victory, Italy, it seemed, had been revealed as a power weaker than little Greece, and Mussolini's a dictatorship that could not match the ramshackle and reactionary government of General Metaxas.

During the previous months Greece had been an on-again, off-again target for the Italians.[153] Once more lacking the ethnic and racial thrust which smoothed the way for Nazi advances, Italy had no irredentist claims on Greece (though its Albanian puppets did). Indeed, the existence of speakers of *grico* (a Greek dialect) in Puglia and Calabria might have made Italy an object of the Greek nationalist 'Great Idea' had the Greek government been sufficiently bold. In practice, Greece was singled out for attack because, in August, the Italians were warned off Yugoslavia by their German allies,[154] because Vichy-ite French politicians had been adroit in persuading their German conquerors that they should not yield too much to the greedy Italians – the acquisition of Savoy, Nice, Corsica, Tunis and Djibouti remained a chimera[155] – and, at least according to De Felice, because Mussolini's scrutiny of the auguries had convinced him that the great conflict was about to end.[156]

Certainly, the idea of a 'parallel war' in the Mediterranean had never got beyond the notional. Only nine days after Italy entered the conflict, Ciano was told by Ribbentrop that Hitler believed firmly that 'the British empire is an element of stability and social order in the world and so of great utility. In the present state of things, it would be impossible to replace it'.[157] Similarly, the Germans had shown little interest in what all but historian De Felice have regarded as far-fetched Italian plans to win over Iraq and other parts of the Arab world to the Axis cause.[158] Reconciling German war aims with Italian ones, should the latter ever be fully developed, continued to appear unlikely. Mussolini had begun by boasting that Italy would attack on 'five' fronts and, in Greece, seemed anxious to increase that number,[159] but the multiplication of effort only concealed the fragmentation of planning. The Italian military went hither and yon, but no one, and certainly not Mussolini, knew why.

And so, on 15 October, came the formal decision to attack Greece.[160] The prompt to action had been a sudden German despatch of a mission to Romania, which Mussolini deemed the equivalent of occupation. 'Hitler perpetually places me before a *fait accompli*', he complained to Ciano. 'This time I'll pay him back in his own coin. He'll learn from the newspapers that I have occupied Greece and so restored the balance between us.'[161]

The defeat in Greece was followed by other losses. In Libya, from late October the armies under General Graziani, who had been timidly ignoring increasingly frequent goads from Mussolini urging him to go onto the attack, were swiftly pushed back by British forces – it was now that Eden observed sarcastically that 'never had so much been surrendered by so many to so few'.[162] Axis forces in Libya only rallied after the Italians were stiffened by German support led by General Erwin Rommel in February 1941. A much touted conquest of British Somaliland[163] was soon succeeded by Italian imperial defeats;[164] Addis Ababa was back in the hands of Emperor Haile Selassie by April 1941. Certainly the superficiality and perhaps the lightness of five fleeting years of Italian rule in Ethiopia was demonstrated by the fact that only fifty-six Italians were murdered in revenge killings.[165] The empire of AOI, celebrated with such exhilaration by almost all Italians in 1936, had collapsed with scarcely a whimper.

These setbacks did result in some sackings. In early December after a protracted process lasting almost a month but initiated by Farinacci – who wrote to argue that people were 'stupified' by events in Greece and that, in the USSR, a host of generals by now would have been shot out of hand[166] – Badoglio finally resigned as Chief of General Staff, to be replaced by Ugo Cavallero, another career officer.[167] In his posthumously published diary, Cavallero said that, on 1 December, Mussolini charged him to build a General Staff based on 'fruitful collaboration' rather than on 'Moslem-style absenteeism', as it had been under his predecessor. To keep him up to the mark, the *Duce* promised to see his military chief every day.[168] Badoglio had been told the same thing (he understood that the *Duce*'s military commentary was to be 'general' rather than specific).[169] But soldiers in the know were already grumbling that Mussolini spent 'every afternoon' with Claretta Petacci and was frequently impossible to contact.[170]

On the Home Front changes had occurred earlier, with Muti being dropped on 30 October. According to police reports, the Party Secretary had favoured the 'demobilisation' of the PNF on the grounds that, after 19 years, being a Fascist and being an Italian ought to have become inextricable.[171] In *Critica Fascista*, Bottai, with some tautology, had similarly urged that war should become 'a way of life for the whole nation, in every aspect and every sector and organisation', but soon went on to argue in contradiction that fighting was 'a religious act', which should be suffused with 'the mystical power of our Fascist faith'.[172] Less ponderous in his lucubrations, similarly Mussolini never quite believed in the identification of party and people; one of the evident failings of his regime's war effort was its inability to merge the nation of Italy and the ideology of Fascism in the minds of the masses. Certainly, in the autumn of 1940, there were plenty of rumours still about endemic corruption – Mussolini himself was told the joke that the best way to assist Hitler to conquer Britain would be to send him 'a dozen party bosses'. They were so thirsty they could lick the Channel dry.[173] Muti's replacement, it was plain, had plenty of work to do. In practice, however, the new Secretary, Adelchi Serena, was a colourless party bureaucrat who had earlier been *podestà* of L'Aquila and Minister for Public Works. He proved to be a competent administrator but, over the next year, did little to arrest the Party's decline.

To be sure, the largely meaningless lists of party card-carriers had continued to fill – in 1942 membership peaked at 4.77 million.[174] However, a year earlier, De Bono had defined the PNF as 'Italy's greatest enemy',[175] and even Mussolini made an effort to distance himself from its evident deficiencies. In January 1941 he announced the mobilisation of his ministers to the Albanian front, prompting what Ciano acidly described as consternation in the waiting room of the Palazzo Venezia.[176] Now even Bottai's wide-eyed belief in his 'inhuman' leader crumbled: 'A terrible solitude. Something which for more than twenty years has made my heart beat, stopped at a blow. A love, a faith, a dedication. Now, I am alone, without my Chief.'[177]

Mussolini, too, was beset by psychological crisis, telling Cavallero that, 'given our tragic situation, . . . the only thing left to do is to place everything in Hitler's hands, because we are incapable of doing anything'.[178] His colleagues noticed his pallor and his insomnia;[179] here was a war leader whose ageing physique was collapsing under the weight of office and the evidence of failure. By 1941 Mussolini, like both Fascism and Italy the Great Power, was fading out of existence in a process which might henceforth have moments of pause, but would never be reversed. Action now came from elsewhere. Mussolini, who still confessed to an ignorance of economic processes and a belief that the military knew their own world best,[180] hoped one day to bring his expertise in things 'political' back into play. But precisely where he might find room to manœuvre was by now a mystery to him and to his associates.

Yet, in many ways, 1941 was the year of triumph for the Axis, the time when the alliance headed by Hitler went nearest to winning the Second World War. In March–April the combined Axis forces advanced again towards the Egyptian–Libyan border and besieged Tobruk (it fell in June 1942) in a campaign which did not turn against them until the Battle of El Alamein in October–November 1942. In April–May 1941 Nazi armies swept across Yugoslavia and Greece; in June they snuffed out the last British defences in Crete. Already in April Pavelić had come to power in Zagreb, and, riding on German coat-tails, the Italians acquired a major administrative role in Slovenia (where the province of 'Lubiana' was annexed to Italy), Croatia, Montenegro and Greece. On 22 June the Nazis began Operation Barbarossa against the Soviets – Mussolini was awoken at his holiday villa at Riccione in the wee hours to be informed of the *Führer*'s decision[181] – and victory after victory followed, with the Nazis reaching the gates of both Leningrad and Moscow before winter blocked their path. On 7 December 1941 the great conflict extended to the Pacific when Japan attacked the United States at Pearl Harbor and, before long, stripped Singapore from its hapless British defenders and bid fair to destroy the empires of Britain, France and the Netherlands in the Asia–Pacific area.

In this gigantic global struggle, Mussolini, from time to time, could claim petty Italian gains, even though, until July 1943, the Italian sacrifice on every front was confined to 205 000 military and 25 000 civilian dead, a toll only about a third of the 650 000 Italians who died

in the First World War. Nor did Italy's casualties approach the cata-
clysmic losses being endured in the USSR, Yugoslavia, Poland,
Germany, China and Japan (and among European Jewry).[182] It may be
true that, from time to time, an element of the *Duce*'s charisma flut-
tered back into existence among the Fascist leadership or the Italian
populace.[183] However, the Greek fiasco and the evident failure of the
Fascist war effort to rally had left the great majority of Italians, and
probably Mussolini himself, sure that their nation and 'revolution'
could no longer aspire to singularity and greatness, but must at best
act as the (ignoble) second of the Nazi Germans.

Non-Italians agreed. The relative 'softness' of Fascist Italy's war did
nothing to restrain the contempt in which all Italians were held by
their German partner – in June 1941 Goebbels commented disgustedly
that 'we have the worst allies that could possibly be imagined',[184]
adding that 'the Italians are the most hated people in the whole of
Europe'.[185] At first Italian generals did ask their *Duce* to dissuade the
Germans from treating them as mere auxiliaries,[186] but they soon abandoned such thoughts of independence and, on most fronts, served the
Germans with the mutinous sullenness of a conscript. In response,
German commanders dismissed the Italians as 'listless', like 'a mass of
... children', 'easily contented [with] coffee, cigarettes and women'.
The Nazis were happy to abandon their woebegone allies when danger
threatened as it eventually did, especially on the Eastern front.[187] Even
Hitler, the Italophile, grew doubtful, by November 1940 suggesting
that Mussolini was 'the only real man' in Italy.[188] Early the following
month he agreed with Goebbels that the Italians amounted to 'a
laughing stock' and added, with somewhat surprising uneasiness,
'now there can be no more doubt about who is to lead Europe, Hitler
or Mussolini'.[189] Then and thereafter the two fascist chiefs continued
to correspond on a regular basis, and there were a number of meetings
for an exchange of views. But Hitler had assumed the position of dominance in these discussions,[190] and it was not a posture which he would
ever have reason to yield. All Mussolini could do was make the occasional rancorous remark off the record to a dutiful Italian listener
about the 'unavoidability' of an eventual conflict between Italy and
Germany, for example over the Alto Adige, before subsiding under the
fear that, in such a battle, too, the Italians would be bound to
surrender.[191]

Mutual incomprehension was also evident between Italian forces
and their murderous Croatian 'friends', despite Pavelić's efforts on
occasion to ingratiate himself in Rome with talk about the triumph of

'Mussolinian policy'.[192] Aimone of Savoy, selected to become King Tomislav II of the new Croatia and dismissed by Mussolini as a 'complete mental defective',[193] was restrained from staging a coronation in Zagreb by stories of 'incomprehensible' *Ustasha* atrocities.[194] Aimone was smart enough to stay in Italy, earning himself the charming title of 'the King who never was'.[195] Events in the Balkans only confirmed Mussolini in the bleakness of his understanding of humankind. Every single inhabitant of the ex-Yugoslavia, he told Cavallero in March 1942, should be regarded as an enemy.[196] To Ciano, he ordered a reprisal rate of two locals to be shot for every Italian wounded and twenty for every one killed, but, as his son-in-law noted disarmingly, 'he won't enforce it'.[197] In reality, he both did and did not. Italian behaviour in those parts of Yugoslavia under Fascist occupation was scarcely mild. General Roatta was later to be accused of war crimes in the area and tens of thousands of 'Slavs' died, quite a number in outright massacres which could extend to women and children and involve the razing of whole villages. Rather as in Libya a decade before, the perpetrators, however, were acting as much as members of the Royal army as they were following the orders of their *Duce*. Mussolini's responsibility arose more from his habitual endorsement of violence and brutality than from any specific command.

The friendship with Spain, which had tempted Franco to enter the war in the summer of 1940, for all the calamitous condition of his country and the fact that his troops were still shooting their republican enemies, began to fray. The Italian assault on Greece coincided with the meeting between the *Caudillo* and Hitler at Hendaye, which convinced the *Führer* that the Spanish were unlikely to join the war.[198] A subsequent visit by Franco and his Foreign Minister Ramón Serrano Suñer to Italy in February 1941 got no further, with Mussolini embarrassed in his efforts to explain away Italian defeats and Franco taking care to emphasise a recent bad harvest and the poverty of his land.[199]

Of course, from June 1941 the 'real' war was fought on the Eastern Front between the Germans and the Soviets. In his letter of explanation of the Nazi attack, Hitler had told Mussolini that he felt 'liberated' by the step which the Germans were taking.[200] At last he had the war he had always wanted. Mussolini's response was on the surface just as enthusiastic. The campaign against communism pleased many elements in Italy – the Church for one[201] – and the ideology of Fascism could revive. The Americans were a nuisance but they could not arrest this crusade. 'The *Stimmung* of the Italian people', he concluded, is now 'very good indeed'. They were ready to march with their German ally 'to the end'. And yet somewhere in the phrases was a hint of doubt. A conflict against the USSR amounted to 'a war against space', the *Duce* warned. No doubt German planes and tanks could conquer the Russian vastness, he hastily added. There was no reason to worry.[202] Or was there? Certainly when, in November 1941, Mussolini tried to suggest that the key to victory was now found in the battles with Britain on the Egyptian border,[203] he got no sensible response from Berlin. Neither Italian national self-interest nor Italian Fascist ideology – after the invasion of the USSR, Mussolini had again talked about how he would make a 'real' revolution once victory was his[204] – counted for much, when compared with the titanic ideological battle in the East.

In this deepening unreality it was easy to welcome the Japanese action that brought the Americans into the war.[205] With its history of emigration, Italy as a country had greater reason than most to plumb the economic power of the USA. Whereas Hitler was a German provincial *petit bourgeois*, whose mental world had little comprehension of wider society, 'Prof. Mussolini' had once aspired to a universal knowledge. None of this mattered as Italy, too, declared war against the American government and people.[206] Back in May 1941 Mussolini had angrily dismissed Roosevelt as a statesman: 'Never in history', he told his son-in-law, 'has a people been ruled by a paralytic. There have been bald kings, fat kings, handsome kings and even stupid ones, but never a king who when he wants to go to the toilet or to dinner must be assisted by other men.'[207] It was a typically brutal outburst. However, by the end of 1941 Mussolini had allowed the underdeveloped Italian economy and fragile and divided Italian society to be pitted against both the USA and the USSR. In such an uneven contest, it was Benito Mussolini who was to learn the meaning (and the cost) of paralysis. And Italy itself would be the collateral damage in this process of understanding.

17

First fall and feeble resurrection, 1942–1943

JAPANESE victories might be praised effusively (especially if there was a chance thereby to arouse German envy).[1] But Christmas 1941 did not bring cheer to Benito Mussolini. Rather his misanthropy deepened yet again. From Germany there was news of the sudden sacking of General Walther Brauchitsch, with its implication that the Soviets were not yet wiped from the map.[2] Was the Eastern Front to prove that Hitler was a *coglione* (prickhead)? – Ciano must have enjoyed writing down the word, although he ascribed its usage to a German diplomat.[3] But the most blatant malice was not guaranteed to raise a smile from his father-in-law these days. Instead Mussolini used the occasion of a meeting to reveal the gall within his soul. From inveighing about the need further to politicise his army (another utterly barren wish on his part), Mussolini switched his hostility to Christmas. He was amazed, he said, that the Germans had not abolished it. The festival recorded 'only the birth of a Jew who presented the world with theories which weakened and emasculated it'. Christ, he complained, had 'especially stuffed Italy given the Papacy's ability to fracture Italian society'. To eradicate such pestiferous influences, the *Duce* boasted, he had prohibited Italian papers from mentioning the birth of Jesus.[4] It was a futile gesture. One look out of the window of the *Sala del Mappamondo*, Ciano commented to the privacy of his diary, and it was plain that the people, bustling around the street outside, 'remembered [Christmas] and loved it still'. Mussolini, it might be concluded, was being thwarted even in his aspirations to be a grinch.

Perhaps some party loyalists did postpone their celebrations until the *Befana fascista* (6 January, Epiphany, or 'last day of Christmas', a traditional time for the exchange of presents in Italy, accorded a Fascist gloss under the dictatorship). Certainly, they were aware by

then that the *Duce* had been keeping a Christmas surprise in store for
his entourage, the party and the nation. On 26 December it was
announced that Serena had lost his job and the new PNF secretary was
to be Aldo Vidussoni. Ciano expressed his amazement: the appointment, he wrote, had gone

> to a certain Vidussoni, who won a gold medal for military valour [in
> Spain] and is twenty-six, with a law degree. Other than that, I don't
> know what to put down. Evidently we are talking about a brave exper-
> iment and let's hope that this time fortune is indeed the companion of
> courage. I don't know the man at all, not even what he looks like.[5]

A day later, Ciano noted the 'general stupour' at the news – from the
humblest caddy at his golf course to the distinguished Giuseppe Volpi,
Count of Misurata, currently president both of *Confindustria* and 'the
Italo-Croat Economic Commission',[6] every Italian was polishing his
sarcasm on the choice. Nor did acquaintance with the new star in the
political firmament end the puzzlement. When Vidussoni had spoken
to 'that environment of old whores which [these days] is the Party',
Ciano recalled bitingly, the young secretary had 'sweated blood'. He
seemed an enthusiast, a true believer, and presumably that was to the
good, but most saw him as one who had 'arisen from the *Duce*'s head',
just as 'Minerva sprang from the head of Jupiter'.[7]

A week later Ciano gained further insight into the mind of this
incarnation of the new generation of Fascists. Vidussoni turned up at
the Ministry of Foreign Affairs to discuss the Balkans and the insta-
bility which continued to plague Italy's north-eastern border, where
guerrilla opposition to Fascist governance was spreading. His ideas
were straightforward. Italy should liquidate all Slovenes. Ciano, in his
robes as statesman and bourgeois, 'permitted himself to note that there
were more than a million of them'. 'No matter', came the reply. 'We
should behave with them as the *ascari* [Italy's black colonial troops
from Eritrea and the Somaliland] do with their enemies, simply exterminate them.'[8] Here, it seemed, was a young man who had indeed
imbibed the spirit of the times in the Axis (though his use of black
models hinted that he, too, had failed to plumb the meaning of 'scientific racism').

De Felice argues that the appointment was a last attempt by
Mussolini to organise the party in his own way,[9] but the selection of
Vidussoni is better seen as a gesture of desperation and despair. The
Duce may have told the Party that youth must have its day (adding

with a hint of apology that the Secretary was actually 28 not 26);[10] Vidussoni could act as his 'apprentice'. Mussolini may have urged a concentration under the new administration on 'politics', by which he meant the education or indoctrination of the people, and not on 'police activities', which as ever he thought better reserved to the 'state'. He may have concluded that a long war had its advantages in that it forced all Italians to dig deep morally until they won their battles at home and abroad.[11] But neither Vidussoni nor Mussolini could paper over the cracks which were by now everywhere spreading in the edifice of Fascism.

The more they examined it, the more the old Fascist elite was affronted by the change. All those who had previously viewed themselves as the special emanations of the *Duce*, in some sense his *alter egos*, were forced to face their own worthlessness and impotence. Farinacci,[12] Ciano,[13] Bottai,[14] each saw a 'cretin', an 'imbecile', suddenly and recklessly raised to be their competitor or superior.[15] Worse still, their judgement was right. Rumour spread that the new Secretary displayed his youth, manliness and submission by regularly sprinting the distance which separated the door of Mussolini's office in the Palazzo Venezia from the *Duce's* desk.[16] Vidussoni may have been able to mouth some Fascist slogans but, as a vehicle of Fascist 'mysticism', the new Secretary was further proof of the failure of Fascism drastically to amend the hearts of men and women, and a demonstration that a career in administration requires some training. In February 1943 a police report summed up Vidussoni's term in office as a disaster, especially owing to 'his lack of organising ability which every day drains away still further the essence of the party'. 'The work of Vidussoni', the commentator ran bitterly on, 'is restricted to visiting the wounded in hospital and turning up at football or boxing matches.' After 14 months in office, Vidussoni had not properly acquainted himself with the leading figures in the party or developed any comprehension of their patterns of behaviour. People who mattered continued to ask what on earth was he doing as Party Secretary and why the *Duce* had brought him from nowhere to his current hollow eminence.[17] In other words, rather than making the PNF finally his own, Mussolini, through this appointment, completed the alienation from himself of his closest followers. By the time Vidussoni finally left office in April 1943, Mussolini's own fall was itself imminent.

In his speech in January 1942 introducing Vidussoni to his new colleagues Mussolini had stated: 'After twenty years of the regime, there are two generations which dispute the government. One is setting, the other rising.' Each cohort, Mussolini added, in words replete with the Darwinism which dominated his understanding of the world, fought with its predecessor.[18] But these were dangerous sentiments. Mussolini had taken office at 39; in 1943 he would turn 60. Most of his colleagues were his juniors, many by 10 years or more, while Ciano was not yet 40. Did they not constitute the 'new generation',[19] who might be destined to oust the old? Propagandists might still write that 'no-one is perennially new and eternal as He is; no-one is born every morning to history, to politics, to the idea, like Him', adding that the people needed 'Him' as they did 'bread and air'.[20] But the credibility of an eternally youthful *Duce* was crumbling.

With every passing day, 'old' was the word which better described the *Duce*. Bottai gave a typical account of his ageing leader after seeing him one evening in October 1942. Mussolini was in clear decline, 'his face ashen, his cheeks shrunken, his mouth turned down bitterly', as if he were in pain from his ulcer or whatever exactly was the matter with him. 'The fact is', Bottai noted in his diary, 'the man is not just tired, disheartened, sad, but he is no longer winning out over his age.' The situation was dismaying 'for those who loved him, and, who, despite everything, love him still. If only he would take our hands into his hands and really talk to us. But he has killed in himself the man who once was'. Even among his entourage, Bottai admitted sadly, Mussolini was now mockingly called *Provolone* (Cheeseball), because of his shiny bald head, 'which once used to radiate with his personal appeal'. 'The man who was always right, now, for most, is always wrong', Bottai declared with his usual desire to find philosophical meaning in the day's events. 'Once any apparent achievements or merits were ascribed to him. Now he is blamed for everything which goes wrong even when it isn't his fault. This is the law of compensation.'[21]

What, then, by 1942–43 was the state of the *Duce*'s health? To what extent was he another war-leader whose failures in command coincided with encroaching physical debility? Ever since the attack in 1925, Mussolini had suffered from a duodenal ulcer.[22] All the same, most of the time a careful diet (though one which doctors, with the knowledge that ulcers are bacterial infections, now say relied too much on milk and other dairy products), an avoidance of meat, alcohol and cigarettes, left him in reasonable form, even though the whitening of his hair by the time he turned fifty belied his official image as an eternally youthful he-man, virile in bed and the master of every sport imaginable. Under the stress of the war, however, the swimming, jogging, horse-riding *Duce* made way for a Mussolini whose health was frequently bad and sometimes rendered him prostrate.

In August 1941 the Mussolinis had their own familial war casualty when Bruno crashed to his death while acting as the test pilot of a bomber in Tuscany.[23] Bruno's widow took pains to collect the sheets and pillowslips on which her husband had slept during his last night at a Pisa hotel and presented them to her mourning mother-in-law.[24] Mussolini had never been close to his elder sons, though it was said that, after Bruno's demise, he tried to spend more time than in the past with Vittorio.[25] Certainly, as with the *Vita di Arnaldo*, through which he had mourned his brother, he now produced a small book entitled *Parlo con Bruno* (I talk with Bruno). Like the earlier work, it is another curious piece, mingling Fascist rigour with maudlin family sentiment.[26] It is also riven with hypocrisy, all but deifying Bruno, while calling him but one of the many committed to victory. Similarly, Mussolini emphasised the privacy of the father–son relationship and of the tomb, while marketing copies to the public with full Fascist propaganda fanfare. In the Fascist hero now somewhat inconsistently being sculptured, acquaintances found little reflection of the 'shy, timid', bullied, wordless and repressed Bruno they had known.[27]

Though never abandoned, the Mussolinis of the Villa Torlonia and the *Rocca delle Caminate* with their everyday uncouthness had never much eased the tension in the *Duce*'s life. Extra-marital satisfaction was also not guaranteed. The affair with Claretta Petacci continued – Ciano and others in the entourage gossiped openly and censoriously about the 'senile passions' of their *Duce*,[28] while Arpinati, back from *confino*, said Claretta was corruptly meddling at Rimini, just as other 'Mussolini women' were known to do in the rest of the Romagna.[29] Although the *Duce* was growing flaccid with age, back in Rome Claretta spent lavishly on her bedroom which featured mirrors and a black marble bathroom *en suite* – even a general remarked severely that it looked 'like an American film set and was of plainly bad taste'.[30] After a hard day at the office, the *Duce* was in the habit of ringing his lover late at night, usually to complain about his work-load and insomnia, and to be assuaged with cheap love-talk. Calls were, for example, recorded on 9 June 1940 and on 22 June 1941 at midnight or after – on the latter occasion Mussolini prophesied disaster from the German attack on the USSR; the Nazis, he said, would win many battles but lose the war.[31] But Claretta was often sick; in 1940 she seems to have suffered from an extra-uterine pregnancy.[32] There were rumours, too, of an abortion and, in December 1941, she was taped telling the *Duce* she was pregnant by him, a statement which drew clichés of pleasure from the *Duce*, although no baby was ever born.[33] In return, Claretta fussed contentedly over her man's health problems, pressing his doctors for assurances that some improvement was in sight.[34] A melancholy shared hypochondria, it may be surmised, was one topic which kept them together.

Similarly Marcello Petacci still caused annoyance. He drew attention to himself by squabbling publicly with a Venetian countess over some real estate.[35] In the summer of 1942 there were also rumours of illegal gold trafficking, with Riccardi commenting on the *Duce*'s humiliation in being forced to admit that peculation was being indulged in by members of his own alternative 'family'.[36] In February 1943 Petacci took his callowness to new depths by sending the *Duce* a master plan to win the war. It was a fantastic scheme, involving organised and coordinated surprise attacks by Spain on the Anglo-American forces in Morocco, by Turkey on the USSR, and by China on Siberia (the Japanese were to be diverted to India and Australia), all to be combined with Vatican support. Should this version not be practical, Petacci added disarmingly, he might be able to get to Stalin through an unnamed friend, or to the British through Sir Samuel Hoare. Plainly some arrangement was needed, since, by Petacci's reckoning, the Anglo-American forces now assembled were steeled with ten times the strength of the Italians.[37]

Scandal was also never far from the career of Claretta's younger sister, Maria, born 1923. By 1940 she had already been launched as a singer, though somewhat hampered by her thin voice. She moved on to risqué film roles, using the art name of Myriam di San Servolo. In June 1942 she found *sistemazione* of a kind, although not that to be expected of a Fascist new woman, by marrying a count.[38] There can be little doubt that the notoriety of the Petaccis helped further to smudge the *Duce*'s charisma – by late 1942 even Bottai was remarking: 'The regime is "Pompadouring" itself; and with what a wretched quality of Pompadour!'[39]

Sexual satisfaction came at a cost, it seemed. Moreoever, by 1942 Claretta had a competitor of a kind in the 19-year-old typist and philosophy student Elena Curti – the topic of her studies especially gratified the *Duce*.[40] Mussolini became accustomed to drop into Curti's flat for afternoon chats[41] and seek there the psychological rewards of being admired by a young female (even at the cost of jealous scenes from Claretta). Mussolini's craving for such solace was no doubt meant to counter that brutal misanthropy which came so easily to his lips when he was at the office – in his search for a soft escape from the cruel public world, Mussolini was doing what many a male executive in his fifties has done before and since. Playing the part of sentimental sugar daddy with Elena and Claretta, he could fudge the grim memoranda piling up on his desk and forget the lack of human content left in his relationships with his colleagues. There he could try to resuscitate a 'real' Mussolini, and forget for a moment the burden of his charisma.

Such distractions were doubtless pleasing but Mussolini continued to experience medical troubles. Already in 1941 his attention to the war effort was becoming distracted by worries about his health. In May 1942 he fell victim to flu and contemporaries began to notice his increased susceptibility to colds and other passing indispositions. In July he returned from a visit to Libya with a recurrence of pain and, over the next months, it only worsened, with both family and doctors debating whether it was caused by the ulcer or by some infection caught in the tropical heat of the empire. By November the spasms had become all but unendurable. The *Duce*'s famous jutting chin, a doctor noted, was gone and Mussolini had become 'pallid, with shrunken cheeks and a withered neck'.[42] The state of his health was so patently bad that he had to endure nostrums from others – his old acquaintance from Forlì, Giacomo Paolucci di Calboli, assured him that a cure based on 'potato juice' was bound to bring rejuvenation.[43]

With his actual doctors, Mussolini was an obedient patient, taking the pills prescribed for him and being scrupulous about his diet. Even on his sick-bed he liked to read philosophy if he could, though he was also typically surrounded by piles of newspapers which, in one doctor's view, he scanned both with relish and with a sense of duty. With pencil in hand, he loved to pick up errors on which he would then loudly and sarcastically comment.[44] Even in July 1943 he was vain enough to enjoy being visited by a manicurist.[45] The *portiere* and housekeeper at the Villa Torlonia, it was noticed, were both from the Romagna[46] – a young visitor more conscious of social proprieties than a mere doctor recorded his shock at finding the manservant wearing tan shoes and an open shirt.[47] As ever, there was an awkward atmosphere in the *Duce*'s home which, to all observers, was not a place of comfort. Ciano gossiped about a dinner at the Villa Torlonia when the *Duce* tried to impress Vittorio with the promise that 'in five years' he would have the Italians 'really jumping', while Rachele, a doughtily

Fascist Red Queen from the provinces, broke in to urge her husband to 'make some heads roll'.[48]

After a brief interlude in which he felt better – it was now that Bottai thought he detected tears in the dictator's eyes after he spoke to officials with something approaching his old panache[49] – the *Duce* fell ill again and, in December 1942, he was forced to send his son-in-law to substitute for him on a scheduled visit to Hitler. His doctors reported that he had shed about a quarter of his body weight over a few months.[50] Although Mussolini had been given a course of daily injections against his stomach troubles, his weight continued to decline and his blood pressure had also fallen noticeably. His medical team, however, seem to have been unsure whether they were treating a physical condition or a psychological one. The *Duce* was manifestly depressed.[51] Over Christmas–New Year 1942–43 he spent most days in bed – now he lacked the strength again to be a grinch. By mid-January one doctor even suggested that he might be suffering from advanced cancer.[52] This diagnosis proved alarmist and, from February to July 1943, Mussolini's condition reverted to being tolerable on most days, although he was still a frequent victim of severe stomach pain. Insomnia also dogged him. Despite a diet which often was mainly liquid, Mussolini had to fight off a tendency to vomit after eating and his weight continued to fluctuate. He was reported to be anaemic and asthenic;[53] a visiting Hungarian politician found him looking 'very ill. His head was bald, his skin yellowish-white, and he was talking quickly and with nervous gestures'.[54] During a trip to Germany in April 1943 Mussolini had another medical crisis and, in May, one night at the *Rocca delle Caminate*, the pain was so great that he rolled on the floor in an effort to relieve it.[55] Even his war wound now acted up.[56] Again the crisis passed and the *Duce* resumed his accustomed work-load, but his habit of loosening his trousers and pressing his hands into his stomach had become an everyday reflex.[57] In his correspondence with Hitler, too, there were now regular exchanges on health matters, with each of the dictators, but especially Mussolini, confessing to the wearing effects of the war.[58]

Behind the physical and psychological pain lay political agony. Except for that loose talk about opening the Atlantic to Italian penetration, Mussolini and the regime had never really defined their war aims. They had, after all, been possessed of a short-war illusion until the setback in Greece and, after that defeat, recognition of the regime's dependence on Germany made any attempt to sketch Italian gains on their own account seem foolish and unrealistic. In his various speeches and writings, Mussolini cast about in an effort to explain what advantage was to be gained from the war. In October 1941, for example, he argued that the superior will of the Axis forces was ensuring that, 'within a few years the world will be fascist'.[59] In January 1942 it was race which was the key issue; the war was allowing the fusion of the Italian provinces to accelerate, so that, within the somewhat loose time-frame of a century, Italians could be sure they had made 'a pure Italian race'. 'Free access to the ocean' would somehow promote this process and the general ideal of Italian unity (and it also signified an avoidance of *giri di valtzer*). [60] By eschewing these sins of the Liberal past and marching with the Germans and Japanese 'to the uttermost', he contended, Italy was earning a good grade in the 'test' of war. In this examination, some nations fell and the others rose, and Italy must include itself in the latter category.[61] Darwinism of the crudest sort still won the *Duce*'s endorsement:

> Struggle lies at the origin of everything because life is full of contrasts. There is love and hatred, white and black, day and night, good and evil. Until these contrasts find a balance, struggle will always be placed at the heart of human nature and will be its supreme destiny.[62]

But what, the question every day more evidently became, if Italy, Fascism and Mussolini belonged to the category of historical losers?

The softness of the bourgeoisie, a sin which, it seemed, could easily be located in all his people, remained a target of the *Duce*'s savage criticism. Italians, he somewhat self-consciously told a meeting of party officials from the Veneto and Alto Adige – that is, the regions bordering the super-efficient Germanic world – must learn to be prompt. They must run their lives on schedule. 'When nine o'clock is the time, we must go at nine o'clock and not at a quarter past nine.' 'We must with utter desperation seek to become a serious people', he added in phrasing which sounded despairing. The laggard and the lackadaisical must be expelled from the Fascist party, while 'we punt resolutely on the young; punt, that is, on the new generations'.[63] The *federali* of the Emilia were objects of a similar lecture: 'We must make the Italians get used to being precise in language, in statements, in facts.' 'Foreigners', Mussolini added, 'see us as people who never arrive on time, who are always vague in our language and undertakings, who are and are not, who are fond of *giri di valtzer*' (once more that embarrassing phrase from the First World War).[64]

Somehow, such preaching always proved unproductive; Italians did not come up to the mark. In May 1942 Mussolini hectored the Party directorate on the troubles of the Home Front. There 'indiscipline, sabotage and passive resistance could be found all along the line'. Fascists were hoarding 'leather, liquor, boiled pears' (this last sounded an unconscious reference to his own diet). In the years between 1915 and 1918 – again that gnawing sense of inadequacy of the Fascist war compared with the Liberal one – Italians had really understood the meaning of self-sacrifice. Now they must be driven to it through 'absolute brutality'. Italian business was especially to blame; it was up to its old tricks and had never yielded to the Fascist revolution.[65] To an industrialist, however, he instead argued that the real blame fell on 'small business men and hoteliers'; they were the ones who had not yet been properly fascistised.[66] One philippic succeeded another, but they never quite spelled out how amendment was meant to proceed and never quite explained why, given that the regime had been in office for twenty years, its achievement had proven so empty. In that regard, Mussolini was perfectly capable of the grossest contradiction. To an assembly of Fascist journalists, the *Duce* said in words which aborted any discussion: 'During its two decades of rule, Fascism has given an exhaustive reply to every question which disturbs contemporary consciousness.' There was not even the most minimal problem with the theory, Mussolini advised. It was just the practice which let Italians down.[67]

All this speechifying was doing nothing to resolve the many dilemmas which the war was bringing. One terrible issue was the fate of the European Jews. As time passed, information about genocide was reaching Rome. In December 1941 Ciano was told 'with a meaningful smile' by the Croatian Minister of War, Slavko Kvaternik, that the number of Jews under his rule was reduced by more than two-thirds, through 'a process of emigration' from which they would not return.[68] The Italian leadership remained highly disgruntled by what Mussolini himself labelled the German overwhelming of Croatia in the economic, military and political fields,[69] and Pavelić's own efforts to play off the two allies only confirmed Mussolini's usual understanding of the ingratitude of self-styled friends. He was also ready to criticise Pavelić directly for his fanaticism, in killing Serbs, for example; the matter, Mussolini remarked, was not just 'inhumane', but a political 'error, a grave error'.[70] To Hitler, however, the *Duce* said little, usually just urging in words he thought the *Führer* would like to hear that the occupying forces in ex-Yugoslavia should adopt 'extreme' measures in pacifying any opposition to the Axis occupation.[71]

From the USSR and the Eastern front still viler reports began to be heard. In March 1942 an Italian diplomat returning from Berlin told colleagues at the Ministry of Foreign Affairs about 'horrors being perpetrated in occupied Polish and Russian territory', with 'systematic massacre, the killing of women and children, forced prostitution, the sending of nuns to brothels etc.'[72] By May–June the Vatican was in receipt of detailed reports of 'the most radical Anti-Semitism' in Axis-occupied territories, with 'millions' of dead,[73] although, at the very same time, Pavelić told Pius XII that, in his Catholic part of that zone, 'the Croat people wants its conduct and its legislation to be wholly inspired by Catholicism'.[74] In response the Pope maintained that ambiguous or culpable silence which had become his way of coping with the tragedies of the war. However, by the summer and autumn of 1942 Italian officials in Yugoslavia, France and Tunis, and anywhere Italian citizenship could save Jews from German barbarity,[75] were initiating the curious Fascist attempt to oppose and divert the Final Solution.[76] They directed towards the Germans those arts of obfuscation and procrastination which had always been part of their bureaucratic armoury and had not been eliminated by the years of Fascist 'rigour'.

Within Italy the wartime politics of race remained confused. The Anti-Semitic press continued its polemics. In a typically paranoid article in September 1942 Preziosi pressed for the 'solution of the Jewish problem', arguing that Italy was much more penetrated by Jews than had so far been acknowledged. 'Crypto-Jews', he was sure, pullulated in Catholic Action and the rest of the Church, while also being responsible for the 'mammonisation [sic] of our bourgeoisie'. A precise scientific tabulation of Italian blood stocks, he stated, should urgently be prepared. Then the country and its revolution could move on.[77] Farinacci, too, if rather more vaguely, declared in a speech at Milan that the Jewish issue needed to be resolved with 'firmness and surgical intelligence'. 'The Jews want to destroy us; we will destroy them.'[78] Other propagandists inveighed against the alleged Jewish domination of the USA and its leader, 'the criminal in the White House',[79] while the most extreme racist cheerfully suggested 'twenty-one million' Jews be 'sacrificed' to cure a problem which cried out for 'extreme measures'.[80]

Despite these brutal words, which could only be expressed with official approval (Mussolini's personal theoretical journal *Gerarchia*, which he had once shared with Margherita Sarfatti, also published diatribes against the Jews),[81] the practice of Anti-Semitism under

Fascism remained relatively benign. Until July 1943 frontier officials were known to permit Jewish refugees from the horrors elsewhere to find sanctuary across Italian borders.[82] If war is meant, like an X-ray, to expose the reality of a society (and certainly the conflict brought into the open the murderousness at the heart of Nazism), the lenience in racial practice in Italian territories and the scepticism in most Italian minds about racial theory indicated that modern racism was an accretion to Fascism and not its epicentre. But was this true of the *Duce* himself, the Italian who, after all, was in perpetual contact with the Germans, as well as the man informed on a number of occasions that he was Hitler's only surviving 'real friend'?[83] What was Mussolini's own position on the 'Final Solution'?

The answer is that, in his attitudes and responses, he was not so different from many Italians. If the Germans pushed, he obeyed them. When, for example, in August 1942 they demanded point-blank the right to join with the Croats in the Italian occupation zone in a sweep against the Jews and to be able to rely on Italian military support until then not forthcoming, the *Duce* minuted his approval. Nothing, he wrote, should stand in the way of this collaboration.[84] Yet he did little to halt continuing Italian efforts to delay and frustrate the Germans. In return the Nazi chiefs did not keep him fully informed. In October, for example, Himmler met Mussolini at the Palazzo Venezia and presented a half-told tale. The Jews, he acknowledged, were being deported east and, in 'Russia', 'quite a lot', including women and children, had been shot, because otherwise they helped the partisans. Mussolini in response nodded that 'this is the only possible solution'. Himmler then enlarged his account to say that more Jews had been worked to death in those parts, mainly because they were so unused to manual labour. The Nazis, he hurried to add mendaciously, kept older Jews alive in some comfort at Theresienstadt or in hospitals in Berlin, Vienna and other places. The remaining Jews they tried to hustle across the front to the Soviets, only to find communist troops firing on them, 'clearly demonstrating that [the Soviets], too, don't want the Jews'.[85]

While certainly not providing his Italian ally with a complete brief about the terrible detail of the Final Solution, Himmler had none the less confirmed that murders were being perpetrated against the Jews and Mussolini had let him ramble on, without serious questioning or objection. A few weeks later Vidussoni returned from a trip to the Eastern Front (he claimed to have insisted virtuously on travelling in an adapted third-class rail compartment) with a similar *mélange* of information and disinformation. The Jews, he reported, were being treated by the Germans with 'absolute rigour', which meant either their massacre or their being worked to death. 'The Italians', he added, were 'impressed by the method of the killing' and by the resignation with which the victims accepted it. Vidussoni's own moral sense and ability to order his prose were too weak for him to say more, and he digressed to such other matters as the Italian soldiery's dislike of the Germans, and his own admiration for Hitler and for the Nazi world where the Party was real.[86] Nevertheless, Vidussoni had said enough to leave his more sophisticated *Duce* a little appalled by what he certainly knew was happening. Here, too, as so often, it was easiest just to be cynical – in November 1942 Mussolini fobbed off complaints by industrialist Alberto Pirelli about German occupation policies in the East by stating: 'They are making them [the Jews] emigrate to another world.'[87] A few weeks later, he told the Fascist parliament that 'you can't make war without hating the enemy' and Italians, he charged, must slough off 'false sentimentality'.[88] Yet he did not use this occasion to condemn the Jews. The massacres in the East, it must be concluded, were in his eyes a terrible part of the war and of the German alliance, but what could he, or Fascism, or Italy, do about it? Until July 1943 Mussolini managed to be a Pontius Pilate in regard to the killing of the Jews. After September 1943 that minimal detachment no longer proved possible.

Meanwhile, as 1942 drew to a close, the weakness of the Axis compared with the huge Allied coalition was plain to see. In the North African sideshow, German assistance could not prevent the second great Allied advance and Cyrenaica was lost by November. In that same month American forces landed in French Morocco and promised to press forward against Tunis, hastily occupied by the Axis. Now the unimaginable battle of puny Italy against the wealth of the USA was indeed joined. Worse, on the Eastern Front Hitler had stubbornly locked his Sixth Army into the siege of Stalingrad – the eventual surrender of Marshal von Paulus in January 1943 came at a cost in German lives from this one battle[89] which almost equalled the whole Italian sacrifice from 1940 to July 1943.[90] In the hellish battles in the East, even Hitler deprecated the assistance his forces received from the Italian allies; Fascist troops, he said, were worse than Romanian ones, (though, still a good Austrian, the *Führer* thought the Hungarians were the worst).[91] Similarly, reports multiplied[92] of German contempt for the Italian guest workers – a further 229 000 of them entered the Reich in 1941, 81 000 in 1942.[93] A 'scientific' study by German time and motion experts reckoned Italian workers were inferior in productivity and discipline even to Soviet POWs; indisciplined and feckless, as might be expected of a 'Southern race', they spent too much time ogling women and playing cards.[94] In every way, the Italians appeared unsatisfactory allies, and, in the spring of 1942, Mussolini nervously repeated what he had heard was a German saying: 'We'll win the war in two months against Russia, in four months against England and in four days against Italy.'[95]

If the Axis partnership worked uneasily in Europe, in North Africa the Allies squeezed the united German–Italian armies from west and east. Libya, greatest of the conquests of Liberal Italy, was lost – by February 1943 Rommel was seeking to barricade his Axis forces on the Tunisian side of the border with Tripolitania, taking over defences prepared by the French in the 1930s. An attempted breakout was thwarted after initial American losses and, by May, 'Army Group Africa' caught between the pincer of British forces advancing from Tripoli and the Americans proceeding from Tunis, capitulated. Some 225 000 Italian and German POWs fell to the Allies. An invasion of Italy was next on the Allied agenda.

Faced with this array of military disasters, Mussolini had no answers. His meetings with the *Führer* followed a regular pattern in which Hitler spoke on and on, most frequently in self-justification of the course of the war in the East (meteorologists, he told the *Duce* in April 1942, were as guilty of bad advice as were theologists).[96] When Mussolini drew attention to Italian needs – for example when he wanted help to blast Malta into surrender[97] – he was fobbed off. In other areas, progress was hard to see. Serrano Suñer might remain a fascist at heart, but the military situation had convinced even him that Spain must preserve its neutrality.[98] By February 1943 Mussolini was left with the tack of warning Franco that the Allies 'will not distinguish Fascism, Falangism and National Socialism', but rather intended to restore 'the Reds'.[99] The Vichy French, too, even after their country was fully occupied by the Axis in November 1942, showed few signs of wishing to ingratiate themselves with the Italians. Most seriously, Mussolini's roundabout and apologetic efforts to diminish Hitler's obsession with the East and persuade him instead that 'the Anglo-Saxons' were the real enemy got nowhere, unsurprisingly since the ideology of Hitler, the Nazis and most of the Germans was so riveted to the titanic racial–ideological battle against 'Judeo-Bolshevism'.[100]

By the spring of 1943 a desperation was becoming evident also at home. In February Mussolini launched another of his sudden and drastic cabinet changes. Now the sackings included Bottai, Riccardi

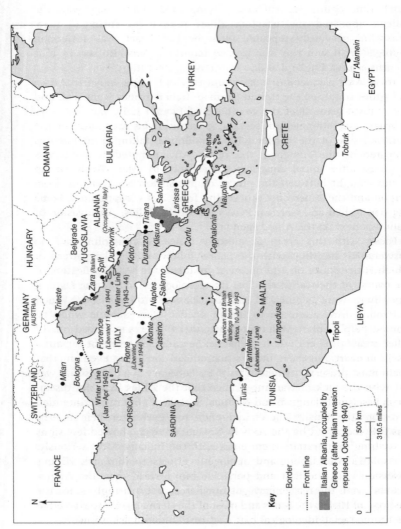

Map 4 Italy's Second World War

and Ciano, this last sent to become ambassador to the Vatican, with a hint that the bourgeois face of Fascism could escape its destiny by negotiating some deal through the Church. As if to reflect this intriguing possibility, Ciano jotted archly into his diary 'the ways which Providence chooses are indeed sometimes mysterious'.[101] Bottai, in his more adolescent way, confessed to trying to seem indifferent to the loss of his Ministry of Education, given that 'the Chief' had been cruelly unmoved when he met him.[102]

Mussolini himself went back to being Minister of Foreign Affairs, but his Under-Secretary was now Giuseppe Bastianini, the man who in 1939–40 had replaced Grandi as ambassador in London and was not badly regarded there.[103] Belatedly Bastianini, returning to the practice once adopted by Suvich, tried to persuade Mussolini to formulate his war aims, helpfully sending him a seven-point list,[104] hoping thus to counter the Atlantic Charter, just issued by Churchill and Roosevelt.[105] For Bastianini, it turned out that the Italians were fighting for the principle of 'ethnic unity'; all states, he wrote, should be permitted to achieve it (Mussolini changed the term to 'homogeneity' and restricted the states involved to 'European ones'), full sovereignty and independence (again Mussolini, evidently scarred by his conflict with the African empire of Ethiopia and the misunderstandings at Stresa, narrowed the matter to Europe), the right of each state to pursue its own domestic system, access to the economic resources of the world (deleted by Mussolini), the right of social justice for peoples (similarly deleted), an affirmation that peace could only come through 'real collaboration' in a host of economic and social fields (Mussolini added that it must be European and 'under the leadership of the Axis'), and freedom of the seas (dropped by the *Duce*). Here was a justification unlikely to meet the approval of Nazi fanatics, while Mussolini's own corrections left a list which resembled *sacro egoismo* rather more than bespeaking a furious fascism. No wonder the *Duce* would now on occasion maintain that 'all the Fascist wars were inevitable' and he himself had just been dragged into them.[106]

In April 1943 Vidussoni finally lost his secretaryship, being replaced by Carlo Scorza, an old Fascist (born 1897)[107] – here was proof that the punting on the young had not brought great returns. Scorza was yet another who promised to revitalise the Fascist party and, despite the evident lateness of the hour, extend its control over society. Having been elevated to Deputy Secretary of the PNF the previous December, Scorza had urged shortly thereafter that class difference in Italy must end and that the party must be purged, although he was careful to suggest that 'the most powerful weapon' which Italy possessed was 'the figure, the thought, the person, the action of the *DUCE*'.[108] Once having achieved the Secretaryship, despite Mussolini's gloomy intimation that he disliked subordinates who were too independent and activist,[109] Scorza proceeded to make a further sounding of the nation and, on 7 June, came up with a devastating report.

After an introduction which emphasised that he was merely trying to be an 'intelligent subordinate', who understood that Mussolini wanted to 'give a completely new direction to the whole life of the nation', Scorza provided his leader with a class analysis of the country (for all that talk of Fascist unity, these categories still made most sense). Among the top people, Scorza advised, 'Anti-Fascism and Anti-Mussolinism' were 'only contained by fear' that the end of the war would bring social collapse and 'Bolshevism'. In the more middling classes, among white-collar workers and professionals, the hostility was less obvious, but it was also hard to locate 'committed Fascists'. Only the *petite bourgeoisie* and others of the 'little people' remained real Fascists and faithful devotees of their *Duce*, and they must form the basis of any political reconstruction. The Party itself was deeply sick, damaged by a numerical 'elephantitis', by corruption and by internecine quarrelling; only the young still believed in it. Furthermore, the state bureaucracy interfered in all aspects of life, including those which were the proper responsibility of the Party, and, especially among the senior ranks, indulged in further corruption. Economically, too, times were bad. Hunger on the one hand and the black market on the other were rampant. Autarchy, with its sponsoring of a slew of semi-governmental bodies, had led to appalling overlap and confusion. Urgent cuts were mandatory. The Army was guilty of 'planning failure, a lack of preparation, incompetence and irresponsibility'. There were five existing 'supreme' organisations running the war, none of which worked. Italians were suspicious of their German allies and needed better and more convincing information about them and their cause. The senior generals must be eliminated at once. In every area, Mussolini should bestir himself, act and be known to act. Only with the rekindling of the Fascist spirit in the country at large could the regime be revived and the war won.[110]

Equally graphic and potentially more influential was a telegram from Edda in May reporting the effect on Palermo of bombing there. 'Here', she said, 'civilians feel themselves abandoned' by the authorities, whether military or Fascist. 'I have been in Albania and Russia but never have I seen such suffering and pain. Generally', she added in words which echo down Italian history whenever a northerner visits the south, 'I have the impression of being dropped who knows where, a least a thousand miles from the *Patria* and civilization.' Medicine, clothes, bread, pasta, all were lacking.[111]

Some of the populist cast of Scorza's phrases should be discounted, but both his report and that of Edda showed just what a failing grade Fascist Italy and its *Duce* were receiving under the test of war. Plainly it was now far too late for anything to be done, and Mussolini himself, in his response to such information, tried to downplay the criticism implied.[112] On 10 July Allied forces landed successfully in Sicily, having severely bombed and then seized the 'impregnable' islands of Pantelleria[113] and Lampedusa, the latter allegedly at the cost to the invaders of one man bitten by a donkey.[114] On 14 July Mussolini, who had received little more than kind words from his regular petitions for German aerial support against the invasion,[115] was left pathetically to ask General Ambrosio if any plan existed to save Sicily, should the Allies begin to penetrate it.[116] The *Duce* must have known there was not.

For at least six months the possibility of Mussolini's overthrow had been mooted. Since the end of 1942, Eden and the SOE had been receiving approaches purporting to come from Badoglio.[117] Ciano, who had long told any who would listen that the war was lost,[118] knew that the monarchy,[119] the Papacy,[120] business leaders,[121] and the police[122] were all ready to listen to any plan to extract Italy from the war. Worse, in March–April Italian workers had courageously gone on strike, the first such instance from within the Nazi–fascist 'New Order'.[123] Mussolini himself took great notice of this event, frightened in his soul by evidence which seemed to confirm the socialism he had ratted on so long ago still sparked the workers,[124] although Volpi tried to comfort him with the line that the protests were 'merely an economic phenomenon'.[125]

Beset by these and other spectres, Mussolini, as his contemporaries noted, was reduced to the Micawberish position of being utterly devoid of plans but hoping somehow that something positive would turn up.[126] For the rest of the elite, the problem was starker. How could they get rid of Mussolini and withdraw from the war without bringing down on themselves and their country German fury, which would be unlikely to stop at personal punishment but would instead entail the loss of large segments of northern Italy? On 19 July Mussolini, despite his poor physical and mental health flying himself part of the way, met

Hitler at a villa near Feltre for one last discussion of the war situation. Bastianini had provided the *Duce* with a desperate memorandum, ascribing the series of Italian military defeats to the paucity of Fascist means and begging yet again for massive help.[127] In the event, Mussolini had difficulty getting a word in edgeways as the *Führer* discoursed about the general war situation, notably in the East, and ended by telling his Italian colleague peremptorily that he must produce more modern weapons and instil better morale in his officers.[128]

While the *Duce* was thus so fruitlessly engaged, Allied forces bombed his capital, inflicting heavy damage on the working-class area near the railway-line and all but destroying San Lorenzo, one of the seven basilicas of Rome. Elsewhere bombing had a mixed record in effectiveness during the Second World and later wars, but the attack on Rome signalled the end for Mussolini. It was reported that 150 000 Romans had fled their city,[129] and there was general agreement that the populace now put their faith in the Church (or the Anglo-Americans) and not in Fascism. Over the next week, Foggia and Bologna were also savagely attacked from the air. Peasants in the countryside, little contaminated by a Fascist understanding of technologised war, took the bombings as further proof that Americans were millionaires every one – how else could they afford to knock things down with such light hearts?[130]

The final act of Mussolini's dictatorship was played out at the 187th and last meeting of the Grand Council on the night of 24–25 July 1943.[131] The Council was another part of the Fascist state grown rusty with age – its members had not assembled since the war began. Under the leadership of the feline Dino Grandi, a majority of the council, including Ciano, Bottai, and 15 others had agreed on a motion to restore military command to the King. Most of those present understood that the implication was that the *Duce* would lose considerable power, though it is unclear how many realised they were provoking his fall and that of the Fascist regime.

The meeting began on a hot Rome summer afternoon at 5.15 p.m. The atmosphere in the somewhat inaptly named *Sala del Papagallo* (Room of the Parrot) in the Palazzo Venezia was oppressive. The asthmatic Suardo's laboured breathing[132] enhanced the tension felt by this sweaty group of ageing politicians. Marinelli was too deaf to understand what was going on, but, to his eventual doom, he voted with the majority anyway.[133] Mussolini,[134] who had allegedly arrived at the meeting with counsel from Rachele to 'arrest them all' ringing in his ears, opened proceedings with a lengthy and incoherent account of the war situation. In a speech lasting more than two hours, he was forced to pause from time to time to press his stomach because of the pain.[135] He did boast, however, perhaps hoping especially to convince himself, that he was still possessed of 'a memory of iron'.[136] Then the attacks, generally embarrassed and diffident, trying to approach the issue tangentially, began – De Bono, for example, responded to Mussolini's remarks by defending the army. Farinacci, who was not one of the nineteen, admitted that he was 'a disappointed soldier and citizen' and, presumably remembering Vidussoni, complained that Mussolini had never paid enough attention to 'us old ones'.[137]

The meeting lurched on as meetings do. At midnight Mussolini moved to adjourn proceedings, but Grandi objected and a half-hour pause was approved. When discussion resumed, Bastianini declared in telling metaphor that 'the Nation has gone on strike against the Party'.[138] Finally, the vote was taken; nineteen for, seven against, with Suardo abstaining, and Farinacci announcing that he could only vote for a motion of his own.[139] It was 3 a.m. when the exhausted Fascist chiefs finally broke up. Mussolini had remarked to Grandi: 'I'm a man of sixty [his birthday was four days off] and I know very well where these matters will end.' After the final vote, he also said: 'Gentlemen, you have opened the crisis of the regime.' He did nothing, however, to encourage sympathisers like Scorza, or Enzo Galbiati of the MVSN,[140] who were perhaps open to the suggestion that they should act violently in his defence, and ignored a suggestion from Galbiati that he fly to Germany to 'consult' Himmler.[141]

Mussolini dragged himself home certainly to rebuke from Rachele and perhaps to his insomnia and depression. The next morning he returned promptly to work, seeing Scorza at 10.30 and the Japanese ambassador at noon (to whom he talked again of the need to win Hitler over to the idea of a separate peace with the USSR).[142] At 5 in the afternoon he kept what traditionally was his bi-weekly appointment with the King, arriving at the Villa Savoia in a rumpled blue suit.[143] Victor Emmanuel III, by contrast, as befitted a geriatric *re soldato*, was wearing uniform. In behaviour which seemed a ghostly repeat of the practices of a Liberal Cabinet crisis, Mussolini informed the King about the success of the Grandi motion. In reply, Victor Emmanuel, after touching on the hot weather, deepened Mussolini's depression with the remark that the *Duce* had become 'the most hated man in Italy'. Given that fact, he had decided, the King said, that Badoglio must take over as Head of Government.[144] The consultation over,

Mussolini headed back towards his own car, but a Captain Paolo Vigneri intercepted him and he was whisked off to a military hospital and imprisonment[145] – Queen Elena, the Montenegrin, feared the infringement of royal hospitality thus involved; no good, she prophesied, would come of discourtesy perpetrated on a guest at the royal house.[146] By 27 July Admiral Franco Maugeri was escorting Mussolini to what was in practice a form of *confino* on the island of Ponza. As Maugeri remembered the scene, Mussolini 'was wearing a baggy, unpressed, shabby, blue-serge suit; it looked as if he had been sleeping in it for several days and he probably had'. The God of a few hours before now seemed 'a wry, sad and even pathetic clown'.[147] So – at least for the first time – fell Fascism and its *Duce*.

On Ponza, Pietro Nenni and Tito Zaniboni, intransigent Anti-Fascists, were still awaiting their release, but Mussolini was put in a dilapidated house away from the main settlement. It had for a time been the place of imprisonment of the Ethiopian Ras Imru. But Ponza was militarily insecure and, on 7 August, Mussolini was moved to the naval base at La Maddalena off Sardinia. Here, too, his stay was brief and, on 28 August, he was transferred to the more redolently named *Campo Imperatore*, a ski resort at the *Gran Sasso*, 2000 metres up in what Mussolini drily defined as 'the highest prison in the world'.[148] Behind these sudden peregrinations lay the new Italian authorities' fear of the Germans. The Nazis were indeed engaged in a hunt for the *Duce* which, in its bathos, foreshadowed the absurd pursuit of Mussolini's corpse in 1946.[149] Himmler engaged an astrologer for what he hoped was useful advice about Mussolini's fate,[150] but the orthodox techniques of the Nazi secret service were more successful in discovering where their old Axis ally was being held. German preparations for his release swung into action.

While confined on Ponza, Mussolini showed signs of a Catholic faith (though perhaps the local priest was the only half-tolerable person with whom he could have a conversation, and the *Duce* had a long record of telling interlocutors what they wanted to hear). Still in part 'Prof. Mussolini', he also settled down to translate Carducci's *Odi barbare* into German.[151] At La Maddalena he welcomed Hitler's (belated) sixtieth birthday present, a complete, 24-volume set of the works of Nietzsche – Mussolini claimed to have read four before other events intervened.[152] The ex-*Duce* also wrote to his family, first asking Rachele for clean underwear and 'some books',[153] but later telling her that his conscience was 'clear': 'I have worked for twenty-one years without a break and with complete disinterest and perfect loyalty.'[154]

His correspondence with his sister was more revelatory, with Edvige being assured that he viewed himself as 'defunct', 'a heap of skin and bones in process of organic decomposition'. He hoped for a Catholic burial, but asked, somewhat unnecessarily in the present circumstances, that he not be granted official honours.[155]

During his captivity, Mussolini's health continued to deteriorate. On Ponza, where he celebrated a melancholy sixtieth birthday, he had endured another severe stomach attack, although some improvement seemed to come thereafter from new medication.[156] Logic suggested that he was a dead man walking.[157] At La Maddalena he also lamented the failing state of his health, claiming that it was being ruined by the Sardinian climate.[158] After transfer to the *Campo Imperatore*, he was lethargic, preferring to play *scopone* rather than to read, dining early at 7 p.m. and becoming most animated when he could expatiate about his physical condition.[159] There were rumours that he planned to slash his wrists rather than allow himself to fall into Allied hands,[160] though his habitual fondness for over-statement leaves doubts about his resolution in carrying through a suicide.[161]

While Mussolini was thus focused on himself, the government of Badoglio and the King was fumbling its attempt to get out of what was now deemed the 'Fascist war'. On 3 September an agreement was reached with Allied negotiators and, five days later, the surrender was made official.[162] Disaster followed, given that the Germans, from July and even before, had been extending their *de facto* control over most of Italy. By the early morning of 9 September Victor Emmanuel and his government, frightened for their lives and unconcerned about the people whom they ruled, fled Rome, abandoning the capital and all Central and Northern Italy to the Nazis. Amidst these chaotic events, on 12 September Mussolini was rescued by an SS glider team headed by the Austrian Colonel Otto Skorzeny, who had been personally entrusted by Hitler with the task shortly after 25 July.[163] The *Duce*'s gaolers had heard nothing from Rome for five days, and in the event no attempt was made to block the Germans. Mussolini was crammed into one of the single-seater planes which took off with difficulty and deposited him at an airport in German hands at Pratica di Mare. Thence he was flown on to Munich for a reunion with his family who had made their way to Nazi sanctuary by diverse routes, and a meeting with Hitler. On 18 September he was sufficiently recovered to broadcast from Munich the news of his survival and his determination to punish the King and his aides. 'Only blood', Mussolini pronounced, 'can cancel so humiliating a page from the history of the *patria*'. The war continued. Traitors of all types must be 'eliminated'. The 'parasitic plutocracy' must meet its fate. Peasants, workers and *petit bourgeois* could unite in the cause of a reinvigorated Fascism.[164] According to the account Mussolini later published in the newspapers, from July to September he had experienced a 'calvary and a resurrection'.[165]

The metaphor may have been hackneyed, but Fascist sympathisers asserted almost at once after 1945[166] that, in response to the events of 8 September, the *Duce* had heroically decided to offer his body to the Italian people to save them from what would otherwise have been a terrible revenge wrought by the Germans upon them for their 'treachery'. In this view, the new republican state established under Mussolini's leadership was 'the necessary republic'.[167] During the 1990s this case was re-presented by serious historians riding the wave of revisionism about the Fascist past.[168] The concept of a leader cleaving to the Nazis in order to shield his people from the terror and the horror is, of course, familiar in the literature about Philippe Pétain and Vichy France. Both in France and Italy, however, it remains unconvincing. No doubt Mussolini accepted the events being visited upon him, both his imprisonment and his release, with the mentality of a sleepwalker. If suicide was ruled out, what could he do but go along with them? This passivity, however, should not be confused with planning or sacrifice. Mussolini accepted the leadership of the RSI not just because there was no help for it, but also because he preserved political ambition, was indeed a Fascist and 'friend of the *Führer*' and still preferred to work with the Nazi Germans rather than actively oppose them. Cheap fear also played a part in his choice. Mussolini talked grandly of how the English would clap him in the Tower or confine him on a desert island[169] – the parallel between himself and that great Frenchman Napoleon sprang automatically to his mind. But behind the words lay a more simple apprehension about trial, humiliation and execution. Better to be with the Germans he knew than with the Anglo-Saxons he could only imagine; better for Mussolini, and bad luck for the rest.

To be sure the *Duce* carried to the north by his rescuer was a 'physical ruin'[170] and at least as battered psychologically. Now he was accorded the assistance of German doctors, under the ultimate control of the *Führer*'s loopy Dr. Theodor Morell. One, Georg Zachariae, wrote his memoirs. On his arrival in Germany, the *Duce*, Zachariae recalled, had been given a battery of clinical tests. They demonstrated that he indeed suffered from a duodenal ulcer, which had in turn enlarged his liver and partially blocked his bowel. Without the use of laxatives, his digestive processes no longer worked. There was no evidence of cancer; the heart and arteries functioned normally, but his blood pressure was rather low. A neurological specialist also examined the *Duce*, but found nothing abnormal. There was no sign of syphilis and, when asked, Mussolini vigorously denied ever having been afflicted by it.[171]

Back in Italy, however, Mussolini again suffered bouts of sickness, depression and insomnia. The new secretary of his office noticed at a first meeting in October 1943 that the *Duce* was sitting with his belt undone and that, during their conversation, he reached down to alleviate the pain.[172] Zachariae now himself came from Germany and was appalled at the condition of the Italian dictator. He found him slumped on a divan, wearing a shirt and a dirty dressing gown, and was greeted by Mussolini muttering: 'Well, you see the state I'm in.'[173] His patient went on to relate that he had endured an ulcer for 'twenty years', but that its effect had worsened since '1940'. 'In the two or three hours after eating and at night he was tormented by cramps, which felt as though someone was punching him in the stomach as hard as they could.' He could not sleep and had grown afraid of the onset of the night. He was forever constipated and the blockage could only be relieved by his taking of strong purgatives. He ate very little, certainly not enough, in the German doctor's opinion, to sustain his workload. He was, in sum, a 'physical wreck, on the edge of the tomb'[174] – perhaps it was true that the habitual biliousness of Mussolini's depiction of the world and humankind owed something to his blocked digestion.

Mussolini's Italian doctors had put him on a regimen of tea, *pane biscottato* (dry toast), a little boiled fruit and milk. Recently he had also been drinking two litres of boiled water daily. But this diet had only worsened his constipation. Zachariae was enough the pupil of Morell to look instead to the gains which might come from vitamins (although in his post-war memoirs he denied that he followed Morell's advice fully).[175] At least by Zachariae's account, the efforts at vitamin enhancement and the elimination of milk from the diet brought immediate improvement to his eminent patient. Indeed, according to the German doctor, by early 1944 the *Duce* was largely back in form, able to enjoy some white meat or fish and limiting the sugar in his regular plates of cooked fruit. Mussolini still took vitamin B and C in considerable dosage, either in pills or by injection. He put on weight, improved his colour, began to ride a bicycle and could play tennis for an hour and a half each morning. Zachariae remembered Mussolini being courteously grateful when his mistakes in using foreign tongues were pointed out to him[176] – can he have been pining to go back to being that Mussolini whose ambition might have been satisfied as a language-teacher? But for a continuing weakness for colds and a lingering tiredness,[177] the *Duce* remained in good health until February 1945, when another decline set in, with weight loss, stomach pain, depression so deep that it almost amounted to apathy, and finally 'a grave nervous attack, a real breakdown'.[178] When he first saw Mussolini, Zachariae had surmised that the dictator's health was so poor that it must have affected his decisions, probably since 1940.[179] In 1945, it seemed, he was again reduced to being a walking corpse.

For the restored *Duce* the family was discomforting. Officials may have busied themselves ensuring that the Villa Feltrinelli had sufficient supplies of coffee, that three wagon-loads of books were delivered there, that the tennis court was spruced up with bags of 'red dust' and that a manicurist kept her appointments with her august client,[180] but the atmosphere in the Mussolini family grew rancid. Rachele was bitterly determined on a vendetta against those who had 'betrayed' her husband in July, and directed her greatest animus against her son-in-law, the yuppy golfer.[181] There was even trouble from young Romano, a jazz pianist in the making. Perhaps taking refuge from his school failures – his teachers in 1942 had suggested that he needed urgent remedial attention to overcome his short attention span[182] – he insisted on playing boogie-woogie in the hearing of his German hosts, ignoring their manifest disapproval. Worse, he publicly told his father he was talking rubbish when the *Duce* claimed to be able to read Nietzsche's Greek quotes in the original.[183] Even at home, the little and the big lies of Fascism were hard to escape. Whichever bleak house the family established itself in did nothing to increase Mussolini's charity towards his political associates; to a man, he remarked in October 1943, they were 'insects', 'creatures who matured in the body of a great animal'.[184] Almost as reflex, Mussolini had resumed his accustomed administrative practices, expending much time on 'audiences'; in any one day, he met a score of his associates in fifteen to thirty minute sessions.[185] The phantom nature of most of the ensuing discussion did little to lift Mussolini's spirits or dispel his misanthropy.

It is therefore no surprise to discover the RSI to be a state riddled with contradiction, corruption and incompetence, while also being an organisation willing to condone and conduct violence of the most barbarous kind. It was now, for example, that the 'banality of good' lost its power and Fascist Italians became direct perpetrators of the Final Solution. Some 7500 Jews were collected, generally by Italians, and despatched to their fate in the East. Six hundred and ten lived.[186] When, in November, those who were supporting the new state met at Verona, they drafted a Manifesto which declared brutally but with a hint of residual confusion: 'Those belonging to the Jewish race are foreigners. During this war they belong to an enemy nationality.'[187] Meanwhile a decree published under the name of Minister of the Interior, Guido Buffarini Guidi, ordered the concentration of all Jews in camps and the sequestration of their property.[188]

The fact that Mussolini did not himself take over the Ministry of the Interior was an indication both of the fragility of his own myth and power in the Social Republic and the failure once again to delineate clearly the relationship between state and party. Such (self-interested) Fascist true believers as Farinacci were loud in their demands that the party now cast off the shackles of the state administration on what they imagined was the model of the Fascism of 1919 and the practice in Nazi Germany. Confronted with conflict, Mussolini again took refuge in words, arguing that 'men' had failed him in the past and that there was nothing wrong with the idea of Fascism – it just needed greater refinement (could Professor Mussolini the Philosopher, he mused, earn a better grade from history than seemed likely to be awarded to the warlord and dictator?).[189] There was much talk of the 'enlarging and perfecting' of 'socialisation',[190] an idea which Mussolini had in the past derided,[191] but which now fitted a desperate populism intended to rally the people behind their returned leadership. An advocacy of a drastic equalisation also had the advantage, certainly understood by Mussolini who slyly savoured the prospect of posthumous revenge, of leaving *mine sociali* (social mines) floating in Italian society,[192] with the potential to cause wounds and terror for any successor state to the Fascist dictatorship.

Some Italians were attracted to the new regime, usually from a mixture of a patriotism outraged by the events of 8 September, a youthful sense of adventure, or a more malevolent commitment to a fascist Europe (each of these motives could sometimes be expressed through a surviving love for the *Duce*).[193] Other Italians, by contrast, were already taking to the hills and joining the first formations of the armed Anti-Fascist resistance. The great majority of the populace belonged to neither side but hoped somehow to prevent the irruption of the general tragedy of war into their individual lives. Almost all took as their first lesson from the events of 1943: 'here, no-one believes in anything'.[194] It was a message which, in the new millennium, can still be traced in Italian souls.

For Mussolini, the chief dilemma had become the simpler one of how to live with himself and the profundity of his failure to find a political third way, nationalise the Italian masses and unequivocally raise the Italian nation to the ranks of the genuinely Great Powers. The exercise of his power had rarely happened without him preserving a sense of manipulation and being aware of the need to cover a possible retreat. Now it seemed that neither he nor any other Italian could aspire to frame independent policy. Mussolini's envious admiration of Hitler could still lead him to tell associates that the *Führer* was 'a mystic at the head of a great, modern, State. What an adventure for Germany!'[195] But he was just as likely to complain again about the fighting qualities of the Italian people. Farinacci, so long tolerated as his appealingly roughneck associate, had tried in September to enlist the Germans in his own cause − and lead the new Italy − only to find the fastidious Hitler taking a personal dislike to him.[196] Farinacci's days of being the man who could tell Mussolini a variety of truth were over; in Mussolini's hearing, he was sarcastically dismissed as 'The *Gauleiter*'.[197] Once he was established at Gargnano, Mussolini found as replacement a last friend in Nicola Bombacci, like himself a socialist 'rat' but a more belated one, and a man who had never totally abandoned socialist ideals.[198] In their regular talks, Mussolini could perhaps convince himself that he, too, had never really been bought and sold by the bourgeoisie.

For the last decade the bourgeois face of Fascism had been most directly embodied for Mussolini by his son-in-law Ciano. In the successes and travails of the regime, the two had formed an odd couple who, contrary to some appearances, managed to associate politically. But now Ciano, the 'traitor of July' most easily within reach, was hated by the Germans and the other leaders of the RSI and, notably, by Pavolini, the secretary of the reconstituted Republican Fascist Party. Because their backgrounds and their attitudes until July had been so similar Pavolini was all the more determined on the death of his old friend. Rachele also demanded her son-in-law's execution. Mussolini tried limply to deflect the criticism, telling his administrative secretary in October that Ciano was really no better and no worse than any other. The ex-Foreign Minister was, he noted insightfully, the target of all because they could not condemn the *Duce* himself.[199] Ciano's failings, he admitted, had been his own.

In reality, Mussolini was guilty of each of the sins of commission and omission which could be attributed to both Ciano and Farinacci. He had preached a revolution which destroyed neither private property nor the family and the hierarchies associated with it. He had tried to be Catholic and non-Catholic, Romagnole, Italian and universal, populist and elitist, orthodox economist and advocate of social welfare, racist and realist. For a while, a long while, the trick had worked. He had experienced an adulation which is nowadays restricted to stars in the sports and entertainment 'industries'. He had been ascribed a limitless charisma. He had created an 'Italian Empire'. And yet somehow, amid the hosannas, personal satisfaction never came. Rachele and Edda increased his unease at home. Claretta might occasionally relieve the body but never the mind. His stomach pain nagged away. And now, in this ersatz new Republic, he had to live in the greyness of the northern lakes, and go through the motions of power while all the time knowing that he was reduced to being, as he put it, a low-grade 'mayor of Gargnano',[200] trying to 'stand erect in quicksands'.[201] Even in that claim, he was again fooling himself. In 1943–44 Mussolini had become a 'puppet dictator', a war leader without credible armies, a Fascist whose ideology had been hijacked by his 'mystical' partner to the north, no more than a historical oxymoron. Now all that loose Fascist talk about the regime's own brand of mysticism, its own perfervid militancy, exacted its cost. This failed Mussolini was the one who, in January 1944, cravenly let his son-in-law go to his death in his own place, and who thereafter presided over the worst part of Italy's war, still only a superficial matter compared with the hell in the East, but killing more than 200 000 Italians. For him, too, in April 1945 the Second World War finally, and mercifully, brought an end. For this man, who had once been first of his class and had never lacked intelligence of a kind, the wages of cynicism and Darwinism, the only ideas which could still survive in the confusion of his mind, had indeed been dishonour and death.

18

The ghost of Benito Mussolini, 1945–2001

AFTER Mussolini and his mistress had been shot at Mezzegra, their bodies, and those of such last associates as Nicola Bombacci, Alessandro Pavolini, Paolo Zerbino and the *Duce*'s personal secretary, Luigi Gatti, were flung onto the back of a truck. It took them through the dead of night the 60 kilometres or so which separates Lago di Como from Milan. According to Sergio Luzzatto, a recent historian: 'In front of the gates of the Villa Belmonte di Giulino, on the afternoon of 28 April 1945, one history closed. It was that of the living body of the *Duce*. Another history opened; that of his corpse.'[1] In Milan, these corpses were united with those of Farinacci,[2] killed while fleeing with a noble mistress, and Starace – the latter had been eking out a pensioner's existence in Milan, dining at the *mensa di guerra* and feebly exhibiting his surviving Fascist *élan* by jogging around the streets, where he was ignored or avoided by all, and could only partially comprehend what was happening to the regime, to the country and to himself.[3] The partisans' destination in the Lombard capital was the Piazzale Loreto near the central railway station, an undistinguished suburban square with a set of petrol bowsers to one side. Today they have disappeared, replaced by a rusting monument to the Resistance, but fans of *il fast* (fast food) can appease their appetites at a McDonald's overseeing the site from a second floor and there contemplate the 'real' victors of all the Second World Wars.

The Piazzale Loreto had not been chosen lightly. On the morning of 10 August 1944, at German command, 15 imprisoned partisans had been shot there in reprisal for Allied bombing and Resistance raids. To the horror of the locals, the corpses were then exposed publicly in the square – some women, it was rumoured, moved to pity at the sight, had strewn flowers on their remains. The authorities of the RSI, publicly and privately, tried to detach themselves from any responsibility for this savagery. One leading official complained that such overt cruelty only helped the Allies.[4] Distant from the action at Salò, Mussolini was reported to have mumbled: 'For the blood of Piazzale Loreto, we shall pay dearly.'[5] Such special pleading after the event cannot be read too literally. The Nazis were in Milan as the friends and allies of the Fascist state, and the *Duce* and his colleagues could scarcely have been surprised by the Nazi liking for condign punishment. In any case, Piazzale Loreto was not the only place in Italy where the Nazis practised public terror, but it was a site which Italians would have a double cause to remember.

The second moment of horror in the Piazzale Loreto was destined to be different from the first. If national stereotypes play any part in history, then it was to be more an 'Italian' than a 'German' event. The truck carrying the bodies of Mussolini and his comrades reached Milan in the early hours of the morning of 29 April, without the Resistance chiefs having worked out what they might do with what to some might seem the holy relics of the dictator. The partisans who had come from Lago di Como had a clearer idea on the subject and proceeded to the Piazzale Loreto. There they flung the bodies down on the dirt of the square, in front of a row of peeling placards advertising local cinematic and theatrical events.[6] The news spread that here was entertainment of a more immediate kind.

In a spring dawn, the people of the neighbourhood, their lives having been so disrupted and afflicted by war, spontaneously began to assemble. The moment had come when they could show what they thought about Mussolini's tyranny, the disaster of the war, great politics, and, most simply, the fall of a dictator. The dead Mussolini at last could be attacked with impunity. Not only did the crowd hurl imprecations at their ex-leader and spit at his remains, they also hit out at the corpse with sticks and their bare hands. Local women, it is claimed, urinated on it. The 15 executed in 1944 were revenged. In every way, the end of the dictator was made humiliating and disgraceful. He was photographed lying almost on top of his mistress but carrying, sceptre-like, a Fascist *gagliardetto* (pennon). In that image, he looked for a moment like a dead or deposed king, clutching hopelessly but unrepentantly the hollow (if phallic) sceptre of power. When, with a certain mercy, his body was strung up beside the bowsers, it was covered with detritus. Brain matter seeped out from wounds which were especially deep on the right side of Mussolini's head. Next to the *Duce* swung the corpse of Claretta Petacci, devoted in her naïve conventionality to her 'Ben' until beyond the end. A 'man of respect', or, according to some, a charitable priest, had tied up her skirts so that, as she swung upside down, she did not expose too much of her charms to the raucous and unforgiving public.

Sergio Luzzatto has moralised about the macabre nature of this scene, depicting it as 'a festival of death', which left a regrettably negative legacy to the Italian Republic.[7] In interpreting events this way, Luzzatto was pursuing a party line. Current conservative Italian historiography is engaged in a campaign to de-ideologise the past, so that it can better fit that de-ideologised present in which we all live, or are meant to live, after 'the end of history'. In 1945 the more self-aware ex-Fascists had similarly been troubled by the 'terrible ferocity' manifested by the people,[8] no doubt half thinking that there but for the grace of God went they. A rival reading of the Piazzale Loreto is, however, possible. Mussolini's end in that square actually had much that was appropriate about it. The boy from Dovia had made it all the way to Predappio, to Forlì, to Milan, and on to Rome and back to Milan, the Lombard city where his brother had worked and died. Before 1914 it had already become his crucial power base. Its bankers and businessmen had given help when needed, fully abandoning their *Duce* only when the war was plainly lost. In 1943-45 Mussolini had hoped that Milan could somehow become the capital of the RSI.[9] Perhaps the architecture of the place was a little too Germanic, too redolent of the days of Habsburg rule, too like the Trentino for the contentment of the *Duce*'s ghost. On the other hand, the city was near to Europe, to Paris, and so to that great world where the young Mussolini had imagined himself questing. Rome, Africa and the rest had turned out to be illusions. Milan was a proper place in which Benito Mussolini should die (or have his death made public).

Nor was the 'spectacle' of Piazzale Loreto as 'unedifying' as Luzzatto thinks. The events of 29 April did not really replay the parades and speeches of the Piazza Venezia in Rome.[10] Rather the death rites of the *Duce* were those that failed tyrants had often expected from history. The people's reactions were doubtless violent but, when compared with what the Fascist regime had done to them, their families and to a whole host of victims, were not especially cruel. The more telling contrast is with the events of Hitler's death in his Berlin bunker. Mussolini's old patron, Giuseppe Prezzolini, who had waited out the Second World War in New York but retained his usual ability to read history awry, commented in his diary on 5 May that 'Hitler is dead with decency and mystery, as suits a god of the Niebelungen.

Thus he seems the opposite of Mussolini, killed as if in a pub brawl.'[11] Certainly, the *Führer* met his end with the fire and technology of war all about, in a sort of *Götterdämmerung*, leaving his teeth as his surest identifying remnant. Mussolini's demise was of a more conventional and recognisable, and less 'modern' kind, as befitted a man who had committed acts of great evil but who did not utterly betray humankind.

Moreover, the people, in their spontaneous and violent contempt, were not the only group to seek their dealings with the dead *Duce*. After its day in the Piazzale Loreto, his corpse was carried to the hospital (the *Istituto di medicina legale*) of the University of Milan.[12] There it was mercifully cleaned and measured – at death, Mussolini had weighed 72 kilograms and was 1.66 metres tall.[13] The body was also subjected to the posthumous insult of autopsy. The American military authorities demanded, as it were, their slice of the action. Clinically precise, despite the crowds of Italians who continued to mill around the corpse even within the hospital, the American doctors removed some brain tissue from the *Duce*'s head and sent it back to their home country for examination. The Americans, troubled by the thought that any could reject the beneficence of their ideals, were convinced that Mussolini was 'mad'. Insanity, they believed, had been brought on by longstanding syphilis (although they had so far spared the *Duce* the sort of psychoanalysis *in absentia* which some of their 'experts' had visited on Hitler during the war).[14] Now they looked to medical science to prove their hypotheses correct.

However, the US soon had a Cold War to organise and manage, and Mussolini rapidly lost ground as a significant figure in their demonology. In any case it was confirmed yet again that he did not suffer from syphilis. Mere science did not have the answer to his politics. This matter resolved, or, rather, the examination of Mussolini's tissue over, the slivers of brain were preserved for years at St Elizabeth's psychiatric hospital in Washington. Eventually, however, perhaps prompted by some desire to spring-clean, it was agreed to get rid of them. On 25 March 1966 the remnants of brain matter were returned to Rachele, 'in six test tubes in a wooden box, with the compliments of the US ambassador in Rome'.[15] Allegedly the English-language tag on the box ascribed the remains to a certain 'Mussolinni'.[16]

Exempted from this American sojourn, the rest of Mussolini's corpse had been moved from the *Istituto di medicina legale* to a hurried and anonymous burial at the Musocco cemetery outside the city of

Milan.[17] The grave was numbered 384, but was otherwise unmarked.[18] The Mussolini family, presently dispersed, was not permitted mourning. But the body was not yet to lie still. At midnight on 22 April 1946 Domenico Leccisi, a Fascist nostalgic, broke into the cemetery aiming, with the help of two friends, to steal the corpse. By his own account, Leccisi admits that his career as a body-snatcher had a bathetic side. Amid some confusion, the actual tomb was not reached until 2.30 a.m. Then the soil proved as hard as stone, the digging was difficult and noisy and it took more than an hour and a half to begin to uncover the *Duce*. Eventually, Leccisi himself jumped into the hole he and his friends had made and prised open the coffin to reveal Mussolini's mouldering head, set, so Leccisi thought, in a sad smile.[19] The ex-dictator's body was wrapped in a sheet and was unwound only with great trouble. It was also heavy and unwieldy – how could it be transported across the wide spaces of the cemetery? Dawn was approaching as the conspirators resolved this problem when they located a gardener's wheelbarrow in which to deposit their treasure. Leccisi recalls his concern because, as the barrow was pushed hurriedly down the cemetery's paths, Mussolini's head lolled out over the side.[20] Leccisi, in his piety or fanaticism, had planned that his escapade should resemble an Easter resurrection and he had aimed to leave the tomb-site marching with the solemnity and good order of a funeral. Actually the final departure was hurried, and some pieces of skin and bone from the decaying *Duce* spilled out on the parapet of the 2-metre cemetery wall.[21] In addition, Leccisi's assistant tripped as he climbed the barrier and tumbled to the ground, dropping the corpse which fell on top of him. Recomposing themselves, and their *Duce*, as best they could, Leccisi and his friends shoved their booty into the back of their car and sped off into the morning light.[22] More in tune with the plan, they had remembered to leave behind some propaganda material for the *Partito fascista democratico* (Fascist democratic party), a tiny group which Leccisi led. A press release was also issued; it read 'Musocco – the dead have taken wings'.[23] It was true that, during the latter stages of the war, an American preacher-man had detected that Mussolini was the Anti-Christ – *Viva il Duce*, he claimed, concealed the number 666, the mark of the beast – and had predicted his resurrection,[24] but he had not foreseen Leccisi's method of assuming Mussolini into the ether.

For all their achievement as body-snatchers, Leccisi and his friends were scarcely destined to rise to power. None the less, the disappearance of even a defunct *Duce* did make an impact on the Italian media, then passionately debating the coming referendum which, on 2 June, decided to expel the Savoy dynasty and at last made Italy a republic. In a farcical re-evocation of the tragic events in 1924 concerning Matteotti, the fate of the corpse became a public matter. In a search which resembled a protracted scene from the *Keystone Cops*, the police and other judicial authorities took a hundred days to rediscover the body, while rumours grew steadily more vivid about its fate. Some believed that Mussolini's corpse would be exposed on the 'Altar of the Fatherland' in Rome and so check the ceremonies of the first anniversary of the end of the war. Others feared Churchill, whose name post-war fancy often bracketed with Mussolini's, had ordered it spirited across the Channel for an unclear reason. The police, overestimating their opponents in a predictable fashion, were sure that the abductors were expert in necrology and medicine, as well as plainly in receipt of considerable finance.[25]

Despite such delusions, the authorities did soon penetrate the thin and inexperienced ranks of the *Partito fascista democratico*, and made some arrests.[26] What they could not do, however, as the date of the referendum neared and then passed, was locate the body. Not until 31 July was Leccisi trapped in Milan, but he did not bend under questioning. Finally, on 11 August two priests with Fascist sympathies, the delightfully named Padre Zucca (Father Pumpkin) and Padre Alberto Parini, brother of Piero Parini, a leading Salò Fascist, confessed that they had helped in the concealment of Mussolini's remains. At first the body had been taken to the Valtellina – again ironies abounded in this belated arrival of the *Duce* at a place which he had sometimes boasted would constitute Fascism's last redoubt. However, the corpse spent only a couple of weeks hidden there before being brought back to Milan and, with the aid of the pious fathers, hidden for a while at the Church of Sant' Angelo.[27] From there it was moved again and, during the last weeks, what was left of the *Duce* had been preserved in the noble and beautiful surrounds of the *Certosa* of Pavia, one of Italy's most distinguished religious sites. Such beauty did not enhance the condition of the corpse, however. It was meanly wrapped in plastic sheeting and crammed into a box which had itself been concealed in a wall-cupboard of a monk's cell on the ground floor of the *Certosa*.[28]

Sergio Luzzatto, historian of these grotesque events, is very inclined to sympathise with Leccisi, whom he regards as 'a genuine person, sincerely devoted to the cult of the *Duce* and to the cause of neo-fascism'. Luzzatto is critical of the reaction of the Italian government to what they treated as a schoolboy prank. Leccisi received a mild gaol term of 6 months for forging counterfeit money (some stocks of it had been found in the raid on the *Partito fascista democratico*), and was allowed to get away scot-free with his kidnapping of the corpse.[29] It might be argued, in reply, that such mercy amounted to an excellent tactic by the authorities, helping the whole affair to be treated with the derision it deserved. Mouldering dictators might have a certain allure, but it was proper that the purloining of Mussolini's corpse did not distract Italians from voting in the Republic and commencing a political process which, over the next decades, brought to the people of the peninsula many and much needed reforms.

While the history of the Republic in its chiaroscuro lay ahead, Mussolini was reburied, this time in the Capuchin chapel at Cerro Maggiore, outside Milan. His bodily remains, lacking the brain slivers and the dropped pieces of skin and bone, were, on this occasion, interred with Christian ceremony, as Catholic charity suggested. Fathers Zucca and Parini had exacted such a concession to dignity or piety before revealing the hideout at the Pavia *Certosa*.[30]

However, another chapter of the saga of Mussolini's corpse was still to be written. In 1957 Mussolini was moved again, on this final occasion home to the San Cassiano cemetery at Predappio, near where Rachele again lived and where, according to her admirers, she was frugally given to cooking bean soup for her surviving friends and relations.[31] The agent of Mussolini's final transfer was Christian Democrat Prime Minister, Adone Zoli, a lawyer now based in Florence and a Catholic Anti-Fascist. More importantly, Zoli also sprang from that same family on whose estates Rachele had been born,[32] and who had provided the counsel to Rosa Maltoni, persuading her to send her son to the Salesians at Faenza,[33] and who had otherwise been useful patrons of the Mussolinis.[34] Naturally, Adone Zoli had retained contacts both with the administration of Predappio and with surviving members of the Mussolini family. Moreover, he may have been pushed towards a new clemency by the preaching, in the early part of the 1950s, of the aged parish priest at Predappio. This charitable prelate was Don Pietro Zoli, a man who remembered with advantages his own training at Rosa Maltoni's school before the First World War.[35]

It was thus no surprise when Adone Zoli issued the necessary government permits which, on 31 August 1957, allowed Mussolini to be buried with some ceremony in the family crypt in his home town.[36] Reviewing the event, a British official commented that 'Italians deeply respect the dead and the feelings of the bereaved, a fact which even the Communists have [had] to take into account in their criticisms of the government.' In any case, he added charitably, 'the memory of the Duce, in spite of his crimes against the Italian nation, no longer arouses violent feelings among the great majority of Italians. If his misdeeds are remembered, so are his early achievements and his efforts to give his people a sense of nationhood'.[37] Mussolini's own spirit might not have been so easily pacified. Although he had avoided thinking about the matter when in office, it may be surmised that, had the dictator died in power, he would have been interred in a grandiose tomb at Rome, the ideal heart of the nation. Perhaps the model suburb of EUR could have provided a suitable place of entombment, given the monumentality of its Fascist architecture. But, in the event, the *Duce*'s final resting place was at the San Cassiano cemetery. Interment there with considerable irony carried deep resonances of micro-history, of the story of the *paese* and the *paesani* of Predappio. Mussolini's fate was to be buried in the world of the Italies and not that of a restored Italian Roman empire. Even posthumously, his ambitions to strut triumphantly in the wider world failed.

Of course in Predappio few locals saw it that way. They remembered instead that, under the regime, their *paese* had blossomed in a modest yet telling way. The most important change to the town was a move in its centre of gravity, down the hill towards the river Rabbi, and to Dovia and the *Casa Natale del Duce*. Predappio vecchio (Old Predappio) slept on its hill, content with its sloping, roughly oval-shaped, *piazza*, its two rival churches and its pastel-painted houses, looking for all the world like a set for the staging of the *Barber of Seville*. Predappio nuovo (New Predappio) exhibited a different sort of architecture, carrying a diverse and more militant message. Already in the mid-1920s New Predappio was a place for pilgrimages. A colonnaded area marked the centre of the place: from there awed Fascist visitors were meant to turn their gaze to the east and see the *Rocca delle Caminate*, castle-residence of the Mussolini family. To the west, just above the colonnades, they could admire the old schoolhouse of Varano, the 'birthplace of the *Duce*', inevitably a sacred site. Into this central area, which also served more prosaically as a market, ran the *Corso Benito Mussolini*, not really as grand a street as the name implied, but the main artery through the town. At the southern end of it was another square, dominated by the new, imposing but ugly Church of Sant'Antonio and the rather more handsome, turreted, *Casa del Fascio*. Scattered along the *Corso* lay a new barracks (for the *Duce*'s personal guard), a new school named after Rosa Maltoni, a new hospital and, perhaps most usefully, a new bank. During the 1930s on some flattish land near the river, a Caproni factory for the construction of aeroplanes was established, and an airfield was bulldozed from the surrounding foothills of the Apennines (although it is said that no planes ever took off from its runway). Some years earlier, the flourishing commune of Predappio had even been permitted to annex the nearby *paese* of Fiumana, in what was doubtless its tiny version of a *Weltpolitik*.[38]

In other words the Fascist regime had been good for Predappio, if in a less than overwhelming fashion. Fascist trade union boss, Edmondo Rossoni, had encouraged rather more lavish spending on his home *paese*, Tresigallo di Ferrara. Actually, the most renowned Mussolini in Predappio and its environs was not Benito, but Rachele. She was the local *padrona*, the *dura*, the 'tough one', whom it was better not to cross; she was *Donna Rachele*, a woman of respect,[39] if, like many another such person, thought not above certainly the exercise of patronage and perhaps the seeking of illicit financial gain.[40] After all Rachele had gone on speaking the local dialect as her language of choice until the end of the regime, thus ignoring its nationalising pretensions.[41] After 1945 she soon renewed her local presence, running the nearby Mussolini family estate at the Villa Carpena and, for a time, presiding over a restaurant in the shadow of the *Rocca delle Caminate*, where she offered her clients rich helpings of *tagliatelle alla bolognese*, the speciality of the region.[42]

There were other ironies in the post-Fascist history of Predappio. With the war over, it at once fell to the Left, with the soul of Alessandro Mussolini thus, in a sense, triumphing over that of his son. As was typical of the Emilia-Romagna, it became a stronghold of the PCI. Writing in the 1950s, Vittore Querel, a Fascist sympathiser, lamented this fact, declaring Predappio (with some exaggeration) 'the poorest and most abandoned, the saddest and most wretched town in all Italy'.[43] He also bewailed the way in which the *Casa Natale* had been sacked by partisans at the end of the war, condemning the degradation then visited on the cemetery at San Cassiano, although he did admit that it had been cleaned up thereafter, allowing it to resume its character as 'one of the most romantic spots in the Romagna'.[44]

Querel had one other great theme, and that was the possibility that Predappio, nourished by tourist monies, could find a remunerated role as a place of pilgrimage to, and remembrance of, the history of the *Duce*. Already, he noted, visitors were arriving; Fascist nostalgics being inclined to gather at the *Bar Sport*.[45] Many then proceeded to the Mussolini crypt, which contained the bodies of Mussolini's parents, of Arnaldo and Bruno, and of Bruno's wife, Gina.[46] Actually, Gina Ruberti's tomb was the only one not adorned with Fascist insignia,[47] perhaps because her death in May 1946 had occurred in a boating accident when she was alone with some English officers. Scandalous and salacious rumours had spread about what such company might have signified.[48]

Querel also mentioned the availability in the crypt of a notebook into which 'humble people, soldiers, Fascists' could inscribe their respect 'for the Man who has fallen and whose corpse has not yet found peace'.[49] Shortly after Querel wrote this account, his implied wish was granted – Mussolini's remains were entombed with those of his relatives. However, a complete peace still escaped the *Duce*. On Christmas night of 1971 at a time of political excitation in Italy, a mysterious bomb blew out the door of the San Cassiano crypt.[50] More broadly, the Mussolini family found it hard to slough off their inheritance from the *Duce* and their own lives were neither happy nor productive. The polio-stricken Anna Maria married, but died without issue in 1968. Her elder sister Edda never forgave her father for his betrayal of her husband and, after 1945, resumed a fecklessly worldly life – some purist Fascists were alarmed by rumours that she bathed nude in the seas off Lipari.[51] She did not die till 1995, but was long a victim of kidney disease, perhaps the result of her drinking. She had watched one of her sons, Fabrizio, run unsuccessfully for parliament as a member of the neo-fascist MSI (*Movimento Sociale Italiano* or Italian Social Movement). He had described himself uneasily as 'the son of a Fascist who got it wrong and paid for it'. After his predictable defeat, he emigrated to Venezuela.[52] Her other son, Marzio, died of alcoholism in 1974.

Vittorio Mussolini, the eldest son of the dictator, also spent many years in Latin America, that region of the world where a migration from the Italies had continued for some generations, but where the national government of Italy had rarely carried much weight. Vittorio had fled to Argentina in December 1946, utilising those Vatican networks which were so helpful to many ex-fascists in the aftermath of the war. In Buenos Aires he was well received by local dictator Juan Peron, a long-time Mussolini admirer who treasured a memory of being in the cheering crowd when, in 1936 victorious in Ethiopia, Mussolini had proclaimed the new Roman empire. Eventually Vittorio began to make occasional visits to Italy, usually to 'defend' his own 'honour' as a soldier and that of the family, before returning for good in 1968. His marriage broke up, but in October 1979, with the death of Rachele, he did assume the title of head of the Mussolini family.[53]

Romano, Vittorio's surviving younger brother, enjoyed a post-war career as a jazz pianist, a somewhat politically incorrect interest for the son of an 'Aryan' Fascist dictator.[54] Like other members of his family, and presumably prompted by journalists on the make, Romano eventually published some memoirs about his father in coffee-table format and particularly anodyne in their content.[55] His greater claim to fame was his marriage, for a time, to the Neapolitan Maria Scicolone, a sister of the actor Sophia Loren, although eventually this marriage, too, ended in divorce.[56] The daughter of this union, the photogenic Alessandra Mussolini, did hit the headlines when, in 1992, she was elected to the Italian chamber of deputies,[57] where, in the new millennium, she remains. She had won her electoral victory as a member of the MSI, now renamed the *Alleanza Nazionale* (National Alliance) and declared by its leader, in 2001 to be Italy's Deputy Prime Minister, Gianfranco Fini, 'post-Fascist'. Alessandra Mussolini's own politics have proved somewhat erratic, while the patriarchal beliefs of many of her fellow AN members have not helped her rise in her party's ranks, all the more given her own dallying with a sort of Fascist feminism. She can, however, always earn press coverage with a ceremony of some kind – a marriage, a baptism, a commemoration – held at the 'Fascist' church of Sant'Antonio at Predappio. She has also striven to preserve a reputation as a 'true believer' in her grandfather. 'I'm called Mussolini', she typically told an interviewer, 'I have a clear identity ... the people love me or hate me'.[58] In reality, the meaning of such phrases is anything but limpid, but, as far as the media is concerned, Alessandra is the Mussolini of the new generation. Additionally, in naming her second daughter Clarissa Benita, Alessandra apparently envisages Mussolinis still bound spiritually to the *Duce* in the generations beyond her own.

Querel's imaginings about a tourist future for Predappio have proven partially correct, although the continuance of leftist administration deflated ambitions to turn the *paese* into a centre of full-blown fascist mysticism. A visitor today can still find the architecture, the crypt and the notebook – it is said that a new one replaces an old every 6 weeks, by which time its pages have been filled with pledges of honour and respect for the *Duce* and with hopeful statements about the imminent resurrection of his ideas. To make the atmosphere more suggestive, an eternal flame burns before the *Duce*'s remains, a frowning marble bust records his facial features, while such relics as his black shirt and one military boot (the other was somehow lost during the abduction of 1946) recall his militancy. An altar is signed with that characteristic 'M', which was once the brief indication that Mussolini had scanned and comprehended a bureaucratic memorandum. In the town itself a tourist can choose between four memorabilia shops. From them, Fascist nostalgics can pick up at a good price teeshirts with salutary messages printed on them, imitation weapons, small statues of the dictator (and of his lineal heirs, the leaders of the MSI and AN) and postcards. The ruling junta of Predappio dreams of better ways to recall the town's most famous son and to appraise his history, perhaps through a 'heritage' museum of Fascism and Anti-Fascism, which could give a satisfactory purpose to the elegant erstwhile *Casa del Fascio*. But such hopes are blasted by the fear that history is too easily twisted into celebration and notoriety. In the streets of Predappio, the ghost of Benito Mussolini is neither quiet nor altogether quietened.

It is clear, then, that until 1957 and even thereafter Mussolini's body may have had trouble mouldering in its grave, but what of his spirit, the ideals of Fascism, the memory of the whole Fascist experience? How deeply was Fascism ingrained in Republican Italy? After 1945, did Mussolini's soul in some way go marching on?

Politically, the answer to these questions is a plain 'yes'. Whereas West Germany, East Germany and Austria, in their different ways, all did their best to fudge and conceal the popularity and ubiquity of Nazi support in Germanic lands, Italy pursued a much more open course about its Fascist past. Even in 1944 the curiously named *Uomo Qualunque* (Everyman) party, headed by radio comedian and journalist Guglielmo Giannini, rallied sympathisers with the fallen regime, especially in Rome and the South, under the slogan *Abbasso tutti* (Down with everything).[59] Not long after, Giannini was destroyed politically by the canniness, or ruthlessness, of PCI leader Palmiro Togliatti. However, Giannini's political demise had already been offset by the creation on 26 December 1946 of the *Movimento Sociale Italiano*, under the guidance of Arturo Michelini.[60] The indirectness of the name 'social movement' was enough to get around Italian laws hostile to the re-establishment of the Fascist party. Those in the know apparently understood that MSI 'really' stood for *Mussolini Sempre Immortale* (Mussolini Always Immortal),[61] although the *Duce* himself, a man who in office loved to point out journalists' errors and solecisms, might have been pained by the tautology.

The MSI soon found a role in the multi-party Italian system, usually garnering fourth place in national elections, behind the Christian Democrats, the PCI, and the socialists. Although there were great regional variations, most of the time the neo-fascist party could aspire to some 8 per cent of the vote. Like its rivals in the Italian parliament, the MSI harboured internal factions. Its history was thus characterised by a succession of disputes between moderates, ready, through some version of *trasformismo*, to accept an entry into the Republican system, and true believers, opposed to such compromise. Giorgio Almirante, leader of the party through the 1970s and 1980s and once a writer for the ponderously Anti-Semitic journal *La difesa della razza*, as well as an official under the Salò regime, could on occasion tack before the political wind. But there can be little doubt that he encouraged such unreconstructed philosophers of neo-fascism as Pino Rauti and Julius Evola, the latter once his colleague on *La difesa della razza*. Moreover, just to the party's right lay a constellation of fascist terrorists. Their actions continued to scar the history of the Italian Republic, most tragically in the bombings of Piazza Fontana at Milan in December 1969, Piazza della Loggia at Brescia in May 1974, and in various attempts to attack the railway line between Florence and Bologna. These schemes culminated in the murderous destruction of Bologna station in August 1980 when more than 80 victims died.

A more humdrum terrorism was common in certain zones of Rome, Milan and other cities, and on university campuses, where, especially during the politically riven period that followed the upheavals of 1968, the equivalent of 'no go' areas were patrolled by fascist thugs.[62] In Italian youth culture, Fascism retained, and presently retains, if now in rather different guise, a prominent role. Football fans regularly parade their masculinity under Fascist banners. More seriously, for some youth flaunting a generic Fascism seems the really radical posture, the only 'diverse' political stance available in a society locked into consensus for the market and its world order, a sort of national fundamentalism. A different sort of nostalgia for the regime has long been common in many areas of southern Italy (always the MSI's largest voting base) and, even more so, in Italian emigrant communities scattered around the world. In Australia, for example, Franco Battistessa, an extremist Fascist whose curious boast was that he had founded the first *fascio* in Bombay, remained a powerful figure in the media of the 'Italian community', a group which welcomed for a time a paper called *La Gente d'Italia* (in order not openly to be named *Il Popolo d'Italia*).[63] A relative lack of education was often accompanied by a sentimental approval of Fascism both among emigrants and among those who had stayed in Italy. As Sergio Luzzatto has noted, those fans of popular culture who, during the 1950s and 1960s, concentrated their reading on pulp magazines, often preferred a popular history yearning for Fascist order, and being decidedly nostalgic about the 'strong man' Mussolini himself.[64] Indro Montanelli, ex-Fascist journalist turned independent radical conservative, satisfied the hunger of that section of this public for actual books with a series of narrative histories with the same theme.[65]

More influentially, in the secret service and business worlds, indeed in all the partially hidden networks of the ruling elites, including those blessed by the American embassy, a residual yen for Fascism had by no means been eliminated. Anti-Communism, Anti-Anti-Fascism and some version of Fascism were not always easy to tease apart. In 1964 and 1970 rightist coups were contemplated in these circles, and there may have been other instances when the downfall of the Republic was plotted. Furthermore, these 'extra-parliamentary' groups always cherished international connections, frequently surfacing as supporters of South American dictators, of *Apartheid* while it lasted in South Africa, of Franco, Salazar and the Greek colonels and, indeed, of anti-democratic forces wherever they might be found.

The only problem is whether the ghost of Mussolini could take much credit for this neo-fascism. Memories of him were often mixed. Such a self-consciously profound thinker as Julius Evola preferred the Romanian Corneliu Codreanu, murdered leader of the 'Legion of the Archangel Michael', who had the advantage of leaving behind a corpus of cloudily mystical writings, and whose verbal extremism had never been dimmed by the compromises common to holders of office. Neo-fascists were rarely ill advised enough to write it down on a piece of paper, but the secret predilection of many was actually for the macabrely Wagnerian 'success' of Hitler and the Germanic right, rather than for the doubtful totalitarianism of Mussolini. The drastic and humiliating nature of the Italian defeat in the Second World War was a heavy legacy fully to deny or overcome.

None the less Mussolini fans did from time to time surface. In the 1960s neo-fascist intellectual Giano Accamè organised in Rome a series of lectures under the title *Incontri romani della cultura di destra* (Roman meetings of right-wing culture). Among Accamè's speakers was the American political scientist, A.J. Gregor, at that stage the only scholar in the Anglo-Saxon world who took Mussolini's thought at all seriously.[66] The MSI could also rely on help from the publisher

Giovanni Volpe, the son of the most prominent historian under the regime, Gioacchino Volpe,[67] an intellectual who made little effort to change his political shirt after 1945. By the 1990s Bruno Bottai, the son of the Fascist minister, had become bureaucratic head of the Italian Ministry of Foreign Affairs,[68] and his contacts were appreciated by that 'De Felice school' which strove to moderate past condemnations of Fascism.

In the English-speaking world, however, Mussolini had been receiving a very bad posthumous press. Historian after historian wrote him off as little more than a joke. A.J.P. Taylor, the most brilliant historical writer of his generation, put this interpretation into the most striking words:

> Fascism never possessed the ruthless drive, let alone the material strength, of National Socialism. Morally it was just as corrupting – or perhaps more so from its very dishonesty. Everything about Fascism was a fraud. The social peril from which it saved Italy was a fraud; the revolution by which it seized power was a fraud; the ability and policy of Mussolini were fraudulent. Fascist rule was corrupt, incompetent, empty; Mussolini himself a vain, blundering boaster without either ideas or aims.[69]

Not too surprisingly, some Italian historians viewed the peremptoriness of this dismissal of a generation of their history as itself coloured by levity or prejudice. And, from the 1960s on, the *Duce's* reputation could boast, if not a champion, then certainly a defender of a kind in his biographer, Renzo De Felice. In successive volumes, the Italian historian became more and more ready to give some credit to Mussolini's achievements or ideals. Moreover, De Felice's work found echo inside Italy, where, during the 1980s, Accamè and De Felice collaborated in a series of exhibitions under the patronage of socialist Prime Minister, Bettino Craxi. Such displays emphasised the feisty originality of Fascism, as manifest, for example, in its consumer goods. They ignored war, tyranny and defeat.[70] At the same time, De Felice won converts in the United States, where some experts, perhaps influenced by their own origins in an emigrant 'community' and conscious of their 'roots', disliked the sarcasm of Taylor and his friends.[71]

Political and cultural events were also favouring a turn in the historiography as the 'non-political' Clifford Geertz and the hard-to-place Michel Foucault jostled for chief guru status. By the 1990s quite a few Italian historians and even more pundits took on the slightly odd task of asking why the nationalisation of the masses in Italy had proved such an inadequate process. In undertaking these investigations, their usual target was the 'parties', by which they frequently meant the PCI, under the Republic. With this focus on the sins of the Left, Fascism began to reacquire a certain lustre. Commentators, including De Felice before his death, took to admitting that the Fascist regime may have had its troubles, but then asking whether they were as bad as those of the Republic?[72]

Most significant was that new, globalised and marketised politics which typically favoured the 'pacification' of the past. The 1990s became the decade of the 'apology' for the sins of the fathers, though usually in the most generic way and with little serious attempt to investigate what had actually occasioned the evil now being so heart-fully, and so cosily, regretted. In Italy, such a process entailed the 'de-ideologisation' of the Fascist dictatorship's history and the cancelling of a moral stance towards the relatively recent events of the past. The dispute between Fascism and Anti-Fascism was now typically portrayed possessing an incomprehensible passion, when the more intelligent present could easily see faults on both sides. Both Fascists and Anti-Fascists had killed fellow Italians, the simple message ran, and so they were morally indistinguishable. In any case, history and heritage were slipping into the same melting pot of info-tainment. In its turbid waters Fascism had the advantage of seeming fascinating with its plethora of parades and uniforms; its propaganda, however feeble compared with that of consumerism, retained a posthumous pizzazz. A whole school of 'culturalist' historians, espe-cially in the USA, entertained themselves, if not always their readers, with lovingly 'thick descriptions' of the 'webs of significance' to be found in this or that arena of the dictatorship.

Mussolini himself was something of an underling in these processes, since the culturalists usually thought that they were portraying history from below. Since they accepted their powerless-ness in the present, they saw no reason to review the exercise of power in the past. As far as they were concerned, Mussolini probably held it; but who cared, when the task of history was to describe not to analyse? A 'pacification' of the Fascist past was thus, on balance, good for the *Duce*. The age of embarrassing questions was over.[73] As early as the 1980s, Mussolini's striding masculine figure had been used to advertise the high-quality Hotel Excelsior in Venice. Any client of its comforts, the rubric then ran, could rely on the fact that, in that estab-lishment, *il cliente ha sempre ragione* (the client is always right).[74] In 1998, an Italian crime writer decided to use the drama of the assassination attempt on Mussolini in 1926 to write a piece of 'faction' under the alluring title of *Mussolini's nose*.[75] An English crime-writer, less respectfully, had earlier introduced into one of his works a character called Benito Mussolini, a photographer, blackmailer and murder victim, but one who proved not nearly as clever as his pet monkey.[76] The further appearance of Mussolini's image in such surrounds may be predicted. To become at last banal may be an odd fate for the *Duce*, but not an altogether unwelcome one, given the more negative conclusions that a rigorous analysis of his life would most likely still yield.[77]

To be reduced to an advertising icon was certainly not what Mussolini had imagined when he embarked so bumptiously on his career. But then, in the new millennium, many of his ideas appear so evidently wrong. In our era of *laissez faire*, the Fascist preference for autarchy must be written off as fundamentally mistaken economics. In a time of globalisation, the petty nationalism of a Fascist Italy, which had never altogether secured its rank as a Great Power and which utterly failed the 'test' of the Second World War, seems antique and irrelevant. With a Europe seemingly ever more united, and with their nation's membership being cheered by Italians rather more than by any other members of the union, Fascist hopes of nationalising the masses look equally ill directed. Still more tellingly, the state which, from around the time of Mussolini's birth until the end of the 1980s, was a credible centre for the exercise of human power and for the spreading of welfare and enlightenment, is now fast disappearing into the dustbin of history. The great enemy of the Fascist view of a state has turned out to be not, as Mussolini generally imagined, some variant of socialist democracy, but rather U.S.-style capitalism. Globalised companies now possess a hegemony so sure and unchallenged, and a propaganda, often boldly marketed as 'information', so pervasive as to make any Fascist rhetoric about their building of an omnipresent *stato totalitario* seem quaint indeed.

Mussolini had been accustomed to boast that Fascism was **the** ideology of the twentieth century. For a time, his various admirers and fellow-travellers, from Hitler to Franco to Pius XII to Peron and other post-war national leaders in the Third World, apparently justified his claim. Moreover, even after 1945 the cause of outright neo-fascism, certainly in Italy, was, as has been seen, by no means dead. However, two generations later, history, despite the occasional surfacings of Haiders, Le Pens and Finis, has proven Mussolini utterly wrong. In the world order of our times, the only way a far right can survive for long or with serious effect is by accommodating itself to globalised capitalism and so by downplaying Fascist ideology, discounting such left-overs from the interwar period as corporatism, autarchy, Anti-Semitism and other forms of racial theoretics, empire, war and the intrusive 'totalitarian' state. In certain places and on certain occasions, deals between the far right and the market are indeed imaginable, as is the occasional despairing indulgence by historical losers in nationalist or other forms of fundamentalism. In neither case, however, will the result be something which can be legitimately defined as Fascism. A confused yearning for a return to national welfarism (at least for some special interest group), a bullying patriarchalism, a rapacity towards a neighbour's goods, especially among those who already possess wealth, a social Darwinian hope in the struggle of the fittest, a linked and contradictory envy at the success of others, a ruthless willingness to kill and to maim in war and not only in war, an unalloyed racism (especially directed against blacks, 'Slavs' and Arabs but extending to Jews), a determination to end the power of trade unions (or to channel it to the advantage of special interest groups), a love of false advertising, all these ideas may survive and flourish. But they should no longer be imagined as constituting a 'Fascist threat'. Rather, Mussolinian Fascism must now be accorded the status of a period piece. Only lingering, but incredible, rhetoric about a 'third way', detached from the market, still carries a hint of the Fascist project, although one the advocates of such a path strenuously ignore or deny.

If his ideology is falling back into the mists of the past, perhaps Mussolini the politician is not. Just as once he tried to appear the most knowledgeable of men, today's leaders on occasion flaunt their own unlikely intellectuality. If Mussolini's fame did not seem to make him happy but rather left him cynical about women, friends, family and nation, his successors continue to grasp for power and then be most often unrequited when it turns out to be hollow. Indeed, the myth-making about the *Duce*'s charisma, in which Mussolini himself so eagerly participated, may well have paved the way to the contemporary world of 'spin', in which the last or most damaging ambition of any sage executive is self-knowledge. Aspects of Mussolinian populism – his alleged fondness for sport, his mingling (most frequently from behind his office desk) with wide groups of his subjects and with foreign admirers, even his public extrusion of his bodily liquids – have tended to become the norm since his death, but were less than usual in the world into which he was born. It may not be altogether clear how much Mussolini really believed that the appearance is the message, but he often acted as though it was, or it might as well be. As a man of image, Mussolini can indeed boast heirs.

In sum, then, it may be agreed that Mussolini was, in some sense, 'a man for all that', a personage who reflected his gender, class, region and nation, a tyrant of course, but not so vicious that history should relegate him, frozen, to the bottommost circle of a Dantesque hell. Yet, perhaps to his greater dismay, Mussolini's story in practice turns out to have been one of sound and fury, possessed of a certain historical significance to Italy and to Europe at a certain historical moment, but with a lasting legacy largely confined to the superficial. In the final analysis, the problem with Benito Amilcare Andrea Mussolini was that, for all his aspirations to exercise power, he turned out to be no more than an ambitious intellectual from the provinces who believed that his will mattered and who thought, as did others, that he was a *Duce* and could lead a state like Italy towards a special sort of modernisation. His propagandists declared that he was always right. However, in the most profound matters which touch on the human condition, he was, with little exception, wrong.

Notes

PREFACE

1. G. Prezzolini, 'Diario di guerra' in A. Soffici and G. Prezzolini, *Diari 1939–1945*, Milan, 1962, p. 246.
2. B. Mussolini, *My autobiography (translated with a foreword by Richard Washburn Child, American ambassador to Italy May 1921 to February 1924)*, London, nd. (My copy indicates that 47 000 volumes had already been sold). In reality the work was largely ghosted in a collaboration between the ambassador and Arnaldo Mussolini, the *Duce*'s younger brother.
3. For my response to the review, see R. Bosworth, 'Italian foreign policy and its historiography' in R. Bosworth and G. Rizzo (eds.), *Altro Polo: intellectuals and their ideas in contemporary Italy*, Sydney, 1983, pp. 65–86.
4. My phrase is borrowed from that extraordinary Australian historian, C.M.H. Clark. This, in spirit, nineteenth century-style forger of a nation somehow still flourished in 1970s Australia and wrote with a biblical and liturgical reference which my own timid preference for irony generally eschews. Despite the antiquated nature of his history-writing, his ghost still affrights the right who, with enduring and baffled malevolence, seek to upbraid him in the worthy pages of the *Brisbane Courier Mail* and *Times Literary Supplement*.

INTRODUCTION

1. For examples, see B. Mussolini, *Corrispondenza inedita* (ed. D. Susmel), Milan, 1972.
2. G. Dolfin, *Con Mussolini nella tragedia: diario del capo della segreteria particolare del Duce 1943–1944*, Milan, 1949, p. 35.
3. See, generally, Y. De Begnac, *Taccuini mussoliniani*, Bologna, 1990.
4. *Ibid.*, p. 321.
5. Archivio Centrale dello Stato (ACS), Rome, Segreteria particolare del Duce, Carteggio riservato (SPDCR) 1, 16 June 1937, Mussolini to Gentile.
6. Y. De Begnac, *Taccuini mussoliniani*, p. 37.
7. The archives indicate that Mussolini could write fluently in French but his English was more doubtful, for example with him on one occasion putting 'niews' for news and 'politice' for practice. See SPD Carte della Cassetta di Zinco 7, May 1929, note.
8. See B. Mussolini, *Corrispondenza inedita*, pp. 114–16; 120–2; 124–7.
9. SPDCR 107, 26 January 1931, Mussolini to Edda.
10. Cited by D. Dutton, *Anthony Eden: a life and reputation*, London, 1997, p. 97.
11. This title was first used by the democratic journalist G. Seldes, *Sawdust Caesar: the untold*

Notes

history of Mussolini and Fascism, London, 1936, during the propaganda battles of the Ethiopian war.

12. M. Mazower, *Dark continent: Europe's twentieth century*, Harmondsworth, 1999, p. 26.
13. D. Mack Smith, *Mussolini's Roman empire*, London, 1976, p. v.
14. His most strident effort was an interview with Pasquale Chessa of Berlusconi's weekly *Panorama*. See R. De Felice, *Rosso e nero* (ed. P. Chessa), Milan, 1995.
15. P. Milza, *Mussolini*, Paris, 1999.
16. See, most notably, S. Fitzpatrick, *Everyday Stalinism: ordinary life in extraordinary times: Soviet Russia in the 1930s*, New York, 1998.
17. P. Preston, *Franco: a biography*, London, 1993, p. xix.
18. *Ibid.*, p. 275.
19. *Ibid.*
20. *Ibid.*, p. 637.
21. I. Kershaw, *Hitler 1936–1945: nemesis*, London, 2000.
22. I. Kershaw, *Hitler 1889–1936: hubris*, London, 1998, p. xii.
23. R.G.L. Waite, *The psychopathic God: Adolf Hitler*, New York, 1977.
24. I. Kershaw, *Hitler 1889–1936: hubris*, p. xxvi.
25. *Ibid.*, pp. xxvi-xxvii.
26. *Ibid.*, pp. xiii, xxix.
27. *Ibid.*, p. 529.
28. I suppose it is a novel story. But cf. Robert Musil's brilliant evocation of pre-1914 Austria-Hungary as the place where every station-master had whiskers identical to those of Emperor Franz Joseph (and vice versa). See R. Musil, *The man without qualities*, London, 1968, vol. 1.
29. I. Kershaw, *Hitler 1889–1936*, p. 553.

CHAPTER 1

1. F. Ciano, *Quando il nonno fece fucilare papà*, Milan, 1991. A strong competitor is G. Pisanò, *Gli ultimi cinque secondi di Mussolini*, Milan, 1996, for which see below.
2. For a description of the squad, see R. Montagna, *Mussolini e il processo di Verona*, Milan, 1949, p. 219. According to Montagna, Gottardi's last words were *Viva il Duce, Viva l'Italia*, while Pareschi and De Bono opted just for *Viva l'Italia*. Ciano was silent, as was Marinelli, who was carried to his execution almost unconscious with fear (p. 220).
3. For a recent journalistic English-language biography, see R. Moseley, *Mussolini's shadow: the double life of Count Galeazzo Ciano*, New Haven, 1999.
4. P. Pisenti, *Una repubblica necessaria (R.S.I.)*, Rome, 1977, p. 93.
5. For a modern biography, see A. Santini, *Costanzo Ciano: il ganascia del fascismo*, Milan, 1993. Galeazzo Ciano was not above half-admitting his father's venality, joking that the Livornese were the 'Australians of Italy', that is, those who exhibited most stubbornly a convict stock. O. Vergani, *Ciano: una lunga confessione*, Milan, 1974, p. 38.
6. A. Santini, *Costanzo Ciano*, p. 176.
7. A biographer reckons that Mussolini had sexual relations with 162 different women, but that Ciano exceeded this total in 7 years as Foreign Minister. See G.B. Guerri, *Galeazzo Ciano: una vita 1903–1944*, Milan, 1979, p. 69. Not even the Acquasanta rough, it seems, was sacred against his lubricity.
8. D. Susmel, *Vita sbagliata di Galeazzo Ciano*, Milan, 1962, p. 56.
9. *Ibid.*, p. 46.
10. G. Bottai, *Diario 1935–1944* (ed. G.B. Guerri), Milan, 1982, p. 167.
11. For the reverently edited ramblings of Bottai as he went through his legionary experience and tried to shrug off his record under Fascism, see G. Bottai, *Diario 1944–1948* (ed. G.B.

Notes

Guerri), Milan, 1988 and, especially, *Quaderno affricano*, Florence, 1995. The revival of Bottai's reputation may have coincided with the rise of his son to be Secretary-General of the Italian Foreign Ministry. See his own memoirs, B. Bottai, *Fascismo famigliare*, Casale Monferrato, 1997.

12. See C. Senise, *Quando ero Capo della Polizia 1940–1943*, Rome, 1946, pp. 234–40, for the killing and the controversy it unleashed.

13. For a sympathetic account of his motives, see R. De Felice, *Mussolini l'alleato 1940–1945 II. La guerra civile 1943–1945*, Turin, 1997, pp. 349–55.

14. For a biography, see A. Petacco, *Il superfascista: vita e morte di Alessandro Pavolini*, Milan, 1998. Pavolini's father was a distinguished (and nationalist) academic. His brother, Corrado, had married a Jew, but also had been an active Fascist.

15. V. Cersosimo, *Dall'istruttoria alla fucilazione: storia del processo di Verona*, Milan, 1961, p. 254.

16. For allegations about Ciano and cocaine, see G. Servadio, *Luchino Visconti: a biography*, London, 1981, p. 31.

17. With Fascist flamboyance, they were named Fabrizio (with journalists finding reference to the *fabbro* or blacksmith, Alessandro, father to Benito) and Marzio or Mars. Edda had put up with a man who liked to phone her with accounts of how bombing raids were literally orgasmic experiences for him. See D. Susmel, *Vita sbagliata di Galeazzo Ciano*, p. 205.

18. V. Cersosimo, *Dall'istruttoria alla fucilazione*, p.15.

19. When under arrest in August 1943, Mussolini himself expressed similar disdain for Ciano's habits in regard to both golf and *contessine*. See F. Maugeri, *From the ashes of disgrace*, New York, 1948, p. 146.

20. B. Spampanato, *Contromemoriale*, Rome, 1952, vol. I, p. 234.

21. *L'Assalto* (Bologna), 1 December 1943. Cf. the issue of 23 March 1944, when Coppola was even more virulently racist towards the black soldiers serving in the US and French armies.

22. For a recent forgiving account, see L. Ganapini, *La repubblica delle camicie nere*, Milan, 1999, pp. 453–84 being specifically devoted to recounting the story of 'the prisoner by the lake'.

23. For the historiographical background, see R.J.B. Bosworth, *The Italian dictatorship: problems and perspectives in the interpretation of Mussolini and Fascism*, London, 1998.

24. L. Bolla, *Perché a Salò: diario della Repubblica Sociale Italiana* (ed. G.B. Guerri), Milan, 1982, p. 158. His interlocutor deemed Vittorio 'one of the biggest louts who has ever existed on the face of this earth'.

25. G. Pini and D. Susmel, *Mussolini: l'uomo e l'opera*, Florence, 1953–55, vol. IV, pp. 336; 343–4.

26. G. Bocca, *La Repubblica di Mussolini*, Bari, 1977, p. 136.

27. G. Dolfin, *Con Mussolini nella tragedia: diario del capo della segreteria particolare del Duce 1943–1944*, Milan, 1949, p. 101.

28. *Ibid.*, pp. 82–3. Cf. G. Zachariae, *Mussolini si confessa*, Milan, 1966, p. 34.

29. G. Dolfin, *Con Mussolini nella tragedia*, p. 183.

30. For her account of this event, full of self-pity and with an absolute lack of awareness of the tragedy tearing her country apart, see C. Petacci, *Il mio diario*, np, 1946. In prison she kept up with world events through the pages of *La Gazzetta dello sport* (p. 48). For a biography, see F. Bandini, *Claretta: profilo di Clara Petacci*, Milan, 1960.

31. R. De Felice, *Mussolini l'alleato 1943–1945*, pp. 527–8.

32. G. Pini and D. Susmel, *Mussolini*, vol. IV, p. 413. In March 1945 Edda rejected one last attempt by her father to appease her (p. 471).

33. For this work, see B. Mussolini, *Opera omnia* (ed. E. and D. Susmel), 44 vols., Florence, 1951–1960, Rome, 1978–1980 [hereafter BMOO], vol. XXXIV, pp. 197–268.

34. E. Amicucci, *1600 giorni di Mussolini (dal Gran Sasso a Dongo)*, Rome, 1948, p. 42.

Notes

35. R. Montagna, *Mussolini e il processo di Verona*, pp. 225–9.
36. G. Pini and D. Susmel, *Mussolini*, vol. IV, pp. 383; 390.
37. R. Montagna, *Mussolini e il processo di Verona*, p. 228.
38. G. Pini and D. Susmel, *Mussolini*, vol. IV, p. 391.
39. G. Dolfin, *Con Mussolini nella tragedia*, p. 200. In his self-pity, he showed Edda's condemnatory letter to Fascist officials, allowing them in a way which would never have been possible before July 1943 to tut-tut about his fate. See R. De Felice, 'Dalle "Memorie" di Fulvio Balisti: un dannunziano di fronte alla crisi del 1943 e alla Repubblica Sociale Italiana', *Storia contemporanea*, 17, 1986, pp. 490–1.
40. BMOO, XXXII, p. 161.
41. G. Pini and D. Susmel, *Mussolini*, vol. IV, p. 390.
42. For the most scabrous account of this last, see the novel about the multiple corruptions of liberated Naples, C. Malaparte, *The Skin*, London, 1952.
43. For boys, see C. Mazzantini, *I Balilla andarono a Salò: l'armata degli adolescenti che pagò il conto della Storia*, Venice, 1995; for girls, cf. M. Fraddosio, 'The Fallen Hero: the myth of Mussolini and Fascist women in the Italian Social Republic (1943–5)', *Journal of Contemporary History*, 31, 1996, pp. 99–124.
44. See, for example, R. Vivarelli, *La fine di una stagione*, Bologna, 2000.
45. By far the most subtle account of these years (and still Anti-Fascist in character) is C. Pavone, *Una guerra civile: saggio storico sulla moralità nella Resistenza*, Turin, 1991.
46. H. Thomas, *The Spanish Civil War*, New York, 1994, pp. 926–7. Thomas believes that Franco's forces killed 110 000 Republicans in battle and another 75 000 behind the lines between 1936 and 1939.
47. G. Gentile, 'Questione morale', *Italia e Civiltà*, 8 January 1944.
48. For examples, see SPDCR 14.
49. A. Soffici, 'La verità', *Italia e Civiltà*, 8 January 1944. Cf. also the writings at this time of the young Giovanni Spadolini, to be a Prime Minister of the Italian republic and an indefatigable bellettrist historian of the liberal Risorgimento. He deplored the failure of the Fascist regime before 1943 to sweep away its enemies as both Hitler and Stalin had done. G. Spadolini, 'Responsabilità', *Italia e Civiltà*, 15 January 1944.
50. The most subtle account of the relationship between the war and the Italian people is R. Absalom, *A strange alliance: aspects of escape and survival in Italy 1943–45*, Florence, 1991.
51. See, for example, SPDCR RSI 50, 25 January 1944, Mussolini to Provincial Chiefs.
52. D.L. Rusinow, *Italy's Austrian heritage 1919–1946*, Oxford, 1969, p. 300.
53. J. Goebbels, *Final entries, 1945: the diaries of Joseph Goebbels* (ed. H.R. Trevor-Roper), New York, 1978, p. 268.
54. R. Graziani, *Ho difeso la patria*, Milan, 1947, pp. 461–5; cf. F.W. Deakin, *The last days of Mussolini*, Harmondsworth, 1962, pp. 184–93.
55. For an account of their fate, see R. Lazzero, *Gli schiavi di Hitler: i deportati italiani in Germania nella seconda guerra mondiale*, Milan, 1996 and, in more scholarly vein, B. Mantelli, 'Camerati di lavoro': i lavoratori italiani emigrati nel Terzo Reich nel periodo dell'Asse 1938–1943*, Florence, 1992.
56. F.W. Deakin, *The last days of Mussolini*, p. 185.
57. See Chapters 16 and 17 for more on this matter.
58. E.F. Moellhausen, *La carta perdente: memorie diplomatiche 25 luglio 1943–2 maggio 1945* (ed. V. Rusca), Rome, 1948, p. 292.
59. F.W. Deakin, *The last days of Mussolini*, p. 193.
60. BMOO, XXXII, pp. 84–5.
61. BMOO, XXXII, pp. 92–4.
62. F.W. Deakin, *The last days of Mussolini*, p. 185.

Notes

63. B. Spampanato, *Contromemoriale*, vol. II, p. 218.

64. BMOO, XXXII, pp. 100–1.

65. R. Graziani, *Ho difeso la patria*, pp. 447–8.

66. For an account, see I. Kershaw, *Hitler 1936–1945: nemesis*, London, 2000, pp. 671–84.

67. E. Dollmann, *The interpreter: memoirs*, London, 1967, p. 321; P. Schmitt, *Hitler's interpreter: the secret history of German diplomacy 1935–1945*, London, 1951, pp. 274–7.

68. B. Spampanato, *Contromemoriale*, vol. II, p. 232.

69. A. Hitler, *Hitler's table talk 1941–1944* (ed. H.R. Trevor-Roper), London, 1953, p. 10, in which Hitler stated 'my dearest wish would be to wander about in Italy as an unknown painter'.

70. F.W. Deakin, *The last days of Mussolini*, p. 215.

71. See, for example, BMOO, XLIII, pp. 161–5.

72. BMOO, XLIII, p. 103.

73. For a summary, see R. De Felice, *Mussolini l'alleato 1943–1945*, pp. 378–9.

74. See, for example, G. Spadolini, 'I nuovi socialisti', *Italia e Civiltà*, 18 March 1944.

75. See Chapter 12.

76. B. Spampanato, *Contromemoriale* vol. II, p. 174.

77. V. Costa, *L'ultimo federale*, pp. 76; 81.

78. *Ibid.*, p. 148.

79. SPDCR RSI 50, 10 March 1944, Mussolini to Provincial Chiefs.

80. N. D'Aroma, *Mussolini segreto*, Rocca San Casciano, 1958, p. 303.

81. BMOO, XXXII, pp. 112–16.

82. SPDCR RSI 50, 5 February 1944, Mussolini to Provincial Chiefs.

83. For the dispute, see R. De Felice, *Mussolini l'alleato 1943–1945*, pp. 452–65. Cf. also G. Buffarini Guidi, *La vera verità: i documenti dell'archivio segreto del Ministro degli Interni Guido Buffarini Guidi dal 1938 al 1945*, Milan, 1970, pp. 117–45.

84. See G. Pansa, *L'esercito di Salò*, Milan, 1970, p. 140.

85. For an account, see R. Lazzero, *La Decima Mas*, Milan, 1984.

86. He had, before 1943, only met the Duce once he would claim, and then in November 1940 when Mussolini was unimpressively dressed in civilian gear and seemed 'tired and upset'. J.V. Borghese, *Decima flottiglia Mas: dalle origini all'armistizio*, Rome, 1950, p. 89.

87. G. Bocca, *La Repubblica di Mussolini*, p. 281.

88. *Ibid.*, pp. 196–217. Claretta Petacci and Buffarini Guidi also tried to mobilise Mussolini against Borghese.

89. E. Amicucci, *I 600 giorni di Mussolini*, pp. 109–15.

90. B. Spampanato, *Contromemoriale*, vol. II, p. 221.

91. For this event and its contested memory, see G. Contini, *La memoria divisa*, Milan, 1997. Cf. the rather similar story at Guardistallo as narrated in P. Pezzino, *Anatomia di un massacro: controversia sopra una strage tedesca*, Bologna, 1997.

92. BMOO, XLIII, pp. 162–5.

93. See, for example, SPDCR RSI 50, 14 March 1944, Mussolini to Provincial Chiefs; 23 May 1944, Mussolini to Rahn; 22 December 1944, Mussolini to Provincial Chiefs.

94. B. Mussolini, *Storia di un anno (il tempo del bastone e della carota)* in BMOO, XXXIV, pp. 301–444.

95. BMOO, XXXII, pp. 126–39.

96. G. Dolfin, *Con Mussolini nella tragedia*, p. 172.

97. V. Costa, *L'ultimo federale*, p. 123.

98. B. Spampanato, *Contromemoriale*, vol. II, pp. 76–7.

99. G. Dolfin, *Con Mussolini nella tragedia*, p. 260 (February 1944); BMOO, XXXII, p. 169 (March 1945).

Notes

100. L. Garibaldi (ed.), *Mussolini e il professore: vita e diari di Carlo Alberto Biggini*, Milan, 1983, p. 362.
101. BMOO, XXXII, p. 191.
102. BMOO, XXXII, p. 170. It is typical of the posthumous allure of the two dictators that Hitler's dogs should have found their (surreal) narrator in Günter Grass, while Mussolini's cats remain ignored. See G. Grass, *Dog years*, Harmondsworth, 1969.
103. BMOO, XXXII, p. 158.
104. BMOO, XXXII, pp. 157–9.
105. BMOO, XXXII, p. 159.
106. BMOO, XXXII, p. 194.
107. BMOO, XXXII, pp. 173–4.
108. BMOO, XXXII, p. 178.
109. C. Silvestri, *Matteotti Mussolini e il dramma italiano*, Milan, 1981, p. 30.
110. G. Pini and D. Susmel, *Mussolini*, vol. IV, pp. 497–8.
111. *Ibid.*, p. 495.
112. V. Costa, *L'ultimo federale*, pp. 220–1.
113. R. Rahn, *Ambasciatore di Hitler a Vichy e a Salò*, Milan, 1950, p. 329. Rahn remembered being partially appeased by the sight of a volume of Mörike's poetry open on the Duce's desk. Mussolini, by contrast, with his usual malice, remarked to a friend that Rahn reminded him of a carpet salesman. See N. D'Aroma, *Mussolini segreto*, Rocca San Casciano, 1958, p. 320.
114. G. Zachariae, *Mussolini si confessa*, pp. 27–8.
115. L. Garibaldi (ed.), *Mussolini e il professore*, p. 320.
116. G. Pini and D. Susmel, *Mussolini*, vol. IV, p. 468.
117. R. Graziani, *Ho difeso la patria*, p. 494.
118. G. Pisanò, *Io, Fascista*, Milan, 1997, p. 25. If that was true when he first arrived on 20 April, Pisanò does claim that some 8000 unrequited admirers of Mussolini had assembled in the valley by 27 April (p. 53). The maps consulted over the *Ridotto alpino* were those drawn by the lay organisation, the *Touring Club Italiano*.
119. B. Spampanato, *Contromemoriale*, vol. II, p. 375.
120. *Ibid.*, vol. II, p. 376.
121. *Ibid.*, vol. II, p. 377.
122. V. Costa, *L'ultimo federale*, pp. 256–8.
123. P. Pisenti, *Una repubblica necessaria*, p. 167. Cf. also Carte B. Spampanato 1, account of talk with Mussolini, April 1945.
124. In English, the best reconstruction of the period is still F.W. Deakin, *The last days of Mussolini*.
125. D. Binchy, *Church and state in Fascist Italy*, Oxford, 1970, pp. 432–3.
126. *Ibid.*, pp. 131–2.
127. R. De Felice, *Mussolini il duce: I. gli anni del consenso 1929–1936*, Turin, 1974, pp. 634–5.
128. D. Binchy, *Church and state in Fascist Italy*, pp. 688–9.
129. *Ibid.*, pp. 624–5.
130. See I. Schuster, *Gli ultimi tempi di un regime*, Milan, 1945.
131. *Ibid.*, p. 162.
132. D. Binchy, *Church and state in Fascist Italy*, p. 624.
133. I. Schuster, *Gli ultimi tempi di un regime*, p. 163. Schuster had similarly invoked Arnaldo when he was in contact with Mussolini on 19 April (pp. 131–2).
134. *Ibid.*, p. 163.
135. See, for example, *ibid.*, pp. 6–7.
136. *Ibid.*, pp. 163–4.
137. *Ibid.*, p. 165.

138. *Ibid.*, pp. 166–8.
139. BMOO, XXXII, p. 213.
140. Also present at Como had been Elena Curti, a young woman in her 20s (see further Chapter 17). B. Spampanato, *Contromemoriale*, vol. III, p. 125.
141. SPDCR 78, 18 September 1937 has a police report that he had still not 'sold out' to Fascism but was ready to collaborate with it 'in the interests of the working class' underscored with Mussolini's red pencil.
142. For a scholarly account of his life, see G. Salotti, *Nicola Bombacci da Mosca a Salò*, Rome, 1986.
143. G. Pini, *Itinerario tragico (1943–1945)*, Milan, 1950, p. 164.
144. For an account of these events, see U. Lazzaro, *Il compagno Bill: diario dell'uomo che catturò Mussolini*, Turin, 1989, pp. 105–6. In English, cf. P.L. Bellini delle Stelle and U. Lazzaro, *Dongo: the last act*, London, 1964.
145. E. Amicucci, *I 600 giorni di Mussolini*, p. 52.
146. U. Lazzaro, *Il compagno Bill*, pp. 107–9.
147. *Ibid.*, pp. 119–20.
148. *Ibid.*, pp. 122–5.
149. *Ibid.*, p.125.
150. *Ibid.*, pp. 129; 136.
151. U. Lazzaro, *Dongo: mezzo secolo di menzogne*, Milan, 1993, pp. 45–6.
152. For a relatively sober account, see A. Petacco, *Dear Benito, Caro Winston: verità e misteri del carteggio Churchill–Mussolini*, Milan, 1985.
153. Remarkably, however, just before his death, Renzo De Felice, revived the idea that there might be something to these rumours. See R. De Felice, *Rosso e nero*, Milan, 1995, pp. 144–5.
154. W. Audisio, *In nome del popolo italiano*, Milan, 1975, pp. 376–9.
155. *Ibid.*, p. 381.
156. For his fullest account, see G. Pisanò, *Gli ultimi cinque secondi di Mussolini*, Milan, 1996.
157. U. Lazzaro, *Dongo*, p.46.
158. H. Woller, *I conti con il fascismo: l'epurazione in Italia 1943–1948*, Bologna, 1997, p. 8.

CHAPTER 2

1. In the terminology of local government, Dovia was a *frazione* of the *comune* of Predappio.
2. L. Kemechey, *'Il Duce': the life and work of Benito Mussolini*, London, 1930, p. 21. An Italian eulogist also provided a horoscope. See A. Gravelli, *Mussolini aneddotico*, Rome, 1951. It being after 1945 the horoscope placed the birth under the 'signs of death' – with a conjunction of the Moon, Mars, Saturn and Gemini.
3. G. Dolcetti, *Le origini storiche della famiglia Mussolini*, Venice, 1928, p. 41.
4. C. Petrie, *Mussolini*, London, 1931, p. 2.
5. G. Pini and D. Susmel, *Mussolini: l'uomo e l'opera*, Florence, 1953–55, vol. I, pp. 11–13.
6. E. Ortona, *Diplomazia di guerra: diari 1937–1943*, Bologna, 1993, p. 242. Perhaps this choice of furnishing was made by Mussolini's wife Rachele, who spent far more time at the *Rocca* than did her husband.
7. I. De Begnac, *Trent'anni di Mussolini 1883–1915*, Rome, 1934, p. 255 traces a purported family tree.
8. V. Proli and S. Moschi (eds), 'Alessandro Mussolini: fabbro-ferraio-uomo politico: raccolta di notizie biografiche', unpublished MSS, Predappio, 1999.
9. V. Emiliani, *I tre Mussolini: Luigi, Alessandro, Benito*, Milan, 1997, p. 20.
10. F. Tempera, *Benito: emulo-superiore di Cesare e di Napoleone*, Rome, 1927, p. i. Another commentator, seeking to explain the *Duce* to Italian children, more simply argued that his

Notes

name really meant 'Benedetto' (the blessed one). See V. Perroni, *Il Mussolini dei bimbi*, Rome, 1929, p. 11.

11. See, for example, G. Ghersi, *Mussolini: fabbro dello stato*, Milan, 1937. The author of this hagiography alleged pompously that the metaphor of the political blacksmith had originated with Vico (p. 141).

12. See, for example, the file in the Archivio di Stato di Forlì, Prefettura, Archivio di Gabinetto (hereafter AFPAG), busta 104, fascicolo 106, dated March 1882. It collected details on local *internazionalisti* and included a certain Alessandro Mussolino (elsewhere called Musolino). The police believed that he and his comrades aimed eventually 'to overthrow the government and proclaim the Internationale'. Another report, of 19 April, defined 'Alessandro Mussolini' as the 'Secretary, President, in fact all' of the local movement.

13. R. De Felice, *Mussolini il rivoluzionario 1883–1920*, Turin, 1965, p. 5.

14. R. Hostetter, *The Italian socialist movement, vol. I Origins (1860–1882)*, Princeton, 1958, p. 331.

15. See the portrait of him given by C. Rossi, *Personaggi di ieri e di oggi*, Milan, 1960, p. 59.

16. V. Proli and S. Moschi (eds), 'Alessandro Mussolini', pp. 18–19.

17. *Ibid.*, p. 11.

18. F. Bonavita, *Il padre del Duce*, Rome, 1933, p. 97.

19. BMOO, III, p. 275.

20. V. Proli and S. Moschi (eds), 'Alessandro Mussolini', pp. 26–8.

21. F. Bonavita, *Il padre del Duce*, p. 162.

22. E. Mussolini, *Mio fratello Benito: memorie raccolte e trascritte da Rosetta Ricci Crisolini*, Florence, 1957, p. 16. Cf. R. De Felice, *Mussolini il rivoluzionario*, p. 15, dates the inheritance to 1900 and says that it allowed young Benito Mussolini to start spending money on books. Mussolini himself, writing in 1911, thought that Alessandro wasted most of the bequest, though he did buy some land. The total inherited was the considerable sum of at least 10 000 lire. Whatever Alessandro's debts and fecklessness, the purchased property was still valued by the bank at 8000 lire at the decade's end. BMOO, XXXIII, p. 241.

23. V. Proli and S. Moschi (eds), 'Alessandro Mussolini', p. 38.

24. *Ibid.*, p. 13.

25. A. Balabanoff, *Il traditore: Mussolini e la conquista del potere*, Rome, 1973, p. 26; G. Pini and D. Susmel, *Mussolini*, vol. I, p. 146.

26. His son published an obituary recalling how the house at Varano had been filled both with socialists and with republicans. See BMOO, III, pp. 274–6.

27. Luigi's own father died in his 30s, Luigi's wife in her early 40s.

28. A. Pensotti, *Rachele: sessant'anni con Mussolini nel bene e nel male*, Milan, 1983, p. 19.

29. V. Benedetti, *Rosa Maltoni Mussolini*, Brescia, 1928, p. 141.

30. A. Pensotti, *Rachele*, p. 15.

31. *Ibid.*, p. 12.

32. I. De Begnac, *Trent'anni di Mussolini 1883–1915*, p. 257.

33. A pertinacious tourist to Predappio Nuovo, built during the Fascist regime, can still find the little church of Santa Rosa and there might note its adornment with a ceramic picture of the Madonna and child known as the 'Madonna of the Fascio' – angels can indeed be seen proffering a bundle of rods and axes to the Queen of Heaven. The picture was given to the church by a Portuguese admirer of the *Duce* in the 1930s. See S. Guidi, A. Gulminelli and G. Carduccini, *Predappio: quello che non vi hanno mai raccontato (o che avete dimenticato)*, San Sevino di Predappio, 1997, p. 28.

34. B. Mussolini, *Testamento spirituale con uno studio di Duilio Susmel*, Milan, 1956, p. ix; G. Fanciulli, *Il Duce del popolo italiano*, Rome, 1928, p. 17.

35. A. Gravelli, *Mussolini aneddotico*, p. 9.

36. E. Della Pura, *Lo scolare Benito Mussolini*, Pisa, 1938, pp. 67–8.

Notes

37. I. De Begnac, *Trent'anni di Mussolini 1883–1915*, p. 258.
38. C. Cucchi in S. Smiles, *Passi scelti del Character con note tolte dai discorsi e dagli scritti del Duce*, Milan, 1938, pp. 5–6.
39. V. Emiliani, *I tre Mussolini*, p. 33.
40. I. De Begnac, *Trent'anni di Mussolini 1883–1915*, p. 2.
41. V. Perroni, *Il Mussolini dei bimbi*, p. 11.
42. For more detail, see L. Passerini, *Mussolini immaginario: storia di una biografia, 1915–1939*, Bari, 1991, pp. 48–50.
43. Edgardo Sulis, *Imitazione di Mussolini*, Milan, 1932 as cited by *ibid.*, p. 90. The title of the book blasphemously invoked *The Imitation of Christ*.
44. See, for example, E. Mussolini, *Mio fratello Benito*, pp. 201–2.
45. A. and B. Mussolini, *Vita di Sandro e di Arnaldo*, Milan, 1934, p. 93; E. Bedeschi, *La giovinezza del Duce: ricordi e luoghi: libro per la gioventù italiana*, Turin, 1939, facing p. 29 has a photo of the bed. They were too poor to have a mattress.
46. P. Pedrazza, *Giornalismo di Mussolini*, Milan, 1937, p. 113.
47. A. and B. Mussolini, *Vita di Sandro e di Arnaldo*, p. 128.
48. V. Mussolini, *Vita con mio padre*, Milan, 1957, p. 18.
49. G. Megaro, *Mussolini in the making*, London, 1938, p. 41.
50. A. and B. Mussolini, *Vita di Sandro e di Arnaldo*, p. 90. The Mussolini family at other times were assisted by domestic help, a necessary boon to the ailing Rosa. See D. Mack Smith, *Mussolini*, London, 1981, p. 2.
51. See, for example, *Il Popolo d'Italia*, 22 December 1931.
52. A. and B. Mussolini, *Vita di Sandro e di Arnaldo*, pp. 109–110.
53. Y. De Begnac, *Palazzo Venezia: storia di un regime*, Rome, 1950, p. 122.
54. L.E. Gianturco, *Arnaldo Mussolini*, Como, 1934, p. 7.
55. G.S. Spinetti, *Mistica fascista nel pensiero di Arnaldo Mussolini*, Milan, 1936, p. 3.
56. V. Mussolini, *Vita con mio padre*, p. 31.
57. It is also true that the regime purveyed this view, particularly after Arnaldo's death. See, for example, *Critica fascista*, X, 1 January 1932, editorial p. 1; C. Di Marzio, 'Dopo la morte di Arnaldo Mussolini: penombre', p. 3.
58. V. Emiliani, *Il paese dei Mussolini*, Turin, 1984, p. 34.
59. E. Sulis (ed.), *Mussolini e il Fascismo*, Rome, 1941, p. viii.
60. V. Emiliani, *I tre Mussolini*, p. 81.
61. For an account of the link between the rise of the modern state and the rise of modern statistics, see S. Patriarca, *Numbers and nationhood: writing statistics in nineteenth century Italy*, Cambridge, 1996.
62. See T. De Mauro, *Storia linguistica dell'Italia unita*, Bari, 1963, p. 38.
63. For further explanation, see R.J.B. Bosworth, *Italy, the least of the Great Powers: Italian foreign policy before the First World War*, Cambridge, 1979 and, more generally, my *Italy and the wider world 1860–1960*, London, 1996.
64. Cited by R. Petrignani, *Neutralità e alleanza: le scelte di politica estera dell'Italia dopo l'Unità*, Bologna, 1987, p. 381.
65. Cited by G. Carocci, *Agostino Depretis e la politica interna italiana dal 1876 al 1887*, Turin, 1956, p. 313.
66. F. Bonavita, *Il padre del Duce*, p. 9.
67. I. De Begnac, *Trent'anni di Mussolini 1883–1915*, p. 2.
68. G. Massani, *Duce e popolo*, Milan, 1942; cf. G. Massani, *La Sua terra*, Bergamo, 1936, p. 8.
69. A.L. Cardoza, *Agrarian elites and Italian Fascism: the province of Bologna 1901–1926*, Princeton, 1982, p. 13.
70. *Ibid.*, p. 54.

Notes

71. For a somewhat eulogistic account of Costa's reckoning with the peasants of the Romagna, see R. Zangheri, 'Andrea Costa e le lotte contadine del suo tempo', in his *Agricoltura e contadini nella storia d'Italia*, Turin, 1977, pp. 241–82.

72. BMOO, I, p. 27. The work was published in the Swiss-Italian socialist journal *L'Avvenire del Lavoratore* (The Worker's Future).

73. See, for example, C. Marroni, *Mussolini se stesso*, Rome, 1941, p. 8; cf. the same claim in I. De Begnac, *Trent'anni di Mussolini 1883–1915*, p. 6.

74. E. Balbo, *Augusto e Mussolini*, Rome, 1937, p. 123. The point of this book was to parallel Mussolini and Augustus, while concluding that Mussolini was the greater.

75. F. Bonavita, *Primavera fascista dall'avvento fascista all'impero africano*, Milan, 1937, p. 47.

76. A. Gravelli, *Mussolini aneddotico*, p. 5.

77. BMOO, III, p. 276.

78. V. Querel, *Il paese di Benito: cronache di Predappio e dintorni*, Rome, 1954, p. 64.

79. I. De Begnac, *Trent'anni di Mussolini 1883–1915*, p. 27.

80. N. D'Aroma, *Mussolini segreto*, Rocca San Casciano, 1958, p. 64.

81. BMOO, XXXIII, p. 222.

82. BMOO, XXXIII, p. 223.

83. BMOO, XXXIII, pp. 228–230.

84. For an account, see R. De Felice, *Mussolini il rivoluzionario 1883–1920*, pp. 11–13.

85. AFPAG 106/B, preserves the formal note from the school admitting Mussolini as a boarder on 6 September 1894.

86. AFPAG 106/B, report for 1900–01.

87. E. Susmel, *Mussolini e il suo tempo*, Milan, 1950, p. 14.

88. AFPAG 106/B, report of 29 October 1899.

89. AFPAG 106/B, 5 May 1940, Mussolini to Forlimpopoli school head; 18 October 1932, report of Mussolini visit to 'his school'.

90. R. De Felice, *Mussolini il rivoluzionario 1883–1920*, p. 14. The ceremonies also included two plays and a flute solo, with songs in Bolognese dialect enlivening the interval. See AFPAG 106/B, for the day of 10 February 1901.

91. BMOO, I, p. 244. The name of the Calabrian bandit Musolino, notorious at the time, doubtless heightened the confusion.

92. AFPAG, 106/B, letter dated 31 May 1901.

93. BMOO, I, p. 204; XXXIII, p. 239.

94. BMOO, I, p. 205.

95. Y. De Begnac, *Palazzo Venezia: storia di un regime*, p. 129.

96. S. Bedeschi and R. Alessi, *Anni giovanili di Mussolini*, Milan, 1939, pp. 24–5; 36; 60–1.

97. BMOO, III, p. 219.

98. BMOO, I, pp. 3–4. The piece was entitled 'Il romanzo russo'. In it Mussolini inveighed against the 'individualist subjectivity' of Italian writers, the 'latent nationalism' of the French and the metaphysics of the Germans, by contrast with the healthy Russian predilection for social criticism.

99. R. Mussolini, *The real Mussolini (as told to A. Zarca)*, Farnborough, 1973, p. 66.

100. BMOO, I, p. 205.

101. I. De Begnac, *Trent'anni di Mussolini 1883–1915*, p. 260.

102. A. Marpicati, *Il Duce e le sue opere*, San Remo, 1938, p. 6.

103. I. De Begnac, *Trent'anni di Mussolini 1883–1915*, pp. 263–4. When dictator, he did not forget his ideal that teachers should be free in their approach and their classes not too big. Y. De Begnac, *Palazzo Venezia: storia di un regime*, p. 363.

104. G. Pini and D. Susmel, *Mussolini*, vol. I, p. 64.

105. R. De Felice, *Mussolini il rivoluzionario 1883–1920*, pp. 20–1.

106. BMOO, I, p. 210.

Notes

107. BMOO, XXXIII, pp. 247–8. By another account he had bitten her. See F. Castellini, *Il ribelle di Predappio: amori e giovinezza di Mussolini*, Milan, 1996, p. 40.
108. BMOO, I, p. 211.
109. BMOO, I, p. 212.

CHAPTER 3

1. For an English-language introduction to the issues involved, see R.J.B. Bosworth, *Italy and the wider world 1860–1960*, London, 1996, pp. 114–36.
2. G. Rosoli, *Un secolo di emigrazione italiana: 1876–1976*, Rome, 1976, p. 350.
3. Y. De Begnac, *Palazzo Venezia: storia di un regime*, Rome, 1950, p. 115; G. Pini, *The official life of Benito Mussolini*, London, 1939, p. 37. Given Mussolini's later flirtation with the Nazi idea of transporting European Jews to Madagascar (without anyone contemplating asking the local population what they thought of the suggestion), there is profound irony in this proposal.
4. BMOO, XXXVIII, p. 2.
5. R. Mussolini, *The real Mussolini (as told to A. Zarca)*, Farnborough, 1973, p. 9.
6. R.J.B. Bosworth, *Italy and the wider world 1860–1960*, p. 118.
7. R. Murri, 'Gl'Italiani nell'America Latina – impressioni di viaggio', *Nuova Antologia*, f. 991, 1 April 1913, p. 437. Mussolini counted Murri, an eventually defrocked priest with a bizarre political itinerary, as a 'friend'. See Y. De Begnac, *Taccuini mussoliniani*, Bologna, 1990, p. 87.
8. For an English-language biography, see J.J. Tinghino, *Edmondo Rossoni from revolutionary syndicalism to Fascism*, New York, 1991, p. 50.
9. A. Dumini, *Diciassette colpi*, Milan, 1958, pp. 11–13.
10. G. Megaro, *Mussolini in the making*, London, 1938, pp. 30–2.
11. BMOO, I, pp. 10; 213.
12. M. Barbagli, *Educating for unemployment: politics, labor markets, and the school system – Italy, 1859–1973*, New York, 1982, p. 18.
13. E. Gentile (ed.), *L'Italia giolittiana: la storia e la critica*, Bari, 1977, p. 154.
14. Quoted by M. Barbagli, *Educating for unemployment*, pp. 22–3.
15. BMOO, I, pp. 9–10.
16. A. Balabanoff, *Il traditore: Mussolini e la conquista del potere*, Rome, 1973, p. 75.
17. The most respectful later commentator is A.J. Gregor, *Young Mussolini and the intellectual origins of Fascism*, Berkeley, 1979.
18. For a review of the issue, concluding that Mussolini probably was there, see R. De Felice, *Mussolini il rivoluzionario 1883–1920*, Turin, 1965, pp. 37–8.
19. O. Dinale, *Quarant'anni di colloqui con lui*, Milan, 1953, p. 37.
20. BMOO, I, p. 212.
21. A Balabanoff, *Il traditore: Mussolini*, pp. 24–5; 131.
22. A. Borghi, *Mussolini: red and black*, London, 1935, pp. 26–7.
23. BMOO, XXXVIII, p. 2. Exaggerating his age, Mussolini in the same letter mused how strange it was for a 20 year old 'not to feel the need to be in love'.
24. BMOO, I, p. 215.
25. BMOO, III, p. 253.
26. O. Dinale, *Quarant'anni di colloqui con lui*, p. 9.
27. BMOO, III, p. 253.
28. BMOO, I, p. 251.
29. BMOO, I, p. 214. Cf. BMOO, XXXV, p. 5. The police, with period decorum and attention to scientific 'fact', officially registered his anthropometric details. See G. Megaro, *Mussolini in the making*, p. 59.

Notes

30. BMOO, I, p. 17.

31. BMOO, I, pp. 21–2.

32. BMOO, I, pp. 31–4.

33. BMOO, I, pp. 58–60. Mussolini was now writing for *L'Avanguardia socialista* (The Socialist vanguard), a weekly with rather more intellectual ambition than the papers which had earlier published his work.

34. It can be found in BMOO, XXXIII, ambitiously entitled *Claudia Particella: l'amante del Cardinale (grande romanzo storico dell'epoca del Cardinale Carlo Emanuele Madruzzo)*, and published in Trento in 1910. An English version also appeared, put out with some malice after the signature of the Lateran Pacts between the Fascist state and the Catholic Church. See B. Mussolini, *The Cardinal's mistress*, London, 1929. An English admirer thought that its prose carried echoes of Dumas *père*. C. Petrie, *Mussolini*, London, 1931, p. 13.

35. BMOO, I, pp. 25–6. The title of the piece was 'Il natale umano' (The Human Christmas).

36. BMOO, I, pp. 37–9.

37. BMOO, XXXV, p. 6.

38. BMOO, XXXVIII, p. 1.

39. G. Megaro, *Mussolini in the making*, pp. 91–7; for Mussolini's own pompous published version of the debate, see BMOO, XXXIII, pp. 1–31 under the title 'L'Uomo e la divinità'.

40. C. Rossi, *Mussolini com'era*, Rome, 1947, pp. 34–5. Can the audience really have been so patient or enthralled?

41. The classic study is E. Weber, *Peasants into Frenchmen: the modernization of rural France, 1870–1914*, Stanford, 1976; In Italian, cf. U. Levra, *Fare gli italiani: memoria e celebrazione nel Risorgimento*, Turin, 1992.

42. BMOO, XXXIII, p. 235.

43. BMOO, XXXIII, p. 248.

44. See, for example, his article on 'Swiss socialism in Switzerland' in *L'Avvenire del Lavoratore*, 22 November 1902. BMOO, I, pp. 23–4.

45. R. De Felice, *Mussolini il rivoluzionario 1883–1920*, p. 33.

46. See especially, A. Balabanoff, *Il traditore Mussolini*; cf. also her *My life as a rebel*, London, 1938; *Impressions of Lenin*, Ann Arbor, 1968.

47. A. Balabanoff, *Il traditore: Mussolini*, p. 142.

48. BMOO, XXXIII, p. 257.

49. Y. De Begnac, *Taccuini mussoliniani*, Bologna, 1990, p. 5.

50. A. Balabanoff, *My life as a rebel*, p. 39.

51. For an English-language account, see J.J. Roth, *The cult of violence: Sorel and the Sorelians*, Berkeley, 1980.

52. BMOO, XXXIII, pp. 254–8; cf. XXXV, p. 6, where he attacked the way conscripts from his own town went off to do their national duty singing. More education in socialism would, he thought, discourage such waywardness.

53. A. and B. Mussolini, *Vita di Sandro e di Arnaldo*, Milan, 1934, p. 99.

54. I. De Begnac, *Trent'anni di Mussolini 1883–1915*, Rome, 1934, p. 265.

55. BMOO, XXXV, p. 205.

56. G. Pini, *The official life of Benito Mussolini*, p. 41.

57. BMOO, XXXV, p. 205.

58. V. Benedetti, *Rosa Maltoni Mussolini*, Brescia, 1928, p. 141.

59. BMOO, I, p. 216.

60. T. Nanni, *Bolscevismo e fascismo al lume della critica marxista Benito Mussolini*, Bologna, 1924, p. 151.

61. BMOO, XXXIII, pp. 262–3.

62. BMOO, XXXIII, pp. 264–5.

63. A. Spinosa, *I figli del Duce*, Milan, 1989, p. 10.

Notes

64. A. Borghi, *Mussolini red and black*, p. 31.
65. BMOO, I, pp. 265–6. The local socialist paper, by contrast, thought that his name was Musolino (p. 266).
66. BMOO, I, pp. 105–6.
67. BMOO, I, p. 130.
68. BMOO, I, pp. 145–6.
69. BMOO, I, p. 102; 105.
70. BMOO, XXXVIII, p. 4.
71. BMOO, I, pp. 159–66.
72. R. De Felice, *Mussolini il rivoluzionario 1883–1920*, pp. 56–8.
73. BMOO, I, p. 184.
74. BMOO, I, pp. 190–2.
75. G. Megaro, *Mussolini in the making*, p. 142.
76. R. De Felice, *Mussolini il rivoluzionario 1883–1920*, p. 62.
77. A. Balabanoff, *My life as a rebel*, p. 123.
78. For a telling example, see BMOO, II, pp. 86–99 and the tale entitled 'Nulla è vero, tutto è permesso' (Nothing is true, everything is allowed) which he published in *Vita trentina*. In this story of suicide, sex, shipping magnates and Masonic conspiracies, the Hero lived with his adoring mother, while the villain departed on a trip on the spanking new *Lusitania*.
79. BMOO, II, pp. 263–4.
80. See, generally, C. Schorske, *Fin de siècle Vienna: politics and culture*, New York, 1980.
81. See I. Kershaw, *Hitler 1889–1936: hubris*, Harmondsworth, 1998, pp. 36–60.
82. *Rivista Mensile del Touring Club Italiano*, May 1910.
83. See, for example, BMOO, II, pp. 141; 182–3.
84. BMOO, II, p. 48.
85. BMOO, II, pp. 6–7.
86. BMOO, II, p. 5.
87. See, for example, D.D. Roberts, *The syndicalist tradition and Italian Fascism*, Manchester, 1979, pp. 12–13. Cf. also the collection of writings of A.O. Olivetti, *Dal sindacalismo rivoluzionario al corporativismo* (ed. F. Perfetti), Rome, 1984.
88. BMOO, II, pp. 123–8.
89. BMOO, II, pp. 163–4.
90. BMOO, II, pp. 248–9.
91. BMOO, II, p. 8.
92. BMOO, II, pp. 30–1.
93. BMOO, II, pp. 120; 169–70.
94. BMOO, II, pp. 119; 238.
95. See, especially, his account 'Il Trentino visto da un socialista', published two years later and as available in BMOO, XXXIII, pp. 149–213. He took special pleasure in denouncing the lies and absurdities of such racist writers as Gobineau and H.S. Chamberlain (pp. 153–8). The situation he then described was complicated, however. He asserted, for example, that 'black-legs' and their ilk were the only Italian-speakers who readily surrendered their culture, while the most self-conscious and politically active workers clung to their Italian speech and habits (p. 207).
96. BMOO, II, pp. 21–2.
97. BMOO, II, p. 23.
98. BMOO, II, pp. 194–5.
99. See G. Prezzolini, *L'Italiano inutile*, Milan, 1983.
100. BMOO, II, pp. 259–60.
101. BMOO, II, pp. 53–5; XXXVIII, p. 5.

Notes

102. BMOO, XXXVIII, pp. 6; 10.
103. Actually this was also the catch phrase of the *Touring Club Italiano*. See R.J.B. Bosworth, 'The *Touring Club Italiano* and the nationalisation of the Italian bourgeoisie', *European History Quarterly*, 27, 1997, p. 383.
104. BMOO, XXXVIII, p. 11.
105. BMOO, XXXV, p. 11.
106. BMOO, II, pp. 209–10.
107. For the English version, see A. Lyttelton (ed), *Italian fascisms from Pareto to Gentile*, London, 1973, pp. 207–21.
108. R. De Felice, *Mussolini il rivoluzionario 1883–1920*, pp. 73–5.
109. BMOO, II, pp. 319–21.
110. BMOO, II, p. 268.
111. M. Terzaghi, *Fascismo e Massoneria*, Milan, 1950, p. 11.
112. BMOO, II, p. 66.
113. F. Bandini, *Claretta: profilo di Clara Petacci e dei suoi tempi*, Milan, 1960, p. 55.
114. BMOO, XXXIII, p. 268.
115. A. Pensotti, *Rachele: sessant'anni con Mussolini nel bene e nel male*, Milan, 1983, p. 16.
116. *Ibid.*, p. 21.
117. BMOO, XXXIII, p. 267.
118. A. Pensotti, *Rachele*, p. 14.
119. G. Zachariae, *Mussolini si confessa*, Milan, 1966, p. 48.
120. BMOO, III, pp. 5–7.
121. BMOO, XXXIII, p. 269.

CHAPTER 4

1. Y. De Begnac, *Taccuini mussoliniani* (ed. F. Perfetti), Bologna, 1990, p. 9.
2. Arnaldo Mussolini sought solace from his family troubles by writing religious–agrarian poems. For an example, see A. and B. Mussolini, *Vita di Sandro e Arnaldo*, Milan, 1934, pp. 148–9.
3. L. Preti, *Mussolini giovane*, Milan, 1982, p. 63.
4. G. Pini and D. Susmel, *Mussolini: l'uomo e l'opera*, Florence, 1953–55, vol. I, p.161.
5. F. Bonavita, *Mussolini svelato: origine, sviluppo e finalità del pensiero mussoliniano*, Milan, 1927, p. 88.
6. G. Pini and D. Susmel, *Mussolini*, vol. I, p. 175.
7. G.A. Fanelli, *Cento pagine su Mussolini e un ritratto politico della 'prima ora'*, Rome, 1931, pp. 78–9; 83.
8. A. Pensotti, *Rachele: sessant'anni con Mussolini nel bene e nel male*, Milan, 1983, p. 44.
9. R. De Felice, *Mussolini il rivoluzionario 1883–1920*, Turin, 1965, p. 57.
10. BMOO, IV, p. 19.
11. BMOO, III, pp. 9–10. It was easy, too, to turn the rhetoric of Ravenna republicans back on themselves, when they accused extremist socialists like Mussolini of behaving in an inquisitorial manner (pp. 28–9).
12. F. Bonavita, *Mussolini svelato*, pp. 124–7.
13. BMOO, III, pp. 14–5.
14. C. Rossi, *Mussolini com'era*, Rome, 1947, p. 50.
15. BMOO, III, pp. 23–4.
16. BMOO, III, pp. 208–11. Actually, the revolutionary faction supported by Mussolini did badly at this congress and Mussolini himself made little impression there. See R. De Felice, *Mussolini il rivoluzionario 1883–1920*, pp. 95–6.
17. BMOO, III, pp. 43–4.

Notes

18. BMOO, III, pp. 336–40.

19. BMOO, III, pp. 122–4.

20. BMOO, III, p. 110.

21. BMOO, III, pp. 5–7.

22. BMOO, III, pp. 404–5.

23. BMOO, III, pp. 187–96 (these thoughts were expressed in two long, successive articles in *La Lotta di Classe*).

24. BMOO, IV, p. 7.

25. BMOO, IV, pp. 19–21. Mussolini was writing for the Rome revolutionary socialist journal *La Soffitta* (The Attic), thus boldly named after Prime Minister Giolitti boasted that he had 'relegated socialism to the attic'.

26. A. Iraci, *Arpinati: l'oppositore di Mussolini*, Rome, 1970, p. 7.

27. BMOO, IV, pp. 5–6.

28. BMOO, III, pp. 271–2.

29. BMOO, III, p. 280.

30. BMOO, IV, p. 16. Mussolini also attacked the 'unexampled brutality' of the American bourgeoisie, those 'brutal dollar people', embodied in their deployment of the electric chair and, indeed, manifest in every aspect of their justice system (pp. 180–1; 239–41).

31. See BMOO, XXXIII, pp. 149–213; XXXVIII, pp. 18–21.

32. BMOO, III, p. 349.

33. R. De Felice, *Mussolini il rivoluzionario 1883–1920*, pp. 99–103.

34. E. Forcella, 'Roma 1911: quadri di una esposizione', in G. Piantoni (ed.), *Roma 1911*, Rome, 1980, p. 27.

35. For a standard account, see M. Abrate, *La lotta sindacale nella industrializzazione in Italia 1906–1926*, Turin, 1967.

36. A.L. Cardoza, *Agrarian elites and Italian Fascism: the province of Bologna 1910–1926*, Princeton, 1982, p. 182.

37. For an introduction, see A. Lyttelton (ed.), *Italian Fascisms from Pareto to Gentile*, London, 1973, pp. 135–63.

38. BMOO, IV, p. 59.

39. BMOO, IV, pp. 61–72.

40. BMOO, IV, p. 75.

41. D. Manetti, *Gente di Romagna: Aldo Oviglio*, Bologna, 1924, pp. 99–100.

42. BMOO, IV, pp. 104–7.

43. For a fuller account, see R. De Felice, *Mussolini il rivoluzionario 1883–1920*, pp. 106–11.

44. BMOO, IV, p. 286.

45. BMOO, IV, p. 288.

46. BMOO, IV, p. 289.

47. BMOO, IV, p. 290. Attendance cost 2.75 lire (p. 289).

48. BMOO, IV, p. 249.

49. As with *The Cardinal's Mistress*, an edition was published with hostile intent in very literal English translation in 1929 to lessen the credit of the Lateran Pacts. See B. Mussolini, *John Huss*, New York, 1929. It was reprinted after 1945. B. Mussolini, *Giovanni Huss il veridico*, Rome, 1948; cf. BMOO, XXXIII, pp. 271–327. The original work was released in 1913 in a series dedicated to 'the martyrs of free thought'.

50. B. Mussolini, *Giovanni Huss*, p. 7.

51. *Ibid.*, pp. 93–124.

52. BMOO, IV, pp. 157–60; cf. R. De Felice, *Mussolini il rivoluzionario 1883–1920*, pp. 112–36.

53. C. Rossi, *Mussolini com'era*, p. 61.

54. On this matter, see, for example, Z. Bauman, *Modernity and the Holocaust*, Oxford, 1989; *Modernity and Ambivalence*, Oxford, 1991.

Notes

55. The word Mussolini actually used was the technical one, phagocyte.

56. BMOO, IV, pp. 161–70.

57. Staunchly anti-Soviet historian Richard Pipes has claimed that 'no prominent European socialist before the First World War resembled Lenin more closely than [did] Benito Mussolini'. But the future *Duce*'s version of being intellectual scarcely possessed the cosmopolitan self-assurance of the Russian theorist. See R. Pipes, *Russia under the Bolshevik regime 1917–1924*, London, 1995, p. 245.

58. R. De Felice, *Mussolini il rivoluzionario 1883–1920*, pp. 127–8.

59. SPDCR 104, 29 July 1912, Mussolini to *sindaco* of Crespellano; 20 June 1913, Mussolini to *sindaco*, belatedly pulling out of the job contest.

60. BMOO, IV, pp. 218–21.

61. G. Bozzetti, *Mussolini: direttore dell'Avanti!*, Milan, 1979, p. 39.

62. G. Pini and D. Susmel, *Mussolini*, vol. I, p. 194.

63. BMOO, V, pp. 5–7; cf. his characteristic final editorial in *La Lotta di Classe* which declared his debt to the 'stern land' of the Romagna and his embodiment of its 'redness' (IV, p. 377).

64. P. Valera, *Mussolini*, Milan, 1975, pp. 3; 10. This work was first published in 1924.

65. BMOO, IV, p. 182.

66. BMOO, IV, pp. 184–90.

67. BMOO, IV, pp. 173–4.

68. BMOO, XXXVIII, pp. 22–3.

69. BMOO, XXXVIII, p. 28.

70. Cf., for example, BMOO, IV, p. 259, where Mussolini argued strongly to a childhood friend against the 'professionalisation' of the journalist's job.

71. G. Borsa, *Memorie di un redivivo*, Milan, 1945, p. 420.

72. C. Rossi, *Trentatre vicende mussoliniane*, Milan, 1958, pp. 14–16.

73. P.V. Cannistraro and B.R. Sullivan, *Il Duce's other woman*, New York, 1993. The authors say (p. 97) that she was certainly his mistress by early 1913.

74. It was translated into English, with a gratified preface from Mussolini himself, and widely distributed. See M. Sarfatti, *The life of Benito Mussolini*, London, 1925. My own copy of the book is an 8th impression, published in 1934.

75. Among her numerous publications, see L. Rafanelli, *Alle madri italiane*, Florence, nd; *Lavoratori!* Milan, 1921; *Donne e femmine: novelle*, Milan, 1921; *Incantamento: romanzo*, Milan, 1921 (she wrote under the pseudonym 'Sahra'); *Bozzetti sociali*, Milan, 1921; 'Prefazio' to C. Albert, *L'amore libero*, Milan, 1921; *L'eroe della folla*, Milan, 1925; translation of E. Gamalier, *L'oasi: romanzo*, Milan, 1929; *La 'castità' clericale*, Rome, 1946.

76. They are collected in BMOO, XXXVIII.

77. L. Rafanelli, *Una donna e Mussolini*, Milan, 1975.

78. *Ibid.*, pp. 8; 13. Rafanelli claimed never to have slept with Mussolini.

79. L. Rafanelli, *Lavoratori!* pp. 7; 24.

80. G. Pini and D. Susmel, *Mussolini*, vol. I, p. 199.

81. L. Rafanelli, *Incantamento*, pp. 6–10; 36–8.

82. BMOO, XXXVIII, p. 29.

83. BMOO, XXXVIII, p. 30.

84. BMOO, XXXVIII, p. 30. He signed himself 'B.'

85. BMOO, XXXVIII, pp. 32–3.

86. BMOO, XXXVIII, p. 38.

87. BMOO, XXXVIII, p. 40.

88. L. Rafanelli, *Una donna e Mussolini*, p. 144.

89. BMOO, XXXVIII, p. 42.

90. BMOO, XXXVIII, p. 44. Again he signed himself 'Tuo B.'

91. BMOO, XXXVIII, p. 48.

92. BMOO, XXXVIII, p. 52.
93. BMOO, XXXVIII, pp. 53–4.
94. BMOO, XXXVIII, pp. 65–6. He was writing during the July crisis.
95. BMOO, XXXVIII, p. 68.
96. BMOO, XXXVIII, p. 39.
97. N. D'Aroma, Mussolini segreto, p. 180.
98. BMOO, V, pp. 355–6; 359–60.
99. BMOO, V, p. 356.
100. BMOO, V, p. 357.
101. G. Bozzetti, Mussolini: direttore dell'Avanti!, pp. 133; 146.
102. BMOO, XXXVIII, p. 56.
103. R. De Felice (ed.), Mussolini giornalista, Milan, 1995, p. v.
104. BMOO, V, p. 46.
105. BMOO, V, pp. 119–21.
106. See, for example, BMOO, V, pp. 75–81.
107. BMOO, VI, pp. 87–94.
108. BMOO, V, p. 383.
109. R. De Felice, Mussolini il rivoluzionario 1883–1920, pp. 185–6.
110. Mussolini's articles can be located in BMOO, V–VI. The whole journal, however, was re-edited by De Felice as B. Mussolini, Utopia: rivista quindicinale del socialismo rivoluzionario italiano, Milan, n.d.
111. Utopia, I, 22 November 1913.
112. BMOO, VI, p. 5.
113. BMOO, V, pp. 154–5.
114. BMOO, VI, p. 48.
115. R. De Felice, Mussolini il rivoluzionario 1883–1920, pp. 175–6.
116. BMOO, VI, pp. 114–15.
117. F. Anfuso, Roma Berlino Salò (1936–1945), Milan, 1950, pp. 85–6.
118. N. D'Aroma, Mussolini segreto, Rocca San Casciano, 1958, p. 180.
119. G. Bottai, Mussolini: costruttore d'impero, Milan, n.d, p. 5.
120. C. Delcroix, Un uomo e un popolo, Florence, 1928, p. 3.
121. As quoted by D. Mack Smith, Storia di cento anni di vita italiana visti attraverso Il Corriere della Sera, Milan, 1978, p. 183.
122. Under the regime, they would be given a mystical character. See, for example, E. Adami, La lingua di Mussolini, Modena, 1939.
123. See L. Passerini, Mussolini immaginario: storia di una biografia 1915–1939, Bari, 1991, pp. 32–4. Nanni invented the splendid term specorizzare (to de-sheepise).
124. BMOO, VI, pp. 209–10; 214; 226.
125. R. De Felice, Mussolini il rivoluzionario 1883–1920, p. 201.
126. A.O. Olivetti, Dal sindacalismo rivoluzionario al corporativismo (ed. F. Perfetti), Rome, 1984, p. 166.

CHAPTER 5

1. For an English language summary, see R.J.B. Bosworth, Italy and the approach of the First World War, London, 1983, pp. 121–41.
2. A. Solmi, 'Carteggio tra Salandra e Sonnino nella prima fase della neutralità italiana', Nuova Antologia, f. 1510, 16 February 1935, p. 487.
3. R. De Felice, Mussolini il rivoluzionario 1883–1920, Turin, 1965, p. 218.
4. Ibid., p. 261. Mussolini was writing in his theoretical journal Utopia.
5. BMOO, VI, pp. 239–40.

Notes

6. BMOO, VI, p. 254.

7. BMOO, VI, p. 264.

8. BMOO, VI, pp. 285–8.

9. BMOO, VI, pp. 297; 305–6; 308.

10. As late as 19 September, he still expressed fears about this eventuality. BMOO, VI, p. 364.

11. BMOO, VI, p. 340; cf. pp. 316–20.

12. BMOO, VI, pp. 335–7.

13. L. Campolonghi, 'Il fascismo italiano raccontato dai fascisti: dall'armistizio alla marcia su Roma', in R. De Felice (ed.), *Benito Mussolini: quattro testimonianze*, Florence, 1976, p. 113.

14. The majority of the movement, however, remained opposed to the war. See W. Thorpe, 'The European syndicalists and war, 1914–1918', *Contemporary European History*, 10, 2001, pp. 11–14.

15. BMOO, XXXV, pp. 29–34.

16. BMOO, VI, pp. 372–3.

17. BMOO, XXXVIII, p. 69.

18. BMOO, VI, p. 393.

19. BMOO, VI, p. 394.

20. BMOO, VI, p. 400.

21. BMOO, VI, p. 402.

22. BMOO, VI, p. 403.

23. See R. De Felice, *Mussolini il rivoluzionario 1883–1920*, pp. 260–8.

24. *Ibid.*, pp. 266–7.

25. BMOO, XXXVIII, p. 71.

26. BMOO, VI, pp. 404–8. Cf., for example, A. Borghi, *Mussolini: red and black*, London, 1935, pp. 73–80, a chapter headed 'how he was bought'.

27. BMOO, VII, p. 40.

28. BMOO, VI, pp. 409–15; 419–23.

29. BMOO, VII, pp. 431–4.

30. BMOO, VI, pp. 430–2. Mussolini may have thought of himself as a socialist still, but this interview contained swipes at 'Marx the war-monger' (p. 431). This choice of language scarcely boded well for Mussolini's return to socialist orthodoxy.

31. *Il Popolo d'Italia*, 15 November 1914.

32. The term is used by G. Bozzetti, *Mussolini direttore dell'Avanti!*, Milan, 1979, p. 244.

33. C. Rossi, *Mussolini com'era*, Rome, 1947, pp. 67–70.

34. D. Manetti, *Gente di Romagna: Aldo Oviglio*, Bologna, 1924, p. 265.

35. R. De Felice, *Mussolini il rivoluzionario 1883–1920*, p. 275.

36. M. Girardon, 'La chiave del segreto di Mussolini', in R. De Felice (ed.) *Benito Mussolini*, pp. 167–8.

37. *Ibid.*, pp. 174–80.

38. For the details, see P. Preston, *Franco: a biography*, London, 1993.

39. W.A. Renzi, 'Mussolini's sources of financial support, 1914–1915', *History*, 56, 1971, pp. 193–5. The Russians also probably provided help.

40. *Ibid.*, p. 205. Drolly, the disbursing agent of the British in Rome seems to have been Sir Samuel Hoare, then working for the secret service, but later Secretary of State for Foreign Affairs at the start of the Ethiopian War and, during the Second World War, British ambassador to Franco.

41. For some background, see R.J.B. Bosworth, *Italy the least of the Great Powers: Italian foreign policy before the First World War*, Cambridge, 1979, p. 82.

42. F. Martini, *Diario 1914–1918* (ed. G. De Rosa), Milan, 1966, p. 162.

43. *Ibid.*, p. 288.

44. *Ibid.*, p. 641.

Notes

45. C. Sforza, *L'Italia dal 1914 al 1944 quale io la vidi*, Milan, 1945, p. 129.

46. P. Valera, *Mussolini*, Milan, 1975, p. 26. He was briefly buoyed up when the socialists of Faenza, if not those of Forlì, for a time supported his views. See BMOO, VI, pp. 443–4.

47. G. Pini and D. Susmel, *Mussolini: l'uomo e l'opera*, Florence, 1953–55, vol. I, p. 264.

48. BMOO, VII, pp. 5–7.

49. BMOO, VII, pp. 13–15.

50. BMOO, XXXV, p. 207.

51. BMOO, XXXVIII, p. 80.

52. BMOO, VII, pp. 25–7.

53. BMOO, VII, pp. 94–6.

54. BMOO, VII, p. 424.

55. BMOO, VII, p. 32.

56. He was fighting a fellow deputy. See C. Seton Watson, *Italy from Liberalism to Fascism 1870–1925*, London, 1967, p. 191.

57. *Il Popolo d'Italia*, 20 December 1914.

58. BMOO, VII, p. 489.

59. C. Rossi, *Trentatre vicende mussoliniane*, Milan, 1958, pp. 29; 34.

60. BMOO, XXXVIII, p. 72; cf. P. Nello, *Dino Grandi: la formazione di un leader fascista*, Bologna, 1987, p. 34.

61. BMOO, VII, pp. 70–1.

62. BMOO, VII, pp. 461–2. Mussolini still cheerfully derided Victor Emmanuel III as 'the numismatic king' (p. 235).

63. BMOO, VII, pp. 117–19.

64. BMOO, VII, pp. 139–41.

65. BMOO, VII, pp. 187–8.

66. BMOO, XXXVIII, p. 83.

67. BMOO, VII, p. 197.

68. BMOO, VII, p. 376.

69. BMOO, XXXVIII, p. 85.

70. BMOO, XXXVIII, p. 85 (in a letter to another intellectual, Ardengo Soffici). Mussolini's brief arrest in Rome on 12 April in the company of Marinetti was re-invoked regularly during the regime, especially when the Futurist was being self-important (as he often was). See F.T. Marinetti, *Futurismo e fascismo*, Foligno, 1924, p. 17.

71. BMOO, VII, pp. 356–8.

72. BMOO, XXXV, p. 42.

73. BMOO, VII, pp. 418–19.

74. *Il Popolo d'Italia*, 6 May 1915.

75. BMOO, VII, pp. 308–10.

76. BMOO, VII, pp. 345–8.

77. BMOO, VII, p. 419.

78. In October 1915 Italy did officially enter the conflict against Turkey.

79. As a prelude to the later historiography, the French military in 1916 were already scoffing at Italian claims that Alpine warfare was different. See N. Brancaccio, *In Francia durante la guerra*, Milan, 1926, pp. 31–2.

80. It also confirmed every non-Italian prejudice about the poor fighting quality of Italians. For further background on such stereotypes, see R.J.B. Bosworth, 'Mito e linguaggio nella politica estera italiana', in R.J.B. Bosworth and S. Romano (eds), *La politica estera italiana (1860–1985)*, Bologna, 1991, pp. 35–67.

81. P. Melograni, *Storia politica della grande guerra, 1915–1918*, Bari, 1969, p. 423. Italian POWs, in great majority peasants, had a very rough war, with some 20 per cent dying while imprisoned, the great majority from diseases occasioned by simple hunger. See G. Procacci,

Notes

Soldati e prigionieri italiani nella grande guerra, Rome, 1993, pp. 150–1. Procacci also emphasises the huge difference in the experience of imprisonment for officers and men, and the massive psychological and class gap between them.

82. P. Melograni, *Storia politica della grande guerra, 1915–1918*, p. 6.
83. *Ibid.*, pp. 93; 112. These sons were numbered among those known derisively as *imboscati* (draft-dodgers but literally 'those gone to the woods').
84. *Ibid.*, pp. 165–6.
85. For an English-language biography, see H. Fornari, *Mussolini's gadfly: Roberto Farinacci*, Nashville, 1971.
86. R. Farinacci, *Storia della rivoluzione fascista*, Cremona, 1937, vol. I, p. 14.
87. He did write a letter to a government minister in July 1915 complaining that his name had not yet come up and threatening to volunteer in France if he was not conscripted soon. See BMOO, XXXVIII, p. 86.
88. BMOO, VIII, p. 195.
89. BMOO, XXXVIII, p. 88.
90. A. Gravelli, *Uno e molti: interpretazioni spirituali di Mussolini*, Rome, 1938, pp. 9–10; 16. For further background, see L. Passerini, *Mussolini immaginario: storia di una biografia, 1915–1939*, Bari, 1991, pp. 15–32.
91. B. Mussolini, *Il mio diario di guerra (1915–1917)*, Milan, 1923.
92. *Ibid.*, p. 13.
93. *Ibid.*, p. 52.
94. *Ibid.*, pp. 71; 80–1.
95. *Ibid.*, p. 124.
96. *Ibid.*, p. 97.
97. *Ibid.*, p. 22.
98. *Ibid.*, p. 37.
99. *Ibid.*, p. 14.
100. *Ibid.*, pp. 57–8.
101. *Il Popolo d'Italia*, 11 November 1918.
102. B. Mussolini, *Il mio diario di guerra (1915–1917)*, p. 74.
103. V. Perroni, *Il Mussolini dei bimbi*, Rome, 1929, p. 84.
104. *Il Popolo d'Italia*, 4 April 1917.
105. Contemporary newspaper accounts differ and the last two sentences may be an embroidering of the event. B. Mussolini, *Il mio diario di guerra (1915–1917)*, pp. 221–2.
106. *Ibid.*, pp. 18; 141.
107. *Ibid.*, p. 133.
108. G. Pini and D. Susmel, *Mussolini*, vol. I, p. 304.
109. *Ibid.*, vol. I, 343. Mussolini exchanged letters with his sister Edvige on a number of occasions during the war. See BMOO, XXXV, pp. 212; 218; 223. Later, Edvige and Arnaldo helped distribute to his family monies which Mussolini had collected.
110. BMOO, X, p. 445.
111. G. Pini and and D. Susmel, *Mussolini*, vol. IV, p. 183 give a death date of 25 June 1942. But for later detail on the affair, see the article entitled 'Mussolini e Ida Dalser: la vera storia del bigamo Benito', *Il Corriere della Sera*, 10 May 2001.
112. For a racy account of these matters, see A. Spinosa, *I figli del Duce*, Milan, 1983, pp. 24–5; 98–102. In 1926 Ida Dalser was confined in a lunatic asylum after she approached a Fascist minister about her cause. Her defenders say she was sane at the time. She died in 1937. Another journalistic account has Mussolini fathering a child on a certain Fernanda Oss in 1910. The baby was called Benito Ribelle (the name seems too good to be true) and, allegedly, soon died. See F. Castellini, *Il ribelle di Predappio: amori e giovinezza di Mussolini*, Milan, 1996, pp. 139–40.

Notes

113. G. Pini and D. Susmel, *Mussolini*, vol. II, p. 421.

114. P.V. Cannistraro and B.R. Sullivan, *Il Duce's other woman*, New York, 1993, pp. 132–66.

115. R. De Felice, *Mussolini il rivoluzionario 1883–1920*, p. 320.

116. BMOO, VIII, pp. 11–15.

117. BMOO, VIII, pp. 23–5.

118. BMOO, VIII, p. 55–7.

119. G. Pini and D. Susmel, *Mussolini*, vol. II, p. 26.

120. BMOO, VIII, p. 297.

121. R. De Felice, *Mussolini il rivoluzionario 1883–1920*, pp. 354–5; 414–5.

122. BMOO, VIII, pp. 354–6.

123. See E. Settimelli, *Gli animatori: Benito Mussolini*, Piacenza 1921.

124. BMOO, IX, pp. 5–8; 188–9. He now noticed the existence of 'Lenine', whom he condemned as a traitor working in the pay of the Germans (pp. 74–6).

125. BMOO, IX, pp. 126–7.

126. BMOO, IX, pp. 82–4.

127. BMOO, IX, pp. 116–19.

128. BMOO, IX, pp. 307–9. Mussolini may have flirted with the idea of a coup in which he would have been the propagandist for such army chiefs as Luigi Cadorna. See O. Dinale, *Quarant'anni di colloqui con lui*, Milan, 1953, pp. 84–5.

129. BMOO, X, pp. 14–16.

130. BMOO, X, pp. 23–5.

131. BMOO, X, pp. 36–8.

132. BMOO, X, pp. 55–7.

133. BMOO, X, pp. 67–8.

134. BMOO, X, pp. 86–8.

135. R. De Felice, *Mussolini il rivoluzionario 1883–1920*, p. 392.

136. BMOO, X, p. 188.

137. BMOO, X, p. 141.

138. BMOO, X, p. 100.

139. BMOO, X, pp. 114–16; 127–9; 430–2.

140. BMOO, XI, pp. 88–90.

141. BMOO, XI, pp. 384–6.

142. BMOO, XII, pp. 100–3; 110–12.

143. *Il Popolo d'Italia*, 17 October 1918; the effect of this enthusiasm was dented a little by the hailing of the 'traditional lies' [sic] which bound the USA and Europe (15 November 1918).

144. BMOO, X, pp. 392–4.

145. BMOO, XI, pp. 8–9.

146. BMOO, XI, pp. 33–6.

147. BMOO, XII, p. 286.

148. BMOO, X, pp. 140–2.

149. BMOO, X, pp. 381–3.

150. BMOO, XI, pp. 241–3.

151. BMOO, X, pp. 433–5. Although Fiume (Rijeka) was 'a highly Italian' place, he did think it could presently be handed over to the Croats (pp. 327–9; 339–41).

152. BMOO, XI, pp. 258–61. He used the English expression.

153. BMOO, XI, pp. 175–8.

154. BMOO, X, p. 327. 'Imperialism', he added in January 1919, was 'the eternal and immutable law of life' (XII, p. 100).

155. BMOO, XI, p. 183.

156. BMOO, XI, pp. 455–7.

157. BMOO, XI, p. 476.

Notes

158. C. Rossi, *Mussolini com'era*, p. 234.

159. BMOO, XII, pp. 3–5.

160. BMOO, XII, pp. 27–9.

161. BMOO, XII, pp. 6–8.

162. BMOO, XII, p. 69.

163. For the complex history of this body, founded in November 1918, see G. Sabbatucci, *I combattenti nel primo dopoguerra*, Bari, 1974.

164. R. De Felice, *Mussolini il rivoluzionario 1883–1920*, p. 476.

165. BMOO, XII, pp. 309–11, advertises the coming event. On 15 March Mussolini had announced the creation of a journal, to be entitled *Ardita* and aimed at viewing the world through the eyes of youth.

166. G. Pini and D. Susmel, *Mussolini*, vol. I, p. 389.

CHAPTER 6

1. S. Maurano, *Ricordi di un giornalista fascista*, Milan, 1973, p. 14.

2. A. Rosato, *Mussolini: colloquio intimo*, Milan, 1923, pp. 12–13; 19; 27–31.

3. P. Pedrazza, *Giornalismo di Mussolini*, Milan, 1937, p. 39.

4. For the full report, see appendix 18 to R. De Felice, *Mussolini il rivoluzionario 1883–1920*, Turin, 1965, pp. 725–37.

5. Mussolini fought at least two duels in 1919 and another in 1920. Perhaps the most notorious that year was a challenge he made to an old acquaintance, the historian Gaetano Salvemini, who was destined to become the most pertinacious of Anti-Fascist publicists. Salvemini had accused Mussolini of diverting to his own advantage monies collected for D'Annunzio at Fiume. See BMOO, XV, pp. 143–6. Cf. also *Il Popolo d'Italia*, 12, 13, 17 August 1920. There, with his accustomed violence, Mussolini painted 'Gastone Slavemini' [sic] as a 'coward' for avoiding the fight. His habits were not unique. One contemporary tallied sixty-seven duels fought by journalists on his paper between 1924 and 1930. See S. Maurano, *Ricordi*, p. 51.

6. R. De Felice, *Mussolini il rivoluzionario 1883–1920*, pp. 734–5.

7. *Ibid.*, p. 734.

8. For a recent example, see P. Milza, *Mussolini*, Paris, 1999, pp. 225–36.

9. See most fulsomely, G. Policastro, *Crispi e Mussolini*, Mantua, 1928.

10. G. Pini and D. Susmel, *Mussolini: l'uomo e l'opera*, Florence, 1953–55, vol. II, p. 38.

11. *Ibid.*, vol. II, p. 110.

12. For background, see R. Wohl, *A passion for wings: aviation and the Western imagination 1908–1918*, New Haven, 1994.

13. P. Milza, *Mussolini*, p. 215.

14. G. Pini and D. Susmel, *Mussolini*, vol II, p. 40.

15. For the context, R.J.B. Bosworth, *Italy and the wider world 1860–1960*, London, 1996, pp. 32–5.

16. BMOO, XII, p. 321.

17. N. D'Aroma, *Mussolini segreto*, Rocca San Casciano, 1958, p. 256.

18. F. Vecchi, *Arditismo civile*, Milan, 1920, p. 31.

19. In *L'Ardito Marinetti* duly argued that the greatest results of the war were the impulses given to science and sport. See F.T. Marinetti, *Futurismo e fascismo*, Foligno, 1924, p. 111.

20. F. Vecchi, *Arditismo civile*, p. 36.

21. *Ibid.*, pp. 55–6; 85; 137.

22. *Ibid.*, p. 139.

23. E. Daquanno, *Vecchia guardia*, Rome, 1934, p. 13.

Notes

24. R. Giuliani, *Gli arditi: breve storia dei reparti d'assalto della Terza Armata*, Milan, 1926, pp. 25–34; 61; 204.

25. M. Carli, *Arditismo*, Rome, 1929, pp. 5; 17; 22; 33.

26. F. Vecchi, *Arditismo civile*, p. 54.

27. M.G. Sarfatti, *Acqua passata*, Rocca San Casciano, 1955, p. 98.

28. For an enthusiastic account of her artistic achievement, see L. Panzera (ed.), *La Futurista: Benedetta Cappa Marinetti*, Philadelphia, 1998.

29. F.T. Marinetti, *Futurismo e fascismo*, p. 111. On other occasion he urged the abolition of the police force on the grounds that a society should be united enough to defend itself (pp. 56–73).

30. *Ibid.*, p. 128.

31. Y. De Begnac, *Taccuini mussoliniani* (ed. F. Perfetti), Bologna, 1990, p. 424.

32. BMOO, XIII, pp. 386–8.

33. F. Vecchi, *Arditismo civile*, p. 29.

34. F.T. Marinetti, *Futurismo e fascismo*, pp. 167–9.

35. BMOO, XIII, pp. 61–3.

36. E. Gentile, *Storia del Partito Fascista 1919–1922: movimento e milizia*, Bari, 1989, pp. 26–39.

37. BMOO, XIII, pp. 12–13.

38. A.O. Olivetti, *Dal sindacalismo rivoluzionario al corporativismo*, Rome, 1984, p. 184.

39. R. De Felice, *Mussolini il rivoluzionario 1883–1920*, pp. 522–3.

40. BMOO, XIII, pp. 62–3.

41. BMOO, XIII, p. 72.

42. BMOO, XIII, p. 89.

43. BMOO, XIII, p. 83.

44. BMOO, XIII, pp. 124–7; 148.

45. BMOO, XIII, pp. 164–5.

46. One of Preziosi's targets in 1918 was Baron Alberto Fassini whom he accused of shady dealings with Jewish businessmen and a general lack of patriotism. From 1922 Fassini was to be Mussolini's accommodating landlord in his quarters at the Palazzo Tittoni in the via Rasella in Rome. Then and thereafter, Fassini played an important part in the regime's financial elite. For the attack, see *La Vita Italiana*, 15 August 1918.

47. BMOO, XIII, pp. 168–70.

48. For a scholarly example, see M. Michaelis, *Mussolini and the Jews: German–Italian relations and the Jewish question in Italy 1922–1945*, Oxford, 1978, pp. 12–13.

49. BMOO, XIII, pp. 188–90. A few weeks later, Mussolini was much more sarcastic about the Hungarian communists, using Bela Kun's flight from Budapest to tell Italian socialists of the idiocy of their reading of both revolution and international affairs (pp. 276–8).

50. BMOO, XIII, pp. 204–5.

51. O. Mosca, *Nessuno volle i miei dollari d'oro*, Naples, 1958, p. 189.

52. BMOO, XIII, p. 296.

53. BMOO, XIII, pp. 273–5.

54. See, for example, BMOO, XIII, pp. 391–5; 402; 407–8; 423–5; 429–31; 437–9, with reiterated articles by G.M. Serrati and others in which Mussolini was frequently called 'the man without a name'.

55. A. Tasca, *The rise of Italian fascism 1918–1922*, New York, 1966, p. 59. For a detailed account of the economics of the time, with their emphasis on the poorer sections of society paying for the war, see D. R. Forsyth, *The crisis of Liberal Italy: monetary and financial policy 1914–1922*, Cambridge, 1993, pp. 195–228.

56. For the words, see G. Vettori (ed.), *Canzoni italiane di protesta (1794–1974)*, Rome, 1974, pp. 133–4.

Notes

57. R. De Felice, *Mussolini il rivoluzionario*, pp. 536–9.

58. See, for example, BMOO, XIII, pp. 17–20; 47.

59. BMOO, XIV, p. 111.

60. N.S. Onofri, *La strage di palazzo d'Accursio: origine e nascita del fascismo bolognese 1919–1920*, Milan, 1980, pp. 10–11. They were the *Fascio liberale*, the *Fascio di resistenza dei movimentisti postali*, the *Fascio libertario bolognese*, the *Fascio socialista comunista*, the *Fascio universitario repubblicano*, the *Fascio universitario del PPI*, the *Fascio dei medici reduci dal fronte*, the *Fascio universitario costituzionale*, the *Fascio dei ferrovieri*, the *Fascio universitario dei partiti nazionalisti*, the *Fascio libertario imolese*, the *Fascio giovanile socialista*, the *Fascio di educazione sociale*, the *Fascio degli studenti delle scuole medie*, the *Fascio di propaganda* and the *Fascio rivoluzionario dei postaltelegrafici*.

61. F. Vecchi, *Arditismo civile*, p. 36.

62. A.J. Rhodes, *The poet as superman: a life of Gabriele D'Annunzio*, London, 1959, p. 184.

63. See R. De Felice (ed.), *La Carta del Carnaro nei testi di Alceste De Ambris e di Gabriele D'Annunzio*, Bologna, 1973.

64. A. De Ambris, 'Mussolini: la leggenda e!l'uomo', in R. De Felice (ed.), *Benito Mussolini: quattro testimonianze*, Florence, 1976, pp. 30; 35; 79.

65. M.A. Ledeen, *D'Annunzio a Fiume*, Bari, 1975, p. 3. Cf. also R. De Felice, *D'Annunzio politico 1918–1938*, Bari, 1978.

66. BMOO, XIV, p. 5.

67. BMOO, XIV, pp. 19–20.

68. BMOO, XIV, pp. 43–5. The word *Cagoia* had been used by D'Annunzio to berate Nitti and seems to have been taken from a Triestine dialect word meaning one who thinks only of his stomach.

69. BMOO, XIV, p. 127. For a tracing of the way in which the words transmogrified into the official Fascist anthem, see A.V. Savona and M.L. Straniero (eds), *Canti dell'Italia fascista (1919–1945)*, Milan, 1979, pp. 53–7; 61–3.

70. BMOO, XIV, p. 133.

71. E. Gentile, *Storia del Partito Fascista 1919–1922*, p. 63.

72. R. De Felice, *D'Annunzio politico*, p. 57.

73. G. Giuriati, *Con D'Annunzio e Millo in difesa dell'Adriatico*, Florence, 1954, p. 56.

74. E. Gentile, *Storia del Partito Fascista 1919–1922*, p. 43.

75. BMOO, XIV, p. 136.

76. BMOO, XIV, p. 169.

77. BMOO, XIV, p. 140.

78. R. De Felice, *Mussolini il rivoluzionario 1883–1920*, pp. 574–7.

79. For his revelatory memoirs, see E. Conti, *Dal taccuino di un borghese*, Cremona, 1946.

80. *La Vita Italiana*, 15 February 1920, pp. 102–12.

81. BMOO, XIV, p. 285.

82. 'Volt', *Dal partito allo stato*, Brescia, 1930, p. 8. Fani Ciotti died in 1927.

83. *Ibid.*, p. 15.

84. *Ibid.*, p. 28.

85. BMOO, XIV, p. 231.

86. R. Riccardi, *Pagine squadristiche*, Rome, 1939, p. 32.

87. *Ibid.*, pp. 41–3.

88. E. Apih, *Italia: fascismo e antifascismo nella Venezia Giulia (1918–1943)*, Bari, 1966, p. 92, reveals that a patriotic Italian group calling themselves *Sursum Corda* went about the city armed and alert from as early as 1908.

89. F. Giunta, *Essenza dello squadrismo*, Rome, 1931, p. 5.

90. F.M. Snowden, *Violence and great estates in the south of Italy: Apulia 1900–1922*, Cambridge, 1986, p. 3.

91. BMOO, XIV, p. 379.

Notes

92. BMOO, XIV, p. 397.

93. BMOO, XV, pp. 57–9.

94. BMOO, XIV, pp. 466–71.

95. R. De Felice, *Mussolini il rivoluzionario 1883–1920*, p. 594.

96. E. Gentile, *Storia del partito fascista 1919–1922*, p. 100.

97. P. Spriano, *The occupation of the factories: Italy 1920*, London, 1975, p. 97.

98. *Ibid.*, p. 99.

99. BMOO, XV, p. 153.

100. BMOO, XV, pp. 182–3.

101. BMOO, XV, p. 152.

102. BMOO, XV, pp. 226–8.

103. BMOO, XIII, p. 303. At this time, Tullio, the brother of Mussolini's long-term fixer, Manlio Morgagni, was killed in an aircrash. See C. Redaelli, *Iniziando Mussolini alle vie del cielo*, Milan, 1933, p. 60. Mourning victims of the air easily adapted itself to the growing Fascist harnessing both the casualties of the war and their own political 'martyrs' into ceremonies of death and renewal.

104. BMOO, XIV, p. 481.

105. BMOO, XV, p. 15.

106. A decade later, Fascist journals were still invoking the 'great flyers' international' which elevated Lindbergh, and the Australians Charles Kingsford-Smith and Bert Hinkler, each to being 'one of us'. See *L'Ala d'Italia*, 22 May 1932.

107. G. Mattioli, *Mussolini aviatore*, Milan, 1942, p. 89.

108. G.B. Guerri, Italo Balbo, Milan, 1984, p. 18.

109. G.C. Segrè, *Italo Balbo: a Fascist life*, Berkeley, 1987, p. 16. For his later career, see also G. Rochat, *Italo Balbo: aviatore e ministro dell'aeronautica 1926–1933*, Ferrara, 1979.

110. G. Mattioli, *Mussolini aviatore*, p. 16–17.

111. BMOO, XIV, p. 480 (in a letter to his early follower Longoni).

112. G. Mattioli, *Mussolini aviatore*, p. 55.

113. R. Cantagalli, *Storia del fascismo fiorentino 1919–1925*, Florence, 1972, p. 75.

114. C. Redaelli, *Iniziando Mussolini*, pp. 27–31. Redaelli, in 1919 at least, charged 100 lire per half hour for joy-flights (p. 21). Formal instruction must have cost more.

115. *Ibid.*, pp. 33; 42.

116. *Ibid.*, pp. 21; 42–3; 77.

117. *Ibid.*, p. 86.

118. G. Pini and D. Susmel, *Mussolini*, vol. IV, p. 356.

119. D. Mack Smith, *Mussolini*, London, 1981, p. 269.

CHAPTER 7

1. For some details, see M. Franzinelli, *I tentacoli dell'OVRA: agenti, collaboratori e vittime della polizia politica fascista*, Turin, 1999, pp. 57–9; 406–7.

2. G. Rizzo, *D'Annunzio e Mussolini: la verità sui loro rapporti*, Rocca San Casciano, 1960, p. 21.

3. For his background as a nationalist radical and *Alpini* captain, see P. Nello, *Dino Grandi: la formazione di un leader fascista*, Bologna, 1987.

4. R. De Felice and E. Mariano (eds), *Carteggio D'Annunzio–Mussolini (1919–1938)*, Milan, 1971, p. xxviii.

5. *Ibid.*, pp. xxxii–xxxiv.

6. E. Gentile, *Storia del Partito Fascista 1919–1922: movimento e milizia*, Bari, 1989, p. 639.

7. The two continued a correspondence which, beneath the lines, can be read for many fine examples of lying and hostility. See R. De Felice and E. Mariano (eds.), *Carteggio D'Annunzio–Mussolini (1919–1938)*.

Notes

8. BMOO, XV, pp. 55–7.

9. BMOO, XV, p. 70.

10. BMOO, XV, p. 184,

11. BMOO, XV, pp. 28–9; 120–2.

12. BMOO, XV, pp. 269–70.

13. *La Vita Italiana*, XVI, 15 August 1920. See also his follow-up pieces in the numbers of 15 September 1920, XVII, 15 January 1921, 15 April 1921. In the issue XIX, 15 March 1922, Preziosi again assumed a Jewish background for 'Loyd George' (*sic*) and the then Italian Foreign Minister, Carlo Schanzer.

14. C. Rossi, *Mussolini com'era*, Rome, 1947, p. 260.

15. The Nationalist, Luigi Federzoni, believed that Mussolini was especially chameleon-like before 1922. See L. Federzoni, *Italia di ieri per la storia di domani*, Milan, 1967, p. 70.

16. BMOO, XVI, pp. 17–19.

17. R. De Felice, *Mussolini il rivoluzionario 1883–1920*, Turin, 1965, pp. 634–46.

18. BMOO, XVI, pp. 5–6.

19. BMOO, XV, pp. 38–9.

20. BMOO, XV, pp. 214–22.

21. BMOO, XV, pp. 226–8.

22. E. Apih, *Italia: fascismo e antifascismo nella Venezia Giulia (1918–1943)*, Bari, 1966, pp. 121–3. Cf. the speeches of an official representative there, later promoted to be a Fascist Minister of Finance and eventual author of blandly justificatory memoirs. A. Mosconi, *I primi anni di governo italiano nella Venezia Giulia: Trieste 1919–1922*, Bologna, 1924; and his *La mia linea politica*, Rome, 1952.

23. F. Giunta, *Essenza dello squadrismo*, Rome, 1931, p. 50.

24. R. De Felice, *Mussolini il rivoluzionario 1883–1920*, p. 662.

25. A. Roveri, *Le origini del fascismo a Ferrara 1918–1921*, Milan, 1974, p. 20.

26. P. Corner, *Fascism in Ferrara 1915–1925*, Oxford, 1975, p. 15

27. A. Roveri, *Le origini del fascismo a Ferrara*, p. 69.

28. P. Corner, *Fascism in Ferrara*, p. 55.

29. *Ibid.*, p. 128 and see more generally, C.G. Segrè, *Italo Balbo: a Fascist life*, Berkeley, 1987.

30. P. Corner, *Fascism in Ferrara*, p. 151.

31. *Ibid.*, p. 172.

32. I. Balbo, *Diario 1922*, Milan, 1932, pp. 11–12.

33. P. Corner, *Fascism in Ferrara*, p. 210.

34. A.L. Cardoza, *Agrarian elites and Italian Fascism: the province of Bologna 1901–1926*, Princeton, 1982, p. 192.

35. *Ibid.*, p. 273.

36. *Ibid.*, p. 297; T. Nanni, *Leandro Arpinati e il fascismo bolognese*, Bologna, 1927, p. 104.

37. For defences of Arpinati, see G. Cantamessa Arpinati, *Arpinati mio padre*, Rome, 1968; A. Iraci, *Arpinati: l'oppositore di Mussolini*, Rome, 1970.

38. BMOO, XVI, pp. 25–6.

39. G. Cantamessa Arpinati, *Arpinati mio padre*, p. 26.

40. T. Nanni, *Leandro Arpinati*, p. 113.

41. A.L. Cardoza, *Agrarian elites and Italian Fascism: the province of Bologna*, p. 326.

42. G. Ricci, *Squadrismo forlivese*, Forlì, 1942, pp. 42; 130; 139.

43. G. Zibordi, *Critica socialista del fascismo*, Bologna, 1922, pp. 16; 19.

44. G. Bergamo, *Il Fascismo visto da un repubblicano*, Bologna, 1921, p. 32.

45. *Ibid.*, p. 11.

46. See L. Ponziani, *Notabili, combattenti e nazionalisti verso il Fascismo*, Milan, 1988, pp. 16–18; 76.

47. *Ibid.*, pp. 131–42; 193.

Notes

48. *Ibid.*, pp. 148; 179.

49. *Ibid.*, p. 177.

50. For his career as a colonialist under-secretary already before 1914, see R.J.B. Bosworth, *Italy the least of the Great Powers: Italian foreign policy before the First World War*, Cambridge, 1979, pp. 26; 54–5.

51. G. Miccichè, *Dopoguerra e fascismo in Sicilia 1919–1927*, Rome, 1976, p. 18. By 1920 his *Partito agrario* possessed its own armed 'squads', determined to do what the government seemed too weak to do (pp. 69–70). Members of the Nationalist Association were also soon organising themselves into squads under a name which hinted at a boy scouts' morality *Sempre Pronti* (Always Prepared) (p. 117).

52. *Ibid.*, p. 73.

53. See, for example, B. Pace, *L'impero e la collaborazione internazionale in Africa*, Rome, 1938. This booklet was published under the auspices of the *Istituto nazionale di cultura fascista*.

54. For an account of the ambiguity of the term, see C. Duggan, *Fascism and the Mafia*, New Haven, 1989, pp. 15–19.

55. G. Miccichè, *Dopoguerra e fascismo in Sicilia*, p. 99.

56. M. Vaini, *Le origini del fascismo a Mantova (1914–1922)*, Rome, 1961, p. 102.

57. R. Cantagalli, *Storia del fascismo fiorentino 1919–1925*, Florence, 1972, p. 198.

58. R. De Felice, *Mussolini il fascista: 1. La conquista del potere 1921–5*, Turin, 1966, p. 7.

59. *Ibid.*, p. 87.

60. J. Busoni, *Nel tempo del fascismo*, Rome, 1975, p. 17.

61. A. Roveri, *Le origini del fascismo a Ferrara*, p. 81. It was at this time that the man who would become the leading Fascist historian, Gioacchino Volpe, made his first approaches to Mussolini, who, impressed by his prestige and anxious that it rub off on him, gave warm welcome. See BMOO, XVI, p. 22.

62. BMOO, XVI, p. 101.

63. BMOO, XVI, pp. 118–21; 126–7.

64. A. Gramsci, *Selections from political writings (1921–1926)*, London, 1978, p. 374.

65. BMOO, XVI, p. 170.

66. BMOO, XVI, p. 181.

67. BMOO, XVI, pp. 186–8.

68. BMOO, XVI, p. 212.

69. BMOO, XVI, pp. 283–5.

70. C. Sforza, *L'Italia dal 1914 al 1944 quale io la vidi*, Milan, 1944, p. 97.

71. E. Gentile, *Storia del Partito Fascista 1919–1922*, p. 206.

72. BMOO, XVI, pp. 358–362. In words probably meant mainly to destabilise Giolitti, he added that they would contemplate joining a government led by Salandra or even one under the aegis of the patriotic Catholic, Filippo Meda. Mussolini made these comments in another of his interviews with *Il Giornale d'Italia*.

73. BMOO, XVI, pp. 373–6.

74. BMOO, XVII, p. 13.

75. BMOO, XVI, pp. 351–2.

76. F. Anfuso, *Roma Berlino Salò (1936–1945)*, Milan, 1950, p. 9.

77. For examples, see C. Pavone (ed.), *Dalle carte di Giovanni Giolitti: quarant'anni di politica italiana vol. III. Dai prodromi della grande guerra al fascismo 1910–1928*, Milan, 1962, pp. 158; 371.

78. P. Milza, *Mussolini*, Paris, 1999, pp. 285–6. He may now have begun a relationship with Angela Curti that produced a daughter, Elena, destined to give Mussolini some personal solace in the dark days of the Second World War.

79. M. Vaini, *Le origini del fascismo a Mantova*, p. 143.

80. BMOO, XVII, pp. 25–9; 43–6. R. De Felice, *Mussolini il fascista 1921–5*, pp. 131–9.

Notes

81. BMOO, XVII, pp. 67–8.
82. H. Fornari, *Mussolini's gadfly: Roberto Farinacci*, Nashville, 1971, p. 46. For Farinacci's own version, cf. R. Farinacci, *Storia della rivoluzione fascista* (2 vols), Cremona, 1937; *Squadrismo: dal mio diario della vigilia 1919–1922*, Rome, 1933.
83. M. Pantaleoni, 'Plutocrazia e bolscevismo sgretolano il fascismo', *La Vita Italiana*, XVIII, 15 July 1921.
84. BMOO, XVII, pp. 80–3.
85. E. Corradini, 'Costruire lo Stato', *La Vita Italiana*, XVIII, 15 August 1921, pp. 89–91.
86. For an introduction, see F. Piva, *Lotte contadine e origini del fascismo, Padova-Venezia: 1919–1922*, Venice, 1977.
87. For a respectful biography, see S. Romano, *Giuseppe Volpi: industria e finanza tra Giolitti e Mussolini*, Milan, 1979.
88. See Y. De Begnac, *Taccuini mussoliniani* (ed. F. Perfetti), Bologna, 1990, pp. 505–8. Marsich had introduced Volpi to Mussolini in 1919.
89. Cited by F. Piva, *Lotte contadine e origini del fascismo*, p. 212.
90. Cited by E. Gentile, *Storia del Partito Fascista 1919–1922*, p. 283.
91. M. Piazzesi, *Diario di uno squadrista toscano 1919–1922*, Rome, 1981, pp. 192–3.
92. *Ibid.*, p. 199.
93. BMOO, XVII, pp. 103–5.
94. See E. Gentile, 'Mussolini's charisma', *Modern Italy*, 3, 1998, p. 222.
95. BMOO, XVII, pp. 112–13.
96. BMOO, XVII, pp. 157–8.
97. BMOO, XVII, pp. 201–3; 431–5.
98. R. De Felice, *Mussolini il fascista 1921–5*, p. 182.
99. P.V. Cannistraro and B.R. Sullivan, *Il Duce's other woman*, New York, 1993, pp. 252–3.
100. R. De Felice, *Mussolini il fascista 1921–5*, pp. 198–9.
101. BMOO, XVII, p. 241.
102. BMOO, XVII, pp. 174–8.
103. BMOO, XVII, p. 220.
104. BMOO, XVII, p. 196.
105. BMOO, XVII, p. 318.
106. D.M. Tuninetti, *La vita di Michele Bianchi*, Rome, 1935, pp. 34; 48; but cf. the less respectful M. Rocca, *Come il fascismo divenne una dittatura*, Milan, 1952, p. 99, who deemed Bianchi both ambitious and weak.
107. BMOO, XVII, p. 415.
108. E. Gentile, *Storia del Partito Fascista 1919–1922*, p. 387; cf. also R.J.B. Bosworth, '*Per necessità famigliare*: hypocrisy and corruption in Fascist Italy', *European History Quarterly*, 30, 2000, pp. 363–5.
109. Mussolini dismissed him as 'my weakness', a man who could not think beyond his virility and his beard. See N. D'Aroma, *Mussolini segreto*, Rocca San Casciano, 1958, p. 68.
110. M. Rocca, *Come il fascismo divenne una dittatura*, p.100; R. Montagna, *Mussolini e il processo di Verona*, Milan, 1949, p. 208. A colleague remembered him as short, fat, sweaty and with a squint. See A. Turati, *Fuori dell'ombra della mia vita: dieci anni nel solco del fascismo*, Brescia, 1973, p. 69.
111. V. De Grazia, *How Fascism ruled women: Italy 1922–1945*, Berkeley, 1992, p. 30.
112. E. Gentile, *Storia del Partito Fascista 1919–1922*, p. 417.
113. *Ibid.*, pp. 423–6.
114. *Ibid.*, p. 518.
115. In English, see especially E. Gentile, *The sacralization of politics in Fascist Italy*, Cambridge, Mass., 1996.
116. E. Gentile, *Storia del Partito Fascista 1919–1922*, pp. 498–9.

117. I. Balbo, *Diario 1922*, Milan, 1932, pp. 109–10. In the aftermath of this raid, Balbo refreshed his manliness with a dashing spot of nude bathing near Ancona at midnight (p. 136).

118. R. De Felice, *Mussolini il fascista 1921–5*, pp. 298; 318.

119. F. Giunta, *Un po' di fascismo*, Milan, 1935, p. 93.

120. E. Settimelli, *Gli animatori: Benito Mussolini*, Piacenza, 1922.

121. I. Balbo, *Diario 1922*, p. 86.

122. R. De Felice, *Mussolini il fascista 1921–5*, pp. 270–2.

123. BMOO, XVIII, pp. 16–18.

124. By September 1922 he had expelled the key Catholic deputy and unionist, Guido Miglioli, from the town. See H. Fornari, *Mussolini's gadfly*, pp. 60–1.

125. See, for example, G. Guidi, *Pius XI*, Milan, 1938, p. 111.

126. G. Acerbo, *Fra due plotoni di esecuzione: avvenimenti e problemi dell'epoca fascista*, Rocca San Casciano, 1968, pp. 267–8.

127. See, for example, BMOO, XVIII, pp. 21–7.

128. BMOO, XVIII, p. 256. In *La Vita Italiana*, 15 July 1922, Preziosi, by contrast, welcomed the murder as visited upon one of the Elders of Zion.

129. BMOO, XVIII, p. 104.

130. BMOO, XVIII, p. 96.

131. BMOO, XVIII, p. 95.

132. BMOO, XVIII, pp. 508–512; some 6 weeks later, he engaged in a celebrated 40-minute duel with journalist Mario Missiroli, a contest which was fought until Missiroli was unable to continue. The duellists were not reconciled (pp. 513–16; 524–6).

133. BMOO, XVIII, pp. 179–80; 274–5.

134. BMOO, XVIII, pp. 368–70.

135. BMOO, XVIII, pp. 389–90.

136. BMOO, XVIII, p. 44.

137. R. De Felice, *Mussolini il fascista 1921–5*, pp. 239–40; 245.

138. L. Salvatorelli and G. Mira, *Storia d'Italia nel periodo fascista* (2 vols), Milan, 1969, vol. I, pp. 230–1.

139. G. Acerbo, *Fra due plotoni di esecuzione*, pp. 174–7.

140. M. Rocca, *Come il fascismo divenne una dittatura*, p. 110.

141. C. Pavone (ed.), *Dalle carte di Giovanni Giolitti*, vol. III, p. 387. Cf. also L. Federzoni, *Italia di ieri per la storia di domani*, pp. 70–1.

142. L. Federzoni, *Italia di ieri per la storia di domani*, p. 83.

143. For a classic account, see A. Repaci, *La marcia su Roma: mito e realtà* (2 vols), Rome, 1963.

144. See, for example, BMOO, XVIII, pp. 138; 321.

145. BMOO, XVIII, p. 416.

146. BMOO, XVIII, pp. 405–10. The masses' puerility, he suggested, made it all the more clear that he and his party had renounced the 'grotesque' enthusiasm of socialists and democrats for the principles of 1789.

147. BMOO, XVIII, pp. 443–4.

148. For an English-language account, see D. Mack Smith, *Italy and its monarchy*, New Haven, 1989, pp. 247–54.

149. For a doubtful denial of his own responsibility while passing it on to General Armando Diaz, see E. Pugliese, *Io difendo l'esercito*, Naples, 1946, pp. 151–2. Pugliese was of Jewish extraction.

150. BMOO, XVIII, pp. 468–9.

151. G. Salvemini, *Carteggio 1922–1926* (ed. E. Tagliacozzo), Bari, 1985, p. 100.

152. P.V. Cannistraro and B.R. Sullivan, *Il Duce's other woman*, p. 281.

Notes

CHAPTER 8

1. See, for example, M. Sarfatti, *The life of Benito Mussolini*, London, 1925, p. 314.
2. In an official message to Bonar Law and Poincaré, Mussolini declared that Victor Emmanuel had acknowledged him as the embodiment of the 'national idealism which lay behind Vittorio Veneto'. See *I Documenti diplomatici italiani* [hereafter DDI], 7th series, vol. I, 7, 31 October 1922.
3. A. Turati, *Fuori dell'ombra della mia vita: dieci anni nel solco del fascismo*, Brescia, 1973, p. 35.
4. I. Kershaw, *Hitler 1889–1936: hubris*, London, 1998, p. 73.
5. See O. Bartov, *Murder in our midst: the Holocaust, industrial killing and representation*, New York, 1996; *Mirrors of destruction: war, genocide and modern identity*, New York, 2000.
6. G. Pini and D. Susmel, *Mussolini: l'uomo e l'opera*, Florence, 1953–55, vol. II, p. 206. For more on A. Volpi, cf. M. Canali, *Il delitto Matteotti: affarismo e politica nel primo governo Mussolini*, Bologna, 1997, pp. 308–9.
7. U. Guspini, *L'orecchio del regime: le intercettazioni telefoniche al tempo del fascismo*, Milan, 1973, p. 28. The phone call was tapped (see below for further examples of this curious feature of life in Fascist Italy).
8. R. Ducci, *La bella gioventù*, Bologna, 1996, p. 81.
9. BMOO, XIX, pp. 187–8.
10. P.V. Cannistraro and B.R. Sullivan, *Il Duce's other woman*, New York, 1993, pp. 265–71.
11. BMOO, XIX, p. 354. He was writing to the impressionable Bottai.
12. L. Federzoni, *Italia di ieri per la storia di domani*, Milan, 1967, p. 84.
13. According to one historian from October 1920 to October 1922 more died in traditional style 'social troubles' in Western Sicily than as a direct cost of Fascism's rise. See M. Clark, 'Squadrismo and contemporary vigilantism', *European History Quarterly*, 18, 1988, p. 35.
14. M. Rocca, *Come il fascismo divenne una dittatura*, Milan, 1952, p. 113.
15. I. Balbo, *Diario 1922*, Milan, 1932, pp. 163–7.
16. M. Rocca, *Come il fascismo divenne una dittatura*, p. 104.
17. L. Federzoni, *Italia di ieri per la storia di domani*, pp. 83–4.
18. These can be consulted notably in the files collected as SPDCR, Autografi del Duce, Carte della Cassetta di Zinco.
19. G. Bastianini, *Uomini cose fatti: memorie di un ambasciatore*, Milan, 1959, p. 23.
20. For a splendid example, see the files on Edgardo Sulis, not altogether naïve author of *Imitazione di Mussolini*, Milan, 1934, in Segreteria particolare del Duce, Carteggio ordinario [hereafter SPDCO] 590534 and DGPS, Confinati politici 986.
21. C. Rossi, *Mussolini com'era*, Rome, 1947, pp. 135–6.
22. For a listing of these and the resultant expenditure, see Carte A. Finzi 1.
23. *La Stampa italiana*, 22 April 1932. For further background, see R.J.B. Bosworth, 'Luigi Mistrorigo and *La Stampa italiana*: the strange story of a Fascist journalist in Perth', *Studies in Western Australian History*, 12, 1991, pp. 61–70. Cf. also R.J.B. Bosworth, 'Renato Citarelli, Fascist Vice Consul in Perth: a documentary note', *Papers in Labor History*, 14, 1994, pp. 91–6.
24. SPDCO 209446, 18 December 1922, Citarelli to Mussolini.
25. R. De Felice, *Mussolini il fascista 1. la conquista del potere 1921–1925*, Turin, 1966, p. 407.
26. M. Salvati, *Il regime e gli impiegati: la nazionalizzazione piccolo-borghese nel ventennio fascista*, Bari, 1992, p. 196. The ban was reiterated twice in the next two years.
27. P. Dogliani, *L'Italia fascista 1922–1940*, Milan, 1999, p. 108.
28. In the archives, a droll letter survives from Fassini to Chiavolini requesting the *portiere* of the Excelsior Hotel in Naples be raised to the rank of *Cavaliere* 'because of his work in the cause of Fascism and *italianità*'. See SPDCO 518/197736, 19 January 1931.

Notes

29. SPDCO 518/197736, 3 April 1923, Fassini to Mussolini, thanking him for sending his photo-graph and urging him to further patriotic action. Later Fassini would have a presumably well-remunerated career in the Fascist tourist business. See R.J.B. Bosworth, 'Tourist plan-ning in Fascist Italy and the limits of a totalitarian culture', *Contemporary European History*, 6, 1997, pp. 16–18.

30. N. D'Aroma, *Vent'anni insieme: Vittorio Emanuele e Mussolini*, Rocca San Casciano, 1957, pp. 105–6.

31. C. Rossi, *Mussolini com'era*, pp. 142–3.

32. G. Pini and D. Susmel, *Mussolini*, vol. III, p. 9.

33. *Carteggio Arnaldo-Benito Mussolini* (ed. D. Susmel), Florence, 1954, p. 9.

34. T.B. Morgan, *Spurs on the boot: Italy under her masters*, London, 1942, p. 82.

35. G. Pini, *Filo diretto con Palazzo Venezia*, Milan, 1967, p. 16.

36. R. De Felice, *Mussolini il duce 1. gli anni del consenso 1929–1936*, Turin, 1974, p. 301.

37. For his own account of his split with Mussolini, see M. Terzaghi, *Fascismo e Massoneria*, Milan, 1950.

38. P. Bruni, *Giuseppe Caradonna e la destra nazionale*, Rome 1996, p. 71. This work is very much one of the 1990s, anxious to give Caradonna his 'voice' and noting, among other achievements, his zealous patronage of Padre Pio (see pp. 108–10).

39. Y. De Begnac, *Taccuini mussoliniani* (ed. F. Perfetti), Bologna, 1990, p. 569.

40. F. Rosso, *Armando Diaz dopo la Marcia su Roma*, Florence, 1934, pp. 82–3.

41. For some examples, see 'G. De Frenzi' [a pseudonym], *Per l'italianità del 'Gardasee'*, Naples, 1909; *L'Italia nell'Egeo*, Rome, 1913; L. Federzoni, *La Dalmazia che aspetta*, Bologna, 1915.

42. L. Federzoni, *Presagi alla nazione: discorsi politici*, Milan, 1924, p. 320.

43. SPDCR 82/R, 21 December 1922, Federzoni to Mussolini.

44. SPDCR 82/R, February 1923, Rocco memorandum.

45. P. Togliatti, *Lectures on Fascism*, London, 1976, p. 36. With suitable classical reference, he thought the Nationalists played the part of Athens to Fascism's Rome.

46. N. D'Aroma, *Mussolini segreto*, Rocca San Casciano, 1958, p. 247.

47. See, for example, A. De' Stefani, 'Vilfredo Pareto', *Gerarchia*, 2, September 1923, pp. 1187–9.

48. F. Marcoaldi, *Vent'anni di economia e politica. Le Carte De' Stefani (1922–1941)*, Milan, 1986, p. 18.

49. *Ibid.*, pp. 86–7; 110–12.

50. BMOO, XIX, pp. 163–4.

51. E.P. Bell, *Italy's rebirth: premier Mussolini tells of Fascismo's purposes*, Chicago, 1924, p. 8. He added the engaging prophesy that, one day, the US would 'lead civilization in the fine arts, dimming even the greatest glories of the past' (p. 10).

52. For an English-language introduction to De' Stefani as economist, see the nuanced account of V. Zamagni, *The economic history of Italy 1860–1990*, Oxford, 1993, pp. 244–7.

53. See, for example, A.M. and E. Nasalli Rocca, *Realismo nazionale: per una coscienza politica dei cattolici italiani*, Rome, 1926, pp. 6–7; 15–17; 77.

54. BMOO, XXXVIII, p. 151.

55. G. Salvemini, *Carteggio 1921–1926* (ed. E. Tagliacozzo), Bari, 1985, p. 104.

56. BMOO, XIX, pp. 17–18.

57. BMOO, XIX, p. 43.

58. BMOO, XIX, pp. 32–4; cf. also pp. 74–6.

59. See BMOO, XIX, pp. 188–9, for his official visit to the seat of the worthily patriotic *Touring Club Italiano* in Milan. He had earlier remembered to salute the super-patriotic Dante Alighieri Society. BMOO, XXXVIII, p. 165.

60. BMOO, XIX, p. 73.

61. BMOO, XIX, pp. 71–2.

Notes

62. BMOO, XIX, pp. 80–1.
63. G. Pini and D. Susmel, *Mussolini*, vol. II, p. 264.
64. BMOO, XIX, pp. 71–2.
65. BMOO, XIX, p. 97.
66. A. Lyttelton, *The seizure of power: Fascism in Italy 1919–1929*, London, pp. 152–3. For a more detailed account, cf. R. De Felice, 'I fatti di Torino del dicembre 1922', as republished in his *Fascismo, Antifascismo, Nazione: note e ricerche* (ed. F. Perfetti), Rome, 1996, pp. 63–104.
67. SPDCR 4, 18 December 1922, Mussolini to De Vecchi.
68. SPDCR 4, 19 December 1922, De Vecchi to Mussolini.
69. BMOO, XXXVIII, p. 523.
70. For the details, see P. Varvaro, *Una città fascista: potere e società a Napoli*, Palermo, 1990. Cf. SPDCR 47, which has a file on Padovani. In a typical letter, Mussolini noted (22 October 1923) that he, too, was 'possessed of a hard temperament' and that he had had enough of Padovani.
71. See the volume of his memoirs directed posthumously at shoring up his 'respectability'. C. De Vecchi di Val Cismon, *Tra Papa, Duce e Re: il conflitto tra Chiesa cattolica e Stato fascista nel diario 1930–1931 del primo ambasciatore del regno d'Italia presso la Santa Sede* (ed. S. Setta), Rome, 1998.
72. See SPDCR 4, 1 May 1923. Mussolini bluntly and even savagely accused De Vecchi of gross incompetence.
73. A few months before Federzoni, still thinking like a Minister in a Liberal administration, threatened resignation if De Vecchi was sent as Governor of Cyrenaica. See SPDCR 82R/2, 22 July 1923, Federzoni to Mussolini.
74. See, for example, G. Ciano, *Diario 1937–1943* (ed. R. De Felice), Milan, 1980, pp. 46–7.
75. For a fascinating, oral history, account, see L. Passerini, *Fascism in popular memory: the cultural experience of the Turin working class*, Cambridge, 1987. Cf. SPDCR 4, Palmieri (the local prefect) to Mussolini, noting critically De Vecchi's bad odour in the circles around Giovanni Agnelli, the owner of Fiat.
76. For this line, see R. De Felice, *Mussolini il fascista 1921–5*, pp. 430–2 and cf. A. Aquarone, *L'organizzazione dello stato totalitario*, Turin, 1965, pp. 17–18.
77. BMOO, XIX, p. 254.
78. A. Aquarone, *L'organizzazione dello stato totalitario*, pp. 19–21.
79. BMOO, XVIII, p. 466.
80. BMOO, XIX, pp. 17–19.
81. *The Times*, 12 August 1922.
82. BMOO, XIX, pp. 3–4.
83. *The Times*, 28 October 1922. For a more developed account, see R.J.B. Bosworth, 'The British press, the conservatives and Mussolini 1920–34', *Journal of Contemporary History*, 5, 1970, pp. 163–82.
84. BMOO, XIX, p. 130.
85. Public Record Office, London [hereafter PRO], FO371/9882/C4593/160/19, 17 March 1924, Graham to MacDonald.
86. FO 371/9946/C2661/2661/22, 14 February 1924, Graham annual report.
87. PRO, MacDonald papers, FO 800/219, 8 February 1924, Graham to MacDonald.
88. E. Di Nolfo, *Mussolini e la politica estera italiana 1919–1933*, Padua, 1960, p. 48.
89. See DDI 7s, 1, 2, 31 October 1922, Contarini to Sforza, for an expression of the Ministry line that precipitate rejection of the Fascists should be avoided.
90. See R.J.B. Bosworth, *Italy, the least of the Great Powers: Italian foreign policy before the First World War*, Cambridge, 1979, p. 106.
91. DDI 7s, 1, 38, 2 November 1922, De Martino to Mussolini.

Notes

92. DDI 7s, I, 50, 3 November 1922, Rosso to Mussolini.

93. M. Luciolli, *Palazzo Chigi: anni roventi. Ricordi di una vita diplomatica italiana dal 1933 al 1948*, Milan, 1976, p. 53.

94. G. Volpe, 'Italiani vicini e lontani: i Corsi', *Gerarchia*, 2, June 1923, pp. 1018–28. By contrast, Mussolini advised that any patriotic Italian activity there should be pursued discretely and covertly. DDI 7s, I, 427, 29 January 1923, Mussolini to De Visart, though he did raise unsuccessfully with Diaz the idea of a masked Foreign Legion of Italophile Corsicans within the national armed forces. 705, 12 April 1923, Mussolini to Diaz. Cf. BMOO, XXXIX, p. 171, in which Mussolini in a letter of 23 May 1924 told Volpe to back-pedal on the Corsican issue (it is also printed in DDI 7s, III, 212).

95. M.G. Sarfatti, *Tunisiaca*, Milan, 1924, pp. 94; 97. In his preface, 'Latinus' talked somewhat obscurely of the 'crystalline simplicity' of the issues in a place where 'Italian faith' could only grow (but where it was not at all clear what should be done about it).

96. For background, see R.J.B. Bosworth, *Italy, the least of the Great Powers*, pp. 299–329.

97. DDI 7s, I, 76, 6 November 1922, De Bosdari to Mussolini.

98. BMOO, XXXVIII, p. 355.

99. BMOO, XXXVIII, p. 458.

100. DDI 7s, II, 186, 28 August 1923, Mussolini to Montagna.

101. For background, see E. Di Nolfo, *Mussolini e la politica estera italiana (1919–1933)*, Padua, 1960, pp. 79–86; or, still more fully, J. Barros, *The Corfu incident of 1923: Mussolini and the League of Nations*, Princeton, 1965.

102. DDI 7s, II, 195, 29 August 1923, Mussolini to Montagna.

103. DDI 7s, II, 244, 1 September 1923, Mussolini to his representatives abroad.

104. DDI 7s, II, 310, 7 September 1923, Giuriati to Mussolini. He did add politely that Mussolini was the only proper judge of the matter.

105. *The Times*, 8 September 1923.

106. DDI 7s, II, 239, 1 September 1923, Mussolini to Della Torretta.

107. J. Barros, *The Corfu incident of 1923*, p. 40. Cf., for example, D. Mack Smith, *Mussolini's Roman empire*, London, 1976, pp. 5–6.

108. A. Cassels, *Mussolini's early diplomacy*, Princeton, 1970, p. 126.

109. F. Gambetti, *Gli anni che scottano*, Milan, 1967, p. 75, remembered that 'public opinion' (such as it was in 1920s Italy) favoured the government line.

110. D. Mack Smith, *Storia di cento anni di vita italiana visti attraverso il Corriere della Sera*, Milan, 1978, pp. 274–5.

111. R. De Felice, *Mussolini il fascista 1921–5*, pp. 562–3.

112. E. Ferrante, 'Un rischio calcolato? Mussolini e gli ammiragli nella gestione della crisi di Corfù', *Storia delle relazioni internazionali*, 5, 1989, pp. 223; 226.

113. A. Foschini, 'A trent'anni dall'occupazione di Corfù', *Nuova Antologia*, f. 1836, December 1953, pp. 401–12. In 1953 Foschini still defended the action which was, he said, merely aiming at making Italy respected.

114. Not for nothing did patriotic historian Volpe endorse the government line. See G. Volpe, 'A crisi superata: constatazione e previsioni', *Gerarchia*, 2, October 1923.

115. See, for example, *Daily Mail*, 8 and 15 September 1923; *Morning Post*, 5, 6 and 12 September 1923; *The Observer*, 2, 9, 16 September 1923.

116. *Headway*, January 1924.

117. E. Ferrante, 'Un rischio calcolato?', p. 235.

118. DDI 7s, II, 397, 23 September 1923, memorandum.

119. DDI 7s, I, 131, 17 November 1923, A. Tedaldi to Mussolini.

120. DDI 7s, II, 474, 10 November 1923, Durini di Monza to Mussolini.

121. S. Ben-Ami, *Fascism from above: the dictatorship of Miguel Primo de Rivera in Spain 1923–1930*, Oxford, 1983, pp. 131–2.

Notes

122. L. Federzoni, *Italia di ieri per la storia di domani*, p. 259.

123. See, for example, G. Salvemini, *Carteggio 1921–6*, p. 239. Salvemini described Mussolini as 'a greater and truer Giolitti', who embodied the fact that 'Italy wants to be governed like this'.

124. R. De Felice, *Mussolini il fascista 1921–5*, pp. 519–26.

125. See, for example, SPDCR 42, 3 July and 4 August 1923, Farinacci to Mussolini.

126. SPDCR 43, 15 August 1923, Farinacci to Mussolini.

127. G.B. Guerri, *Giuseppe Bottai: un fascista critico: ideologia e azione del gerarca che avrebbe voluto portare l'intelligenza nel fascismo e il fascismo alla liberalizzazione*, Milan, 1976, p. 27.

128. *Critica Fascista*, 1, June 1923. The journal's title also represented a swipe at *Critica Socialista*, for a generation a key source of the debates of Italian Marxism, especially of the more moderate kind.

129. *Critica Fascista*, 2, 1 April 1924.

130. *Critica Fascista*, 1, 1 July 1923.

131. *Critica Fascista*, 1, 15 July 1923.

132. BMOO, XX, p. 40.

133. *Critica Fascista*, 1, 1 December 1923.

134. B. Mussolini, 'Preludio al Machiavelli', *Gerarchia*, 3, April 1924.

135. BMOO, XX, pp. 163–4.

136. *Carteggio Arnaldo-Benito Mussolini*, p. 18.

137. R. De Felice, *Mussolini il fascista 1921–5*, pp. 577–83.

138. *Ibid.*, pp. 591–613.

139. For further detail, see M. Canali, *Il delitto Matteotti*, pp. 23–59.

140. G. Matteotti, *Scritti e discorsi scelti*, Parma, 1974, p. 272.

141. M. Canali, *Il delitto Matteotti*, pp. 87–303.

142. *Ibid.*, pp. 112–27.

143. *Ibid.* pp. 218–19. Finzi's brother Gino worked helpfully for Westinghouse, while Finzi had gained financial connections through his own marriage to a Cardinal's niece.

CHAPTER 9

1. See, for example, BMOO, XXXIX, p. 55, letter to E. De Nicola; p. 136, letter to B. Scelsi (agent of V.E. Orlando); p. 156, letter to P. Boselli.

2. BMOO, XXIX, p. 123.

3. BMOO, XXIX, p. 6.

4. See, for example, D. Mack Smith, *Mussolini*, London, 1981, p. 65.

5. G. Salvemini, *Carteggio 1921–1926* (ed. E. Tagliacozzo), Bari, 1985, p. 238.

6. For the fundamental exploration of this theme, but in a German context, see G. Mosse, *The nationalisation of the masses: political symbolism and mass movements from the Napoleonic wars through the Third Reich*, New York, 1975.

7. R. De Felice, *Mussolini il fascista I. La conquista del potere 1921–1925*, Turin, 1966, pp. 380–4.

8. *Ibid.*, pp. 598–613. Indeed, in late June, D'Aragona and Mussolini were still discussing whether the socialist union, the *Confederazione generale del lavoro*, could somehow advise the state (pp. 614–15).

9. *Ibid.*, pp. 622–3.

10. M. Canali, *Il delitto Matteotti: affarismo e politica nel primo governo Mussolini*, Bologna, 1997, p. 412.

11. *Ibid.*, p. 354.

12. Some of his speeches are available in English as G. Matteotti, *The Fascisti exposed: a year of Fascist domination*, New York, 1969 (first published 1924).

Notes

13. M. Canali, *Il delitto Matteotti*, p. 119.

14. *Ibid.*, pp. 318–21.

15. SPDCR 97, 25 May 1929, A.N. Norchi to Mussolini.

16. SPDCR 97, 18 June 1934, Volpi to Mussolini; 19 June 1934, D. Ghetti to Sebastianini.

17. SPDCR 84, November 1939, report to Bocchini.

18. SPDCR 84, 19 December 1929, Dumini to Mussolini.

19. SPDCR 84, 21 November 1928, Dumini to his wife Bianca.

20. SPDCR 84, 23 July 1932, Jessie Wilson to Mussolini.

21. G. Rossini (ed.), *Il delitto Matteotti tra Viminale e l'Aventino: dagli atti del processo De Bono davanti all'Alta Corte di Giustizia*, Bologna, 1966, p. 385.

22. For Dumini's own post-war account, see A. Dumini, *Diciassette colpi*, Milan, 1958, pp. 79–80.

23. M. Canali, *Il delitto Matteotti*, pp. 577–99.

24. Their telephone calls were tapped. See U. Guspini, *L'orecchio del regime: le intercettazioni telefoniche al tempo del fascismo*, Milan, 1973, pp. 46–9.

25. Contarini was at pains to assure the diplomatic world that Mussolini was not personally involved in the killing. See, for example, PRO MacDonald papers, FO 800/219, 17 June 1924, Graham to MacDonald.

26. *The Times*, 21 June 1924.

27. *The Times*, 21 June 1924; cf. comments from its Rome correspondent 16, 17, 18 June 1924.

28. *The Times*, 14 August 1924, 13 November 1924, 25 April 1927.

29. Quoted by C. Seton Watson, *Italy from Liberalism to Fascism 1870–1925*, London, 1967, p. 656.

30. N. D'Aroma, *Vent'anni insieme: Vittorio Emanuele e Mussolini*, Rocca San Casciano, 1957, pp. 140–1.

31. *Ibid.*, p. 163.

32. *Ibid.*, pp. 167–9.

33. G. Rochat, *L'esercito italiano da Vittorio Veneto a Mussolini (1919–1925)*, Bari, 1967, pp. 441–2.

34. P. Melograni, *Gli industriali e Mussolini: rapporti tra Confindustria e Fascismo dal 1919 al 1929*, Milan, 1972, pp. 86–7.

35. *Ibid.*, p. 79.

36. *Ibid.*, p. 109.

37. R. De Felice, *Mussolini il fascista 1921–1925*, p. 653.

38. BMOO, XX, pp. 326–9.

39. R. De Felice, *Mussolini il fascista 1921–1925*, p. 632.

40. Simultaneously Fascist Chief of Police De Bono stood down, being replaced by the colourless (but pro-Nationalist) functionary, Francesco Crispo Moncada. See R. De Felice, *Mussolini il fascista 1921–1925*, p. 650.

41. A. Gramsci, *Selections from political writings (1921–1926)* (ed. Q. Hoare), London, 1978, pp. 267–70. The communists had themselves abandoned the Aventine only a week after its creation.

42. See, for example, P. Nenni, *La battaglia socialista contro il fascismo 1922–1944* (ed. D. Zucàro), Milan, 1977, pp. 110; 118.

43. S. Colarizi, *I democratici all'opposizione: Giovanni Amendola e l'Unione nazionale (1922–1926)*, Bologna, 1973, p. 67.

44. D. Mack Smith, *Storia di cento anni di vita italiana visti attraverso il Corriere della Sera*, Milan, 1978, pp. 277–82.

45. J.N. Molony, *The emergence of political catholicism in Italy: partito popolare 1919–1926*, London, 1977, p. 185.

46. R. Farinacci, *Andante mosso 1924–25*, Milan, p. 22.

Notes

47. *Ibid.*, p. 35.
48. *Ibid.*, p. 48.
49. BMOO, XXXIX, pp. 186–9.
50. BMOO, XXI, pp. 1–2. He was seconded by the more dutiful sections of the Fascist press. Bottai typically wrote that the murder was 'the most cruel, inhuman and stupid' of crimes, amounting to a 'criminal degeneration of political behaviour'. *Critica Fascista*, 2, 15 June 1924.
51. BMOO, XXI, pp. 12–17.
52. BMOO XXI, pp. 21–9.
53. BMOO, XXI, pp. 56–9.
54. BMOO, XXI, pp. 59–65. Mussolini was being interviewed by the conservative paper, *Il Giornale d'Italia*.
55. SPDCR 41, 6 September 1924, Mussolini to Farinacci.
56. R. Farinacci, *Andante mosso*, pp. 104–6.
57. *Ibid.*, p. 133.
58. BMOO, XXI, p. 90.
59. BMOO, XXI, pp. 100–1.
60. BMOO, XXXIX, p. 280.
61. BMOO, XXXIX, p. 296; XXI, pp. 188–9.
62. See, for example, BMOO, XXI, pp. 105–7; 120–1.
63. BMOO, XXI, pp. 194–207.
64. R. Farinacci, *Andante mosso*, pp. 164–73.
65. G. Rossini (ed.), *Il delitto Matteotti*, pp. 7; 305. Finzi had allegedly given his brother a letter, only to be opened on the occasion of his premature death.
66. *Ibid.*, p. 302.
67. R. De Felice, *Mussolini il fascista 1921–1925*, pp. 702–4.
68. G. Salotti, *Giuseppe Giulietti: il sindacato dei marittimi dal 1910 al 1953*, Rome, 1982, p. 210.
69. R. Farinacci, *Andante mosso*, p. 165.
70. R. De Felice, *Mussolini il fascista 1921–1925*, pp. 711–14.
71. BMOO, XXXIX, pp. 319.
72. P. Orano, *Mussolini da vicino*, Rome, 1935, pp. 84–8.
73. R. De Felice, *Mussolini il fascista 1921–1925*, pp. 717–25.
74. BMOO, XXI, pp. 235–41.
75. L. Federzoni, *Italia di ieri per la storia di domani*, Milan, 1967, p. 99.
76. S. Romano, *Giuseppe Volpi: industria e finanza tra Giolitti e Mussolini*, Milan, 1979, p. 197; 249–55 (for the list of companies).
77. See A. Lessona, *Memorie*, Rome, 1963, pp. 82–7; 107; *Un ministro di Mussolini*, Milan, 1973, pp. 70–7.
78. SPDCR 87, 11 April 1938, Lessona to Mussolini.
79. BMOO, XXXIX, pp. 395–6; 421.
80. R. De Felice, *Mussolini il fascista II. l'organizzazione dello stato fascista 1925–1929*, Turin, 1968, p. 57.
81. See, for example, *La Vita Italiana*, 15 December 1924.
82. For a highly typical combination of themes, see, for example, R. Farinacci, *La Chiesa e gli ebrei*, Milan, 1938.
83. Mussolini's personal files reported that Farinacci, as late as 1928, had duelled with the Fascist journalist and constructor of the *Duce*'s charisma, Emilio Settimelli, despite the regime's discouragement by then of such public violence. See SPDCR 42, 6 January 1928, Guadagnini to Mussolini.
84. For his speech, see R. Farinacci, *Il processo Matteotti alle Assise di Chieti: l'arringa di Roberto Farinacci*, n.p., 1927. Cf. also his predictably pompous publication of his speeches while Party Secretary. R. Farinacci, *Un periodo aureo del Partito Nazionale Fascista: raccolta di discorsi e dichiarazioni*, Foligno, 1927.

Notes

85. SPDCR 40, 8 July 1926, Farinacci to Mussolini.
86. Mussolini's files saved a telephone tap recording Farinacci's boast in 1932 that he was earning 700 000 lire per annum as a lawyer. SPDCR 43, October 1932 note.
87. See SPDCR 40, 42, 43.
88. G. Rochat, *L'esercito italiano da Vittorio Veneto a Mussolini*, p. 137.
89. *Ibid.*, pp. 295–343.
90. *Ibid.*, p. 407.
91. *Ibid.*, pp. 477–8. Cf. Carte A. Finzi 1, 11 January 1924, Mussolini to Diaz.
92. G. Rochat, *L'esercito italaino da Vittorio Veneto a Mussolini*, pp. 474; 513.
93. P. Pieri and G. Rochat, *Pietro Badoglio*, Turin, 1974, p. 19.
94. S. Cilibrizzi, *Pietro Badoglio rispetto a Mussolini e di fronte alla storia*, Naples, n.d., pp. 18–52.
95. P. Pieri and G. Rochat, *Pietro Badoglio*, p. 468.
96. *Ibid.*, pp. 508–10.
97. *Ibid.*, p. 513.
98. For a typical example, see SPDCR 64, 17 February 1937, note.
99. G. Rochat, *L'esercito italiano da Vittorio Veneto a Mussolini*, pp. 586; 590.
100. SPDCR 104, 15 February 1925, medical file.
101. PRO, GFM 36/13, 3 March 1925, police report.
102. R. Zangrandi, *Il lungo viaggio attraverso il fascismo: contributo alla storia di una generazione*, Milan, 1962, p. 22.
103. See, for example, BMOO, XLIV, pp. 155–60, interview with Alice Rohe of the New York *Sun*.
104. SPDCR 113, 15 October 1928, Mussolini to Edda.
105. G. Pini and D. Susmel, *Mussolini: l'uomo e l'opera*, Florence, 1953–5, vol. III, p. 5.
106. See reports in *Il Corriere della Sera*, *The Guardian*, 1 September 2001.
107. V.J. Bordeux, *Benito Mussolini – the man*, London, nd, p. 287.
108. *Gerarchia*, 4, February 1925, pp. 69–75.
109. G. Pini and D. Susmel, *Mussolini*, vol. II, p. 361.
110. V. Emiliani, *Il paese dei Mussolini*, Turin, 1984, pp. 46–7.
111. *Ibid.*, pp. 48–9.
112. SPDCR 106, 12 October 1926, Mussolini press release.
113. C. Ipsen, *Dictating demography: the problem of population in Fascist Italy*, Cambridge, 1996, pp. 178–80 tallies a reproduction rate by 1937 of members of the Grand Council of 1.9. The *Duce* himself was easily the most prolific.
114. SPDCR 113, 1 November 1925, Mussolini to School Director urging (unconvincingly) that he expected that Edda would be treated exactly the same as her fellow pupils.
115. SPDCR 113, 15 September 1929, police report of her trip to Bologna to meet an unsuitable boy, when she had said she was going to Cesenatico to be with friends.
116. SPDCR 113, 29 January 1929, Mussolini to Edda, affectionately welcomed her back. Cf. 11 August 1929, Mussolini to Edda sending her Carlo Formichi's not too taxing *India e indiani* to keep up her interests in the East.
117. SPDCR 113, 2 August 1929, Chiavolini to Prefect at Forlì; 12 August 1929, Mussolini to Chiavolini.
118. A. Gravelli, *Mussolini aneddotico*, Rome, 1951, p. 172.
119. N. D'Aroma, *Mussolini segreto*, Rocca San Casciano, 1958, p. 352.
120. V. Mussolini, *Vita con mio padre*, Milan, 1957, p. 19.
121. See, for example, a note by Federzoni in January 1927 that, when he consulted the *Duce* over a ministerial matter, Mussolini was suffering 'atrociously' from stomach pain and could hardly speak. L. Federzoni, *1927: diario di un ministro del fascismo* (ed. A. Macchi), Florence, 1993, p. 27.

Notes

122. A. Turati, *Fuori dell'ombra della mia vita: dieci anni nel solco del fascismo*, Brescia, 1973, p. 35.

123. G. Pini, *Filo diretto con Palazzo Venezia*, Milan, 1967, pp. 33–4.

124. L. Passerini, *Mussolini immaginario: storia di una biografia 1915–1939*, Bari, 1991, pp. 132–5.

125. D. Darrah, *Hail Caesar!* Boston, 1936, p. 100.

126. G. Pini and D. Susmel, *Mussolini*, vol. III, p. 86.

127. F. Ciarlantini, *Mussolini immaginario*, Milan, 1933, pp. 48; 75.

128. His biographer goes further in suggesting that Bottai was one of the most intelligent Cabinet Ministers ever to serve in Italy. See G.B. Guerri, preface to G. Bottai, *Diario 1935–1944*, Milan, 1982, p. 18.

129. SPDCR 4, 23 July 1924, Bottai to Mussolini. Cf. also *Critica Fascista*, 3, 15 January 1925 where Bottai claimed he had never approved excessive adulation, but ... the 'Chief' was an extraordinary figure.

130. SPDCR 82R, 26 May 1925, Federzoni to Mussolini.

131. SPDCR 42, 22 October 1925, Farinacci to Mussolini.

132. SPDCR 42, 21 October 1925, Farinacci to Mussolini.

133. For some examples, see V. De Grazia, *The culture of consent: mass organization of leisure in Fascist Italy*, Cambridge, 1981.

134. C. Dall'Ungaro, *Mussolini e lo sport*, Mantua, 1928, p. 8.

135. *Ibid.*, pp. 10; 15.

136. *Ibid.*, pp. 26–7.

137. *Ibid.*, pp. 28; 36.

138. *Lo sport fascista*, I, June 1928; cf. L. Ferretti, *Il libro dello sport*, Rome, 1928, p. 7.

139. G. Seldes, *Sawdust Caesar: the untold history of Mussolini and Fascism*, London, 1936, p. 365.

140. E. Sturani, *Otto milioni di cartoline per il Duce*, Turin, 1995, pp. 20; 25.

141. *Ibid.*, p. 39.

142. A. Petacco, *L'archivio segreto di Mussolini*, Milan, 1997, pp. 127–9.

143. P. Ardali, *San Francesco e Mussolini*, Mantua, 1926.

144. K. Pinkus, *Bodily regimes: Italian advertising under Fascism*, Minneapolis, 1995, p. 17.

145. The maximum claims were made well after the event in the post-war era. The ghosted memoirs of Mussolini's batman claimed that the *Duce* had his way with a different woman almost every day, but that he usually only spent two or three minutes in the act. See Q. Navarra, *Memorie del cameriere di Mussolini*, Milan, 1946, pp. 199–200. Navarra's ghosts were Indro Montanelli and Leo Longanesi. See S. Luzzatto, *Il corpo del Duce: un cadavere tra immaginazione, storia e memoria*, Turin, 1998, p. 122.

146. See, for example, E. Settimelli, *Mussolini visto da Settimelli*, Rome, 1929, p. 252.

147. Y. De Begnac, *Palazzo Venezia: storia di un regime*, Rome, 1950, p. 134.

148. See, for example, C. Scorza, *Il segreto di Mussolini*, Lanciano, 1933, p. 253.

149. G. Boatti (ed.), *Caro Duce: lettere di donne italiane a Mussolini 1922–1943*, Milan, 1989, p. 61.

150. Cited by J. Ridley, *Mussolini*, London, 1997, p. 179.

151. *Il Popolo d'Italia*, 20 August 1924.

152. DDI 7s, IV, 443, 30 September 1926, Mussolini memorandum of talk with A. Chamberlain. Mussolini met the Chamberlains on at least four private occasions in these years. See P.G. Edwards, 'The Austen Chamberlain–Mussolini meetings', *Historical Journal*, 14, 1971, pp. 153–64. Cf. also SPDCR 100, with some letters from Lady Chamberlain to Mussolini.

153. Mussolini, in turn, told a visiting female aristocrat that he admired Lady Sybil. 'She was his conception of a great lady with her fair hair and quiet manner.' Duchess of Sermoneta, *Sparkle distant worlds*, London, 1947, p. 17.

Notes

154. M.G. Sarfatti, *Acqua passata*, Rocca San Casciano, 1955, pp. 172–3.
155. For Mussolini's own endorsement, see BMOO, XXI, pp. 342–4.
156. O. Danese, *Vittorio Emanuele III: il re fascista*, Mantua, 1923, pp. 22–3.
157. R. Forges Davanzati, *Il balilla Vittorio: racconto*, Rome, 1938, p. 111.
158. *Ibid.*, pp. 92; 96; 181; 287. 'Vittorio' even felt the charisma of Crown Princess, and later alleged Anti-Fascist, Maria José (p. 152). Cf., too, the attempt to inscribe charisma on Queen Elena. A. Lumbroso, *Elena di Montenegro: regina d'Italia*, Florence, 1935.
159. A bracketing of the two in charismatic greatness survived the Second World War. See G. De' Rossi dell'Arno, *Pio XI e Mussolini*, Rome, 1954.
160. See, for example, *Lo sport fascista*, II, March 1929. Pius published some *Scritti alpinistici*, which a reviewer noted solemnly were full of 'Latin values'. Not Victor Emmanuel but other members of the royal family could be hailed as real or potential sports stars. *Lo sport fascista* of December 1929 was sure that Maria José was brilliant at tennis and skating and so, along with Crown Prince Umberto, made up 'the most handsome sporting couple in the world'. The Duke of the Abruzzi, disappointed in his love for an American millionaire Jewess, spent much time exploring and climbing until his death in 1933, a loss which was with some ambiguity fascistised. For recent admiring studies, see M. Tenderini and M. Shandrick, *The Duke of the Abruzzi: an explorer's life*, Seattle, 1997; G. Speroni, *Il Duca degli Abruzzi*, Milan, 1991.
161. E. Settimelli, *Mussolini visto da Settimelli*, p. 289.
162. P. Ardali, *Mussolini e Pio XI*, Mantua, 1926, p. 25.
163. See A.R. Fusilli, *Giampaoli*, Rome, 1928.
164. See T. Nanni, *Leandro Arpinati e il fascismo bolognese*, Bologna, 1927.
165. SPDCR 41, 18 July 1925, Mussolini to prefects.
166. For an official account of one on Salvemini, see SPDCR 48, 13 July 1925, Palmieri to Mussolini. The radical Fascist theoretician, Sergio Panunzio, with typical if somewhat ambiguous phrases, telegrammed Mussolini in November about his desire to dissociate 'my Molfetta' from an Anti-Fascist statement by Salvemini, also a son of that town (28 November 1925, Panunzio to Mussolini).
167. See M.L. Salvadori, *Gaetano Salvemini*, Turin, 1963, pp. 31–4.
168. The standard English-language account of Anti-Fascism remains C.F. Delzell, *Mussolini's enemies: the Italian anti-Fascist resistance*, Princeton, 1961 and see pp. 27–9 (Gobetti) and 24–5 (Amendola).
169. For his account, see A. Rocco, *La trasformazione dello stato: dallo stato liberale allo stato fascista*, Rome, 1927.
170. For the agreement, see A. Aquarone, *L'organizzazione dello stato totalitario*, Turin, 1965, p. 439.
171. SPDCR 79, 21 June 1923, Barella to Mussolini.
172. R. De Felice, *Mussolini il fascista 1925–1929*, pp. 138–9.
173. SPDCR 100, 8 December 1925, M. Crespi to Mussolini.
174. See, for example, SPDCR 82R, 24 December 1925, Federzoni to Mussolini on the case of *Mattino* in Naples.
175. BMOO, XXII, pp. 36–7.
176. See, for example, DDI 7s, III, 349, 27 June 1924, Mussolini to Romano Avezzana (Paris). Mussolini had swiftly instructed his representatives abroad that they must follow the official line in any comment on the Matteotti murder.
177. DDI 7s, 797, III, 11 April 1925, Mussolini to Farinacci.
178. See, for example, DDI 7s, III, 2 May 1924, Mussolini to MacDonald.
179. For a summary of the continuity in Fascist diplomacy to Russia, see G. Petracchi, *Da San Pietroburgo a Mosca: la diplomazia italiana in Russia 1861–1941*, Rome, 1993.
180. M.L. Napolitano, *Mussolini e la conferenza di Locarno (1925): il problema di sicurezza nella politica estera italiana*, Urbino, 1996, p. 200.

Notes

181. See, for example, DDI 7s, IV, 21, 8 June 1925, Mussolini to his major ambassadors.
182. BMOO, XXII, p. 36.
183. See R. De Felice, *Mussolini il fascista 1925–1929*, pp. 42–4.
184. For perhaps the most wholehearted example, see composer Pietro Mascagni, once a 'socialist'. SPDCR 102, 24 June 1926, Mascagni to Mussolini. SPDCR 14, the file on Ardengo Soffici offers strong competition.
185. BMOO, XXI, pp. 362–3. He now boasted that never in his life had he read a page of Croce (p. 358).
186. BMOO, XXI, p. 425.

CHAPTER 10

1. BMOO, XXXIX, p. 476.
2. V. Perroni, *Il Duce ai Balilla: brani e pensieri dei discorsi di Mussolini, ordinati e illustrati per i bimbi d'Italia*, Rome, 1930, pp. 30–1.
3. R. De Felice, *Mussolini il duce: 1. gli anni del consenso 1929–1936*, Turin, 1974, p. 20.
4. F. Anfuso, *Da Palazzo Venezia al Lago di Garda (1936–1945)*, Rome, 1996, p. 71.
5. BMOO, XL, p. 71.
6. BMOO, XL, p. 5.
7. BMOO, XXIII, p. 159. When he made these remarks, Mussolini was addressing the Senate (5 June 1928).
8. A. Lyttelton, *The seizure of power: Fascism in Italy 1919–1929*, London, 1973, p. 482.
9. SPDCR 43, 16 November 1925, Mussolini to Farinacci.
10. See further SPDCR 64.
11. BMOO, XXII, pp. 107–10.
12. BMOO, XXII, p. 111.
13. U. Guspini, *L'orecchio del regime: le intercettazioni telefoniche al tempo del fascismo*, Milan, 1973, p. 70.
14. R. De Felice, *Mussolini il fascista: II l'organizzazione dello stato fascista 1925–1929*, Turin, 1968, p. 200.
15. *La Vita Italiana*, 15 April 1926.
16. See further SPDCR 64.
17. For a splendidly evocative ethnography, see B. Dalla Casa, *Attentato al duce: le molte storie del caso Zamboni*, Bologna, 2000.
18. M.L. Salvadori, *Gaetano Salvemini*, Turin, 1963, p. 32.
19. R. De Felice, *Mussolini il fascista 1925–1929*, pp. 211–12.
20. C. Rossi, *Personaggi di ieri e di oggi*, Milan, 1960, p. 207.
21. M. Franzinelli, *I tentacoli dell'Ovra: agenti, collaboratori e vittime della polizia politica fascista*, Turin, 1999, p. 27.
22. C. Rossi, *Personaggi di ieri e di oggi*, p. 209.
23. For an example of Mussolini's approval of his work there, see BMOO, XXXIX, p. 1.
24. G. Leto, *OVRA: fascismo-antifascismo*, Rocca San Casciano, 1952, p. 31.
25. C. Rossi, *Personaggi di ieri e di oggi*, p. 219.
26. E. Dollmann, *The interpreter: memoirs*, London, 1967, p. 180.
27. C. Rossi, *Personaggi di ieri e di oggi*, pp. 245–6.
28. *Ibid.*, p. 244.
29. M. Franzinelli, *I tentacoli dell'Ovra*, p. 28.
30. *Ibid.*
31. See *Carteggio Arnaldo-Benito Mussolini* (ed. D. Susmel), Florence, 1954, p. 53 for Arnaldo's complaint in November 1926 about the matter.
32. G. Leto, *OVRA*, p. 162.

Notes

33. *Ibid.*, p. 211–12; M. Franzinelli, *I tentacoli dell'Ovra*, p. 374.

34. G. Leto, *OVRA*, p. 200; M. Franzinelli, *I tentacoli dell'Ovra*, p. 376.

35. D.R. Gabaccia, *Italy's many diasporas*, Seattle, 2000, p. 65.

36. M. Franzinelli, *I tentacoli dell'Ovra*, p. 4.

37. BMOO, XXII, p. 371.

38. BMOO, XXII, pp. 371–80.

39. See above, Chapter 1. Bocchini was succeeded by Carmine Senise, a Neapolitan of very similar attitudes, practices and class, as well as an old client and junior of Bocchini. They had worked together in the Press Office during the First World War. For his account of himself, see C. Senise, *Quando ero Capo della Polizia 1940–1943*, Rome, 1946.

40. M. Franzinelli, *I tentacoli dell'Ovra*, p. 63.

41. R. Zangrandi, *Il lungo viaggio attraverso il fascismo: contributo alla storia di una generazione*, Milan, 1962, p. 36.

42. M. Frazinelli, *I tentacoli dell'Ovra*, p. 388.

43. One *confinato* recalled in his memoirs that the remote islands had been used for a similar purpose by the Bourbons since 1752. Toilets, he found, were scarcely available there, while savage pigs wandered around, often sleeping with their owners. See J. Busoni, *Nel tempo del fascismo*, Rome, 1975, pp. 138–140. Dumini also spent time at Tremiti, complaining bitterly about the loss of civilisation entailed.

44. *Ibid.*, p. 150. Cf. M. Giua, *Ricordi di un ex-detenuto politico 1935–1943*, Turin, 1945, p. 53. The classic account of an incomprehension between the peasant and political worlds is C.Levi, *Christ stopped at Eboli: the story of a year*, New York, 1947.

45. For background, see Q. Navarra, *Memorie del cameriere di Mussolini*, Milan, 1946.

46. DGPS, Confinati politici 598, case of Don Francesco Malalan.

47. Carte Volpi 2/15, 2 June 1927, Mussolini to Volpi.

48. M. Franzinelli, *I tentacoli dell'Ovra*, p. 627.

49. C.F. Delzell, *Mussolini's enemies: the Italian anti-Fascist resistance*, Princeton, 1961, p. 40.

50. Still the best short, English-language, summary of his ideas and life is J. Joll, *Gramsci*, Glasgow, 1977.

51. For the background, see G. Fiori, *Vita di Antonio Gramsci*, Bari, 1973, pp. 334–7.

52. For the debate about Gramsci, see G. Liguori, *Gramsci conteso: storia di un dibattito 1922–1996*, Rome, 1996.

53. BMOO, XXII, p. 92. Mussolini was orating about a law confirming the social role of Fascist unions.

54. BMOO, XXII, p. 30.

55. For an English-language example, see D.D. Roberts, *The syndicalist tradition and Italian Fascism*, Manchester, 1979, p. 309. The interpretation is also a given for most of the De Felice school.

56. BMOO, XXII, p. 287.

57. Rocco was another who was politely ready to acknowledge his leader's 'infallible instinct'. See A. Rocco, *La trasformazione dello stato: dallo stato liberale allo stato fascista*, Rome, 1927, p. 9.

58. R. De Felice, *Mussolini il fascista 1925–1929*, pp. 267–74.

59. In his Ascension Day speech he actually asserted that it had already come into existence and then, ignoring the evident contradiction, went on to discuss the processes by which it might occur. See BMOO, XXII, pp. 388–9.

60. See, for example, BMOO, XXII, pp. 270–1; 281–3.

61. For the text, see A. Aquarone, *L'organizzazione dello stato totalitario*, Turin, 1965, pp. 477–81.

62. R. De Felice, *Mussolini il fascista 1925–1929*, p. 293.

63. A. Aniante, 'Imitare la maniera di vita di Mussolini', *Critica fascista*, 5, 15 May 1927.

Notes

64. G. Bottai, 'Significato della "Carta del Lavoro"', *Gerarchia*, 7, May 1927, pp. 322–4.
65. R. De Felice, *Mussolini il fascista 1925–1929*, pp. 295–6.
66. J.J. Tinghino, *Edmondo Rossoni*, New York, 1991, pp. 208–9.
67. See the files in SPDCR 91.
68. SPDCR 91, report of 26 April 1937.
69. SPDCR 41, 9 August 1925, Mussolini to Prefect at Cremona; BMOO, XL, p. 71.
70. R. De Felice, *Mussolini il fascista 1925–1929*, p. 230.
71. G.G. Migone, *Gli Stati Uniti e il fascismo: alle origini dell'egemonia americana in Italia*, Milan, 1980, p. 105.
72. *Ibid.*, pp. 130–51.
73. BMOO, XXXIX, p. 479.
74. DDI 7s, IV, 387, 8 August 1926, Mussolini to Volpi.
75. *Ibid.* Also in BMOO, XL, pp. 110–18.
76. BMOO, XXII, pp. 196–8.
77. BMOO, XXIII, pp. 82–4. For critical English-language analyses, see R. Sarti, 'Mussolini and the Italian industrial leadership in the battle for the lira 1925–1927', *Past and Present*, 47, 1970, pp. 97–112; J.S. Cohen, 'The 1927 revaluation of the lira: a study in political economy', *The Economic History Review*, 25, 1972, pp. 642–654; V. Zamagni, *The economic history of Italy 1860–1990*, Oxford, 1993, pp. 251–2.
78. For a typical example of an industrialist's effort to divert the *Duce* through praise, see Carte Volpi, 6/46, 4 June 1927, Pirelli to Volpi.
79. G.G. Migone, *Gli Stati Uniti e il fascismo*, pp. 189–90.
80. R. Sarti, 'Mussolini and the industrial leadership', p. 111.
81. W.G. Welk, *Fascist economic policy: an analysis of Italy's economic experiment*, Cambridge, Mass., 1938 (republished, New York, 1968), p. 164.
82. In English, see especially, A.J. Gregor, *Italian Fascism and developmental dictatorship*, Princeton, 1979.
83. For an analysis, see J. Morris, 'Retailers, Fascism and the origins of social protection of shopkeepers in Italy', *Contemporary European History*, 5, 1996, pp. 285–318; 'The Fascist "Disciplining" of the Italian retail sector, 1922–1940', *Business History*, 40, 1998, pp. 138–64. So mild was Fascist legislation and so happy were shopkeepers with Fascist institutions in their sector, that both the laws and the organisations were carried over into the Republic.
84. V. Castronovo, *Storia di una banca: La Banca Nazionale del Lavoro e lo sviluppo economico italiano 1913–1983*, Turin, 1983, pp. 167–95.
85. The initial police reports which Mussolini received on him were duly negative. See SPDCR 11, 24 February 1926, Pericoli to Mussolini.
86. V. Castronovo, *Storia di una banca*, pp. 98–108.
87. *Ibid.*, p. 108.
88. With typical bluntness, Farinacci tried to defend Osio after his sacking. See SPDCR 11, 20 February 1942, Farinacci to Mussolini.
89. V. Castronovo, *Storia di una banca*, p. 231. His departure made it all the easier for him to transform into Anti-Fascism from 1943.
90. J.P. Morgan was polite enough to send a message of regret at the news. ACS, Carte Volpi 2/20/2, 12 July 1928, J.P. Morgan to Volpi.
91. A. Mosconi, *La mia linea politica*, Rome, 1952, pp. 17–19; 23–4.
92. G. Belluzzo, 'L'Italia è povera di materie prime?', *Gerarchia*, 7, January 1927, pp. 4–11.
93. G. Carocci, *Italian Fascism*, Harmondsworth, 1975, p. 115.
94. BMOO, XXI, p. 38.
95. BMOO, XXI, p. 356. For the background, cf. R. De Felice, *Mussolini il fascista 1925–1929*, pp. 80–2.

Notes

96. BMOO, XXII, pp. 366–7.
97. ACS, Ministry of the Interior, Direzione Generale di Pubblica Sicurezza (hereafter DGPS), 8/64, 10 June 1922, Inspector Adinolfi to Under-Secretary for Interior.
98. DGPS 1/8, 30 March 1923, Porro to Mussolini.
99. C.G. Chapman, *Milocca: a Sicilian village*, London, 1973, p. 4. Cf., for example, the almost exactly similar report of a police official about Fascism at Catanzaro by 1925. DGPS 1/119, 10 July 1925, report.
100. C.G. Chapman, *Milocca*, p. 155.
101. *Ibid.*, pp. 155–6.
102. *Ibid.*, p. 218.
103. SPDCR 4, 18 September 1924, Acerbo to Mussolini.
104. SPDCR 4, 11 November 1924, Acerbo to Mussolini.
105. Carte M. Bianchi, 1/2, 16 June 1924, Bianchi to Mussolini.
106. SPDCR 100, 17 August 1929, report. Bianchi's death in 1930 did elevate him to the Fascist pantheon and gain him a eulogy which, somewhat contrary to these charges, emphasised his complete moral inflexibility, as well as his unswerving attachment to the native soil of Calabria. See D.M. Tuninetti, *La vita di Michele Bianchi*, Rome, 1935.
107. See, for example, Carte M. Bianchi, 1/8; 1/7, 2 April 1924, Maraviglia to Bianchi.
108. C. Mori, *Con la Mafia ai ferri corti*, Milan, 1932, p. 230.
109. *Ibid.*, pp. 81; 242.
110. C. Duggan, *Fascism and the Mafia*, New Haven, 1989, p. 85.
111. *Ibid.*, p. 266.
112. BMOO, XXVIII, pp. 239–42.
113. D. Detragiache, 'Le fascisme féminin de San Sepolcro à l'affaire Matteotti', *Revue d'histoire moderne et contemporaine*, 30, 1983, pp. 368–72.
114. See, for example, BMOO, XIII, p. 17.
115. BMOO, XIX, pp. 215; 226–8.
116. BMOO, XIX, p. 357.
117. The best general study of the topic is V. De Grazia, *How Fascism ruled women: Italy 1922–1945*, Berkeley, 1992.
118. For the relevant legislation, see A. Aquarone, *L'organizzazione dello stato totalitario*, pp. 412–15.
119. V. De Grazia, *How Fascism ruled women*, pp. 7–8; 60–9.
120. BMOO, XXII, pp. 363–5.
121. V. De Grazia, *How Fascism ruled women*, p. 43.
122. A. Turati, *Il partito e i suoi compiti*, Rome, 1928, p. 189.
123. Cf. V. De Grazia, *How Fascism ruled women*, for the way Italian women actually utilised the opportunity of such space.
124. Y. De Begnac, *Palazzo Venezia: storia di un regime*, Rome, 1950, p. 134.
125. N. D'Aroma, *Mussolini segreto*, Rocca San Casciano, 1957, p. 28.
126. E. Ludwig, *Talks with Mussolini*, London, 1932, pp. 115; 168.
127. M. Ostenc, 'Una tappa della fascistizzazione: la scuola e la politica del 1925 al 1928', *Storia contemporanea*, 4, 1973, pp. 497–8.
128. T.M. Mazzatosta, *Il regime fascista tra educazione e propaganda (1935–1943)*, Bologna, 1978, p. 94.
129. R. Cantalupo, 'La classe dirigente e il suo Duce', *Gerarchia*, 6, January 1926, pp. 3–13.
130. SPDCR 81, 8 January 1928, Mussolini to Bodrero. Mussolini did add more disarmingly that Bodrero could say that the *Duce* indeed possessed a weakness for philosophy and, especially, the history of philosophy, and had just been reading some Plato.
131. SPD Carte della Cassetta di Zinco 6, 9 February 1927, note.
132. See, for example, Carte R. Farinacci 31, 12 September 1932, Farinacci to Mussolini, blaming Turati for 'five years of persecution'.

Notes

133. Carte R. Farinacci 31, has a file of letters exchanged with Arnaldo; cf. SPDCR 40, 8 July 1926, Farinacci to Mussolini.

134. SPDCR 40, 10 July 1926, Mussolini to Farinacci.

135. A. Turati, *Il partito e i suoi compiti*, pp. 157; 203.

136. See A. Turati, *Ragioni ideali di vita fascista*, Rome, 1926.

137. See A. Turati and G. Bottai (eds.), *La Carta del Lavoro: illustrato e commentato*, Rome, 1929, p. 59.

138. A. Turati, *Ragioni ideali*, p. 35.

139. A. Turati, *Una rivoluzione e un capo*, Rome, 1927, p. 124.

140. See R. De Felice, *Mussolini il fascista 1925–1929*, pp. 301–14.

141. SPDCR 43, 16 January 1926, Mussolini to Farinacci.

142. 'Critica Fascista', 'Mussolini, dittatore del partito', *Critica Fascista*, 4, 18 September 1926, pp. 342–4.

143. *Il 1919*, 2, January 1926.

144. SPDCR 46, 9 October 1926, A. Mussolini to Giampaoli; 41, 27 November 1926, A. Mussolini to Farinacci.

145. SPDCR 46, memorandum of 30 September 1927. Cf. 20 November 1928, A. Mussolini to Giampaoli.

146. SPDCR 46, police reports, 16 January, 18 December 1928.

147. SPDCR 46, telephone tap, 25 December 1928.

148. SPDCR 46, note, 19 December 1928. In case he was a coming man, a file was already growing on him, with allegations of a series of sexual misdemeanours, including homosexuality and rape, of corruption including the use of cocaine, of Masonic friendships, and of being hen-pecked. See 94, notes, 13, 16 October 1928, 12 October 1932.

149. SPDCR 46, Giampaoli to Sebastiani. There are also a series of letters in 1929, in which Giampaoli, in words very like those of Dumini during his travails, appealed about family misfortunes. He suffered from an ill grandmother, the alleged fact that his own hair had turned white overnight, and financial difficulties, while he also highlighted his past loyalty and contribution.

150. SPDCR 46, note, 17 February 1940.

151. SPDCR 46, police reports, 9 September 1940, 20 April 1942.

152. SPDCR 46, Giampaoli to Mussolini, 1 May 1943.

153. SPDCR 42, Farinacci to Mussolini, 6 June 1927.

154. SPDCR 43, Farinacci to Mussolini, 3 May 1927.

155. SPDCR 42, Farinacci to Mussolini, 1 September 1927.

156. For another example, see SPDCR 41, Arnaldo Mussolini to Mussolini, 14 February 1927. Arnaldo had carpeted Farinacci over his attacks on Turati and the party status quo to be told that Volpi and Balbo were disloyal and Turati also, while Costanzo Ciano and Giuriati were present friends.

157. For a telling example, see SPDCR 87, report on F. Lantini, 5 May 1928. The police noted that Lantini was favoured by Turati but opposed by Farinacci, Rossoni, Balbo and Bottai.

158. SPDCR 43, Mussolini to Farinacci, 16 November 1925.

159. P. Scoppola, *La Chiesa e il Fascismo: documenti e interpretazioni*, Bari, 1971, pp. 4–5; 32.

160. For an example of such rhetoric, see P. Zama, *Fascismo e religione*, Milan, 1923, pp. 7–10. Zama was published by Imperia, the PNF party publishers.

161. BMOO, XXII, pp. 400–1; cf. C.A. Biggini, *Storia inedita della Conciliazione*, Milan, 1942, pp. 72–3.

162. R. De Felice, *Mussolini il fascista 1925–1929*, p. 403.

163. *Ibid.*, pp. 403; 422.

164. F. Pacelli, *Diario della Conciliazione con verbali e appendice di documenti* (ed. M. Maccarrone), Città del Vaticano, 1959, pp. 113–24.

Notes

165. Nogara took the moment to revive an idea, discussed before 1914, of the institution of a national bank of credit, which could be swung behind patriotic initiatives abroad and thus ally Church and State in the imperial cause. See DDI 7s, VII, 188, 18 January 1929, Nogara to Mussolini.

166. For an account of the effect on Vatican finance, see J.F. Pollard, 'The Vatican and the Wall Street crash: Bernardino Nogara and papal finances in the early 1930s', *Historical Journal*, 42, 1999, pp. 1077–91.

167. For an English-language summary, see J.F. Pollard, *The Vatican and Italian Fascism, 1929–1932: a study in conflict*, Cambridge, 1985, pp. 46–7.

168. *Il Popolo d'Italia*, 12 February 1929.

169. J.F. Pollard, *The Vatican and Italian Fascism*, pp. 49–50.

170. P. Scoppola, *La Chiesa e il Fascismo*, p. 196.

171. P.C. Kent, *The Pope and the Duce: the international impact of the Lateran Agreements*, London, 1981, p. 193.

172. G. Guidi, *Pio XI*, Milan, 1938, p. 158.

173. SPDCR 6, 13 February 1929, police report.

174. *The Tablet*, 30 March, 18 May, 15 June 1929.

175. *The Times*, 13 February 1929.

176. *The Economist*, 15 June 1929. The pacts even earned Rachele Mussolini a gushing article in the *Girl's Own Annual* of 1929. See I. Phayre, 'The romance of Rachele Mussolini: from milkmaid and farmhand to "Caesar's wife" and "Cousin of the King"', pp. 414–16.

177. C.A. Biggini, *Storia inedita della conciliazione*, pp. 9; 411.

178. G. Cresciani, *Fascism, Anti-Fascism and Italians in Australia 1922–1945*, Canberra, 1980, p. 210.

179. R. De Felice, *Mussolini il duce 1929–1936*, p. 3.

180. For an account of its history, accompanied by telling photographs of the castle, before its reconstruction reduced by earthquake and the other wear and tear of time to a stump, see P. Mastri, *La Rocca delle Caminate (Il Castello del Duce)*, Bologna, 1927.

181. G. Pini and D. Susmel, *Mussolini: l'uomo e l'opera*, Florence, 1953–5, vol. III, p. 111.

182. *Carteggio Arnaldo-Benito Mussolini*, p. 30.

183. For example in his Ascension Day speech, BMOO XXI, p. 370. After 1927 the building of Predappio as a Fascist sacred site did slow.

184. SPDCR 116 has an extensive file.

CHAPTER 11

1. P. Einzig, *The economic foundations of Fascism*, London, 1933, pp. vi–vii; 10; 100.

2. Y. De Begnac, *Palazzo Venezia: storia di un regime*, Rome, 1950, p. 353.

3. His propagandists naturally agreed. See G. Gennaioli, *Mussolini e Napoleone I*, San Sepolcro, 1926.

4. For a relatively moderate example, see G. Volpe, *Storia della Corsica italiana*, Milan, 1939, who self-effacingly notes that it was the French after 1815 who tried to write Napoleon off as an Italian (p. 70).

5. See, for example, F. Tempera, *Benito: emulo-superatore di Cesare e di Napoleone*, Rome, 1927.

6. G. Viganoni, *Mussolini e i Cesari*, Milan, 1933, p. 237. The author stated that he saw Mussolini for the first time in October 1932 and was spontaneously moved to murmur: 'Ave, Caesar Imperator' (p. 10).

7. For an English-language text, see B. Mussolini and G. Forzano, *Napoleon: the hundred days*, London, 1932.

8. See G. Forzano, 'Introduzione: la mia collaborazione teatrale con Benito Mussolini', in his *Mussolini: autore drammatico*, Florence, 1954.

Notes

9. B. Mussolini and G. Forzano, *Napoleon*, p. 87. Napoleon was prophetically addressing his mother.

10. R. De Felice, *Mussolini il fascista II. L'organizzazione dello stato fascista 1925–1929*, Turin, 1968, p. 438.

11. L. Passerini, *Mussolini immaginario: storia di una biografia 1915–1939*, Bari, 1991, p. 141.

12. For an account of these events, see A. Cederna, *Mussolini urbanista: lo sventramento di Roma negli anni del consenso*, Bari, 1979.

13. R. Ducci, *La bella gioventù*, Bologna, 1996, p. 65–6. It was 1941!

14. L. Passerini, *Mussolini immaginario*, p. 139.

15. For an evocative, star-struck, account of visiting Mussolini there, see V. Brancati, 'La mia visita a Mussolini', *Critica Fascista*, 9, 1 August 1931, pp. 292–3.

16. In 1935 one commentator, with skills in the archaeology of voice, decided the two were the same because they spoke in the same way. N. Sigillino, *Mussolini visto da me*, Rome, 1935, p. 24.

17. See, for example, V.J. Bordeux, *Benito Mussolini*, London, n.d., p. 284.

18. Y. De Begnac, *Palazzo Venezia: storia di un regime*, p. 649.

19. B. Bottai, *Fascismo famigliare*, Casale Monferrato, 1997, p. 17.

20. See *L'Illustrazione italiana*, 26 March 1933, for an unguarded picture of a greying Mussolini.

21. S. Colarizi, *L'opinione degli italiani sotto il regime 1929–1943*, Bari, 1991, p. 25.

22. SPDCR 75, police report, May 1927.

23. Y. De Begnac, *Taccuini mussoliniani*, p. 471. Mussolini liked to maintain to selected audiences that Turati was innocent of the charges, which had been drummed up by Farinacci, but he did nothing either to save his ex-colleague or to give him the opportunity of further government office.

24. A. Turati, *Fuori dell'ombra della mia vita: dieci anni nel solco del fascismo* (ed. A. Frappani), Brescia, 1973, p. 37.

25. T. Cianetti, *Memorie dal carcere di Verona* (ed. R. De Felice), Milan, 1983, pp. 146–7.

26. *Ibid.*, p. 213.

27. Cf. here E.N. Peterson, *The limits of Hitler's power*, Princeton, 1969.

28. For the two most direct examples, see G.T. Garratt, *Mussolini's Roman Empire*, Harmondsworth, 1938; D. Mack Smith, *Mussolini's Roman Empire*, London, 1976. The title of the Italian translation of Mack Smith's book is indeed *Le guerre del Duce*.

29. M. Knox, *Common destiny: dictatorship, foreign policy, and war in Fascist Italy and Nazi Germany*, Cambridge, 2000, p. 66.

30. M. Knox, *Hitler's Italian allies: Royal armed forces, Fascist regime, and the war of 1940–1943*, Cambridge, 2000, p. 5.

31. E. Di Nolfo, *Mussolini e la politica estera italiana (1919–1933)*, Padua, 1960, pp. 245–6.

32. P.G. Edwards, 'The Austen Chamberlain–Mussolini meetings', *Historical Journal*, 14, 1971, p. 163.

33. For a detailed account of one sector, see L. Tosi, *Alle origini della FAO: le relazioni tra l'Istituto internazionale di Agricoltura e la Società delle Nazioni*, Milan, 1989.

34. BMOO, XXIII, p. 271.

35. See, for example, DDI 7s, VI, 391, 8 June 1928, Mussolini to De Martino.

36. BMOO, XXII, pp. 66–7.

37. However, according to one young diplomat, the initiative for the change came from Grandi. See M. Luciolli, *Palazzo Chigi: anni roventi. Ricordi di vita diplomatica italiana dal 1933 al 1948*, Milan, 1976, p. 51.

38. See, for example, DDI 7s, V, 256, 8 June 1927, Grandi to Turati, explaining that Mussolini desired the entry of 'war heroes' and 'authentic Fascists'. For Mussolini's announcement of the change, see BMOO, XXIII, pp. 190–1.

Notes

39. L.V. Ferraris, 'L'amministrazione centrale del Ministero degli Esteri italiano nel suo sviluppo storico (1848–1954)', *Rivista di studi politici internazionali*, 21, 1954, p. 457. For further background about the Liberal ministry, its social and patronage patterns, see R.J.B. Bosworth, *Italy, the least of the Great Powers: Italian foreign policy before the First World War*, Cambridge, 1979, pp. 95–126.

40. For a distinguished example and his explanation of his decision in September 1943, see L. Bolla, *Perché a Salò: diario della Repubblica Sociale Italiana* (ed. G.B. Guerri), Milan, 1982.

41. H. Fornari, *Mussolini's gadfly: Roberto Farinacci*, Nashville, 1971, p. 175. Franco Farinacci was notably pessimistic about the chances of the Axis in the war.

42. See *Annuario diplomatico e delle carriere direttive*, Rome, 1980, p. 593.

43. In the 1980s Grandi in old age was blessed by members of the De Felice school, who respectfully edited some of his memoirs. See D. Grandi, *Il mio paese: ricordi autobiografici* (ed. R. De Felice), Bologna, 1985; *La politica estera dell'Italia dal 1929 al 1932* (ed. P. Nello), 2 vols, Rome, 1985. For some of the complications involved, cf. M. Knox, 'I testi "aggiustati" dei discorsi segreti di Grandi', *Passato e Presente*, 13, 1987, pp. 97–117.

44. D. Grandi, *Giovani*, Bologna, 1941, pp. 147; 225.

45. P. Nello, *Dino Grandi: la formazione di un leader fascista*, Bologna, 1987, p. 250.

46. DDI 7s VIII, 19, 26 September 1929, Grandi to Mussolini.

47. Mussolini's file on Grandi, inevitably, included a charge in 1929 of corrupt real estate deals, shrugged off by the Under Secretary, who used the occasion to request a doubling and more of his salary. See SPDCR 14, 17 June 1929, Grandi to Mussolini.

48. For an account of the revival of ambitions there before 1914 (the defeat at Adowa had by no means persuaded all Liberals for ever to stay out of Ethiopia), see R.J.B. Bosworth, *Italy, the least of the Great Powers*, pp. 329–36.

49. DDI 7s, IV, 397, 27 August 1926, Mussolini to his major ambassadors.

50. See A. Cassels, *Mussolini's early diplomacy*, pp. 300–2.

51. See, for example, DDI 7s, VI, 186, 26 March 1928, Mussolini to Cora, where Mussolini's phrasing suggests that he thought that his diplomatic representative might be surprised at the news. On the agreement, cf. also G. Cora, 'Il trattato italo-etiopico del 1928', *Rivista di studi politici internazionali*, 15, 1948, pp. 205–26.

52. G. Cora, 'Un diplomatico durante l'era fascista', *Storia e politica*, 5, 1966, pp. 88–9.

53. R. De Felice, *Mussolini il duce I. gli anni del consenso 1929–1936*, Turin, 1974, pp. 396–7.

54. For his own account, see R. Guariglia, *Ricordi 1922–1946*, Naples, 1949.

55. R. De Felice, *Mussolini il duce 1929–1936*, pp. 397–400. Guariglia repeated his advice the next year. See DDI 7s, XII, 222, 26 August 1932, Guariglia to Mussolini; 223, 27 August 1932, Guariglia to Mussolini.

56. The puppet nature of Zog's regime is exemplified in its acceptance of Italian command of its armed forces should there be war. See DDI 7s, VI, 611, military agreements of 31 August 1928.

57. Cf. Grandi's automatic assumption that an Italian economic presence in Albania, even in regard to the state petrol company A.G.I.P., would naturally be at the cost of the Italians. See DDI 7s, VIII, 170, 19 November 1929, Grandi to Bottai. The businessmen involved were happy to adapt to such attitudes. See X, 104, 3 March 1931, Giarratana to Grandi. For a further general comment on the subsidies expended there, cf. XII, 60, 25 May 1932, Grandi to Bottai.

58. See, for example, DDI 7s, IX, 395, 22 November 1930, Grandi to Auriti.

59. DDI 7s, IV, 448, 2 October 1926, Mussolini to Badoglio.

60. See, for example, DDI 7s, VI, 641, 11 September 1928, Mussolini to Rochira.

61. J.J. Sadkovich, *Italy's support for Croatian separatism 1927–1937*, New York, 1987, p. 33.

62. R. De Felice, *Mussolini il duce 1929–1936*, p. 515.

63. DDI 7s, VII, 249, 13 February 1929, Auriti to Mussolini. Auriti put a '*sic*' after his description of the suggestion.

Notes

64. DDI 7s, VIII, 129, October 1929, Grandi to Mussolini.
65. B. Mussolini, *Corrispondenza inedita* (ed. D. Susmel), Milan, 1972, p. 107.
66. See, for example, 'Lettera aperta a Bottai di Georges Valois', *Critica Fascista*, 4, 1 August 1926; A. Pavolini, 'Le cose di Francia e l'universalità del fascismo', *Critica Fascista*, 4, 15 January 1926, pp. 25–7.
67. See DDI 7s, V, 48, 4 March 1927, Primo De Rivera to Mussolini. The Spanish general expressed the profundity of his 'admiration for the great work of world-ranging value in which you are engaged'. Cf. VII, 600, 21 August 1929, Mussolini to Medici, rejecting an invitation from Primo to advise him constitutionally.
68. See, for example, DDI 7s, VII, 17, 3 October 1928, Auriti to Mussolini; VIII, 101, 22 October 1929, Grandi to Auriti (enthusing about the idea of the *Heimwehr* reaching government).
69. DDI 7s, IV, 551, 18 December 1926, Bastianini to Mussolini with the news that the *Duce* was taken by them as their 'spiritual chief'.
70. See issues of *Critica Fascista*, 3, 1 April and 1 May 1925.
71. *La Vita Italiana*, March 1925, hailed James Strachey Barnes. For his views, see further J.S. Barnes, *Io amo l'Italia: memorie di un giornalista inglese*, Milan, 1939.
72. 'Il premier australiano è fascista', *Critica Fascista*, 4, 1 March 1926, p. 92.
73. See J.S. Barnes, *The universal aspects of Fascism*, London, 1928. Cf. also his *Fascism*, London, 1931.
74. M.G. Sarfatti, 'Il fascismo visto dall'estero', *Gerarchia*, 9, June 1929, pp. 436–43.
75. BMOO, XXIII, p. 122.
76. A. Mussolini, *Scritti e discorsi*, Milan, 1934, vol. II, pp. 18–20.
77. For his work, see B. Ricci, *Avvisi*, Florence, 1943; *La rivoluzione fascista: antologia di scritti politici* (eds A. Cucchi and G. Galante), Milan, 1996.
78. For an English-language account, see M.A. Ledeen, *Universal Fascism: the theory and practice of the Fascist International 1928–1936*, New York, 1972.
79. M.G. Sarfatti, 'L'universalità della politica italiana', *Gerarchia*, 12, January 1932, pp. 39–40.
80. *Le Vie d'Italia*, XXXIV, February 1928.
81. A. Pavolini, 'Il Rotary', *Critica Fascista*, 7, 15 January 1929, pp. 22–4.
82. DDI 7s, VII, 348, 2 April 1929, memorandum of talk held at Florence.
83. See, for example, DDI 7s, VIII, 304, 10 January 1930, Mussolini to Grandi; 343, 3 February 1930, Mussolini to Grandi.
84. DDI 7s, VIII, 362, 13 February 1930, Grandi to Mussolini.
85. DDI 7s, X, 174, 28 April 1931, Badoglio to Grandi.
86. BMOO, XXIV, p. 281. He then went on to deny that he had ever said that Fascism was not for export. It was rather 'spiritually' universal (p. 283).
87. DDI 7s, IX, 122, 29 June 1930, Grandi to Mussolini.
88. F. Suvich, *Memorie 1932–1936* (ed. G. Bianchi), Milan, 1984, p. 10.
89. E. Di Nolfo, *Mussolini e la politica estera italiana*, p. 309, concludes that no striking policy position had been achieved at this time, while Fulvio D'Amoja argues that such normality continued in 1933–34. See F. D'Amoja, *Declino e prima crisi dell'Europa di Versailles: studio sulla diplomazia italiana ed europea (1931–1933)*, Milan, 1967, p. 105.
90. The metaphor lingered into Fascism and beyond. See, for example, A. Lessona, *La missione dell'Italia in Africa*, Rome, 1936, p. 9; M. Gianturco, *La guerra degli imperi capitalisti contro gli imperi proletari*, Florence, 1940, p. 6. Gianturco, a sometime collaborator on *La Vita Italiana*, re-emerged after 1945 as a government advisor on migration.
91. For the figures, see G. Rosoli (ed.), *Un secolo di emigrazione italiana 1876–1976*, Rome, 1978, p. 346.
92. See C.G. Segrè, *Fourth shore: the Italian colonization of Libya*, Chicago, 1974.
93. See, for example, *Il Legionario*, 2, 18 July 1925.

Notes

94. E. Gentile, 'La politica estera del partito fascista. Ideologia e organizzazione dei Fasci italiani all'estero (1920–1930)', *Storia contemporanea*, 26, 1995, pp. 897–956.

95. For one example, see R. and M. Bosworth, *Fremantle's Italy*, Rome, 1993, pp. 87–91.

96. BMOO, XXI, p. 221.

97. BMOO, XXII, pp. 150–1.

98. BMOO, XXIII, pp. 89–91. Cf. pp. 124–5, where Mussolini, in an interview with the *Chicago Daily News*, renounced any serious idea of blocking the assimilation of Italians in the USA.

99. A. Del Boca, *Gli italiani in Libia: Tripoli bel suol d'amore 1860–1922*, Bari, 1986, p. 453.

100. *Ibid.*, p. 153.

101. A. Del Boca, *Gli italiani in Libia dal fascismo a Gheddafi*, Bari, 1988, p. 5.

102. For Graziani's general memoirs, see R. Graziani, *Ho difeso la patria*, Milan, 1948. He also wrote a series of accounts of his 'Roman' victories in Libya. They are summarised in R. Graziani, *Pace romana in Libia*, Milan, 1937.

103. A. Del Boca, *Gli italiani in Libia dal fascismo al Gheddafi*, pp. 25–55.

104. See, for example, R. Graziani, *Pace romana*, pp. 265; 338.

105. C.M. De Vecchi, *Orizzonti d'impero: cinque anni in Somalia*, Milan, 1935.

106. Racial legislation was extended there in 1938 and orthodox schools were banned in 1939. See C. Marongiu Buonaiuti, *La politica religiosa del fascismo nel Dodecaneso*, Naples, 1979, pp. 95–106.

107. For an account from below, see N. Doumanis, *Myth and memory in the Mediterranean: remembering Fascism's empire*, London, 1997. De Vecchi's better regarded predecessor was the ex-Nationalist, Mario Lago.

108. For a full account, see A. Del Boca, *Gli italiani in Libia dal fascismo al Gheddafi*, pp. 174–232.

109. *Ibid.*, p. 180.

110. *Ibid.*, p. 183.

111. *Ibid.*, p. 189.

112. *Ibid.*, p. 207.

113. *Ibid.*, pp. 191–7.

114. G. Rochat, 'L'impiego di gas nella guerra d'Etiopia 1935–6', *Rivista di storia contemporanea*, 17, 1988, p. 79.

115. A. Del Boca, *Gli italiani in Libia dal fascismo al Gheddafi*, p. 191.

116. For fine accounts of the reticences of Italian imperial historiography, see A. Del Boca (ed.), *I gas di Mussolini: il fascismo e la guerra d'Etiopia*, Rome, 1996; A. Del Boca (ed.), *Adua: le ragioni di una sconfitta*, Bari, 1997.

117. See, for example, O. Bartov, *The Eastern Front, 1941–45: German troops and the barbarisation of warfare*, New York, 1986.

118. A. Del Boca, *Gli italiani in Libia dal fascismo al Gheddafi*, p. 198.

119. For further discussion, see Chapter 14.

120. For a detailed account of the bureaucratic disputes, see R.J.B. Bosworth, 'Tourist planning in Fascist Italy and the limits of a totalitarian culture', *Contemporary European History*, 6, 1997, pp. 1–25.

121. For more detail, see R.J.B. Bosworth, 'The *Touring Club Italiano* and the nationalisation of the Italian bourgeoisie', *European History Quarterly*, 27, 1997, pp. 371–410.

122. R.J.B. Bosworth, 'The *Touring Club Italiano*', p. 396.

123. BMOO, XXV, p. 148.

124. BMOO, XXIV, pp. 45–90.

125. D. Binchy, *Church and state in Fascist Italy*, Oxford, 1941, pp. 496–8.

126. See *Critica Fascista*, 9, 15 July 1931, editorial. Cf. the more openly critical B. Spampanato, 'Stato e Chiesa: distanze e funzioni', in the same issue (pp. 264–6).

Notes

127. C.M. De Vecchi di Val Cismon, *Tra Papa, Duce e Re: il conflitto tra Chiesa cattolica e Stato fascista nel diario 1930–1931 del primo ambasciatore del Regno d'Italia presso la Santa Sede* (ed. S. Setta), p. 210.

128. J.F. Pollard, *The Vatican and Italian Fascism, 1929–1932*, Cambridge, 1985, p. 145.

129. C.M. De Vecchi di Val Cismon, *Tra Papa, Duce e Re*, p. 294.

130. *Ibid.*, pp. 182; 294.

131. *Ibid.*, p. 89.

132. For Mussolini's report of the meeting, see DDI 7s, XI, 205, 11 February 1932, Mussolini to King Victor Emmanuel III.

133. For one tiff, see SPDCR 14, 14 August 1932, Mussolini to Grandi; 4 and 20 August 1932, Grandi to Mussolini, in which Grandi agreed in the end simply to accept that Balbo was 'a poor coward'.

134. For his account, see G. Giuriati, *La parabola di Mussolini nei ricordi di un gerarca* (ed. E. Gentile), Bari, 1981.

135. For his own accounts, see G. Giuriati, *La vigilia (gennaio 1913–maggio 1915)*, Milan, 1930; *Con D'Annunzio e Millo in difesa dell'Adriatico*, Florence, 1954.

136. G. Giuriati, *La parabola di Mussolini*, p. 43.

137. *Ibid.*, p. 50.

138. *Ibid.*, p. 51. For an example, cf. the file on profound corruption at the University of Naples medical school involving Pietro Castellini. In 1933, on Castellini's death, Mussolini nonetheless sent a letter of condolence to his son, eulogising Pietro's life-long dedication to science and the university. See SPDCR 38.

139. SPDCR 43, 10 October 1934.

140. SPDCR 47, 29 October 1930, Giuriati to PNF officials.

141. G. Giuriati, *La parabola di Mussolini* p. 130. Giuriati also aspired to restore Latin as the language of international diplomacy (p. 150).

142. SPDCR 47, 22 February 1931, Giuriati to Mussolini.

143. G. Giuriati, *La parabola di Mussolini*, p. 156.

144. A. Spinosa, *Starace*, Milan, 1981, p. 292.

145. *Ibid.*, p. 63.

146. See A. Starace, *La marcia su Gondar della colonna celere A.O. e le successive operazioni nella Etiopia occidentale*, Milan, 1936.

147. G. Bottai, *Diario 1935–1944* (ed. G.B. Guerri), Milan, 1989, p. 102.

148. R. De Felice, *Mussolini il duce 1929–1936*, pp. 216–17.

149. SPDCR 40, 6 February 1932, Starace to Mussolini. On 20 January 1932 Farinacci had sent the *Duce* a twenty-seven page letter of complaint at his present treatment.

150. BMOO, XXV, p. 50.

151. R. De Felice, *Mussolini il duce 1929–1936*, p. 217.

152. *Ibid.*, p. 221.

153. After his death, Arnaldo composed a sentimental account of that event which began 'Daddy is writing to you'. A. and B. Mussolini, *Vita di Sandro e di Arnaldo*, Milan, 1934, p. 11. Among the remedies tried on Sandro was holy water from Lourdes (p. 45).

154. For an account, see G. Sofri, *Gandhi in Italia*, Bologna, 1988.

155. G. Pini and D. Susmel, *Mussolini: l'uomo e l'opera*, Florence, 1953–5, vol. III, pp. 239–40.

156. The grovelling novelist, Ada Negri, who was trying to prompt Mussolini into nominating her for a Nobel prize, typically wrote privately to him to say that she found the book 'wonderful, fine and chaste from the first to the last line, with a density and intensity which can even hurt in the way that a hand pressed strongly on your heart can'. See SPDCR 14, 21 February 1933, A. Negri to Mussolini.

157. R. Farinacci, 'Matrimonio d'amore', *La Vita Italiana*, XXXVIII, 15 July 1931, pp. 1–2. Farinacci thereafter wrote a monthy column for the journal.

Notes

158. A. Assante, 'Arnaldo Mussolini', *La Vita Italiana*, XXXIX, 15 January 1932, pp. 11–15.

159. *Carteggio Arnaldo-Benito Mussolini* (ed. D. Susmel), Florence, 1954, p. 184.

160. *Ibid.*, p. 216.

161. G. Bottai, 'Il cammino segreto', *Critica Fascista*, 7, 15 September 1929, p. 350. Radical Fascist philosopher, Ugo Spirito, claimed later that Mussolini, with a certain contradiction, told him to think independently. U. Spirito, *Memorie di un incosciente*, Milan, 1977, p. 174.

162. G. Gamberini, 'Il dovere di discutere', *Critica Fascista*, 8, 15 March 1930, pp. 103–4.

163. See, for example (Spampanato was insistent on the theme), B. Spampanato, 'Equazioni rivoluzionarie: dal bolscevismo al fascismo', *Critica Fascista*, 8, 15 April 1930, pp. 152–4.

164. G. Bottai, 'La rivoluzione permanente: quarto anniversario', *Critica Fascista*, 4, 1 November 1926, pp. 391–2.

165. G. Bottai, 'Il partito non è superato', *Critica Fascista*, 9, 15 September 1931, p. 341.

166. A. Gravelli, *Mussolini aneddotico*, Rome, 1951, p. 206.

167. It was rapidly made available in English as B. Mussolini, 'The political and social doctrine of Fascism', *Political Quarterly*, 4, 1933, pp. 341–56. See also BMOO, XXXIV, pp. 117–38.

168. N. D'Aroma, *Mussolini segreto*, Rocca San Casciano, 1958, p. 68.

169. E. Ludwig, *Talks with Mussolini*, London, 1932, p. 37.

170. *Ibid.*, pp. 14; 32; 37.

171. *Ibid.*, p. 70.

172. *Ibid.*, p. 191.

173. *Ibid.*, pp. 73–4.

174. *Ibid.*, p. 220.

175. *Ibid.*, p. 217.

176. N. D'Aroma, *Mussolini segreto*, p. 24.

177. For a useful English-language account of the event indicating that the populace were not merely passive consumers, but tried to manipulate it to their own 'corrupt' advantage, see M. Stone, 'Staging Fascism: the Exhibition of the Fascist Revolution', *Journal of Contemporary History*, 28, 1993, pp. 215–43.

178. For an able summary, see R. De Felice, *Mussolini il duce 1929–1936*, pp. 56–74.

179. For an example, preaching a retention of freeish trade and rejecting 'autarchy', while praising Mussolini's admirable harnessing of factional interests, see E. Conti, 'Difendiamo il lavoro italiano!', *Gerarchia*, 12, April 1932, pp. 271–5. Cf. also the not dissimilar A. De' Stefani, 'Lo Stato e la vita economica', *Gerarchia*, 12, June 1932, pp. 462–8. The ex-Minister argued that 'no single design' could solve the dilemma of the economy.

180. O. Dinale, *La rivoluzione che vince (1914–1934)*, Rome, 1934, pp. 143–53.

181. F. Ciarlantini, *Mussolini immaginario*, Milan, 1933, pp. 6; 48.

182. G. Cavacciocchi, *Mussolini*, Florence, 1932, p. 65.

183. SPDCR 113 has an extensive file on the wedding including cards formally printed to say that Benito and Rachele Mussolini were 'at home' at certain times.

184. See BMOO, XLI, pp. 467; 473; XLII, p. 2; 8–13; 22. Within a month his grandfather had arranged an honorary membership card in the Balilla for him. SPDCR 114, 20 November 1931, Mussolini to Edda.

185. G. Pini and D. Susmel, *Mussolini*, vol. III, p. 259.

186. C. Rossi, *Trentatre vicende mussoliniane*, Milan, 1958, pp. 371–2.

CHAPTER 12

1. L. Garibaldi (ed.), *Mussolini e il professore: vita e diarii di Carlo Alberto Biggini*, Milan, 1983, p. 361. Cf. Chapter 1 above.

Notes

2. Ironically, a pair of science fiction writers did locate Mussolini literally in Hell, though, another Virgil, he became their guide there and they eventually admitted that, unlike Hitler, he was not all bad, but a man of originally good intentions. Had he not, after all, dished the communists? See L. Niven and J. Pournelle, *Inferno*, New York, 1976.

3. For further background, see R.J.B. Bosworth, *The Italian dictatorship: problems and perspectives in the interpretation of Mussolini and Fascism*, London, 1998, especially pp. 205–30.

4. I. Kershaw, *Hitler 1889–1936: hubris*, London, 1998, pp. 131; 183–4.

5. A. Cassels, *Mussolini's early diplomacy*, Princeton, 1970, pp. 168–74.

6. DDI 7s, I, 131, 17 November 1922, Tedaldi to Mussolini.

7. A. Tamaro, 'Il fascismo in Germania e nell'Europa centrale', *Critica Fascista*, 3, 16 March 1925, pp. 103–5. Cf. reports in the same journal in 1926 that Hitler's movement was on the wane. O. Randi, 'Il fascismo bavarese', *Critica Fascista*, 4, 1 February 1926, pp. 48–9.

8. M. Michaelis, *Mussolini and the Jews: German–Italian relations and the Jewish question in Italy 1922–1945*, Oxford, 1978, pp. 37–8. Nazi ideologue Alfred Rosenberg apparently believed him (p. 38).

9. Hitler still used this word to describe Mussolini in April 1942. See A. Hitler, *Hitler's table talk*, p. 437.

10. A. Hitler, *Mein Kampf* (ed. D.C. Watt), London, 1969, p. 566.

11. *Ibid.*, pp. 571–4.

12. *Ibid.*, p. 581.

13. See, for example, BMOO, XXII, p. 71. Mussolini declared the Germans of the region to be 'not a national minority but an ethnic left-over' (p. 73).

14. See R.J.B. Bosworth, *Italy and the wider world 1860–1960*, London, 1996, pp. 43–5.

15. A. Hitler, *Hitler's secret book* (ed. T. Taylor, 1961), p. 3.

16. *Ibid.*, p. 74.

17. *Ibid.*, p. 167.

18. A. Hitler, *Hitler's table talk 1941–1944* (ed. H.R. Trevor-Roper), London, 1953, p. 10.

19. I. Kershaw, *Hitler 1889–1936*, pp. 182–5.

20. Joseph Goebbels took a while to surrender to Hitler's charisma because that step involved him accepting the idea of an alliance with Italy (and Britain). See J. Goebbels, *Diaries* (ed. L.P. Lochner), London, 1948, p. xx.

21. DDI 7s, V, 206, 17 May 1927, Summonte to Mussolini.

22. DDI 7s, V, 673, 14 December 1927, Aldrovandi to Mussolini. It may be assumed that the press *attaché* had secret funds at his disposal. For background, see G. Carocci, *La politica estera dell'Italia fascista (1925–1928)*, Bari, 1969, pp. 196–7.

23. See, for example, DDI 7s, V, 168, 27 April 1927, Ricciardi to Mussolini.

24. DDI 7s, VII, 413, 8 May 1929, Morreale note.

25. DDI 7s, IX, 193, 4 August 1930, Fani to Orsini Barone, forwarding 15 July, report by Renzetti to Turati.

26. G. Bevione, 'Il trionfo di Hitler', *Gerarchia*, 10, September 1930, pp. 705–9.

27. DDI 7s, IX, 289, 4 October 1930, Morreale to Mussolini (with enclosed report of meeting of 28 September).

28. DDI 7s, X, 287, 23–4 May 1931, Grandi to Mussolini.

29. DDI 7s, X, 305, 1 June 1931, Mussolini note.

30. See, for example, DDI 7s, 56, XI, 23 October 1931, Sebastiani note.

31. DDI 7s, XI, 79, 20 November 1931; 110, 7 December, both Renzetti to Mussolini.

32. For examples, see DDI 7s, XII, 87, 12 June; 108, 21 June; 324, 11 October 1932, Renzetti to Mussolini. On this last occasion Hitler, at least according to Goering, had expressed a desire to see the museums and displays of the *Decennale*.

33. DDI 7s, XII, 364, 25 October 1932, Renzetti to Mussolini.

Notes

34. Ciarlantini's articles were published in successive issues of *Augustea* from August to October 1932 and then collected as F. Ciarlantini, *Hitler e il fascismo*, Florence, 1933, p. 10.
35. *Ibid.*, p. 8.
36. *Ibid.*, pp. 9; 19.
37. G. Bortolotto, *Fascismo e nazionalsocialismo*, Bologna, 1933, p. 29. Cf. also P. Solari, *Hitler e il Terzo Reich*, Milan, 1932.
38. See R. Farinacci, 'Rilievi mensili', *La Vita Italiana*, XL, 15 September, 15 November 1932.
39. See, for example, G. Preziosi, 'Hitler', *La Vita Italiana*, XXXVI, 15 September 1930, pp. 209–13; J. Evola, 'L'Internazionale ebraica e la profezia della nuova guerra mondiale secondo Ludendorff', *La Vita Italiana*, XL, 15 November 1932, pp. 544–6.
40. See, for example, A. Gravelli (ed.), *Razzismo*, Rome, n.d., p. 333.
41. G. Renzetti, 'Hindenburg e Hitler', *Gerarchia*, 12, March 1932, pp. 233–7. In 1933 Renzetti continued to report sympathetically about the Nazis for this semi-official journal. Cf. the more gushing articles by Mario Da Silva in *Critica Fascista*, 10, 15 May, 1 June 1932.
42. BMOO, XXXVII, pp. 398–9.
43. DDI 7s, XII, 401, [November 1932], draft letter, Suvich to Renzetti. Suvich wanted him to work through the Italian ambassador in Berlin, Vittorio Cerruti, whose wife, like Renzetti's, was Jewish. For her account of these years, see E. Cerruti, *Ambassador's wife*, London, 1952.
44. BMOO, XLII, p. 36.
45. BMOO, XLII, p. 58.
46. See above, Chapters 6 and 7.
47. See, for example, DDI 7s, IV, 476, 5 November 1926, Grandi to Scalea.
48. SPDCR 1, 17 February 1934, Mussolini to Ercole.
49. BMOO, XXIII, p. 74.
50. DDI 7s, XI, 205, 11 February 1932, Mussolini to King Victor Emmanuel III.
51. R. De Felice, *Mussolini il duce I. Gli anni del consenso 1929–1936*, Turin, 1974, p. 155.
52. Primo Levi, the magnificently honest Anti-Fascist recounter of Auschwitz, does after all say, without comment, that those of his suffering colleagues who gave up the fight and, like zombies, made ready to die, were known as *Muselmann* (Moslems). They were 'the weak, the inept and those doomed to selection'. P. Levi, *'If this is a man' and 'The truce'* (ed. S.J. Woolf), Harmondsworth, 1979, p. 94. Cf. also the liberal-democrat, F.S. Nitti, *The decadence of Europe: the paths of reconstruction*, London, 1923, p. 123, where he deplores the French sending of black troops into Germany and the resultant playing of 'African melodies' in the 'land of Mozart and Beethoven', a country which was one of the 'most cultured on earth'.
53. N. D'Aroma, *Mussolini segreto*, Rocca San Casciano, 1958, p. 128.
54. *Ibid.*, p. 48.
55. L. Frassati, *Il destino passa per Varsavia*, Milan, 1985, p. 139.
56. See, for example, BMOO, XXIX, pp. 51–2.
57. For a graphic example, see P.V. Cannistraro, 'Mussolini, Saccco-Vanzetti, and the anarchists: the transatlantic context', *Journal of Modern History*, 68, 1996, pp. 31–62.
58. Carte B. Spampanato 1, diary 27 January 1939.
59. BMOO, XXVI, p. 4. It was the Nationalists who had started calling them Italy's 'step-sister', a label repeated under the regime. See S. Maurano, *Francia la sorellastra*, Milan, 1939.
60. BMOO, XXIII, p. 74.
61. One of the visitors who especially appealed to Mussolini was Jackie Coogan. See P. Orano, *Mussolini da vicino*, Rome, 1935, pp. 100–2. Cf. also Grandi's sententious view that the Americans were a medley of 'titans and children', who could be 'won' or 'lost' by 'almost nothing'. DDI 7s, XI, 100, 2 December 1931, Grandi to Mussolini.
62. BMOO, XXIII, p. 74.
63. Y. De Begnac, *Palazzo Venezia: storia di un regime*, Rome, 1950, p. 643.

Notes

64. L. Frassati, *Il destino passa per Varsavia*, p. 34.

65. BMOO, XXII, p. 138.

66. L. Frassati, *Il destino passa per Varsavia*, p. 35. Cf. his use of almost the same words to the journalist Amicucci 10 years earlier. BMOO, XXIV, p. 350.

67. For an example of regime propaganda in that regard, see G. Massani, *La sua terra*, Bergamo, 1936.

68. See, for example, his typifying of Volpi and Giuriati in Y. De Begnac, *Taccuini mussoliniani* (ed. F. Perfetti), Bologna, 1990, pp. 481; 505–8.

69. *Ibid.*, p. 299. Cf. the view of the (Tuscan) radical Fascist, Berto Ricci, that his time in Ethiopia was fun, since he served among 'the best people in the world – Tuscans'. P. Buchignani, *Un fascismo impossibile: l'eresia di Berto Ricci nella cultura del Ventennio*, Bologna, 1994, p. 277.

70. BMOO, XXIII, p. 304. Cf. XXIII, p. 298, when he told Arnaldo that he agreed with him that Naples was a place of 'much beauty and little substance'.

71. G. Bottai, *Diario 1935–1944* (ed. G.B. Guerri), Milan, 1989, p. 115. Cf., by contrast, Mussolini's claim to a visiting foreign journalist that he himself had utterly united Italians spiritually, and ended any distinction between northerners and southerners. BMOO, XLIV, p. 101.

72. G. Ciano, *Ciano's diary 1939–1943* (ed. M. Muggeridge), London, 1947, p. 392.

73. The whole issue of *Gerarchia*, 13, June 1933, was devoted to praise of the agreement. Among others, Oswald Mosley, a pensioner of the Italian government's secret funds, declared the pact both 'virile' and proof that Fascism did not mean war.

74. For a full archival narrative, see G. Giordano, *Il patto a quattro nella politica estera di Mussolini*, Bologna, 1976.

75. BMOO, XXVI, pp. 36–8.

76. G. Giordano, *Il patto a quattro*, p. 53.

77. PRO FO371/16800/C7361, 5 August 1933, Graham to Simon.

78. BMOO, XXVI, pp. 19–20.

79. His footnotes reveal his continual reliance on her in both volumes of *Mussolini il duce*.

80. R. Quartararo, *Roma tra Londra e Berlino: la politica estera fascista dal 1931 al 1940*, Rome, 1980, p. 28. In this case, she was quoting British Permanent Under-Secretary, Robert Vansittart.

81. For a typical Grandi usage, see DDI 7s, X, 272, 17 May 1931, Grandi to Mussolini.

82. R. Quartararo, *Roma tra Londra e Berlino*, p. 38.

83. See, for example, A.J.P. Taylor, *The origins of the Second World War*, Harmondsworth, 1964, pp. 107–8.

84. Cf., for example, Mussolini's ridiculing of the idea that the powers of the Little Entente together constituted a 'fifth' Great Power. BMOO, XXV, pp. 221–4.

85. See a Mussolini attack on these, sarcastically entitled 'Adagio con Walhalla', in BMOO, XXVI, pp. 6–7.

86. BMOO, XXXVII, 12 April 1933, Mussolini note.

87. F. Suvich, *Memorie 1932–1936* (ed. G. Bianchi), Milan, 1984, pp. 91–4.

88. *Ibid.*, p. 187.

89. For details, see F. D'Amoja, *Declino e prima crisi dell'Europa di Versailles: studio sulla diplomazia italiana ed europea (1931–1933)*, Milan, 1967, pp. 382–391. Cf. BMOO, XXVI, pp. 61–3.

90. R. Quartararo, *Italia-URSS 1917–1941: i rapporti politici*, Naples, 1997, pp. 125–8.

91. For an English-language study of the Italian Navy, confident that its intent was aggressive, see R. Mallett, *The Italian Navy and Fascist expansionism 1935–1940*, London, 1998.

92. For a recent review of these ideas, see P.L. Bassignana, *Fascisti nel paese dei Soviet*, Turin, 2000.

93. R. De Felice, *Mussolini l'alleato 1940–1945 I. l'Italia in guerra 1940–1943*, Turin, 1990, pp. 1175; 1256–71. Cf. Chapters 1 and 17.

94. BMOO, XXVI, pp. 20–1.

95. For a summary, see E. Gentile, 'Impending modernity: Fascism and the ambivalent image of the United States', *Journal of Contemporary History*, 28, 1993, pp. 7–29.

96. BMOO, XXVI, p. 10.

97. BMOO, XXVI, pp. 22–4; 43–5. Cf., for example also, P. Sacerdoti, 'L'America verso il fascismo?', *Gerarchia*, 13, November 1933, pp. 933–43; B. De Ritis, 'L'America si scopre se stessa: lettera dal America del Nord', *Critica Fascista*, 11, 1 June 1933, pp. 212–13; E. Brunetta, 'Esperimento di Roosevelt', *Critica Fascista*, 11, 1 November 1933, pp. 334–5.

98. For an instance of Ciano's preference of the Chinese, among whom he was stationed, to the Japanese, see DDI 7s, XII, 441, 19 November 1932, Ciano to Mussolini.

99. BMOO, XXVI, pp. 154–6.

100. DDI 7s, XV, 376, 10 June 1934, Mussolini to Boscarelli.

101. T. Cianetti, *Memorie dal carcere di Verona* (ed. R. De Felice), Milan, 1983, p. 278.

102. BMOO, XLII, p. 61.

103. F. Bandini, *Claretta: profilo di Clara Petacci e dei suoi tempi*, Milan, 1960, pp. 13–15.

104. M. Petacci, *Chi ama è perduto: mia sorella Claretta*, Gardolo di Trento, 1988, p. 45.

105. F. Bandini, *Claretta*, pp. 22–7.

106. *Ibid.*, pp. 30–2.

107. There are rumours about a sultry affair with a French journalist, Magda Fontages. See G. D'Aurora, *La maschera e la volta di Magda Fontages*, Milan, 1946. She alleged that Mussolini used his violin as a key element in seduction (p. 15). A telephone tap in June 1934 recorded Mussolini's conversation with another mistress, Cornelia Tanzi. See U. Guspini, *L'orecchio del regime: le intercettazioni telefoniche al tempo del fascismo*, Milan, 1973, p. 122. By then, contemporaries noticed that Margherita Sarfatti was in disgrace. See C. Alvaro, *Quasi una vita: giornale di uno scrittore*, Milan, 1950, p. 121.

108. R. De Felice, *Mussolini il duce 1929–1936*, p. 803.

109. F. Bandini, *Claretta*, pp. 40–2.

110. U. Guspini, *L'orecchio del regime*, p. 143.

111. Her younger sister, briefly a film actor under the regime, claims that Federici beat her. See M. Petacci, *Chi ama è perduto*, p. 89.

112. U. Guspini, *L'orecchio del regime*, p. 143.

113. *Ibid.*, p. 151.

114. F. Caplan, *Gore Vidal: a biography*, New York, 1999, p. 96.

115. Her biographer, by contrast, says that she had naturally curly hair (and a big bust). See F. Bandini, *Claretta*, p. 11.

116. E. Cerruti, *Ambassador's wife*, p. 224.

117. In 1934 he boasted to a foreign journalist that he had kept up with outdoor swims of half an hour or more until 25 October, despite the encroaching cold. See BMOO, XLIV, p. 100.

118. E. Caviglia, *Diario (aprile 1925–marzo 1945)*, Rome, 1952, p. 122.

119. See, for example, *Il Popolo d'Italia*, 26 January 1934.

120. F. Anfuso, *Roma Berlino Salò (1936–1945)*, Milan, 1950, p. 141. Anfuso also remarked that there were too many photos and other reproductions of the *Duce* in the more public rooms, although Mussolini seemed not to notice them (p. 142).

121. V. Mussolini, *Vita con mio padre*, Milan, 1957, p. 41.

122. SPDCR 108 has regular reports on such matters.

123. S. Petrucci, *In Puglia con Mussolini*, Rome, 1935, pp. 32–5.

124. F. Ciano, *Quando il nonno fece fucilare papà*, Milan, 1991, pp. 36–7. The grandchildren of Mussolini had a German governess (p. 31).

125. N. D'Aroma, *Mussolini segreto*, p. 121.

Notes

126. *Ibid.*, p. 108.

127. Y. De Begnac, *Palazzo Venezia*, pp. 11–13.

128. R. De Felice, *Mussolini il fascista II. l'organizzazione dello stato fascista 1925–1929*, Turin, 1968, p. 313.

129. SPDCR 3, 22 October 1934, report saying that Balbo blamed Starace and was determined to organise a coterie of friends to plot against him. Among these were thought to be the Venetians, Volpi and Giorgio Cini.

130. SPDCR 79, 26 July 1934, D'Andrea to Bocchini.

131. SPDCR 79, 24 July 1934, Prefect of Bologna to Mussolini.

132. His term was extended by 5 years in 1939 because he refused to acknowledge any guilt on his part. See SPDCR 79, 19 July 1939, Benigni to Mussolini. There is a graphic file of letters from Arpinati to his family in DGPS, Confinati politici 40. They ostentatiously eschew direct political reference.

133. SPDCR 94, 23 October 1934, note.

134. Y. De Begnac, *Palazzo Venezia*, p. 557.

135. SPDCR 49, 3 May 1933, Starace to Mussolini.

136. SPDCR 79, 17 October 1933, Martignoni to Starace.

137. SPDCR 49, 3 May 1933, Starace to Mussolini.

138. SPDCR 25, 10 September 1934, Starace to Mussolini.

139. SPDCR 25, 10 September 1934, Starace to Mussolini; 49, 15 September 1934, Starace to Mussolini.

140. Starace warned him against an amnesty for Arpinati and his friends. SPDCR 49, 15 September 1934, Starace to Mussolini.

141. As he began his affair with Petacci, Mussolini may have been amused by the regular reports he received on Farinacci's truck with Gianna Pederzini, an opera singer, who was eventually recorded saying loudly that the only thing the two had in common was bed. See SPDCR 40.

142. SPDCR 40, 3 August 1933, Farinacci to Mussolini.

143. SPDCR 79, 10 June 1940, Arpinati to Mussolini.

144. Even Starace expressed doubts about morale in Bologna. See SPDCR 49, 15 September 1934, Starace to Mussolini.

145. SPDCR 94, 11 May 1933, report. In 1932 Starace had also tried to get off a speeding charge by telling the *carabiniero* who stopped him that he was the *Duce*'s nephew. In a later telephone call Starace was recorded as saying that the traditionally monarchist *carabinieri* were no more than 'brigands'. See SPDCR, 20, 23 August 1932, reports.

146. See, for example, *Augustea*, 10, 15 June 1934.

147. BMOO, XXVI, p. 188.

148. R. Farinacci, 'Rilievi mensili', *La Vita Italiana*, XLIII, 15 March 1934, pp. 264–9. Cf., for example, M. Sertoli, 'L'Austria è una Nazione', *Critica Fascista*, 12, 1 February 1934, p. 52.

149. BMOO, XXVI, pp. 232–3.

150. G. Sommi Picenardi, 'Rosenberg, l'Anticristo', *La Vita Italiana*, 43, 15 June 1934, pp. 668–77.

151. F. Anfuso, *Roma Berlino Salò (1936–1945)*, p. 42.

152. See R.J.B. Bosworth, 'Golf and Italian Fascism', in M.R. Farrally and A.J. Cochran (eds), *Science and Golf III*, London, 1999, pp. 346–7.

153. E. Cerruti, *Ambassador's wife*, p. 149.

154. The Fascist press had long exulted in the *Duce*'s alleged ability to switch into four languages while speaking. See *Il Popolo d'Italia*, 9 September 1927.

155. For accounts of the well-known exchanges, see D. Mack Smith, *Mussolini's Roman Empire*, London, 1976, pp. 53–4; R. De Felice, *Mussolini il duce 1929–1936*, pp. 494–7.

156. DDI 7s, XV, 419, 19–20 June 1934, Renzetti to Mussolini.

Notes

157. DDI 7s, 396, 13 June 1934, Renzetti to Mussolini. Sweetly, Renzetti added that one happy result of the meeting would be the arrival of more German tourists in Italy. 401, 14 June 1934, Renzetti to Mussolini.

158. DDI 7s, XV, 411, 13 June 1934, Suvich to Dollfuss.

159. DDI 7s, XV, 430, 22 June 1934, Mussolini to De Vecchi; 469, 2 July 1934, memorandum of De Vecchi–Mussolini talk.

160. I. Kershaw, *Hitler 1889–1936*, pp. 512–17.

161. *Augustea*, 10, 13 July 1934, pp. 385–6.

162. DDI 7s, XV, 528, 15 July 1934, Mussolini to Grazzi.

163. DDI 7s, XV, 458, 27–8 June 1934, Dollfuss to Suvich.

164. SPDCR 71, 1, 2 July 1934 police reports of the preparations for this event.

165. R. De Felice, *Mussolini il duce 1929–1936*, pp. 499–500.

166. See, for example, R. Farinacci, 'Rilievi mensili', *La Vita Italiana*, XLIV, 15 August 1934, pp. 137–142, noting that Mussolini had reacted so swiftly because he understood the German temperament and, in so doing, he had 'interpreted the thoughts of civilised Europe'. Oddly, Preziosi took the occasion to hail Farinacci as alone among the Fascist chiefs in remaining sceptical against the widespread 'hosannas' for the Nazis in Italy. See *La Vita Italiana*, 15 September 1934, p. 370. Cf. U. Nanni, 'La questione dell' "Anschluss"', *Gerarchia*, 14, September 1934, pp. 757–65, which warned that 'seventy-five million' Germans on the Italian border would be bound to unleash 'Pan-German' ambition against Italy itself.

167. R. De Felice, *Mussolini il duce 1929–1936*, p. 501.

168. SPDCR 71, 21 March 1938, A. Dollfuss to Mussolini.

169. SPDCR 71, August 1934 report.

170. M. Stone, *The patron state: culture and politics in Fascist Italy*, Princeton, 1998, p. 77.

171. BMOO, XXVI, pp. 309–10.

172. BMOO, XXVI, pp. 327–8.

173. BMOO, XXVI, p. 315.

174. BMOO, XXVI, pp. 318–20. Predictably, Mussolini was seconded by the press. See, for example, G. Selvi, 'Il mito della razza', *Gerarchia*, 14, October 1934, pp. 803–7. Cf., in the same issue, N. Goldmann, 'La crisi dell'ebraismo', pp. 851–4, worrying about Zionism but emphasising that Italy was a place where Jews kept 'legal equality'. With his usual personal interest in Napoleon, Mussolini's reading of a new study by Louis Madelin convinced him, somewhat paradoxically, that the emperor had been a 'pure blooded Italian'. See BMOO, XXVI, p. 377.

175. BMOO, XXVI, 1 July, 9 September 1933, Mussolini to Dollfuss; DDI 7s, XV, 180, 3 May 1934, Mussolini to Dollfuss.

176. For background, see J. Rothschild, *East Central Europe between the two world wars*, Seattle, 1974, pp. 171–6.

177. R. Guariglia, *Ricordi 1922–1946*, Naples, 1949, pp. 192–203.

178. DDI 7s, XV, 54, 31 March 1934, minute of meeting; cf. 100, 14 April 1934, Balbo to Mussolini. Cf. XVI, 16, 3 October 1934, agreement between the PNF and the 'Persian Nationalist Party', with the Italians offering money, arms, ammunition and training.

179. See, for example, DDI 7s, XV, 825, 18 September 1934, Mussolini to Galli, with an example of a Croat paper which had said that a hundred Croats could rout ten thousand Italians.

180. R. De Felice, *Mussolini il duce 1929–1936*, pp. 514–18.

181. DDI 7s, XVI, 112, 6 November 1934, memorandum of Mussolini–Gömbös meeting.

182. DDI 7s, XVI, 157, 17 November 1934, memorandum of Mussolini–Schuschnigg meeting.

183. For the case of a subtle Swiss, see R. Joseph, 'The Martignoni affair: how a Swiss politician deceived Mussolini', *Journal of Contemporary History*, 9, 1974, pp. 77–90.

Notes

184. R.J.B. Bosworth, *Italy the least of the Great Powers: Italian foreign policy before the First World War*, Cambridge, 1979, pp. 119–26.
185. For Guariglia's account, see R. Guariglia, *Ricordi*.
186. See, for example, DDI 7s, X, 329, 11 June 1931, De Bono to Mussolini.
187. DDI 7s, XII, 393, 5 November 1932, memorandum of meeting at Ministy of Colonies; 534, 12 December 1932, De Bono to Mussolini.
188. For a narrative of developments, see R. De Felice, *Mussolini il duce 1929–1936*, pp. 597–610.
189. DDI 7s, XV, 219, 12 May 1934, Badoglio to De Bono.
190. DDI 7s, XV, 686, 10 August 1934, Mussolini to De Bono and others. The note can also be found in BMOO, XLII, pp. 84–5.
191. *The Scotsman*, 23, 28 August 1934.
192. DDI 7s, XVI, 358, 30 December 1934, Mussolini directive. Also available in BMOO, XXXVII, pp. 141–3.

CHAPTER 13

1. DDI 7s, XVI, 358, 30 December 1934, Mussolini directive.
2. R. Trevisani of the University of Trieste in preface to E. Ronchi, *Mussolini: economista della rivoluzione*, Rome, 1930.
3. E. Ronchi, *Mussolini: creatore d'economia*, Rome, 1936, pp. 10; 15.
4. F. Suvich, *Memorie 1932–1936* (ed. G. Bianchi), Milan, 1984, pp. 4–6.
5. A. Aquarone, 'Italy: the crisis and the corporative economy', *Journal of Contemporary History*, 4, 1969, p. 38.
6. O. Mosca, *Nessuno volle i miei dollari d'oro*, Naples, 1958, p. 252.
7. S. La Francesca, *La politica economica del fascismo*, Bari, 1976, pp. 48; 71.
8. R. De Felice, *Mussolini il duce I. gli anni del consenso 1929–1936*, Turin, 1974, p. 63.
9. *Ibid.*, p. 74.
10. R.J.B. Bosworth, 'Tourist planning in Fascist Italy and the limits of a totalitarian culture', *Contemporary European History*, 6, 1997, p. 17. The Vatican's own finances were troubled, with a solution only being found later in the 1930s through increased reliance on the USA. This shift in Vatican investments had damaging potential for the Italian economy. See J.F. Pollard, 'The Vatican and the Wall Street crash: Bernardino Nogara and papal finances in the early 1930s', *Historical Journal*, 42, 1999, pp. 1086–91.
11. S. La Francesca, *La politica economica del fascismo*, p. 48.
12. *Ibid.*, p. 77.
13. C.S. Maier, *In search of stability: explorations in historical political economy*, Cambridge, 1987, p. 91.
14. For table, see V. Zamagni, *The economic history of Italy 1860–1990*, Oxford, 1993, p. 246.
15. F. Guarneri, *Battaglie economiche fra le due guerre* (ed. L. Zani), Bologna, 1988, p. 457.
16. R. De Felice, *Mussolini il duce 1929–1936*, pp. 175–6.
17. BMOO, XXVII, pp. 241–8.
18. S. La Francesca, *La politica economica del fascismo*, p. 85.
19. SPDCR 4, 6 February 1933, 10 March 1934, both Mussolini to Jung.
20. N. D'Aroma, *Mussolini segreto*, Rocca San Casciano, 1958, p. 120.
21. Y. De Begnac, *Taccuini mussoliniani* (ed. F. Perfetti), Bologna, 1990, p. 241.
22. See L. Passerini, *Fascism in popular memory: the cultural experience of the Turin working class*, Cambridge, 1987, p. 195.
23. BMOO, XXVI, p. 401.
24. G. Bottai, 'La rivoluzione nella Rivoluzione', *Critica Fascista*, 11, 15 December 1933, pp. 461–2.

Notes

25. For an optimistic account by one Fascist union boss, convinced that social progress was indeed occurring, see P. Capoferri, *Venti anni col fascismo e con i sindacati*, Milan, 1957.

26. BMOO, XXVI, pp. 89–96.

27. BMOO, XXVI, p. 362.

28. For examples, see M. Isnenghi (ed.), *I luoghi della memoria* (3 vols), Bari, 1996–7.

29. V. De Grazia, *The culture of consent: mass organization of leisure in fascist Italy*, Cambridge, 1981, p. 24.

30. *Ibid.*, p. 91.

31. *Ibid.*, pp. 37–9.

32. *Ibid.*, pp. 54–5.

33. BMOO, XXVI, pp. 16–18.

34. The key analyst here is J. Herf, *Reactionary modernism: technology, culture and politics in Weimar and the Third Reich*, Cambridge, 1986.

35. *Il Popolo d'Italia*, 6 May 1924.

36. C. Langobardi, *Land-reclamation in Italy: rural revival in the building of a nation*, London, 1936, p. iv. The other chief new centre in the Pontine area was called, with Fascist compromise, Sabaudia, after the ruling dynasty.

37. R. De Felice, *Mussolini il duce 1929–1936*, pp. 142–7.

38. O. Gaspari, *L'emigrazione veneta nell'Agro Pontino durante il periodo fascista*, Brescia, 1985, p. 21.

39. F.M. Snowden, '"Fields of death": malaria in Italy, 1861–1962', *Modern Italy*, 4, 1999, pp. 25–57.

40. For an account of life in the Tuscan Alps, where the writ of Fascist government scarcely ran, see R. Sarti, *Long live the strong: a history of rural society in the Apennines mountains*, Amherst, 1985.

41. N. Revelli, *Il mondo dei vinti: testimonianze di vita contadina*, Turin, 1977, vol. II, p. 98.

42. *Ibid.*, vol. I, p. 47.

43. M. Salvati, *Il regime e gli impiegati: la nazionalizzazione piccolo-borghese nel ventennio fascista*, Bari, 1992, p. 134.

44. Y. De Begnac, *Palazzo Venezia: storia di un regime*, Rome, 1950, p. 394.

45. A. De' Stefani, *Una riforma al rogo*, Rome, 1963, pp. 9–12.

46. BMOO, XXIV, p. 119.

47. M. Salvati, *Il regime e gli impiegati*, p. 215.

48. Y. De Begnac, *Taccuini mussoliniani*, p. 436.

49. Y. De Begnac, *Palazzo Venezia*, p. 116.

50. See, for example, BMOO, XXIII, pp. 291–2; XXIV, p. 329.

51. BMOO, XXIV, pp. 108–9. He was speaking at the opening of the Seventh National Philosophy Conference.

52. T.M. Mazzatosta, *Il regime fascista tra educazione e propaganda (1935–1943)*, Bologna, 1978, p. 23.

53. By 1939 so pervasive was Mussolini's thought alleged to be that an entrepreneurial Fascist published a dictionary of it, offered to the market 'as a manual of genuine practical utility for every individual and business concern'. See B. Biancini (ed.), *Dizionario mussoliniano: mille affermazioni e definizioni del Duce*, Milan, 1939. In 1941 a bibliography of studies of Mussolini's thought ran to eighty-one pages. See E. Sulis (ed.), *Mussolini e il Fascismo*, Rome, 1941.

54. A. Lodolini, *La storia della razza italiana da Augusto a Mussolini dedicata agli italiani di Mussolini e specialmente ai giovani e alle scuole*, Rome, 1939, p. 312.

55. O. Tesini, *Il grande educatore dell'Italia nuova*, Palermo, 1931, p. 9.

56. N. Mezzetti, *Mussolini e la questione sociale*, Rome, 1931, p. 100.

57. For a typical enthusing about this, see F. Mezzasoma, *Essenza del GUF*, Cremona, 1937.

Notes

58. F. Gambetti, *Gli anni che scottano*, Milan, 1967, p. 118.

59. See the long, and typically pompous, C. De Vecchi di Val Cismon, *Bonifica fascista della cultura*, Milan, 1937.

60. For an account of this organisation, see P.V. Cannistraro, *La fabbrica del consenso: fascismo e mass media*, Bari, 1975, pp. 101–66.

61. BMOO, XXV, p. 104.

62. BMOO, XXV, p. 143.

63. BMOO, XXV, p. 136.

64. D. Marchesini, 'Un episodio della politica culturale del regime: la scuola di mistica fascista', *Rivista di storia contemporanea*, 1, 1972, p. 92. Cf. further D. Marchesini, *La scuola dei gerarchi: mistica fascista: storia, problemi, istituzioni*, Milan, 1976.

65. D. Marchesini, 'Un episodio della politica culturale del regime', p. 91.

66. Y. De Begnac, *Taccuini mussoliniani*, pp. 375–6.

67. G.P. Brunetta, *Storia del cinema italiano 1895–1945*, Rome, 1979, p. 297.

68. *Ibid.*, p. 242.

69. *Ibid.*, p. 308.

70. V. De Grazia, 'Mass culture and sovereignty: the American challenge to European cinemas', *Journal of Modern History*, 61, 1989, p. 73.

71. J. Hay, *Popular film culture in Fascist Italy: the passing of the* Rex, Bloomington, 1987, p. 96.

72. S. Falasca-Zamponi, *Fascist spectacle: the aesthetics of power in Mussolini's Italy*, Berkeley, 1997, pp. 7; 148.

73. *Ibid.*, p. 148.

74. E. Gentile, *The sacralization of politics in Fascist Italy*, Cambridge, Mass., 1996, p. ix.

75. P. Orano, *Mussolini, fondatore dell'impero*, Rome, 1936, p. 14.

76. M. Stone, *The patron state: culture and politics in Fascist Italy*, Princeton, 1998, p. 54.

77. SPDCR 102, 12 June 1934, Mascagni letter.

78. R. Zangrandi, *Il lungo viaggio attraverso il fascismo: contributo alla storia di una generazione*, Milan, 1964, p. 15. For a wonderfully self-interested article, urging government intervention to provide more jobs for intellectuals (like himself), see R. Zangrandi, 'Un giovane per i giovani: il problema della disoccupazione intellettuale', *Gerarchia*, 18, October 1937, pp. 706–8.

79. R. De Felice, *Mussolini il duce 1929–1936*, pp. 610–14.

80. One of the more important works of the time was F. Marconcini, *Culle vuote: il declino delle nascite in Europa: sviluppo–cause–rimedi*, Como, 1935. The spirit of empire could fill the 'empty cots'.

81. For a narrative of these matters, see R.J.B. Bosworth, *Italy, the least of the Great Powers: Italian foreign policy before the First World War*, Cambridge, 1979, pp. 127–95.

82. BMOO, XXVII, p. 3.

83. For an account of this deterioration, highly critical of the French, see D. Bolech Cecchi, *Non bruciare i ponti con Roma: le relazioni fra l'Italia, la Gran Bretagna e la Francia dall'accordo di Monaco allo scoppio della seconda guerra mondiale*, Milan, 1986.

84. DDI 7s, XVI, 391, 5 January; 399, 6 January 1935, Mussolini–Laval talks.

85. BMOO, XXVII, p. 9. For the actual accords, see DDI 7s, XVI, 403, 7 January 1935. With his love of philosophy-speak, Mussolini now took the moment to attack the German mystical nationalist, Ernst Jünger, for his sarcasm about Italy's effort in the First World War (BMOO, XXVII, pp. 9–10).

86. For a French denial, see G. Bonnet, *Quai d'Orsay*, Douglas, 1965, pp. 118–19. On the Italian side, Guariglia was convinced that Mussolini did believe that he had gained full French support. R. Guariglia, *Ricordi 1922–1946*, Naples, 1949, pp. 220–1.

87. R. Quartararo, *Roma tra Londra e Berlino: la politica estera fascista dal 1931 al 1940*, Rome, 1980, pp. 118–31.

Notes

88. C.A. Micaud, *The French Right and Nazi Germany 1933–1939: a study of public opinion*, New York, 1964, p. 10.

89. R. De Felice, *Mussolini il duce 1929–1936*, p. 615.

90. The best-known example was Germanophobe Permanent Under-Secretary, Robert Vansittart, who believed that Rome was worth a mass. For his own rococo account, see R. Vansittart, *The mist procession: autobiography*, London, 1958. For an analysis, cf. A.L. Goldman, 'Sir Robert Vansittart's search for Italian co-operation against Hitler 1933–36', *Journal of Contemporary History*, 9, 1974, pp. 93–130.

91. DDI 7s, XVI, 694, 4 March 1935, Cavagnari to Mussolini.

92. G. Rochat, *Militari e politici nella preparazione della campagna d'Etiopia: studio e documenti 1932–1936*, Milan, 1971, p. 129.

93. E. Caviglia, *Diario (aprile 1925–marzo 1945)*, Rome, 1952, p. 133.

94. P.V. Cannistraro and B.R. Sullivan, *Il Duce's other woman*, New York, 1993, p. 467.

95. For his own grandiloquent account, made available also in English, see E. De Bono, *Anno XIIII [sic]: the conquest of an empire*, London, 1937. In De Bono's view, only he and his *Duce* knew what was going to happen (p. 13).

96. G. Rochat, *Militari e politici nella preparazione della campagna d'Etiopia*, p. 269.

97. DDI 7s, XVI, 492, 25 January 1935, Mussolini to Grandi.

98. DDI 7s, XVI, 523, 1 February 1935, Grandi to Mussolini.

99. DDI 7s, XVI, 545, 4 February 1935, Grandi to Mussolini.

100. DDI 7s, XVI, 626, 20 February 1935, Grandi to Mussolini. At this time Mussolini wrote ingratiatingly to his ambassadors in Washington, Moscow and Tokyo, assuring the governments of the USA, USSR and Japan that Italy planned them no harm. See, for example, 659, 676, 682.

101. DDI 7s, XVI, 770, 8 March 1935, Mussolini to De Bono.

102. One Italian account, however, suggests that there were some disadvantages in operating in the provinces. MacDonald broke his only pair of glasses on arrival at Stresa and they could only be replaced in Milan. He thus wandered around the meeting in short-sighted bewilderment. See P. Quaroni, *Diplomatic bags: an ambassador's memoirs*, London, 1966, p. 8.

103. BMOO, XXVII, p. 53.

104. The phrase *la paix de l'Europe* was indeed there. See DDI 7s, XVI, 922, 14 April 1935, Stresa resolution.

105. A.J.P. Taylor, *The origins of the Second World War*, Harmondsworth, 1964, p. 120.

106. R. Guariglia, *Ricordi*, p. 229.

107. DDI 8s, I, 247, 18 May 1935, Mussolini to De Bono.

108. See, for example, D. Mack Smith, *Mussolini's Roman empire*, London, 1976, pp. 59–71.

109. DDI 8s, I, 60, 20 April 1935, Mussolini to Grandi.

110. BMOO, XXVII, p. 78.

111. For a classic example, see the paperback A. Lavagetto, *La vita eroica del capitano Bottego (1893–1897)*, Milan, 1934.

112. For an endorsement of the line that this was indeed Mussolini's purpose, see R. Mallett, 'Fascist foreign policy and official Italian views of Anthony Eden in the 1930s', *Historical Journal*, 43, 2000, pp. 157–87.

113. DDI 8s, I, 114, 30 April 1935, SIM to Mussolini.

114. W. Phillips, *Ventures in diplomacy*, London, 1955, p. 80.

115. Quoted by G.W. Baer, *Test case: Italy, Ethiopia and the League of Nations*, Stanford, 1976, p. 62.

116. For a detailed English-language account, see G.W. Baer, *The coming of the Italian-Ethiopian war*, Cambridge Mass., 1967, pp. 190–200.

117. R.J.B. Bosworth, *Italy, the least of the Great Powers*, p. 334.

Notes

118. After 1945, Guariglia was still affronted by the inadequacy of the British offer. See R. Guariglia, *Ricordi*, p. 246.
119. DDI 8s, I, 431, 24 June 1935, second Mussolini–Eden talk.
120. DDI 8s, I, 433, 25 June 1935, third Mussolini–Eden talk.
121. DDI 8s, I, 419, 21 June 1935, Renzetti to Ciano.
122. *The Times*, 5 July 1935.
123. DDI 8s, I, 475, 2 July 1935, Grandi to Mussolini.
124. D. Dutton, *Anthony Eden: a life and reputation*, London, 1997, pp. 47; 69; 97.
125. *Ibid.*, p. 394.
126. D. Darrah, *Hail Caesar!* Boston, 1936, p. 100.
127. For the recollections of Darrah of the *Chicago Herald Tribune* in this regard, see *ibid.*, pp. 315–21.
128. G. Seldes, *Sawdust Caesar: the untold history of Mussolini and Fascism*, London, 1936, p. 381.
129. *Ibid.*, p. 86.
130. *Evening Standard*, 19 October 1935.
131. *Evening Standard*, 6 July 1935.
132. See, for example, E. Polson Newman, *The Mediterranean and its problems*, London, 1927.
133. See E. Polson Newman, *Ethiopian realities*, London, 1936; *Italy's conquest of Ethiopia*, London, 1937.
134. L. Goglia, 'La propaganda italiana a sostegno della guerra contro l'Etiopia svolta in Gran Bretagna nel 1935–36', *Storia contemporanea*, 15, 1984, pp. 845–906.
135. DDI 8s, I, 657, 3 August 1935, Mussolini to Grandi.
136. DDI 8s, I, 548, 16 July 1935, Mussolini–Chambrun talk.
137. DDI 8s, II, 13, 2 September 1935, Mussolini–Chambrun talk.
138. G.W. Baer, *The coming of the Italian-Ethiopian war*, p. 327.
139. DDI 8s, II, 146, 19 September 1935, Grandi to Mussolini.
140. DDI 8s, II, 202, 29 September 1935, Mussolini to De Bono.
141. For a highly typical article written by a young man destined to become both an Anti-Fascist and a patriotic historian of empire, see C. Zaghi, 'Da Assab ad Adua', *Meridiani*, 2, October–November 1935, pp. 46–52.
142. BMOO, XXVII, p. 159.
143. BMOO, XXXVIII, p. 138.
144. SPDCR 87, 26 May 1935, Lanzillo to Mussolini.
145. A. Pirelli, *Taccuini 1922–1943* (ed. D. Barbone), Bologna, 1984, pp. 133–4.
146. *Ibid.*, p. 147. De' Stefani, by contrast, declared that Italy had been savaged by sanctions for years as its emigration history demonstrated. See A. De' Stefani, *Garanzie di potenza: saggi economici*, Bologna, 1936, p. 178.
147. The establishment journal, *Nuova Antologia*, provides endless examples.
148. G. Bottai, 'Abissinia: impresa rivoluzionaria', *Critica Fascista*, 13, 15 July 1935, pp. 357–9.
149. F. Guarneri, *Battaglie economiche*, p. 504.
150. For a review of these matters, see R. Mallett, *The Italian navy and Fascist expansionism 1935–1940*, London, 1998, pp. 7–47.
151. For a typical example, see the interview he gave to a journalist from the ultra-conservative and pro-Italian *Morning Post* of London in BMOO, XXVII, pp. 139–41.
152. DDI 8s, II, 331, 13 October 1935, Mussolini to Cerruti; 357, 16 October 1935, Mussolini–Chambrun talk.
153. DDI 8s, II, 335, 13 October 1935, Pignatti to Mussolini.
154. DDI 8s, II, 437, 20 October 1935, Mussolini to De Bono.
155. DDI 8s, II, 660, 18 November 1935, Suvich to Mussolini.
156. DDI 8s, II, 795, 4 December 1935, Mussolini to Grandi.

Notes

157. G.M. Gathorne-Hardy, *A short history of international affairs 1920–1939*, Oxford, 1950, pp. 416–17.

158. *The Times*, 13, 16 December 1935.

159. *The Evening Standard*, 30 December 1935. Others of his cartoons readily invoked stereotypes of Italian inferiority. Fascist troops were depicted (30 November) as cursing their want of 'hair-oil'; while Mussolini appeared with monkey and organ, begging charity for 'forty million children' (28 December).

160. See, for example, BMOO, XXVII, pp. 205–6.

161. Badoglio estimated Ethiopian forces confronting him at 350 000 men. Typically of a colonial war, neither he nor so all-embracing a historian as De Felice have bothered to estimate the Ethiopian death toll during the war which must have run into the tens of thousands. Up to 40 per cent of 'Italian' troops, were 'colonial soldiers', that is, black ones, notably from Eritrea and Somalia. See Badoglio's account of the war, with a subsidised English translation made available as P. Badoglio, *The war in Abyssinia*, London, 1937, pp. 8–11. The book came complete with a preface by Mussolini. Badoglio's juniors praised his military achievement effusively raising 'Him' to the level of those who could rate capital letters when 'The Man' was mentioned. See Q. Armellini, *Con Badoglio in Etiopia*, Milan, pp. 10; 257.

162. Italy used 1597 gas bombs weighing 317 tonnes. See A. Del Boca (ed.), *I gas di Mussolini: il fascismo e la guerra d'Etiopia*, Rome, 1996, p. 20. Mussolini had also authorised Graziani to use gas 'as a last resort' in December 1935. See R. De Felice, *Mussolini il duce 1929–1936*, p. 707. Suvich advised gas should only be used in 'military necessity'. DDI 8s, III, 36, 10 January 1936, Suvich to Mussolini.

163. A. Del Boca, *The Ethiopian war 1935–1941*, Chicago, 1969, p. 113.

164. For his grovelling early views on 'Fascism and history', see *Il Popolo d'Italia*, 22 May 1934.

165. A droll controversy had broken out over the popular song, *Faccetta nera* (Little black face), a ditty which implied some kind of love between Italian soldier and Ethiopian maid. By May 1936, however, it was decided, in the name of Mussolini, that the words were inappropriate and the song 'stupid'. See C. Savoia, 'Appunti del buon gusto', *Meridiani*, 2, April–May 1936, pp. 19–20.

166. I. Montanelli, 'Dentro la guerra', *Civiltà Fascista*, 3, January 1936, pp. 38–9.

167. SPDCR 108, 17 April 1936, Mussolini to Vittorio and Bruno.

168. V. Mussolini, *Voli sulle Ambe*, Florence, 1937, pp. 27–8.

169. *Ibid.*, p. 147.

170. His diary entries throughout his stint in Africa are in G. Bottai, *Diario 1935–1944* (ed. G.B. Guerri), Milan, 1989, pp. 53–105.

171. *Ibid.*, pp. 102–3. Bottai had greeted Farinacci's arrival with some pleasure, since he was such a man of the people, even if, Bottai added wrily, his career as a lawyer had made him a devil's advocate indeed, and a well-paid one (p. 90). After his return 'wounded' to Italy, Farinacci kept Mussolini up with the efforts of Bologna doctors to construct a 'special prosthesis' for him. SPDCR 44, 6 June 1936, Farinacci to Mussolini.

172. R. De Felice, *Mussolini il duce 1929–1936*, p. 758.

173. The papers of Anthony Eden, PRO FO 954/13A/It/36/9, 30 May 1936, Drummond to Eden.

174. G. Gentile, 'Dopo la fondazione dell'impero', *Civiltà Fascista*, 3, May 1936, pp. 321–34.

175. A. Del Boca, *The Ethiopian war*, p. 212.

176. R. De Felice, *Mussolini il duce 1929–1936*, p. 642.

177. G.W. Baer, *Test case*, p. 79.

178. It was now that he was elevated to become Duke of Addis Ababa. Hearing that he had also acquired an honorary doctorate, Farinacci wondered if he could be made a canon or a cardinal as well. SPDCR 67, 22 January 1937, Farinacci to Mussolini.

179. G. Bottai, *Diario 1935–1944*, pp. 78–9.

Notes

180. *Ibid.*, p. 61.
181. *Ibid.*, p. 66 gives the example of Bottai and his friends being convinced that Badoglio's gain over De Bono had been plotted by Balbo and Lessona.
182. The classic case was the philosopher of universal Fascism, Asvero Gravelli. See *ibid.*, p. 77.
183. See *ibid.*, p. 90 on his *circoletto*.
184. In January 1936, Suvich reported that he had been playing up rumours that Italy intended to switch to the German side to impress foreign diplomats. DDI 8s, III, 131, 29 January 1936, Suvich to Mussolini. Hitler let Suvich know that he was sure the Italians would win. 241, 17 February 1936, Suvich–Hassell talk.
185. See, for example, DDI 8s, III, 564, 2 April; 763, 26 April 1936, both Mussolini to Attolico.
186. For the details, see F. Minniti, 'Il problema degli armamenti nella preparazione militare italiana dal 1935 al 1943', *Storia contemporanea*, 9, 1978 and as summarised in R. Mallett, *The Italian navy*, p. 60. Expenditure in 1936–37 was almost four times the total in 1934–35.
187. G. Bottai, *Diario 1935–1944*, p. 57.
188. BMOO, XXVII, p. 268.

CHAPTER 14

1. P. Orano, *Mussolini, fondatore dell'impero*, Rome, 1936, appendix of Mussolinian writing under the caption *pagine apostoliche*.
2. A. Gravelli, *Uno e molti: interpretazioni spirituali di Mussolini*, Rome, 1938, p. 55.
3. *Ibid.*, p. 106.
4. *Ibid.*, p. 31.
5. A. Lodolini, *La storia della razza italiana da Augusto a Mussolini dedicata agli italiani di Mussolini e specialmente ai giovani e alle scuole*, Rome, 1939, p. 290.
6. U. Burani, *Ineluttabilità mussoliniana*, Rome, 1939, pp. 43; 71; 78.
7. G. Villaroel, *Realtà e mito di Mussolini*, Turin, 1938, p. 192.
8. Returning from service in Ethiopia, Bottai found himself greeted by 'a statue and not a man'. See G. Bottai, *Diario 1935–1944* (ed. G.B. Guerri), Milan, 1989, pp. 109–10.
9. For a narrative, see A. Spinosa, *I figli del Duce*, Milan, 1983, pp. 115–17. In Mussolini's private files, the most personal letter of regret over the illness was written by Farinacci. SPDCR 43, 10 July 1936, Farinacci to Mussolini.
10. A. Lessona, *Un ministro di Mussolini racconta*, Milan, 1973, p. 174.
11. See, for example, V. Mussolini (ed.), *Anno XIII – Ludi Iuvenalis*, Rome, 1935.
12. A. Spinosa, *I figli del Duce*, p. 155.
13. Y. De Begnac, *Taccuini mussoliniani* (ed. F. Perfetti), Bologna, 1990, p. 423.
14. G. Ansaldo, *Il giornalista di Ciano: diarii 1932–1943*, Bologna, 2000, p. 121.
15. SPDCR 109, 12 October 1938, police report.
16. See, for example, *L'Illustrazione italiana*, 14 February 1937.
17. SPDCR 109, 6 April 1938, police report.
18. SPDCR 109, 7 November 1936, police report on Gina. For images of this marriage, see the full coverage in *L'Illustrazione italiana*, 6 February 1938.
19. SPDCR 109, 12 January 1940 note. Marina Mussolini was born on 6 March 1940.
20. G. Pini and D. Susmel, *Mussolini: l'uomo e l'opera*, Florence, 1953–55, vol. III, p. 183.
21. Somewhat ironically a nostalgic *Duce*'s cookbook was published in 1988, evidencing the revival of Mussolini's reputation in Italy. See V. Luchinat and G.F. Borelli (eds), *Le ricette del Duce*, Modena, 1988. Many of its recipes would not have been approved by the *Duce*'s doctors.
22. N. D'Aroma, *Mussolini segreto*, Rocca San Casciano, 1958, p. 45.
23. F. Bandini, *Claretta: profilo di Clara Petacci e dei suoi tempi*, Milan, 1960, p. 21.

Notes

24. M. Petacci, *Chi ama è perduta: mia sorella Claretta*, Gardolo di Trento, 1988, p. 32.

25. For background, see the diaries of Giovanni Ansaldo, sometimes an Anti-Fascist, sometimes a Fascist and, most often, confused, but also from 1936 the editor of *Il Telegrafo*: G. Ansaldo, *L'antifascista riluttante: memorie del carcere e del confino 1926–1927*, Bologna, 1992; *Diario di prigionia* (ed. R. De Felice), Bologna, 1993; *Il giornalista di Ciano*.

26. G.B. Guerri, *Galeazzo Ciano: una vita 1903–1944*, Milan, 1979, p. 18.

27. D. Susmel, *Vita sbagliata di Galeazzo Ciano*, Milan, 1962, p. 18.

28. G.B. Guerri, *Galeazzo Ciano*, pp. 34–5; 41.

29. A. Lessona, *Un ministro di Mussolini*, p. 135.

30. R. Ducci, *La bella gioventù*, Bologna, 1996, p. 144. Fabrizio and Marzio addressed their grandfather as *nonno-duce*. See O. Vergani, *Ciano: una lunga confessione*, Milan, 1974, p. 40.

31. G. Bottai, *Diario 1935–1944*, p. 90. Ironically, but typical of the weakness of the man, Bottai was often a member.

32. It was rumoured he held 40 per cent of the shares of the *Azienda Italiana Petroli Albanesi*. F. Bojano, *In the wake of the goose-step*, London, 1944, p. 110.

33. F. Maugeri, *From the ashes of disgrace*, New York, 1948, p. 89.

34. The best edition is G. Ciano, *Diario 1937–1943* (ed. R. De Felice), Milan, 1980.

35. I am borrowing from the title of R. Moseley, *Mussolini's shadow: the double life of Galeazzo Ciano*, New Haven, 1999.

36. He told a friend that he despised the pomposity and humourlessness of the minor Party hierarchs. See N. D'Aroma, *Mussolini segreto*, p. 119. His son says he loved Rossini, a composer rather more inclined to poke fun at ponderous gods than was, say, Wagner. See V. Mussolini, *Vita con mio padre*, Milan, 1957, p. 43.

37. Y. De Begnac, *Palazzo Venezia: storia di un regime*, Rome, 1950, p. 567.

38. BMOO, XXVIII, pp. 136–9; XLIV, p. 199.

39. Y. De Begnac, *Palazzo Venezia*, p. 650.

40. BMOO, XLIV, pp. 67–70.

41. He also overstated their number, tallying them in the hundreds of thousands! See Y. De Begnac, *Palazzo Venezia*, p. 651. One Anti-Fascist commentator thought that the constant interview was the basis of his rule. See C. Berneri, *Mussolini: psicologia di un dittatore* (ed. P.C. Masini), Milan, 1966, p. 58.

42. For an example, see U. Spirito, *Memorie di un incosciente*, Milan, 1977, p. 173.

43. See, among other sources, Q. Navarra, *Memorie del cameriere di Mussolini*, Milan, 1946, p. 55. In the 1920s, when matters may have been more disciplined, a French journalist claimed that she had to give five Roman salutes to get to the door of Mussolini's office and then made another one to him. See V.J. Bordeux, *Benito Mussolini – the man*, London, n.d., pp. 279–82.

44. A. Lessona, *Un ministro di Mussolini*, p. 179.

45. V. Panunzio, *Il 'secondo fascismo' 1936–1943: la reazione della nuova generazione alla crisi del movimento e del regime*, Milan, 1988, p. 63. Panunzio noticed that the *Duce* was keeping himself informed about military progress in Spain, by marking a map provided by the great tourist organisation, the *Touring Club Italiano*.

46. A. Lessona, *Un ministro di Mussolini*, p. 179.

47. Q. Navarra, *Memorie*, pp. 60–1.

48. V. Panunzio, *Il 'secondo fascismo'*, p. 63.

49. As Mussolini himself complained in August 1939. See Y. De Begnac, *Palazzo Venezia*, p. 651.

50. Quoted by J.F. Coverdale, *Italian intervention in the Spanish Civil War*, Princeton, 1975, p. 38.

51. See, for example, Guariglia's account of his instructions on being posted to Madrid. R. Guariglia, *Ricordi 1922–1946*, Naples, 1949, pp. 193–9.

52. Even after the rising occurred, his habitual underlining of diplomatic papers which was extensive did not include reports on Spain; it is quite likely that he did not read them.

Notes

53. R. Guariglia, *Ricordi*, p. 203.
54. J.F. Coverdale, *Italian intervention in the Spanish Civil War*, p. 55.
55. The Consul in San Sebastian earned the ire of Pedrazzi by reporting a month early that Sanjurjo and the Army had risen. See DDI 8s, IV, 341, 22 June 1936, Paternò to Ciano; 414, 30 June 1936, Pedrazzi to Ciano.
56. DDI 8s, IV, 516, 13 July 1936, Pedrazzi to Ciano.
57. DDI 8s, IV, 565, 18 July 1936, Pedrazzi to Ciano.
58. DDI 8s, IV, 570, 20 July 1936, Luccardi to Ministry of War.
59. DDI 8s, IV, 577, 20 July 1936, Alfonso XIII to Mussolini.
60. DDI 8s, IV, 596, 23 July 1936, Luccardi to Ministry of War.
61. DDI 8s, IV, 582, 21 July 1936, Roatta to Ciano.
62. J.F. Coverdale, *Italian intervention in the Spanish Civil War*, pp. 70–2.
63. DDI 8s, IV, 599, 23 July 1936, De Rossi (the consul at Tangiers) to Ciano.
64. J.F. Coverdale, *Italian intervention in the Spanish Civil War*, pp. 73–4.
65. DDI 8s, IV, 610, 24 July 1936, Ciano to De Rossi.
66. DDI 8s, IV, 634, 27 July 1936, SIM to Mussolini.
67. G. Bonnet, *Quai d'Orsay*, Douglas, 1965, p. 156.
68. BMOO, XXVIII, p. 191.
69. DDI 8s, IV, 661, 31 July 1936, De Rossi to Ciano.
70. R. De Felice, *Mussolini il duce II. lo stato totalitario 1936–1940*, Turin, 1981, p. 376.
71. *Ibid.*, p. 364.
72. DDI 8s, IV, 685, 5 August 1936, SIM to Ministry of Foreign Affairs.
73. Rather typically, early Italian reports suggested that the capital would fall quickly and ascribed the imminent victory to Italian arms and prowess. See DDI 8s, V, 363, 6 November 1936, Anfuso to Ciano.
74. R. De Felice, *Mussolini il duce 1936–1940*, pp. 390–1.
75. *Ibid.*, p. 465.
76. See, for example, DDI 8s, V, 546, 6 December 1936, Mussolini meeting with Ciano, his military under-secretaries and Canaris report.
77. M. Knox, *Mussolini unleashed 1939–1941: politics and strategy in Fascist Italy's last war*, Cambridge, 1982, p. 6.
78. Duchess of Atholl, *Searchlight on Spain*, Harmondsworth, 1938, p. 147.
79. G. Jackson, *The Spanish republic and the civil war 1931–1939*, Princeton, 1967, p. 352.
80. J.F. Coverdale, *Italian intervention in the Spanish Civil War*, p. 255.
81. See the complete file in SPDCR 72.
82. BMOO, XLII, p. 184.
83. R. De Felice, *Mussolini il duce 1936–1940*, p. 421.
84. E. Santarelli, preface to S. Trentin, *Dieci anni di fascismo in Italia: dall'istituzione del Tribunale speciale alla proclamazione dell'Impero (1926–1936)*, p. 13.
85. See, for example, Trentin in *ibid.*, p. 232.
86. For a good English-language introduction to his life and thought, see S.G. Pugliese, *Carlo Rosselli: socialist heretic and Antifascist exile*, Cambridge, Mass., 1999.
87. E. Lussu, *Emilio Lussu e 'Giustizia e Libertà'*, Cagliari, 1976, p. 155.
88. For an appraisal of the situation within Italy, see R. De Felice, *Mussolini il duce 1936–1940*, pp. 156–68.
89. For a detailed account, see S.G. Pugliese, *Carlo Rosselli*, pp. 221–2.
90. *Ibid.*, pp. 223–6.
91. SPDCR 44, 5 March 1937, Farinacci to Mussolini. Even quite early in the war, Mussolini, robed as a statesman, had tried to persuade Franco not to cut all bridges with the Basques. See DDI 8s, V, 667, 26 December 1936, Mussolini to Roatta.
92. Cf. also P. Quilici, *Spagna*, Rome, 1938. The distinguished author of this manual, published

Notes

for the *Istituto nazionale di cultura fascista*, was ready to believe that the Spanish were naturally cruel: 'the Spaniard always has the sense of walking on tombs' (p. 62). Cf. also M.M. Morandi, 'Contro il terrore', *Critica Fascista*, 15, 1 March 1937, pp. 133–5, who, echoing Farinacci, deplored the terror appearing in both the USSR and Spain, contrasting such places with 'civilised' Italy, where the revolution in 1921–22 had cost only 'a thousand deaths'.

93. BMOO, XXVIII, pp. 145–6. For a typical example of the propagandising of this event, see E.M. Gray, *Il Duce in Libia: che cosa ha detto, che cosa ha visto*, Milan, 1937.

94. R. De Felice, *Mussolini il duce 1936–1940*, p. 336.

95. BMOO, XXVIII, p. 92.

96. A. Mockler, *Haile Selassie's war: the Italian–Ethiopian campaign 1935–1941*, New York, 1984, p. 175.

97. A. Sbacchi, *Ethiopia under Mussolini: Fascism and the colonial experience*, London, 1985, p. 192.

98. R. De Felice, *Mussolini il duce 1936–1940*, p. 336.

99. For a biography, see E. Borra, *Amedeo di Savoia: terzo duca d'Aosta e vicerè d'Etiopia*, Milan, 1985.

100. *Ibid.*, p. 66, with the allegation, too, that he had been the choice of Alessandro Lessona. As a boy Aosta had spent some months at a Scottish school, but reportedly disliked the food, the cold baths and the rugby (p. 16).

101. L. Calabrò, *Intermezzo africano: ricordi di un Residente di Governo in Etiopia (1937–1941)*, Rome, 1988, p. 89. He was especially scathing about the Under-Secretary and then Minister of Colonies, Attilio Teruzzi, a man whom Mussolini, too, regarded as an oversexed crook, incapable of 'thinking beyond his beard and his virility'. N. D'Aroma, *Mussolini segreto*, p. 68; cf. also P.M. Masotti, *Ricordi d'Etiopia di un funzionario coloniale*, Milan, 1981, p. 23.

102. L. Calabrò, *Intermezzo africano*, p. 38. They were thus rather like the populace of Sicily.

103. SPDCR 44, 25 December 1938, Farinacci to Mussolini.

104. SPDCR 98, 21 July 1942, report.

105. SPDCR 98, 12 June 1942, report on Boattini.

106. Cf. the account of historian and by then Anti-Fascist, Corrado Zaghi, whose doctor friends organised comfortable hospital billets for him for eight and a half months in 1943, on the specious grounds that he had eye problems. C. Zaghi, *Terrore a Ferrara durante i 18 mesi della repubblica di Salò*, Bologna, 1992, p. 16.

107. SPDCR 98, 3 August 1942, police report.

108. SPDCR 87, 24 June 1930, police report. Lessona had not joined the party until 1923, but was another who organised the back-dating of his membership. See report of 27 December 1927, as well as 15 September 1937, Lessona to Starace.

109. For Lessona's own accounts of himself, see A. Lessona, *Memorie*, Rome, 1963; *Un Ministro di Mussolini racconta*.

110. SPDCR 3, 28 February 1937, Mussolini memorandum.

111. SPDCR 3, 8 July 1937, De Bono to Mussolini.

112. SPDCR 3, 4 September 1937, De Bono to Mussolini.

113. N. D'Aroma, *Mussolini segreto*, p. 68. (He was speaking in December 1933.)

114. SPDCR 87, 2 December 1937, telephone tap; 19 November 1938, note.

115. See, for example, SPDCR 87, 15 September 1938, Lessona to Mussolini, complaining that De Bono continued to pursue a vendetta against him.

116. SPDCR 87, 28 February 1937, report.

117. Y. De Begnac, *Taccuini mussoliniani*, pp. 426; 446; 497; 507; 617.

118. SPDCR 38, 11 February 1937, police report.

119. Notable among them was evidence of the corruption and vanity of Badoglio and his family.

The general had been adamant about the need to be made Duke of Addis Ababa, and had also managed to extract a gift of 3 million lire from a variety of government institutions, in order to fund a palatial house in Rome. See SPDCR 67, 2 July 1936, Fedele to Mussolini; 5 April 1937, Lessona to Colonna; 28 July 1937, where the source of the most malicious rumours was said to be De Bono and his friends. For a comparison with Hitler's much more politically tailored corruption of his leading generals, cf. N.J.W. Goda, 'Black marks: Hitler's bribery of senior officers during World War II', *Journal of Modern History*, 72, 2000, pp. 413–52. Cf. also evidence that Starace was trying to impose on the *dopolavoro* the compulsory purchase of his *Marcia su Gondar*, the grandiloquent and highly unreliable account of the Party Secretary's alleged military triumphs in Ethiopia. SPDCR 94, 7 January 1937, telephone tap.

120. N. D'Aroma, *Mussolini segreto*, p. 217.

121. *Ibid.*, p. 33.

122. SPDCR 4, 17 February 1936, Acerbo to Mussolini, in a 14-page letter, reminded the *Duce* of just how pressing was the issue of leaving Italy a Great Power in Europe.

123. DDI 8s, IV, 805, 28 August 1936, Mussolini to Boscarelli. Cf. V, 154, 4 October 1936, Mussolini to De Rossi, similarly urging Franco to make sure his 'authoritarian' regime was also 'popular and social'.

124. DDI 8s, IV, 55, 15 May 1936, Mussolini to Salata.

125. DDI 8s, IV, 37, 14 May 1936, Suvich to Mussolini.

126. DDI 8s, IV, 192, 5 June 1936, Mussolini–Schuschnigg meeting report.

127. DDI 8s, IV, 208, 7 June 1936, Mussolini to Attolico.

128. Cf. DDI 8s, IV, 503, 11 July 1936, Mussolini–Hassell meeting report, where Mussolini repeated his phrase about applauding a *modus vivendi* but tried to delay unilateral German recognition of Italian Ethiopia. Cf. V, 101, 23 September 1936, Mussolini–Frank talk report in which the *Duce*, somewhat less abruptly, still counselled the Germans against providing recognition too precipitately.

129. Churchill College, Cambridge, Vansittart papers, 2/29, 17 May 1936, Vansittart minute.

130. BMOO, XXVIII, p. 25 in an interview with H.R. Knickerbocker of the Hearst press. Cf. p. 5, where he said the same to a correspondent of the London *Daily Telegraph*.

131. BMOO, XLIV, p. 188.

132. DDI 8s, V, 67, 15 September 1936, Mussolini–Schmidt talk report.

133. DDI 8s, V, 101, 23 September 1936, Mussolini–Frank meeting report. Mussolini took the occasion to urge the Nazis to lessen their anti-Catholic zeal since, he warned, warring against religion was like warring against fog.

134. DDI 8s, V, 277, 24 October 1936, Ciano–Hitler talk report (and summary of accompanying dossier).

135. BMOO, XXVIII, pp. 67–72.

136. See, for example, P. Pastorelli in R. De Felice (ed.), *L'Italia fra tedeschi e alleati: la politica estera fascista e la seconda guerra mondiale*, Bologna, 1973, p. 103.

137. M. Knox, *Common destiny: dictatorship, foreign policy and war in Fascist Italy and Nazi Germany*, Cambridge, 2000, pp. 142–3.

138. G. Ciano, *Diario 1937–1943*, p. 35.

139. *Ibid.*, p. 175.

140. *Ibid.*, pp. 82–3.

141. For a detailed study of the background, see R. De Felice, *Il Fascismo e l'Oriente: arabi, ebrei e indiani nella politica di Mussolini*, Bologna, 1988.

142. G. Bottai, *Diario 1935–1944*, p. 115.

143. G. Ciano, *Diario 1937–1943*, p. 28, boasted that he had extracted secret funds of 60 million lire to foster the process.

144. *Ibid.*, p. 135. Earlier, they discussed violating Swiss neutrality in order to attack France (pp. 99–100).

Notes

145. *Ibid.*, pp. 34; 116–17.

146. *Ibid.*, pp. 56–7.

147. *Ibid.*, p. 96.

148. See, for example, DDI 8s, VIII, 87, 2 February 1938, Mussolini to Franco.

149. G. Bottai, *Diario 1935–1944*, p. 115.

150. M. Knox, *Mussolini unleashed 1939–1941*, p. 15.

151. *Ibid.*, pp. 30–1.

152. See, for example, G. Ciano, *Diario 1937–1943*, p. 54. Cf. BMOO, XXIX, p. 251.

153. BMOO, XXVIII, pp. 154–6.

154. R. Quartararo, *Italia-URSS, 1917–1941: i rapporti politici*, Naples, 1997, p. 198.

155. See, for example, A. Nasti, 'L'Italia, il bolscevismo, la Russia', *Critica Fascista*, 15, 15 March 1937, pp. 162–3.

156. G. Ciano, *Diario 1937–1943*, pp. 54–5, wondered if it could be widened to include Spain, Brazil and Poland, this last not a country likely to be welcomed for ever by Nazi Germany as a member of such a group. On 15 February 1938 Mussolini came up with the bright idea that Austria should join and so display its independence (p. 99).

157. *Ibid.*, pp. 67; 256.

158. DDI 8s, III, 598, 6 April 1936, Mussolini to Grandi.

159. See, for example, DDI 8s, VII, 85, 16–17 July 1937, Ciano–Dingli talks report.

160. DDI 8s, VII, 127, 27 July 1937, Grandi to Ciano.

161. DDI 8s, VII, 136, 28 July 1937, N. Chamberlain to Mussolini. Less adroitly, Chamberlain recalled happy youthful holidays in Italy.

162. DDI 8s, VII, 155, including 31 July 1937, Mussolini to N. Chamberlain.

163. See, for example, a statement of continuing openness to a 'totalitarian' accord in DDI 8s, VIII, 105, 8 February 1938, Ciano to Grandi; cf. also 203, 22 February 1938, Grandi to Ciano.

164. BMOO, XXIX, p. 33.

165. BMOO, XXVIII, p. 252. In some sections of the Fascist press, however, hopes sprouted of a revival of the Four Power Pact. See P. Solari, 'Ritorno al Patto a Quattro', *Critica Fascista*, 15, 15 October 1937, pp. 411–13. Bottai was still nostalgic about it in an editorial published after the *Anschluss*. *Critica Fascista*, 16, 15 April 1938, pp. 188–9.

166. For an account, see I. Kershaw, *Hitler 1936–1945: nemesis*, London, 2000, pp. 44–5.

167. *Ibid.*, p. 45.

168. BMOO, XXIX, p. 1.

169. G. Bottai, *Diario 1935–1944*, p. 115.

170. DDI 8s, VI, 500, 22–23 April 1937, Mussolini–Schuschnigg talk report. Cf. VII, 27, 6 July 1937, Mussolini to Bossi, where the *Duce* tried to persuade Franco to be merciful to the Basques after their surrender, given that they were 'Catholics who got things wrong but they are, almost totally, people who could be recuperated for Your Spain'.

171. G. Ciano, *Diario 1937–1943*, p. 98.

172. The Hungarian leader, István Bethlen, had told the *Duce* in January that 80 per cent of Austrians were Nazis and the rest also backed an *Anschluss*. DDI 8s, VIII, 15, 5 January 1938, Mussolini–Bethlen talks report.

173. DDI 8s, VIII, 235, 27 February 1938, Mussolini memorandum.

174. G. Ciano, *Diario 1937–1943*, p. 100.

175. DDI 8s, VII, 393, 4 October 1937, Mussolini to Victor Emmanuel III.

176. DDI 8s, VIII, 296, 11 March 1938, Hitler to Mussolini.

177. DDI 8s, VIII, 312, 13 March 1938, Hitler to Mussolini.

178. DDI 8s, VIII, 316, 14 March 1938, Mussolini to Hitler.

179. F. Anfuso, *Roma Berlino Salò*, p. 65.

180. BMOO, XXIX, p. 71.

Notes

181. G. Ciano, *Diario 1937–1943*, p. 112.
182. R. De Felice, *Mussolini il duce 1936–1940*, p. 471.
183. G. Ciano, *Diario 1937–1943*, pp. 113–14.
184. A. Lessona, *Un ministro di Mussolini*, p. 217.
185. W. Phillips, *Ventures in diplomacy*, London, 1955, p. 119.
186. G. Ciano, *Diario 1937–1943*, p. 120.
187. B. Spampanato, *1938: l'anno decisivo*, Naples, 1938, pp. 111; 122.
188. With some ambiguity, Bottai explained that the Axis was close because it was built not so much on ideological affinity as a commonality of interests. See his editorial, 'L'Asse Roma-Berlino e l'Europa', *Critica Fascista*, 16, 15 May 1938, pp. 210–11.
189. A. Petacco, *Regina: la vita e i segreti di Maria José*, Milan, 1997, p. 132.
190. A. Hitler, *Hitler's table talk 1941–1944* (ed. H. Trevor-Roper), London, 1953, p. 267.
191. DDI 8s, VIII, 461, 7 April 1938, Pignatti to Ciano.
192. E. Dollmann, *The interpreter: memoirs*, London, 1967, p. 110.
193. R. De Felice, *Mussolini il duce 1936–1940*, p. 479.
194. G. Ciano, *Diario 1937–1943*, pp. 131–3.
195. *Ibid.*, p. 166.
196. BMOO, XXIX, p. 156.
197. G. Ciano, *Diario 1937–1943*, p. 179.
198. *Ibid.*, p. 184.
199. *Ibid.*
200. *Ibid.*, p. 188. Earlier he had joked with his son-in-law about the ludicrous English habit of being nice to animals (p. 187).
201. *L'Illustrazione italiana*, 9 October 1938.
202. R. De Felice, *Mussolini il duce 1936–1940*, pp. 530–50.
203. It was called the *passo romano*, or 'Roman step', on the grounds that geese had saved the Capitol from the Gauls and so were plainly Roman birds.
204. BMOO, XXIX, p. 53.

CHAPTER 15

1. For a detailed assessment of the contribution of Italian social and medical 'science' to Italian racism, see G. Israel and P. Nastasi, *Scienza e razza nell'Italia fascista*, Bologna, 1998.
2. G. Bottai, *Diario 1935–1944* (ed. G.B. Guerri), Milan, 1989, p. 125.
3. BMOO, XLIV, p. 72. Mussolini was speaking in October 1933.
4. F. Bojano, *In the wake of the goose-step*, London, 1944, p. 41.
5. R. De Felice, *Storia degli ebrei italiani sotto il fascismo*, Turin, 1961, p. 158.
6. G. Mosse, *Confronting history*, London, 2000, pp. 108–9.
7. G. Bottai, *Diario 1935–1944*, p. 115.
8. DDI, 8s, III, 715, 20 April 1936, Mussolini to Grandi. Preziosi took the chance to affirm that criticism of Italy during the Libyan war had also been sponsored by the Jews. See G. Preziosi, *Giudaismo-bolscevismo plutocrazia massoneria*, Milan, 1941, p. 228.
9. For the humiliating circumstances, see S.G. Pugliese, *Carlo Rosselli: socialist heretic and Antifascist exile*, Cambridge, Mass., 1999, p. 194.
10. Meanwhile, Preziosi hammered away at the idea that Blum was 'possessed of a conception of the world which is wholly Jewish'. See his editorial in *La Vita Italiana*, 49, 15 April 1937, p. 486.
11. G. Miccoli, 'Santa Sede e chiesa italiana di fronte alle leggi antiebraiche del 1938', *Studi storici*, 29, 1988, p. 851. For a more developed study, cf. his *I dilemmi e i silenzi di Pio XII*, Milan, 2000.
12. A commentator in *La Vita Italiana* had then typically maintained that the racial element

Notes

predominating in the unhappy 'moral and religious' character of the English was the Jewish. See G. Pisitello, 'Il fondamento etico-religioso della politica inglese', *La Vita Italiana*, 47, 15 January 1936, pp. 16–24. In the same issue, Ezra Pound, 'Moneta fascista' (pp. 33–7), waxed enthusiastic about a Fascist resistance to the omnivorous banks and other by implication Jewish capitalist firms which lay behind Geneva and sanctions.

13. See, for example, the argument of racist philosopher, Julius Evola, that the 'bolshevising' of Spain at the hands of Jews and Freemasons was intended to be universal. J. Evola, 'Sulla storia segreta della rivoluzione spagnola', *La Vita Italiana*, 52, 15 July 1938, pp. 30–7.
14. E. Morelli, 'Giuseppe Mazzini e Antonio Gallenga', *La Vita Italiana*, 48, 15 July 1936, p. 49.
15. G. Ciano, *Diario 1937–1943* (ed. R. De Felice), Milan, 1980, p. 86.
16. SPD, Carte della Cassetta di Zinco 10, 18 November 1937, Mussolini to Duke of Aosta.
17. L. Goglia, 'Note sul razzismo coloniale fascista', *Storia contemporanea*, 19, 1988, pp. 1231–2.
18. See, further, L. Goglia, 'Una diversa politica razziale coloniale in un documento inedito di Generale Pollena del 1937', *Storia contemporanea*, 16, 1985, pp. 1071–91. Goglia notes that, among the stauncher racists in the empire, were those officials who regarded themselves as the least 'Fascist'.
19. R. De Felice, *Ebrei in un paese arabo*, Bologna, 1978, pp. 21–2.
20. *Ibid.*, p. 111.
21. G. Ciano, *Diario 1937–1943*, pp. 64–5.
22. N. D'Aroma, *Mussolini segreto*, Rocca San Casciano, 1958, p. 86. The *Duce* was speaking in November 1934.
23. G. Ciano, *Diario 1937–1943*, p. 95.
24. G. Bottai, *Diario 1935–1944*, p. 125.
25. G. Ciano, *Diario 1937–1943*, p. 99. Another straw in the wind was the publication of P. Orano, *Gli ebrei in Italia*, Rome, 1937.
26. M. Michaelis, *Mussolini and the Jews: German–Italian relations and the Jewish question in Italy 1922–1945*, Oxford, 1978, p. 141.
27. G. Ciano, *Diario 1937–1943*, p. 99.
28. M. Michaelis, *Mussolini and the Jews*, p. 142.
29. BMOO, XXIX, pp. 99–102.
30. BMOO, XXIX, pp. 120–1.
31. G. Ciano, *Diario 1937–1943*, p. 156.
32. An English translation can be found in C. Delzell (ed.), *Mediterranean fascism 1919–1945*, New York, 1970, pp. 174–6.
33. BMOO, XXIX, pp. 125–6.
34. G. Preziosi, 'Era mussoliniana', *La Vita Italiana*, 52, 15 August 1938, pp. 133–6.
35. *La Vita Italiana*, 52, 1 September 1938, p. 374, editorial note.
36. The imperial theme was advanced most fully by an anonymous 'Historicus', 'Razzismo e giudaismo nell'Europa moderna', *Civiltà Fascista*, 5, September 1938, pp. 784–803, in which it was argued that the Anglo-Saxons had traditionally been the most racist of peoples and that such racism went with imperialism. Before long, one leading journalist was condemning Roosevelt as the 'super-Jew', attacking Fascists for having flirted with his New Deal and placing the USA among Italy's racial enemies. See E. Canevari, 'Rivendicazioni italiane e isterismi americani', *La Vita Italiana*, 53, 15 January 1939, pp. 7–13.
37. [G. Bottai], 'Politica fascista della razza', *Critica Fascista*, 16, 1 August 1938, pp. 210–11.
38. Bottai reiterated these matters in a succession of issues of his journal. See *Critica Fascista*, 16, 15 August 1938, pp. 306–7; 1 September 1938, pp. 322–3; 15 September 1938, pp. 338–9; 15 October 1938, pp. 370–1; 15 December 1938, pp. 50–1.
39. S. Colarizi, *L'opinione degli italiani sotto il regime 1929–1943*, Bari, 1991, p. 242.
40. For accounts of the equivocal wartime history of Italian camps, see C.S. Capogreco,

Notes

Ferramonti: la vita e gli uomini del più grande campo d'internamento fascista (1940–1945), Florence, 1987 and K. Voigt, *Il rifugio precario: gli esuli in Italia dal 1933 al 1945* (2 vols), Florence, 1996. Cf. J. Walston, 'History and memory of the Italian concentration camps', *Historical Journal*, 40, 1997, pp. 169–83. Walston shows that the most punitive policies were pursued against Slovenes, Italy's or Fascism's 'real' enemies in a way no other people were.

41. R. Pommerin, 'Le controversie di politica razziale nei rapporti dell'Asse Roma-Berlino (1938–1943)', *Storia contemporanea*, 10, 1979, pp. 925–40.

42. G. Ciano, *Diario 1937–1943*, p. 149.

43. *Ibid.*, p. 163.

44. *Ibid.*, p. 170.

45. W. Skof Newby, *Tra pace e guerra: una ragazza slovena nell'Italia fascista*, Bologna, 1994, p. 85.

46. BMOO, XXIX, pp. 145–6.

47. E. Momigliano, *Storia tragica e grottesca del razzismo fascista*, Milan, 1946, p. 67.

48. There, according to Ciano, Balbo, De Bono and Federzoni had opposed the new line but Bottai had staunchly backed it. See G. Ciano, *Diario 1937–1943*, p. 193. Acerbo was another old leader who disliked the move to racial politics. See G. Acerbo, *Fra due plotoni di esecuzione: avvenimenti e problemi dell'epoca fascista*, Rocca San Casciano, 1968, pp. 284–5.

49. G. Bottai, *Diario 1935–1944*, p. 136.

50. BMOO, XXIX, pp. 185–96.

51. G. Ciano, *Diario 1937–1943*, p. 211.

52. S. Colarizi, *L'opinione degli italiani sotto il regime*, p. 256.

53. G. Ciano, *Diario 1937–1943*, p. 212.

54. Again, it is available in English in C. Delzell (ed.), *Mediterranean fascism*, pp. 178–83.

55. For an account of the way in which the majority of non-Jewish academics gave the exclusion of their colleagues their at least passive support, see R. Finzi, *L'università italiana e le leggi antiebraiche*, Rome, 1997.

56. For his views, see T. Interlandi, *Pane bigio: scritti politici*, Bologna, 1927; *Contro Judaeos*, Rome, 1938.

57. T. Interlandi, *Contra Judaeos*, p. 132.

58. For some of his divagations, see G. Almirante, 'Una razza alla conquista di un continente', *La difesa della razza*, 2, 5 November 1938, pp. 20–1; 'Giornalismo', 5 July 1939, pp. 24–7; 'Storia razziale della zona di Arsia', 3, 5 May 1940, pp. 38–41. Guido Landra, the anthropologist, knew scientifically that both Corsicans and Maltese were full of Aryan blood. See the issues of 20 November 1938, pp. 8–10; 5 January 1939, pp. 8–10. Apart from support from leading intellectuals, the paper happily received advertising from such important business concerns as Fiat, Shell and the major national banks. Cf. also P. Orano (ed.), *Inchiesta sulla razza*, Rome, 1939, in which such prominent Fascist journalists as Giorgio Pini lined up to express racist thoughts. Pini argued that classical Rome had declined and fallen because it had become racially bastardised (p. 192). Virginio Gayda was convinced of the imperial face of the issue, urging that, for racial reasons, 'we must give Italians in Africa Italian women' (p. 118).

59. SPDCR 44, 3 August 1938, Farinacci to Mussolini.

60. SPDCR 44, 5 August 1938, Farinacci to Mussolini.

61. SPDCR 44, 6 June 1938, Farinacci to Mussolini.

62. See, for example, Ciano on the subject at the height of the 1938 campaign. G. Ciano, *Diario 1937–1943*, p. 211.

63. See J. Steinberg, *All or nothing: the Axis and the Holocaust 1941–1943*, London, 1990.

64. Y. De Begnac, *Palazzo Venezia: storia di un regime*, Rome, 1950, p. 643.

65. N. D'Aroma, *Mussolini segreto*, p. 250. Mussolini was speaking in April 1942.

Notes

66. P.V. Cannistraro and B.R. Sullivan, *Il Duce's other woman*, New York, 1993, pp. 518; 528.

67. M. Michaelis, *Mussolini and the Jews*, pp. 254–5, notes that bans were extended in the summer of 1939 to Jewish journalists and notaries, and that harsher inheritance provisions were also now applied. However, another law gave the *Duce* the right to 'Aryanise' whomever he liked, thus at a stroke undermining any concept that the 'Jewish race' could be defined scientifically.

68. Cf. D. Goldhagen, *Hitler's willing executioners: ordinary Germans and the Holocaust*, New York, 1996.

69. See classically, G. Pisanò, *Mussolini e gli ebrei*, Milan, 1967.

70. Gypsies were viewed unfavourably in Fascist Italy from the 1920s, but were treated as a 'crime' problem. See G. Boursier, 'La persecuzione degli zingari nell'Italia fascista', *Studi storici*, 37, 1996, pp. 1065–82.

71. L. Salvatorelli and G. Mira, *Storia d'Italia nel periodo fascista*, Milan, 1969, vol. 2, p. 318.

72. R. De Felice, *Mussolini il duce: lo stato totalitario 1936–1940*, Turin, 1981, p. 101. In his speech of 25 October 1938, Mussolini gave this change his imprimatur. See BMOO, XXIX, pp. 189–90.

73. Archives (Milan), *Touring Club Italiano*, 100/1, 19 July 1937, Bonardi draft letter.

74. For this example and further background, see R.J.B. Bosworth, *Italy and the wider world 1860–1960*, London, 1996, p. 177.

75. R. De Felice, *Mussolini il duce 1936–1940*, p. 120.

76. G. Bottai, *La carta della scuola*, Milan, 1939.

77. *Ibid.*, p. 33.

78. *Ibid.*, p. 94.

79. G. Bottai, 'Concetto mussoliniano della "rivoluzione permanente"', *Critica Fascista*, 19, September 1939, pp. 592–9.

80. For the fullest study of these complex matters, see R. Ben-Ghiat, *Fascist modernities: Italy, 1922–1945*, Berkeley, 2001.

81. A. Spinosa, *I figli del Duce*, Milan, 1989, p. 88. The first Coca Cola ad. appeared in *Il Popolo d'Italia* (and the rest of the press) on 30 July 1930. Cf. D. Forgacs, *Italian culture in the industrial era 1880–1980: cultural industries, politics and the public*, Manchester, 1990, p. 76.

82. In real terms it still beset almost half of the population of the South and the islands. See M. Knox, *Hitler's Italian allies: royal armed forces, Fascist regime, and the war of 1940–1943*, Cambridge, 2000, p. 23. In 1931 an estimated 3 per cent of Italy's university students came from the working class (a figure which had fallen since 1911). See M. Barbagli, *Educating for unemployment: politics, labor markets, and the school system – Italy 1850–1973*, New York, 1982, p. 138.

83. G. Acerbo, *Fra due plotoni di esecuzione*, p. 386.

84. M. Barbagli, *Educating for unemployment*, p. 180, reports that, despite a low production rate of engineers at least for a serious industrial power, an estimated 50 per cent of them were unemployed in 1935.

85. V. Panunzio, *Il 'secondo fascismo' 1936–1943: la reazione della nuova generazione alla crisi del movimento e del regime*, Milan, 1988, pp. 52–6; 132–3.

86. The *Tribunale Speciale* condemned 310 Anti-Fascists in 1938 and 365 in 1939, higher numbers than from 1932 to 1937, but less than in the 1920s. See R. De Felice, *Mussolini il duce 1936–1940*, pp. 45–6.

87. P. Melograni, *Rapporti segreti della polizia fascista*, Bari, 1979, p. 35.

88. C. Alvaro, *Quasi una vita: giornale di uno scrittore*, Milan, 1950, pp. 204; 215.

89. For another example, see G. Pini, 'Ritratto di Mussolini', *Gerarchia*, 19, April 1939, pp. 249–55. Pini also noted that the *Duce* had small hands and ears.

90. F. Bandini, *Claretta: profilo di Clara Petacci e i suoi tempi*, Milan, 1960, p. 48.

91. C. Petacci, *Il mio diario*, n.p., 1946, pp. 63–4.

Notes

92. See the file in SPDCR 103 and R.J.B. Bosworth, 'Per necessità famigliare: hypocrisy and corruption in Fascist Italy', European History Quarterly, 30, 2000, p. 369.

93. SPDCR 103, 14 August 1939, report.

94. For a detailed account of these matters, see F. Perfetti, La Camera dei fasci e delle corporazioni, Rome, 1991, pp. 7–233.

95. Ibid., p. 208.

96. G. Bottai, Diario 1935–1944, p. 125.

97. N. D'Aroma, Venti anni insieme: Vittorio Emanuele e Mussolini, Rocca San Casciano, 1957, p. 244.

98. For a detailed description of the nomination and its reception, see R. De Felice, Mussolini il duce 1936–1940, pp. 23–38.

99. Ibid., p. 39.

100. SPDCR 105, 2 April 1938, S. Romano memorandum and accompanying note, Mussolini to Victor Emmanuel III.

101. N. D'Aroma, Vent'anni insieme, p. 155.

102. A. Petacco, Regina: la vita e i segreti di Maria José, Milan, 1997, p. 83.

103. C.M. De Vecchi di Val Cismon, Il quadrumviro scomodo: il vero Mussolini nelle memorie del più monarchico dei fascisti, Milan, 1983, p. 116.

104. R. De Felice, Mussolini il duce 1936–1940, p. 40.

105. G. Ciano, Diario 1937–1943, pp. 250–1.

106. Ibid., p. 259. However, a deal between the PNF and Catholic Action in July 1938 was assessed by De Felice as a success for the Church. See R. De Felice, Mussolini il duce 1936–1940, p. 145.

107. One writer thought him an enemy of 'the judaeo-bolshevik cyclone'. See G. Aureli, 'Pio XII', La Vita Italiana, 53, 15 March 1939, pp. 273–87.

108. G. Ciano, Diario 1937–1943, p. 209. Among those who now described alleged French perfidy was the distinguished historian, Ettore Rota. See his Italia e Francia davanti alla storia: il mito della Sorella Latina, Milan, 1939.

109. U. Guspini, L'orecchio del regime: le intercettazioni telefoniche al tempo del fascismo, Milan, 1973, p. 157.

110. According to Rachele Mussolini, the King was pained by Mussolini's relative lack of interest in 'regaining' Savoy. See R. Mussolini, The real Mussolini (as told to A. Zarca), Farnborough, 1973, p. 185.

111. G. Ciano, Diario 1937–1943, pp. 218–19.

112. Ibid., p. 221.

113. Ibid., p. 296.

114. Ibid., p. 228. At least one young diplomat claimed that he was profoundly alienated by the crudely manipulative nature of the campaign. See E. Ortona, Diplomazia di guerra: diari 1937–1943, Bologna, 1993, p. 55. Milan opinion was also reported to be unimpressed by the tirades against France. See P. Melograni, Rapporti segreti, pp. 23–4.

115. N. D'Aroma, Mussolini segreto, p. 25.

116. P. Stafford, 'The Chamberlain–Halifax visit to Rome: a reappraisal', English Historical Review, 98, 1983, p. 64.

117. Ibid., p. 91. According to Ciano, Chamberlain's eyes grew misty when the English colony burst into 'For he's a jolly good fellow' at his departure ceremony in Rome, while Mussolini turned to Grandi and asked belligerently what the song was. G. Ciano, Diario 1937–1943, p. 240.

118. PRO FO 371/23784/R502, 18 January 1939, Cabinet report.

119. G. Ciano, Diario 1937–1943, p. 239.

120. Ibid., pp. 233; 237; 241.

121. R. De Felice, Mussolini il duce 1936–1940, p. 581.

Notes

122. G. Ciano, *Diario 1937–1943*, p. 262.

123. *Ibid.*, p. 265.

124. *Ibid.*, pp. 266–7.

125. Cf., for example, BMOO, XXIX, p. 251.

126. G. Bottai, *Diario 1935–1944*, pp. 142–4.

127. R. De Felice, *Mussolini il duce 1936–1940*, p. 266.

128. For the details, see M. Toscano, *The origins of the Pact of Steel*, Baltimore, 1967, pp. 127–8.

129. For their history, see B. Mantelli, *'Camerati del lavoro': i lavoratori italiani emigrati nel Terzo Reich nel periodo dell'Asse 1938–1943*, Florence, 1992. Or, in English-language summary, B. Mantelli, 'Italians in Germany, 1938–1945: an aspect of the Rome–Berlin Axis', in R.J.B. Bosworth and P. Dogliani (eds), *Italian Fascism: history, memory and representation*, London, 1999, pp. 45–63.

130. See B. Mantelli, *'Camerati del lavoro'*, p. 54 for the application of the term.

131. G. Gafencu, *The last days of Europe: a diplomatic journey in 1939*, London, 1947, p. 128.

132. As a model of some sort, Liberal Italy had invaded the waterless island of Saseno on Christmas Day, 1914.

133. G. Ciano, *Diario 1937–1943*, p. 277. For further background, see the memoirs of the Italian minister in Tirana (and close friend and business associate of Ciano), F. Jacomoni di San Savino, *La politica dell'Italia in Albania*, Rocca San Casciano, 1965.

134. G. Ciano, *Diario 1937–1943*, p. 284.

135. F. Anfuso, *Roma Berlino Salò (1936–1945)*, Milan, 1950, p. 115.

136. BMOO, XXIX, pp. 252–3.

137. G. Ciano, *Diario 1937–1943*, p. 290.

138. *Ibid.*, p. 305.

139. F. Guarneri, *Battaglie economiche fra le due guerre*, Bologna, 1988, p. 97.

140. *Ibid.*, p. 749.

141. *Ibid.*, p. 910.

142. *Ibid.*, p. 847.

143. R. De Felice, *Mussolini il duce 1936–1940*, pp. 617–18.

144. De Felice argues that the decision was taken suddenly and only after Ribbentrop had spoken of a considerable period of peace (pp. 621–5).

145. G. Ciano, *Diario 1937–1943*, p. 301.

146. *Ibid.*, p. 306.

147. DDI 8s, XII, 59, 30 May 1939, Mussolini to Hitler.

148. DDI 8s, XII, 403, 29 June 1939, Rosso to Ciano.

149. DDI 8s, XII, 480, 5 July 1939, Viola to Ciano.

150. DDI 8s, XII, 488, 6 July 1939, Mussolini to Franco. Ciano met Franco and was alarmed to find his forces still shooting '250 per day in Madrid, 150 at Barcelona and 80 at Seville', a cruelty, he surmised, which expressed 'the Spanish mentality'. Still Franco had declared ingratiatingly that he was a convert to the Mussolinian formula of attaching the people to his regime. 611, 19 July 1939, Ciano–Franco meeting report.

151. DDI 8s, XII, 505, 7 July 1939, Mussolini to Ciano. Cf. also 662, 24 July 1939, Mussolini to embassy in Berlin through Magistrati.

152. G. Ciano, *Diario 1937–1943*, p. 324.

153. *Ibid.*, p. 326.

154. *Ibid.*, p. 327.

155. See DDI 8s, XIII, I, 1 and 4, both 12 August 1939, Ciano reports.

156. G. Ciano, *Diario 1937–1943*, p. 328.

157. They therefore fit the argument of the De Feliceans that his policy remained spurred most by a fear of Germany. The extreme position is that of Rosaria Quartararo, who has argued that it was Britain which deliberately converted the crisis over Danzig into war. See R.

Notes

Quartararo, *Roma tra Londra e Berlino: la politica estera fascista dal 1931 al 1940*, Rome, 1980, p. 500.

158. G. Ciano, *Diario 1937–1943*, p. 330.
159. E. Canevari, *Graziani mi ha detto*, Rome, 1947, p. 149.
160. G. Bottai, *Diario 1935–1944*, p. 152.
161. See, for example, G. Ciano, *Diario 1937–1943*, pp. 331–2.
162. DDI 8s, XIII, 136, 21 August 1939, Mussolini to Hitler.
163. An explanation arrived from Hitler on 25 August. See DDI 8s, XIII, 245, 25 August 1939, Hitler to Mussolini.
164. V. Mussolini, *Vita con mio padre*, Milan, 1957, p. 99. The Anti-Fascist leadership in exile was equally shocked and appalled by the news. See, for example, P. Spriano, *Storia del partito comunista italiano*, Turin, 1970, vol. 3, p. 312.
165. G. Ciano, *Diario 1937–1943*, p. 332.
166. *Ibid.*, p. 333. Mussolini formally told the King that 'at least in the first phase of the conflict', Italy 'will limit itself to a purely demonstrative attitude'. DDI 8s, XIII, 209, 25 August 1939, Mussolini to King Victor Emmanuel III.
167. DDI 8s, XIII, 250, 25 August 1939, Mussolini to Hitler. 293, 26 August 1939, Mussolini to Hitler, contains the full details of the materials requested.
168. In fact, Hitler offered to meet some but not all of the Italian demands. See DDI 8s, XIII, 298, 26 August 1939, Hitler to Mussolini.
169. G. Ciano, *Diario 1937–1943*, p. 335.
170. DDI 8s, XIII, 304, 26 August 1939, Mussolini to Hitler.
171. DDI 8s, XIII, 329, 27 August 1939, Hitler to Mussolini.
172. See, for example, DDI 8s, XIII, 414, 29 August 1939, Ciano to Attolico.
173. G. Ciano, *Diario 1937–1943*, p. 336.
174. *Ibid.*, p. 337.
175. *Records and documents of the Holy See relating to the Second World War* (ed. G. Noel), Dublin, 1968, p. 245.
176. G. Bottai, *Diario 1935–1944*, pp. 153–4.
177. See DDI 8s, XIII, 128, 21 August 1939, Roncalli to Ciano; 485, 31 August 1939, Mameli to Ciano.
178. G. Ciano, *Diario 1937–1943*, p. 341.
179. *Ibid.*, p. 342.

CHAPTER 16

1. G. Ciano, *Diario 1937–1943* (ed. R. De Felice), Milan, 1980, p. 328.
2. G. Ansaldo, *Il giornalista di Ciano: diari 1932–1943*, Bologna, 2000, p. 230. It was Ciano who had reported this phrase to him.
3. G. Ciano, *Diario 1937–1943*, p. 341.
4. M. Legnani, 'Guerra e governo delle risorse: strategie economiche e soggetti sociali nell'Italia 1940–1943', *Italia contemporanea*, 179, 1990, p. 239.
5. G. Ciano, *Diario 1937–1943*, p. 343.
6. DDI 9s, I, 6, 4 September 1939, Ciano to Pignatti; 650, 7 October 1939, Pignatti to Ciano.
7. G. Ciano, *Diario 1937–1943*, p. 343.
8. SPDCR 87, 9 September 1939, Lanzillo to Mussolini.
9. SPDCR 44, 13 September 1939, Farinacci to Mussolini. The letter characteristically ran to 13 pages.
10. See, for example, DDI 9s, I, 60, 6 September 1939, Grazzi to Ciano; 85, 7 September 1939, Gambara to Ciano.
11. DDI 9s, I, 22, 4 September 1939, Magistrati to Ciano.

Notes

12. G. Ciano, *Diario 1937–1943*, p. 347.

13. *Ibid.*, pp. 341; 347.

14. DDI 9s, I, 138, 10 September 1939, Mussolini to Attolico.

15. *Ibid.*

16. *La Vita Italiana* was naturally convinced that the war was the fault of the Jews, but it also foresaw an early peace. See, for example, E. Canevari, 'La guerra giudaica', *La Vita Italiana*, 54, 15 September 1939.

17. G. Ciano, *Diario 1937–1943*, pp. 356–7.

18. See F. Marzari, 'Projects for an Italian-led Balkan bloc of neutrals, September–October 1939', *Historical Journal*, 13, 1970, pp. 767–88; H. Cliadakis, 'Neutrality and war in Italian policy 1939–40', *Journal of Contemporary History*, 9, 1974, pp. 171–90.

19. G. Ciano, *Diario 1937–1943*, pp. 358–9.

20. BMOO, XXIX, p. 316.

21. DDI 9s, I, 523, 30 September 1939, Mussolini to King Victor Emmanuel III. By contrast, a writer in *Gerarchia* justified Nazi 'sterilisation' policy, claiming that it included lots of safeguards and entailed a great deal of consultation with the public. See L. Cipriani, 'Le scienze antropologiche nella Germania hitleriana', *Gerarchia*, 19, December 1939, pp. 787–91.

22. P. Melograni, *Rapporti segreti della polizia fascista*, Bari, 1979, p. 46.

23. See, for example, DDI 9s, II, 443, 4 December 1939, Bonarelli to Ciano. Cf. I, 817, 20 October 1939, Ciano to Attolico.

24. DDI 9s, II, 633, 17 December 1939, Ciano to Bonarelli.

25. DDI 9s, II, 646, 18 December 1939, Anfuso to Ciano.

26. DDI 9s, I, 796, 18 October 1939, Anfuso to Rosso.

27. DDI 9s, II, 207, 13 November 1939, Rosso to Anfuso.

28. DDI 9s, II, 208, 13 November 1939, Rosso to Anfuso.

29. M. Toscano, *Storia diplomatica della questione dell'Alto Adige*, Bari, 1967, p. ix. Toscano, a Jew, a Nationalist, and a patriotic 'old-fashioned diplomatic historian', is a case study in the continuities of Italian academic life through Fascism into the Republic.

30. A.E. Alcock, *The history of the South Tyrol question*, Geneva, 1970, p. 38.

31. *Ibid.* Cf. also the bitterly critical account of an emigré, E. Reut-Nicolussi, *Tyrol under the axe of Italian Fascism*, London, 1930. He condemned the Italian regime for persecuting German-speakers by chipping German names from gravestones (p. 264), seeking to ban the Christmas tree (pp. 228–9) and corrupting local Germanic women through the advocacy of 'advanced' sexual practices, a charge which appears to prove that all matters are relative (p. 211).

32. M. Toscano, *Storia diplomatica dell'Alto Adige*, pp. 145–6.

33. G. Aly, *'Final Solution': Nazi population policy and the murder of the European Jews*, London, 1999, p. 25.

34. R. De Felice, *Il problema dell'Alto Adige nei rapporti italo-tedeschi dall'Anschluss alla fine della seconda guerra mondiale*, Bologna, 1973, pp. 15–29.

35. G. Aly, *'Final Solution'*, pp. 25–6.

36. R. De Felice, *Il problema dell'Alto Adige*, p. 54.

37. *Ibid.*, p. 57.

38. G. Ciano, *Diario 1937–1943*, p. 362.

39. R. De Felice, *Mussolini il duce II. lo stato totalitario 1936–1940*, Turin, 1981, p. 705.

40. SPDCR 12, 8 October 1927, police report.

41. G. Ciano, *Diario 1937–1943*, p. 363. Alas, by the end of December, Ciano was complaining that Muti was following his own course, believing that he had Mussolini on side (p. 379).

42. Shortly after Starace's fall, Mussolini defended the Party Secretary's work on Fascist style to Bottai and claimed that it would be a lasting legacy. See G. Bottai, *Diario 1935–1944* (ed. G.B. Guerri), Milan, 1989, p. 168.

Notes

43. See SPDCR 94, for example, 24 December 1941, Starace to Mussolini, in which he talked about still going horse-riding because the *Duce* preferred it as a sport, even though the unemployed Starace could no longer really afford such an upper-class activity. Or 28 October 1942, Starace to Mussolini, in which Starace confessed to being spiritually downcast, awaiting some recognition that he was still the *Duce*'s 'old legionnaire'.

44. P. Melograni, *Rapporti segreti*, p. 50. Cf., by comparison, the typical efforts by Bottai to talk up the PNF as still an utterly 'intransigent' body. [G. Bottai], 'Il Partito quindici anni dopo il 3 gennaio', *Critica Fascista*, 18, 1 January 1940.

45. P. Melograni, *Rapporti segreti*, p. 51.

46. A. Petacco, *Il superfascista: vita e morte di Alessandro Pavolini*, Milan, 1998, p. 87.

47. G. Ciano, *Diario 1937–1943*, p. 364.

48. See, for example, R. Riccardi, *Economia fascista: sanzioni, commercio estero, autarchia*, Rome, 1939. Secret reports later claimed that Riccardi (another 'friend' of Ciano) was notoriously corrupt in the granting of import–export licences. Moreover, it was said that he played tennis regularly with Osio of the *Banca Nazionale del Lavoro* for a purse of 1000 lire and Osio made every effort to lose. See SPDCR 91, 28 January 1943, report. He also allegedly had no compunction about continuing to work through Oscar Morpurgo, a bankrupt Jew.

49. Soddu provided a splendid aphorism about how to survive the military life: 'When you have a fine plate of *pasta* guaranteed for life, and a little music, you don't need anything more.' It seemed to indicate an incomplete conversion to Fascist rigour. See M. Knox, *Mussolini unleashed 1939–1941: politics and strategy in Fascist Italy's last war*, Cambridge, 1982, p. 57.

50. For his later effort at self-exculpation, see F. Pricolo, *Ignavia contro eroismo: l'avventura italo-greca*, Rome, 1946.

51. G. Ciano, *Diario 1937–1943*, p. 371.

52. *Ibid.*, p. 378.

53. *Ibid.*, p. 355.

54. DDI 9s, II, 118, 6 November 1939, Attolico to Ciano.

55. G. Ciano, *Diario 1937–1943*, p. 374.

56. *Ibid.*, p. 380.

57. DDI 9s, III, 33, 5 January 1940, Mussolini to Hitler. It is also found in BMOO, XXIX, pp. 423–7.

58. DDI 9s, III, 40, 6 January 1940, Mussolini to Ciano.

59. G. Ciano, *Diario 1937–1943*, p. 380.

60. A telephone tap confirmed Badoglio's hostility to war entry and his enhanced distrust of the Fascist Party. See SPDCR 67, 29 December 1939, report to Sebastiani.

61. G. Ciano, *Diario 1937–1943*, pp. 385–6.

62. *Ibid.*, p. 400.

63. *Ibid.*, pp. 386; 395.

64. G. Bottai, *Diario 1935–1944*, p. 174. A certain unreality was evident in discussion in *Gerarchia* around this time of the fruitfulness to the national economy of tourism. See F. Pullé, 'Turismo e finanziamento', *Gerarchia*, 20, January 1940, pp. 25–30. Bottai had similarly tried to escape current conundrums by suggesting that, though modern war depended on economics, it was not just production but 'organisation' which really mattered and, in this regard, Fascist Italy was a model. See [G. Bottai], 'Guerra e economia', *Critica Fascista*, 17, 1 October 1939, pp. 362–3.

65. G. Ciano, *Diario 1937–1943*, pp. 401–2.

66. DDI 9s, III, 78, 10 January 1940, Attolico to Ciano, enclosing a report from Magistrati.

67. DDI 9s, III, 137, 16 January 1940, Attolico to Ciano.

68. G. Ciano, *Diario 1937–1943*, p. 391.

Notes

69. DDI 9s, III, 194, 23 January 1940, Ciano–Pavelić talk report.

70. G. Ciano, *Diario 1937–1943*, p. 387.

71. *Ibid.*, p. 394. Ciano added a little defensively: 'He does not distinguish one class from another, but rather lumps in as "people" all those who prefer to vegetate in their lives.'

72. S. Welles, *The time for decision*, London, 1944, p. 81.

73. *Ibid.*, pp. 84–5. For the Italian version, see DDI 9s, III, 395, 26 February 1940, Mussolini–Welles talk report.

74. S. Welles, *The time for decision*, pp. 135–43.

75. DDI 9s, III, 570, 16 March 1940, Mussolini–Welles talk report.

76. DDI 9s, III, 492, 8 March 1940, Hitler to Mussolini.

77. DDI 9s, III, 524, 11 March 1940, Mussolini–Ribbentrop talk report. Cf. also 512, 10 March 1940, Mussolini–Ribbentrop talk report.

78. A. Petacco, *L'archivio segreto di Mussolini*, Milan, 1997, pp. 152–3.

79. For a review of this visit, see M. Knox, *Mussolini unleashed*, pp. 81–6.

80. G. Ciano, *Diario 1937–1943*, p. 406. Or so Ciano thought he understood from a conversation at Acquasanta golf club with Duke Pietro Acquarone, the Minister of the Royal House.

81. *Ibid.*, p. 407.

82. DDI 9s, III, 578, 18 March 1940, Mussolini–Hitler talk report.

83. G. Ciano, *Diario 1937–1943*, p. 408.

84. DDI 9s, III, 669, 31 March 1940, Mussolini to King Victor Emmanuel III and others. It is also in BMOO, XXIX, pp. 364–7.

85. DDI 9s, IV, 16, 9 April; 31, 10 April; 130, 18 April; 218, 26 April 1940, all Hitler to Mussolini.

86. DDI 9s, III, 700, 4 April and 726, 8 April 1940, Mussolini to Franco.

87. G. Ciano, *Diario 1937–1943*, pp. 417–18.

88. DDI 9s, IV, 37, 11 April 1940, Mussolini to Hitler.

89. G. Ciano, *Diario 1937–1943*, p. 416.

90. *Ibid.*, p. 326.

91. *Ibid.*, p. 419.

92. *Ibid.*, p. 421.

93. E. Ortona, *Diplomazia di guerra: diari 1937–1943*, Bologna, 1993, p. 83.

94. G. Bottai, *Diario 1935–1944*, p. 187.

95. G. Ciano, *Diario 1937–1943*, p. 426.

96. DDI 9s, IV, 348, 9 May 1940, Hitler to Mussolini. Cf. 353, 10 May 1940, Mussolini to Hitler, with the *Duce* still stressing that only the Italian Navy was really ready.

97. G. Ciano, *Diario 1937–1943*, pp. 428–9.

98. *Ibid.*, pp. 429–30. Cf. also DDI 9s, IV, 189, 24 April 1940, Pius XII to Mussolini; 232, 28 April 1940, Mussolini to Pius XII, in which the Pope still looked for some sort of compromise peace.

99. G. Ciano, *Diario 1937–1943*, p. 432.

100. BMOO, XXIX, pp. 393–5. Earlier in May, Mussolini had berated his prefect at Cremona (and no doubt, behind him, Farinacci) with complaints about that sluggish demographic growth which left Italy with only '45 million' against '250 million Slavs' and '100 million Germans'. The comment is proof of both the *Duce*'s habitual statistical imprecision and his surviving fear that the epicentre of the war would not actually be in the Mediterranean. See BMOO, XLIII, 3 May 1940, Mussolini to Prefect at Cremona.

101. He reported that the Albanian collaborators liked the idea of war since it could deliver Kosovo (and parts of northern Greece) to them. See G. Ciano, *Diario 1937–1943*, p. 433.

102. G. Bottai, *Diario 1935–1944*, p. 191.

103. P. Badoglio, *Italy in the Second World War: memoirs and documents*, London, 1948, p. 15. Badoglio maintained that he warned it would amount to 'suicide'.

Notes

104. DDI 9s, IV, 642, 29 May 1940, Mussolini meeting with military chiefs report. It is also in BMOO, XXIX, pp. 396–8.
105. DDI 9s, IV, 680, 30 May 1940, Mussolini to Hitler.
106. See DDI 9s, IV, 694, 1 June 1940, Badoglio to Mussolini; 829, 9 June 1940, Favagrossa to Mussolini.
107. R. De Felice, *Mussolini il duce 1929–1936*, p. 839.
108. BMOO, XXIX, pp. 403–5.
109. DDI 9s, IV, 847, 10 June 1940, Franco to Mussolini.
110. G. Ciano, *Diario 1937–1943*, p. 442.
111. D. Varè, *The two imposters*, London, 1949, p. 217.
112. See R. De Felice, *Mussolini il duce 1936–1940*, pp. 843–4.
113. For an account of Milanese opinion confirming this view, see P. Melograni, *Rapporti segreti*, pp. 65–92. More generally, see the conclusion of S. Colarizi, *L'opinione degli italiani sotto il regime 1929–1943*, Bari, 1991, pp. 336–8, discerning a general change in 'mid-May'. Cf. also A. Padrone, 'Le reazioni dell'opinione pubblica italiana all'intervento nella seconda guerra mondiale', *Rivista di storia della storiografia moderna*, 6, 1985, pp. 57–90. The old Fascist historian, Attilio Tamaro, claimed after the war that, by 29 May, 'the historic moment could not have been more favourable' and that the great majority of Italians were by then willing and ready to follow their *Duce*. See A. Tamaro, *Venti anni di storia 1922–1943*, Rome, 1953, vol. III, p. 409.
114. A. Padrone, 'Le reazioni dell'opinione pubblica italiana', pp. 83–6.
115. Among the smaller combatants, the natural addition to this list is communist, and more likely than not Serb, Yugoslavia, a state which would eventually learn that the fine-print of history was not offering long-term 'victory'.
116. F.H. Hinsley, *British intelligence in the Second World War: its influence on strategy and operations*, London, 1979, pp. 200–5.
117. P. Melograni, *Rapporti segreti*, pp. 101; 122.
118. *Ibid.*, pp. 102–3.
119. M. Knox, *Mussolini unleashed*, pp. 126–33.
120. For an English-language account, see C.G. Segrè, *Italo Balbo: a Fascist life*, Berkeley, 1987, pp. 392–401.
121. N. D'Aroma, *Mussolini segreto*, Rocca San Casciano, 1958, p. 229.
122. For introduction to such social divisions, see G. Rochat, 'Qualche dato sugli ufficiali di complemento dell'esercito nel 1940', *Ricerche storiche*, 23, 1993, pp. 607–35.
123. F. Rossi, *Mussolini e lo stato maggiore: avvenimenti del 1940*, Rome, 1951, p. 9.
124. L. Sorrentino, *Da Bel Ami a Lili Marlene: quello che il corrispondente di guerra non scrisse*, Milan, 1980, p. 50. Among the exempt categories were sportsmen and actors.
125. M. Knox, *Mussolini unleashed*, pp. 159; 193.
126. See R.J.B. Bosworth, *Italy and the wider world 1860–1960*, London, 1996, p. 71.
127. M. Knox, *Hitler's Italian allies: Royal armed forces, Fascist regime, and the war of 1940–1943*, Cambridge, 2000, pp. 17–18.
128. R. Graziani, *Ho difeso la patria*, Milan, 1948, p. 283.
129. G. Bottai, *Diario 1935–1944*, pp. 215; 275.
130. M. Legnani, 'Guerra e governo delle risorse', p. 245.
131. C. Favagrossa, *Perché perdemmo la guerra: Mussolini e la produzione bellica*, Milan, 1946, p. 69.
132. G. Pini and D. Susmel, *Mussolini: l'uomo e l'opera*, Florence, 1953–55, vol. IV, p. 159.
133. For a typical example, see GFM 36/6, meeting of 1 October 1942.
134. F. Anfuso, *Roma, Berlino Salò (1936–1945)*, Milan, 1950, p. 146.
135. M. Legnani, 'Guerra e governo delle risorse', p. 240.
136. A. Cassels, *Fascist Italy*, London, 1969, p. 99.

Notes

137. V. Ronchi, *Guerra e crisi alimentare in Italia: 1940–1950 ricordi ed esperienze*, Rome, 1977, pp. 26–7.

138. *Ibid.*, p. 51.

139. M. Clark, *Modern Italy 1871–1982*, London, 1984, p. 288.

140. A.S. Milward, *War, economy and society 1939–1945*, Harmondsworth, 1987, p. 97.

141. B. Mantelli, 'Camerati del lavoro': *i lavoratori italiani emigrati nel Terzo Reich nel periodo dell'Asse 1938–1943*, Florence, 1992, p. 43.

142. M. Knox, *Hitler's Italian allies*, pp. 51–67, gives a devastating account of Italian inadequacies in this regard, being specially sardonic about what he calls Italy's 'tankette'. Cf. also the memory of Nuto Revelli, eventually to be a marvellous recounter of the horror of Italian armies on the Eastern Front. An entrant to officers' school in 1939 when still a believing Fascist, Revelli says that in his training he never saw a tank. N. Revelli, *La guerra dei poveri*, Turin, 1962, p. 5.

143. G. Bottai, *Diario 1935–1944*, p. 220.

144. R. De Felice, *Mussolini l'alleato 1940–1945 I. L'Italia in guerra 1940–1943*, Turin, 1990, pp. 98–9.

145. G. Bottai, *Diario 1935–1944*, p. 211.

146. Q. Armellini, *Diario di guerra: nove mesi al Comando Supremo*, Milan, 1946, p. 52.

147. R. and E. Packard, *Balcony empire: Fascist Italy at war*, London, 1943, pp. 100–2.

148. *Ibid.*, p. 103. Cf. the similar description in R.G. Massock, *Italy from within*, London, 1943, p. 208, again emphasising the solecisms in dress and the underarm serve from within the court.

149. As the Italian army leadership never ceased to complain. See, for example, F. Pricolo, *Ignavia contro eroismo*, pp. 7–8.

150. J. Steinberg, *All or nothing: the Axis and the Holocaust 1941–1943*, London, 1990, p. 19.

151. F. Pricolo, *Ignavia contro eroismo*, pp. 38–43.

152. *Ibid.*, p. 80.

153. For a bitter account of the levity of Italian diplomacy on the matter, see E. Grazzi, *Il principio della fine (L'impresa di Grecia)*, Rome, 1945.

154. G. Ciano, *Diario 1937–1943*, p. 458.

155. See, for example, DDI 9s, V, 200, 7 July 1940, Ciano to Mussolini.

156. R. De Felice, *L'Italia in guerra 1940–1943*, pp. 302–3.

157. DDI 9s, V, 65, 19 June 1940, Ciano to Mussolini.

158. R. De Felice, *L'Italia in guerra 1940–1943*, pp. 223–68.

159. See, for example, DDI 9s, V, 467, 22 July 1940, Mussolini directive; 753, 19 October 1940, Mussolini to Hitler, in which the *Duce* generously said he was willing to forego Djibouti since it was only a 'desert'. Mussolini also lightly observed that there was no need to worry about the USA, since the Americans were already doing all that they could do to assist their *de facto* allies. See 677, 4 October 1940, Mussolini–Hitler talk report.

160. DDI 9s, V, 728, 15 October 1940, Mussolini meeting with Ciano, Jacomoni and military chiefs report.

161. G. Ciano, *Diario 1937–1943*, p. 470.

162. M. Knox, *Mussolini unleashed*, p. 256.

163. See, for example, DDI 9s, V, 516, 29 August 1940, Ciano to Mussolini, conveying congratulations from Hitler.

164. See DDI 9s, VI, 107, 14–5 November 1940, Badoglio–Keitel talk, in which the Italian typically told his German colleagues that he had no preoccupations about the situation there.

165. A. Sbacchi, *Ethiopia under Mussolini: Fascism and the colonial experience*, London, 1985, p. 215.

166. SPDCR 44, 9 November 1940, Farinacci to Mussolini.

167. For an example of the corruption allegations which soon were directed at him, see SPDCR 67, 10 January 1942, memo.

Notes

168. U. Cavallero, *Comando supremo: diario 1940–43*, Bologna, 1948, p. 8.
169. Q. Armellini, *Diario di guerra*, pp. 8–12.
170. *Ibid.*, p. 183.
171. Some hungry intellectuals were, however, still ready to adapt their prose to the times. See, for example, L. Meneghello, 'Razza e costume nella formazione della coscienza fascista', *Gerarchia*, 19, June 1940, pp. 311–13. In the same issue, *Littoriale* Mario Capuana expatiated on 'Il contributo dell'impero all'autarchia nazionale'.
172. [G. Bottai], 'Verità universale del fascismo', *Critica Fascista*, 18, 1 April 1940, pp. 178–9; 'Guerra di principi', *Critica Fascista*, 18, 1 June 1940, pp. 242–3.
173. SPDCR 47, 31 October 1940, report on Muti.
174. R. De Felice, *L'Italia in guerra 1940–1943*, p. 969.
175. *Ibid.*, p. 973.
176. G. Ciano, *Diario 1937–1943*, pp. 499–500.
177. G. Bottai, *Diario 1935–1944*, p. 246.
178. R. De Felice, *L'Italia in guerra 1940–1943*, p. 369.
179. G. Bottai, *Diario 1935–1944*, p. 245.
180. As is acknowledged by R. De Felice, *L'Italia in guerra 1940–1943*, pp. 536–7.
181. G. Ciano, *Diario 1937–1943*, pp. 526–7. When, in early June, Hitler intimated to his colleague the probable future, Mussolini had responded with the typical jealous hope that the Germans would lose 'plenty of feathers' there (p. 522). In the confusion of the actual invasion, Rosso, the Italian ambassador, who had learned the news of the war by listening to the radio, spent a week locked in a train on the frontier. See M. Toscano, 'L'intervento dell'Italia contro l'Unione Sovietica nel 1941 visto dalla nostra Ambasciata a Mosca (con documenti inediti)', *Nuova Antologia f.*, 1935–36, March–April 1962, pp. 299–312; 445–62.
182. M. Knox, *Hitler's Italian allies*, p. 21.
183. De Felice strenuously argues this case in *L'Italia in guerra*, but he reduces its credibility by his absurd endorsement of the continuing Mussolinian, and Italian, wish that the war find its epicentre in the Mediterranean. Perhaps for a few months in 1940, it was possible to think of a war won through the expulsion of Britain from the Mediterranean but, even then, the Nazis' 'real' war faced east not south or west.
184. R. De Felice, *L'Italia in guerra 1940–1943*, p. 566.
185. J. Goebbels, *The Goebbels diaries 1939–1941* (ed. F. Taylor), London, 1982, p. 405. Earlier, a letter on the 'South Tyrol' had brought blood rushing to his head (p. 208).
186. For an example in Greece, see S. Pelagalli, 'Le relazioni militari italo-germaniche nelle carte del generale Marras addetto militare a Berlino (giugno–settembre 1943)', *Storia contemporanea*, 21, 1990, p. 30.
187. The words are those of Field Marshal Albert Kesselring, quoted by J.J. Sadkovich, 'Of myths and men: Rommel and the Italians in North Africa, 1940–1942', *International History Review*, 13, 1991, p. 311.
188. J. Goebbels, *The Goebbels diaries 1939–1941*, p. 165.
189. *Ibid.*, p. 191.
190. See, for example, reports of the meeting at the Berghof in January 1941 in DDI 9s, VI, 471 and 473, 19 and 20 January 1941. Cf. VII, 503, 25 August, 511, 26 August 1941, meeting on the slowing progress in the USSR, where Mussolini virtually did not add a word, but Hitler grew misty-eyed at the thought that he could retire to Florence after victory was won.
191. G. Ciano, *Diario 1937–1943*, pp. 529; 531.
192. See, for example, DDI 9s, VI, 935, 18 April 1941, Pavelić to Mussolini.
193. N. D'Aroma, *Mussolini segreto*, p. 224.
194. G.N. Amoretti, *La vicenda italo-croata nei documenti di Aimone di Savoia (1941–1943)*,

Notes

195. S.K. Pavlowitch, 'The King who never was: an instance of Italian involvement in Croatia, 1941–3', *European Studies Review*, 8, 1978, pp. 465–87.
196. U. Cavallero, *Comando supremo*, p. 239.
197. G. Ciano, *Diario 1937–1943*, p. 555.
198. See DDI 9s, VI, 18, 30 October 1940, Franco to Mussolini, for the Spanish account of 'friendship' preserved.
199. DDI 9s, VI, 568, 12 February 1941, Mussolini–Franco–Serrano Suñer talk report.
200. DDI 9s, VII, 288, 21 June 1941, Hitler to Mussolini.
201. See, for example, R. De Felice, *L'Italia in guerra 1940–1943*, pp. 749–56.
202. DDI 9s, VII, 299, 23 June 1942, Mussolini to Hitler.
203. DDI 9s, VII, 722, 6 November 1941, Mussolini to Hitler.
204. R. De Felice, *L'Italia in guerra 1940–1943*, pp. 538–9.
205. See, for example, DDI 9s, VII, 808, 3 December 1941, Mussolini–Horikiri talk report.
206. According to Ciano, the King also welcomed the attack. G. Ciano, *Diaries 1937–1943*, p. 564.
207. *Ibid.*, p. 517.

CHAPTER 17

1. G. Ciano, *Diario 1937–1943* (ed. R. De Felice), Milan, 1980, p. 595.
2. For the background of this event, which did indeed mark a change in Hitler's position, see I. Kershaw, *Hitler 1936–1945: nemesis*, London, 2000, pp. 450–3.
3. G. Ciano, *Diario 1937–1943*, p. 569.
4. *Ibid.*, p. 570.
5. *Ibid.*, p. 571.
6. For his own cringing efforts to propagandise the war effort and the link with Germany, see G. Volpi di Misurata, 'L'industria e la guerra', *Civiltà Fascista*, 9, January 1942 (also published in *Nuova Antologia*, f. 1677, 1 February 1942). Volpi preached the Darwinian message that, in war, some forces were destined to conquer and others to die.
7. G. Ciano, *Diario 1937–1943*, p. 572.
8. *Ibid.*, p. 578.
9. R. De Felice, *Mussolini l'alleato 1940–1945 I. L'Italia in guerra 1940–1943*, Turin, 1990, p. 1011.
10. But Cianetti remembered him as 25, as well as seeing proof in the appointment of the profundity of Mussolini's contempt for his entire entourage. See T. Cianetti, *Memorie dal carcere di Verona* (ed. R. De Felice), Milan, 1983, p. 349.
11. BMOO, XXX, pp. 152–7.
12. Eventually, in November 1942, Farinacci sent his leader a long letter warning him about public discontent and urging drastic action. 'The Party', he added, 'is completely absent from everything'; Vidussoni 'a brave boy, but just a boy'.
13. The son-in-law was especially outraged when Vidussoni talked polemically about closing golf courses for the duration of the war, remarking disgustedly that he sounded like a socialist thug from 1920–21. See G. Ciano, *Diario 1937–1943*, pp. 617–18. Ciano was equally appalled by the thought of swingeing penal sanctions for tax evaders (p. 628).
14. G. Bottai, *Diario 1935–1944* (ed. G.B. Guerri), Milan, 1989, p. 305, thought that Vidussoni had trouble reading scripts when confronted by his betters and was then a prey to panic attacks.
15. R. De Felice, *L'Italia in guerra 1940–1943*, pp. 1014–15.
16. C. Senise, *Quando ero Capo della Polizia 1940–1943*, Rome, 1946, p. 97.
17. SPDCR 50, 16 February 1943, A. Caruso to Mussolini.
18. BMOO, XXX, p. 153.

Notes

19. Bottai's journal applauded Vidussoni somewhat enigmatically as the embodiment of the 'youngest generation'. See *Critica Fascista*, 20, 1 January 1942.
20. E. Sulis (ed.), *Mussolini e il Fascismo*, Rome, 1941, p. ix.
21. G. Bottai, *Diario 1935–1944*, pp. 327–8.
22. For a review of these matters, see R. De Felice, *L'Italia in guerra 1940–1943*, pp. 1077–86.
23. *Ibid.*, pp. 1076–8.
24. SPDCR 110, August 1941, report.
25. F. Anfuso, *Roma Berlino Salò (1936–1945)*, Milan, 1950, p. 234.
26. It can be found in BMOO, XXXIV, pp. 193–269.
27. N. D'Aroma, *Mussolini segreto*, Rocca San Casciano, 1958, p. 350.
28. The phrase was duly recorded in a telephone tap available to Mussolini. See U. Guspini, *L'orecchio del regime: le intercettazioni telefoniche al tempo del fascismo*, Milan, 1973, p. 190.
29. G. Ciano, *Diario 1937–1943*, p. 641.
30. R. De Felice, *L'Italia in guerra 1940–1943*, p. 1537.
31. *Ibid.*, p. 189.
32. P. Milza, *Mussolini*, Paris, 1999, p. 796.
33. A. Petacco, *L'archivio segreto di Mussolini*, Milan, 1987, p. 156. This matter was given a special air of hypocrisy since F.S. Petacci, the father and papal doctor, published in *Il Messaggero* a typically overblown piece hailing Fascism for the way it had purified young Italian womanhood, both spiritually and physically. See SPDCR 104, article of 16 November 1937.
34. G. Zachariae, *Mussolini si confessa*, Milan, 1966, p. 36.
35. SPDCR 103, 1942 report.
36. G. Ciano, *Diario 1937–1943*, pp. 632–4.
37. SPDCR 103, 21 February 1943, Petacci plan.
38. F. Bandini, *Claretta: profilo di Clara Petacci e dei suoi tempi*, Milan, 1960, pp. 103–11. The most notorious affair of Fascism at war was, however, that of Alessandro Pavolini with the more successful and more scandalous film actor, Doris Duranti. This last was proud of being the first to exhibit her breasts nude on film (although her claim was contested). See SPDCR 48, 4, 25 March 1942, reports; 26 May 1942, Pavolini pro-memoria. Cf. her version, D. Duranti, *Il romanzo della mia vita* (ed. G.F. Venè), Milan, 1987 and the more sceptical A. Petacco, *Il superfascista: vita e morte di Alessandro Pavolini*, Milan, 1998.
39. G. Bottai, *Diario 1935–1944*, p. 337.
40. SPDCR 117 has a file of correspondence between Mussolini and Angela Curti, Elena's mother.
41. SPDCR 117, 7 August 1941, E. Curti to Mussolini.
42. A. Pozzi, *Come li ho visti io: dal diario di un medico*, Milan, 1947, p. 116.
43. SPDCR 103, 14 February 1943, Paolucci di Calboli to Mussolini.
44. A. Pozzi, *Come li ho visti io*, pp. 118–19.
45. *Ibid.*, p. 164.
46. *Ibid.*, p. 115.
47. E. Ortona, *Diplomazia di guerra: diari 1937–1943*, Bologna, 1993, p. 182.
48. G. Bottai, *Diario 1935–1944*, p. 376.
49. *Ibid.*, p. 340.
50. SPDCR 104, 29 November 1942, Frugoni to De Cesare.
51. R. De Felice, *L'Italia in guerra 1940–1943*, pp. 1083–4.
52. *Ibid.*, p. 1085.
53. G. Pini and D. Susmel, *Mussolini: l'uomo e l'opera*, Florence, 1953–5, vol. IV, p. 221.
54. N. Kalláy, *Hungarian premier: a personal account of a nation's struggle in the Second World War*, London, 1954, p. 146.
55. G. Pini and D. Susmel, *Mussolini*, vol. IV, pp. 227–8.

Notes

56. *Ibid.*, vol. IV, p. 227.

57. De Felice, with his usual effort to be positive about the *Duce*, argues that his health was actually on the mend in July 1943, adding that the improvement demonstrates that the cause was not psychosomatic. R. De Felice, *L'Italia in guerra 1940–1943*, p. 1086. Modern medicine has identified peptic ulcers as produced by a germ called *Helicobacter pylori* and is doubtful of the ameliorative value of the so-called SIPPI diet of milk, cream and boiled food, which seems to have been visited on Mussolini. Stress is no longer thought to be the direct cause, but nervous exhaustion does make it harder for a sufferer to control the symptoms. Mussolini's other ailments may indicate that he had a mild case of Hepatitis C, which was common in Italy. Also the ageing process very likely was seeing his duodenal ulcer extend to a gastric one. Finally, his evident depression may have worsened his whole condition. I owe this advice to Barry J. Marshall of the Australian National Health and Medical Research Council Laboratory, linked to the University of Western Australia.

58. See, for example, DDI 9s, X, 31, 16 February 1943, Hitler to Mussolini; 95, 9 March 1943, Mussolini to Hitler. On this occasion, he shrugged off the damage to his 'nerves' from 'forty-three years' of politicking, by assuring the *Führer*: 'Little personal troubles are as nothing compared with the sickness which the demo-plutocracies and Judaism have inflicted on humankind.'

59. BMOO, XLIV, pp. 268–9.

60. BMOO, XXXI, p. 5.

61. BMOO, XXXI, pp. 16; 21.

62. BMOO, XXXVII, p. 477.

63. BMOO, XXXI, pp. 23–6.

64. BMOO, XXXI, pp. 32–4. Mussolini rather spoiled the emphasis on an iron-hard unity by indulging in local patriotism, telling his audience that people from the region which produced the Mussolinis were 'through all time, decisive in Italian history' (p. 33).

65. BMOO, XXXI, pp. 71–6.

66. A. Pirelli, *Taccuini 1922–1943* (ed. D. Barbone), Bologna, 1984, p. 348.

67. BMOO, XLIV, p. 284.

68. DDI 9s, VIII, 26, 15 December 1941, Ciano–Pavelić talk report. Cf. 195, 23 January 1942, Ambrosio to Cavallero, in which the Chief of General Staff was told of *Ustasha* 'crimes'; 536, 12 May 1942, Giustiniani to Ciano, stating that only 6000 of an original 40 000 Jews remained alive under *Ustasha* rule.

69. DDI 9s, VIII, 29, 16 December 1941, Lanza d'Ajeta to Farace.

70. DDI 9s, X, 24, 15 February 1943, Casertano to Bastianini.

71. See, for example, DDI 9s, VIII, 79, 29 December 1941, Mussolini to Hitler.

72. DDI 9s, VIII, 368, 14 March 1942, Luciolli to Lanza d'Ajeta. Luciolli then went on to attack German policies in general, both during the war and in any coming peace. The message Ciano drew from Luciolli's reports was that one day 'a small but efficient army' (like the Italian) could 'decide the destinies of Europe', by implication in a short, sharp campaign against the Nazis. See G. Ciano, *Diario 1937–1943*, pp. 602–3.

73. G. Miccoli, *I dilemma e i silenzi di Pio XII*, Milan, 2000, pp. 6–13.

74. *Ibid.*, p. 64.

75. For an example, see an effort to save Italian Jews in the Baltic states. DDI 9s, X, 20, 14 February 1943, Bastianini to Alfieri.

76. For the most recent detailed accounts, see J. Steinberg, *All or nothing: the Axis and the Holocaust 1941–3*, London, 1990; D. Carpi, *Between Mussolini and Hitler: the Jews and the Italian authorities in France and Tunisia*, Hanover, 1994.

77. G. Preziosi, 'Per la soluzione del problema ebraico', *La Vita Italiana*, 60, 15 September 1942, pp. 221–4.

Notes

78. R. Farinacci, 'Il problema giudaico da un punto da vista storico-politico', *La Vita Italiana*, 60, 15 July 1942, pp. 3–14.

79. E. Canevari, 'All'inizio dell'anno nuovo', *La Vita Italiana*, 61, 15 January 1943, pp. 3–9; cf., for example, L. Villari, 'I profittatori della guerra americana', *La Vita Italiana*, 61, 15 March 1943, pp. 228–34; 'La delinquenza negli Stati Uniti', issue of 15 May 1943, pp. 445–51. Cf., too, the journal *La Svastica*, from May 1941 a joint publication of the propaganda ministries of the Axis allies.

80. G. Mastrojanni, *Marte e Israele: perchè si combatte*, Bologna, 1943, pp. 276–8.

81. See, for example, R. Pavese, 'Il problema ebraico in Italia', *Gerarchia*, 21, June 1942, pp. 256–8.

82. M. Michaelis, *Mussolini and the Jews: German–Italian relations and the Jewish question in Italy 1922–1945*, Oxford, 1978, p. 303.

83. For an example of the reporting of such sentiments, see DDI 9s, VIII, 307, 23 February 1942, Alfieri to Ciano.

84. For the text, see J. Steinberg, *All or nothing*, p. 2.

85. BMOO, XLIV, 11 October 1942.

86. SPDCR 50, 24 October 1942, Vidussoni to Mussolini.

87. A. Pirelli, *Taccuini 1922–1943*, p. 364.

88. BMOO, XXXI, p. 130.

89. According to Kershaw, the Germans lost around 100 000 outright, while 113 000 were taken prisoner, of whom only a few thousand ever returned home. See I. Kershaw, *Hitler 1936–1945*, p. 550.

90. As if to paper over the difference, Bottai had written at length on the primacy of Italy's contribution to the social and ideological side of the Axis. 'Racial characteristics', he declared, ensured that 'the victorious standards of Italy do not degrade peoples we have defeated but rather associate them in the destiny of our Empire'. G. Bottai, 'Contributi dell'Italia fascista al "nuovo ordine"', *Civiltà Fascista*, 8, December 1941, pp. 6–25.

91. I. Kershaw, *Hitler 1936–1945*, p. 549.

92. See, for example, DDI 9s, VIII, 429, 4 April 1942, Scorza to De Cesare.

93. B. Mantelli, *'Camerati del lavoro': i lavoratori italiani emigrati nel Terzo Reich nel periodo dell'Asse 1938–1943*, Florence, 1992, p. 33.

94. E.L. Homze, *Foreign labor in Nazi Germany*, Princeton, 1967, pp. 61–2; 242.

95. G. Ciano, *Diario 1937–1943*, p. 606.

96. DDI 9s, VIII, 492, 29 April 1942, Mussolini–Hitler talk report.

97. DDI 9s, VIII, 495, 30 April 1942, Mussolini–Hitler talk report. Cf. also 638, 20 June 1942, Mussolini–Hitler talk report.

98. DDI 9s, VIII, 633, 15–19 June 1942, Ciano–Serrano Suñer talk report.

99. DDI 9s, X, 21, 14 February 1943, Mussolini to Franco.

100. For an example, see DDI 9s, X, 95, 9 March 1943, Mussolini to Hitler; 159, 26 March 1943, Mussolini to Hitler.

101. G. Ciano, *Diario 1937–1943*, p. 696.

102. G. Bottai, *Diario 1935–1944*, p. 361. Cf. his meandering defence of his own role as a 'critical Fascist', G. Bottai, 'Funzione rivoluzionaria della critica: nostri vent'anni', *Critica Fascista*, 21, 15 May 1943, pp. 169–75.

103. For the continuation of this sympathy in the historiography, see O. Chadwick, 'Bastianini and the weakening of the Fascist will to fight the Second World War' in T.C.W. Blanning and David Cannadine (eds), *History and biography: essays in honour of Derek Beales*, Cambridge University Press, 1996, pp. 227–42.

104. DDI 9s, X, 198, 6 April 1943, Bastianini to Mussolini.

105. DDI 9s, X, 185, 3 April 1943, Bastianini to Mussolini.

106. Y. De Begnac, *Taccuini mussoliniani* (ed. F. Perfetti), Bologna, 1990, p. 551.

Notes

107. For some of his own expositions of Fascism, see C. Scorza, *Il segreto di Mussolini*, Lanciano, 1933. Later he wrote an account of the *Duce*'s fall, C. Scorza, *La notte del Gran Consiglio*, Milan, 1968.

108. SPDCR 50, 9 February 1943, memorandum. The duty to type the word *DUCE* in capital letters had been instilled by Starace.

109. N. D'Aroma, *Mussolini segreto*, p. 272.

110. SPDCR 49, 7 June 1943, Scorza to Mussolini.

111. SPDCR 115, [May 1943], Edda to Mussolini.

112. BMOO, XXXI, pp. 185–97.

113. In his later self-justification, Mussolini wrote of being especially disgusted by the military failure here. B. Mussolini, *Memoirs 1942–1943 with documents relating to the period* (ed. R. Klibansky), London, 1949, pp. 22–5.

114. Lord Strabolgi, *The conquest of Italy*, London, 1944, p. 30.

115. See, for example, DDI 9s, X, 499, 12 July 1943, Mussolini to Hitler; 505, 13 July 1943, Hitler to Mussolini.

116. DDI 9s, X, 509, 14 July 1943, Mussolini to Ambrosio.

117. PRO Eden papers, FO 954/13B/It/43–1, 14 January 1943, memorandum.

118. E. Ortona, *Diplomazia di guerra*, p. 196.

119. See, for example, DDI 9s, X, 406, 9 June 1943, Vitetti–Acquarone talk report.

120. See, for example, DDI 9s, X, 310, 12 May 1943, Ciano to Mussolini; 382, 1 June 1943, Ciano to Mussolini (in this case with the news that Cardinal Montini – later Paul VI – had warned that the Allies would bomb Rome unless something was done soon).

121. G. Frediani, *La pace separata di Ciano*, Rome, 1990, p. 127. For the specific case of Pirelli, see G. Ciano, *Diario 1937–1943*, p. 687.

122. C. Senise, *Quando ero Capo della Polizia*, p. 141.

123. For an English-language account, see T. Mason, 'The Turin strikes of March 1943', in T. Mason (ed.), *Nazism, Fascism and the working class*, Cambridge, 1995, pp. 274–94.

124. C. Senise, *Quando ero Capo della Polizia*, pp. 171–2.

125. E. Ortona, *Diplomazia di guerra*, p. 211.

126. *Ibid.*, p. 237. De Felice argues a case for the defence that Mussolini was responsibly trying to avoid being a Samson and pulling down the house on his people. The Germans, he was convinced, could never accept an Italian defection. R. De Felice, *L'Italia in guerra 1940–1943*, pp. 1130; 1304.

127. DDI 9s, X, 516, 16 July 1943, Bastianini to Mussolini.

128. DDI 9s, X, 531, 19 July 1943, Mussolini–Hitler talk report.

129. G. Bonacina, *Obiettivo Italia: i bombardamenti aerei delle città italiane dal 1940 al 1945*, Milan, 1970, p. 213.

130. S. Hood, *Carlino*, Manchester, 1985, p. 26.

131. For the fullest account, see R. De Felice, *L'Italia in guerra 1940–1943*, pp. 1089–410.

132. C. Scorza, *La notte del Gran Consiglio*, p. 148.

133. E. Galbiati, *Il 25 luglio e la M.V.S.N.*, Milan, 1950, p. 219.

134. P. Milza, *Mussolini*, p. 822.

135. E. Galbiati, *Il 25 luglio e la M.V.S.N.*, p. 219.

136. C. Scorza, *La notte del Gran Consiglio*, p. 23.

137. *Ibid.*, pp. 72–3.

138. *Ibid.*, p. 107.

139. For the full list of voters, see R. De Felice, *L'Italia in guerra 1940–1943*, p. 1382.

140. He thought these events a 'political thunderbolt'. E. Galbiati, *Il 25 luglio e la M.V.S.N.*, p. 9.

141. *Ibid.*, p. 236.

142. DDI 9s, X, 551, 25 July 1943, Mussolini–Hidaka talk report.

Notes

143. G. Pini and D. Susmel, *Mussolini*, vol. IV, p. 260.

144. R. De Felice, *L'Italia in guerra*, pp. 1397–400.

145. For Mussolini's own account of these events and those that followed, see his *Storia di un anno*, available in BMOO, XXXIV, pp. 301–444.

146. G. Pini and D. Susmel, *Mussolini*, vol. IV, p. 262.

147. F. Maugeri, *From the ashes of disgrace*, New York, 1948, p. 129.

148. R. De Felice, *Mussolini l'alleato 1940–1945 II. La guerra civile 1943–1945*, Turin, 1997, p. 14.

149. See next chapter.

150. R. De Felice, *La guerra civile 1943–1945*, p. 7.

151. BMOO, XXXIV, p. 361.

152. BMOO, XXXIV, p. 364.

153. BMOO, XXXI, p. 264.

154. BMOO, XXXI, p. 265.

155. BMOO, XXXI, pp. 267–8.

156. G. Pini and D. Susmel, *Mussolini*, vol. IV, p. 284.

157. R. De Felice, *La guerra civile 1943–1945*, p. 19.

158. *Ibid.*, p. 21.

159. F. Iurato, 'With Mussolini at the Campo Imperatore', in B. Mussolini, *Memoirs 1942–1943*, p. 247.

160. R. De Felice, *La guerra civile 1943–1945*, p. 26. Cf. also A. Tamaro, *Due anni di storia*, Rome, 1981, vol. I, p. 592.

161. A Fascist journalist claimed that, towards the end of 1944, he again contemplated suicide. See E. Amicucci, *I 600 giorni di Mussolini (dal Gran Sasso a Dongo)*, Rome, 1948, p. 729.

162. The event has been much debated in Italy, especially in recent years, with the De Feliceans seeing it as the worst moment of wartime Italian history. For a patriotic account made available in English, see E. Aga Rossi, *A nation collapses: the Italian surrender of September 1943*, Cambridge, 2000.

163. For his own account, see O. Skorzeny, *Skorzeny's special missions*, London, 1957. Skorzeny wrote that personally he had never forgiven the Italians for their theft of the South Tyrol (p. 46). After the success of his mission, he was accorded the honour of an invitation to take midnight tea with the *Führer* (for his description of this ceremonial event, see p. 90).

164. BMOO, XXXII, pp. 1–5.

165. BMOO, XXXIV, p. 437.

166. For an example, see L. Villari, *Affari esteri 1943–1945*, Rome, 1948, p. 35. He claims Mussolini ordered him to help 'save the saveable'.

167. See the memoirs of one of its servants who used exactly this title. P. Pisenti, *Una Repubblica necessaria (R.S.I.)*, Rome, 1977.

168. For futher on this interpretation, see R.J.B. Bosworth, *The Italian dictatorship: problems and perspectives in the interpretation of Mussolini and Fascism*, London, 1998, pp. 180–204.

169. See G. Dolfin, *Con Mussolini nella tragedia: diario del capo della segreteria particolare del Duce 1943–1944*, Milan, 1949, p. 24.

170. A. Tamaro, *Due anni di storia*, vol. I, p. 591.

171. G. Zachariae, *Mussolini si confessa*, pp. 11–12.

172. G. Dolfin, *Con Mussolini nella tragedia*, p. 34. The stage furniture of the office again included works by Socrates and Plato, open on his desk.

173. G. Zachariae, *Mussolini si confessa*, p. 17.

174. *Ibid.*, pp. 17–19.

175. *Ibid.*, pp. 21–2.

176. *Ibid.*, p. 57.

177. *Ibid.*, p. 123.

Notes

178. *Ibid.*, pp. 23–8.
179. *Ibid.*, p. 20.
180. SPDCR 105, 19 December 1943, Dolfin to Rachele; 2 January 1944, Dolfin to German Counsellor; 20 January 1944, Dolfin note; 4 August 1944, Dolfin to Ditta Capretti Fausto at Brescia.
181. E. Amicucci, *I 600 giorni di Mussolini*, p. 81.
182. SPDCR 112, 5 November 1942, report.
183. F. Anfuso, *Da Palazzo Venezia al Lago di Garda (1936–1945)*, Rome, 1996, p. 350.
184. N. D'Aroma, *Mussolini segreto*, p. 278.
185. Lists of these are preserved in SPDCR RSI.
186. R. De Felice, *Storia degli ebrei italiani sotto il fascismo*, Turin, 1961, p. 524. For further on the Anti-Semitism of Salò and the activities, for example, of Giovanni Preziosi, in March 1944 made head of the *Ispettorato generale per la razza*, see L. Ganapini, *La repubblica delle camicie nere*, Milan, 1999, pp. 132–56.
187. The Manifesto is available in full in R. De Felice, *La guerra civile 1943–1945*, pp. 610–13.
188. L. Ganapini, *La repubblica delle camicie nere*, p. 136.
189. B. Spampanato, *Contromemoriale*, Rome, 1952, vol. 2, p. 33.
190. *Ibid.*
191. Y. De Begnac, *Palazzo Venezia: storia di un regime*, Rome, 1950, p. 392.
192. L. Ganapini, *La repubblica delle camicie nere,* p. 453.
193. For an English-language account of some such women, see M. Fraddosio, 'The Fallen Hero: the myth of Mussolini and Fascist women in the Italian Social Republic (1943–5)', *Journal of Contemporary History*, 31, 1996, pp. 99–124.
194. N. Revelli, *La guerra dei poveri*, Turin, 1962, p. 118.
195. B. Spampanato, *Contromemoriale*, vol. 2, p. 130.
196. I. Kershaw, *Hitler 1936–1945*, pp. 594–7.
197. V. Cerosimo, *Dall'istruttoria alla fucilazione: storia del processo di Verona*, Milan, 1961, p. 189.
198. G. Pini, *Itinerario tragico (1943–1945)*, Milan, 1950, p. 164. An attempted reconciliation with the similar figure of Arpinati had failed (p. 36).
199. G. Dolfin, *Con Mussolini nella tragedia*, p. 29.
200. A. Gravelli, *Mussolini aneddotico*, Rome, 1951, p. 283.
201. G. Dolfin, *Con Mussolini nella tragedia*, p. vii.

CHAPTER 18

1. S. Luzzatto, *Il corpo del duce: un cadavere tra immaginazione, storia e memoria*, Turin, 1998, p. 57.
2. For his end, see H. Fornari, *Mussolini's gadfly: Roberto Farinacci*, Nashville, 1971, p. 214.
3. R.J.B. Bosworth, '*Per necessità famigliare*: hypocrisy and corruption in Fascist Italy', *European History Quarterly*, 30, 2000, pp. 364–5.
4. V. Costa, *L'ultimo federale: memorie della guerra civile 1943–1945*, Bologna, 1997, p. 109.
5. Quoted by S. Luzzatto, *Il corpo del duce*, p. 61.
6. *Ibid.*, pp. 63–4.
7. *Ibid.*, p. 57.
8. See, for example, G. Ansaldo, *Diario di prigionia* (ed. R. De Felice), Bologna, 1993, p. 361.
9. See B. Spampanato, *Contromemoriale*, Rome, 1952, vol. 1, p. 338.
10. S. Luzzatto, *Il corpo del duce*, pp. 57; 70. Going way over the rhetorical top, Luzzatto argues that the events in Piazzale Loreto carried echoes of the crucifixion of Christ (p. 64) and of the Jewish sacrifices in the Holocaust (p. 84).
11. A. Soffici and G. Prezzolini, *Diari 1939–1945*, Rome, 1962, p. 347.

Notes

12. S. Luzzatto, *Il corpo del duce*, pp. 67–8.
13. G. Pisanò, *Gli ultimi cinque secondi di Mussolini*, Milan, 1996, pp. 179–83.
14. See W.C. Langer, *The mind of Adolf Hitler*, London, 1973.
15. See J.P. Diggins, *Mussolini and Fascism: the view from America*, Princeton, 1972, p. xv.
16. A. Pensotti, *Rachele: sessant'anni con Mussolini nel bene e nel male*, Milan, 1983, p. 200.
17. S. Luzzatto, *Il corpo del duce*, pp. 84–5.
18. D. Leccisi, *Con Mussolini prima e dopo Piazzale Loreto*, Rome, 1991, p. 247.
19. *Ibid.*, pp. 252–61.
20. *Ibid.*, pp. 262–3.
21. S. Luzzatto, *Il corpo del duce*, pp. 100–1; 103.
22. D. Leccisi, *Con Mussolini prima e dopo Piazzale Loreto*, pp. 263–5.
23. *Ibid.*, p. 266.
24. W.S. McBirnie, *What the bible says about Mussolini*, Norfolk, Va, 1944, pp. 85; 108. McBirnie, another given to mathematical certainties, knew that the *Duce* had so far committed 44 of the acts of the Anti-Christ and in the proper order. He had 10 to complete.
25. S. Luzzatto, *Il corpo del duce*, pp. 101; 103–4.
26. *Ibid.*, p. 105.
27. D. Leccisi, *Con Mussolini prima e dopo Piazzale Loreto*, p. 294.
28. S. Luzzatto, *Il corpo del duce*, p. 108.
29. *Ibid.*, p. 111.
30. *Ibid.*, p. 120. After brief imprisonment, the two priests were sent off to work among emigrants in South America where, according to Leccisi, they were welcomed with open arms. See D. Leccisi, *Con Mussolini prima e dopo Piazzale Loreto*, p. 326.
31. B. D'Agostini, *Colloqui con Rachele Mussolini*, Rome, 1946, p. 9. After the war, for a while the family had stayed in a villa on the island of Ischia, but soon moved back to the Villa Carpena.
32. V. Emiliani, *I tre Mussolini*, Milan, 1997, p. 148.
33. BMOO, XXXIII, p. 222.
34. I. De Begnac, *Trent'anni di Mussolini 1883–1915*, Rome, 1934, pp. 265–6.
35. *Ibid.*, p. 179.
36. S. Luzzatto, *Il corpo del duce*, p. 212.
37. PRO, FO 371/130456, 9 September 1957, Burnett to Selwyn Lloyd.
38. V. Emiliani, *Il paese dei Mussolini*, Turin, 1984, pp. 38–9; 99.
39. *Ibid.*, pp. 52; 76–7.
40. According to post-war accounts, Arpinati had annoyed Mussolini by opposing, in 1933, Rachele's dabbling in contracts at the nearby spa of Castrocaro Terme. See A. Iraci, *Arpinati: l'oppositore di Mussolini*, Rome, 1970, pp. 181–2.
41. G. Dolfin, *Con Mussolini nella tragedia: diario del capo della segreteria particolare del Duce 1943–1944*, Milan, 1949, p. 82.
42. V. Emiliani, *Il paese dei Mussolini*, p. 120.
43. V. Querel, *Il paese di Benito: cronache di Predappio e dintorni*, Rome, 1954, p. 22.
44. *Ibid.*, pp. 33; 61.
45. *Ibid.*, pp. 38–9.
46. G. Zachariae, *Mussolini si confessa*, Milan, 1966, p. 34. Perhaps, among the quarrelling family, she reminded him, in her *petit bourgeois* ordinariness and conformism, of Claretta Petacci.
47. V. Querel, *Il paese di Benito*, p. 74.
48. A. Spinosa, *I figli del Duce*, Milan, 1989, p. 239.
49. V. Querel, *Il paese di Benito*, p. 75.
50. V. Mussolini, *Mussolini: the tragic women in his life*, London, 1973, p. 125.
51. Perhaps the graver part of the charge was that men were watching. See E. Settimelli, *Edda*

Notes

contro Benito: indagine sulla personalità del Duce attraverso un memoriale autografo di Edda Ciano Mussolini qui riprodotto, Rome, 1952, p. 64.

52. A. Spinosa, *I figli del Duce*, p. 233.

53. *Ibid.*, p. 244.

54. And one of which it was said his father had disapproved. See G. Zachariae, *Mussolini si confessa*, p. 34.

55. Romano Mussolini, *Benito Mussolini: apologia di mio padre*, Bologna, 1969. Vittorio Mussolini had ghosted for him some pot-boiler memoirs. See, in English, V. Mussolini, *Mussolini, the tragic women in his life*, London, 1973.

56. A. Spinosa, *I figli del Duce*, pp. 257–67.

57. A copy writer in the London *Times* no doubt enjoyed heading a story about her 'Mussolini declares for election'. See *The Times*, 23 November 1993.

58. C. Valentini, 'Il mio duce è il Cavaliere', *L'Espresso*, XLV, 24 February 2000.

59. S. Setta, *L'Uomo qualunque, 1944–1948*, Bari, 1975, p. 3.

60. P. Ignazi, *Il polo escluso: profilo del Movimento Sociale Italiano*, Bari, 1989, p. 15.

61. S. Luzzatto, *Il corpo del duce*, p. 112.

62. For a repentant autobiography of one such thug, see G. Salierno, *Autobiografia di un picchiatore fascista*, Turin, 1976.

63. *Gente* and *popolo* both mean people, although the first term is the vaguer. For more on Battistessa before 1945, see G. Cresciani, *Fascism, Anti-Fascism and Italians in Australia 1922–1945*, Canberra, 1980.

64. S. Luzzatto, *Il corpo del duce*, p. 194. Luzzatto thinks that this culture was 'hegemonic' and, in a praiseworthy manner, flourished without state subsidy (p. 198).

65. See further, R.J.B. Bosworth, *The Italian dictatorship: problems and perspectives in the interpretation of Mussolini and Fascism*, London, 1998, p. 180.

66. P. Ignazi, *Il polo escluso*, p. 150, f.n. 39.

67. *Ibid.*, p. 152. G. Volpe published the MSI's 'theoretical' journal *La Torre* and also the appendix of eight volumes of Mussolini's works (BMOO XXXVII –XLIV), which came out in Rome between 1978 and 1980.

68. For his memoirs, see B. Bottai, *Fascismo famigliare*, Casale Monferrato, 1997.

69. A.J.P. Taylor, *The Origins of the Second World War*, Harmondsworth, 1964, pp. 84–5. For further on the context of this comment, cf. R.J.B. Bosworth, *The Italian dictatorship*, pp. 82–105.

70. For a deconstruction, see T. Mason, 'The great economic history show', *History Workshop*, 21, 1986; 'Italy and modernization: a montage', *History Workshop*, 25, 1988.

71. In England, too, there was the curious case of Richard Lamb. See his laudatory introduction to B. Mussolini, *My rise and fall*, New York, 1998, p. xi.

72. For a belated example, see R. De Felice, *Rosso e nero* (ed. P. Chessa), Milan, 1995.

73. For a typical example of the new moderation, see P. Milza, *Mussolini*, Paris, 1999.

74. For a reproduction of the image, see R.J.B. Bosworth, 'Italian foreign policy and its historiography' in R.J.B. Bosworth and G. Rizzo (eds), *Altro polo: intellectuals and their ideas in contemporary Italy*, Sydney, 1983, p. 66.

75. See L. Trevisan, *Il naso di Mussolini*, Milan, 1998. Similarly, there was brief excitement in the 1990s over some forged Mussolini diaries. See B. Mussolini, *I diari del mistero*, Milan, 1994. As early as 1950, one author imagined a Mussolini rendered victorious in the Second World War after it turned out that the Axis had the Bomb. M. Ramperti, *Benito I Imperatore*, Rome, 1950. It is typical, however, that the more commercial imaginings of Robert Harris have dealt with Hitler and Stalin, but not Mussolini.

76. T. Holme, *The devil and the dolce vita*, New York, 1982.

77. For all his debt to contemporary 'revisionism', A. Campi, *Mussolini*, Bologna, 2001 is still a little perturbed by the possibility that Mussolini's ghost can afflict the Italians.

Select bibliography

ARCHIVAL MATERIAL

Archivio centrale dello stato (Rome):
Segreteria particolare del Duce: carteggio riservato
Segreteria particolare del Duce: carteggio ordinario (selected *buste*)
Segreteria particolare del Duce: carte della cassetta di zinco
Segreteria particolare del Duce: carte della valigia
Segreteria particolare del Duce: carteggio riservato 1943–1945 (selected *buste*)
Ministero della Cultura Popolare. Direzione Propaganda (selected *buste*)
Ministero dell'Interno. Direzione Generale di Pubblica Sicurezza (selected *buste*)
Ministero dell'Interno: Direzione Generale di Pubblica Sicurezza: Divisione Affari generali e riservati: Confinati politici (selected *buste*)
Carte M. Bianchi
Carte E. De Bono
Carte R. Farinacci
Carte A. Finzi
Carte B. Spampanato
Carte G. Volpi

Archivio di stato di Forlì:
Archivio di gabinetto

Archivio del Touring Club Italiano (Milan)

Public Record Office (London):
Foreign Office FO 371 files on Italy
Selected FO 800 files from the papers of Lord Curzon, Lord Halifax, S. Hoare, R. MacDonald, J. Simon and A. Eden (FO 954)
The papers of Austen Chamberlain
GFM 36 captured Italian files from 'Mussolini's handbag' (material also available at ACS, Rome in SPD files)

Churchill College Cambridge:
The papers of R. Vansittart

Select bibliography

PUBLISHED GOVERNMENT MATERIAL

Documents on British foreign policy 1919–1939, 2nd and 3rd series
Documents on German foreign policy 1918–1945, series C and D
I documenti diplomatici italiani serie 7, 8, 9, 10
Records and documents of the Holy See relating to the Second World War

JOURNALS

L'Ala d'Italia
L'Assalto
Augustea
Civiltà Cattolica
Civiltà Fascista
Clio
Critica Fascista
La Difesa della razza
L'Economia nazionale
The Economist
The Evening Standard
I Fasci italiani all'estero (from June 1925 entitled *Il Legionario*)
Fascismo
Il Gazzettino
Italia contemporanea
Gerarchia
Headway
L'Idea di Roma
L'Illustrazione italiana
Italia e Civiltà
Meridiani
Nuova Antologia
Nuova Storia contemporanea
L'Oltremare
Passato e presente
Politica
Il Popolo d'Italia
Ricerche storiche
Rivista d'Albania
Rivista di politica economica
Rivista di storia contemporanea
Rivista di viaggi
Rivista storica italiana
Rivista storica del Risorgimento
Romana
The Scotsman
Lo Sport fascista
Storia contemporanea
Storia delle relazioni internazionali
Studi storici
Survey of International Affairs
La Svastica

Select bibliography

The Tablet
The Times
Le Tre Venezia
Le Vie d'Italia
La Vita italiana all'estero

BIOGRAPHICAL ACCOUNTS OF MUSSOLINI

Adami, E. *La lingua di Mussolini*, Società Tipografica Modenese, Modena, 1939.

Aniente, A. *Mussolini*, Grasset, Paris, 1932.

Ardali, P. *Mussolini e Pio XI*, Edizioni Paladino, Mantua, 1926.

Ardali, P. *San Francesco e Mussolini*, Edizioni Paladino, Mantua, 1927.

Balabanoff, A. *Il traditore: Mussolini e la conquista del potere*, Universale Napoleone, Rome, 1973.

Balbo, E. *Augusto e Mussolini*, Casa Editrice Pinciana, Rome, 1937.

Barzini, L. 'B. Mussolini', *Encounter*, 23, 1964.

Bedeschi, E. *La giovinezza del Duce: ricordi e luoghi mussoliniani: libro per la gioventù italiana*, Società Editrice Internazionale, Turin, 1939.

Bedeschi, S. and Alessi, R. *Anni giovanili di Mussolini*, Mondadori, Milan, 1939.

Bell, E.P. *Italy's rebirth: Premier Mussolini tells of Fascismo's purpose*, Chicago Daily News, Chicago, 1924.

Benedetti, V. *Rosa Maltoni Mussolini*, Vittorio Gatti editore, Brescia, 1928.

Berneri, C. *Mussolini: psicologia di un dittatore* (ed. P.C. Masini), Edizioni Azione Comune, Milan, 1966.

Biancini, B. (ed.), *Dizionario mussoliniano: mille affermazioni e definizioni del Duce*, Hoepli, Milan, 1939.

Biondi, D. 'Come nacque il mito del Duce', *Nuova Antologia*, f. 1997, 1967.

Bitelli, G. *Benito Mussolini*, G. Paravia, Turin, 1938.

Boatti, G (ed.) *Caro Duce: lettere di donne italiane a Mussolini 1922–1943*, Rizzoli, Milan, 1989.

Bocca, G. *Mussolini socialfascista*, Garzanti, Milan, 1983.

Bonavita, F. *Mussolini svelato: origine, sviluppo e finalità del pensiero mussoliniano*, Sonzogno, Milan, 1927.

Bonavita, F. *Il padre del Duce*, Casa Editrice Pinciana, Rome, 1933.

Bonavita, F. *Primavera fascista dall'avvento fascista all'impero africano*, Gontrano Martucci, Milan, 1937.

Bond, J. *Mussolini: the wild man of Europe*, Independent Publishing Company, Washington, D.C., 1929.

Bordeux, V.J. *Benito Mussolini – the man*, Hutchinson, London, n.d.

Borghi, A. *Mussolini: red and black*, Wishart books, London, 1935.

Bottai, G. *Mussolini: costruttore d'impero*, Edizioni Paladino, Mantua, n.d.

Bozzetti, G. *Mussolini: direttore dell'Avanti!* Feltrinelli, Milan, 1979.

Brancati, R. *Il Duce*, Studio Editoriale Moderno, Catania, 1934.

Buonamici, M. *Duce nostro*, Nemi, Florence, 1933.

Burani, U. *Ineluttabilità mussoliniana*, P. Maglione editore, Rome, 1939.

Campi, A. *Mussolini*, Il Mulino, Bologna, 2001.

Cannistraro P.V. and Sullivan, B.R. *Il Duce's other woman*, William Morrow, New York, 1993.

Castellini, F. *Il ribelle di Predappio: amori e giovinezza di Mussolini*, Mursia, Milan, 1996.

Cavacciocchi, G. *Mussolini: sintesi critiche*, Vallecchi, Florence, 1932.

Ciarlantini, F. *Mussolini immaginario*, Sonzogno, Milan, 1933.

Collier, R. *Duce! the rise and fall of Benito Mussolini*, Collins, London, 1971.

D'Agostini, B. *Colloqui con Rachele Mussolini*, O.E.T. Edizioni del Secolo, Rome, 1946.

Select bibliography

D'Andrea, U. *Mussolini: motore del secolo*, Hoepli, Milan, 1937.

D'Aroma, N. *Vent'anni insieme: Vittorio Emanuele e Mussolini*, Cappelli, Rocca San Casciano, 1957.

D'Aroma, N. *Mussolini segreto*, Cappelli, Rocca San Casciano, 1958.

D'Aurora, G. *La maschera e il volto di Magda Fontages*, Celes, Milan, 1946.

De Begnac, Y. *Palazzo Venezia: storia di un regime*, Editrice la Rocca, Rome, 1950.

De Begnac, I. [sic] *Trent'anni di Mussolini 1883–1915*, Arte Grafiche Menaglia, Rome, 1934.

De Begnac, Y. *Taccuini mussoliniani* (ed. F. Perfetti), Il Mulino, Bologna, 1990.

De Felice, R. *Mussolini il rivoluzionario 1883–1920*, Einaudi, Turin, 1965.

De Felice, R. *Mussolini il fascista: I. la conquista del potere 1921–1925*, Einaudi, Turin, 1966.

De Felice, R. *Mussolini il fascista: II. l'organizzazione dello stato fascista 1925–1929*, Einaudi, Turin, 1968.

De Felice, R. and Mariano, E. (eds), *Carteggio D'Annunzio–Mussolini (1919–1938)*, Mondadori, Milan, 1971.

De Felice, R. *Mussolini il duce: I. gli anni del consenso 1929–1936*, Einaudi, Turin, 1974.

De Felice, R. (ed.) *Benito Mussolini: quattro testimonianze – Alceste De Ambris, Luigi Campolonghi, Mario Girardon, Maria Rygier*, La Nuova Italia, Florence, 1976.

De Felice, R. (ed.) *Utopia: rivista quindicinale del socialismo rivoluzionario italiano – direttore Benito Mussolini*, Feltrinelli reprint, Milan, 1976.

De Felice, R. *Mussolini il duce: II. lo stato totalitario 1936–1940*, Einaudi, Turin, 1981.

De Felice, R. and Goglia, L. *Mussolini il mito*, Laterza, Bari, 1983.

De Felice, R. *Mussolini l'alleato 1940–1945: I. l'Italia in guerra 1940–1943*, Einaudi, Turin, 1990.

De Felice, R. (ed.) *Mussolini giornalista*, Rizzoli, Milan, 1995.

De Felice, R. *Mussolini l'alleato 1940–1945: II. la guerra civile 1943–1945*, Einaudi, Turin, 1997.

De Fiori, V.E. *Mussolini: the man of destiny*, Dent, London, 1919.

Dei Gaslini, M. *Mussolini in Africa*, Edizioni Paladino, Mantua, n.d.

Delcroix, C. *Un uomo e un popolo*, Vallecchi, Florence, 1928.

Della Pura, E. *Lo scolare Benito Mussolini*, Edizione Via dell'Impero U. Giardini, Pisa, 1938.

De Renzis, R. *Mussolini musicista*, Edizioni Paladino, Mantua, 1927.

De' Rossi dell'Arno, G. *Pio XI e Mussolini*, Corso editore, Rome, 1954.

Dinale, O. *Quarant'anni di colloqui con lui*, Ciarrocca, Milan, 1953.

Dolcetti, G. *Le origini storiche della famiglia Mussolini*, Casa Editrice Pietro Brasolini, Venice, 1928.

Dombrowski, R. *Mussolini: twilight and fall*, Heinemann, London, 1956.

Emiliani, V. *Il paese dei Mussolini*, Einaudi, Turin, 1984.

Emiliani, V. *I tre Mussolini: Luigi, Alessandro, Benito*, Baldini e Castoldi, Milan, 1997.

Fanciulli, G. *Il Duce del popolo italiano*, Segreteria Generale dei Fasci all'Estero, Rome, 1928.

Fanelli, G.A. *Cento pagine su Mussolini e un ritratto politico della 'prima ora'*, P. Maglione editore, Rome, 1931.

Fermi, L. *Mussolini*, University of Chicago Press, 1966.

Fisher, G. and McNair-Wilson, M. *Blackshirt: the decline and fall of a dictator*, Belmont, New York, 1961.

Forzano, G. *Mussolini: autore drammatico con fascimili di autografi inediti: Campo di Marte-Villafranca-Cesare*, G. Barbèra editore, Florence, 1954.

Gallo, M. *Mussolini's Italy: twenty years of the Fascist era*, Abelard-Schuman, London, 1974.

Gennaiolo, G. *Mussolini e Napoleone I*, Tipografia S. Boncampagni, San Sepolcro, 1926.

Ghersi, G. *Mussolini: fabbro dello stato*, La Tradizione, Milan, 1937.

Ghignoni, A. *Universalità di Mussolini*, Casa Editrice Ambrosiana, Milan, 1941.

Gianturco, L.E. *Arnaldo Mussolini*, Edito della Federazione dei Fasci di Combattimento, Como, 1934.

Grana, S. *Mussolini spiegato ai bimbi: facili conversazioni sull'opera del Duce di prima o dopo la Marcia su Roma rivolte alle piccole e utili ai grandi*, Paravia, Turin, 1937.

Select bibliography

Gravelli, A. *Uno e molti: interpretazioni spirituali di Mussolini*, Nuova Europa, Rome, 1938.

Gravelli, A. *Mussolini aneddotico*, Casa Editrice Latinità, Rome, 1951.

Gray, E.M. *Il Duce in Libia: che cosa ha detto, che cosa ha visto*, Il Consultore, Milan, 1937.

Gregor, A.J. *Young Mussolini and the intellectual origins of Fascism*, University of California Press, Berkeley, 1979.

Hibbert, C. *Benito Mussolini*, Longmans, London, 1962.

Jones, S. *Benito Mussolini: an introduction to the study of Fascism*, Hunter and Longhurst, London, 1927.

Kemechey, L. *'Il Duce': the life and work of Benito Mussolini*, Williams and Norgate, London, 1930.

Kirkpatrick, I. *Mussolini: study of a demagogue*, Odhams books, London, 1964.

Ludwig, E. *Talks with Mussolini*, George Allen and Unwin, London, 1932.

Ludwig, E. 'Mussolini: the Italian autocrat', in *Leaders of Europe*, Ivor Nicholson and Watson, London, 1934.

Luzzatto, S. *Il corpo del Duce: un cadavere tra immaginazione, storia e memoria*, Einaudi, Turin, 1998.

Macartney, M.H.H. *One man alone: the history of Mussolini and the Axis*, Chatto and Windus, London, 1944.

Mack Smith, D. 'Mussolini: artist in propaganda', *History Today*, 9, 1959.

Mack Smith, D. *Mussolini*, Weidenfeld and Nicolson, London, 1981.

Malaparte, C. *Muss: Il grande imbecille*, Luni editrice, Milan, 1999.

'Marga', *Aneddoti e giudizi su Mussolini con lettera*, Bemporad, Florence, 1925.

Marpicati, A. *Il Duce e le sue opere: conferenza tenuta nel teatro dell'opera del Casino Municipale nell' 'Annuale' della Fondazione dei Fasci di Combattimento*, San Remo, 1938.

Marroni, C. *Mussolini se stesso*, G.B. Palumbo editore, Palermo, 1939.

Martinelli, F. *Mussolini ai raggi X*, Giovanni De Vecchi editore, Milan, 1964.

Masciangioli, L. *Mussolini da lontano*, Stabilimento Tipografico Editoriale Angeletti, Sulmona, 1937.

Masini, P.C. *Mussolini: la maschera del dittatore*, Biblioteca Franco Serantini, Milan, 1999.

Massani, G. *La sua terra*, Istituto Italiano d'Arti Grafiche, Bergamo, 1936.

Massani, G. *Duce e Popolo*, Il Rubicone, Milan, 1942.

Mastri, P. *La Rocca delle Caminate (Il Castello del Duce)*, Zanichelli, Bologna, 1927.

Mattioli, G. *Mussolini aviatore*, Mondadori, Milan, 1942.

Megaro, G. *Mussolini in the making*, George Allen and Unwin, London, 1938.

Mezzetti, N. *Mussolini e la questione sociale*, Casa Editrice Pinciana, Rome, 1931.

Micheli, G. *Mussolini: versi romaneschi*, Casa Editrice Ausonia, Rome, 1930.

Milza, P. *Mussolini*, Fayard, Paris, 1999.

Monelli, P. *Mussolini, piccolo borghese*, Garzanti, Milan, 1950.

Montanelli, I. *Il buonanimo Mussolini*, Edizioni Riunite, Milan, 1947.

Mussolini, B. *Il mio diario di guerra (1915–1917)*, Imperia, Milan, 1923.

Mussolini, B. *My autobiography*, Hutchinson, London, n.d.

Mussolini, B. *John Huss*, Albert and Charles Boni, New York, 1929.

Mussolini, B. *The cardinal's mistress*, Cassell, London, 1929.

Mussolini, B. *La dottrina del fascismo: con una storia del movimento fascista di Gioacchino Volpe*, Treves-Treccani-Tuminelli, Rome, 1932.

Mussolini, B. and Forzano, G. *Napoleon: the hundred days (adapted from the Italian for the English stage by John Drinkwater)*, Sidgwick and Jackson, London, 1932.

Mussolini, B. 'The political and social doctrine of Fascism', *Political Quarterly*, 4, 1933.

Mussolini, B. *Memoirs 1942–1943 with documents relating to the period*, Weidenfeld and Nicolson, London, 1949.

Mussolini, B. *Opera omnia* (eds E. and D. Susmel), 36 vols, La Fenice, Florence, 1951–62.

Select bibliography

Mussolini, B. *Testamento spirituale con uno studio di Duilio Susmel*, Edito a cura di Comitato Repubblica Sociale Italiana, Milan, 1956.

Mussolini, B. *Corrispondenza inedita* (ed. D. Susmel), Edizioni del Borghese, Milan, 1972.

Mussolini, B. *The Corporate state*, H. Fertig, New York, 1975.

Mussolini, B. *Opera omnia* (eds E. and D. Susmel) *Appendici I–VIII* (vols 37–44), Giovanni Volpe editore, Florence, 1978–1980.

Mussolini, B. *Scritti politici* (ed. E. Santarelli), Feltrinelli, Milan, 1979.

Mussolini, B. *My rise and fall* (ed. R. Lamb), Da Capo press, New York, 1998.

['Mussolini, B.'] *I diari del mistero: piccola antologia di manoscritti attribuiti a Mussolini dalla presa di potere all'entrata in guerra*, Mondadori, Milan, 1994.

Mussolini, E. *Mio fratello Benito: memorie raccolte e trascritte da Rosetta Ricci Crisolini*, La Fenice, Florence, 1957.

Mussolini Ciano, E. *My truth (as told to Albert Zarca)*, Weidenfeld and Nicolson, London, 1977.

Mussolini, Rachele *My life with Mussolini*, Robert Hale, London, 1959.

Mussolini, Rachele *The real Mussolini (as told to A. Zarca)*, Saxon House, Farnborough, 1973.

Mussolini, Romano *Benito Mussolini: apologia di mio padre*, Collana di studi storici a cura di Rivista Romana, Bologna, 1969.

Mussolini, V. *Voli sulle Ambe*, Sansoni, Florence, 1937.

Mussolini, V. *Vita con mio padre*, Mondadori, Milan, 1957.

Mussolini, V. *Mussolini: the tragic women in his life*, NEL, London, 1973.

'Mussoliniana', *Mussolini e lo sport*, Edizioni Paladino, Mantua, 1928.

Orano, P. *Mussolini da vicino*, Casa Editrice Pinciana, Rome, 1935.

Orano, P. *Mussolini: fondatore dell'impero*, Casa Editrice Pinciana, Rome, 1936.

Passerini, L. *Mussolini immaginario: storia di una biografia 1915–1939*, Laterza, Bari, 1991.

Pedrazza, P. *Giornalismo di Mussolini*, Casa Editrice Oberdan Zucchi, Milan, 1937.

Pellegrino, C. *Benito Mussolini e la ricostruzione nazionale per i fanciulli d'Italia*, Società Editrice Dante Alighieri, Milan, 1928.

Pensotti, A. *Rachele: sessant'anni con Mussolini nel bene e nel male*, Bompiani, Milan, 1983.

Perroni, V. *Il Mussolini dei bimbi*, Libreria del Littorio, Rome, 1929.

Perroni, V. *Il Duce ai Balilla: brani e pensieri dei discorsi di Mussolini, ordinati e illustrati per i bimbi d'Italia*, Libreria del Littorio, Rome, 1930.

Petacco, A. *Dear Benito, Caro Winston: verità e misteri del carteggio Churchill–Mussolini*, Mondadori, Milan, 1985.

Petacco, A. *L'archivio segreto di Mussolini*, Mondadori, Milan, 1997.

Petrie, C. *Mussolini*, Holme Press, London, 1931.

Petrie, C. 'Mussolini' in his *Great contemporaries*, Cassell, London, 1935.

Petrucci, S. *In Puglia con Mussolini: cronache e note di un inviato speciale con il testo integrale dei discorsi editi e inediti pronunciati dal Duce nelle giornate pugliesi del settembre XII*, Società Editrice di 'Novissima', Rome, 1935.

Pierson, L. [Forest, E.] *Mussolini visto da una scrittrice olandese*, Anonimo Tipografico Editoriale Libraria, Rome, 1933.

Pini, G. *The official life of Benito Mussolini*, Hutchinson, London, 1939.

Pini, G. and Susmel, D. *Mussolini: l'uomo e l'opera* 4 vols, La Fenice, Florence, 1953–5.

Pisanò, G. *Gli ultimi cinque secondi di Mussolini*, Il Saggiatore, Milan, 1996.

Policastro, G. *Crispi e Mussolini*, Edizioni Paladino, Mantua, 1928.

Policastro, G. *Mussolini e la Sicilia*, Edizioni "Mussoliniana", Mantua, 1929.

Preti, L. *Mussolini giovane*, Rusconi, Milan, 1982.

Proli, V. and Moschi, S. (eds), 'Alessandro Mussolini: fabbro ferraio-uomo politico: raccolti di notizie biografiche', unpublished MS, Predappio, 1999.

Quaranta di San Severino, B. *Mussolini as revealed in his political speeches*, Dent, London, 1923.

Querèl, V. *Il paese di Benito: cronache di Predappio e dintorni*, Corso editore, Rome, 1954.

Select bibliography

Rafanelli, L. *Una donna e Mussolini* (ed. P.C. Masini), Rizzoli, Milan, 1975.

Ramperti, M, *Benito I Imperatore*, Scirè, Rome, 1950.

Redaelli, C. *Iniziando Mussolini alle vie del cielo*, Fratelli Magnani, Milan, 1933.

Ridley, J. *Mussolini*, Cassell, London, 1997.

Ronchi, E. *Mussolini: economista della rivoluzione*, Casa Editrice Pinciana, Rome, n.d.

Ronchi, E. *Mussolini: creatore d'economia*, Casa Editrice Pinciana, Rome, 1936.

Rossato, A. *Mussolini: colloquio intimo*, Modernissima Casa Editrice Italiana, Milan, 1923.

Rossi, C. *Mussolini com'era*, Ruffolo editore, Rome, 1947.

Rossi, C. *Trentatre vicende mussoliniane*, Casa Editrice Ceschina, Milan, 1958.

Rossi, C. *Personaggi di ieri e oggi*, Casa Editrice Ceschina, Milan, 1960.

Rossi, F. *Mussolini e lo stato maggiore: avvenimenti del 1940*, Regionale, Rome, 1951.

Rossi, G. *Al sublime artefice fondatore dell'impero ed agli eroi della gesta gloriosa italiana in Africa Orientale: poesia*, Tipografia Grifani-Donati, Città di Castello, 1937.

Rossi, L. *Uomini che ho conosciuto: Mussolini*, Trevi editore, Rome, 1982.

Rossi, R. *Mussolini nudo alla meta*, Edizioni 'La Rinascita d'Italia', Rome, 1944.

Sandri, S. *La vita del Duce dall'infanzia fino ad oggi*, Società Tipografica Editrice Siciliana, Catania, n.d.

Santoro, N. *I cinque giorni del Duce a Milano*, Lettura italiana, Milan, 1937.

Sapori, F. *L'Arte e il Duce*, Mondadori, Milan, 1932.

Sapori, F. (ed.) *Il Duce nel mondo: giudizi tradotti e presentati*, Società Editrice di 'Novissimo', Rome, 1938.

Sardo, A. *Mussolini: libro dedicato ai giovani*, Società Editrice Dante Aligheri, Milan, 1927.

Sarfatti, M. *The life of Benito Mussolini*, T. Butterworth, London, 1934.

Scorza, C. *Il segreto di Mussolini*, Gino Carabba editore, Lanciano, 1933.

Seldes, G. *Sawdust Caesar: the untold history of Mussolini and Fascism*, A. Barker, London, 1936.

Settimelli, E. *Gli animatori: Benito Mussolini*, Società Tipografica Editoriale Porta, Piacenza, 1922.

Settimelli, E. *Mussolini visto da Settimelli*, Casa Editrice Pinciana, 1929.

Settimelli, E. *Edda contro Benito: indagine sulla personalità del Duce attraverso un memoriale autografo di Edda Ciano Mussolini qui riprodotto*, Casa Editrice Libraria Corso, Rome, 1952.

Sigillino, N. *Mussolini visto da me*, Edizioni Casa del Libro, Rome, 1935.

Silvestri, C. *Matteotti, Mussolini e il dramma italiano*, Cavallotti editori, Milan, 1981.

Smiles, S. *Passi scelti del Character con note tolte dei discorsi del Duce* (ed. C. Cucchi), Società Anonima Editrice Dante Alighieri, Milan, 1938.

Somma, L. *Mussolini morto e vivo*, Vito Bianco editore, Naples, 1960.

Speciale, F. *Augusto fondatore dell'impero romano: Il Duce fondatore dell'impero italiano*, Società Anonima Tipografia Editrice Trevigiana, Treviso, 1937.

Spinetti, E. *Sintesi di Mussolini: raccolta di brani di scritti e discorsi di Mussolini, ordinati secondo un criterio logico in ordine cronologico*, Cappelli, Rocca San Casciano, 1950.

Spinetti, G.S. *Mistica fascista nel pensiero di Arnaldo Mussolini*, Hoepli, Milan, 1936.

Spinosa, A. *I figli del Duce*, Rizzoli, Milan, 1983.

Sulis, E. *Imitazione di Mussolini*, Casa editrice 'Novecentesca', Milan, 1934.

Sulis, E. (ed.) *Mussolini e il fascismo*, Istituto nazionale per le relazioni culturali con l'estero, Rome, 1941.

Sulis, E. (ed.) *Mussolini contro il mito di Demos: dagli 'Scritti e Discorsi' del Duce*, Hoepli, Milan, 1942.

Susmel, D. (ed.) *Carteggio Arnaldo-Benito Mussolini*, La Fenice, Florence, 1954.

Susmel, E. *Le giornate fiumane di Mussolini*, Sansoni, Florence, 1937.

Susmel, E. *Mussolini e il suo tempo*, Garzanti, Milan, 1950.

Svanoni, G. *Mussolini e gli arditi*, Casa editrice Carnaro, Milan, 1938.

Tempera, F. *Benito: emulo-superatore di Cesare e di Napoleone*, Casa Editrice Italia Imperiale, Rome, 1927.

Select bibliography

Tesini, O. *Il grande educatore dell'Italia nuova*, Società Editrice I.R.E.S., Palermo, 1931.

Trevisan, L. *Il naso di Mussolini*, Milan, 1998.

Tripodi, N. *Il fascismo secondo Mussolini*, Le Edizioni del Borghese, Milan, 1971.

Valera, P. *Mussolini* (ed. E. Guidetti), Longanesi, Milan, 1975.

Venturini, D. *Dante Alighieri e Benito Mussolini*, Casa Editrice 'Nuova Italia', Rome, 1927.

Viganoni, G. *Mussolini e i Cesari*, Edizioni 'Ultra', Milan, 1933.

Villani, C. *Stile di Mussolini: nella terra e fra la gente del Duce*, S.E.I., Turin, 1939.

Villaroel, G. *Realtà e mito di Mussolini*, Edizioni Chiantore, Turin, 1938.

Volpicelli, L. *Motivi su Mussolini*, Istituto nazionale fascista di cultura, Rome, 1935.

Weber, M. *On charisma and institution building: selected papers* (ed. S.N. Eisenstadt), University of Chicago Press, 1968.

Zachariae, G. *Mussolini si confessa*, Garzanti, Milan, 1966.

Zamboni, A. *Personalità di Mussolini*, Nistri-Lischi editore, Pisa, 1941.

FASCIST (AND ANTI-FASCIST) PUBLICATIONS

Alberti, M. *L'irredentismo senza romanticismi*, Cavalleri, Como, 1936.

Alvaro, C. *Terra nuova*, Istituto nazionale fascista di cultura, Rome, 1934.

Amicucci, E. *La stampa della rivoluzione e della regime*, Mondadori, Milan, 1938.

Angell, N. *Peace with the dictators? A symposium and some conclusions*, Hamish Hamilton, London, 1938.

Appelius, M. *Parole dure e chiare*, Mondadori, Milan, 1942.

Arcuno, I. *Abissinia ieri ed oggi*, Cooperativa Editrice Libraria, Naples, 1934.

Arena, C. *Italiani per il mondo: politica nazionale dell'emigrazione*, Alpes, Milan, 1927.

Associazione Nazionale Volontari di Guerra, *Il Decennale*, Florence, 1929.

Avancini, M. *Entità e svolgimento del traffico turistico in Italia: dati e congetture*, Tipografia del Senato, Rome, 1925.

Avancini, M. *La pubblicità alberghiera*, Federazione nazionale fascista alberghi e turismo, Rome, 1932.

Avarna di Gualtieri, C. *La politica giapponese del 'Nuovo Ordine'*, Casa Editrice Giuseppe Principato, Milan, 1940.

Barnes, J.S. *The universal aspects of Fascism*, Williams and Norgate, London, 1928.

Barnes, J.S. *Fascism*, T. Butterworth, London, 1931.

Barzini, L. *Il Giappone in armi*, Casa Editrice Apuana, Piacenza, 1935.

Baskerville, B. *What next o Duce?* Longmans, London, 1937.

Becker, W. *Italian Fascism and its great originator: a summary of events, aims, principles and results*, The Continental Weekly, Monte Carlo, 1926.

Belluzzo, G. *Economia fascista*, Libreria del Littorio, Rome, 1928.

Bergamo, G. *Il Fascismo visto da un repubblicano*, Cappelli, Bologna, 1921.

Bodrero, E. *La fine di un'epoca*, Cappelli, Bologna, 1933.

Bollati, A. *La campagna italo-etiopica nella stampa militare estera (previsioni, critiche, riconoscimenti e deduzioni)*, Istituto poligrafico dello stato, Rome, 1938.

Bompiani, G. and Prepositi, C. *Le ali della guerra*, Mondadori, Milan, 1931.

Bonomi, I. *From socialism to Fascism: a study of contemporary Italy*, Martin Hopkinson, London, 1924.

Booth, C.D. and I.B. *Italy's Aegean possessions*, Arrowsmith, London, 1928.

Bottai, G. 'Corporate state and N.R.A.', *Foreign Affairs*, 13, 1935.

Bottai, G. *La carta della scuola*, Mondadori, Milan, 1939.

Bovolo, M. *Agricoltura fascista: nozioni di agraria e di computisteria rurale per gli istituti magistrali*, Paravia, Turin, 1942.

Broad, L. and Russell, L. *The way of the dictators*, Hutchinson, London, 1934.

Select bibliography

Canevari, E. *Il generale Tommaso Salsa e le sue campagne coloniali: lettere e documenti*, Mondadori, Milan, 1935.

Cantalupo, R. *L'Italia musulmana*, La Voce, Rome, 1928.

Cantalupo, R. *Fuad: primo re d'Egitto*, Garzanti, Milan, 1940.

Cappuccio, L. *U.R.S.S.: precedenti storici, organizzazione interna, politica estera*, ISPI, Milan, 1940.

Carli, M. *Arditismo*, Augustea, Rome, 1929.

'Cassius', *The trial of Mussolini*, V. Gollancz, London, 1943.

Castagna, G.C. *L'ora di Giappone*, Libreria Emiliana editrice, Venice, 1932.

Catalano, M.C. *L'era del Pacifico: i problemi dell'Estremo Oriente. contributo dell'Italia alla loro soluzione*, Fratelli Bocca, Milan, 1939.

Cataluccio, F. *Italia e Francia in Tunisia (1878–1939)*, Istituto nazionale di cultura fascista, Rome, 1939.

Cataluccio, F. *La 'nostra' guerra: L'Italia nella guerra mondiale*, Istituto nazionale di cultura fascista, Rome, 1940.

Cermelj, L. *Life and death struggle of a national minority (the Jugoslavs in Italy)*, Jugoslav Union of the League of Nations, Ljubljana, 1936.

Cian, V. *Luigi Federzoni: profilo*, La Società Tipografica Editoriale Porta, Piacenza, 1924.

Ciarlantini, F. *Hitler e il fascismo*, Bemporad, Florence, 1933.

Ciasca, R. *Storia coloniale dell'Italia contemporanea da Assab all'impero*, Hoepli, Milan, 1938.

Cippico, A. *Italy: the central problem of the Mediterranean*, Yale University Press, New Haven, Conn., 1926.

Colli, R. *Fascismo: dramma di propaganda in 4 atti*, Tipografia Sigheri e Gasperetti, Barga, 1923.

Coote, C.R. *Italian town and country life*, Methuen. London, 1925.

Coppola, F. 'Italy in the Mediterranean', *Foreign Affairs*, 1, 1923.

Coppola, F. *Fascismo e Bolscevismo*, Istituto nazionale di cultura fascista, Rome, 1938.

Cora, G. *Il Giappone e la 'più grande Asia Orientale'*, Sansoni, Florence, 1942.

Corradini, E. *Pagine degli anni sacri*, Treves, Milan, 1920.

Corradini, E. *Discorsi politici (1902–1924)*, Vallecchi, Florence, 1925.

Corselli, R. *Cadorna*, Corbaccio, Milan, 1937.

Corsi, M. *Il teatro all'aperto in Italia*, Rizzoli, Milan, 1939.

Andrea Costa, Imola 1910–1960: cinquant'anni fa, La Lotta, Imola, 1960.

Cresswell, C.M. *The keystone of Fascism*, Methuen, London, 1929.

Curcio, C. *L'eredità del Risorgimento*, La Nuova Italia, Florence, 1931.

Currey, M. *Italian foreign policy 1918–1932*, Nicholson and Watson, London, 1932.

Danese, O. *Vittorio Emanuele III: il re fascista*, Franco Paladino, Mantua, 1923.

Daquanno, E. *Riscossa artigiana*, Casa Editrice Pinciana, Rome, 1929.

Daquanno, E. *Vecchia guardia*, Edizioni Ardita, Rome, 1934.

De Begnac, I. *L'arcangelo sindacalista (Filippo Corridoni)*, Mondadori, Milan, 1943.

De Falco, G. *Il Fascismo milizia di classe: commenti alla cronaca*, Cappelli, Bologna, 1921.

De Francisci, P. *Augusto e l'impero*, Istituto nazionale di cultura fascista, Rome, 1937.

De Francisci, P. *Civiltà romana*, Istituto nazionale di cultura fascista, Rome, 1939.

Delcroix, C. *Il nostro contributo alla vittoria degli alleati*, Vallecchi, Florence, 1931.

De Michaelis, G. *La crisi economica mondiale*, C. Colombo, Rome, 1930.

De Michaelis, G. *Alimentazione e giustizia sociale*, Istituto nazionale di cultura fascista, Rome, 1937.

De Ruggiero, G. *Scritti politici 1912–1926* (ed. R. De Felice), Cappelli, Rocca San Casciano, 1963.

De' Stefani, A. *Colpi di vaglio: commenti sulla finanza del 1927*, Treves, Milan, 1928.

De' Stefani, A. *Garanzie di potenza: saggi economici*, Zanichelli, Bologna, 1936.

De Vecchi di Val Cismon, C. M. *Bonifica fascista della cultura*, Mondadori, Milan, 1937.

Diehl, L. *'Behold our new empire': Mussolini*, Hurst and Blackett, London, 1939.

Select bibliography

Dinale, O. *Tempo di Mussolini*, Mondadori, Milan, 1934.

Dinale, O. *La rivoluzione che vince (1914–1934)*, Franco Campitelli, Rome, 1934.

Dobbert, G. (ed.) *L'economia fascista: problemi e fatti*, Sansoni, Florence, 1935.

Ducci, G. *Il Pacifico*, La Nuova Italia, Florence, 1939.

Einzig, P. *The economic foundations of Fascism*, Macmillan, London, 1933.

Einzig, P. 'Signor Mussolini's dilemma' in *Bankers, Statesmen and Economists*, Macmillan, London, 1935.

Elliott, W.Y. *The pragmatic revolt in politics: a study of syndicalism, fascism and the constitutional state*, Macmillan, New York, 1928.

Elwin, W. *Fascism at work*, Martin Hopkinson, London, 1934.

Fabietti, E. *Cesare Battisti: l'anima, la vita*, Vallecchi, Florence, 1928.

Fani Ciotti, V. ('Volt'), *Programma della destra fascista*, Società Anonima Editrice 'La Voce', Florence, 1924.

Fani Ciotti, V. ('Volt'), *Dal partito allo stato*, Vittorio Gatti editore, Brescia, 1930.

Farinacci, R. *Andante mosso 1924–25*, Mondadori, Milan, 1925.

Farinacci, R. *Il processo Matteotti alle Assise di Chieti: l'arringa di Roberto Farinacci*, n.p., n.d.

Farinacci, R. *Un periodo aureo del Partito Nazionale Fascista: raccolta di discorsi e dichiarazioni* (ed. R. Bacchetta), Franco Campitelli editore, Foligno, 1927.

Farinacci, R. *Storia della rivoluzione fascista* (2 vols), Società Editrice 'Cremona Nuova', Cremona, 1937.

Farinacci, R. *La Chiesa e gli ebrei: discorso inaugurale dell'anno accademico 1938–9 XVII della sezione di Milano dell'Istituto nazionale di cultura fascista*, Milan, 1938.

Farinacci, R. *Realtà storiche*, Società Editrice 'Cremona Nuova', Cremona, 1939.

Federzoni, L. *Presagi alla nazione: discorsi politici*, Editrice Imperia del PNF, Milan, 1924.

Federzoni, L. *Paradossi di ieri*, Mondadori, Milan, 1926.

Federzoni, L. 'Hegemony in the Mediterranean', *Foreign Affairs*, 14, 1936.

Ferretti, L. *Il libro dello sport*, Libreria del Littorio, Rome, 1928.

Finer, S.H. *Mussolini's Italy*, V. Gollancz, London, 1935.

Fiorentino, A.R. *La corporazione del turismo*, Grafia, Rome, 1932.

Fiorentino, V. *Renato Ricci*, Casa Editrice Pinciana, Rome, 1928.

Forges Davanzati, R. *Fascismo e cultura*, Bemporad, Florence, 1926.

Forges Davanzati, R. *Il balilla Vittorio: il libro della V classe elementare*, La Libreria dello Stato, Rome, 1939.

Formigari, F. *Rapporto di Mogadiscio*, Istituto nazionale di cultura fascista, Rome, 1938.

Fox, F. *Italy to-day*, H. Jenkins, London, 1927.

Franzero, C.M. *Inside Italy*, Hodder and Stoughton, London, 1941.

Fredo, M.A. *Mussolini and the progress of the Italian state*, Ausonia, Boston, 1935.

Fusilli, A.R. *Giampaoli*, Casa Editrice Pinciana, Rome, 1928.

Gadda, C.E. *Eros e Priapo (da furore a cenere)*, Garzanti, Milan, 1967.

Garratt, G.T. *Mussolini's Roman Empire*, Penguin, Harmondsworth, 1938.

Gayda, V. *Italia e Francia: problemi aperti*, Giornale d'Italia, Rome, 1939.

Gayda, V. *Che cosa vuole l'Italia?* Giornale d'Italia, Rome, 1940.

Giannini, A. *I concordati postbellici*, Società Editrice 'Vita e Pensiero', Milan, 1929.

Giannini, A. *I rapporti italo-inglesi*, Istituto nazionale fascista di cultura, Rome, 1936.

Giannini, A. *L'Albania dall'indipendenza all'unione con l'Italia*, ISPI, Milan, 1940.

Giannini, A. *L'ultima fase della questione orientale (1913–1939)*, ISPI, Milan, 1941.

Giannini, A. *Uomini politici del mio tempo*, ISPI, Rome, 1942.

Gianturco, M. *La guerra degli imperi capitalisti contro gli imperi proletari*, Le Monnier, Florence, 1940.

Gianturco, M. *Costituzione della Camera dei Fasci e delle Corporazioni*, Edizioni IRCE, Rome, 1940.

Select bibliography

Giglio, C. *The triumph of Barabbas*, Angus and Robertson, Sydney, 1937.

Giuliani, R. *Gli arditi: breve storia dei rapporti dei reparti d'assalto della Terza Armata*, Treves, Milan, 1926.

Giuliani, S. *Le 19 provincie create dal Duce: la ricostruzione di Reggio e di Messina*, Tipografia Popolo d'Italia, Milan, 1928.

Giunta, F. *Essenza dello squadrismo*, Libreria del Littorio, Rome, 1931.

Giunta, F. *Un po' di fascismo*, Consalvo editore, Milan, 1935.

Goad, H. *The making of the corporate state: a study of Fascist development*, Christophers, London, 1932.

Goad, H. 'The Corporate State', *International Affairs*, 12, 1933.

Goad, H.E. and Currey, M. *The working of the corporate state (a study of national cooperation)*, Ivor Nicolson and Watson, London, 1934.

Godden, G.M. *Mussolini: the birth of a new democracy*, Burns Oates and Washbourne, London, 1923.

Gonella, G. *Verso la seconda guerra mondiale: cronache politiche: 'Acta Diurna', 1933–1940* (ed. F. Malgeri), Laterza, Bari, 1979.

Gorgolini, P. *The Fascist movement in Italian life*, T. Fisher Unwin, London, 1923.

Gramsci, A. *The modern prince and other writings*, International publishers, New York, 1959.

Gramsci, A. *Selections from the Prison notebooks* (ed. Q. Hoare and G. Nowell Smith), Lawrence and Wishart, London, 1971.

Gramsci, A. *Letters from prison* (ed. L. Lawner), Harper and Row, New York, 1973.

Gramsci, A. *Selections from political writings* (ed. Q. Hoare), Lawrence and Wishart, London, 1978.

Gramsci, A. *Selections from cultural writings* (ed. D. Forgacs and G. Nowell Smith), Lawrence and Wishart, London, 1985.

Gramsci, A. *Pre-prison writings* (ed. R. Bellamy), Cambridge University Press, 1994.

Gravelli, A. *Verso l'internazionale fascista*, Nuova Europa Libreria editrice, Rome, 1932.

Gravelli, A. (ed.) *Razzismo*, Nuova Europa, Rome, 1933.

Gravelli, A. *Panfascismo*, Casa Editrice 'Nuova Europa', Rome, 1935.

Gray, E.M. *Il turismo aereo: relazione al IV congresso internazionale di navigazione aerea*, C.I.T., Rome, 1927.

Gray, E.M. *Crescendo di certezze*, Casa Editrice Pinciana, Rome, 1930.

Gray, E.M. (ed.) *Il Duca d'Aosta: cittadino della riscossa italica*, Ente Autonomo Stampa, Milan, 1931.

Gray, E.M. *I problemi dell'italianità nel mondo*, Palazzo di Firenze, Rome, 1932.

Gray, E.M. *Credenti nella patria*, Mondadori, Milan, 1935.

Gray, E.M. *L'Italia ha sempre ragione*, Mondadori, Milan, 1936.

Gray, E.M. *La chiesa anglicana contro Roma fascista e cristiana*, Casa Editrice Il Consultore, Milan, 1937.

Gray, E.M. *Noi e tunisi: come perdemmo Tunisi, come costruimmo la Tunisia*, Mondadori, Milan, 1939.

Gray, E.M. *La loro civiltà*, Edizioni della Gazzetta del Popolo, Turin, 1941.

Gray, E.M. *Ramazza: cronache dette e non dette*, Mondadori, Milan, 1942.

Gray, E.M. *Il filo di Arianna*, Rizzoli, Milan, 1942.

Gray, E.M. *Lecturae Ducis: tre commenti*, Edizioni Latium, Rome, 1942.

Gray, E.M. *Dopo vent'anni: il fascismo e l'Europa*, PNF, Rome, 1943.

Gray, E.M. *Chi è colonello Poletti*, Edizioni della Gazzetta del Popolo, Turin, 1944.

Gualco, S. *La bonifica della razza e l'alimentazione ittica*, Ufficio Stampa Grande Pesca, Rome, 1940.

Guerin, D. *Fascism and big business*, Anchor, New York, 1973.

Guidi, G. *Pio XI*, Tipografia Editoriale Lucchi, Milan, 1938.

Select bibliography

Guidi, M. *Aspetti e problemi del mondo islamico*, Istituto nazionale di cultura fascista, Rome, 1937.

Interlandi, T. *Pane bigio: scritti politici*, L'Italiano editore, Bologna, 1927.

Interlandi, T. *Contro Judaeos*, Tumminelli editori, Rome, 1938.

Istituto nazionale di cultura fascista (ed.) *Ragioni di questa guerra*, Rome, 1941.

Hambloch, E. *Italy militant*, Duckworth, London, 1941.

Hayek, F.A. *The road to serfdom*, University of Chicago Press, 1944.

Hentze, M. *Pre-Fascist Italy: the rise and fall of the parliamentary regime*, George Allen and Unwin, London, 1939.

Hollis, C. *Italy in Africa*, Hamish Hamilton, London, 1941.

Howard, M.W. *Fascism: a challenge to democracy*, F.H. Revell, New York, 1928.

Istituto Coloniale Fascista, *Nozioni coloniali per le organizzazioni femminili del Partito Nazionale Fascista*, Castaldi, Rome, n.d.

Istituto per gli studi di politica internazionale, *Albania*, ISPI, Milan, 1940.

Jones, S.A. *Is Fascism the answer? Italy's law of unions compared with the N.R.A.* Hamish Hamilton, Ottawa,1933.

Labriola, A. *Polemica antifascista*, Ceccoli, Naples, 1925.

Langobardi, C. *Land-reclamation in Italy: rural revival in the building of a nation*, P.S. King, London, 1936.

Lantini, F. *Il metodo corporativo per raggiungere l'autarchia*, Società italiana per il progresso delle scienze, Rome, 1939.

Lavagetto, A. *La vita eroica del capitano Bottego (1893–1897)*, Mondadori, Milan, 1934.

Le Bon, G. *The crowd: a study of the popular mind*, T. Fisher Unwin, London, 1922.

Lessona, A. *Scritti e discorsi coloniali*, Editoriale 'Arte e Scienza', Milan, 1935.

Lessona, A. *La missione dell'Italia in Africa*, Istituto nazionale fascista di cultura, Rome, 1936.

Lischi, D. *Alessandro Lessona*, Casa Editrice Pinciana, Rome, 1929.

Lodolini, A. *La storia della razza italiana da Augusto a Mussolini dedicato agli italiani di Mussolini e specialmente ai giovani e alle scuole*, Unione Editoriale d'Italia, Rome, 1939.

Lumbroso, A. *Elena di Montenegro: Regina d'Italia*, Edizioni de 'La Fiamma Fedele' e di 'Fiamme Gialle d'Italia', Florence, 1935.

Lupi, D. *Nel solco dell'idea*, Libreria del Littorio, Rome, 1928.

Mancini, A. *La donna fascista nell'irrobustimento della razza*, V. Ferri, Rome, 1937.

Manetti, D. *Gente di Romagna: Aldo Oviglio*, Cappelli, Bologna, 1924.

Marconini, F. *Culle vuote: il declino delle nascite in Europa: sviluppo-cause-rimedi*, Casa Editrice Emo Cavalleri, Como, 1935.

Marinetti, F. *Futurismo e fascismo*, Franco Campitelli editore, Foligno, 1924.

Mariotti, A. *L'industria del forestiero in Italia*, Zanichelli, Bologna, 1923.

Mariotti, A. *L'importanza economica del turismo*, Edizioni AESTI, Florence, 1931.

Mariotti, A. *Corso di economia turistica*, De Agostini, Rome, 1933.

Mariotti, A. *Lezioni di economia turistica per gli studenti della Facoltà di economia e commercio*, Società Editrice Nuovissima, Rome, 1941.

Mariotti, G. *Il turismo fra le due guerre*, Edizioni Mercurio, Rome, 1941.

Martelli, G. *Italy against the world*, Chatto and Windus, London, 1937.

Mastrojanni, G. *Marte e Israele: perchè si combatte*, Cappelli, Bologna, 1943.

Maurano, S. *Francia la sorellastra*, Casa Editrice Ceschina, Milan, 1939.

Mazzucconi, R. *La giornata di Adua (1896)*, Mondadori, Milan, 1935.

McBirnie, W.S. *What the Bible says about Mussolini*, McBirnie publications, Norfolk, Virginia, 1944.

Meenan, J. *The Italian corporative system*, Cork University Press, 1944.

Mezzasoma, F. *Essenza del G.U.F.*, GUF, Genoa, 1937.

Select bibliography

Michels, R. *L'imperialismo italiano: studi politico-demografici*, Società Editrice Libraria, Milan, 1914.

Ministero delle Colonie, *Le colonie italiane di diretto dominio*, Ministero delle Colonie, Rome, 1929.

Ministero della Cultura Popolare, *Che cosa hanno fatto gli inglesi in Cirenaica*, Ministero della Cultura Popolare, Rome, 1941.

Miserocchi, M. *Australia: continente minorenne*, Garzanti, Milan, 1940.

Missiroli, M. *Date a Cesare: la politica religiosa di Mussolini con documenti inediti*, Libreria del Littorio, Rome, 1929.

Missiroli, M. *L'Italia d'oggi*, N. Zanichelli, Bologna, 1932.

Missiroli, M. *Italia e Germania nelle relazioni culturali*, Stabilimento Tipografico F. Canello, Rome, 1941.

Mondaini, G. *La legislazione coloniale italiana nel suo sviluppo storico e nel suo stato attuale (1881–1940)*, 2 vols, ISPI, Milan, 1941.

Montemaggiori, A. *Dizionario della dottrina fascista*, Paravia, Turin, 1934.

Moore, M. *Fourth shore: Italy's mass colonization of Libya*, George Routledge, London, 1940.

Moran, H.M. *Letters from Rome: an Australian's view of the Italo-Abyssinian question*, Angus and Robertson, Sydney, 1935.

Morgan, T.B. *Spurs on the boot: Italy under her masters*, Harrap, London, 1942.

Mosca, O. *Volpi di Misurata*, Casa Editrice Pinciana, Rome, 1928.

Munro, I.S. *Through Fascism to world power: a history of the revolution in Italy*, Alexander Maclehose, London, 1933.

Mussolini, A. *Forlì*, Edizioni Tiber, Rome, 1929.

Mussolini, A. *Ammonimenti ai giovani e al popolo*, Libreria del Littorio, Rome, 1931.

Mussolini, A. *Terra di Romagna*, Treves-Treccani-Tuminelli, Rome, 1932.

Mussolini, A. *Scritti e discorsi* (3 vols), Hoepli, Milan, 1934.

Mussolini, A. *Tripolitania*, Istituto coloniale fascista, Rome, n.d.

Mussolini, V. *Anno XIII – Ludi Iuvenalis*, Tipografia Luzzatti, Rome, 1935.

Nanni, T. *Bolscevismo e fascismo al lume della critica marxista Benito Mussolini*, Cappelli, Bologna, 1924.

Nanni, T., *Leandro Arpinati e il fascismo bolognese*, Edizioni 'Autarchia', Bologna, 1927.

Nasalli Rocca, A.M. and E. *Realismo nazionale: per una coscienza politica dei cattolici italiani*, G. Marino editore, Rome, 1926.

Newman, E.P. *The Mediterranean and its problems*, Philpott, London, 1927.

Niceforo, A. *Il movimento dei forestieri in Italia*, Tipografia del Senato, Rome, 1923.

Occhini, P.L. *La lotta di classe delle nazioni*, Le Monnier, Florence, 1929.

Olivetti, A.O. *Dal sindacalismo rivoluzionario al corporativismo* (ed. F. Perfetti), Bonacci, Rome, 1984.

Orano, P. *Gli ebrei in Italia*, Casa Editrice Pinciana, Rome, 1937.

Orano, P. (ed.) *Inchiesta sulla razza*, Pinciana, Rome, 1939.

Pace, B. *L'impero e la collaborazione internazionale in Africa*, Istituto nazionale di cultura fascista, Rome, 1938.

Padellaro, N. *Giovinezza nel mondo*, Istituto nazionale fascista di cultura, Rome, 1936.

Padellaro, N. *Fascismo educatore*, Cremonese, Rome, 1938.

Pagliari, E. *Ferrovie e alberghi d'Italia nell'industria turistica*, Echi e commenti, Rome, 1931.

Paladini, V. *Arte nella Russia dei Soviets: il padiglione dell'URSS a Venezia*, Edizioni de 'La Bilancia', Rome, 1925.

Panunzio, S. *Lo stato fascista*, Cappelli, Bologna, 1925.

Pareto, V. *Trasformazione della democrazia* (ed. F. Perfetti), Giovanni Volpe editore, Rome, 1975.

Pareti, L. *I due imperi di Roma*, Vincenzo Miglio editore, Catania, 1938.

Pareti, L. *Tre secoli di ingerenze inglesi*, Edizioni Latium, Rome, 1941.

Select bibliography

Parini, P. (ed.) *Sole d'Italia: letture classe quinte*, Libreria dello Stato, Rome, 1931.

Partito Nazionale Fascista, *Il Gran Consiglio nei primi anni dell'era fascista*, Libreria del Littorio, Rome, 1927.

Partito Nazionale Fascista, *Dizionario politico* (4 vols), Istituto della Enciclopedia Italiana, Rome, 1940.

Pascazio, N. *La crisi sociale dell'impero britannico: studio compiuto in Inghilterra*, Garzanti, Milan, 1941.

Pavolini, A. *Disperata*, Vallecchi, Florence, 1937.

Pegolotti, B. *Corsica Tunisia Gibuti (dal taccuino di un 'inviato speciale')*, Vallecchi, Florence, 1939.

'Pentad', *The remaking of Italy*, Penguin, Harmondsworth, 1941.

Petrie, C. *Lords of the inland sea: a study of the Mediterranean powers*, Lovat Dickson, London, 1937.

Pettinato, C. *La Francia vinta*, ISPI, Milan, 1941.

Phillips, P. *The 'Red Dragon' and the Black Shirts: how Fascist Italy found her soul: the true story of the Fascisti movement*, Carmelite House, London, 1923.

Piazza, G. *La fiamma bilingue: momenti del dissidio ideale 1913–1923*, Edizioni 'Corbaccio', Milan, 1924.

Pirelli, A. *Economia e guerra* (2 vols), ISPI, Milan, 1940.

Pitigliani, F. *The Italian Corporative State*, P.S. King, London, 1933.

Po, G. *Il Grande Ammiraglio Paolo Thaon di Revel*, S. Lattes, Turin, 1936.

Por, O. *Fascism*, Labour, London, 1923.

Por, O. *Materie prime ed autarchia*, Istituto nazionale di cultura fascista, Rome, 1937.

Pound, E. *Jefferson and/or Mussolini: l'idea statale. Fascism as I have seen it*, S. Nott, London, 1935.

Preti, L. *Gli inglesi a Malta: una politica errata, la cui fine contribuirebbe a migliorare i rapporti anglo-italiani*, Fratelli Bocca, Milan, 1934.

Preziosi, G. *Giudaismo bolscevismo plutocrazia massoneria*, Mondadori, Milan, 1941.

Prezzolini, G. *Fascism*, Methuen, London, 1926.

Quaranta, F. *Ethiopia: an empire in the making*, P.S. King, London, 1939.

Quartara, G. *L'Italia tradita*, Fratelli Bocca, Milan, 1941.

Quilici, N, *Spagna*, Istituto nazionale di cultura fascista, Rome, 1938.

Rafanelli, L. *Alle madri italiane*, Libreria Editrice G. Nerbia, Florence, n.d.

Rafanelli, L. *Lavoratori!* Tipografia Appiano, Turin, 1959 (first published by Libreria Editrice Sociale, Milan, 1921).

Rafanelli, L. *Donne e femmine: novelle*, Casa Editrice Sociale, Milan, 1921.

'Sahra' [L. Rafanelli] *Incantamento: romanzo*, Casa Editrice Italiana 'Modernissima', Milan, 1921.

Rafanelli, L. 'Prefazio' to C. Albert, *L'amore libero*, Casa Editrice Sociale, Milan, 1921.

Rafanelli, L. *Bozzetti sociali*, Casa Editrice Sociale, Milan, 1921.

Rafanelli, L. *L'eroe della folla: romanzo*, Casa Editrice Sociale, Milan, 1925.

Rafanelli, L. translation of E. Gamalier, *L'oasi: romanzo arabo*, Casa Editrice Monanni, Milan, 1929.

Rafanelli, L. *La 'castità' clericale*, La Rivolta, Rome, 1946.

Rava, L. *Per la 'Dante Alighieri' (trent'anni di propaganda: discorsi e ricordi 1900–1931)*, Società Dante Alighieri, Rome, 1932.

Repaci, A. *La marcia su Roma: mito e realtà* (2 vols), Canesi, Rome, 1963.

Reut-Nicolussi, E. *Tyrol under the axe of Italian Fascism*, George Allen and Unwin, London, 1930.

Riccardi, R. *Economia fascista: sanzioni, commercio estero, autarchia*, Unione Editoriale d'Italia, Rome, 1939.

Ricci, B. *Avvisi*, Vallecchi, Florence, 1943.

Select bibliography

Ricci, B. *La rivoluzione fascista: antologia di scritti politici* (eds A. Cucchi and G. Galante), Società Editrice Barbarossa, Milan, 1996.

Ricci, G. *Squadrismo forlivese*, Sezione editoriale 'Via Consolare' del GUF di Forlì, Forlì, 1942.

Ridley, F.A. *The Papacy and Fascism: the crisis of the twentieth century*, Secker Warburg, London, 1937.

Ritucci-Chini, F. *Il corporativismo nella storia con speciale riferimento all'Abruzzo*, G. Guzzetti, Vasto, 1932.

Rocco, A. *La trasformazione dello stato: dallo stato liberale allo stato fascista*, 'La Voce' Anonima Editrice, Rome, 1927.

Romagnoli, E. *Nel Decennale della Rivoluzione Fascista*, Zanichelli, Bologna, 1933.

Romagnoli, E. *Discorsi critici*, Zanichelli, Bologna, 1934.

Rosso, F. *Armando Diaz dopo la Marcia su Roma*, Vallecchi, Florence, 1934.

Rota, E. *Italia e Francia davanti alla storia: il mito della Sorella Latina*, ISPI, Milan, 1939.

Rotary International (ed.), *Terza conferenza regionale Europa–Africa–Asia Minore*, Stamperia Zanetti, Venice, 1936.

Ruinas, S. *Figure del fascismo sardo*, Cremonese editore, Rome, 1930.

Salata, F. *Il patto Mussolini: storia di un piano politico e di un negoziato diplomatico*, Mondadori, Milan, 1933.

Salata, F. *Il nodo di Gibuti*, ISPI, Milan, 1939.

Salvatorelli, L. *Nazionalfascismo*, Einaudi, Turin, 1977.

Salvemini, G. *The Fascist dictatorship in Italy*, H. Holt, New York, 1927.

Salvemini, G. *Under the axe of Fascism*, V. Gollancz, London, 1936.

Salvemini, G. 'Can Italy live at home' *Foreign Affairs*, 14, 1936.

Salvemini, G. *Italian Fascism*, V. Gollancz, London, 1938.

Salvemini, G. and La Piana, G. *What to do with Italy*, V. Gollancz, London, 1943.

Sarfatti, M. *Tunisiaca*, Mondadori, Milan, 1924.

Scarfoglio, C. *Il popolo dei cinque pasti (brindisi a Mr Asquith)*, Mondadori, Milan, 1923.

Schmidt, C. *The Corporate State in action: Italy under Fascism*, Gollancz, London, 1939.

Schneider, H.W. *Making the Fascist state*, Oxford University Press, New York, 1928.

Schneider, H.W. and Clough, S. *Making Fascists*, University of Chicago Press, 1929.

Scorza, C. *Tipi..tipi..tipi*, Vallecchi, Florence, 1942.

Segrè, C. *Itinerari di stranieri in Italia*, Mondadori, Milan, 1938.

Sencourt, R. *Italy*, Arrowsmith, London, 1938.

Sertoli Salis, R. *Le isole italiane dell'Egeo dall'occupazione alla sovranità*, Vittoriano, Rome, 1939.

Sertoli Salis, R. *Italia Europa Arabia*, ISPI, Milan, 1940.

Settimelli, E. *Antinglese*, Casa Editrice Pinciana, Rome, 1936.

Sforza, C. *Diplomatic Europe since the Treaty of Versailles*, Yale University Press, New Haven, 1928.

Sforza, C. *European dictatorships*, Libraries Press, New York, 1931.

Sforza, C. *Europe and the Europeans: a study in historical psychology and international politics*, Harrap, London, 1936.

Sforza, C. *Panorama europeo: apparenze politiche e realtà psicologiche*, Einaudi, Turin, 1945.

Sforza, C. *Costruttori e distruttori*, Donatello da Luigi, Rome, 1945.

Sforza, C. *Italy and Italians*, F. Muller, London, 1948.

Sighele, S. *Il nazionalismo e i partiti*, Treves, Milan, 1911.

Sillani, T. (ed.) *L'Italia di Vittorio Emanuele III*, La Rassegna Italiana, Rome, 1926.

Sillani, T. (ed.) *What is Fascism and why?* E. Benn, London, 1931.

Sillani, T. (ed.) *La Libia in venti anni di occupazione: studi e documenti*, La Rassegna Italiana, Rome, 1932.

Sillani, T. (ed.) *L'Italia e il Levante: studi e documenti*, La Rassegna Italiana, Rome, 1934.

Sillani, T. (ed.) *L'Italia e l'Oriente medio ed estremo: studi e documenti*, La Rassegna Italiana, Rome, 1935.

Select bibliography

Silva, P. *Il Mediterraneo dall'unità di Roma all'unità d'Italia*, Mondadori, Milan, 1927.

Silva, P. *Italia–Francia–Inghilterra nel Mediterraneo*, ISPI, Milan, 1936.

Silva, P. *Figure e momenti di storia italiana*, ISPI, Milan, 1939.

Siracusa Cabrini, E. *Da Zeila alle frontiere del Kaffa (Antonio Cecchi)*, Paravia, Turin, 1930.

Soffici, A. *Battaglia fra due vittorie*, Società Anonima Editrice "La Voce", Florence, 1923.

Solari, L. *Marconi nell'intimità e nel lavoro*, Mondadori, Milan, 1940.

Solari, P. *Hitler e il Terzo Reich*, Casa Editrice Giacomo Agnelli, Milan, 1932.

Solaro del Borgo, V. *Giornate di guerra del re soldato*, Mondadori, Milan, 1931.

Solmi, A. *Discorsi sulla storia d'Italia*, La Nuova Italia, Florence, 1933.

Solmi, A. (ed.) *Egitto moderno e antico*, ISPI, Milan, 1941.

Spampanato, B. *Idee e baionette*, Alberto Morano, Naples, 1932.

Spampanato, B. *Sguardo all'Europa*, Politica Nuova, Rome, 1935.

Spampanato, B. *1938: l'anno decisivo*, Politica Nuova, Naples, 1938.

Starace, A. *La marcia su Gondar della colonna celere A.O. e le successive operazioni nella Etiopia occidentale*, Mondadori, Milan, 1936.

Starace, A. *Gioventù italiana del Littorio*, Mondadori, Milan, 1939.

Steiner, H.A. *Government in Fascist Italy*, McGraw-Hill, New York, 1938.

Sturzo, L. *Italy and Fascismo*, Faber and Faber, London, 1926.

Sturzo, L. *Italy and the new world order*, Macdonald, London, 1944.

Sulis, E. (ed.) *Processo alla borghesia*, Edizioni Roma, Rome, 1939.

Sulis, E. *Rivoluzione ideale*, Vallecchi, Florence, 1939.

Tamaro, A. *La lotta delle razze nell'Europa danubiana*, Zanichelli, Bologna, 1923.

Tasca, A. *The rise of Italian Fascism 1918–1922*, H. Fertig, New York, 1966.

Tittoni, T. *International economic and political problems of the day and some aspects of Fascism (1919–1926)*, Simpkin, Marshall, Hamilton, Kent and Co., London, 1926.

Tittoni, T. *Questione del giorno*, Treves, Milan, 1928.

Togliatti, P. *Lectures on Fascism*, Lawrence and Wishart, London, 1976.

Torre, A. *Alla vigilia della guerra mondiale 1914–8*, ISPI, Milan, 1942.

Traversi, L. *l'Italia e l'Etiopia da Assab a Ual-ual*, Cappelli, Bologna, 1935.

Trevelyan, G.M. *The historical causes of the present state of affairs in Italy*, Oxford University Press, London, 1923.

Truffi, R. (ed.) *Precursori dell'Impero Africano: lettere inedite*, Edizioni Roma, Rome, 1936.

Tuninetti, D.M. *La vita di Michele Bianchi*, Casa Editrice Pinciana, Rome, 1935.

Turati, A. *Ragioni ideali di vita fascista*, Casa Editrice G. Barbutti, Rome, 1926.

Turati, A. *Una rivoluzione e un capo*, Libreria del Littorio, Rome, 1927.

Turati, A. *Un popolo, un'idea, un uomo*, Istituto fascista di cultura, Milan, 1927.

Turati, A. *Il partito e i suoi compiti*, Libreria del Littorio, Rome, 1928.

Turati, A. *Un anno di vita del partito*, Libreria d'Italia, Milan, 1929.

Turati, A. and Bottai, G. (eds) *La Carta del Lavoro: illustrata e commentata*, Edizioni del Diritto del Lavoro, Rome, 1929.

Turcotti, E. (ed) *Fascist europe/Europa fascista: an Anglo-Italian symposium*, Istituto nazionale di cultura fascista di Pavia, Milan, 1939.

Vannutelli, G. *Il Mediterraneo e la civiltà mondiale dalle origini all'impero fascista della Nuova Italia*, Cappelli, Bologna, 1936.

Varè, D. 'British foreign policy through Italian eyes', *International Affairs*, 15, 1936.

Vecchi, F. *Arditismo civile*, Libreria Editrice de l'Ardito, Milan, 1920.

Villa, C. *L'ultima Inghilterra*, Casa editrice Oberdan Zucchi, Milan, 1936.

Villari, L. *The Fascist experiment*, Faber and Gwyer, London, 1926.

Villari, L. *The expansion of Italy*, Faber and Faber, London, 1930.

Villari, L. 'The economics of Fascism' in G.S. Counts (ed.) *Bolshevism, Fascism and capitalism: an account of the three economic systems*, Yale University Press, New Haven, 1932.

Select bibliography

Villari, L. *On the roads from Rome*, A. Maclehose, London, 1932.

Villari, L. *The war on the Italian front*, Calder-Sanderson, London, 1932.

Villari, L. 'Italian foreign policy', *International Affairs*, 14, 1935.

Villari, L. *Storia diplomatica del conflitto italo-etiopico*, Zanichelli, Bologna, 1943.

Volpe, G. *Guerra dopoguerra fascismo*, La Nuova Italia, Venice, 1928.

Volpe, G. *L'Italia in cammino: l'ultimo cinquantennio*, Treves, Milan, 1928.

Volpe, G. *Pacifismo e storia*, Istituto nazionale fascista di cultura, Rome, 1934.

Volpe, G. *L'Italia nella Triplice Alleanza 1882–1915*, ISPI, Milan, 1939.

Volpe, G. *Storia della Corsica italiana*, ISPI, Milan, 1939.

Volpe, G. *Vittorio Emanuele III*, ISPI, Milan, 1939.

Volpe, G. *Il popolo italiano tra la pace e la guerra (1914–1915)*, ISPI, Milan, 1940.

Volpi, G. 'Italy's financial policy', *International Conciliation*, 234, November 1927.

Volpi, G. *Finanza fascista: Anno VII*, Libreria del Littorio, Rome, 1929.

Volpi, G. *Economic progress of Fascist Italy*, Usila, Rome, 1937.

Volpi, G. *Venezia antica e moderna*, ATENA, Rome, 1939.

Ward, B. *Italian foreign policy*, Clarendon, Oxford, 1941.

Weil, L. *Orrori e miserie della schiavitù in Abissinia*, Edizioni SACSE, Milan, 1935.

Welk, W.G. *Fascist economic policy: an analysis of Italy's economic experiment*, Russell and Russell, New York, 1968.

Zaghi, C. *Le origini della colonia Eritrea*, Cappelli, Bologna, 1934.

Zama, P. *Fascismo e religione*, Imperia Casa Editrice del PNF, Milan, 1923.

Zanette, G. *Tempeste sulle alpi albanesi*, Casa Editrice Pinciana, Rome, 1942.

Zappa, P. *Singapore: porto del Pacifico*, Corbaccio, Milan, 1941.

Zibordi, G. *Critica socialista del fascismo*, Cappelli, Bologna, 1922.

Zingarelli, I. *I paesi danubiani e balcanici*, ISPI, Milan, 1938.

MEMOIRS

Acciarini, F. *Autobiografia di un socialista (da Torino a Mauthausen)*, Silva editore, Rome, 1970.

Acerbo, G. *Fra due plotoni di esecuzione: avvenimenti e problemi dell'epoca fascista*, Cappelli, Rocca San Casciano, 1968.

Acton, H. *Memoirs of an aesthete*, Methuen, London, 1948.

Agnelli, S. *We always wore sailor suits*, Weidenfeld and Nicolson, London, 1975.

Alfieri, D. *Dictators face to face*, Elek, London, 1954.

Allason, B. *Memorie di una antifascista 1919–1940*, Edizioni Avanti!, Milan, 1961.

Almirante, G. *Autobiografia di un "fucilatore"*, Edizioni del Borghese, Milan, 1974.

Alvaro, C. *Quasi una vita: giornale di uno scrittore*, Bompiani, Milan, 1950.

Amendola, G. *Una scelta di vita*, Rizzoli, Milan, 1976.

Amicucci, E. *I 600 giorni di Mussolini (dal Gran Sasso a Dongo)*, Edizioni 'Farò', Rome, 1948.

Anfuso, F. *Roma Berlino Salò (1936–1945)*, Garzanti, Milan, 1950.

Anfuso, F. *Da Palazzo Venezia al Lago di Garda (1936–1945)*, Settimo Sigillo, Rome, 1996.

Ansaldo, G. *L'Antifascista riluttante: memorie del carcere e del confino 1926–1927* (ed. M. Staglieno), Il Mulino, Bologna, 1992.

Ansaldo, G. *Diario di prigionia* (ed. R. De Felice), Il Mulino, Bologna, 1993.

Ansaldo, G. *Il giornalista di Ciano: diari 1932–1943*, Il Mulino, Bologna, 2000.

Antongini, T. *D'Annunzio*, Heinemann, London, 1938.

Armellini, Q. *Con Badoglio in Etiopia*, Mondadori, Milan, 1937.

Armellini, Q. *Diario di guerra: nove mesi al Comando Supremo*, Garzanti, Milan, 1946.

Associazione degli industriali nel 40 anniversario di Porto Marghera e del Rotary Club di Venezia nel 35 anniversario della sua fondazione (eds), *Giuseppe Volpi: ricordi e testimonianze*, Venice, 1959.

Select bibliography

Audisio, W. *In nome del popolo italiano*, Teti editore, Milan, 1975.

Badoglio, P. *The war in Abyssinia*, Methuen, London, 1937.

Badoglio, P. *Italy in the Second World War*, Oxford University Press, 1948.

Balabanoff, A. *My life as a rebel*, Hamish Hamilton, London, 1938.

Balbo, I, *Stormi in volo sull'oceano*, Mondadori, Milan, 1931.

Balbo, I. *Diario 1922*, Mondadori, Milan, 1932.

Barnes, G.S. *Io amo l'Italia: memorie di un giornalista inglese*, Garzanti, Milan, 1939.

Bastianini, G. *Uomini cose fatti: memorie di un ambasciatore*, Vitagliano, Milan, 1959.

Bellini delle Stelle, P.L. and Lazzaro, U., *Dongo: the last act*, MacDonald, London, 1964.

Benuzzi, F. *No picnic on Mount Kenya*, W. Kimber, London, 1953.

Benzoni, G. *La vita ribelle: memorie di un'aristocratica italiana fra belle époque e repubblica*, Il Mulino, Bologna, 1985.

Bermani, C. *Novara 1922: battaglia al fascismo*, Nuove Edizioni Operaie, Rome, 1978.

Bernotti, R. *Cinquant'anni nella Marina Militare*, Mursia, Milan, 1971.

Biggini, C.A. *Storia inedita della Conciliazione*, Garzanti, Milan, 1942.

Bisach, G. *Pertini racconta: gli anni 1915–1945*, Mondadori, Milan, 1983.

Blasetti, A. *Scritti sul cinema* (ed. A. Aprà), Marsilio, Venice, 1982.

Bobbio, N. *Autobiografia* (ed. A. Papuzzi), Laterza, Bari, 1997.

Bojano, F. *In the wake of the goose-step*, Cassell, London, 1944.

Bolla, L. *Perché a Salò: diario della Repubblica Sociale Italiana* (ed. G.B. Guerri), Bompiani, Milan, 1982.

Bonnet, G. *Quai d'Orsay*, Times Press, Douglas Isle of Man, 1965.

Borghese, J.V. *Decima Flottiglia Mas: dalle origini all'armistizio*, Garzanti, Rome, 1950.

Borsa, M. *Memorie di un redivivo*, Rizzoli, Milan, 1945.

Bottai, B. *Fascismo famigliare*, Piemme, Casale Monferrato, 1997.

Bottai, G. *Vent'anni e un giorno (24 luglio 1943)*, Garzanti, Milan, 1977.

Bottai, G. *Diario 1935–1944* (ed. G.B. Guerri), Rizzoli, Milan, 1982.

Bottai, G. *Diario 1944–1948* (ed. G.B. Guerri), Rizzoli, Milan, 1988.

Bottai, G. *Quaderno affricano*, Giunti, Florence, 1995.

Bottai, G. *Quaderni giovanili 1915–1920*, Fondazione Arnaldo e Alberto Mondadori, Missaglia, 1996.

Bottai, G. and G. De Luca, *Carteggio 1940–1957* (ed. R. De Felice and R. Moro), Edizioni di storia e letteratura, Rome, 1989.

Bova Scoppa, R. *Colloqui con due dittatori*, Ruffolo editore, Rome, 1949.

Brignoli, P. *Santa messa per i miei fucilati: le spietate rappresaglie italiane contro i partigiani in Croazia dal diario di un cappellano*, Longanesi, Milan, 1973.

Buchanan, M. *Ambassador's daughter*, Cassell, London, 1958.

Buffarini Guidi, G. *La vera verità*, Sugar, Milan, 1970.

Buitoni, G. *Storia di un imprenditore*, Longanesi, Milan, 1972.

Bullotta, A. *La Somalia sotto due bandiere*, Garzanti, Milan, 1949.

Calabrò, L. *Intermezzo africano: ricordi di un Residente di Governo in Etiopia (1937–1941)*, Bonacci, Rome, 1988.

Canevari, E. *Graziani mi ha detto*, Magi-Spinetti editore, Rome, 1947.

Capello, L. *Caporetto, perché?: la seconda armata e gli avvenimenti dell'ottobre 1917*, Einaudi, Turin, 1967.

Capoferri, P. *Venti anni col fascismo e con i sindacati*, Gastaldi editore, Milan, 1957.

Carboni, G. *Memorie segrete 1935–1948: 'Più che il dovere'*, Parenti editore, Florence, 1955.

Castellano, G. *Come firmai l'armistizio di Cassibile*, Mondadori, Milan, 1945.

Cavallero, U. *Comando supremo: diario 1940–43 del Capo di S.M.G.*, Cappelli, Bologna, 1948.

Cersosimo, V. *Dall'istruttoria alla fucilazione: storia del processo di Verona*, Garzanti, Milan, 1961.

Select bibliography

Cerutti, E. *Ambassador's wife*, George Allen and Unwin, London, 1952.

Chiesa, E. *La mano nel sacco e altri scritti editi e inediti* (ed. M.T. Chiesa), Tarantella editore, Milan, 1946.

Churchill, W.S. *The gathering storm*, Penguin, Harmondsworth, 1962.

Cianetti, T. *Memorie del carcere di Verona* (ed. R. De Felice), Rizzoli, Milan, 1983.

Ciano, F. *Quando il nonno fece fucilare papà* (ed. D. Cimagalli), Mondadori, Milan, 1991.

Ciano, G. *Ciano's diary 1937–1938* (ed. A. Mayor), Methuen, London, 1952.

Ciano, G. *Ciano's diary 1939–1943* (ed. M. Muggeridge), Heinemann, London, 1947.

Ciano, G. *Diplomatic papers* (ed. M. Muggeridge), Odhams, London, 1948.

Ciano, G. *Diario 1937–1943* (ed. R. De Felice), Rizzoli, Milan, 1980.

Colombi, A. *Nelle mani del nemico*, Riuniti, Rome, 1971.

Conti, E. *Dal taccuino di un borghese*, Garzanti, Milan, 1946.

Cora, G. 'Un diplomatico durante l'era fascista', *Storia e Politica*, 5, 1966.

Corvo, M. *The O.S.S. in Italy 1942–1945: a personal memoir*, Praeger, New York, 1990.

Costa, V. *L'ultimo federale: memorie della guerra civile 1943–1945*, Il Mulino, Bologna, 1997.

Croce, B. *Croce, the King and the Allies: extracts from a diary July 1943–June 1944*, George Allen and Unwin, London, 1950.

Croce, B. *Scritti e discorsi politici (1943–1947)*, Laterza, Bari, 1963.

Dall'Ora, F. *Intendenza in A.O.*, Istituto Nazionale Fascista di Cultura, Rome, 1937.

Darrah, D. *Hail Caesar*, Flint, Boston, 1936.

De Bono, E. *Nell'esercito nostro prima della guerra*, Mondadori, Milan, 1931.

De Bono, E. *La guerra come e dove l'ho vista e combattuta io*, Mondadori, Milan, 1935.

De Bono, E. *Anno XIIII: the conquest of an empire*, Cresset Press, London, 1937.

De Dampierre, 'Dix années de politique française a Rome (1925–1935)', *Revue des Deux Mondes*, 21, 1953.

De Rosa, G. (ed.) *Giolitti e il fascismo in alcune sue lettere inedite*, Edizioni di storia e letteratura, Rome, 1957.

De' Stefani, A. *Baraonda bancaria*, Le edizioni del Borghese, Milan, 1960.

De' Stefani, A. *Una riforma al rogo*, Giovanni Volpe editore, Rome, 1963.

De Vecchi, C.M. *Orizzonti d'impero: cinque anni in Somalia*, Mondadori, Milan, 1935.

De Vecchi, C.M. *Il Quadrumviro scomodo: il vero Mussolini nelle memorie del più monarchico dei fascisti* (ed. L. Romersa), Mursia, Milan, 1983.

De Vecchi, C.M. *Tra Papa, Duce e Re: il conflitto tra Chiesa Cattolica e Stato fascista nel diario 1930–1931 del primo ambasciatore del Regno d'Italia presso la Santa Sede* (ed. S. Setta), Jouvence, Rome, 1998.

Devoto, G. *La parentesi: quasi un diario*, La Nuova Italia, Florence, 1974.

Di Nolfo, E. *Le paure e le speranze degli italiani (1943–1953)*, Mondadori, Milan, 1986.

Dolfin, G. *Con Mussolini nella tragedia: diario del capo della segreteria particolare del Duce 1943–1944*, Garzanti, Milan, 1949.

Dollmann, E. *The interpreter: memoirs*, Hutchinson, London, 1967.

Ducci, R. *La bella gioventù*, Il Mulino, Bologna, 1996.

Dumini, A. *Diciassette colpi*, Longanesi, Milan, 1958.

Duranti, D. *Il romanzo della mia vita* (ed. G. F. Venè), Mondadori, Milan, 1987.

Eden, A. *Memoirs* (3 vols), Cassell, London, 1960–65.

Fanelli, G.A. *Agonia di un regime (gennaio–luglio 1943)*, Giovanni Volpe editore, Rome, 1971.

Farinacci, R. *Squadrismo: dal mio diario della vigilia 1919–1922*, Edizioni Ardita, Rome, 1933.

Favagrossa, C. *Perché perdemmo la guerra: Mussolini e la produzione bellica*, Rizzoli, Milan, 1946.

Federzoni, L. *Italia di ieri per la storia di domani*, Mondadori, Milan, 1967.

Federzoni, L. *1927: diario di un ministro del fascismo* (ed. A. Macchi), Passigli, Florence, 1993.

Ferraris, E. *La Marcia su Roma veduta dal Viminale*, Edizioni Leonardo, Rome, 1946.

Foschini, A. 'A trent'anni dall'occupazione di Corfu', *Nuova Antologia*, f. 1836, 1953.

Select bibliography

Fragnito, G. 'I miei debutti nella carriera', *Rivista di studi politici internazionali*, 39, 1972.

Frassati, L. *Il destino passa per Varsavia*, Bompiani, Milan, 1985.

Frediani, G. *La pace separata di Ciano*, Bonacci, Rome, 1990.

Gafencu, G. *The last days in Europe: a diplomatic journey in Europe*, Frederick Muller, London, 1947.

Galbiati, E. *Il 25 luglio e la M.V.S.N.*, Editrice Bernabò, Milan, 1950.

Galli, C. 'Jugoslavia tragica (1928–1934)', *Nuova Antologia*, f. 1830, 1953.

Gambetti, F. *Gli anni che scottano*, Mursia, Milan, 1967.

Garibaldi, L. (ed.), *Mussolini e il professore: vita e diarii di Carlo Alberto Biggini*, Mursia, Milan, 1983.

Giua, M. *Ricordi di un ex-detenuto politico 1935–1943*, Chiantore, Turin, 1945.

Giuriati, G. *La vigilia (gennaio 1913–maggio 1915)*, Mondadori, Milan, 1930.

Giuriati, G. *Con D'Annunzio e Millo in difesa dell'Adriatico*, Sansoni, Florence, 1954.

Giuriati, G. *La parabola di Mussolini nei ricordi di un gerarca* (ed. E. Gentile), Laterza, Bari, 1981.

Goebbels, J. *Diaries* (ed. L.P. Lochner), Hamish Hamilton, London, 1948.

Goebbels, J. *Final entries 1945: diaries* (ed. H. Trevor-Roper), Putnam, New York, 1978.

Goebbels, J. *The Goebbels diaries 1939–1941* (ed. F. Taylor), Hamish Hamilton, London, 1982.

Grandi, D. *Giovani*, Zanichelli, Bologna, 1941.

Grandi, D. 'Il diario della marcia su Roma', *Epoca*, 15 October 1972.

Grandi, D. *Il mio paese: ricordi autobiografici* (ed. R. De Felice), Il Mulino, Bologna, 1985.

Grandi, D. *La politica estera dell'Italia dal 1929 al 1932* (2 vols) (ed. P. Nello), Bonacci, Rome, 1985.

Graziani, R. *Pace romana in Libia*, Mondadori, Milan, 1937.

Graziani, R. *Ho difeso la patria*, Garzanti, Milan, 1947.

Grazzi, E. *Il principio della fine (L'impresa di Grecia)*, Editrice Faro, Rome, 1945.

Guariglia, R. *Ricordi, 1922–1946*, Edizioni scientifiche italiane, Naples, 1950.

Guariglia, R. *Primi passi in diplomazia e rapporti dall'ambasciata di Madrid 1932–1934* (ed. R. Moscati), Edizioni scientifiche italiane, Naples, 1972.

Guariglia, R. *Scritti 'storico-eruditi' e documenti diplomatici (1936–1940)*, Edizioni scientifiche italiane, Naples, 1981.

Guarneri, F. *Battaglie economiche fra le due guerre* (ed. L. Zani), Il Mulino, Bologna, 1988.

Hitler, A. *Hitler's table talk 1941–1944* (ed. H. Trevor-Roper), Weidenfeld and Nicolson, London, 1953.

Hitler, A. *Hitler's secret book* (ed. T. Taylor), Grove Press, New York, 1961.

Hitler, A. *Mein Kampf* (ed. D.C. Watt), Hutchinson, London, 1972.

Hoare, S. *Nine troubled years*, Collins, London, 1954.

Jacomoni di San Savino, F. *La politica dell'Italia in Albania*, Cappelli, Rocca San Casciano, 1965.

Kallay, N. *Hungarian premier: a personal account of a nation's struggle in the Second World War*, London, 1954.

Kirkpatrick, I. *The inner circle*, Macmillan, London, 1959.

Lazzaro, U. *Il compagno Bill: diario dell'uomo che catturò Mussolini*, Società Editrice Internazionale, Turin, 1989.

Leccisi, D. *Con Mussolini prima e dopo Piazzale Loreto*, Edizioni Settimo Sigillo, Rome, 1991.

Lessona, A. *Verso l'impero: memorie per la storia politica del conflitto italo-etiopico*, Sansoni, Florence, 1939.

Lessona, A. *Memorie*, Edizioni Lessona, Rome, 1963.

Lessona, A. *Un ministro di Mussolini racconta*, Edizioni Nazionali, Milan, 1973.

Leto, G. *OVRA: fascismo–antifascismo*, Cappelli, Rocca San Casciano, 1952.

Levi, C. *Christ stopped at Eboli: the story of a year*, Cassell, London, 1948.

Levi, P. *If this is a man*, New English Library, London, 1969.

Longo, L. *Un popolo alla macchia*, Riuniti, Rome, 1965.

Select bibliography

Luciolli, M. *Palazzo Chigi: anni roventi. Ricordi di vita diplomatica italiana dal 1933 al 1948*, Rusconi, Milan, 1976.

Lussu, E. *Enter Mussolini: observations and adventures of an Anti-Fascist*, Methuen, London, 1936.

Lussu, E. *Essere a sinistra: democrazia, autonomia e socialismo in cinquant'anni di lotte*, Mazzotta, Milan, 1976.

Lussu, E. *Il cinghiale del diavolo e altri scritti sulla Sardegna*, Einaudi, Turin, 1976.

Magistrati, M. 'L'Anschluss austro-tedesco visto da Berlino', *Rivista di studi politici internazionali*, 15, 1948.

Magistrati, M. *L'Italia a Berlino (1937–1939)*, Mondadori, Milan, 1956.

Magistrati, M. *Il prologo del dramma: Berlino 1934–1937*, Mursia, Milan, 1971.

Malaparte, C. *Kaputt*, A. Redman, London, 1948.

Marchesi, L. *Come siamo arrivati a Brindisi*, Bompiani, Milan, 1969.

Marcoaldi, F. (ed.), *Vent'anni di economia e politica. Le carte De' Stefani (1922–1941)*, Franco Angeli, Milan, 1986.

Martini, F. *Diario 1914–1918* (ed. G. De Rosa), Mondadori, Milan, 1966.

Masotti, P.M. *Ricordi d'Etiopia di un funzionario coloniale*, Pan, Milan, 1981.

Massock, R.G. *Italy from within*, Macmillan, London, 1943.

Matteotti, G. *The Fascisti exposed: a year of Fascist domination*, H. Fertig, New York, 1969.

Matteotti, G. *Scritti e discorsi scelti*, Guanda editore, Parma, 1974.

Maugeri, F. *From the ashes of disgrace*, Reynal and Hitchcock, New York, 1948.

Maugeri, F. *Ricordi di un marinaio: la marina italiana dai primi del Novecento al secondo dopoguerra nelle memorie di uno dei suoi capi*, Mursia, Milan, 1980.

Maurano, S. *Ricordi di un giornalista fascista*, Casa editrice Ceschina, Milan, 1973.

Moellhausen, E.F. *La carta perdente: memorie diplomatiche 25 luglio 1943–2 maggio 1945* (ed. V. Rusca), Sestante, Rome, 1948.

Montagna, R. *Mussolini e il processo di Verona*, Edizioni Omnia, Milan, 1949.

Moran, H.M. *In my fashion: an autobiography of the last ten years*, P. Davis, London, 1946.

Mori, C. *Con la Mafia ai ferri corti*, Mondadori, Milan, 1932.

Mosca, O. *Nessuno volle i miei dollari d'oro*, E. Scarfoglio, Naples, 1958.

Mosconi, A. *I primi anni di governo italiano nella Venezia Giulia: Trieste 1919–1922*, Cappelli, Bologna, 1924.

Mosconi, A. *La mia linea politica*, Studio Tipografico De Biase, Rome, 1952.

Musmanno, M.A. *La guerra non l'ho voluta io*, Vallecchi, Florence, 1947.

Natta, A. *L'altra Resistenza: i militari italiani internati in Germania*, Einaudi, Turin, 1997.

Navarra, Q. *Memorie del cameriere di Mussolini*, Longanesi, Milan, 1946.

Nenni, P. *Ten years of tyranny in Italy*, George Allen and Unwin, London, 1932.

Nenni, P. *Storia di quattro anni (1919–1922)*, G. Einaudi, Rome, 1946.

Nenni, P. *La battaglia socialista contro il fascismo 1922–1944* (ed. D. Zucàro), Mursia, Milan, 1977.

Newby, E. *Love and war in the Apennines*, Hodder and Stoughton, London, 1971.

Newby, W. *Peace and war: growing up in Fascist Italy*, Collins, London, 1991.

Nicholson, H. *Some people*, Oxford University Press, London, 1983.

Nitti, F.S. *Peaceless Europe*, Cassell, London, 1922.

Nitti, F.S. *The decadence of Europe: the paths of reconstruction*, T. Fisher Unwin, London, 1923.

Nobile, U. *With the 'Italia' to the North Pole*, George Allen and Unwin, London, 1930.

Nobile, U. *My polar flights: an account of the voyages of the airships 'Italia' and 'Norge'*, F. Muller, London, 1961.

Ortona, E. 'L'esodo da Londra dell'ambasciata italiana nel 1940', *Storia contemporanea*, 21, 1990.

Ortona, E. *Diplomazia di guerra: diari 1937–1943*, Il Mulino, Bologna, 1993.

Select bibliography

Pacelli, F. *Diario della Conciliazione con verbali e appendice di documenti* (ed. M. Maccarrone), Libreria Editrice Vaticana, Città del Vaticano, 1959.

Packard, R. and E. *Balcony empire: Fascist Italy at war*, Chatto and Windus, London, 1943.

Pajetta, G. *Douce France: diario 1941–1942*, Riuniti, Rome, 1971.

Pajetta, G. *Ricordi di Spagna: diario 1937–1939*, Riuniti, Rome, 1977.

Pajetta, G. *Il ragazzo rosso va alla guerra*, Mondadori, Milan, 1986.

Panunzio, V. *Il 'secondo fascismo' 1936–1943: la reazione della nuova generazione alla crisi del movimento e del regime*, Mursia, Milan, 1988.

Paolucci, R. *Il mio piccolo mondo perduto*, Cappelli, Bologna, 1947.

Pavese, C. *This business of living*, World Distributors, London, 1964.

Pertini, S. *Sei condanne, due evasioni* (ed. U. Faggi), Mondadori, Milan, 1978.

Pesce, G. *And no quarter: an Italian partisan in World War II*, Ohio University Press, Columbus, 1972.

Petacci, C. *Il mio diario*, Editori Associati, n.p., 1946.

Petacci, M. *Chi ama è perduto: mia sorella Claretta* (ed. S. Corvaja), Luigi Reverdito editore, Gardolo del Trento, 1988.

Phillips, W. *Ventures in diplomacy*, J. Murray, London, 1955.

Piazzesi, M. *Diario di uno squadrista toscano 1919–1922*, Bonacci, Rome, 1981.

Pini, G. *Itinerario tragico (1943–1945)*, Edizioni Omnia, Milan, 1950.

Pini, G. *Filo diretto con Palazzo Venezia*, Edizioni FPE, Milan, 1967.

Pintor, G. *Doppio diario 1936–1943* (ed. M. Serri), Einaudi, Turin, 1978.

Pirelli, A. *Taccuini 1922–1943* (ed. D. Barbone), Il Mulino, Bologna, 1984.

Pisanò, G. *Io, Fascista*, Il Saggiatore, Milan, 1997.

Pisenti, P. *Una repubblica necessaria (R.S.I.)*, G. Volpe editore, Rome, 1977.

Pizzoni, A. *Alla guida del CLNAI: memorie per i figli*, Il Mulino, Bologna, 1995.

Pozzi, A. *Come li ho visti io: dal diario di un medico*, Mondadori, Milan, 1947.

Prezzolini, G. *L'Italiano inutile*, Rusconi, Milan, 1983.

Pricolo, F. *Ignavia contro eroismo: l'avventura italo-greca: ottobre 1940–aprile 1941*, Nicola Ruffolo editore, Rome, 1946.

Pugliese, E. *Io difendo l'esercito*, Rispoli editore, Naples, 1946.

Quaroni, P. *Diplomatic bags: an ambassador's memoirs*, Weidenfeld and Nicolson, London, 1966.

Rahn, R. *Ambasciatore di Hitler a Vichy e a Salò*, Garzanti, Milan, 1950.

Renzi, R. *Da Starace ad Antonioni: diario critico di un ex balilla*, Marsilio, Padua, 1964.

Riccardi, R. *Pagine squadristiche*, Unione Editoriale d'Italia, Rome, 1939.

Ridomi, C. *La fine dell'ambasciata a Berlino 1940–1943*, Longanesi, Milan, 1952.

Roatta, M. *Otto milioni di baionette: l'esercito italiano in guerra dal 1940 al 1944*, Mondadori, Milan, 1946.

Rocca, M. (Tancredi, L.) *Come il fascismo divenne una dittatura*, ELI, Milan, 1952.

Romualdi, P. *Fascismo repubblicano* (ed. M. Viganò), SugarCo, Varese, 1992.

Ronchi, V. *Guerra e crisi alimentare in Italia: 1940–1950 ricordi e esperienze*, Vittorio Ronchi, Rome, 1977.

Rossi, E. *Miserie e splendori del confino di polizia: lettere da Ventotene 1939–1943* (ed. M. Magini), Feltrinelli, Milan, 1981.

Rossoni, G. (ed.) *Il delitto Matteotti tra il Viminale e l'Aventino: dagli atti del processo De Bono davanti all'Alta Corte di Giustizia*, Il Mulino, Bologna, 1966.

Sacerdoti, G. *Ricordi di un ebreo bolognese: illusioni e delusioni 1929–1945* (ed. R. De Felice), Bonacci, Rome, 1983.

Salvadori, M. *The Labour and the wounds: a personal chronicle of one man's fight for freedom*, Pall Mall Press, London, 1958.

Salvemini, G. *Memorie di un fuoruscito*, Feltrinelli, Milan, 1960.

Select bibliography

Salvemini, G. *Carteggio 1921–1926* (ed. E. Tagliacozzo), Laterza, Bari, 1985.
Sapelli, A. *Memorie d'Africa (1883–1906)*, Zanichelli, Bologna, 1935.
Sapori, A. *Mondo finito*, Leonardo, Rome, 1946.
Sarfatti, M. *Acqua passata*, Cappelli, Rocca San Casciano, 1955.
Schuster, I. *Gli ultimi tempi di un regime*, La Via, Milan, 1945.
Scaroni, S. *Con Vittorio Emanuele III*, Mondadori, Milan, 1954.
Scof Newby, W. *Tra pace e guerra: una ragazza slovena nell'Italia fascista*, Il Mulino, Bologna, 1994.
Scorza, C. *La notte del Gran Consiglio*, Palazzi editore, Milan, 1968.
Segre, D.V. *Memoirs of a fortunate Jew: an Italian story*, Paladin, London, 1987.
Senise, C. *Quando ero capo della polizia 1940–1943*, Ruffolo, Rome, 1946.
Sforza, C. *L'Italia dal 1914 al 1944 quale io la vidi*, Mondadori, Milan, 1944.
Silva, P. *Io difendo la monarchia*, De Fonseca, Rome, 1946.
Simoni, L. *Berlino ambasciata d'Italia 1939–1943*, Migliaresi, Rome, 1946.
Soffici, A. and Prezzolini, G. *Diari 1939–1945*, Le edizioni del Borghese, Milan, 1962.
Sogno, E. *La Franchi: storia di un'organizzazione partigiana*, Il Mulino, Bologna, 1996.
Soleri, M. *Memorie*, Einaudi, Rome, 1949.
Spampanato, B. *Contromemoriale* (3 vols), Edizione di 'Illustrato', Rome, 1952.
Spirito, U. *Memorie di un incosciente*, Rusconi, Milan, 1977.
Strabolgi, Lord *The conquest of Italy*, Hutchinson, London, 1944.
Stuparich, G. *Un anno di scuola e ricordi istriani*, Einaudi, Turin, 1961.
Suvich, F. *Memorie 1932–1936* (ed. G. Bianchi), Rizzoli, Milan, 1984.
Tamaro, A. *Venti anni di storia 1922–1943* (3 vols), Editrice Tiber, Rome, 1953.
Tamaro, A. *Due anni di storia*, Giovanni Volpe editore, Rome, 1981.
Terzaghi, M, *Fascismo e Massoneria*, Editrice Storica, Milan, 1950.
Toeplitz, L. *Il banchiere: al tempo in cui nacque, crebbe e fiorì la Banca Commerciale Italiana*, Edizioni Milano Nuovo, Milan, 1963.
Toeplitz, L. *Ciak a chi tocca*, Edizioni Milano Nuovo, Milan, 1964.
Trabucchi, A. *I vinti hanno sempre torto*, Francesco De Silva, Turin, 1947.
Trentin, S. *Dieci anni di fascismo totalitario in Italia: dall'istituzione del Tribunale speciale alla proclamazione dell'Impero (1926–1936)*, Riuniti, Rome, 1975.
Treves, P. *What Mussolini did to us*, Gollancz, London, 1940.
Tripodi, N. *Italia fascista in piedi! Memorie di un littore*, Le Edizioni del Borghese, Rome, 1960.
Tripodi, N. *Fascismo così: problemi di un tempo ritrovato*, Ciarrapico editore, Rome, 1984.
Turati, A. *Fuori dell'ombra della mia vita: dieci anni nel solco del fascismo* (ed. A. Frappani), Centro Bresciano di iniziative culturali, Brescia, 1973.
Vailati, V. *Badoglio risponde*, Rizzoli, Milan, 1958.
Valiani, L. *Dall'antifascismo alla Resistenza*, Feltrinelli, Milan, 1959.
Valiani, L. *Sessant'anni di avventure e battaglie: riflessioni e ricordi* (ed. M. Pini), Rizzoli, Milan, 1983.
Valiani, L. *Tutte le strade conducono a Roma* (ed. N. Matteucci), Il Mulino, Bologna, 1983.
Vansittart, R. *The mist procession*, Hutchinson, London, 1958.
Varè, D. *Laughing diplomat*, J. Murray, London, 1938.
Varè, D. *The two impostors*, J. Murray, London, 1949.
Varè, D. *Ghosts of the Spanish steps*, J. Murray, London, 1955.
Vergani, O. *Ciano: una lunga confessione*, Longanesi, Milan, 1974.
Vicentini, R.A. *Il movimento fascista veneto attraverso il diario di uno squadrista*, Società Stamperia Zanetti, Venice, 1935.
Visconti Prasca, S. *Io ho aggredito la Grecia*, Rizzoli, Milan, 1946.
Vivarelli, R. *La fine di una stagione: memoria 1943–1945*, Il Mulino, Bologna, 2000.
Volpe, G. *Ritorno al paese (Paganica): memorie minime*, AGE, Rome, 1963.

Select bibliography

Volpi, G. 'Ricordi e orizzonti balcanici', *Rassegna di politica internazionale*, 4, 1937.

Von Hassell, U. *The Von Hassell diaries 1938–1944*, Hamish Hamilton, London, 1948.

Ward-Price, G. *I know these dictators*, Harrap, London, 1937.

Waterfield, L. *Castle in Italy: an autobiography*, J. Murray, London, 1961.

Welles, S. *The time for decision*, Hamish Hamilton, London, 1944.

Zaghi, C. *Terrore a Ferrara durante i 18 mesi della repubblica di Salò*, Istituto regionale 'Ferruccio Parri' per la storia del movimento di liberazione e dell'età contemporanea in Emilia-Romagna, Bologna, 1992.

Zangrandi, R. *Il lungo viaggio attraverso il fascismo: contributo alla storia di una generazione*, Feltrinelli, Milan, 1964.

Zaniboni, T. *Testamento spirituale: ricominciamo a vivere (se vi pare)*, Baldini and Castoldi, Milan, 1949.

Zucaro, D. *Lettere di una spia*, Sugar, Milan, 1977.

SELECT SECONDARY SOURCES

Books

Abrate, M. *Ricerche per la storia dell'organizzazione sindacale dell'industria in Italia dalle origini al patto di Palazzo Vidoni*, Scuola d'amministrazione industriale dell'università di Torino, Turin, 1966.

Abrate, M. *La lotta sindacale nella industrializzazione in Italia 1906–1926*, F. Angeli, Turin, 1967.

Absalom, R. *A strange alliance: aspects of escape and survival in Italy 1943–45*, Olschki, Florence, 1991.

Addis Saba, M. *Gioventù italiana del littorio: la stampa dei giovani nella guerra fascista*, Feltrinelli, Milan, 1973.

Adamson, W.L. *Avant-garde Florence from modernism to Fascism*, Harvard University Press, Cambridge, Mass., 1993.

Adler, F.H. *Italian industrialists from liberalism to fascism: the political development of the industrial bourgeoisie 1906–1934*, Cambridge University Press, 1995.

Agarossi, E. and Smith, B.F. *La resa tedesca in Italia*, Feltrinelli, Milan, 1980.

Agarossi, E. *L'Italia nella sconfitta: politica interna e situazione internazionale durante la seconda guerra mondiale*, Edizioni scientifiche italiane, Naples, 1985.

Agarossi, E. *Una nazione allo sbando: l'armistizio italiano del settembre 1943*, Il Mulino, Bologna, 1993.

Alatri, P. *Le origini del fascismo*, Riuniti, Rome, 1962.

Alcock, A.E. *The history of the South Tyrol question*, Michael Joseph, Geneva, 1970.

Allio, R. *L'organizzazione internazionale del lavoro e il sindacalismo fascista*, Il Mulino, Bologna, 1973.

Alvazzi del Frate, P., Andreini, R. and Bellini, V. *et al. La ricerca storica: teorie, techniche, problemi*, Università degli studi di Roma, Rome, 1981.

Ambri, M. *I falsi fascismi*, Jouvence, Rome, 1980.

Amendola, G. *Fascismo e movimento operaio*, Riuniti, Rome, 1975.

Amendola, G. *Intervista sull'antifascismo* (ed. P. Melograni), Laterza, Bari, 1976.

Amoretti, G.N. *La vicenda italo-croata nei documenti di Aimone di Savoia (1941–1943)*, Editrice Ipotesi, Rapallo, 1979.

Apih, E. *Italia fascismo e antifascismo nella Venezia-Giulia (1918–1943)*, Laterza, Bari, 1966.

Aquarone, A. *L'organizzazione dello stato totalitario*, Einaudi, Turin, 1965.

Argentieri, M. Baldassare, A. and Crainz, G. *et al. Fascismo e antifascismo negli anni della repubblica*, F. Angeli, Milan, 1986.

Select bibliography

Arlacchi, P. *Mafia, peasants and great estates: society in traditional Calabria*, Cambridge University Press, 1983.

Arnaldi, G., Caracciolo, A. and Carandini, A. *et al. Incontro con gli storici*, Laterza, Bari, 1986.

Asante, S.K.B. *Pan-African protest: West Africa and the Italo-Ethiopian crisis 1934–1941*, Longmans, London, 1977.

Baer, G.W. *The coming of the Italo-Ethiopian war*, Harvard University Press, Cambridge Mass., 1967.

Baer, G.W. *Test case: Italy, Ethiopia and the League of Nations*, Hoover Institution Press, Stanford, 1976.

Bandini, F. *Claretta: profilo di Clara Petacci e dei suoi tempi*, Sugar editore, Milan, 1960.

Barker, A.J. *The civilizing mission: the Italo-Ethiopian war 1935–6*, Cassell, London, 1968.

Barros, J. *The Corfu incident of 1923: Mussolini and the League of Nations*, Princeton University Press, 1965.

Bassignana, P.L. *Fascisti nel paese dei Soviet*, Bollati Boringhieri, Turin, 2000.

Basso, L. *Fascismo e Democrazia Cristiana: due regimi del capitalismo italiano*, Mazzotta, Milan, 1975.

Battaglia, R. *Storia della resistenza italiana (8 settembre 1943–25 aprile 1945)*, Einaudi, Turin, 1953.

Ben-Ghiat, R. *Fascist modernities: Italy, 1922–1945*, University of California Press, Berkeley, 2001.

Berezin, M. *Making the Fascist self: the political culture of interwar Italy*, Cornell University Press, Ithaca, 1997.

Bernabei, A. *Esuli ed emigrati italiani nel Regno Unito 1920–1940*, Mursia, Milan, 1997.

Berselli, A. *L'opinione pubblica inglese e l'avvento del fascismo (1919–1925)*, F. Angeli, Milan, 1971.

Bersellini, G. *Il riscatto 8 settembre–25 aprile: le tesi di Renzo De Felice: Salò – La Resistenza – L'identità della nazione*, F. Angeli, Milan, 1998.

Bertoldi, S. *Vittorio Emanuele III*, UTET, Turin, 1970.

Bessel, R. (ed.) *Fascist Italy and Nazi Germany: comparisons and contrasts*, Cambridge University Press, 1996.

Binchy, D.A. *Church and state in Fascist Italy*, Oxford University Press, London, 1970.

Bocca, G. *La repubblica di Mussolini*, Laterza, Bari, 1977.

Bolech Cecchi, D. *Non bruciare i ponti con Roma: le relazioni fra l'Italia, la Gran Bretagna e la Francia dall'accordo di Monaco allo scoppio della seconda guerra mondiale*, Giuffrè, Milan, 1986.

Bolla, N. *Il segreto di due re*, Rizzoli, Milan, 1951.

Bonacina, G. *Obiettivo Italia: I bombardamenti aerei delle città italiane dal 1940 al 1945*, Club degli editori, Milan, 1970.

Borra, E. *Amedeo di Savoia: terzo Duca d'Aosta e Viceré d'Etiopia*, Mursia, Milan, 1985.

Bortolotti, L. *Storia della politica edilizia in Italia: proprietà, imprese edili e lavori pubblici dal primo dopoguerra ad oggi (1919–1970)*, Riuniti, Rome, 1978.

Bosworth, R.J.B. *Italy, the least of the Great Powers: Italian foreign policy before the First World War*, Cambridge University Press, 1979.

Bosworth, R. and Rizzo, G. (eds), *Altro polo: intellectuals and their ideas in contemporary Italy*, F. May Foundation, Sydney, 1983.

Bosworth, R.J.B. 'Italy's historians and the myth of Fascism' in R. Langhorne (ed.), *Diplomacy and intelligence during the Second World War; essays in honour of F.H. Hinsley*, Cambridge University Press, 1985.

Bosworth, R.J.B. and Romano, S. (eds) *La politica estera italiana (1860–1985)*, Il Mulino, Bologna, 1991.

Bosworth, R.J.B. *Italy and the wider world 1860–1960*, Routledge, London, 1996.

Select bibliography

Bosworth, R.J.B. *The Italian dictatorship: problems and perspectives in the interpretation of Mussolini and Fascism*, Arnold, London, 1998.

Bosworth, R.J.B. and Dogliani, P. (eds), *Italian fascism: history, memory and representation*, Macmillan, London, 1999.

Bracalini, R. *Il re 'vittorioso': la vita, il regno e l'esilio di Vittorio Emanuele III*, Feltrinelli, Milan, 1980.

Bravo, A. and Bruzzone, A.M. *In guerra senza armi: storie di donne 1940–1945*, Laterza, Bari, 1995.

Brunetta, G.P. *Storia del cinema italiano 1895–1945*, Riuniti, Rome, 1979.

Bruni, P. *Giuseppe Caradonna e la destra nazionale*, Serarcangeli editore, Rome, 1996.

Bruzzone, A.M. 'Women in the Italian Resistance', in P. Thompson (ed.) *Our common history: the transformation of Europe*, Pluto Press, London, 1982.

Buchignani, P. *Un fascismo impossibile: l'eresia di Berto Ricci nella cultura del Ventennio*, Il Mulino, Bologna, 1994.

Burgwyn, H.J. *Il revisionismo fascista: la sfida di Mussolini alle grandi potenze nei Balcani e sul Danubio 1925–1933*, Feltrinelli, Milan, 1979.

Burgwyn, H.J. *Italian foreign policy in the interwar period 1918–1940*, Praeger, Westport, Conn., 1997.

Busoni, J. *Nel tempo del fascismo*, Riuniti, Rome, 1975.

Cagnetta, M. *Antichisti e impero fascista*, Dedalo, Bari, 1979.

Cambria, A. *Maria José*, Longanesi, Milan, 1966.

Canali, M. *Il dissidentismo fascista: Pisa e il caso Santini 1923–1925*, Bonacci, Rome, 1983.

Canali, M. *Il delitto Matteotti: affarismo e politica nel primo governo Mussolini*, Il Mulino, Bologna, 1997.

Cannistraro, P.V. *La fabbrica del consenso: fascismo e mass media*, Laterza, Bari, 1975.

Cannistraro, P.V. (ed.) *Historical dictionary of Fascist Italy*, Greenwood Press, Westport, Conn., 1982.

Cantagalli, R. *Storia del fascismo fiorentino 1919–1925*, Vallecchi, Florence, 1972.

Cantalupo, R. *Vita di Salvatore Contarini*, Sesante, Rome, 1947.

Cantamessa Arpinati, G. *Arpinati mio padre*, Casa Editrice Il Sagittario, Rome, 1968.

Capogreco, C.S. *Ferramonti: la vita e gli uomini del più grande campo d'internamento fascista (1940–1945)*, La Giuntina, Florence, 1987.

Caracciolo, N. *Gli ebrei e l'Italia durante la guerra 1940–1945*, Bonacci, Rome, 1986.

Cardoza, A. *Agrarian elites and Italian Fascism: the province of Bologna 1901–1926*, Princeton University Press, 1982.

Cardoza, A. *Aristocrats in bourgeois Italy: the Piedmontese nobility 1861–1930*, Cambridge University Press, 1997.

Carlotti, A.L. *Storia del partito fascista sammarinese*, Celuc, Milan, 1973.

Carocci, G. *La politica estera dell'Italia fascista (1925–1928)*, Laterza, Bari, 1969.

Carocci, G. *Italian Fascism*, Penguin, Harmondsworth, 1975.

Caroleo, A. *Le banche cattoliche dalla prima guerra mondiale al fascismo*, Feltrinelli, Milan, 1976.

Carpi, D. *Between Mussolini and Hitler: the Jews and the Italian authorities in France and Tunisia*, Brandeis University Press, Hanover, 1994.

Carsten, F.L. *The rise of fascism*, Batsford, London, 1967.

Casali, A. *Storici italiani fra le due guerre: La 'Nuova Rivista Storica' 1917–1943*, Guida, Naples, 1980.

Cassels, A. *Fascist Italy*, Routledge and Kegan Paul, London, 1969.

Cassels, A. *Mussolini's early diplomacy*, Princeton University Press, 1970.

Castronovo, V. *Giovanni Agnelli: la Fiat dal 1899 al 1945*, Einaudi, Turin, 1977.

Castronovo, V. *Storia di una banca: La Banca Nazionale del Lavoro e lo sviluppo economico italiano 1913–1983*, Einaudi, Turin, 1983.

Select bibliography

Cavazza, S. *Piccole patrie: feste popolari tra regione e nazione durante il fascismo*, Il Mulino, Bologna, 1997.

Cederna, A. *Mussolini urbanista: lo sventramento di Roma negli anni del consenso*, Laterza, Bari, 1979.

Ceplair, L. *Under the shadow of war: Fascism, Anti-Fascism and Marxists 1918–1937*, Columbia University Press, New York, 1987.

Cervelli, I. *Gioacchino Volpe*, Guida, Naples, 1977.

Cervi, M. *The hollow legions: Mussolini's blunder in Greece 1940–1941*, Doubleday, New York, 1971.

Chabod, F. *A history of Italian Fascism*, Weidenfeld and Nicolson, London, 1963.

Chadwick, O. *Britain and the Vatican during the Second World War*, Cambridge University Press, 1986.

Chapman, G.C. *Milocca: a Sicilian village*, George Allen and Unwin, London, 1973.

Chiaretti, T., Drudi Demby, L. and Mingozzi, G. *Gli ultimi tre giorni: 1926. Attentato Zamboni: un'occasione per le leggi speciali*, Cappelli, Bologna, 1977.

Cilibrizzi, S. *Pietro Badoglio rispetto a Mussolini e di fronte alla storia*, Conte, Naples, n.d.

Clarke, J. Calvitt III, *Russia and Italy against Hitler: the Bolshevik–Fascist rapprochement of the 1930s*, Greenwood Press, Westport, Conn., 1991.

Colarizi, S. *Dopoguerra e fascismo in Puglia (1919–1926)*, Laterza, Bari, 1971.

Colarizi, S. *I democratici all'opposizione: Giovanni Amendola e l'Unione nazionale (1922–1926)*, Il Mulino, Bologna, 1973.

Colarizi, S. *L'opinione degli italiani sotto il regime 1929–1943*, Laterza, Bari, 1991.

Consiglio, A. *Vita di Vittorio Emanuele III*, Rizzoli, Milan, 1950.

Contini, G. *La memoria divisa*, Rizzoli, Milan, 1997.

Contini, M. *Maria José: la regina sconosciuta*, Eli, Milan, 1955.

Corner, P. *Fascism in Ferrara 1915–1925*, Oxford University Press, London, 1975.

Coverdale, J.F. *Italian intervention in the Spanish Civil War*, Princeton University Press, 1975.

Craig, G.A. and Gilbert, F. (eds), *The diplomats 1919–39*, Oxford University Press, London, 1953.

Cresciani, G. *Fascismo, antifascismo e gli italiani in Australia 1922–1945*, Bonacci, Rome, 1979.

Dalla Casa, B. *Attentato al duce: le molte storie del caso Zamboni*, Il Mulino, Bologna, 2000.

Damiani, C. *Mussolini e gli Stati Uniti 1922–1935*, Cappelli, Bologna, 1980.

D'Amoja, F. *Declino e prima crisi dell'Europa di Versailles: studio sulla diplomazia italiana ed europa (1931–1933)*, Giuffrè, Milan, 1967.

Da Rold, E. *Turismo e sport nella provincia di Belluno durante il fascismo: economia, ideologia, società e consenso*, Istituto Bellunese di ricerche sociali e culturali, Belluno, 1994.

Davis, J.A. *Gramsci and Italy's passive revolution*, Croom Helm, London, 1979.

Deakin, F.W. *The brutal friendship: Mussolini, Hitler and the fall of Fascism*, Penguin, Harmondsworth, 1966.

Deakin, F.W. *The last days of Mussolini*, Penguin, Harmondsworth, 1966.

De Felice, R. *Storia degli ebrei sotto il fascismo*, Einaudi, Turin, 1961 (rev. edn., 1988).

De Felice, R. *Le interpretazioni del fascismo*, Laterza, Bari, 1969 (English version *Interpretations of Fascism*, Harvard University Press, Cambridge, Mass., 1977).

De Felice, R. (ed.) *La Carta del Carnaro nei testi di Alceste De Ambris e di Gabriele D'Annunzio*, Il Mulino, Bologna, 1973.

De Felice, R. *Il problema dell'Alto Adige nei rapporti italo-tedeschi dall'Anschluss alla fine della seconda guerra mondiale*, Il Mulino, Bologna, 1973.

De Felice, R. (ed.) *L'Italia fra tedeschi e alleati: la politica estera fascista e la seconda guerra mondiale*, Il Mulino, Bologna, 1973.

De Felice, R. *Intervista sul fascismo* (ed. M. Ledeen), Laterza, Bari, 1975 (English version *Fascism: an informal introduction*, Transaction Books, New Brunswick, N.J., 1977).

Select bibliography

De Felice, R. (ed.) *Antologia sul fascismo: il giudizio storico*, Laterza, Bari, 1976.

De Felice, R. (ed.) *Antologia sul fascismo: il giudizio politico*, Laterza, Bari, 1976.

De Felice, R. *D'Annunzio politico 1919–1938*, Laterza, Bari, 1978.

De Felice, R. (ed.) *Autobiografia del fascismo: antologia di testi fascisti 1919–1945*, Minerva Italica, Bergamo, 1978.

De Felice, R. *Ebrei in un paese arabo*, Il Mulino, Bologna, 1978 (English version *Jews in an Arab land*, University of Texas Press, Austin, 1985).

De Felice, R. 'Italian Fascism and the middle classes' in S.U. Larsen *et al*. (eds), *Who were the fascists: social roots of European fascism*, Univerzitetsforlaget, Bergen, 1980.

De Felice, R. and Goglia, L. *Storia fotografica del fascismo*, Laterza, Bari, 1982.

De Felice, R. *Intellettuali di fronte al fascismo: saggi e note documentarie*, Bonacci, Rome, 1985.

De Felice, R. (ed.) *Futurismo, cultura e politica*, Fondazione G. Agnelli, Turin, 1988.

De Felice, R. *Il fascismo e l'Oriente: arabi, ebrei e indiani nella politica di Mussolini*, Il Mulino, Bologna, 1988.

De Felice, R. (ed.) *Bibliografia orientativa del fascismo*, Bonacci, Rome, 1991.

De Felice, R. *Rosso e nero* (ed. P. Chessa), Baldini e Castaldi, Milan, 1995.

De Felice, R. *Fascismo, Antifascismo, Nazione: note e ricerche*, Bonacci, Rome, 1996.

De Felice, R. *Intervista sul fascismo* (ed. M. Ledeen), rev. edn., Laterza, Bari, 1997.

Degl'Innocenti, M. *Il socialismo italiano e la guerra di Libia*, Riuniti, Rome, 1976.

De Grand, A.J. *The Italian Nationalist Association and the rise of Fascism in Italy*, University of Nebraska Press, Lincoln, 1978.

De Grand, A.J. *Italian Fascism: its origins and development*, University of Nebraska Press, Lincoln, 1982.

De Grand, A.J. *Fascist Italy and Nazi Germany: the 'fascist' style of rule*, Routledge, London, 1995.

De Grazia, V. *The culture of consent: mass organization of leisure in Fascist Italy*, Cambridge University Press, 1981.

De Grazia, V. *How Fascism ruled women: Italy 1922–1945*, University of California Press, Berkeley, 1992.

Del Boca, A. *The Ethiopian war 1935–1941*, Univeristy of Chicago, Press, 1969.

Del Boca, A. *Gli italiani in Africa orientale dall'unità alla marcia su Roma*, Laterza, Bari, 1976.

Del Boca, A. *Gli italiani in Africa orientale: la conquista dell'impero*, Laterza, Bari, 1979.

Del Boca, A. *Gli italiani in Africa orientale: la caduta dell'impero*, Laterza, Bari, 1982.

Del Boca, A. *Gli italiani in Africa orientale: nostalgia delle colonie*, Laterza, Bari, 1984.

Del Boca, A. *Gli italiani in Libia: Tripoli bel suol d'amore 1860–1922*, Laterza, Bari, 1986.

Del Boca, A. *Gli italiani in Libia dal fascismo al Gheddafi*, Laterza, Bari, 1988.

Del Boca, A., Legnani, M. and Rossi, M.G. (eds), *Il regime fascista: storia e storiografia*, Laterza, Bari, 1995.

Del Boca, A. (ed.) *I gas di Mussolini: il fascismo e la guerra d'Etiopia*, Riuniti, Rome, 1996.

Del Buono, O. *Eia, Eia, Eia, Alalà: la stampa italiana sotto il fascismo 1919–43*, Feltrinelli, Milan, 1971.

Del Carria, R. *Proletari senza rivoluzione: storia delle classi subalterne italiane dal 1860 al 1950*, Edizioni Oriente, Milan, 1966.

De Luna, G. *Donne in oggetto: l'antifascismo nella società italiana 1922–1939*, Bollati Boringhieri, Turin, 1995.

Delzell, C.F. *Mussolini's enemies: the Italian anti-Fascist resistance*, Princeton University Press, 1961.

Delzell, C.F. (ed.) *Mediterranean fascism 1919–1945*, Harper and Row, New York, 1970.

De Marco, M. *Il Gazzettino: storia di un quotidiano*, Marsilio, Venice, 1976.

Diggins, J.P. *Mussolini and Fascism: the view from America*, Princeton University Press, 1972.

Di Nolfo, E. *Mussolini e la politica estera italiana 1919–1933*, Cedam, Padua, 1960.

Select bibliography

Di Nolfo, E., Rainero, R.H. and Vigezzi, B. (eds), *L'Italia e la politica di potenza in Europa (1938–1940)*, Marzorati editore, Milan, 1986.

Di Nucci, L. *Fascismo e spazio urbano: le città storiche dell'Umbria*, Il Mulino, Bologna, 1992.

Dogliani, P. *L'Italia fascista 1922–1940*, Sansoni, Milan, 1999.

Domenico, R.P. *Italian Fascists on trial 1943–1948*, University of North Carolina Press, Chapel Hill, 1991.

Doumanis, N. *Myth and memory in the Mediterranean: remembering Fascism's empire*, Macmillan, London, 1997.

Duggan, C. *Fascism and the Mafia*, Yale University Press, New Haven, 1989.

Dunnage, J. *The Italian police and the rise of Fascism: a case study of the province of Bologna 1897–1925*, Praeger, Westport, Conn., 1997.

Eatwell, R. *Fascism: a history*, Chatto and Windus, London, 1995.

Ercolani, A. *La fondazione del fascio di combattimento a Fiume tra Mussolini e D'Annunzio*, Bonacci, Milan, 1996.

Evola, J. *Il fascismo: saggio di una analisi critica dal punto di vista della Destra*, Giovanni Volpe editore, Rome, 1964.

Falasca-Zamponi, S. *Fascist spectacle: the aesthetics of power in Mussolini's empire*, University of California Press, Berkeley, 1997.

Ferrarotto, M. *L'Accademia d'Italia: intellettuali e potere durante il fascismo*, Liguori, Naples, 1977.

Finzi, R. *L'università italiana e le leggi antiebraiche*, Riuniti, Rome, 1997.

Foley, C. *Commando extraordinary*, Pan, London, 1954.

Forgacs, D. (ed.) *Rethinking Italian Fascism: capitalism, populism and culture*, Lawrence and Wishart, London, 1986.

Fornari, H. *Mussolini's gadfly: Roberto Farinacci*, Vanderbilt University Press, Nashville, 1971.

Forgacs, D. *Italian culture in the industrial era 1880–1980: cultural industries, politics and the public*, Manchester University Press, 1990.

Forsyth, D. *The crisis of Liberal Italy: monetary and financial policy 1914–1922*, Cambridge University Press, 1993.

Francini, M. *Primo dopoguerra e origini del fascismo a Pistoia*, Feltrinelli, Milan, 1976.

Franzinelli, M. *Il riarmo dello spirito: i cappellani militari nella seconda guerra mondiale*, Pagus edizioni, Padua, 1991.

Franzinelli, M. *I tentacoli dell'Ovra: agenti, collaboratori e vittime della polizia politica fascista*, Bollati Boringhieri, Turin, 1999.

Friedrich, C.J and Brzezinski, Z. *Totalitarian dictatorship and autocracy*, Harvard University Press, Cambridge, Mass., 1956.

Gabaccia, D.R. *Italy's many diasporas*, University of Washington Press, Seattle, 2000.

Gaeta, F. *Nazionalismo italiano*, Edizioni scientifiche italiane, Naples, 1965.

Gaeta, F. (ed.) *La stampa nazionalista*, Cappelli, Rocca San Casciano, 1965.

Galli della Loggia, E. *La morte della patria: la crisi dell'idea della nazione tra Resistenza, antifascismo e Repubblica*, Laterza, Bari, 1996.

Ganapini, L. *La Repubblica delle camicie nere: i combattenti, i politici, gli amministratori, i socializzatori*, Garzanti, Milan, 1999.

Gaspari, O. *L'emigrazione veneta nell'Agro Pontino durante il periodo fascista*, Morcelliana, Brescia, 1985.

Gat, M. *Britain and Italy, 1943–1949*, Sussex Academic Press, Brighton, 1996.

Gentile, E. *Le origini dell'ideologia fascista (1918–1925)*, Laterza, Bari, 1975.

Gentile, E. *Il mito dello stato nuovo dall'antigiolittismo al fascismo*, Laterza, Bari, 1982.

Gentile, E. *Storia del Partito Fascista 1919–1922: movimento e milizia*, Laterza, Bari, 1989.

Gentile, E. *Il culto del littorio: la sacralizzazione della politica nell'Italia fascista*, Laterza, Bari, 1993.

Select bibliography

Gentile, E. *La via italiana al totalitarismo: il partito e lo stato nel regime fascista*, La Nuova Italia Scientifica, Rome, 1995.

Gentile, E. *The sacralization of politics in Fascist Italy*, Harvard University Press, Cambridge, Mass., 1996.

Gentile, E. *La Grande Italia: ascesa e declino del mito della nazione nel ventesimo secolo*, Mondadori, Milan, 1997.

Germino, D. *The Italian Fascist party in power: a study in totalitarian rule*, University of Minnesota Press, Minneapolis, 1959.

Ghirado, D. *Building new communities: New Deal America and Fascist Italy*, Princeton University Press, 1989.

Gianeri, E. *Il piccolo re: Vittorio Emanuele nella caricatura*, Fiorini, Turin, 1946.

Giordano, G. *Il patto a quattro nella politica estera di Mussolini*, Forni, Bologna, 1976.

Gleason, A. *Totalitarianism: the inner history of the Cold War*, Oxford University Press, New York, 1995.

Goglia, L. and Grassi, F. *Il colonialismo italiano da Adua all'Impero*, Laterza, Bari, 1981.

Goglia, L. *Storia fotografica dell'Impero fascista 1935–1941*, Laterza, Bari, 1985.

Golsan, R.J. (ed.) *Fascism, aesthetics and culture*, University of New England Press, Hanover, 1992.

Gregor, A.J. *The ideology of fascism: the rationale of totalitarianism*, The Free Press, New York, 1969.

Gregor, A.J. *The fascist persuasion in radical politics*, Princeton University Press, 1974.

Gregor, A.J. *Interpretations of fascism*, General Learning Press, Morristown, N.J., 1974.

Gregor, A.J. *Sergio Panunzio: il sindacalismo ed il fondamento razionale del fascismo*, Giovanni Volpe editore, Rome, 1978.

Gregor, A.J. *Italian Fascism and developmental dictatorship*, Princeton University Press, 1979.

Griffin, R. *International fascism: theories, causes and new consensus*, Arnold, London, 1998.

Grifone, P. *Il capitale finanziario in Italia*, Einaudi, Turin, 1971.

Guerri, G.B. *Giuseppe Bottai, un fascista critico: ideologia e azione del gerarca che avrebbe voluto portare l'intelligenza nel fascismo e il fascismo alla liberalizzazione*, Feltrinelli, Milan, 1976.

Guerri, G.B. *Galeazzo Ciano: una vita 1903–1944*, Bompiani, Milan, 1979.

Guerri, G.B. *L'arcitaliano: vita di Curzio Malaparte*, Bompiani, Milan, 1980.

Guerri, G.B. *Italo Balbo*, Garzanti, Milan, 1984.

Guerri, G.B. *Fascisti: gli italiani di Mussolini, il regime degli italiani*, Mondadori, Milan, 1995.

Guidi, S., Gulminelli, A. and Carduccini, G. *I percorsi della memoria: Predappio – quello che non vi hanno mai raccontato (o che avete dimenticato)*, Società Eco Più, San Savino di Predappio, 1997.

Guspini, U. *L'orecchio del regime: le intercettazioni telefoniche al tempo del fascismo*, Mursia, Milan, 1973.

Halperin, S.W. *Mussolini and Italian Fascism*, Van Nostrand, New York, 1964.

Hamilton, A. *The appeal of Fascism: a study of intellectuals and Fascism*, Anthony Blond, London, 1971.

Hardie, F. *The Abyssinian crisis*, Batsford, London, 1974.

Harris, B. *The United States and the Italo-Ethiopian crisis*, Stanford University Press, 1964.

Harris, H.S. *The social philosophy of Giovanni Gentile*, University of Illinois Press, Urbana, 1960.

Hay, J. *Popular film culture in Fascist Italy: the passing of the Rex*, Indiana University Press, Bloomington, 1987.

Hayes, P.M. *Fascism*, George Allen and Unwin, London, 1973.

Hoepke, K-P. *La destra tedesca e il fascismo*, Il Mulino, Bologna, 1971.

Horn, D. *Social bodies: science, reproduction and Italian modernity*, Princeton University Press, 1994.

Hostetter, R. *The Italian Socialist Movement*, Van Nostrand, Princeton, 1958.

Hughes, H.S. *The United States and Italy*, W.W. Norton, New York, 1968.

Select bibliography

Hughes, H.S. *Prisoners of hope: the silver age of the Italian Jews 1924–1974*, Harvard University Press, Cambridge, Mass., 1983.

Hughes, S. 'Men of steel: dueling, honor and politics in Liberal Italy', in P. Spierenburg (ed.), *Gender, honor, and rituals in Modern Europe and America*, Ohio University Press, Columbus, 1998.

Iacovetta, F., Perin, R. and Principe, A. (eds), *Enemies within: Italian and other internees in Canada and abroad*, University of Toronto Press, 2000.

Ignazi, P. *Il polo escluso: profilo del Movimento Sociale Italiano*, Il Mulino, Bologna, 1989.

Imbriani, A.M. *Gli italiani e il Duce: il mito e l'immagine di Mussolini negli anni del fascismo (1938–1943)*, Liguori, Naples, 1992.

Innocenti, M. *I gerarchi del fascismo: storia del ventennio attraverso gli uomini del Duce*, Mursia, Milan, 1992.

Ipsen, C. *Dictating demography: the problem of population in Fascist Italy*, Cambridge University Press, 1996.

Isnenghi, M. *Il mito della grande guerra da Marinetti a Malaparte*, Laterza, Bari, 1973.

Isnenghi, M. *L'educazione dell'italiano: il fascismo e l'organizzazione della cultura*, Cappelli, Bologna, 1979.

Isnenghi, M. *Intellettuali militanti e intellettuali funzionari: appunti sulla cultura fascista*, Einaudi, Turin, 1979.

Isnenghi, M. *Le guerre degli italiani: parole, immagini, ricordi 1848–1945*, Mondadori, Milan, 1989.

Isnenghi, M. (ed.) *I luoghi della memoria: simboli e miti dell'Italia unita*, Laterza, Bari, 1996.

Isnenghi, M. (ed.) *I luoghi della memoria: strutture ed eventi dell'Italia unita*, Laterza, Bari, 1997.

Isnenghi, M. (ed.) *I luoghi della memoria: personaggi e date dell'Italia unita*, Laterza, Bari, 1997.

Iraci, A. *Arpinati: l'oppositore di Mussolini*, M. Bulzoni editore, Rome, 1970.

Israel, G. and Nastasi, P. *Scienza e razza nell'Italia fascista*, Il Mulino, Bologna, 1998.

Jacobelli, J. *Il fascismo e gli storici oggi*, Laterza, Bari, 1988.

Kallis, A.A. *Fascist ideology: territory and expansionism in Italy and Germany, 1922–1945*, Routledge, London, 2000.

Kelikian, A.A. *Town and country under Fascism: the transformation of Brescia 1915–26*, Clarendon, Oxford, 1986.

Kent, P.C. *The Pope and the Duce: the international impact of the Lateran Pacts*, Macmillan, London, 1981.

Kershaw, I. *Hitler 1889–1936: hubris*, Allen Lane, London, 1998.

Kershaw, I. *Hitler 1936–1945: nemesis*, Allen Lane, London, 2000.

Kitchen, M. *Fascism*, Macmillan, London, 1976.

Knox, M. *Mussolini unleashed 1939–1941: politics and strategy in Fascist Italy's last war*, Cambridge University Press, 1982.

Knox, M. 'Fascist Italy assesses its enemies' in E.R. May (ed.), *Knowing one's enemies: intelligence assessment before the two world wars*, Princeton University Press, 1984.

Knox, M. *Common destiny: dictatorship, foreign policy and war in Fascist Italy and Nazi Germany*, Cambridge University Press, 2000.

Knox, M. *Hitler's Italian allies: Royal Armed Forces, Fascist Regime, and the war of 1940–1943*, Cambridge University Press, 2000.

Koon, M. *Believe, obey, fight: the political socialization of youth in Fascist Italy 1922–1943*, University of North Carolina Press, Chapel Hill, 1985.

La Francesca, S. *La politica economica del fascismo*, Laterza, Bari, 1972.

Lajolo, L. *Gramsci: un uomo sconfitto*, Rizzoli, Milan, 1980.

Lamb, R. *War in Italy: a brutal story*, J. Murray, London, 1993.

Lamb, R. *Mussolini and the British*, J. Murray, London, 1997.

Landy, M. *Fascism in film: the Italian commercial cinema 1931–1943*, Princeton University Press, 1986.

Select bibliography

Laqueur, W. (ed.) *Fascism: a reader's guide: analysis, interpretations, bibliography*, Penguin, Harmondsworth, 1979.

Lazzaro, U. *Dongo: mezzo secolo di menzogne*, Mondadori, Milan, 1993.

Lazzero, R. *La Decima Mas*, Rizzoli, Milan, 1984.

Lazzero, R. *Gli schiavi di Hitler: i deportati italiani in Germania nella seconda guerra mondiale*, Mondadori, Milan, 1996.

Ledeen, M. *Universal Fascism: the theory and practice of the Fascist International 1928–1936*, H. Fertig, New York, 1972.

Ledeen, M. *D'Annunzio a Fiume*, Laterza, Bari, 1975.

Lubasz, H. (ed.) *Fascism: three major regimes*, John Wiley, New York, 1973.

Ludovici, M. (ed.) *Fascismi in Emilia Romagna*, Società Editrice 'il Ponte Vecchio', Cesena, 1998.

Lyttelton, A. (ed.) *Italian fascisms from Pareto to Gentile*, Jonathan Cape, London, 1973.

Lyttelton, A. *The seizure of power: Fascism in Italy 1919–1929*, Weidenfeld and Nicolson, London, 1973.

Mack Smith, D. 'Anti-British propaganda in Fascist Italy', in *Inghilterra e Italia nel 1900: atti del convegno di Bagni di Lucca ottobre 1972*, La Nuova Italia, Florence, 1973.

Mack Smith, D. *Mussolini's Roman empire*, Longmans, London, 1976.

Mack Smith, D. *Storia di cento anni di vita italiana visti attraverso il Corriere della Sera*, Rizzoli, Milan, 1978.

Mack Smith, D. *Italy and its monarchy*, Yale University Press, New Haven, Conn., 1989.

Maier, C.S. *Recasting bourgeois Europe: stabilization in France, Germany and Italy in the decade after World War I*, Princeton University Press, 1975.

Mallett, R. *The Italian navy and Fascist expansionism 1935–1940*, F. Cass, London, 1998.

Mantelli, B. *'Camerati del lavoro': i lavoratori italiani emigrati nel Terzo Reich nel periodo dell'Asse 1938–1943*, La Nuova Italia, Florence, 1992.

Marchesini, D. *La scuola dei gerarchi: mistica fascista: storia, problemi, istituzioni*, Feltrinelli, Milan, 1976.

Marongiu Buonaiuti, *La politica religiosa del Fascismo nel Dodecanneso*, Giannini Editore, Naples, 1979.

Masella, L. *Tra corporativismo e modernizzazione: le classi dirigenti pugliesi nella crisi dello stato liberale*, Milella, Lecce, 1983.

Mason, T. *Nazism, Fascism and the working class* (ed. J. Caplan), Cambridge University Press, 1995.

Mazzantini, C. *I balilla andarono a Salò: l'armata degli adolescenti che pagò il conto della Storia*, Marsilio, Venice, 1995.

Mazzatosta, T.M. *Il regime fascista tra educazione e propaganda (1935–1943)*, Cappelli, Bologna, 1978.

Mazzatosta, T.M. and Volpi, C. *L'Italietta fascista (lettere al potere 1936–1943)*, Cappelli, Bologna, 1980.

Meldini, P. *Sposa e madre esemplare: ideologia e politica della donna e della famiglia durante il fascismo*, Guaraldi, Florence, 1975.

Meldini, P. (ed.), *Un monumento al Duce? Contributo al dibatto sul fascismo*, Guaraldi, Florence, 1976.

Melograni, P. *Storia politica della grande guerra 1915–1918*, Laterza, Bari, 1969.

Melograni, P. *Gli industriali e Mussolini: rapporti tra Confindustria e Fascismo dal 1919 al 1929*, Longanesi, Milan, 1972.

Melograni, P. *Rapporti segreti della polizia fascista 1938–1940*, Laterza, Bari, 1979.

Miccichè, G. *Dopoguerra e fascismo in Sicilia 1919–1927*, Riuniti, Rome, 1976.

Miccoli, G. *I dilemmi e i silenzi di Pio XI*, Rizzoli, Milan, 2000.

Michaelis, M. *Mussolini and the Jews: German–Italian relations and the Jewish question in Italy 1922–1945*, Clarendon, Oxford, 1978.

Select bibliography

Migone, G.G. *Gli Stati Uniti e il fascismo: alle origini dell'egemonia americana in Italia*, Feltrinelli, Milan, 1980.

Milza, P. *L'Italie fasciste devant l'opinion française 1920–1940*, Colin, Paris, 1967.

Minerbi, S.I. *The Vatican and Zionism: conflict in the Holy Land 1895–1925*, Oxford University Press, New York, 1990.

Missori, M. *Gerarchi e statuti del PNF: Gran Consiglio, Direttorio nazionale, Federazioni provinciali: quadri e biografie*, Bonacci, Rome, 1986.

Mockler, A. *Haile Selassie's war: the Italian–Ethiopian campaign 1935–1941*, Random House, New York, 1984.

Mola, A.A. *Storia della Massoneria italiana dall'unità alla Repubblica*, Bompiani, Milan, 1976.

Molony, J.N. *The emergence of political catholicism in Italy: partito popolare 1919–1926*, Croom Helm, London, 1977.

Momigliano, E. *Storia tragica e grottesca del razzismo fascista*, Mondadori, Milan, 1946.

Morgan, P. *Italian Fascism 1919–1945*, St. Martin's Press, New York, 1995.

Morris, J. *The political economy of shopkeeping in Milan 1886–1922*, Cambridge University Press, 1993.

Moseley, R. *Mussolini's shadow: the double life of Count Galeazzo Ciano*, Yale University Press, New Haven, Conn., 1999.

Mureddu, M. *Il Quirinale del re*, Feltrinelli, Milan, 1977.

Napolitano, M.L. *Mussolini e la conferenza di Locarno (1925): il problema della sicurezza nella politica estera italiana*, Editrice Montefeltro, Urbino, 1996.

Negash, T. *Italian colonialism in Eritrea 1882–1941: policies, practice and impact*, Almquist and Wiksell, Uppsala, 1987.

Neglie, P. *Fratelli in camicia nera: comunisti e fascisti dal corporativismo alla CGIL (1928–1948)*, Il Mulino, Bologna, 1996.

Nello, P. *L'avanguardismo giovanile alle origini del fascismo*, Laterza, Bari, 1978.

Nello, P. *Dino Grandi: la formazione di un leader fascista*, Il Mulino, Bologna, 1987.

Nello, P. *Un fedele disubbidiente: Dino Grandi da Palazzo Chigi al 25 luglio*, Il Mulino, Bologna, 1993.

Neri Serneri, S. *Classe, partito, nazione: alle origini della democrazia italiana 1919–1948*, P. Lacaita editore, Manduria, 1995.

Nolte, E. *Three faces of fascism: Action Française, Italian Fascism, National Socialism*, Mentor, New York, 1969.

Nolte, E. *Marxism, Fascism and Cold War*, Van Gorcum, Assen, 1982.

Novak, B.C. *Trieste 1941–1951: the ethnic, political and ideological struggle*, University of Chicago Press, 1970.

Nozzoli, G. *I ras del regime: gli uomini che disfecero gli italiani*, Bompiani, Milan, 1972.

Onofri, N.S. *La strage di palazzo d'Accursio: origine e nascita del fascismo bolognese 1919–1920*, Feltrinelli, Milan, 1980.

Onofri, N.S. *Il triangolo rosso (1943–1947): la verità sul dopoguerra in Emilia-Romagna attraverso i documenti d'archivio*, Sapere 2000, Rome, 1994.

Orlando, F. *I 45 giorni di Badoglio*, Bonacci, Rome, 1994.

Pansa, G. *L'esercito di Salò*, Mondadori, Milan, 1970.

Pansini, A.J. *The Duce's dilemma: an analysis of the tragic events associated with Italy's part in World War II*, Greenvale Press, Waco, Tex., 1997.

Papa, E.R. *Fascismo e cultura*, Marsilio, Padua, 1975.

Passato e presente della Resistenza: 50 anniversario della Resistenza e della Guerra di Liberazione, Presidenza del Consiglio dei Ministri, Dipartimento per l'informazione e l'editoria, Rome, 1994.

Passerini, L. 'Work ideology and working class attitudes to Fascism', in P. Thompson (ed.), *Our common history: the transformation of Europe*, Pluto, London, 1982.

Passerini, L. *Torino operaio e fascismo: una storia orale*, Laterza, Bari, 1984.

Select bibliography

Pavone, C. *Una guerra civile: saggio storico sulla moralità nella Resistenza*, Bollati Boringhieri, Turin, 1991.

Payne, S.G. *A history of fascism 1914–1945*, University of Wisconsin Press, Madison, Wisc., 1995.

Perco Jacchia, C. *Un paese, La resistenza: testimonianze di uomini e donne di Lucinico/Gorizia*, Del Bianco editore, Udine, 1981.

Perfetti, F. *Il nazionalismo italiano dalle origini alla fusione col fascismo*, Cappelli, Bologna, 1977.

Perfetti, F. *Fascismo monarchico: i paladini della monarchia assoluta fra integralismo e dissidio*, Bonacci, Rome, 1988.

Perfetti, F. *La Camera dei fasci e delle corporazioni*, Bonacci, Rome, 1991.

Petacco, A. *Il superfascista: vita e morte di Alessandro Pavolini*, Mondadori, Milan, 1998.

Petacco, A. *Regina: la vita e segreti di Maria José*, Mondadori, Milan, 1997.

Petracchi, G. *Da San Pietroburgo a Mosca: la diplomazia italiana in Russia 1861–1941*, Bonacci, Rome, 1983.

Pezzino, P. *Anatomia di un massacro: controversie sopra una strage tedesca*, Il Mulino, Bologna, 1997.

Pickering-Iazzi, R. (ed.) *Mothers of invention: women, Italian Fascism and culture*, University of Minnesotsa Press, Minneapolis, 1995.

Pieri, P. and Rochat, G. *Pietro Badoglio*, UTET, Turin, 1974.

Pinkus, K. *Bodily regimes: Italian advertising under Fascism*, University of Minnesota Press, Minneapolis, 1995.

Pisanò, G. *Mussolini e gli ebrei*, Edizioni FPE, Milan, 1967.

Piva, F. *Lotte contadine e origini del fascismo, Padova–Venezia 1919–1922*, Marsilio, Venice, 1977.

Piva, F. *Contadini in fabbrica: Marghera 1920–1945*, Edizioni lavoro, Rome, 1991.

Pizzigallo, M. *Mediterraneo e Russia nella politica estera italiana 1922–1924*, Giuffrè, Milan, 1983.

Pollard, J.F. *The Vatican and Italian Fascism 1929–1932: a study in conflict*, Cambridge University Press, 1985.

Ponziani, L. *Notabili, combattenti e nazionalisti. L'Abruzzo verso il fascismo*, F. Angeli, Milan, 1988.

Poulantzas, N. *Fascism and dictatorship: the Third International and the problem of fascism*, NLB, London, 1974.

Preziosi, A.M. *Borghesia e fascismo in Friuli negli anni 1920–1922*, Bonacci, Rome, 1980.

Pugliese, S.G. *Carlo Rosselli: socialist heretic and Antifascist exile*, Harvard University Press, Cambridge, Mass., 1999.

Quartararo, R. *Roma tra Londra e Berlino: la politica estera fascista dal 1931 al 1940*, Bonacci, Milan, 1980.

Quartararo, R. *Italia–URSS 1917–1941: i rapporti politici*, Edizioni scientifiche italiane, Naples, 1997.

Quartararo, R. *I rapporti italo-americani durante il fascismo (1922–1941)*, Edizioni scientifiche italiane, Naples, 1999.

Quartermaine, L. *Mussolini's last republic: propaganda and politics in the Italian Social Republic (R.S.I.) 1943–45*, Elm Book Publications, Exeter, 2000.

Quazza, G. *Resistenza e storia d'Italia: problemi e ipotesi di ricerca*, Feltrinelli, Milan, 1976.

Quazza, G., Collotti, E., and Legnani, M. *et al. Storiografia e fascismo*, F. Angeli, Milan, 1985.

Rabel, R.G. *Between East and West: Trieste, the United States and the Cold War 1941–1954*, Duke University Press, Durham, N.C., 1988.

Rauti, G. *Le idee che mossero il mondo*, Centro editoriale nazionale, Rome, 1965.

Rauti, G. *L'immane conflitto. Mussolini, Roosevelt, Stalin, Churchill, Hitler*, Centro editoriale nazionale, Rome, 1966.

Select bibliography

Rauti, P. and Sermonti, R. *Storia del fascismo* (5 vols), Centro editoriale nazionale, Rome, 1976–77.

Reich, W. *The mass psychology of fascism*, Condor, New York, 1970.

Revelli, N. *La guerra dei poveri*, Einaudi, Turin, 1962.

Revelli, N. *Il mondo dei vinti: testimonianze di vita contadina* (2 vols), Einaudi, Turin, 1977.

Rizzo, G. *D'Annunzio e Mussolini: la verità sui loro rapporti*, Cappelli, Rocca San Casciano, 1960.

Rizzo, V. *Attenti al Duce: storie minime dell'Italia fascista*, Vallecchi, Florence, 1981.

Roberts, D.D. *The syndicalist tradition and Italian Fascism*, Manchester University Press, 1979.

Robertson, E.M. *Mussolini as empire builder: Europe and Africa 1932–6*, Macmillan, London, 1977.

Rochat, G. *L'esercito italiano da Vittorio Veneto a Mussolini (1919–1925)*, Laterza, Bari, 1967.

Rochat, G. *Militari e politici nella preparazione della campagna d'Etiopia: studio e documenti 1932–1936*, F. Angeli, Milan, 1971.

Rochat, G. *Italo Balbo: aviatore e ministro dell'aeronautica 1926–1933*, Italo Bovolenta editore, Ferrara, 1979.

Rochat, G. *Guerre italiane in Libia e in Etiopia: studi militari 1921–1939*, Pagus editore, Padua, 1991.

Rochat, G. *L'esercito italiano in pace e in guerra: studi di storia militare*, RARA, Milan, 1991.

Rogger, H. and Weber, E. (eds), *The European right: a historical profile*, Weidenfeld and Nicolson, London, 1965.

Romano, S. *Giuseppe Volpi: industria e finanza tra Giolitti e Mussolini*, Bompiani, Milan, 1979.

Romeo, R. *L'Italia unita e la prima guerra mondiale*, Laterza, Bari, 1978.

Rosengarten, F. *The Italian Anti-Fascist press (1919–1945) from the legal opposition press to the underground newspapers of World War II*, Case Western University Press, Cleveland, Ohio, 1968.

Rossi, C. *Il Tribunale Speciale: storia documentata*, Casa editrice Ceschina, Milan, 1952.

Rossi, E. *Padroni del vapore e fascismo*, Laterza, Bari, 1966.

Rossini, G. *Il movimento cattolico nel periodo fascista*, Edizioni cinque lune, Rome, 1966.

Roth, J.J. *The cult of violence: Sorel and the Sorelians*, University of California Press, Berkeley, 1980.

Roveri, A. *Le origini del fascismo a Ferrara 1918–1921*, Feltrinelli, Milan, 1974.

Rumi, G. *Alle origini della politica estera fascista (1918–1923)*, Laterza, Bari, 1968.

Rusconi, G.E. *Resistenza e postfascismo*, Il Mulino, Bologna, 1995.

Rusinow, D.L. *Italy's Austrian heritage 1919–1946*, Clarendon, Oxford, 1969.

Sabbatucci, G. *I combattenti nel primo dopoguerra*, Laterza, Bari, 1974.

Sabbatucci, G. (ed.) *La crisi italiana del primo dopoguerra*, Laterza, Bari, 1976.

Sachs, H. *Music in Fascist Italy*, W.W. Norton, New York, 1988.

Sadkovitch, J.J. *Italian support for Croatian separatism 1927–1937*, Garland, New York, 1987.

Sadkovitch, J.J. *The Italian navy in World War II*, Greenwood Press, Westport, Conn., 1994.

Salotti, G. *Giuseppe Giulietti: il sindacato dei marittimi dal 1910 al 1953*, Bonacci, Rome, 1982.

Salotti, G. *Nicola Bombacci da Mosca a Salò*, Bonacci, Rome, 1986.

Salvadori, M. *Gaetano Salvemini*, Einaudi, Turin, 1963.

Salvati, M. *Il regime e gli impiegati: la nazionalizzazione piccolo-borghese nel ventennio fascista*, Laterza, Bari, 1992.

Salvatorelli, L. and Mira, G. *Storia d'Italia nel periodo fascista* (2 vols), Mondadori, Milan, 1969.

Salvemini, G. *Prelude to World War II*, V. Gollancz, London, 1953.

Salvemini, G. *Italian Fascist activities in the United States*, Centre for Migration Studies, New York, 1977.

Santarelli, E. *Fascismo e neofascismo: studi e problemi di ricerca*, Riuniti, Rome, 1974.

Santini, A. *Costanzo Ciano: il ganascia del fascismo*, Camuria, Milan, 1993.

Santinon, R. *I fasci italiani all'estero*, Edizioni Settimo Sigillo, Rome, 1991.

Select bibliography

Santoro, C.M. *La politica estera di una media potenza: l'Italia dall'unità ad oggi*, Il Mulino, Bologna, 1991.

Sarti, R. *Fascism and the industrial leadership in Italy 1919–1940: a study in the expansion of private power under Fascism*, University of California Press, Berkeley, 1971.

Sarti, R. (ed.) *The Ax within: Italian Fascism in action*, New Viewpoints, New York, 1974.

Sarti, R. *Long live the strong: a history of rural society in the Apennine mountains*, University of Massachusetts Press, Amherst, 1985.

Sbacchi, A. *Ethiopia under Mussolini: Fascism and the colonial experience*, Zed Books, London, 1985.

Schnapp, J. *18BL and the theater of masses for masses*, Stanford University Press, Stanford, Calif., 1996.

Scoppola, P. *La Chiesa e il fascismo: documenti e interpretazioni*, Laterza, Bari, 1971.

Scotto di Luzio, A. *L'appropriazione imperfetta: editori, biblioteche e libri per ragazzi durante il fascismo*, Il Mulino, Bologna, 1996.

Sebastian, P. *I servizi segreti speciali britannici e l'Italia (1940–1945)*, Bonacci, Rome, 1986.

Sechi, S. *Dopoguerra e fascismo in Sardegna: il movimento autonomistico nella crisi dello stato liberale (1918–1926)*, Einaudi, Turin, 1969.

Segrè, C.G. *Fourth shore: the Italian colonization of Libya*, University of Chicago Press, 1974.

Segrè, C.G. *Italo Balbo: a Fascist life*, University of California Press, Berkeley, 1987.

Serra, M. *La ferità della modernità: intellettuali, totalitarismo e immagine del nemico*, Il Mulino, Bologna, 1992.

Seton-Watson, C. *Italy from Liberalism to Fascism 1870–1925*, Methuen, London, 1967.

Setta, S. *Renato Ricci. Dallo squadrismo alla Repubblica Sociale Italiana*, Il Mulino, Bologna, 1986.

Shorrock, W.I. *From ally to enemy: the enigma of Fascist Italy in French diplomacy 1920–1940*, Kent State University Press, Kent, Ohio, 1988.

Slaughter, J. *Women and the Italian Resistance 1943–1945*, Arden Press, Denver, Colo., 1997.

Sluga, G. *The problem of Trieste and the Italo-Yugoslav border: difference, identity, and sovereignty in twentieth-century Europe*, State University of New York Press, 2001.

Smyth, H. McG. *Secrets of the Fascist era: how Uncle Sam obtained some of the top-level documents of Mussolini's period*, Southern Illinois University Press, Carbonale and Edwardsville, Ill., 1975.

Snowden, F.M. *Violence and the great estates: Apulia 1900–1922*, Cambridge University Press, 1986.

Snowden, F.M. *The Fascist revolution in Tuscany 1919–1922*, Cambridge University Press, 1989.

Sofri, G. *Gandhi in Italia*, Il Mulino, Bologna, 1988.

Sorrentino, L. *Da Bel Ami a Lili Marlene: quello che il corrispondente di guerra non scrisse*, Bompiani, Milan, 1980.

Speroni, G. *Il Duca degli Abruzzi*, Rusconi, Milan, 1991.

Spinosa, A. *Starace*, Rizzoli, Milan, 1981.

Spriano, P. *The occupation of the factories: Italy 1920*, Pluto, London, 1975.

Spriano, P. *Antonio Gramsci and the party: the prison years*, Lawrence and Wishart, London, 1979.

Steinberg, J. *All or nothing: the Axis and the Holocaust 1941–3*, Routledge, London, 1990.

Stille, A. *Benevolence and betrayal: five Jewish families under Fascism*, Penguin, New York, 1993.

Stone, M.S. *The patron state: culture and politics in Fascist Italy*, Princeton University Press, 1998.

Sturani, E. *Otto milioni di cartoline per il Duce*, Centro Scientifico editore, Turin, 1995.

Susmel, D. *La vita sbagliata di Galeazzo Ciano*, Aldo Palazzi editore, Milan, 1962.

Tamagna, F.M. *Italy's interests and policies in the Far East*, Institute of Pacific Relations, New York, 1941.

Tamaro, A. *La condanna dell'Italia nel trattato di pace*, Cappelli, Rocca San Casciano, 1952.

Select bibliography

Tannenbaum, E.R. *Fascism in Italy: society and culture 1922–1945*, Allen Lane, London, 1973.

Taylor, A.J.P. *The origins of the Second World War*, Penguin, Harmondsworth, 1964.

Tenderini, M. and Shandrick, M. *The Duke of the Abruzzi: an explorer's life*, The Mountaineers, Baton Wicks, Seattle, Wash., 1997.

Tinghino, J.J. *Edmondo Rossoni from revolutionary syndicalism to Fascism*, P. Lang, New York, 1991.

Toscano, M. 'Eden's mission to Rome on the eve of the Italo-Ethiopian conflict', in A.O. Sarkissian (ed.), *Studies in diplomatic history and historiography in honour of G.P. Gooch*, Longmans, London, 1961.

Toscano, M. *Dal 25 luglio all'8 settembre*, Le Monnier, Florence, 1966.

Toscano, M. *Storia diplomatica della questione dell'Alto Adige*, Laterza, Bari, 1967.

Toscano, M. *The origins of the Pact of Steel*, Johns Hopkins University Press, Baltimore, Md., 1967.

Toscano, M. *Designs in diplomacy: pages from European diplomatic history in the twentieth century*, Johns Hopkins Press, Baltimore, Md., 1970.

Tranfaglia, N. *Carlo Rosselli dall'interventismo a 'Giustizia e Libertà'*, Laterza, Bari, 1965.

Tranfaglia, N. (ed.) *L'Italia unita nella storiografia del secondo dopoguerra*, Feltrinelli, Milan, 1980.

Tranfaglia, N. *Labirinto italiano: radici storiche e nuove contraddizioni*, Celid, Turin, 1984.

Tranfaglia, N. *Un passato scomodo: fascismo e postfascismo*, Laterza, Bari, 1996.

Treves, A. *Le migrazioni interne nell'Italia fascista*, Einaudi, Turin, 1976.

Turner, H.A. (ed.) *Reappraisals of fascism*, New Viewpoints, New York, 1975.

Ungari, P. *Alfredo Rocco e l'ideologia giuridica del fascismo*, Morcelliana, Brescia, 1963.

Vaini, M. *Le origini del fascismo a Mantova (1914–1922)*, Riuniti, Rome, 1961.

Vajda, M. *Fascism as a mass movement*, Allison and Busby, London, 1976.

Vannoni, G. *Massoneria, fascismo e chiesa cattolica*, Laterza, Bari, 1980.

Varvaro, P. *Una città fascista: potere e società a Napoli*, Sellerio, Palermo, 1990.

Venè, G.F. *Mille lire al mese: la vita quotidiana della famiglia nell'Italia fascista*, Mondadori, Milan, 1988.

Venè, G.F. *Coprifuoco: vita quotidiana degli italiani nella guerra civile 1943–1945*, Mondadori, Milan, 1989.

Veneruso, D. *L'Italia fascista 1922–1945*, Il Mulino, Bologna, 1984.

Vigezzi, B. (ed.) *1919–1925: dopoguerra e fascismo: politica e stampa in Italia*, Laterza, Bari, 1965.

Villari, Lucio *Le avventure di un capitano d'industria*, Einaudi, Turin, 1991.

Villari, Lucio *Il capitalismo italiano del novecento*, Laterza, Bari, 1992.

Villari, Luigi *Affari esteri 1943–1945*, Magi-Spinetti, Rome, 1948.

Villari, Luigi *The liberation of Italy 1943–1947*, C.C. Nelson, Appleton, Wisc., 1959.

Villari, Luigi *Italian foreign policy under Mussolini*, Holborn Publishing Company, London, 1959.

Vivarelli, R. *Il dopoguerra in Italia e l'avvento del fascismo (1918–1922) vol. I dalla fine della guerra all'impresa di Fiume*, Istituto italiano per gli studi storici, Naples, 1967.

Vivarelli, R. *Il fallimento del liberalismo: studi sulle origini del fascismo*, Il Mulino, Bologna, 1981.

Vivarelli, R. *Storia delle origini del fascismo: l'Italia dalla grande guerra alla marcia su Roma*, vol. II, Il Mulino, Bologna, 1991.

Voigt, K. *Il rifugio precario: gli esuli in Italia dal 1933 al 1945* (2 vols), La Nuova Italia, Florence, 1996.

Volpe, G. *Gabriele D'Annuzio: l'Italiano, il Politico, il Comandante*, Giovanni Volpe editore, Rome, 1981.

Volpe, G. *Nel regno di Clio: (nuovi 'Storici e Maestri')*, Giovanni Volpe editore, Rome, 1977.

Waley, D. *British public opinion and the Abyssinian war 1935–6*, M. Temple Smith, London, 1975.

Select bibliography

Ward, D. *Antifascisms: cultural politics in Italy 1943–46: Benedetto Croce and the Liberals, Carlo Levi and the 'Actionists'*, Farleigh Dickinson University Press, Madison, Wis., 1996.

Waterfield, G. *Professional diplomat: Sir Percy Loraine of Kirkharle Bt. 1880–1961*, J. Murray, London, 1973.

Watt, D.C. *How war came: the immediate origins of the Second World War 1938–1939*, Heinemann, London, 1989.

Webster, R.A. *L'imperialismo industriale italiano 1908–1915: studi sul pre-fascismo*, Einaudi, Turin, 1974.

Weinberg, G.L. *The foreign policy of Hitler's Germany: diplomatic revolution in Europe 1933–1936*, University of Chicago Press, 1970.

Weinberg, G.L. *The foreign policy of Hitler's Germany: starting World War II 1937–1939*, Chicago University Press, 1980.

Weiss, J. *The fascist tradition: radical right-wing extremism in modern Europe*, Harper and Row, New York, 1967.

Whittam, J. 'The Italian General Staff and the coming of the Second World War', in A. Preston (ed.), *General staffs and diplomacy before the Second World War*, Croom Helm, London, 1978.

Whittam, J. *Fascist Italy*, Manchester University Press, 1995.

Wilhelm, M. de B. *The other Italy: Italian resistance in World War II*, W.W. Norton, New York, 1988.

Wiskemann, E. *The Rome–Berlin Axis*, Oxford University Press, London, 1949.

Wiskemann, E. *Fascism in Italy*, Macmillan, London, 1969.

Wohl, R. *The generation of 1914*, Weidenfeld and Nicolson, London, 1980.

Wohl, R. *A passion for wings: aviation and the Western imagination 1908–1918*, Yale University Press, New Haven, Conn., 1994.

Woller, H. *I conti con il fascismo: l'epurazione in Italia 1943–1948*, Il Mulino, Bologna, 1997.

Woolf, S.J. (ed.) *The nature of fascism*, Weidenfeld and Nicolson, London, 1968.

Woolf, S.J. (ed.) *Fascism in Europe*, Methuen, London, 1981.

Zamagni, V. *The economic history of Italy 1860–1990*, Clarendon, Oxford, 1993.

Zani, L. *Italia libera: il primo movimento antifascista clandestino (1923–1925)*, Laterza, Bari, 1975.

Zanni Rosiello, I. (ed.) *Gli apparati statali dall'unità al fascismo*, Il Mulino, Bologna, 1976.

Zuccotti, S. *The Italians and the Holocaust: persecution, rescue and survival*, Basic Books, New York, 1987.

Articles (English language only)

Absalom, R. 'Hiding history: the Allies, the Resistance and the others in Occupied Italy 1943–1945', *Historical Journal*, 38, 1995.

Adamson, W.L. 'Benedetto Croce and the death of ideology', *Journal of Modern History*, 55, 1983.

Adamson, W.L. 'Fascism and culture: avant-gardes and secular religion in the Italian case', *Journal of Contemporary History*, 24, 1989.

Adamson, W.L. 'Modernism and Fascism: the politics of culture in Italy, 1903–1922', *American Historical Review*, 95, 1990.

Adamson, W.L. 'The language of opposition in early twentieth century Italy: rhetorical continuities between pre-war Florentine avant-gardism and Mussolini's Fascism', *Journal of Modern History*, 64, 1992.

Adamson, W.L. 'The culture of Italian Fascism and the Fascist crisis of modernity: the case of *Il Selvaggio*', *Journal of Contemporary History*, 30, 1995.

Allardyce, G. 'What fascism is not: thoughts on the deflation of a concept', *American Historical Review*, 84, 1979.

Select bibliography

Aquarone, A. 'Italy: the crisis of the corporative economy', *Journal of Contemporary History*, 4, 1969.

Azzi, S.C. 'The historiography of Fascist foreign policy', *Historical Journal*, 36, 1993.

Ben-Ghiat, R. 'Fascism, writing and memory: the realist aesthetic in Italy 1930–1950', *Journal of Modern History*, 67, 1995.

Ben-Ghiat, R. 'Italian Fascism and the aesthetics of the "third way"', *Journal of Contemporary History*, 31, 1996.

Bernardini, G. 'The origins and development of racial Anti-Semitism in Fascist Italy', *Journal of Modern History*, 49, 1977.

Blatt, J. 'The battle of Turin 1933–1936: Carlo Rosselli, Giustizia e Libertà, OVRA and the origins of Mussolini's Anti-Semitic campaigns', *Journal of Modern Italian Studies*, 1, 1995.

Bosworth, R.J.B. 'The British press, the conservatives and Mussolini 1920–1934', *Journal of Contemporary History*, 5, 1970.

Bosworth, R.J.B. 'Renato Citarelli, Fascist Vice Consul in Perth: a documentary note', *Papers in Labor History*, 14, 1994.

Bosworth, R.J.B. 'Tourist planning in Fascist Italy and the limits of a totalitarian culture', *Contemporary European History*, 6, 1995.

Bosworth, R.J.B. 'The *Touring Club Italiano* and the nationalisation of the Italian bourgeoisie', *European History Quarterly*, 27, 1997.

Bosworth, R.J.B. 'Venice between Fascism and international tourism, 1911–1945', *Modern Italy*, 4, 1999.

Bosworth, R.J.B. '*Per necessità famigliare*: hypocrisy and corruption in Fascist Italy', *European History Quarterly*, 30, 2000.

Braun, E. 'Expressionism as Fascist aesthetic', *Journal of Contemporary History*, 31, 1996.

Brunetta, G.P. 'The conversion of the Italian cinema to Fascism in the 1920s', *Journal of Italian History*, 1, 1978.

Burdett, C. 'Journeys to the *other* spaces of Fascist Italy', *Modern Italy*, 5, 2000.

Burdett, C. 'Journeys to Italian East Africa 1936–1941: narrations of settlement', *Journal of Modern Italian Studies*, 5, 2000.

Cammett, J.M. 'Communist theories of Fascism', *Science and Society*, 31, 1967.

Cannistraro, P.V. 'Mussolini's cultural revolution', *Journal of Contemporary History*, 7, 1972.

Cannistraro, P.V. 'Fascism and Italian-Americans in Detroit', *International Migration Review*, 9, 1975.

Cannistraro, P.V. and Rosoli, G. 'Fascist emigration policy in the 1920s: an interpretative framework', *International Migration Review*, 13, 1979.

Cannistraro, P.V. 'Mussolini, Sacco-Vanzetti, and the anarchists: the transatlantic context', *Journal of Modern History*, 68, 1996.

Cassels, A. 'Mussolini and German nationalism', *Journal of Modern History*, 35, 1963.

Cassels, A. 'Fascism for export: Italy and the United States in the twenties', *American Historical Review*, 72, 1964.

Chapman, J.W.M. 'Tricycle recycled: collaboration among the secret intelligence services of the Axis states, 1940–41', *Intelligence and National Security*, 7, 1992.

Ciruzzi, R.J. 'The Federazione universitaria cattolica italiana: Catholic students in Fascist Italy', *Risorgimento*, 3, 1982.

Clark, M. 'Italian squadrism and contemporary vigilantism', *European History Quarterly*, 18, 1988.

Cliadakis, H. 'Neutrality and war in Italian policy 1939–1940', *Journal of Contemporary History*, 9, 1974.

Cohen, J.S. 'The 1927 revaluation of the lira: a study in political economy', *The Economic History Review*, 25, 1972.

Select bibliography

Cohen, J.S. 'Was Italian Fascism a developmental dictatorship? Some evidence to the contrary', *Economic History Review*, 91, 1988.

Corner, P. 'Women in Fascist Italy. Changing family roles in the transition from an agricultural to an industrial society', *European History Quarterly*, 23, 1993.

Coverdale, J.F. 'The battle of Guadalajara, 8–22 March 1937', *Journal of Contemporary History*, 9, 1974.

Csöppus, J. 'The Rome pact and Hungarian agricultural exports to Italy (1920–1944)', *Journal of European Economic History*, 11, 1982.

Davis, J. 'Remapping Italy's path to the twentieth century', *Journal of Modern History*, 66, 1994.

De Caprariis, L. 'Fascism for export? The rise and eclipse of the Fasci Italiani all'Estero', *Journal of Contemporary History*, 35, 2000.

De Felice, R. 'Fascism and culture in Italy: outlines for further study', *Stanford Italian Review*, 8, 1990.

De Grand, A.J. 'Curzio Malaparte: the illusion of the Fascist revolution', *Journal of Contemporary History*, 7, 1972.

De Grand, A.J. 'Cracks in the facade: the failure of Fascist totalitarianism in Italy 1935–9', *European History Quarterly*, 21, 1991.

Delzell, C.F. 'Benito Mussolini; a guide to the biographical literature', *Journal of Modern History*, 35, 1963.

Delzell, C.F. 'Mussolini's Italy: twenty years after', *Journal of Modern History*, 38, 1966.

Delzell, C.F. 'Pius XII, Italy and the outbreak of war', *Journal of Contemporary History*, 2, 1967.

Dogliani, P. 'Sport and Fascism', *Journal of Modern Italian Studies*, 5, 2000.

Edwards, P.G. 'The Foreign Office and Fascism 1924–29', *Journal of Contemporary History*, 5, 1970.

Edwards, P.G. 'The Austen Chamberlain–Mussolini meetings', *Historical Journal*, 14, 1971.

Evans, A.R. 'Assignment to Armageddon: Ernst Jünger and Curzio Malaparte on the Russian front 1941–1943', *Central European History*, 14, 1981.

Fogu, C. 'Fascism and *historic* representation: the 1932 Garibaldian celebrations', *Journal of Contemporary History*, 31, 1996.

Fogu, C. '*Il Duce taumaturgo*: modernist rhetorics in Fascist representations of history', *Representations*, 57, 1997.

Foot, J.M. 'White bosheviks? The catholic left and the socialists in Italy, 1919–1920', *Historical Journal*, 40, 1997.

Foot, J. 'The tale of San Vittore: prisons, politics, crime and Fascism in Milan, 1943–1946', *Modern Italy*, 3, 1998.

Fraddosio, M. 'The Fallen Hero: the myth of Mussolini and Fascist women in the Italian Social Republic (1943–5)', *Journal of Contemporary History*, 31, 1996.

Fuller, M. 'Wherever you are, there you are: Fascist plans for the colonial city of Addis Ababa and the colonizing suburb of EUR '42', *Journal of Contemporary History*, 31, 1996.

Gatt, A. 'Futurism, proto-Fascist Italian culture and the sources of Douhetism', *War and Society*, 15, 1997.

Gentile, E. 'The problem of the party in Italian Fascism', *Journal of Contemporary History*, 19, 1984.

Gentile, E. 'Fascism in Italian historiography: in search of an individual historical identity', *Journal of Contemporary History*, 21, 1986.

Gentile, E. 'Fascism as political religion', *Journal of Contemporary History*, 25, 1990.

Gentile, E. 'Impending modernity: Fascism and the ambivalent image of the United States', *Journal of Contemporary History*, 28, 1993.

Gentile, E. 'Renzo De Felice; a tribute', *Journal of Contemporary History*, 32, 1997.

Gentile, E. 'Mussolini's charisma', *Modern Italy*, 3, 1998.

Ghirardo, D. 'Città fascista: surveillance and spectacle' , *Journal of Contemporary History*, 31, 1996.

Select bibliography

Goldman, A.L. 'Sir Robert Vansittart's search for Italian cooperation against Hitler 1933–36', *Journal of Contemporary History*, 9, 1974.

Gregor, A.J. 'Professor Renzo De Felice and the Fascist phenomenon', *World Politics*, 30, 1978.

Griffin, R. 'The sacred synthesis: the ideological cohesion of Fascist cultural policy', *Modern Italy*, 3, 1998.

Gumbrecht, H.U. '*I redentori della vittoria*: on Fiume's place in the genealogy of Fascism', *Journal of Contemporary History*, 31, 1996.

Hurst, M. 'What is fascism?' *Historical Journal*, 11, 1968.

Ipsen, C. 'The organization of demographic totalitarianism: early population policy in Fascist Italy', *Social Science History*, 17, 1993.

Joseph, R. 'The Martignoni affair: how a Swiss politician deceived Mussolini', *Journal of Contemporary History*, 9, 1974.

Kent, P.C. 'A tale of two Popes: Pius XI, Pius XII and the Rome–Berlin Axis', *Journal of Contemporary History*, 23, 1988.

Kent, P.C. 'Between Rome and London: Pius XI, the Catholic Church and the Abyssinian crisis of 1935–1936', *International History Review*, 11, 1989.

Keserich, C. 'The British Labour press and Italian Fascism 1922–25', *Journal of Contemporary History*, 10, 1975.

Knox, M. 'Conquest, foreign and domestic, in Fascist Italy and Nazi Germany', *Journal of Modern History*, 56, 1984.

Knox, M. 'The Fascist regime, its foreign policy and its wars: an Anti-Anti-Fascist orthodoxy?' *Contemporary European History*, 4, 1995.

La Rovere, L. 'Fascist groups in Italian universities: an organisation at the service of the totalitarian state', *Journal of Contemporary History*, 34, 1999.

Lasansky, D.M. 'Tableau and memory: the Fascist revival of the Medieval/Renaissance festival in Italy', *The European Legacy*, 4, 1999.

Ledeen, M. 'Italian Fascism and youth', *Journal of Contemporary History*, 4, 1969.

Ledeen, M. 'The evolution of Italian Fascist Antisemitism', *Jewish Social Studies*, 37, 1975.

Ledeen, M. 'Renzo De Felice and the controversy over Italian Fascism', *Journal of Contemporary History*, 11, 1976.

Lepschy, G.C. 'The language of Mussolini', *Journal of Italian History*, 1, 1978.

Levy, C. 'Fascism, National Socialism and conservatives in Europe, 1914–1945: issues for comparitivists', *Contemporary European History*, 8, 1999.

Lisenmayer, W.S. 'Italian peace feelers before the fall of Mussolini', *Journal of Contemporary History*, 16, 1981.

Logan, O. 'Pius XII: *romanità*, prophesy and charisma', *Modern Italy*, 3, 1998.

Luzzatto, S. 'The political culture of Fascist Italy', *Contemporary European History*, 8, 1999.

Lyttelton, A. 'Fascism in Italy: the second wave', *Journal of Contemporary History*, 1, 1966.

MacDonald, C.A. 'Radio Bari: Italian wireless propaganda in the Middle East and British counter measures 1934–1938', *Middle Eastern Studies*, 13, 1977.

Mack Smith, 'Benedetto Croce: history and politics', *Journal of Contemporary History*, 8, 1973.

Mack Smith, D. 'Mussolini: reservations about Renzo De Felice's biography', *Modern Italy*, 5, 2000.

Mallett, R. 'Fascist foreign policy and official Italian views of Anthony Eden in the 1930s', *Historical Journal*, 43, 2000.

Marks, S. 'Mussolini and Locarno: Fascist foreign policy in microcosm', *Journal of Contemporary History*, 14, 1979.

Marzari, F. 'Projects for an Italian-led Balkan bloc of neutrals September–December 1939', *Historical Journal*, 13, 1970.

Mason, T. 'The Great Economic History Show', *History Workshop*, 21, 1986.

Mason, T. 'Italy and modernization: a montage', *History Workshop Journal*, 25, 1988.

Select bibliography

Melograni, P. 'The cult of the Duce in Mussolini's Italy, *Journal of Contemporary History*, 11, 1976.

Michaelis, M. 'Fascism, totalitarianism and the Holocaust: reflections on current interpretations of National Socialist Anti-Semitism', *European History Quarterly*, 19, 1989.

Millman, B. 'Canada, sanctions and the Abyssinian crisis of 1935', *Historical Journal*, 40, 1997.

Morris, J. 'Retailers, Fascism and the origins of the social protection of shopkeepers in Italy', *Contemporary European History*, 5, 1996.

Morris, J. 'The Fascist "disciplining" of the Italian retail sector, 1922–1940', *Business History*, 40, 1998.

Mosse, G. 'The political culture of Italian Futurism: a general perspective', *Journal of Contemporary History*, 25, 1990.

Neri Serneri, S. 'A past to be thrown away? Politics and history in the Italian Resistance', *Contemporary European History*, 4, 1995.

Noether, E.P. 'Italian intellectuals under Fascism' *Journal of Modern History*, 43, 1971.

O'Brien, A.C. 'Italian youth in conflict: Catholic Action and Fascist Italy 1929–1931', *Catholic Historical Review*, 68, 1982.

Painter, B. 'Renzo De Felice and the historiography of Italian Fascism', *American Historical Review*, 95, 1990.

Passerini, L. 'Italian working class culture between the wars: consensus to Fascism and work ideology', *International Journal of Oral History*, 1, 1980.

Pavlowitch, S.K. 'The king who never was: an instance of Italian involvement in Croatia 1941–3', *European Studies Review*, 8, 1978.

Paxton, R. 'The five stages of fascism', *Journal of Modern History*, 70, 1998.

Pesman Cooper, R. 'Australian tourists in Fascist Italy', *Journal of Australian Studies*, 27, 1990.

Pesman Cooper, R. '"We want a Mussolini": views of Fascist Italy in Australia', *Australian Journal of Politics and History*, 39, 1993.

Petracarro, D. 'The Italian army in Africa 1940–1943: an attempt at historical perspective', *War and Society*, 9, 1991.

Petracchi, G. 'Ideology and *realpolitik*: Italo-Soviet relations 1917–1932', *Journal of Italian History*, 2, 1979.

Pollard, J.F. 'The Vatican and the Wall Street crash: Bernardino Nogara and papal finances in the early 1930s', *Historical Journal*, 42, 1999.

Procacci, G. 'Italy: from interventionism to fascism 1917–19', *Journal of Contemporary History*, 3, 1968.

Pugliese, S.G. 'Death in exile: the assassination of Carlo Rosselli', *Journal of Contemporary History*, 32, 1997.

Reece, J.E. 'Fascism, the Mafia and the emergence of Sicilian separatism (1919–1943)', *Journal of Modern History*, 45, 1973.

Renzi, W.A. 'Mussolini's sources of financial support 1914–1915', *History*, 56, 1971.

Roberts, D.D. 'Croce and beyond: Italian intellectuals and the First World War', *International History Review*, 3, 1981.

Roberts, D.D. 'How not to think about fascism and ideology, intellectual antecedents and historical meaning', *Journal of Contemporary History*, 35, 2000.

Robertson, E.M. 'Race as a factor in Mussolini's policy in Africa and Europe', *Journal of Contemporary History*, 23, 1988.

Robertson, J.C. 'The Hoare–Laval pact', *Journal of Contemporary History*, 10, 1975.

Roth, J.J. 'The roots of Italian Fascism: Sorel and *Sorelismo*', *Journal of Modern History*, 39, 1967.

Sadkovitch, J.J. 'Aircraft carriers and the Mediterranean 1940–1943: rethinking the obvious', *Aerospace Historian*, 34, 1987.

Select bibliography

Sadkovitch, J.J. 'Understanding defeat: reappraising Italy's role in World War II', *Journal of Contemporary History* 24, 1989.

Sadkovitch, J.J. 'Of myths and men: Rommel and the Italians in North Africa 1940–1942', *International History Review*, 13, 1991.

Sadkovitch, J.J. 'The Italo-Greek war in context: Italian priorities and Axis diplomacy', *Journal of Contemporary History* 28, 1993.

Sadkovitch, J.J. 'Italian morale during the Italo-Greek war of 1940–1941', *War and Society*, 12, 1994.

Salvemini, G. 'Pietro Badoglio's role in the Second World War', *Journal of Modern History*, 21, 1949.

Salvemini, G. 'Economic conditions in Italy 1919–22', *Journal of Modern History*, 23, 1951.

Sarti, R. 'Fascist modernization in Italy: traditional or revolutionary?' *American Historical Review*, 75, 1970.

Sarti, R. 'Mussolini and the Italian industrial leadership in the battle of the lira 1925–1927', *Past and Present*, 47, 1970.

Schnapp, J.T. '*18BL*: Fascist mass spectacle', *Representations*, 43, 1993.

Schnapp, J.T. 'Fascinating fascism', *Journal of Contemporary History* 31, 1996.

Scriba, F. 'The sacralization of the Roman past in Mussolini's Italy. Erudition, aesthetics and religion in the exhibition of Augustus' bimillenary in 1937–38', *Storia della Storiografia*, 30, 1996.

Segrè, C.G. 'Italo Balbo and the colonization of Libya' *Journal of Contemporary History*, 7, 1972.

Segrè, C.G. 'Douhet in Italy: prophet without honor?' *Aerospace Historian*, 26, 1979.

Settembrini, D. 'Mussolini and the legacy of revolutionary socialism' *Journal of Contemporary History*, 11, 1976.

Shorrock, W.I. 'France and the rise of Fascism in Italy 1919–1923', *Journal of Contemporary History*, 10, 1975.

Sluga, G. 'The Risiera di San Sabba: Fascism, anti-Fascism and Italian nationalism', *Journal of Modern Italian Studies*, 1, 1996.

Snowden, F. '"Fields of death": malaria in Italy 1861–1962', *Modern Italy*, 4, 1999.

Stafford, P. 'The Chamberlain–Halifax visit to Rome: a reappraisal', *English Historical Review*, 98, 1983.

Stone, M. 'Staging Fascism: the exhibition of the Fascist revolution', *Journal of Contemporary History*, 28, 1993.

Sullivan, B.R. 'A fleet in being: the rise and fall of Italian sea power 1861–1943', *International History Review*, 10, 1988.

Sullivan, B.R. '"A highly commendable action": William J. Donovan's intelligence mission for Mussolini and Roosevelt December 1935–February 1936', *Intelligence and National Security*, 6, 1991.

Suzzi Valli, R. 'The myth of *squadrismo* in the Fascist regime', *Journal of Contemporary History*, 35, 2000.

Tannenbaum, E.R. 'The goals of Italian Fascism', *American Historical Review*, 74, 1969.

Thorpe, W. 'The European syndicalists and war 1914–1918', *Contemporary European History*, 10, 2001.

Trifokovic, S. 'Rivalry between Germany and Italy in Croatia 1942–1943', *Historical Journal*, 36, 1993.

Turi, G. 'Giovanni Gentile: oblivion, remembrance, and criticism', *Journal of Modern History*, 70, 1998.

Varsori, A. 'Italy, Britain and the problems of a separate peace during the Second World War', *Journal of Italian History*, 1, 1978.

Ventura, A. 'Anna Kuliscioff, Filippo Turati and Italian socialism during the postwar crisis (1919–1925)', *Journal of Italian History*, 1, 1978.

Select bibliography

Verna, F.P. 'Notes on Italian rule in Dalmatia under Bastianini 1941–1943', *International History Review*, 12, 1990.

Visser, R. 'Fascist doctrine and the cult of *romanità*', *Journal of Contemporary History*, 27, 1992.

Vivarelli, R. 'Interpretations of the origins of Fascism', *Journal of Modern History*, 63, 1991.

Von Henneberg, K. 'Imperial uncertainties: architectural syncretism and improvisation in Fascist colonial life', *Journal of Contemporary History*, 31, 1996.

Walston, J. 'History and memory of the Italian concentration camps', *Historical Journal*, 40, 1997.

Wanrooij, B. '"Il Bo" 1935–1944: Italian students between Fascism and Anti-Fascism', *Risorgimento*, 3, 1982.

Wanrooij, B. 'The rise and fall of Italian Fascism as a generational revolt', *Journal of Contemporary History*, 22, 1987.

Watt, D.C. 'The Rome-Berlin Axis 1936–40: myth or reality', *Review of Politics*, 22, 1960.

Watt, D.C. 'Hitler's visit to Rome and the May weekend crisis: a study in Hitler's response to external stimuli', *Journal of Contemporary History*, 9, 1974.

Weber, E. 'Revolution? Counterrevolution? What revolution?', *Journal of Contemporary History*, 9, 1974.

Whealey, R.H. 'Mussolini's ideological diplomacy: an unpublished document', *Journal of Modern History*, 39, 1967.

Whittam, J. 'Drawing the line: Britain and the emergence of the Trieste question 1941–May 1945', *English Historical Review*, 106, 1991.

Wildgen, J.K. 'The liberation of the Valle d'Aosta 1943–1945', *Journal of Modern History*, 42, 1970.

Willson, P.R. 'Flowers for the doctor: pro-natalism and abortion in Fascist Milan', *Modern Italy*, 1, 1996.

Woolf, S.J. 'Mussolini as revolutionary', *Journal of Contemporary History*, 1, 1966.

Yavetz, Z. 'Caesar, Caesarism and the historians', *Journal of Contemporary History*, 6, 1971.

Zapponi, N. 'Fascism in Italian historiography 1986–93: a fading national identity', *Journal of Contemporary History*, 29, 1994.

Index

Abruzzi 153, 190, 229

Accamè, Giano 423–4

Acerbo, Giacomo 153, 167, 177, 190, 229–30

Addis Ababa 26, 247, 306, 308, 320, 333, 336, 376

Adowa 63, 126, 247, 305

Adriatic Sea 48, 108, 132, 138, 146, 148, 178, 188, 239, 346, 375

Aegean Sea 178

Africa (African Empire) 11, 21, 26, 34, 47, 56, 63–4, 92, 186, 227, 247–8, 253–4, 284–5, 287, 295, 297, 299–302, 304–10, 319–321, 324, 335–6, 338, 372, 376, 394–5, 397, 409, 412

Agnelli family 182

Agnelli, Giovanni 141, 289

Aimone of Savoy 380

Airforce 342, 352, 355, 372

Agro Pontino 80

Albania 146–7, 186, 204, 242, 248–9, 312, 327, 349, 352–3, 361, 368, 375, 377, 398

Albanian Fascist Party 352

Albertini, Luigi 150, 188, 200–1, 215, 237

Alessandria 154

Alexander, King 248, 283

Alfieri, Dino 203

Alfonso XIII, King 189, 316

Algeria 96

Alleanza Nazionale 3, 420–1

Allied Military Government 18–19, 413

Almirante, Giorgio 342, 422

Alto Adige (South Tyrol) 24, 69, 164, 266–7, 269, 360, 379, 390

Amarcord 346

Ambrosio, Vittorio 399

Amedeo, Duke of Aosta 320, 336

Amendola, Giovanni 160, 200–1, 204, 214, 218, 253–4

Anarchism 40, 48–9, 64, 74, 80, 82, 91, 134, 152, 160, 182, 189

Ancona 98, 138

Anfuso, Filippo 318

Anglo-German Naval Agreement 299

Ansaldo 118

Anschluss 215, 248, 268–9, 275, 280–1, 298–9, 324, 328–32, 360

Anti-Comintern Pact 328, 350

Aosta, Emanuele Filiberto, Duke of 168

Aprilia 338

Arcore 143

Ardeatine caves 24

Arditismo Civile 129–30, 136, 138, 145, 150

Arezzo 154

Argentina 38

Armaments 251, 255, 337, 353, 355

Chemical weapons 255

Armenian Genocide 59

Army 47, 58, 65, 100, 114–15, 118, 146, 149, 164, 168, 182–3, 187, 198–9, 201–2, 205–7, 241, 246, 254, 256, 259, 315, 317–18, 327, 342, 353, 355, 368, 371–2, 398

Conscription 45, 56, 65, 113–14

Index

Arpinati, Leandro 80, 152, 203, 208, 210, 213, 219, 259, 279–80, 386
Asmara 322
Aspromonte 40
Asquith, Lady 212
Associazione Lombarda dei Giornalisti 90
Associazione Nazionale dei Combattenti 122, 153
Associazione Nazionalista Italiana 8, 81, 111, 128, 148, 151, 156, 178, 185, 188, 190–1, 199, 204, 232, 246, 248, 251, 254, 256, 311, 337, 339, 344, 356
Atatürk, Kemal 166
Athens 186–7, 375
Atlantic Charter 397
Attolico, Bernardo 362, 364
Audisio, Walter 33
Augustea 269
Auschwitz 34, 170, 342
Australia 10, 174, 249, 387, 422
Austria 45–7, 56, 68–70, 73, 100–2, 104, 111–12, 116, 166, 187, 223, 244, 248–9, 268, 275, 280–3, 285, 302–3, 325, 328–31, 337, 357, 365
Autarchy 11, 325, 340, 353, 398, 426
Avanti! 7, 52, 54, 79, 80, 86, 88–91, 95, 97–8, 103–5, 107, 109, 131, 136, 148, 162
Aventine Secession 199, 200, 208, 219
Axis 10, 15, 19–20, 22, 25, 27–8, 30, 227, 267, 275–6, 327–8, 330–2, 335, 339–42, 344, 346–8, 351, 354–5, 358, 360–1, 365, 369, 376, 378, 383, 390–2, 394–5, 397, 411

Babeuf, Gracchus 50, 96
Bacon, Francis 62
Badoglio, Pietro 25, 168, 206–7, 228, 230, 240, 251, 254–6, 284, 299, 305, 307–8, 322, 348, 363, 367–8, 370, 376–7, 399, 401, 403
Baku 137
Bakunin, Michael 40
Balabanoff, Angelica 64–5, 68, 88
Balbo, Italo 142–3, 146, 151, 155, 164–5, 172, 177, 181, 190, 203, 233, 237, 254–5, 279, 315, 323, 336, 340, 371
Baldwin, Stanley 212

Balilla 28, 145, 217, 237
Balkans 96, 101–2, 146, 148, 170, 186, 359, 380, 383
Ball, Sir Joseph 328
Banca d'Italia 227, 237
Banca di Roma 179, 237
Banca di Sicilia 227
Banca Italiana di Sconto 163
Banca Nazionale del Lavoro e della Cooperazione 227
Banco di Napoli 227
Barboni family 61
Barboni, Tito 58
Bari 282
Barracu, Francesco 32
Barrera, Emilio 283
Barthou, Louis 283, 298
Bartov, Omer 255
Bastianini, Giuseppe 162, 181, 190, 397, 400–1
Battistessa, Franco 422
Battisti, Cesare 68, 71, 103
Bauer, Otto 69
Bavaria 189
Bechstein, Frau 268
Beethoven, Ludwig van 232
Belgium 62, 102, 104, 110, 327, 331
Belluzzo, Giuseppe 228
Benedict, Saint 29
Benedict XV, Pope, 100, 165
Beneduce, Alberto 288–9
Benevento 220–1
Benigni, Roberto 373
Benni, A.S. 279
Berchtesgaden 326
Berlin 34, 250, 265, 268–9, 273–4, 301–2, 306, 316, 325–6, 329, 331, 353, 355, 358, 364, 381, 392–3, 412
Berlusconi, Silvio 3, 95
Berti, Cesare 95
Bertinoro 52, 164
Bianchi, Michele 110, 150, 162, 164, 177, 181, 190, 203, 230
Biennale, Venice 281–2
Biggini, Carlo 238
Bissolati, Leonida 78, 83, 87–8
Bizet, Georges 296
Blanqui, Auguste 90, 96, 106

Index

Blériot, Louis 71, 142
Blum, Léon 212, 316–17, 335
Boattini, Ferdinando 321
Bocchini, Arturo 24, 219–22, 229–30, 240,
    273, 318, 324, 332, 356, 358, 362
Bocconi University 201
Bodrero, Emilio 232
Bolin, Luis 316
Bologna 15, 24, 37–9, 49–52, 65–6, 76, 80,
    84, 87, 105, 107, 137, 142, 145–6,
    150–1, 159–60, 163, 210, 219–20, 279,
    321, 373, 400, 422
Bombacci, Nicola 9, 31–2, 34, 408, 410–11
Bombay 422
Bonomi, Ivanoe 87, 158, 163
Bonservizi, Nicola 108
Bordiga, Amadeo 103–4
Borghese, Junio Valerio 24
Bottai, Bruno 424
Bottai, Giuseppe xiv, 14, 142, 190–2, 203,
    210, 224, 227, 233, 260–1, 271, 290,
    295, 305, 307, 309, 312, 339, 345, 348,
    350, 355, 358, 364, 367–8, 372, 374,
    377, 384–5, 387, 389, 395, 397, 400
Brauchitsch, Walther 382
Braun, Eva 332
Brazil 58
Brenner frontier 360, 366
Brescia 220, 422
Brest Litovsk, Treaty of 120
Brigate Nere 23, 27
Bruno, Giordano 62, 67
Brussels 103
Budapest 242
Buenos Aires 253
Bufali, Orsola 311
Buffarini Guidi, Guido 23, 279, 407
Bukharin, Michael 279
Bulgaria 298

Cabrini, Angelo 87
Cagliari 122
Cairo 256
Calabria 110–1, 150, 174, 197, 228, 375
Calvo Sotelo, José 316
Camera dei fasci e delle corporazioni 347
Campanella, Thomas 96
Canali, Mauro 195–6

Canossa 258
Cantalupo, Roberto 232, 256
Cape Matapan 372
Capello, Luigi 214, 218
Caporetto 45, 112, 114–15, 119, 128, 168,
    191, 205–6, 266
Capri 178
Caradonna, Giuseppe 177
Carducci, Giosuè 52, 402
Carducci, Valfredo 52, 54
Carocci, Cesira 175, 240
Carrà, Carlo 91
Carta del Carnaro (Carnaro charter) 134–5,
    345
Casale 174
Casalini, Armando 201
Caucasus 137
Cavallero, Ugo 376–8, 380
Cavallotti, Felice 109
Cavazzoni, Stefano 179
Cavour, Camillo Benso di 47, 194, 366
Cervantes, Miguel de 88, 149
Cesena 31, 45, 164
Chamberlain, Ivy 212
Chamberlain, Neville 328–9, 349–50
Chamberlain, Austen 212, 245, 250, 329
Chambrun, Charles 304
Chaplin, Charles 278
Chiavolini, Alessandro 108, 122, 174
Chicago Daily News 179
China 276, 387
Churchill, Clementine 212
Churchill, Winston xiv, 33, 369, 397, 415
Cianetti, Tullio 244–5
Ciano, Costanzo 13–14, 311–12, 347
Ciano, Fabrizio 13, 263, 278, 419
Ciano, Galeazzo 8–9, 13–17, 221, 227, 273,
    294, 309, 311–13, 316, 318, 324,
    326–8, 330–3, 335–7, 340–1, 345,
    348–50, 352, 354–69, 376–7, 380,
    382–6, 388, 391, 397, 399–400, 406,
    408–9, 419
    Diary 336–7, 354, 358, 369–70, 382
    Execution 13–17, 19
    on Germans 14–15, 354–5
Ciano, Maria 17, 361
Ciano, Marzio 419
Ciardi, Livio 94

Index

Ciarlantini, Franco 269
Cinema 311
Cini, Vittorio 321
Cipriani, Amilcare 39–40, 61–2, 88, 105
Citarelli, Renato 174–5, 246
Civitavecchia 164
Civiltà Cattolica 238, 335
Clemenceau, Georges 112, 121
Clinton, William 425
Coca Cola 345
Codreanu, Corneliu 423
Cold War 413
Comitato di Liberazione Nazionale 33
Communism 2, 18, 22, 25, 28, 33–4, 50,
    104, 139, 141, 155, 158, 164, 178, 190,
    198, 215, 315, 348, 380, 417–18, 425–6
  Italian Communist Party 2, 31, 103, 155,
    200, 418, 421–2, 414
Como 30–1, 61
Confederazione delle Corporazioni fasciste
    214, 223
Confederazione generale del lavoro 85, 159
Confederazione nazionale dei Sindicati
    fascisti 223
Confindustria 84, 133, 160, 214, 383
Consiglio tecnico nazionale 161
Consociazione Turistica Italiana see
    Touring Club Italiano
Constantinople 236
Contarini, Salvatore 187, 246
Conti, Ettore 137
Coppola, Goffredo 15, 32
Corfu 186–9, 215
Corgini, Ottavio 152
Corpo truppo volontario (CTV) 317–18
Corporate State 26, 241, 256, 258, 262, 426
Corporatism, see under
    Fascism–Corporatism
Corradini, Enrico 85, 117, 128, 132, 159,
    190–1
Corridoni, Filippo 94, 103
Corruption 107
  in Liberal Italy 40, 47, 78, 83, 107, 157
  in Fascist Italy 9, 18, 106–7, 177, 193,
    244, 259, 321–2, 347, 398, 418,
    424
Corsica 111, 186, 242, 349, 375
Cortese, Guido 320

Costa, Andrea 39–40, 48, 61–2, 78, 109,
    152
Counter Reformation 68
Craxi, Bettino 424
Cremona 114, 137, 158, 165, 190, 205, 235,
    246, 260, 296, 319, 342–3
Cremona nuova 200, 206
Crespi family 215
Crete 40, 378
Crispi, Francesco 48, 54, 63, 126–7, 194,
    246, 305, 309, 340
Critica Fascista 190–1, 224, 249, 258,
    260–1, 266, 290, 377
Croatia 248, 283, 354–5, 359, 364, 378–80,
    391–2
Croce, Benedetto 199, 216, 237, 308
Cufra 255
Cuneo 159
Cuore 67
Curti, Elena 387–8
Cyrenaica, *see also* under Libya 83, 253–5,
    394
Czechoslovakia 86–7, 266, 274, 324 331–3,
    337, 341, 350

D'Annunzio, Gabriele 117, 122, 128,
    134–6, 142, 145, 146–8, 153, 180
D'Aragona, Ludovico 193
Da Brescia, Arnaldo 44–5
Daily Mail 188, 313
Dainelli, Giotto 344
Dalmatia 111, 120, 354–5
Dalser, Ida Irene 116–17
Dante Alighieri 53, 55, 69, 121, 129, 142,
    149, 151, 201, 427
Danube River 269
Danzig 346, 350, 354–6
Darwin, Charles 71, 90, 121, 134, 171
Darwinism 7–8, 143, 171, 196, 235, 385,
    390, 427
Da Vinci, Leonardo, 293
De Ambris, Alceste 96, 103, 110, 134–5
De Amicis, Edmondo 67
De Bono, Emilio 13, 181, 202–3, 254–6,
    284, 300–1, 305–7, 322–3, 377,
    401
Debra Lebanos 320
Decennale 244, 257, 261–2

Index

De Felice, Renzo 3–4, 8–10, 101, 119, 125, 195, 224, 259–60, 265, 274, 276–7, 296–7, 299, 308, 370, 375–6, 383, 386, 424–5
De Feo, Luciano 311
De Gasperi, Alcide 70, 200
De Lieto Vollaro, Maria Letizia 220
De Martino, Giacomo 185
De Vecchi, Cesare Maria (di Val Cismon) 174, 181–3, 207, 254, 258, 281, 293, 323, 345
De' Stefani, Alberto 178–9, 202–3, 206, 225, 292
Delardinelli, Mario 374
Depretis, Agostino 47–8, 194
Dessié 307
Di Giorgio, Antonino 206
Di Nolfo, Ennio 245
Di San Giuliano, Antonino 106
Di San Servolo, Myriam *see* Petacci, Maria
Diaz, Armando178, 206
Dinale, Ottavio 108
Dingli, Adrian 328
Direzione Generale del Turismo 256
Disperata 14
Djibouti 349, 375
Dodecanese Islands 186, 188, 253–4
Dogali 305
Dollfuss, Engelbert 275, 281–2, 284, 325
Dongo 32–4
Dopolavoro 252, 290–1
Dovia 37, 42, 51, 58, 62, 412, 417
Drexler, Anton 266
Dumini, Amerigo 58, 193, 196–7, 205

Economist 238
Eden, Anthony 1, 302–4, 312, 325, 328, 376, 399
Egypt 91, 132, 256, 304, 327, 378, 381
Einzig, Paul 241, 355
Eire 132
El Alamein
El Krim, Abd 285
Elena, Queen 308, 340, 402
El-Mukhtar, Omar 255
Emigration 10–1, 21, 45, 55–8, 60–1, 71, 80, 82, 115, 161, 186, 193, 251–2, 288–9, 336–7, 343, 351, 356, 381, 419, 422, 424

Emilia-Romagna, see also Romagna 39, 48, 58, 80, 152–3, 160, 390
Empoli 154
Enciclopedia Italiana 270
Engels, Friedrich 118
Enlightenemnt, the 192, 338, 426
Eritrea 47, 107, 253, 284, 301, 321, 383
Esposizione Universale Romana 3, 417
Essenes 257
Ethiopia 9, 19, 26, 28, 31, 34–5, 47, 63–4, 158, 170, 227, 247–8, 253–5, 249, 284–5, 291, 295–300, 302–4, 306–10, 315, 317–18, 320–2, 324–5, 335, 338, 353, 376, 397, 402
Evening Standard 304
Evola, Julius 422–3

Facta, Luigi 163, 166, 168
Faenza 51–2, 416
Faisceau 249
Falangism 395
Fani Ciotti, Vincenzo ('Volt') 138
Farinacci, Franco 246–7, 251
Farinacci, Roberto 9, 29, 113–14, 122, 158, 164–5, 177, 190, 200–5, 207, 210–11, 214–15, 217–18, 225, 227, 232–4, 236–7, 259–60, 270, 280, 293, 296, 307, 313, 319, 321, 342–4, 358, 376, 384, 392, 401, 407–11
Fasci italiani all'estero 252
Fasci d'azione rivoluzionaria 110, 118
Fasci di combattimento 122, 128–9, 131, 134, 136, 160, 231
Fascio parlamentare di difesa nazionale 119
Fasci per la Costituente 121
Fascism 17, 19, 21, 28, 30, 32–3, 35, 108, 110, 121–2, 129, 134–5, 137, 143, 145–6, 156, 163, 170–1, 173–4, 184, 190, 193, 196, 199–201, 204, 206, 210, 212, 214, 216, 222–4, 229–30, 232–3, 236, 238, 243, 248–9, 251, 253, 265–7, 269–71, 273, 280–1, 288–90, 292–6, 298–9, 302–3, 312, 314, 318–19, 324, 326, 329, 331, 342, 358–9, 362, 367, 369–70, 378, 384, 391, 393, 394–5, 397, 400, 402–3, 415, 417, 419, 421–2, 427

Index

Fascism – *continued*

Agrarian Fascism 150, 153, 155, 167, 194, 198, 201–2

Anti-Anti-Fascism 3, 423

Anti-Fascism 3, 11, 18, 28, 30, 35, 51–2, 60, 104, 145, 152, 168–9, 178, 180, 183, 187, 193–4, 196, 198–200, 202, 207–8, 214–16, 218–22, 241–2, 244, 247, 271, 308, 319, 330, 335, 339–40, 346, 348, 358, 398, 402, 407, 410–13, 416, 421, 424–6

Border Fascism 148–9, 153, 156, 249–51, 341

Clerical fascism 46, 213, 275, 350, 356, 415

Concentration camps 255–6, 338–9

Corporatism 135, 229, 241, 256, 258, 262, 290, 323, 426

Cultural policy 91, 243, 294–6, 345

Education 232–3, 237, 257, 271–2, 293, 339, 341–2, 345

Factionalism 182–3, 190, 229, 235, 241–2, 247, 258, 318, 358, 422

Foreign policy 170, 183, 189, 215–16, 218, 222, 227, 241, 245–58, 261, 272, 274–6, 280–5, 287, 291, 295–309, 317–20, 324–3, 335–41, 344–812, 383, 387, 389–90, 393–5, 397, 407

Grand Council 13, 27, 180–2, 191, 201, 279, 300, 341, 346, 350, 400

Ideology 2, 60, 129–32, 134, 136, 141–3, 152–3, 155–6, 161–3, 167, 170, 172, 174, 178, 181, 184–5, 188, 192, 194, 198, 201, 204–5, 214–16, 219–21, 223, 231–2, 235, 241–2, 245–7, 249–62, 265, 290, 292–3, 295, 308, 312–13, 324–7, 333–49, 351, 353, 355–6, 360 365–7, 370–1, 377, 380–1, 414, 420–1, 423–7

International fascism 8, 28, 189, 249–50, 268, 275, 282, 315, 324–5, 330, 352–4, 356, 367, 423

MVSN (and squads) 58, 138–9, 143, 151, 153–6, 158, 162–5, 171–2, 174, 182–3, 187–90, 193–4, 196, 214, 236, 319

Neo-fascism (post-fascism) 3, 23, 34, 231, 342, 344, 404, 413–15, 418–24, 426

Racial legislation 91, 336, 341–5, 348, 353

Ritual 14, 145, 172, 260–2, 344, 412, 414, 417–18, 420–1, 425

Unions 151, 181, 191, 201, 214, 223–4, 244, 418

Violence 149–55, 158, 163–4, 168, 170, 172, 180, 182, 184, 187, 190, 192–3, 196–8, 206, 214, 219, 244, 248, 253–6, 259, 319–20, 323, 330–6, 340–4, 356, 364, 380, 383, 391, 401, 406

and women 15, 42–4, 162–3, 231, 258, 345, 361, 384, 387, 420, 427

Fassini, Alberto 175

Favagrossa, Carlo 367–8, 371

Fedele, Pietro 232

Federici, Riccardo 277

Federterra 50, 84

Federzoni, Luigi 117, 167, 178, 191, 199, 201–2, 207, 210, 219–20, 233, 254, 358

Fellini, Federico 346

Feltre 400

Feminism 91, 162, 420

Fera, Luigi 107

Ferrara 49, 57, 122, 142, 145, 150–1, 190, 371

Ferraris, Dante 132–3, 151

Ferrer, Francisco 77

Fiat 141, 179, 182, 289, 321

Fichte, Johann Gottlieb 64

Filippelli, Filippo 196

Financial Times 241

Fini, Gianfranco 3, 420, 426

Finland 246, 359, 363

Finzi, Aldo 143, 148, 161, 177, 181, 193, 196, 202

FIOM 139–140

Fitzpatrick, Sheila 4

Fiume (Rijeka) 132, 134–7, 140, 142, 145–7

Flandin, Pierre-Etienne 301

Florence 14, 19, 22, 72, 80–1, 96, 122, 129, 136, 145, 150, 154, 160, 192, 209, 256, 273, 334, 416, 422

Index

Foà, Jolé 343

Foggia 400

Ford, Henry 281

Forges Davanzati, Roberto 191, 213

Forlì 31, 37–8, 41–2, 49–54, 68–9, 73,
    75–88, 90, 95, 97, 109, 321, 388, 412

Forlimpopoli 52–4, 75, 152, 176

Fortunato, Giustino 58

Forzano, Giovacchino 242

Foschini, Antonio 188

Foucault, Michel 424

Four Power Pact 273–6

France 56, 63–8, 71, 81–2, 85, 87, 96, 100,
    102, 104–7, 110, 118, 121, 127, 135,
    137, 186, 188, 232, 242, 245–6, 248–9,
    251–2, 256, 272–4, 283, 285,
    298–302, 304, 306, 310, 317–18,
    324–5, 327, 333–5, 338–9, 344, 350,
    353, 355–7, 359, 364–5, 367, 370–1,
    378, 392, 395, 404

    Vichy regime 20, 375, 395, 404

Francis Ferdinand of Habsburg-Este,
    Archduke 99, 101

Franco, Francisco 5–7, 18, 107, 197, 203,
    212, 316–19, 327, 335, 353, 356, 358,
    367, 369, 380, 395, 423, 426

Francis of Assisi, Saint 212

Franz Joseph, Emperor 73

Fratelli Damerini 76–8

Free Masons 25, 47, 79, 100, 112, 177, 179,
    236, 267, 338

Freud, Sigmund 69

Functionalism (structuralism) 4–5, 35, 145,
    214, 241–2, 244–6, 255–6, 305, 370,
    425

Futurism

Gaggioli, Olao 150–1

Galbiati, Enzo401

Galileo, Galilei 62

Gallipoli 221, 259

Gamelin, Maurice 302

Gandhi, Mahatma 260

Gargnano 24–5, 32, 408–9

Garibaldi Brigades 31, 33, 318

Garibaldi, Giuseppe 40, 111, 118, 129, 134,
    229, 318

Gasparri, Pietro 237

Gatti, Luigi 410–1

Gazzetta dell'Aviazione 143

Gazzetta Ferrarese 155

Geertz, Clifford 424

Gemelli, Agostino 77

Geneva 188, 250–1, 302, 306–7

Genoa 82, 220, 273, 337, 373

Gentlemen's Agreement 329

Gentile, Emilio 163, 295

Gentile, Giovanni 18, 177–8, 191, 216, 261,
    308

Georgia 164

Geraldine, Queen 352

Gerarchia 161, 166, 186, 192, 208, 232,
    268, 270, 392

Germany 56, 63–4, 68, 71, 82, 100, 104,
    109, 111–12, 130, 153, 160, 166, 170,
    178, 215, 225, 232, 250, 264, 288,
    301–2, 317–18, 324–7, 329, 334,
    341–2, 344, 350–1, 357–9, 361–8, 373,
    376, 379–80, 382, 411–12, 324

    Imperial Germany 46, 63, 102–3, 118,
        267

    Nazi Germany 6–8, 10, 14, 18–20, 28,
        30, 170, 197, 235, 245, 248, 250,
        252–3, 255–6, 264, 276, 280–2,
        295, 297–9, 324–6, 330–2, 334–7,
        339–44, 346–60, 370–1, 375, 378,
        386–7, 389, 391, 393–4, 398,
        403–5, 407, 410–11, 421, 423–4

        See also under Nazism and under
        Fascism–Fascist Italy and Nazi
        Germany, relationship between

    Weimar Republic 166, 250, 268

Giampaoli, Mario 122, 213, 234–5

Giannini, Guglielmo 421

Giardino, Gaetano 206

Gibson, Violet 218–19, 254

Gimenez Caballero, Ernesto 283

Gioda, Mario 122, 182–3

Giolitti, Giovanni 48, 72, 79, 82–5, 87, 98,
    100–1, 103, 110–11, 113, 140–1, 146,
    148, 153, 155–7, 160, 163, 167–8, 174,
    177, 190, 194, 206–7, 237, 284, 297–8,
    300, 305

Giovanni Huss il veridico

Gioventù Universitaria Fascista

Girardon, Mario 106

Index

Giuliani, Sandro 108, 177

Giunta, Francesco 139, 149, 181, 190, 203, 207

Giurati, Giovanni 187, 258–9

Giustizia e Libertà 318, 335

Globocnik, Odilo 24

Gobetti, Piero 214

Gobineau, Arthur de 334

Goering, Hermann 24, 142, 269, 331, 360, 364

Goethe, Johann von 149

Goglia, Luigi 336

Goldmann, Cesare 118

Gömbös, Gyula 283

Gorgolini, Pietro 182–3

Gottardi, Luciano 13

Graham, Ronald 184, 189, 274

Graham, Sybil 212

Gramsci, Antonio 104, 140, 155, 182, 200, 223

Grandi, Dino 110, 146, 152, 160–2, 177, 181, 191, 203, 246–8, 250–1, 269, 300–4, 306, 328, 328, 397, 400–1

Gravelli, Asvero 270, 310

Gray, Ezio Maria 191, 323

Graziani, Rodolfo 20–1, 23, 27, 254–5, 305, 307, 320, 372, 376

Grazioli, Francesco Saverio 207

Great Britain 14, 20, 38, 82, 85, 95, 100, 104, 107, 110, 121, 127, 132, 166, 184–5, 187–9, 211, 219, 238, 245, 249, 256, 334–6, 339, 347, 349–50, 353–7, 359, 363, 365, 367, 372, 376–8, 387, 395, 400, 404, 416, 419, 426

Greco, Paolo 182

Greece 10, 40, 102, 166, 186–9, 206, 253, 375–6, 378–80, 389, 423

Gregor, A.J. 423

Guadalajara 317–9

Gualtieri Emilia 54–5

Guardia Nazionale Repubblicana 23

Guariglia, Raffaele 247–8, 284, 301, 315–16

Guarneri, Felice 305, 352, 362

Guesde, Jules 96

Guest Workers 20, 351, 356

Guggenheim, Samuel 193

Guidi, Anna 89, 176, 208

Guidi, Giovanna 208

Guidi, Pina 208

Guidi Mussolini, Rachele 9, 15–16, 31, 41–2, 54, 56, 74–6, 80, 89, 91, 94, 116–17, 126, 138, 143, 176, 198, 208–9, 217, 239–40, 278, 292, 311, 313, 321, 388–9, 400–2, 406, 408–9, 413, 416, 418, 420

Habsburg Empire 19, 37, 39, 46, 69–70, 73, 99, 101–2, 139, 412

Haider, Jorg 426

Haile Selassie I, Emperor 247, 285, 297, 304, 306, 376

Halifax, Edward 312, 347

Hamburg 247

Hegel, Georg W.F. 64

Heimwehr 249, 268

Helsinki 359

Hendaye 380

Heydrich, Reinhard 221

Himmler, Heinrich 205, 221, 393, 401

Hindenburg, Paul von 112, 360

Hiroshima 34

Hitler, Adolf 2–8, 10–11, 19, 21–2, 35, 69, 74, 143–4, 170, 172, 189, 197, 203, 212, 217, 223, 245, 250–1, 255, 263–72, 276, 297, 299, 303, 326, 331–2, 334, 343–4, 349–51, 354–6, 358–60, 362, 364, 366, 376, 378, 382, 389, 394, 401, 408, 412–13, 423

and Mussolini 20–2, 143–4, 245, 264–72, 280–2, 314, 333–4, 343–4, 349–41, 353, 355–7, 359, 361–3, 365–8, 373, 376–7, 379–81, 391, 393, 395, 399–400, 402–4, 408, 426

on Italy 19–20, 245, 266–70, 332, 354

death of 412–13

Hoare, Samuel 304, 306, 387

Homosexuality 231, 244

Hotel Balkan 149

Hungary 37, 133, 283, 332, 335, 357

Huss, Jan 86

Il Bersagliere 41, 75

Il Corriere della Sera 25, 105, 150, 188, 190, 200, 215

Il Corriere Italiano 196

Il Fascio 134

Index

Il Giornale d'Italia 109, 131

Il Legionario 252

Il Messaggero 347

Il Mondo

Il Pensiero Romagnolo 68

Il Popolo 68

Il Popolo d'Italia 105–6, 108–11, 114, 117–18, 120–2, 123–6, 129, 132, 134–5, 143, 149, 159, 166, 172, 176–7, 200, 239, 260, 268–70, 279, 299, 317, 338

Il Proletario 62

Il Regime Fascista 251

Il Resto del Carlino 52, 76, 80, 105, 110, 142, 152, 355

Il Secolo 105, 214

Il Telegrafo 312

Imperia 114

Imru, Ras 402

India 121, 209, 326, 387

Informazione diplomatica 337

Innsbruck 73

Integralism 138

Intentionalism 4–5, 35, 145, 241–2, 244–6, 255–6, 305, 369–70, 425

Interlandi, Telesio 342

Iraq 304, 376

Irredentism 153, 349

Ischia 187

Isonzo 115, 205

Istituti coloniali italiani 252

Istituto di Riconstruzione Industriale 289

Istituto Luce 311

Italian Boxing Federation 311

Italy and the 'Italies' 4, 10, 17–19, 25, 27, 33–5, 40, 46, 64, 71, 82–3, 159, 165, 169–70, 173, 192, 201, 211, 215, 218–28, 231, 233–6, 238, 242–4, 247, 253, 265–9, 272–5, 283–5, 287–90, 292–3, 295, 298, 300, 302–10, 315, 318–9, 324–30, 333, 343–5, 350, 357–9, 361–75, 377–83, 390, 392–413, 415–19, 421, 424, 427

  Banks 141, 179, 225, 241, 288–9, 342, 348, 412, 417

  Bureaucracy 100, 112–13, 140, 185, 187, 241–2, 246–8, 251–2, 256–7, 314, 320, 322–3, 342, 344, 347, 368, 372, 392, 398, 421, 424

Constitution 190, 264

  Family 57, 130, 176, 242

  Language 46, 53, 64, 69, 251, 344–5, 351, 371, 390, 418

  Regional identity 49, 57, 80, 83, 116, 242, 418

  the South 56, 83, 89, 101, 103, 136, 139, 167, 174–5, 177, 189, 190–2, 197, 218, 222, 246, 259, 273, 291, 353, 421–2

James, William 293

Japan 25, 138, 249, 276, 285, 328, 333, 365, 378–9, 381–2, 387, 401

Jazz 314, 420

Jews 18, 24–5, 38, 91, 118, 132–3, 143, 148, 151, 159, 166, 234, 238, 250, 261, 272–3, 276, 334–44, 358, 379, 392–3, 426–7

  Anti-Semitism 69, 132–3, 147–8, 159, 166, 234, 250, 261, 266–71, 274, 334–44, 363, 382, 392–3, 426–7

  Holocaust 18, 24, 34, 133, 170, 276, 342–4, 391–4, 407

  Zionism 91, 147, 268, 271, 337

Jieshi, Jiang 276

Juan, Don 5

Jung, Guido 288

Kant, Immanuel 293

Kautsky, Karl 64

Kellogg-Briand Peace Pact 245, 250

Kershaw, Ian 5–8, 10, 170, 255, 267

Klessheim 20–1

Klimt, Gustav 69

Klopstock, Friedrich Gottlieb 68

Knox, Macgregor 245, 327, 330

Kosovo 364

Kristallnacht 341–2

Kropotkin, P.A. 64

Kurds 59

Kvaternik, Slavko 391

L'Anno Santo 210, 236

L'Aquila 153, 377

L'Ardito 129

L'Assalto

L'Avvenire del Lavoratore 58–9, 61–2, 68, 70, 72–4

Index

La carta della scuola 345
La difesa della razza 343, 422
La felicità di Amleto 312
La Folla 89
La Gente d'Italia 422
La Libertà 91
La Lima 67
La Lotta di Classe
La Maddalena 402–3
La Soffitta 86
La Tribuna 61
La Vita Italiana 132, 137, 147, 158, 204,
    219, 253, 260, 270–1, 280, 339
La Voce 71–2, 78, 81, 96, 103, 105
Labour Charter 224
Lamont, T.W. 225
Lampedusa 399
Landra, Guido 337, 343
Lanza di Scalea, Pietro 154, 254
Lanzillo, Agostino 96, 305, 358
Lateran Pacts, *see* Roman Catholic Church–
    Lateran pacts; Mussolini –
    religion
Laurel and Hardy 278
Lausanne 58, 60, 62
Laval, Pierre 20, 247, 284, 298, 300–1,
    304, 306
Lazzari, Costantino 88
Lazzaro, Urbano 32
League of Nations 121, 187–9, 245, 247,
    250, 274, 299, 301, 303–4, 306, 329
Leccisi, Domenico 414–16
Le Figaro 73
Legion of the Archangel Michael 423
Leibniz, Gottfried von 62
Lenin, Vladimir I. 64, 88, 120, 132, 212
Leningrad 378
Leo XIII, Pope 47
Le Pen, Jean-Marie 426
Lessona, Alessandro 203, 310, 322–3
L'Humanité 88
Liberalism 47–8, 72, 76, 79, 83, 96, 113,
    119, 137, 150, 154, 170–2, 177, 179,
    181, 184, 194, 197–201, 203, 216, 236,
    244, 254, 261, 274, 287, 290, 315, 324,
    339, 422
Libya (Tripolitania and Cyrenaica) 34–5,
    83–5, 87, 96, 170, 253–5, 264, 284,
    297, 319, 323–4, 336, 340, 353, 371,
    376, 378, 380, 388, 395
L'Idea Nazionale
Liguria 66, 158
Lindbergh, Charles 142
Lipari islands 222, 280
Liszt, Franz 116
Lithuania 249, 274
Lloyd George, David 112, 147, 317
Locarno, Treaty of 215, 298
Lombardi, Anna 41
Lombardy 165, 257, 334, 410, 412
London 38, 147, 184–5, 187–8, 193, 247,
    274, 300, 304, 306, 326, 397, 399
Longanesi, Leo 210
Longobuco 197
Longoni, Attilio 131
L'Ordine Nuovo 182
Loren, Sophia 420
Lo sport fascista 211
Lourdes 77
Low, David 304
Lucetti, Gino 219
Ludwig, Emil 261
Lueger, Karl 69
Lugano 61
L'Unità 103
L'Universale 250
Lusignoli, Aldo 244–5
Lusignoli, Alfredo 148
Lussu, Emilio 318
Luzzatto, Sergio 410, 412, 415–16, 423

MacDonald, James Ramsay 215, 301
Macedonia 38
Machiavelli, Niccolò 192, 276, 293, 339
Madagascar 56
Madrid 315, 317–18
Mafia 154, 230
Magistrati, Massimo 358
Malaparte, Curzio xiv, 11, 202, 204
Malta 111, 132, 258, 327, 395
Maltoni, Rosa 37, 41–5, 50–1, 53, 55,
    60–1, 64–6, 70, 74, 243, 416–17, 419
Mancini, Pasquale Stanislao 47
Manchukuo 304
Manifesto of Racial Scientists 338
Mannix, Daniel 238

Index

Mantua 67, 154, 280
Marat, Jean-Paul 87
Marche 138–9
Marchetti, Ugo 108
Marinelli, Giovanni 13, 110, 122, 162, 196, 400
Marinetti, Filippo Tommaso 73, 117, 122, 129–31, 135, 137–8, 140, 256
Marseilles 283
Marsich, Pietro 160–1
Martini, Ferdinando 107–8
Marx, Karl 40, 49, 53, 64, 67, 71, 78, 87–8, 104, 118, 121, 147, 171, 335
Marxism 40, 58, 63–4, 69, 75, 85, 104–5, 119–20, 143–4, 182, 223, 252, 267
Marzabotto 24
Mascagni, Pietro 296
Massawa 47, 322
Matteotti, Giacomo 26, 58, 171, 193, 197–8, 200, 202–5, 207, 209, 214, 225, 230, 316, 322–3, 369, 415
Maugeri, Franco 402
Maurras, Charles 68
Maximalism
Maximilian, Emperor 39
Mazzini, Giuseppe 25, 105, 201, 339, 360
McDonald's 410
Mediterranean 170, 178, 189, 266, 276, 306, 326, 328–9, 335, 365, 371, 375
Mein Kampf 172, 267, 282
Meldola 39, 85
Mellon, Andrew 193
Menelik II, Emperor 64
Merlino, Lino 109
Messina 122, 154
Metaxas, Ioannis 324, 358, 375
Metchnikoff, Elie 88
Mexico 39, 193, 271
Mezzasoma, Ferdinando 32
Mezzegra 33–4, 410
Michelini, Arturo 421
Michels, Roberto 71
Milan 24–5, 27–8, 33–4, 37, 40, 49, 72, 78–80, 82, 84, 87, 89–92, 94–7, 106, 112, 116, 118, 122, 123–6, 129–31, 133, 136–7, 139–41, 143, 148, 151, 160, 165, 168, 172, 176, 184, 196, 201–2, 209, 219, 227, 234, 244, 240,

257, 260, 294, 326, 353, 371, 373, 392, 410–6, 422
Milizia Volontaria per la Sicurezza Nazionale (MVSN), see under Fascism – MVSN
Miller, Webb 313
Milza, Pierre 4
Minghetti, Marco 48
Minzoni, Giovanni 190
Missiroli, Mario 96
Missouri 193
Misurata, Count of, see Volpi, Giuseppe
Mit brennender Sorge 348
Modena 145, 150
Modernisation and Technology 11, 47, 57, 83, 95, 133, 150, 227, 253, 353, 361, 413, 428
Modernity 35, 47, 63, 69, 82, 103, 142–3, 149, 192, 256, 336, 338, 340, 413, 426
Mola, General Emilio 319
Molotov, Vyacheslav 312
Monarchy and Monarchism 111, 113, 126, 132, 135, 138, 140, 168, 178, 182, 198–9, 202–3, 206–7, 213, 241, 244, 246, 300, 305, 322, 340, 347–9, 352–3, 355, 362, 364, 366–8, 370–1, 399–401, 403, 415
Montagna, Giulio Cesare 186
Montanelli, Indro 307, 423
Montenegro 378
Monza 143, 231
Monzogoio, Erlado 374
Morell, Theodor 404–5
Morelli, Emilia 335
Morgagni, Manlio 108, 114, 118
Morgan, J.P. 193, 226
Mori, Cesare 230
Morning Post 188
Morocco 285, 304, 316–17, 387, 394
Morsano 45
Mosconi, Angelo 228
Moscow 233, 378
Mosse, George 334
Movimento Sociale Italiano (MSI) 342, 419–23
Munich 267, 270, 275, 332–3, 340–1, 349, 354, 356, 359, 403
Murdoch, Rupert 95

Index

Musocco 413–14

Musso 31–2

Mussolini, Alessandra 420

Mussolini, Alessandro 37, 39–44, 51, 54–5, 58, 62, 68, 73, 75, 78, 81, 86, 89, 138, 243, 418–19

Mussolini, Anna Maria 17, 209, 310, 419

Mussolini, Arnaldo 26, 28–9, 44–5, 53, 60, 65, 116–17, 171, 176–7, 192–3, 196, 208, 210, 218, 233–5, 237–9, 249–50, 260, 263, 294, 412, 419

Mussolini, Benito Albino 116–7

Mussolini, Benito Amilcare Andrea
and agriculture 228–30, 291–2
assassination attempts on 218–19, 254, 425
as aviator 142–4, 211, 418
biographers 38–9, 42–4, 46, 50, 52, 68, 91, 98, 101, 115, 117, 119, 125, 242, 339
and Britain 20, 132, 166, 187, 189, 223, 272, 299, 301, 304, 306, 314, 327–9, 331, 333–4, 341, 349–50, 355, 363, 381
charisma 2, 7–8, 10, 24–5, 32, 77, 97–8, 125, 135, 139, 146, 155, 160, 165, 192, 207, 210, 212, 239, 242–4, 251, 341, 349, 354, 379, 387–8, 409, 427
(his) class 37–8, 51–2, 72, 74, 76–7, 79–81, 85, 87, 89–90, 106, 108, 115, 117, 119, 121, 128, 133, 135, 138, 176, 428
as corpse 410–17, 419, 421
death execution 11, 26–7, 33–4, 263, 340, 404, 410, 412–13, 427
as dictator xiv, 7, 9, 11, 16, 19, 34–5, 97, 116–17, 120, 143, 148, 162, 173, 179, 181, 188, 194, 197–8, 203, 205–6, 217, 230, 232–6, 241–64, 279–80, 290, 292, 300, 303, 305, 308–10, 313–15, 318, 320, 324, 333–4, 338, 340–1, 344–6, 349, 351–6, 373, 374, 383, 388, 391, 393, 395, 400, 402, 409, 411, 414, 416–17, 419–21, 425
as *Duce* 2, 7, 9–10, 27, 29–30, 35, 77, 97–8, 114, 118–19, 129, 138–9, 142, 145–6, 150, 154–7, 162, 164, 193–5,

197–202, 204–5, 208–11, 213, 217–8, 229, 232, 236, 238–64, 269, 272–4, 278–80, 290–2, 295–6, 300, 303, 305, 308–10, 313–15, 318, 320, 324, 333–49, 351–6, 361, 364, 371–4, 379, 383–5, 388, 390–1, 393, 395, 398, 400, 402, 412–15, 417–21, 424–6, 428
and economics 155, 161–2, 179, 194, 199, 203, 225–8, 241, 247–8, 254, 256, 262, 287–90, 305, 308, 325, 338, 351–3, 355–6, 361, 363–4, 378, 409, 426
education 51–3, 66, 76, 409
family life 7, 13–17, 31, 37, 55–6, 60, 64–6, 70, 74–5, 80–1, 86, 89, 92, 94, 116–17, 123, 126, 138, 143, 171, 173, 176–7, 198, 207–10, 239–40, 143–4, 260, 263, 278, 307, 310–11, 313, 334, 340, 346, 354, 386–8, 402–3, 406, 409, 413–14, 416–20, 427
and France 223, 242, 245–6, 272, 298–9, 301, 306, 314–17, 333–5, 338, 341, 349–50, 355, 364, 404
and friendship 31, 96, 98, 108–10, 125, 142, 148, 160, 169, 176–8, 212, 233, 240, 243–4, 262, 323, 334, 344, 427
and Germany 19–20, 22–3, 25–6, 28, 30, 71–2, 87, 102, 111, 118, 166, 189, 245, 251, 255, 265, 270–1, 273, 275, 282, 301, 308, 314, 325–7, 329–34, 337, 339–44, 346, 349–51, 353–6, 359, 361–3, 366, 370, 382, 386, 389, 391, 393–4, 399, 404, 411
health 7, 15–7, 26–7, 50, 60, 68, 86, 109, 115–18, 125–6, 143, 207, 210, 212, 263, 313–14, 346–7, 350, 362, 364–5, 385–9, 399, 401, 403–6, 409, 413
and Hitler 245, 251, 255, 263–72, 276, 280–2, 314, 331, 333–4, 343–4, 349–51, 353–7, 359, 361–3, 365–8, 373, 376–81, 389, 391, 393, 395, 399–400, 402–4, 408
image 1, 2, 7, 10, 16, 25, 50–2, 97–8, 114, 118, 126, 164, 173, 189, 192, 194, 211–12, 218, 241–4, 251–2,

258–60, 262–3, 310, 337, 346, 350, 425, 427–8

and industry/business 155, 178–9, 199, 214, 224–5, 228, 241, 254, 256, 260, 288–90, 338, 351, 353, 373–4, 391, 412

as intellectual 1, 8–9, 11, 23, 26–7, 30, 50–1, 58–73, 75–9, 81, 86, 88, 90, 94, 906, 107, 109, 111, 122, 125, 128, 149, 171–2, 191–2, 259, 261, 293, 314, 338–9, 347, 356, 388, 421, 427–8

as journalist 7, 26, 49, 54, 58–9, 61–2, 67–8, 70, 72, 74–81, 85–90, 92, 95–8, 101–11, 114–16, 118, 121, 123–6, 129, 132, 134, 136, 142–3, 155, 158–9, 165–6, 173, 176, 337–8

as migrant (and on migration) 27, 55–73, 251–2, 336–7, 343–4

and military 70, 81, 85, 102, 119, 136, 162, 172–3, 181, 186, 189, 205, 241, 244–5, 248, 250–6, 261, 285, 287, 302–3, 305–9, 318, 320, 327–8, 333, 335, 337, 341, 343, 345, 348–50, 352–6, 361, 368–9, 371, 373, 375–8, 380–2, 384, 386–8, 393, 395, 399–401

oratory 8, 20–1, 23, 25, 50, 52–3, 62, 66–8, 78–80, 85–91, 96–7, 125, 136, 149, 157, 162, 165, 172–3, 179, 181, 184, 200–3, 221, 244–5, 249, 330, 337–8, 340–1, 412, 419

on race 11, 20–1, 30, 59, 71, 132–3, 142, 147–9, 166, 186, 231, 249–50, 253–6, 261–2, 271–6, 280, 282, 304, 330, 334–44, 382, 390, 393, 409

as Romagnole 78, 80–1, 84, 117, 128, 273, 361, 368, 409, 428

and religion 28–30, 43, 51–2, 54, 62–3, 66–7, 70, 74, 77, 80, 85–7, 95, 117–18, 128, 132, 140, 165, 171, 179–80, 182, 218, 236–41, 244, 257–8, 269, 280, 330, 340, 342, 348–9, 353, 368, 382, 402–3, 414, 416

and Republicanism 62, 77, 80–1,

110–11, 132, 135–6, 140, 156, 161, 170, 175, 180, 241–3, 340, 347–8, 353

and Russia (USSR) 149, 215, 272, 328, 333, 363, 381, 386, 395

and socialism 22, 26, 28, 50–1, 58–73, 75–82, 84–5, 87–90, 92, 95, 99, 101–5, 107–9, 111–12, 116–20, 125, 128, 132–4, 136–42, 148, 150, 152, 155, 158–9, 173, 193–5, 218, 223, 247, 252, 275–6, 328, 335, 347, 399

as soldier 65–6, 70, 114–17, 123–6, 136, 157, 244

and sport 211, 278, 346, 374–5, 386, 427

as teacher 42, 53–5, 60, 66–9, 88, 406

and USA 81, 120, 132, 152, 211, 223, 225, 272, 276, 327, 333, 363, 365, 368, 380–1

and women 43–4, 55, 57, 90–4, 96, 116–17, 120, 169–70, 176, 186, 198, 205, 207, 212, 231–2, 250, 258, 263, 276–8, 311, 344, 346, 348–9, 366, 377, 386–8, 409–12, 427–8

and writings 25, 45, 50, 54, 58–9, 61–2, 66–8, 70–81, 85–7, 89, 92, 96, 98, 101–4, 108–9, 111, 114–6, 118–21, 123–6, 132, 136, 155, 159, 172, 191–2, 208, 242, 260–1, 338

The Cardinal's Mistress 62

Complete works 129, 172

Doctrine of Fascism 261–2

Giovanni Huss il veridico 86–7

Napoleon 242

Utopia 96–7

Vita di Arnaldo 260

Mussolini, Bruno 17, 31, 116, 126, 143, 176, 209, 278, 307, 311, 386, 419

Mussolini, Clarissa Benita 420

Mussolini, Edda 13–17, 74, 80, 89, 94, 116, 143, 176, 207, 209, 263, 276, 311–12, 321, 334, 345, 398–9, 409, 419

Mussolini, Edvige 41, 44, 66, 116, 263, 403

Mussolini, Francesco 38

Mussolini, Jacobus Antonius 38

Mussolini, Luigi 38–9

Mussolini, Pietro 39

Mussolini, Rachele, *see* Guidi Mussolini, Rachele

Index

Mussolini, Romano 17, 209, 406, 420
Mussolini, Sandro 28, 260
Mussolini, Vito 16, 176–7, 294, 311
Mussolini, Vittorio 16, 44, 116, 176, 209,
    295–6, 307, 310–11, 334, 354, 386,
    388, 419
Muti, Ettore 14, 361, 367, 377

Naldi, Filippo 105–8, 143
Nanni, Torquato 98
Naples 19, 104, 122, 167, 182, 185, 216,
    220, 234, 273, 332
Nasser, Gamal Abdel 303
NATO 248
Navy 178, 186, 188–9, 259, 327–8, 342,
    352–3, 355, 371–2
Nazism (National Socialism) 2, 4, 10, 15,
    17, 19, 24, 27–8, 31–2, 72, 133, 170,
    189, 204, 221, 225, 248, 250–3, 255–6,
    265–76, 280–2, 297, 313, 332,
    334–44, 348, 351–2, 354–6, 358, 363,
    393, 395, 410–11, 421, 423–4
Negri, Giuseppe 32
Nenni, Pietro 85, 402
Netherlands 378
New Caledonia 40
New York 91, 147, 253, 412
Newman, E. Polson 304
Nice 349, 375
Nietzsche, Friedrich 68, 89–90, 92, 293,
    355, 402, 406
Night of the Long Knives 197, 281
Nitti, Francesco Saverio 125, 133–7, 140,
    143, 206, 214
Nogara, Bernardino 237
Normandy 318
Northcliffe, Lord Alfred 95
Norway 367

Observer 188
Ogaden Desert 302
Olivetti, Angelo Oliviero 70, 99, 132
Olivetti, Gino 166, 199, 214
Olympics, Berlin 256
Oneglia 66–7, 69, 109
*Opera nazionale per la maternità ed
    infanzia* (ONMI) 231
Orlando, Vittorio Emanuele 107, 119, 127,
    167–8, 190, 308
Ortona, Egidio 38
Osio, Arturo 227, 240
Osservatore Romano 198, 238, 317
Ostia 276
Ottoman Empire 59
Ovra, 222

Pace, Biagio 154
Pacelli, Francesco 237, 258
Pact of Steel 353, 361
Padovani, Aurelio 182
Pagine libere 68, 78
Palazzo Vidoni Pact 214
Palermo 154, 321, 398
Palestine 257, 337
Pantaleoni, Maffeo 132, 158–9, 253
Pantelleria 366, 399
Panunzio, Sergio 70, 96, 103, 191
Panunzio, Vito 346
Paolucci di Calboli, Giacomo 388
Pareschi, Carlo 13
Pareto, Vilfredo 60, 132
Pariani, Alberto 333
Parini, Piero 415–16
Paris 37, 40, 50, 69, 72, 91, 130, 132, 135,
    169, 185, 306, 318, 335, 338, 412
Pasella, Umberto 122, 131, 136, 162
Passerini, Luisa 243
Pavelic, Ante 248, 283, 364, 378–9, 391–2
Pavia 415–6
Pavolini, Alessandro 14–5, 23, 27, 31,
    33–4, 362, 375, 408, 410–11
Pavolini, Corrado 122
Pearl Harbour 378
Peasants/Peasantry 33, 38–9, 41, 45,
    48–50, 63, 69, 74, 76, 83–4, 89, 100,
    112–15, 119, 126, 140, 150, 152, 155,
    171, 229, 241, 291–2, 320, 336, 345,
    372, 400, 404
Pedrazzi, Orazio 316
Pelloux, Luigi 82
Peron, Juan 419, 426
Perth 174, 246
Pertini, Sandro 33
Perugia 168
Pesaro 226
Pescara 153

Index

Petacci family 227, 276–7, 346, 387
Petacci, Claretta 16, 31, 33–4, 211, 263,
    276–8, 311, 346–7, 349, 366, 377,
    386–8, 410–12
Petacci, Francesco Saverio 276
Petacci, Marcello Cesare Augusto 31, 33,
    311, 347, 387
Petacci, Maria 387
Pétain, Philippe 404
Phillips, William 331
Piacenza 145
Piave River 112
Piazzale Loreto 24, 139, 410–13
Piazzesi, Mario 160
Piedmont 141, 154, 163, 182, 206, 273
Pieve Saliceto 54
Pini, Giorgio 3, 177
Pirelli, Alberto 305, 394
Pisa 386
Pisanò, Giorgio 34
Pisenti, Piero 181
Pistoia 91
Pistoia, Duke of 323
Pius IX, Pope 39, 47, 236
Pius XI, Pope 165, 179, 213, 237–8, 257–8,
    271, 276–7, 332, 340, 342, 348
Pius XII, Pope 237, 258, 348–9, 392, 426
Plato 96, 293
Po 38, 48–9, 55, 150, 154, 280, 353
Podrecca, Guido 87
Poe, Edgar Alan 68
Poland 38, 266, 274, 332, 335, 350, 354–6,
    358–9, 362–3, 370, 373, 379, 392
Police 24, 40, 57, 61, 64, 68–9, 73, 85, 125,
    131, 137, 149, 158, 164, 177, 180–1,
    221, 241, 244, 246, 335, 346, 415
Ponza 29, 402–3
Portugal 344, 356, 423
Pound, Ezra 323
Prague 352
Pravda 88
Predappio 37–42, 46, 51, 54, 57, 69, 79,
    90, 128, 152, 167, 173, 208–9, 239–40,
    295, 321, 412, 416–8, 420–1
Premilcuore 66
Press, British 147, 184, 187–8, 284, 297,
    303, 424
  French 317

Italian 24, 31, 105, 130, 179, 181, 193,
    207, 211, 214, 217, 222, 249, 260,
    267, 269, 276, 280–1, 392, 414–15,
    420
  Foreign 335, 350, 422
Preston, Paul 5–6
Preziosi, Giovanni 132–3, 147, 204, 271,
    323, 339, 342, 392
Prezzolini, Giuseppe 71–2, 81, 90, 96, 98,
    103–5, 110–11, 412
Pricolo, Francesco 362
Primo de Rivera, José Antonio 189, 315–16
Primo de Rivera, Miguel 249, 270
Prisoners of War, Italian 20, 112
Protestants 250
Protocols of the Elders of Zion 147
Prussia 21–2, 59, 102, 111, 340
Puccini, Giacomo 107, 202
Puglia 89, 139, 154, 177, 375

Quartararo, Rosaria 274
Queipo de Llano, Gonzalo 318
Querel, Vittore 418–20

Rabbi River 41, 51, 417–18
Race and Racism 2, 11, 18, 28, 59, 71, 87,
    91, 132–3, 139, 186, 249, 252–4, 256,
    266, 270–2, 274, 330, 334–44, 348,
    351, 353, 393, 427
Anti-Slav 71, 139, 142, 149, 153, 249, 266,
    276, 427
'Arabism'/Pan-Arab nationalism 91, 272,
    336, 376, 427
Italianità 27, 46, 71, 129–31, 134, 163, 186,
    249, 252–4, 256, 307, 327, 334–6,
    340–2, 383, 390, 392–3
Mediterranean/Latin 334, 341
'Nordics'/'Aryans' 334, 336, 338, 341–3,
    420
'Racial science' 337–40, 342–3, 427
Romanità 334
Rafanelli, Leda 91–5, 107
Ragusa (Dubrovnik)
Rahn, Rudolf 22, 24
Rapallo, Treaty of 146, 148, 248
Rastenburg 21–2
Rathenau, Walter 166
Ratti, Achille, see Pius XI

Index

Rauti, Pino 422
Ravenna 79, 99, 151, 361
Red Sea 47
'Red Week' 98–9, 101–2
Reggio Emilia 87–90, 152
Renaissance 46, 242, 256
Renner, Karl 69
Renzetti, Giuseppe 268–71, 281, 303
Repubblica Sociale Italiana, see Salò
Republicanism 49, 77, 97, 109, 138, 153, 335, 415
Rerum Novarum 47–8
Resistance 19, 28, 30, 410–11
   myth of 2
   Nazi reprisals 24, 410–11
   Partisans 19, 24, 31–4, 410–11, 418
Rexists 327
Rhineland 299
Ribbentrop, Joachim von 312, 328, 332, 350, 353–4, 364–6, 376
Ribbentrop-Molotov Pact 354, 359, 363
Riccardi, Raffaello 138–9, 362–3, 387, 395
Ricci, Berto 250
Ricci, Renato 23
Riccione 239, 282, 340, 346, 378
Rimini 164, 346, 386
Roatta, Mario 317, 380
Robespierre. Maximilien 62
Rocca delle Caminate 38, 239, 325, 386, 389, 417–18
Rocca, Massimo 181, 191
Rocco, Alfredo 178, 191, 214, 219, 224, 237
Rochat, Giorgio 207
Röhm, Ernst 281
Romagna 31, 37–8, 46, 48, 50, 52, 60, 67, 77–8, 80, 82–3, 86, 98–9, 164, 176, 209, 273, 280, 368, 386, 388, 409
Romagnole Revolutionary Socialist Party 48
Roman Catholic Church 10–11, 28–30, 39, 41, 43, 45–8, 62, 68, 83, 100, 128, 136, 138, 140, 165, 179, 182, 187, 190, 198–200, 208, 211–13, 218, 223, 227, 229, 235–9, 241–2, 257–8, 271, 306, 315, 330, 332, 335, 340, 342, 348, 350, 361, 368, 370, 380, 392, 397, 399, 400, 409, 412, 415–16
   Anti-clericalism 39, 45, 47, 62–3, 67–8,

77, 80, 91, 129, 131, 165, 190, 257, 340, 342, 348
   Catholic Trade Unions 140, 149
   Catholic Press 317, 335
   German Catholics 342
   Inquisition 77
   Jesuits 335
   Lateran Pacts 28–9, 237–9, 241, 244, 257–8
   Vatican 38, 47, 49, 130, 140, 165, 179, 190, 236–7, 258, 269, 288, 295, 332, 342, 348, 353, 356, 358, 387, 392, 397, 419
Roman Club of Fascist Flyers 142
Romania 133, 298, 332, 335, 351, 376, 423
Romano, Ruggero 32
Rome 21, 26, 37–8, 46–7, 49, 61, 72–3, 78–80, 82, 84, 85–7, 93, 111, 131, 148–9, 156–8, 160–2, 164–5, 167–9, 173, 175–6, 179, 184, 187, 189–90, 192–4, 196–7, 199–201, 210, 213, 217–18, 220, 223, 225, 229, 232–3, 237, 240, 243, 247, 250, 254, 257, 260, 263, 265, 268, 276, 291–2, 295, 298, 300–3, 306, 308, 311–12, 315–17, 320, 323, 326, 328, 332, 347, 349, 354, 365–6, 379–80, 386, 391, 400, 403, 412–13, 415, 417, 421–3
   abandonment by King and Badoglio 30, 403
   bombing of 24
   classical Rome 57, 121, 132, 243, 245, 253, 282, 341, 417, 419
   fall of 19, 21
   March on 28, 167–170, 172, 174, 178, 181–2, 206, 216, 243–4, 257, 265, 267
   myth of 21, 49
Rommel, Erwin 376, 395
Roosevelt, Franklin Delano 212, 276, 352, 364, 381, 392, 397
Roosevelt, Theodore 297
Rosenberg, Alfred 280
Rosselli, Carlo 318–19, 335
Rosselli, Nello 318–19
Rossi, Cesare 122, 145, 181, 191, 196
Rossini, Gioachino 314
Rosso, Augusto 360

Index

Rossoni, Edmondo 57, 181, 191, 223–5, 227, 290, 418
Rotary 250
Rothermere, Harold Sidney 95
Rovereto 73
Rovigo 96, 193
Ruberti, Gina 17, 311, 419
Rubicon River 152, 368
Russia (USSR) 64, 109, 120, 133–4, 137, 149, 152, 258, 261, 271–2, 275, 279–80, 328, 333, 353, 393, 395, 398
   Bolshevik Revolution 112, 127, 133, 141, 249
   Soviet regime 20, 149, 197, 258, 261, 345, 348, 359–60, 365–6, 371, 378–82, 387, 392, 401

Salandra, Antonio 101, 107, 112–13, 119, 167–8, 188, 190, 198, 207
Salazar, Oliveira 356, 423
Salvemini, Gaetano 96, 103, 128, 169, 180, 195, 214, 219
Salò Republic 13–6, 18–25, 29–30, 32, 34, 143, 177, 246, 279, 404, 406–10, 412, 415, 422
Salzburg 20, 354, 357
San Sepolcro 122, 128–9, 131, 150, 158, 162, 182
Sanjurjo, José 283
Sansanelli, Nicola 181
Sant'Arcangelo 164
Santissima Annunziata 209
Sarajevo 99, 101
Sardinia 317–18, 402–3
Sarfatti, Margherita 91, 96, 108, 117, 126, 148, 161, 169, 171, 186, 198, 213, 232, 249–50, 300, 344, 392
Sarfatti, Roberto 117
Sarzana 158, 163
Sassari Brigade 153
Savignano 164
Savoy 349, 375
Schallmayer, Lieutenant 31–2
Schönberg, Arnold 69
Schuschnigg, Kurt von 283, 325, 329
Schuster, Ildefonso 28–30, 33
Scicolone, Maria 420

Scorza, Carlo 397–9, 401
Scuola di Mistica Fascista Sandro Mussolini 28, 294
Seldes, George 303
Sempre Pronti 178, 183
Senigallia 138
Senise, Carmine 273
Sennett, Mack 278
Serbia 38, 101–2, 111, 187, 298
Serena, Adelchi 153, 378, 383
Serrano Suñer, Ramón 380, 395
Serrati, Giacinto Menotti 64, 67–8, 88
Serrati, Lucio 67
Settimelli, Emilio 164
Seville 247
Sforza, Carlo 108, 148, 156, 185, 216
Shakespeare, William 149, 171
Shanghai 345
Siberia 387
Sicily 126, 128, 134, 154, 167, 187, 229–31, 291, 352, 361, 366, 399
Simon, John 299–302
Sinclair Oil 193
Singapore 378
Sinigaglia, Oscar 132, 136–7
Sironi, Mario 323
Skorzeny, Otto 403
Slovakia 350
Slovenia 341, 378, 383
Smiles, Samuel 43
Socialism 25–6, 31, 39–41, 48–50, 59, 68, 73, 77, 84, 91, 96, 107–8, 128, 131, 133–4, 136–41, 150, 154, 156, 159, 183, 190–1, 193, 198–200, 218, 236, 290, 315, 347, 399, 418, 424–6
   anti-socialism 48, 122, 127, 129, 133–4, 138–43, 147, 149–51, 153–5, 157, 160, 163–5, 171, 174, 179, 187, 191, 193, 206, 261, 265–8, 274–6, 326, 328, 335, 348, 350, 359–60, 363, 380, 398, 423
   Austro-socialism 69
   in Germany 63, 71
   maximalism 61, 64, 82, 200
   reformism 61, 63–4, 78, 82–3, 85, 87–8, 90, 104, 113, 151, 193, 200
   and religion 62–3, 165, 179

Index

Socialism – *continued*
  and religion – *continued*
    Socialist Party (congresses) 28, 40, 58,
      61, 63, 70, 75, 78–9, 81–2, 87–9,
      98–9, 105, 109, 133–4, 136, 155–6,
      422
    Strikes 67, 84–5, 98–9, 134, 137, 140–1,
      149–51
    and Trade Unions 134, 140–1, 149, 159,
      193, 214
    Syndicalism 65, 68, 70, 78, 80, 90, 96,
      99, 103, 110, 122, 131–2, 134, 138,
      150, 154, 191, 223, 225, 229, 290–1
    and war 84–5, 100, 102–4, 107–8, 127,
      136
Socrates 21, 86
Soddu, Ubaldo 362
Soffici, Ardengo 18
Somalia 183, 253–4, 305, 321, 340
Somaliland 284, 302, 376, 383
Sonnino, Sidney 47, 101, 112–13, 127, 180
Sorel, Georges 65, 70, 81, 85, 88, 106
Spain 18, 34–5, 77, 107, 189, 197, 227, 249,
      270–1, 283, 315–19, 323–4, 326–30,
      335, 340, 344, 353–4, 363, 369, 380,
      383, 387, 395, 423
Spalato (Split) 111
Spampanato, Bruno 22–3, 27–8, 261
SS (*Schutzstaffeln*) 13, 24, 30
Stahlhelm 268
Stalin, Josef 2, 4, 20, 35, 74, 197, 203, 212,
      275, 353, 359–60, 387
Stalinism 23
Stalingrad 394
Starace, Achille 34, 162, 181, 221, 229,
      234–5, 259–60, 278–80, 287, 294,
      314, 340, 344, 347–8, 356, 361,
      410–11
Stauffenberg, Klaus von 21
Steinberg, Jonathan 343
St Louis 58, 193
Stojadinovic, Milan 330
Stresa 301–2, 397
Stringher, Bonaldo 237
Sturzo, Luigi 128, 179, 200–1
Suardo, Giacomo 279, 400–1
Suckert, Curzio see Malaparte, Curzio
Suez Canal 301

Surveillance 177, 259
Susmel, Duilio 3
Suvich, Fulvio 203, 251, 271, 275, 281–2,
      301, 306, 325, 397
Sweden 288, 324
Switzerland 16, 27, 30–1, 45, 55–6, 58–9,
      64–6, 106, 111, 184, 223, 282, 306,
      327, 331

Tablet 238
Tafari Makonnen see Haile Selassie I
Taglialatela, Alfredo 62
Tamaro, Attilio 266–7
Tardini, Silvia 311
Taylor, A.J.P. 424
Tell, William 55
Tellini, Enrico 186
Teramo 153
Terni 164
Teruzzi, Attilio 162, 181, 203, 254
Teruzzi, Paolo 227
Terza Italia 154
Terzaghi, Michele 177
Thaon di Revel, Paolo 178, 188–9, 363–4
Theresienstadt 393
Ticino 111, 327, 349
Times 147, 184, 187, 198, 238, 303,
      306
Tiso, Jozef 350
Tobruk 371, 378
Togliatti, Palmiro 178, 188
Tokyo 142, 277
Tolmezzo 66–7, 69
Tolstoy, Leon 149
Tomislav II, King 380
Totalitarianism 8–9, 11, 15–16, 176, 183,
      195, 197, 216–18, 229, 232, 235–7,
      239, 241, 244, 249, 252, 256, 258,
      261–2, 289–90, 295, 319, 324, 345,
      348, 351–2, 365, 423, 426–7
Totila, King 29
Touring Club Italiano 201, 257, 344
Tourism 37, 256–7, 288–9, 305, 337, 353,
      418, 420–1
Trade Unions 140–1, 149–50, 219, 223,
      241, 427
Trasformismo 47, 126, 137, 193, 422
Tremiti islands 222

Index

Trentino 19, 39, 46, 56, 68, 72, 77, 81, 111, 116, 164, 412
Trento 68–72
Treves, Claudio 82, 88, 109
Trieste 19–20, 24, 27, 39, 46, 72, 103, 111, 137, 139, 148–50, 164, 249, 251, 266, 341
Triple Alliance 46–7, 70, 100, 102, 266
Triple Entente 101, 103–4, 109, 120–1, 127, 266
Tripoli, see also under Libya 83–4, 160, 204, 253–5, 279, 283, 297, 319, 336, 395
Trotsky, Leon 147
Tunis 93, 186, 349, 375, 392, 394–5
Tunisia 298, 395
Turati, Augusto 201, 220, 231–5, 242–3, 245, 258, 291
Turati, Filippo 61, 82–3, 87, 193
Turin 49, 82, 137, 140, 174, 182–3, 289, 335
Turkey 38, 40, 83–4, 166, 253, 297, 387
Tuscany 24, 37–8, 91, 101, 107, 150, 154, 160, 219, 279, 334, 386

Udine 66–7
Umberto I, King 41, 82
Umberto, Crown Prince 320
Umbria 150, 154, 244
United Press 313
United States of America 21, 26, 56–8, 81–2, 115, 120, 127, 176, 185, 193, 211, 223, 225–6, 228, 231, 241, 252, 272, 276, 327, 333, 344–5, 350, 352, 363, 368, 372, 378, 380–1, 387, 392, 394–5, 400, 413–14, 423–6
Universities 15, 293, 372
Uomo Qualunque 421
USSR, see Russia
Ustasha 283, 380

Valera, Paolo 89
Valmy 118
Valois, Georges 249
Valona (Vlora) 147
Valtellina 27, 29–30, 415
Vandervelde, Emile 62
Varano 42, 44, 417

Vasto 153
Vatican, *see* under Roman Catholic Church – the Vatican
Vecchi, Ferruccio 122, 129–31, 134, 137–8, 140, 182
Velluti, Teresa 311
Veneto 45, 153, 291, 390
Venezia Giulia 142, 148–9, 154, 249
Venice 38, 59, 91, 112, 122, 137, 142, 151, 159–61, 256, 273, 280–1, 373, 425
Vercelli 174
Verdi, Giuseppe 52, 314
Verona 13, 145, 407
Versailles 113, 266, 274, 306
Versailles, Treaty of 113, 127, 132, 147, 245, 247, 299
Victor Emmanuel III, King 7, 9, 25, 78, 87, 100, 113, 116, 168, 170, 175, 178, 180, 190, 198–9, 202–3, 207, 213, 300, 305, 309, 332–3, 340, 347–9, 352–3, 355, 362, 364, 366–8, 370, 400–1, 403
Vidussoni, Aldo 383–5, 393–4, 397, 401
Vienna 37, 69, 135, 268, 282, 302, 393
Vigneri, Paolo 402
Villelli, Gennaro 154
Vita trentina 68
Vittorio Veneto, battle, day 14
Volpe, Gioacchino 186, 423–4
Volpe, Giovanni 423
Volpi, Albino 170, 196–7
Volpi, Asmara Norchi 196
Volpi, Giuseppe 160, 204, 222, 225–8, 253–4, 281, 305, 321, 323, 383, 399
von Paulus, Friedrich 394
Vyshinsky, Andrei 279

Wagner, Richard 71, 93, 314, 423
Ward Price, George 313
Warsaw 147, 271
Weber, Max 6
Washington 185, 413
Welles, Sumner 364–5
Wilhelm II, Kaiser 357
Willikens, Werner 6
Wilson, Woodrow 113, 120, 127, 132, 274
Wolff, Karl 30
World War I 8, 14, 24, 27–8, 31, 33, 48, 53, 58–9, 65, 93, 95, 98, 105, 108–9,

Index

World War I – *continued*
114–17, 119, 121–2, 126–8, 135–6,
141, 166, 171–2, 174, 178, 184, 187–8,
193, 195, 203, 215, 249, 253, 259, 266,
284, 331, 341, 347, 356–7, 374, 390,
416
  Italian entry 93, 98, 100–1, 103–4,
    110–12, 114, 117, 121–2, 132,
    135–6, 139, 152–3, 160, 188, 357
  Neutralism 100–4, 110–1, 113–14, 136,
    140, 158, 165, 193, 356
  Reparations 184, 225
War effort 112–3, 128, 132, 378–9, 391
World War II 7–8, 14–15, 17–18, 25–7, 30,
    34–5, 70, 116, 129, 256–7, 267, 276,
    341, 343, 349, 358, 381, 387, 389–90,
    395, 400, 403, 409–13, 415, 418–19,
    423
  Mediterranean front 3, 13, 17–18, 22,
    343
  Outbreak 350–7
  Pacific theatre 382
  Russian Front 3, 20, 255, 343, 382,
    386–7, 392–5, 398–9

X Mas 24

Yagoda, Henryk 279
Yemen 247
Yugoslavia 146, 149, 248–9, 251, 272, 276,
    327, 330, 375, 378–80, 391–2

Zachariae, Georg 404–6
Zagreb 378, 380
Zamboni, Anteo 219
Zaniboni, Tito 204, 402
Zara (Zadar) 111
Zeila 302
Zerbino, Paolo 34, 410–11
Zog I, King 204, 242, 248
Zoli family 51, 416
Zoli, Adone 416
Zoli, Don Pietro 416
Zoli, Temistocle 65
Zoppi, Ottavio 259
Zucca, Padre 415–16
Zurich 93